International Issues in Early Intervention
Series Editor: Michael J. Guralnick

ISEI

THE DEVELOPMENTAL SYSTEMS
APPROACH TO EARLY INTERVENTION

A book series from the
International Society on Early Intervention

Other books in this series:

Early Intervention Practices Around the World
edited by Samuel L. Odom, Ph.D., Marci J. Hanson, Ph.D.,
James A. Blackman, M.D., M.P.H., and Sudha Kaul, Ph.D.

Interdisciplinary Clinical Assessment
of Young Children with Developmental Disabilities
edited by Michael J. Guralnick, Ph.D.

ISEI

THE DEVELOPMENTAL SYSTEMS APPROACH TO EARLY INTERVENTION

edited by

Michael J. Guralnick, Ph.D.
University of Washington, Seattle

·P A U L·H·
BROOKES
PUBLISHING CO.®

Baltimore • London • Sydney

MT

Paul H. Brookes Publishing Co.
Post Office Box 10624
Baltimore, Maryland 21285-0624

www.brookespublishing.com

Typeset by International Graphic Services, Inc.,
Newtown, Pennsylvania.
Manufactured in the United States of America by
Edwards Brothers, Inc., Ann Arbor, Michigan.

The stories in this book are based on the authors' experiences. Some of the vignettes
represent actual people and circumstances. Individuals' names and identifying
details have been changed to protect their identities. Other vignettes are composite
accounts that do not represent the lives or experiences of specific individuals, and
no implications should be inferred.

Library of Congress Cataloging-in-Publication Data

The developmental systems approach to early intervention / edited by Michael
J. Guralnick.
    p.   cm.—(International issues in early intervention)
Includes bibliographical references and index.
ISBN 1-55766-797-7 (hardcover)
1. Developmental disabilities—Treatment—Cross-cultural studies.   2. Develop-
mentally disabled children—Rehabilitation—Cross-cultural studies.   3. Develop-
mentally disabled children—Services for—Cross-cultural studies.   I. Guralnick,
Michael J.   II. Series.

RJ135.D49   2004
618.92'8588—dc22   2004029096

British Library Cataloguing in Publication data are available from the British
Library.

6/9/05

Contents

Series Preface viii
About the Editor ix
Contributors x
Preface xiv
Acknowledgments xvi

Section I   Principles

Chapter 1   An Overview of the Developmental Systems
               Model for Early Intervention
               Michael J. Guralnick 3

Chapter 2   Service Coordination and Integration in a
               Developmental Systems Approach
               to Early Intervention
               Mary Beth Bruder 29

Chapter 3   Inclusion as a Core Principle in the
               Early Intervention System
               Michael J. Guralnick 59

Section II   Practices: National Perspectives

Chapter 4   Screening and Surveillance
               in Early Intervention Systems
               Walter S. Gilliam, Samuel J. Meisels,
               and Linda C. Mayes 73

Chapter 5   Designing an Integrated Point of Access
               in the Early Intervention System
               Gloria L. Harbin 99

Chapter 6   The Role of Comprehensive Interdisciplinary
               Assessments in the Early Intervention System
               Mark L. Wolraich, Robin H. Gurwitch,
               Mary Beth Bruder, and Laura A. Knight 133

Chapter 7   Assessing the Information Needs of Families
               in Early Intervention
               Donald B. Bailey, Jr., and Traci Powell 151

Chapter 8   Assessing Interpersonal and Family Distress
               and Threats to Confident Parenting in the
               Context of Early Intervention
               Gael I. Orsmond 185

Chapter 9   Assessing the Resource Needs of Families
               in the Context of Early Intervention
               R.A. McWilliam 215

Chapter 10   Assessing Family Characteristics Relevant
               to Early Intervention
               *Jean F. Kelly, Cathryn Booth-LaForce, and
               Susan J. Spieker* 235

Chapter 11   Developing and Implementing Preventive
               Intervention Programs for Children at Risk:
               Poverty as a Case in Point
               Dale Clark Farran 267

Chapter 12   Developing and Implementing Early
               Intervention Programs for Children
               with Established Disabilities
               *Donna Spiker, Kathleen Hebbeler, and
               Sangeeta Mallik* 305

Chapter 13   Monitoring and Evaluation in Early
               Intervention Programs
               *Marji Erickson Warfield and
               Penny Hauser-Cram* 351

Chapter 14   Ensuring Effective Transitions in Early
               Intervention
               Marci J. Hanson 373

Section III **Practices: International Perspectives**

Chapter 15   Early Intervention in Australia:
               The Challenge of Systems Implementation
               Coral Kemp and Alan Hayes 401

Chapter 16   A Developmental Communications Model
               within the Early Intervention System
               in Austria
               Manfred Pretis 425

Chapter 17   The Infant Development Program's Early
              Assessment and Early Intervention Model
              in British Columbia
              Hillel Goelman, Dana Brynelsen,
              Mari Pighini, and Gerard M. Kysela 439

Chapter 18   Early Intervention in the United Kingdom:
              Current Policy and Practice
              Barry Carpenter and Philippa Russell 455

Chapter 19   Early Intervention Services in Greece:
              Present Situation and Future Prospects
              Efthalia N. Kaderoglou and
              Maria Drossinou 481

Chapter 20   Early Childhood Intervention in Israel
              Michal Al-Yagon and Malka Margalit 503

Chapter 21   Early Intervention for Children with Special
              Needs: The Italian Paradigm
              Ennio Del Giudice, Michele Bottos,
              Beatrice Dalla Barba, Lorenzo Pavone,
              Martino Ruggieri, and Salvatore Ottaviano 521

Chapter 22   Early Intervention in Spain: An Overview
              of Current Practices
              Climent Giné Giné, M. Teresa García-Díe,
              Marta Gràcia Garcia, and
              Rosa Vilaseca Momplet 543

Chapter 23   Early Intervention in Sweden:
              A Developmental Systems Perspective
              Eva Björck-Åkesson and Mats Granlund 571

Chapter 24   Early Intervention and Children with
              Special Needs in Developing Countries
              Henning Rye and Karsten Hundeide 593

Author Index 621
Subject Index 635

SERIES PREFACE

The *International Issues in Early Intervention* book series was created in recognition of the fact that problems and advances relevant to early intervention transcend national boundaries. Indeed, providing effective early intervention programs for vulnerable children and their families constitutes one of the most important challenges for all contemporary societies. The rapidly expanding knowledge base of early intervention is the product of contributions from researchers, clinicians, program developers, and policy makers from numerous countries. The diverse and creative approaches taken to address early intervention within the historical and cultural contexts of one's own country provide the international community with unique and valuable insights.

Yet, international early intervention collaborations and sharing of knowledge are far from adequate. Accordingly, the *International Issues in Early Intervention* series is designed to enhance awareness and knowledge of international efforts in early intervention and serve as well as a catalyst for collaborations at many levels. Of importance, this book series is one component of the International Society on Early Intervention (ISEI), whose primary purpose is to provide a framework and forum for professionals from around the world to communicate about advances in the field of early intervention (see http://depts.washington.edu/isei for additional information). The membership of ISEI is composed of basic and clinical researchers relevant to the field of early intervention representing a diverse array of biomedical and behavioral disciplines, as well as clinicians and policy makers in leadership positions. Every effort has been made to ensure that this book series will be of interest to all involved and that the information will advance the field of early intervention and improve the development and well-being of vulnerable children and their families.

About the Editor

Michael J. Guralnick, Ph.D., is Director of the Center on Human Development and Disability (CHDD) and Professor of Psychology and Pediatrics at the University of Washington, Seattle. Comprising both a University Center for Excellence in Developmental Disabilities and a Mental Retardation and Developmental Disabilities Research Center, CHDD is one of the largest interdisciplinary research and training centers in the United States addressing issues directly related to developmental disabilities. More than 600 faculty and staff members as well as doctoral and post-doctoral students operate within the four CHDD buildings on the campus of the University of Washington and in community sites to conduct basic and applied research, to provide clinical services to individuals and their families, to provide interdisciplinary clinical research and training, and to provide technical assistance and outreach training to practitioners and community agencies.

Dr. Guralnick has directed research and development projects in the fields of early childhood intervention, inclusion, peer relationships, and pediatric education. He has published approximately 125 articles, book chapters, and books (including seven edited volumes). Dr. Guralnick's publications have appeared in a diverse group of well-respected journals, including *Child Development, Pediatrics, American Journal on Mental Retardation, Journal of Early Intervention, Developmental Psychology, Journal of Developmental and Behavioral Pediatrics, Journal of Applied Developmental Psychology,* and *Development and Psychopathology.* He recently completed a major research project supported by the National Institute of Child Health and Human Development designed to determine the effectiveness of a comprehensive early intervention program in promoting the peer-related social competence of young children with developmental delays.

Dr. Guralnick received the 1994 Research Award from the American Association on Mental Retardation and the 1997 Distinguished Research Award from The Arc of the United States. He is a past president of the Association of University Centers on Disabilities, the Academy on Mental Retardation, and the Council for Exceptional Children's Division for Early Childhood. He is a former chair of the Mental Retardation and Developmental Disabilities Research Center Directors. Dr. Guralnick is currently Chair of the International Society on Early Intervention and Editor of the journal *Infants and Young Children.*

Contributors

Michal Al-Yagon, Ph.D.
Director of Research
Special Education Laboratory
School of Education
Tel Aviv University
Tel Aviv, Israel

Donald B. Bailey, Jr., Ph.D.
Director
FPG Child Development Institute
W.R. Kenan, Jr., Distinguished
 Professor of Education
University of North Carolina at
 Chapel Hill
Chapel Hill, North Carolina, USA

Eva Björck-Åkesson, Ph.D.
Professor in Education
Department of Social Sciences
Mälardalen University
Västerås, Sweden

Cathryn Booth-LaForce, Ph.D.
Professor
Department of Family and Child
 Nursing
University of Washington
Seattle, Washington, USA

Michele Bottos, M.D.
Former Director
Child Neuromotor Disabilities
 Center
Azienda USL di Bologna, Italy

Mary Beth Bruder, Ph.D.
Professor of Pediatrics
Director
A.J. Pappanikou Center for
 Excellence in Developmental
 Disabilities Education,
 Research, and Service
University of Connecticut School
 of Medicine
Farmington, Connecticut, USA

Dana Brynelsen, L.L.D.
Provincial Advisor
Infant Development Program of
 British Columbia
Vancouver, British Columbia,
 Canada

Barry Carpenter, Ph.D., O.B.E.
Professor
Chief Executive, Sunfield School
Stourbridge, Worcester, United
 Kingdom

Beatrice Dalla Barba, M.D.
Department of Pediatrics
University of Padua
Padua, Italy

Ennio Del Giudice, M.D.
Professor of Child
 Neuropsychiatry
Department of Pediatrics
Section of Child Neuropsychiatry
Federico II University
Naples, Italy

Maria Drossinou, Ph.D.
Deputy Counsellor of Special
 Educational Needs
Department of Special Needs
Pedagogical Institute
Agia Paraskevi, Greece

Dale Clark Farran, Ph.D.
Professor
Department of Teaching and
 Learning
Peabody College/Vanderbilt
 University
Nashville, Tennessee, USA

Marta Gràcia Garcia, Ph.D.
Professor
University of Barcelona
Barcelona, Spain

M. Teresa García-Díe, Ph.D.
Professor of Child Clinical
Psychology
Ramon Llull University, Faculty
of Psychology
Barcelona, Spain

Walter S. Gilliam, Ph.D.
Assistant Professor of Child
Psychiatry and Psychology
Yale Child Study Center
New Haven, Connecticut, USA

Climent Giné Giné, Ph.D.
Dean, Facultat de Psicologia
Ciències de l'Educació i de
l'Esport Blanquerna
Universitat Ramon Llull
Barcelona, Spain

Hillel Goelman, Ph.D.
Professor and Associate Director
Human Early Learning
Partnership
University of British Columbia
Vancouver, British Columbia,
Canada

Mats Granlund, Ph.D.
Professor of Psychology
Department of Social Sciences
Mälardalen University
Västerås, Sweden

Robin H. Gurwitch, Ph.D.
Associate Professor
Department of Pediatrics
University of Oklahoma Health
Sciences Center
Oklahoma City, Oklahoma, USA

Marci J. Hanson, Ph.D.
Professor
Department of Special Education
San Francisco State University
San Francisco, California, USA

Gloria L. Harbin, Ph.D.
Scientist
FPG Child Development Institute
Research Associate Professor
School of Education
University of North Carolina at
Chapel Hill
Carrboro, North Carolina, USA

Penny Hauser-Cram, Ed.D.
Professor of Developmental and
Educational Psychology
Lynch School of Education
Boston College
Chestnut Hill, Massachusetts,
USA

Alan Hayes, Ph.D. *Macq.*,
FAPsS, FAmPsyS
Professor
Australian Centre for Educational
Studies
Macquarie University
Bowral, NSW, Australia

Kathleen Hebbeler, Ph.D.
Program Manager
Community Services and
Strategies
SRI International
Center for Education and Human
Services
Menlo Park, California, USA

Karsten Hundeide, Ph.D.
Department of Psychology
University of Oslo
Oslo, Norway

Efthalia N. Kaderoglou, M.Ed.
Special Educator
Early Intervention Advisor
General Secretary of the Hellenic
  Union of Special Educators
Thessaloniki, Greece

Jean F. Kelly, Ph.D.
Research Professor
Department of Family and Child
  Nursing
University of Washington
Seattle, Washington, USA

Coral Kemp, Ph.D.
Academic Team Leader
Early Years Initiative
Macquarie University Special
  Education Centre
Macquarie University
Sydney, NSW, Australia

Laura A. Knight, M.S.
Graduate Student
Department of Psychology
Oklahoma State University
Stillwater, Oklahoma, USA

Gerard M. Kysela, Ph.D.
Professor Emeritus
University of Alberta
Family Centered Practices Group
Vancouver, British Columbia,
  Canada

Sangeeta Mallik, Ph.D.
Senior Research Associate
SRI International
Center for Education and Human
  Services
Menlo Park, California, USA

Malka Margalit, Ph.D.
Dean, Constantiner School of
  Education
Tel Aviv University
Tel Aviv, Israel

Linda C. Mayes, M.D.
Arnold Gesell Associate Professor
  of Child Psychiatry, Pediatrics,
  and Psychology
Yale Child Study Center
New Haven, Connecticut, USA

R.A. McWilliam, Ph.D.
Professor of Pediatrics
Director, Center for Child
  Development
Vanderbilt University Medical
  Center
Nashville, Tennessee, USA

Samuel J. Meisels, Ed.D.
President
Erikson Institute
Chicago, Illinois, USA

Rosa Vilaseca Momplet, Ph.D.
Professor
University of Barcelona
Barcelona, Spain

Gael I. Orsmond, Ph.D.
Assistant Professor
Sargent College of Health and
  Rehabilitation Sciences
Boston University
Boston, Massachusetts, USA

Salvatore Ottaviano, M.D.
Professor
Department of Child
  Neurological and Psychiatric
  Sciences
La Sapienza University
Rome, Italy

Lorenzo Pavone, M.D.
Professor and Chairman
Department of Pediatrics
University of Catania
Catania, Italy

Mari Pighini, M.A.
Research Coordinator
CHILD Project
Human Early Learning
  Partnership
University of British Columbia
Vancouver, British Columbia,
  Canada

Traci Powell, Ph.D.
Postdoctoral Fellow
FPG Child Development Institute
University of North Carolina at
  Chapel Hill
Chapel Hill, North Carolina, USA

Manfred Pretis, Ph.D.
Clinical Psychologist
Special Pedagogue
S.I.N.N. Social Innovative
  Network
Graz, Austria

Martino Ruggieri, M.D., Ph.D.
Senior Lecturer and Assistant
  Professor
Department of Pediatrics
University of Catania
Institute of Neurological Science
Italian National Research Council
Catania, Italy

Philippa Russell, Ph.D., CBE
Disability Rights Commissioner
Special Policy Adviser on
  Disability
National Children's Bureau
Honorary Fellow
Royal College of Paediatrics and
  Child Health
London, United Kingdom

Henning Rye, Ph.D.
Professor
Department of Special Needs
  Education
Faculty of Education
University of Oslo
Oslo, Norway

Susan J. Spieker, Ph.D.
Professor
Department of Family and Child
  Nursing
University of Washington
Seattle, Washington, USA

Donna Spiker, Ph.D.
Program Manager
Early Childhood Programs
SRI International
Center for Education and Human
  Services
Menlo Park, California, USA

Marji Erickson Warfield, Ph.D.
Social Scientist
Heller School for Social Policy
  and Management
Brandeis University
Waltham, Massachusetts, USA

Mark L. Wolraich, M.D.
CMRI/Shaun Walters Professor
  of Pediatrics
Child Study Center
University of Oklahoma
Oklahoma City, Oklahoma, USA

PREFACE

Advances in the field of early intervention in the United States since the passage of the Education of the Handicapped Act Amendments of 1986 (PL 99-457) have been truly remarkable. With federal support and guidance, states and local communities have worked diligently to develop a coherent and systematic array of early intervention services representing the best practices possible, while serving an ever increasing number of vulnerable children and families. Although some communities have succeeded in doing so, the task of incorporating the rapidly expanding knowledge generated by the developmental science of normative development, the developmental science of risk and disability, and intervention science into community practices has been almost overwhelming. When combined with changing philosophical approaches regarding the role of families, the importance of natural environments, and many other issues that alter, in some cases radically, the very principles upon which early intervention practices are based, it is little wonder that communities are having difficulty creating and maintaining state-of-the-art early intervention programs. Further complicating matters are issues related to the adequacy of resources, difficulties associated with professional training, the absence of leadership in many instances, limited access to new knowledge, and the ongoing problems surrounding collaborations among agencies so necessary if programs are to be effective. One result of these circumstances is a highly diverse set of community-based early intervention programs, varying dramatically in focus, quality, approaches, and organization.

This volume constitutes an attempt to address many of these perplexing issues. The central argument here is that a *systems* mechanism must be universally applied across community-based early intervention programs. Any system must articulate a clear organizational structure, carefully outlining its components and interrelationships, as well as presenting a set of principles that together readily translate into a functioning and coherent system of early intervention practices. One such systems approach, referred to as the Developmental Systems Model, is presented in this volume. This model offers a framework that seeks to integrate contemporary thinking about development, intervention science, and practices into a system that is both feasible and state of the art. The proposed system identifies a set of structural components, each of which is treated in a separate chapter in the book. The principles of early intervention's underlying practices are also articulated and embedded in the recommendations presented by individual chapter authors.

The specific goals of this volume are twofold. First, it is intended to encourage the early intervention field to adopt a systems perspective. In the absence of a formal system, along with its assumptions and practices carefully articulated for all to review and critique, the unevenness and inconsistencies across communities will remain. The second goal is to offer one model both as an example of such a systems approach and as a means of encouraging communities at any level of development to seriously consider the specific structural components, principles, and corresponding recommendations for practice articulated in the Developmental Systems Model.

It is important to point out that communities wishing to pursue these suggestions and design a new system or modify a current one consistent with the Developmental Systems Model will not simply be able to directly apply the information in this volume. In essence, although both a framework and specific recommendations can be found in the various chapters, they constitute only *guidelines*, which must now be translated into systems-based practices by communities. To be sure, this will require leadership and resources, but mainly leadership at local, community, or state levels. The outcomes of this process will hardly eliminate the diversity of programs (nor is this a goal) because communities will make their own interpretations of the recommendations and tailor their programs to local circumstances. Yet, thoughtful application of the Developmental Systems Model, or any other well-developed model, is certain to bring about a more consistent, coherent, and simply better system of early intervention for vulnerable children and their families.

ACKNOWLEDGMENTS

To the contributors to the various chapters addressing both the principles (Section I) and practices in the United States of America (Section II), I owe an enormous debt of gratitude. Each brought his or her expertise, experience, and wisdom to the task of trying to make each structural component and principle accessible to readers and to outline specific recommendations for procedures and protocols that would be of value to communities seeking to improve their early intervention service system. As the book evolved through discussions with the chapter authors, I could see the model and approach being transformed for the better.

The United States perspective on the organizational structure, principles, and practices of the Developmental Systems Model is complemented by international commentaries found in Section III. These insightful chapters were intended to examine the similarities and differences of approaches to early intervention through markedly different cultural, historical, and political vantage points. I owe a similar debt of gratitude to these international leaders for sharing their views about the relevance of the Developmental Systems Model to their early intervention programs. The strong international contributions to this volume are a result of collaborations established in the context of the International Society on Early Intervention (http://depts.washington.edu/isei). This is the third volume in the ISEI series sponsored by Paul H. Brookes Publishing Co.

Finally, it is important to acknowledge the extraordinarily high level of editorial assistance provided by Tennessee Dickenson and Carolyn Hamby. Through their efforts, each of the chapters in this volume has been improved immeasurably. Correspondingly, the staff of Paul H. Brookes Publishing Co. have maintained their highly professional publication standards. Brookes's support and encouragement, particularly that provided by Heather Shrestha, has been critical to the successful completion of this work. Moreover, Brookes's support of the International Society on Early Intervention has been very gratifying and has further contributed to advances in the field of early intervention.

Section 1

Principles

CHAPTER 1

An Overview of the Developmental Systems Model for Early Intervention

MICHAEL J. GURALNICK

The recent history of early intervention services for children who are vulnerable and their families in the United States has certainly been one of progressive expansion and refinement. The model projects operating in select communities or university settings and the beginnings of more widespread programs in the 1960s and 1970s have been transformed into a vibrant and visible national program providing early intervention services and supports to which all eligible young children with established disabilities have access (see Guralnick, 2000a, in press-b). Preventive intervention programs for children at risk for developmental disabilities have exhibited considerable growth as well, although these programs lack the many legislative mandates and the coherence of programs for children with established disabilities.

Numerous factors working together created the conditions for these transformations as well as for the continuing support for further advances in contemporary systems of early intervention programs. Historical accounts of these factors, including philosophical shifts, knowledge gained from the developmental science of normative development and the developmental science of risk and disability, the results of intervention science, information derived from clinical practice, increased support for early childhood development programs for all children, and major legislative events can be found elsewhere (Gilliam & Zigler, 2001; Guralnick, 1997b; Meisels & Shonkoff, 2000; National Research Council and Institute of Medicine, 2000; Smith & McKenna, 1994). Taken together, what has emerged from all of these efforts is a strong commitment to make early intervention, in all of its forms, work. Moreover, as programs in each state and local community have become more visible and prominent, the expectations for early intervention programs have increased considerably. Ensuring the availability of well-coordinated, highly effective early intervention programs in every community, each representing contemporary principles and practices, is held to be a reasonable goal by policy makers, parents, and professionals. It is further thought that the absence of uniformly high-quality early intervention programs can jeopardize the health and optimal development of our nation's vulnerable children and pose increasing challenges to the ability of families to function effectively.

This systems-level thinking was central to the Education of the Handicapped Act Amendments of 1986 (PL 99-457) and related early intervention legislative changes articulating a national agenda. In particular, focusing on the birth-to-3 age group, the purpose of this legislation was " . . . to develop and implement a statewide, comprehensive, coordinated, multidisciplinary, interagency system that provides early intervention services for infants and toddlers with disabilities and their families" (Individuals with Disabilities Education Act [IDEA] Amendments of 1997, PL 105-17, Section 631). States could also serve children at risk for developmental delays through this mechanism if they elected to do so. The law identified a number of *structural components* required for such a statewide system including establishing criteria for eligibility for services, ensuring that timely and appropriate assessments occurred, developing a process so that a family's needs and priorities were identified systematically, creating a proactive early identification and referral mechanism, establishing a procedure for developing a specific plan for comprehensive intervention, and ensuring that transitions from one program to another were carried out effectively and seamlessly.

Three- to five-year-old children were served under different provisions of the law. Although differences between the systems serving infants and toddlers and those serving preschool children were often substantial (e.g., less of an emphasis on family involvement for preschoolers), the basic elements remained intact. Accordingly, these requirements were intended to ensure both the existence of a well-coordinated and integrated early intervention system in each state and to ensure the consistency of the systems' structural components across states and communities. Nevertheless, much was left to the discretion of states to interpret and implement the systems they developed. In this manner, states could build on existing relationships and structures, including financing mechanisms, to meet federal requirements. Yet, despite considerable degrees of discretion accorded each state within the structure put forward, the reasonable expectation was that, over time, states would become more and more similar in their early intervention service and support systems. This would be brought about through national leadership and a common recognition by states and communities of the most effective approaches for each component of the system, gained through formal evaluations of the systems in effect and through informal communication channels. Of course, many differences would remain, but common fundamental components and corresponding practices would eventually come to characterize a national system. After all, the design of structural components of systems, such as those for effective screening and referral mechanisms or for multidisciplinary child assessments that could be conducted to obtain needed information, was based on common sources of knowledge provided by researchers and clinicians in the field. Similarly, it is reasonable to anticipate that neighboring states would soon see the value of establishing common eligibility criteria. Perhaps more difficult to achieve than the expected convergence with respect to structural components would be convergence with respect to various specific practices and service guidelines and even philosophical perspectives. But even here, it seemed reasonable that considerable agreement would evolve over time as approaches were clarified and evidence accumulated as to what were the most effective and efficient practices in meeting the needs of children who are vulnerable and their families.

Despite these expectations, analyses have revealed surprisingly large variations across states for many components of statewide early intervention systems. More specifically, substantial differences in practice have been found with respect to criteria for eligibility for services, ways in which families gain access to the system (points of access, transitions from program to program), and the comprehensiveness of the available services (Harbin, McWilliam, & Gallagher, 2000; Spiker, Hebbeler, Wagner, Cameto, & McKenna, 2000). Moreover, only limited state-level leadership has been apparent with respect to promoting systems-level issues. As the authors of a comprehensive study of infant and toddler early intervention systems, referred to as the National Early Intervention Longitudinal Study (NEILS), observed, "The early intervention professionals we interviewed in conducting the NEILS enrollment and those around the country with which we discussed the NEILS have been surprised that there was so much variation in early intervention systems" (Spiker et al., 2000, p. 205). Of importance, considerable variation was found not only across states but also within states.

This general concern about early childhood intervention at the systems level was shared in a comprehensive report from the Committee on Integrating the Science of Early Childhood Development of the National Academy of Sciences. Their analysis indicated that

> Early childhood policies and practices are highly fragmented, with complex and confusing points of entry that are particularly problematic for underserved segments of the population and those with special needs. . . . The time is long overdue for state and local decision makers to take bold actions to design and implement coordinated, functionally

effective infrastructures to reduce the long-standing fragmentation of early childhood policies and programs. (National Research Council and Institute of Medicine, 2000, pp. 309, 402)

PRINCIPLES OF EARLY INTERVENTION

As suggested, it was reasonable to anticipate not only that some common ground would emerge with respect to the various structural components of an early intervention system (e.g., points of access, eligibility, transition planning) but also that a set of common principles and corresponding practices governing systems design and implementation would emerge. That is, structural components and principles should jointly determine practices of the components and of the system as a whole. Indeed, certain principles were embedded in the legislation itself, which called for the early intervention system to center on families (maintain a strong developmental orientation), to maximize the participation of children and families in natural environments, to foster interactions with children without disabilities (inclusion), and to integrate and coordinate activities at all levels of the system. The press for child-find systems as a structural component reflected the principle of the importance of early identification. Moreover, the principle of individualization of intervention was found in many places in the legislation but especially in connection with the design of individualized family service plans (IFSPs) and individualized education programs (IEPs).

These and other principles that seem well accepted by the field are presented in Table 1.1. Nevertheless, as might be expected from the

Table 1.1. Principles of early intervention relevant to the Developmental Systems Model

A *developmental framework* informs all components of the early intervention system and *centers on families.*

Integration and coordination at all levels is apparent. This includes interdisciplinary assessments, assessments for program planning, developing and implementing comprehensive intervention plans, and systems level integration.

The *inclusion* and participation of children and families in typical community programs and activities are maximized.

Early detection and identification procedures are in place.

Surveillance and monitoring are an integral part of the system.

All parts of the system are *individualized.*

A strong *evaluation and feedback process* is evident.

It is recognized that *true partnerships with families* cannot occur without *sensitivity to cultural differences* and an *understanding of their developmental implications.*

There is a belief that recommendations to families and practices must be *evidence-based.*

A *systems perspective* is maintained, recognizing interrelationships among all components.

variability found in the implementation of the structural components, despite an apparent acceptance of these principles at a general level, considerable variability also exists with respect to the implementation of these principles in practice (Guralnick, in press-b; Harbin et al., 2000). Differences in interpretations, access to information, and resource availability, or variations in commitment to certain principles and corresponding values, may account for much of this cross-community variability. As discussed next, variability is perhaps most apparent for what might best be referred to as core principles (i.e., developmental framework, inclusion, integration, and coordination). Although all of the principles listed in Table 1.1 could legitimately be considered "core," these four principles have been most prominent in the field, with important implications for concepts, values, and practices in early intervention systems.

IMPLEMENTATION OF PRINCIPLES

The most fundamental principle is that a developmental orientation should be represented in each structural component and corresponding practice of every early intervention system (Guralnick, 1998; National Research Council and Institute of Medicine, 2000; Sameroff & Fiese, 2000). The most critical feature of this developmental orientation principle is that interventions center on families. This principle includes concepts related to parent empowerment, the establishment of parent–professional partnerships, and recognition of the significance of family patterns of interaction to children's development and well-being. Yet, even when latitude is given with respect to interpretations of this principle and the diversity of practice settings, the general consensus is that the field of early intervention has not yet embraced a developmental framework as reflected in actual practice (see Bruder, 2000; Guralnick, in press-b; and Harbin et al., 2000, for details). The same can be said for the principle of inclusion, although most subscribe to this principle at a conceptual level. Similar to the difficulties encountered for the principle of maintaining a developmental framework, universal access to inclusive programs is far from a reality, practices differ radically from community to community without any apparent rationale, and controversy is common across states with respect to how to interpret and apply the concept of natural environments (see Guralnick, 2001c, for a detailed review). In short, widely different practices exist with respect to maximizing the participation of children and their families in typical community settings and activities. Of note, the extraordinary compatibility of the core principles of inclusion and developmental framework is only now being recognized fully, given that integrating early interventions within family routines (Bernheimer & Keogh, 1995) and community learning activities (Bruder, 2001; Dunst, 2001) also support inclusive practices.

Evidence also indicates that the core principle of integration and coordination has yet to be effectively applied to many components of the early intervention system. For example, at the systems level, interagency coordination approaches take many forms in different states, and these variations are associated with differing levels of comprehensiveness of services and set limits on the types of integration that can occur (Harbin et al., 2000; Spiker et al., 2000). Leadership through decision making and training mechanisms to establish policies to improve integration and coordination are similarly lacking across states (Spiker et al., 2000). It comes as little surprise that families frequently identify service coordination as a major concern (Harbin et al., 2000). Moreover, available evidence suggests that interdisciplinary teams designed to provide comprehensive assessments, as well as to deliver services, often lack the degree of integration and coordination needed to take full advantage of the benefits of interdisciplinary activities (Bruder, 1996; see Guralnick, 2000c). The importance of cross-discipline collaboration poses additional challenges as collaborative consultation models are emerging as best practices in the field (McWilliam, 1996). This approach has the potential to integrate many disparate discipline-specific services into a coherent package of interventions that have considerable functional value for children and families (Dunst, Trivette, Humphries, Raab, & Roper, 2001; Hanft & Pilkington, 2000). As a consequence, when fully implemented, the collaborative consultation approach is consistent not only with the principle of integration and coordination but also with the other two core principles of developmental framework and inclusion.

The other principles listed in Table 1.1 that guide systems of early intervention, however, have not been fully realized in practice. Exemplary models that represent some of the principles do indeed exist, but they constitute only isolated examples in a context of enormous variability in comprehensiveness and effectiveness. For example, few communities have comprehensive systems to identify children at risk as early as possible. In particular, it is difficult to coordinate approaches designed to identify children at substantial risk for developmental delays. Professional organizations continue to develop guidelines for early identification (e.g., American Academy of Pediatrics, 2001), but numerous barriers remain in the design of comprehensive systems, including costs (Dobrez et al., 2001) and general problems associated with interagency coordination. Moreover, sophisticated procedures for early identification of children with specific disorders such as autism are now emerging, posing additional challenges to effectively implementing the principle of early identification (Filipek et al., 2000). Similarly, communication and professional training mechanisms are not yet available to ensure that practices are fully evidence based. The importance of this principle of evidence-based practices has certainly been recognized, and progress continues to be made to develop appropriate practice guidelines (New York State Department of Health, 1999; Sandall, McLean, & Smith, 2000). Yet, the research-to-practice gap remains a major concern, (e.g., Bruder, 2000; Rule, Losardo, Dinnebeil, Kaiser, & Rowland, 1998). Indeed, considering possible future difficulties in narrowing the research-to-practice gap, the Committee on Integrating the Science of Early Childhood Development reached the following conclusion: "As the rapidly evolving science of early childhood development continues to grow, its complexity will increase and the distance between the working knowledge of service providers and the cutting edge of science will be staggering" (National Research Council and Institute of Medicine, 2000, p. 402). Clearly, much needs to be done to implement the principle regarding evidence-based practices in early intervention.

PROSPECTS FOR SYSTEMS CHANGE

These many systems issues constitute legitimate concerns, and their impact on the effectiveness of early intervention programs should not be underestimated. At the same time, it is important to recognize the sources of this variability and to avoid the tendency to simply criticize the system and identify its inadequacies. After all, this variability may well be an intrinsic part of the evolution of the system of early intervention as it passes through various stages of development and refinement (see Guralnick, 2000a). The fact is, there has been a considerable increase in the number of children and families entering the early intervention system over the years. Services are provided annually to more than 800,000 children from birth to 5 years under IDEA '97 (U.S. Department of Education, 2001). The array of services provided is complex and diverse (Guralnick, in press-b; U.S. Department of Education, 2001), and families seem generally satisfied with those services. Nevertheless, increasing complexity poses a formidable challenge to any system, as does the rapid pace of knowledge and demands of professional training. Moreover, some of the variability can be traced to the fact that new systems should experiment with different models and try to work out the best approaches. Given the history of different working relationships and financing patterns, it is not surprising that communities would start at different points with different approaches.

Consequently, these differences found in states and communities with respect to both systems structure and adherence to generally accepted early intervention principles are understandable, at least to a certain degree. Yet, there do not appear to be any systematic efforts under way to examine these differences to determine the most effective strategies or to address the many problems that have been identified. Admittedly, the complexity of the task can easily overwhelm even the most dedicated of professionals. It is not that these problems are unrecognized but that there appears to be no framework to provide guidance for improving the system. To improve the system, the components of an "ideal" system need to be identified or clarified, consideration must be given as to how the principles of early intervention can be applied to relevant structural components, and processes and protocols to guide specific practices consistent with systems components and principles must be available. Should this occur, and communities move to adopt such a system, consistency of early intervention programs across communities should increase substantially, and early intervention systems will be better able to effectively meet the needs of children and families.

It is important to point out at the outset that uniformity of early intervention systems across states and communities is not and should not be expected. Legitimate differences of opinion on early intervention approaches do exist and will continue to exist. In fact, the absence of definitive information with respect to many practice aspects of early intervention will ensure that differences across communities and communities' interpretations of existing knowledge and principles will remain. As noted previously, however, professionals' knowledge has advanced so that systems components, principles, and practices can now be identified in sufficient detail to generate a rational framework for the design of a comprehensive early intervention system. One such approach, the Developmental Systems Model (Guralnick, 2001b), is discussed next and is the basis for the conceptual and organizational framework for this volume.

DEVELOPMENTAL SYSTEMS MODEL

The remainder of this chapter outlines the overarching framework for the Developmental Systems Model. This framework provides a rationale for many structural components and principles, with a strong developmental orientation. Next, each structural component of the model is discussed and its relationship to core and related principles as well as to the overarching framework is highlighted. This is followed by a discussion of steps and the type of leadership that will be required for this system to be developed and established. The final section discusses international perspectives for early intervention systems and the insights that such perspectives can provide with respect to the Developmental Systems Model or to other frameworks that may be put forward.

Overarching Framework

When considering the major experientially based influences on child development, the developmental science of normative development has identified that three types of family patterns of interaction are critical: 1) the quality of parent–child transactions, 2) family-orchestrated child experiences, and 3) health and safety provided by the family (Guralnick, 1998, see Figure 1.1). Constructs associated with parent–child transactions have been extensively investigated, with demonstrated links either singly or in concert with child developmental outcomes. Most well established are the relationship constructs of reciprocating, being sensitive, providing affectively warm social exchanges, having discourse-based interactions, and avoiding intrusiveness (e.g., Guralnick, in press-a; Landry, Smith, Swank, Assel, & Vellet, 2001; Landry, Smith, Swank, & Miller-Loncar, 2000; National Research Council and Institute of Medicine, 2000). Constructs in which families orchestrate specific experiences for their children also have been identified and have been consistently associated with child developmental outcomes. Providing developmentally appropriate materials, organizing activities compatible with the child's special interests or special needs, choosing quality child care, incorporating the child into family

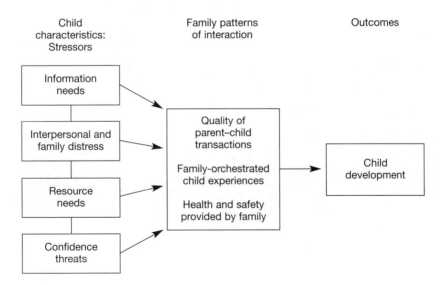

Figure 1.1. The relationships among potential stressors on families due to child characteristics, family patterns of interaction, and child developmental outcomes for children with a biological risk or those with established disabilities. (From Guralnick, M.J. [2000a]. Early childhood intervention: Evolution of a system. In M. Wehmeyer & J.R. Patton [Eds.], *Mental retardation in the 21st century* [p. 40]. Austin, TX: PRO-ED; adapted by permission.)

routines, and organizing social activities especially in connection with peers are examples of this family pattern of interaction (Bernheimer & Keogh, 1995; Bradley, Corwyn, Burchinal, McAdoo, & Coll, 2001; Ladd, Profilet, & Hart, 1992; NICHD Early Child Care Research Network, 2001).

The third family pattern of interaction addresses the health and safety needs of children. Parents are responsible for ensuring their children's well-being, the absence of which also poses significant challenges to other family patterns of interaction. Obtaining immunizations, providing adequate nutrition, and ensuring protection from harm are vital parental roles that have a potentially major impact on child developmental outcomes (Cicchetti & Lynch, 1995; Osofsky, 1995; Taylor, Zuckerman, Harik, & Groves, 1994).

Variations in family patterns of interaction can be considerable, and many reasonable pathways offer optimal developmental outcomes (Guralnick, in press-a; National Research Council and Institute of Medicine, 2000). Nevertheless, these relationships between family patterns of interaction and child developmental outcomes provide important details to guide the core principle of maintaining a developmental orientation in the Developmental Systems Model. More specifically, this orientation suggests that the central goal of early intervention for children who are at risk is to optimize these three family patterns of interaction. Child-focused therapeutic activities may be needed but are best considered among the experiences orchestrated by families. Relatedly, this overarching developmental framework for the Developmental Systems Model clearly indicates that it centers on families and that any interventions must similarly place families at the center.

Stressors to Family Interaction Patterns

When a child is born with a biological risk, such as being born prematurely with low birth weight, or when a child with an established disability enters a family, the developmental science of risk and disability indicates that stress is placed on most if not all aspects of these three family patterns of interaction. As illustrated in Figure 1.1, the child-generated stressors that can perturb family patterns of interaction can take many forms. Information needs about a child's diagnosis and likely developmental patterns are of paramount concern to families early in the process. Accurate information and proper resolution of these issues are essential to ensure the quality of parent–child transactions as well as to maintain other aspects of family patterns of interaction (e.g., Barnett, Clements, Kaplan-Estrin, & Fialka, 2003; Pianta, Marvin, Britner, & Borowitz, 1996). Later in the process, parents must make numerous decisions regarding intervention programs and activities and identify specialists sensitive to their needs (e.g., establish a medical home for their child). Evaluating these intervention options in the context of family life and routines is an important role for families, which can substantially affect family patterns of interaction (Bernheimer & Keogh, 1995). Similarly, interpersonal and family distress in the form of social isolation of the family, shared stigma, or negative emotional effects on families due to their child's developmental and behavioral problems can adversely affect numerous aspects of family patterns of interaction (Goffman, 1963; Krauss, 1993; Roach, Orsmond, & Barratt, 1999). Moreover, a child with a biological risk or one with an established disability can require substantially increased resources. Financial stability can be affected, even with the availability of government-sponsored programs. Furthermore, families may confront considerable challenges with respect to caregiving and established family routines (Dyson, 1993; Gallimore, Weisner, Bernheimer, Guthrie, & Nihira, 1993). Clearly, this category of child-generated stressors, referred to as resource needs, can adversely affect family patterns of interaction. Finally, the cumulative impact of these child-related stressors can undermine the confidence of families in their ability to competently address the many child-specific and larger family issues that exist now or will arise in the future. Should such an attitude take hold in the family, it could have a pervasive and highly damaging influence on family patterns of interaction.

These are only a few examples of the challenges that families may contend with as a consequence of a child with a biological risk or one with an established developmental disability. Information needs, interpersonal and family distress, resource needs, and confidence threats can independently or jointly be of sufficient magnitude to stress one or more family patterns of interaction. When this occurs, optimal child developmental outcomes, above and beyond other factors influencing development, are compromised (see Guralnick, 1998, in press-a).

The operation of these processes is especially apparent for children with an established disability such as Down syndrome. The development of these children will clearly be adversely affected under any circumstances, but, as indicated, nonoptimal family patterns of interaction (i.e., due to stressors associated with child characteristics) can further contribute to children's developmental problems. Consequently, within this framework, the task of the early intervention system is to minimize or prevent these stressors from creating nonoptimal family patterns of interaction, thereby maintaining a family's strengths. This can be accomplished by first assessing stressors and then, where appropriate, working together with families to develop and implement an array of resource supports, social supports, and information and services. If carried out properly, then families will be strengthened in a manner that permits them to maintain as optimal a level of family patterns of interaction as possible (see Guralnick,

2004). When this occurs, evidence from intervention science suggests that child developmental outcomes improve substantially (see Guralnick, 1997a, 1998).

The Developmental Systems Model attempts to be consistent with this framework. The assessment of stressors is a major component of the model, as is the provision of resource supports, social supports, and information and services linked to those assessments. The comprehensiveness of the early intervention program is especially critical, as the success of intervention will depend on the ability of the system to address the numerous issues that can stress family patterns of interaction. It is the cumulative impact that matters (see Guralnick, 2001a).

Environmental Risk

To this point, an assumption has been made that families possess the ability to generate optimal family patterns of interaction in the absence of stressors due to child characteristics. But, of course, many families are not so fortunate. Indeed, many family characteristics themselves can function to stress all aspects of family interaction patterns. Figure 1.2

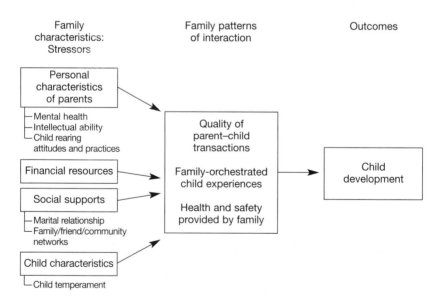

Figure 1.2. The relationship among potential stressors due to family characteristics, family patterns of interaction, and child developmental outcomes for children at environmental risk. (From Guralnick, M.J. [2001b]. A developmental systems model for early intervention. *Infants and Young Children, 14*[2], 3. Copyright © 2001 by Lippincott, Williams & Wilkins; reprinted by permission.)

illustrates this point. As indicated, personal characteristics of the family can be of considerable significance. More specifically, if a parent's mental health is compromised, especially if the mother is depressed; if a parent's intellectual abilities are diminished; or if nonoptimal, usually intergenerationally transmitted, child-rearing practices are evident, then family patterns of interaction will clearly be perturbed (e.g., Feldman, 1997). Poverty, the absence of social supports, and even difficult child characteristics unrelated to the child's risk status or disability could create similar adverse effects (Crnic & Stormshak, 1997; Linver, Brooks-Gunn, & Kohen, 2002).

These family characteristics that can affect the three family patterns of interaction are often referred to as "risk factors" (Burchinal, Roberts, Hooper, & Zeisel, 2000; Sameroff, Seifer, Barocas, Zax, & Greenspan, 1987), suggesting that preventive intervention programs might be capable of at least minimizing adverse child developmental outcomes. The Developmental Systems Model includes a preventive intervention component. It also includes an assessment of stressors in connection with these family characteristics. Of importance, a comprehensive intervention program related to family characteristics has the same components as that for child characteristics that function as stressors to family interaction patterns (i.e., the provision of resource supports, social supports, and information and services). However, because of the unusual difficulties associated with adverse family characteristics, particularly difficulties in addressing serious parental mental health problems or issues related to chronic poverty, it is clear that interventions under these circumstances may well take substantially different forms. Primary among these approaches is intervention-oriented child care (Guralnick, 2000b). Nevertheless, the goal of strengthening families to maximize family patterns of interaction remains unchanged. Given the increasing association between adverse family characteristics, such as poverty and childhood disability (Bowe, 1995; Park, Turnbull, & Turnbull, 2002; Hanson & Carta, 1995), a comprehensive assessment of stressors stemming from both child and family characteristics will be needed in any early intervention system and will require a correspondingly comprehensive intervention program.

In summary, this section has attempted to integrate the developmental science of normative development and the developmental science of risk and disability into a coherent overarching developmental framework that has served as the foundation for the Developmental Systems Model. Experientially based mediators of child developmental outcomes (i.e., family patterns of interaction) have been identified and provide direction for early intervention systems design when those patterns are stressed either by child or family characteristics. The intent of the Developmental Systems Model (see the following summary of components) is to generate an approach consistent with the overarching developmental framework just described as well as with the core and related principles discussed previously in this chapter.

COMPONENTS OF THE DEVELOPMENTAL SYSTEMS MODEL

The key structural components and relationships among the components of the Developmental Systems Model are presented in Figure 1.3. Diamonds represent decision points, and rectangles represent activities. Each of the major components constitutes its own microsystem involving relationships with other components, a process to follow in order to establish and carry out goals and activities, and protocols and related tools to gather information and to guide decision making. As noted, each structural component is intended to be compatible with and to some degree represent the overarching developmental framework as well as the core and related principles. This section briefly considers each component (see Guralnick, 2001b, for additional details) from an organizational perspective. Of note, the term *community* is used here in its most general sense and can be applied to an entire state, a single county, a designated service area, or any entity capable of incorporating all systems components. The central point here is that the Developmental Systems Model is intended to provide an overall framework for communities, including an organizational structure and corresponding principles, capable of guiding actual practices. There are issues and concerns associated with each component that must be addressed to properly implement the Developmental Systems Model from a practice perspective, and those are discussed next. For this model or any other approach to become a reality, however, the detailed functions of each component must be established and achieve some reasonable level of consensus. Accordingly, a major purpose of this volume is to begin that process with respect to the Developmental Systems Model.

Screening Program and Referral

The Screening Program and Referral component of the model is quite complex and is intended to be consistent with the principle regarding the importance of early detection and identification. For a variety of reasons, including the difficult task of integrating health, educational, and social services agencies in the process of screening and referral; concerns about the psychometric properties and cultural relevance of many screening tools; and the absence of a coherent cross-discipline approach to screening, community-based programs are highly variable (see Belcher, 1996). Important tools relying on parent reports are available (Bricker & Squires,

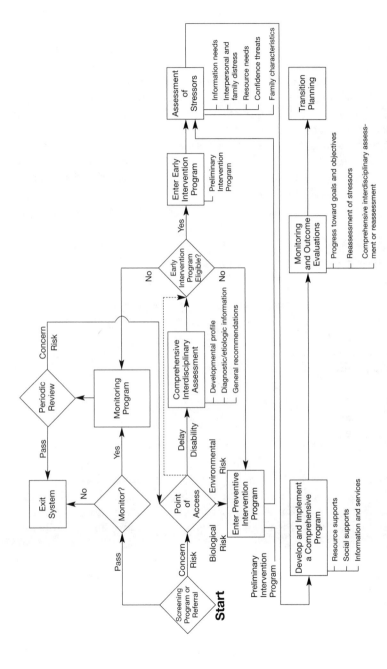

Figure 1.3. A developmental systems model for early intervention for vulnerable children and their families. (From Guralnick, M.J. [2001b]. A developmental systems model for early intervention. *Infants and Young Children, 14*[2], 4. Copyright © 2001 by Lippincott, Williams, & Wilkins; reprinted by permission.)

1999; Glascoe, 1998) as are well-developed protocols focusing on specific disabilities such as autism spectrum disorders (Filipek et al., 2000). Risk indices also are useful and available for the screening and referral process, despite considerable statistical uncertainty (Burchinal et al., 2000). Nevertheless, evidence-based practices certainly can be developed to guide the design of this microsystem for individual communities.

The creation of an effective and efficient community-based Screening Program and Referral component will require an extraordinary level of cooperation among relevant parties to reach decisions and implement practices regarding even fundamental issues such as whether to emphasize targeted or universal screening. How to best involve primary care health providers, what algorithms should be established to guide decisions for referral, and which instruments and related protocols should be selected to direct the entire activity remain key issues requiring resolution by communities.

Monitoring and Surveillance

A similar set of issues is relevant to the Monitoring and Surveillance component of the Developmental Systems Model. For children screened who do not meet referral criteria or who maintain some risk status, a decision must be made as to the degree of Monitoring (i.e., frequency, form, cost) and Surveillance required. Given the variability and ongoing vulnerabilities in children's development, decisions must be made on an individualized basis in accordance with well–thought-through protocols. Such comprehensive protocols remain to be developed.

Point of Access

When a concern about development reaches some criterion (including parental concerns resulting in self-referral) or risks to development are deemed high enough, entry to the next component in the model occurs in the form of a Point of Access to the early intervention system. At some location, the process of gathering, integrating, and coordinating information occurs, and families are introduced to the possible services and supports the system can provide. In addition, the way the Developmental Systems Model is currently constructed, a distinction is made at this point between children at biological and environmental risk for developmental problems and those already exhibiting developmental delays or disabilities. This distinction reflects current practice as systems for preventive interventions for risk conditions largely are functionally separate from systems focusing on children with documented delays or disabilities. This is not necessarily an ideal structure, and efforts are under way to address this issue at many levels. This distinction further suggests usually different Points of Access for these two groups of children and perhaps for other subgroups as well, even within local communities. Indeed, determining how many Points of Access should be available is an important community decision as Points of Access will vary with respect to size, complexity, comprehensiveness, family friendliness, and the like. Available evidence suggests that very few comprehensive community programs exist, including the component related to Points of Access, that thoroughly integrate child and family services for all children at this early stage in the process (Harbin et al., 2000). This includes both preventive and early intervention activities. Of note, the way communities address Points of Access serves as an index of the overall level of integration and coordination of the service system in general—a core principle.

Comprehensive Interdisciplinary Assessment

For children with possible delays or disabilities, whatever the Point of Access, an important responsibility is to organize a Comprehensive Inter- disciplinary Assessment to obtain a general developmental profile for chil- dren, to evaluate aspects of family functioning, to gather information for diagnostic/etiologic purposes, and to make general recommendations (Guralnick, 2000c). This extremely valuable and complex assessment is often temporarily bypassed due to the need to move forward quickly or the limited availability of such comprehensive assessment teams in communities. In this case, a more streamlined assessment occurs with focused teams, often at the Point of Access. More formal interdisciplinary or single discipline assessments will follow as the need arises.

In view of the demands on the system for Comprehensive Interdisci- plinary Assessments, communities must find ways to increase availability and increase the efficiency of teams. Moreover, the development of spe- cialty teams for autism (Filipek et al., 2000) or metabolic disorders such as phenylketonuria (Trahms, Leavitt, Heffernan, & Garretson, 2000) must be included to optimize the effectiveness of this microsystem.

Eligibility

Whatever path is taken (see Figure 1.3), Eligibility decisions are made based on community-determined criteria, the next component of the model. This is the case for children entering the early intervention program (children with delays or disabilities) or those entering the preventive intervention program (based on biological and environmental risk factors). Two issues are important here. The first concerns the need for communities to ensure that those children not meeting Eligibility criteria remain in the system through the Monitoring and Surveillance component noted previously. Second, strong consideration should be given toward establishing consistent Eligibility criteria across states and certainly within states. To be sure, this decision will carry important financial implications, but having common Eligibility criteria is compatible with the spirit of IDEA '97 and addresses important issues of equity.

Assessment of Stressors

Once families enter the Intervention component (either preventive or early intervention), they will usually begin to receive services and supports immediately based on available information in what is generally referred to as a preliminary intervention program. This program, however, is modified and refined as the Assessment of Stressors component is implemented. In many respects, this component is at the heart of the Developmental Systems Model and embraces many of its principles. It most clearly reflects the overarching developmental framework, especially the focus on families; it sets the stage for the highly individualized nature of the Comprehensive Intervention Program to come; and it tests our ability in a very direct way to be sensitive to cultural differences in the formation of parent–professional partnerships. For this component to be effective, processes and protocols must be available to guide professionals in their interactions with families. Determining families' information needs, possible interpersonal and family distress, resource needs, or threats to their confidence to parent appropriately, as well as obtaining information about relevant family characteristics, is a complex and challenging task. If not carried out well, however, then the entire early intervention enterprise is jeopardized because the Assessment of Stressors is the key to ultimately supporting families to enable them to create optimal family patterns of interaction.

Develop and Implement a Comprehensive Program

Discussions between families and professionals about service options during the Assessment of Stressors component (information needs) certainly require knowledge of evidence-based practices. But this principle is most critical when families and professionals become involved in the component of the model referred to as Develop and Implement a Comprehensive Program. Together, a plan specifying resource supports, social supports, and information and services thoughtfully tailored to the stressors identified earlier must be developed in an effort to minimize the stress on family patterns of interaction. If carried out properly, then the plan will fit well within family routines and maximize active family participation where appropriate. Professionals must be particularly thoughtful here in applying the core principles of developmental framework, inclusion, and integration and coordination for this component to be effective. Much can be lost in the implementation phase. The availability of decision-rules for individualizing would be helpful as well, but substantial deviations from this principle are not likely by this point in the process.

Monitoring and Outcome Evaluations

Ensuring the effectiveness of any early intervention system requires an array of well-designed monitoring and evaluation approaches. As the principle requiring a strong evaluation and feedback process indicates, evaluation must occur at many levels, including evaluating progress toward goals and objectives, determining when it is necessary to reassess stressors, and deciding when comprehensive interdisciplinary assessments or reassessments are needed. Structurally, this constitutes the Monitoring and Outcome Evaluations component of the Developmental Systems Model.

Evaluation at the systems level is also important as effectiveness depends on the ability of the components of the system to link together. It is also critical to validate whether the core and related principles are being realized for each of the systems components. Parent reports, self-evaluation protocols for administrators and early intervention professionals, or external evaluations are relevant strategies for this important component of the Developmental Systems Model. Much needs to be developed for this component of the model.

Transition Planning

The final component of the model is Transition Planning. Such plans are essential because the developmental and behavioral patterns of children who are vulnerable are highly fragile and easily disrupted. Ensuring continuity and creating as seamless a transition as possible are vital. Transition can take many forms, including the shift from infant–toddler to preschool programs, when children move to an inclusive child care program, or when the transition is made from preschool to kindergarten. Numerous strategies are now available to maximize the effectiveness of this component (Pianta & Cox, 1999; Sainato & Morrison, 2001) but need to be developed further to enable communities to adopt and adapt these strategies to meet their needs.

PURPOSE OF THIS BOOK

Prior publications presented the conceptual foundations (Guralnick, 1998) and the organizational structure and supporting principles (Guralnick,

2001b) for the Developmental Systems Model. This volume enables communities to begin to apply the model in practice to their system of early intervention. The conceptual framework, organizational structure, and guiding principles provide an invaluable context for practical application, but of course, the translation process remains a highly complex undertaking. Numerous reasonable practice alternatives exist for each decision point (diamond) and activity (rectangle) in the model (see Figure 1.3), and clinical experience must always be factored into all decisions. However, because early intervention practices in far too many communities do not appear to have evolved into coherent systems, the availability of a specific approach such as the Developmental Systems Model may at least serve as a catalyst for communities to examine carefully their own approaches and practices. Considerations by communities, clusters of communities, state-level agencies, and even national organizations of strategies to improve the system of early intervention services and supports will certainly be to the advantage of children who are vulnerable and their families.

Accordingly, the purpose of this volume is to provide the next level of specificity for the Developmental Systems Model for early intervention. In Section I, *Principles*, the core principles of the Developmental Systems Model are discussed, including the overarching developmental framework, coordination and integration (see Chapter 2), and inclusion (see Chapter 3). In Section II, *Practices: National Perspectives*, each of the key components of the Developmental Systems Model is discussed to provide more specific guidance for communities in the United States wishing to further develop a particular component or to examine their current practices. In some instances, broad guidance is provided; in others, specific protocols and instruments are suggested. Efforts to build on and integrate knowledge, along with specific recommendations for communities, can be found for each structural component.

The component now referred to as Screening and Surveillance in early intervention systems (a combination of the screening and monitoring components illustrated in Figure 1.3) is addressed in the first chapter in Section II (see Chapter 4). This is followed by discussions of Points of Access (see Chapter 5) and Comprehensive Interdisciplinary Assessments (see Chapter 6). Given the central role of assessing stressors that may perturb family patterns of interaction in the Developmental Systems Model, four separate chapters focus on different stressors. This includes the child-related stressors of Information Needs of Families (see Chapter 7), Interpersonal and Family Distress as well as Threats to Confident Parenting (see Chapter 8), and the Resource Needs of Families (see Chapter 9). The Assessment of Family Characteristics that can serve as stressors completes this group of chapters (see Chapter 10). The final four chapters (Chapters 11–14) are concerned with the actual intervention features of the early intervention system. Chapters include Developing and Implementing Preventive Intervention Programs for Children at Risk, Developing and Implementing Early Intervention Programs for Children with Established Disabilities, Monitoring and Evaluation in Early Intervention Programs, and Ensuring Effective Transitions in Early Intervention.

It is important to emphasize that the information contained in this volume is merely designed to provide additional guidance for communities and will require considerable decision making and further development by individual communities for proper translations to practice to occur. For those communities interested in pursuing this model at the detailed implementation level, a process should be initiated among all relevant constituencies to examine their own practices using the Developmental Systems Model as a framework. If leadership were provided at the state level, then existing State Interagency Coordinating Councils would be most appropriate. If not, then local communities or clusters of communities around which early intervention services are organized could provide the leadership. It is hoped that when these planning groups complete their work, they will have selected specific protocols, instruments, and processes for each of the system components and ensured that the early intervention principles are thoroughly integrated within each component. It also is hoped that many of the suggestions made by experts in the various chapters of this volume will be of value and translate well to this next implementation level. But even if specific recommendations are not selected, communities in their deliberations certainly should consider the rationale for these suggestions.

Clearly, such a process will not result in a uniform set of services and supports across all communities. As noted previously, that is not the goal of the Developmental Systems Model, nor is it desirable. Yet, explicit or implicit adherence to specific conceptual approaches, organizational structures, and principles matters, as together these approaches, structures, and principles constitute a system of early intervention that influences the developmental course of young children who are vulnerable. Consequently, thoughtful development of a system of early intervention should be a high priority for every community.

Section III of this volume, *Practices: International Perspectives*, provides a discussion of various aspects of the Developmental Systems Model from international viewpoints. Leaders in early intervention in their respective countries have agreed to describe critical components of their early intervention systems and to relate them, wherever possible, to the conceptual framework, organizational structure, and principles of the Developmental Systems Model. Differences in history and culture make this country-by-country analysis especially interesting and instructive. Experts from Australia (Chapter 15), Austria (Chapter 16), Canada (Chapter 17), the

United Kingdom (Chapter 18), Greece (Chapter 19), Israel (Chapter 20), Italy (Chapter 21), Spain (Chapter 22), Sweden (Chapter 23), and developing countries (Chapter 24) provide unique insights into the design of early intervention systems. Nowhere is the need for flexibility in systems more apparent than in these chapters.

Despite vast differences in early intervention systems across countries, efforts are under way to bring professionals around the world together to share ideas and debate the issues. Perhaps the major forum for this is the International Society on Early Intervention (ISEI; http://depts.washing ton.edu/isei/), now representing professionals from 75 countries. Because many of the chapter authors in this section are active in ISEI, further discussions of global approaches to early intervention are assured, as this will continue to remain a topic of considerable importance as part of ISEI's Internet communications network, its formal publications (of which this volume is a part), and its conferences that bring people together for more intensive discussions. This exchange of ideas will certainly inform the Developmental Systems Model or other systems approaches to early intervention.

REFERENCES

American Academy of Pediatrics, Committee on Children with Disabilities. (2001). Developmental surveillance and screening of infants and young children. *Pediatrics, 108*, 192–196.

Barnett, D., Clements, M., Kaplan-Estrin, M., & Fialka, J. (2003). Rebuilding new dreams: Supporting parents' adaptation to their child with special needs. *Infants and Young Children, 3*, 184–200.

Belcher, H.M.E. (1996). Developmental screening. In A.J. Capute & P.J. Accardo (Eds.), *Developmental disabilities in infancy and childhood: Vol. I. The spectrum of developmental disabilities* (2nd ed., pp. 323–340). Baltimore: Paul H. Brookes Publishing Co.

Bernheimer, L.P., & Keogh, B.K. (1995). Weaving interventions into the fabric of everyday life: An approach to family assessment. *Topics in Early Childhood Special Education, 15*, 415–433.

Bowe, F.G. (1995). Population estimates: Birth-to-5 children with disabilities. *The Journal of Special Education, 20*, 461–471.

Bradley, F.H., Corwyn, R.F., Burchinal, M., McAdoo, H.P., & Coll, C.G. (2001). The home environments of children in the United States, Part II: Relations with behavioral development through age thirteen. *Child Development, 72*, 1868–1886.

Bricker, D., & Squires, J., with assistance from Mounts, L., Potter, L., Nickel, R., Twombly, E., & Farrell, J. (1999). *Ages & Stages Questionnaires® (ASQ): A parent-completed, child-monitoring system* (2nd ed.). Baltimore: Paul H. Brookes Publishing Co.

Bruder, M.B. (1996). Interdisciplinary collaboration in service delivery. In R.A. McWilliam (Ed.), *Rethinking pull-out services in early intervention* (pp. 27–48). Baltimore: Paul H. Brookes Publishing Co.

Bruder, M.B. (2000). Family-centered early intervention: Clarifying our values for the new millennium. *Topics in Early Childhood Special Education, 20*, 105–115.

Bruder, M.B. (2001). Inclusion of infants and toddlers: Outcomes and ecology. In M.J. Guralnick (Ed.), *Early childhood inclusion: Focus on change* (pp. 229–251). Baltimore: Paul H. Brookes Publishing Co.

Burchinal, M.R., Roberts, J.E., Hooper, S., & Zeisel, S.A. (2000). Cumulative risk and early cognitive development: A comparison of statistical risk models. *Developmental Psychology, 36,* 793–807.

Cicchetti, D., & Lynch, M. (1995). Failures in the expectable environment and their impact on individual development: The case of child maltreatment. In D. Cicchetti & D.J. Cohen (Eds.), *Developmental psychopathology: Vol. 2. Risk, disorder, and adaptation* (pp. 33–71). New York: John Wiley & Sons.

Crnic, K., & Stormshak, E. (1997). The effectiveness of providing social support for families of children at risk. In M.J. Guralnick (Ed.), *The effectiveness of early intervention* (pp. 209–225). Baltimore: Paul H. Brookes Publishing Co.

Dobrez, D., Sasso, A.L., Holl, J., Shalowitz, M., Leon, S., & Budetti, P. (2001). Estimating the cost of developmental and behavioral screening of preschool children in general pediatric practice. *Pediatrics, 108,* 913–922.

Dunst, C.J. (2001). Participation of young children with disabilities in community learning activities. In M.J. Guralnick (Ed.), *Early childhood inclusion: Focus on change* (pp. 307–333). Baltimore: Paul H. Brookes Publishing Co.

Dunst, C.J., Trivette, C.M., Humphries, T., Raab, M., & Roper, N. (2001). Contrasting approaches to natural learning environment interventions. *Infants and Young Children, 14*(2), 48–63.

Dyson, L.L. (1993). Response to the presence of a child with disabilities: Parental stress and family functioning over time. *American Journal on Mental Retardation, 98,* 207–218.

Education of the Handicapped Act Amendments of 1986, PL 99-457, 20 U.S.C. §§ 1400 *et seq.*

Feldman, M.A. (1997). The effectiveness of early intervention for children of parents with mental retardation. In M.J. Guralnick (Ed.), *The effectiveness of early intervention* (pp. 171–191). Baltimore: Paul H. Brookes Publishing Co.

Filipek, P.A., Accardo, P.J., Ashwal, S., Baranek, G.T., Cook, E.H., Jr., Dawson, G., et al. (2000). Practice parameter: Screening and diagnosis of autism. *Neurology, 55,* 468–479.

Gallimore, R., Weisner, T.S., Bernheimer, L.P., Guthrie, D., & Nihira, K. (1993). Family responses to young children with developmental delays: Accommodation activity in ecological and cultural context. *American Journal on Mental Retardation, 98,* 185–206.

Gilliam, W.S., & Zigler, E.F. (2001). A critical meta-analysis of all evaluations of state-funded preschool from 1977 to 1998: Implications for policy, service delivery and program evaluation. *Early Childhood Research Quarterly, 15,* 441–473.

Glascoe, F.P. (1998). *Parents' evaluations of developmental status (PEDS).* Nashville: Ellsworth & Vandermeer.

Goffman, E. (1963). *Stigma.* Upper Saddle River, NJ: Prentice Hall.

Guralnick, M.J. (Ed.). (1997a). *The effectiveness of early intervention.* Baltimore: Paul H. Brookes Publishing Co.

Guralnick, M.J. (1997b). Second generation research in the field of early intervention. In M.J. Guralnick (Ed.), *The effectiveness of early intervention* (pp. 3–22). Baltimore: Paul H. Brookes Publishing Co.

Guralnick, M.J. (1998). The effectiveness of early intervention for vulnerable children: A developmental perspective. *American Journal on Mental Retardation, 102,* 319–345.

Guralnick, M.J. (2000a). Early childhood intervention: Evolution of a system. In M. Wehmeyer & J.R. Patton (Eds.), *Mental retardation in the 21st century* (pp. 37–58). Austin, TX: PRO-ED.

Guralnick, M.J. (2000b). The early intervention system and out-of-home child care. In D. Cryer & T. Harms (Eds.), *Infants and toddlers in out-of-home care* (pp. 207–234). Baltimore: Paul H. Brookes Publishing Co.

Guralnick, M.J. (2000c). Interdisciplinary team assessment for young children: Purposes and processes. In M.J. Guralnick (Ed.), *Interdisciplinary clinical assessment for young children with developmental disabilities* (pp. 3–15). Baltimore: Paul H. Brookes Publishing Co.

Guralnick, M.J. (2001a). Connections between developmental science and intervention science. *Zero to Three, 21*(5), 24–29.

Guralnick, M.J. (2001b). A developmental systems model for early intervention. *Infants and Young Children, 14*(2), 1–18.

Guralnick, M.J. (2001c). A framework for change in early childhood inclusion. In M.J. Guralnick (Ed.), *Early childhood inclusion: Focus on change* (pp. 3–35). Baltimore: Paul H. Brookes Publishing Co.

Guralnick, M.J. (2004). Family investments in response to the developmental challenges of young children with disabilities. In A. Kalil & T. Deleire (Eds.), *Family investments in children's potential: Resources and behaviors that promote success* (pp. 119–137). Mahwah, NJ: Lawrence Erlbaum Associates.

Guralnick, M.J. (in press-a). Family influences on the development of young children's competence. In K. McCartney & D. Phillips (Eds.), *The Blackwell handbook of early childhood development.* Oxford, UK: Blackwell Publishers.

Guralnick, M.J. (in press-b). The system of early intervention for children with developmental disabilities: Current status and challenges for the future. In J.W. Jacobson & J.A. Mulick (Eds.), *Handbook of mental retardation and developmental disabilities.* New York: Plenum.

Hanft, B.E., & Pilkington, K.O. (2000). Therapy in natural environments: The means or end goal for early intervention? *Infants and Young Children, 12*(4), 1–13.

Hanson, M.J., & Carta, J.J. (1995). Addressing the challenges of families with multiple risks. *Exceptional Children, 62,* 201–212.

Harbin, G.L., McWilliam, R.A., & Gallagher, J.J. (2000). Services for young children with disabilities and their families. In J.P. Shonkoff & S.J. Meisels (Eds.), *Handbook of early childhood intervention* (2nd ed., pp. 387–415). New York: Cambridge University Press.

Individuals with Disabilities Education Act (IDEA) Amendments of 1997, PL 105-17, 20 U.S.C. §§ 1400 *et seq.*

Krauss, M.J. (1993). Child-related and parenting stress: Similarities and differences between mothers and fathers of children with disabilities. *American Journal on Mental Retardation, 97,* 393–404.

Ladd, G.W., Profilet, S.M., & Hart, C.H. (1992). Parents' management of children's peer relations: Facilitating and supervising children's activities in the peer culture. In R.D. Parke & G.W. Ladd (Eds.), *Family-peer relationships: Modes of linkage* (pp. 215–253). Mahwah, NJ: Lawrence Erlbaum Associates.

Landry, S.H., Smith, K.E., Swank, P.R., Assel, M.A., & Vellet, S. (2001). Does early responsive parenting have a special importance for children's development or is consistency across early childhood necessary? *Developmental Psychology, 37,* 387–403.

Landry, S.H., Smith, K.E., Swank, P.R., & Miller-Loncar, C.L. (2000). Early maternal and child influences on children's later independent cognitive and social functioning. *Child Development, 71,* 358–375.

Linver, M.R., Brooks-Gunn, J., & Kohen, D.E. (2002). Family processes as pathways from income to young children's development. *Developmental Psychology, 38,* 719–734.

McWilliam, R.A. (Ed.). (1996). *Rethinking pull-out services in early intervention: A professional resource.* Baltimore: Paul H. Brookes Publishing Co.

Meisels, S.J., & Shonkoff, J.P. (2000). Early childhood intervention: A continuing evolution. In J.P. Shonkoff & S.J. Meisels (Eds.), *Handbook of early childhood intervention* (2nd ed., pp. 3–31). New York: Cambridge University Press.

National Research Council and Institute of Medicine. (2000). *From neurons to neighborhoods: The science of early child development.* Committee on Integrating the Science of Early Childhood Development. Board on Children, Youth, and Families, Commission on Behavioral and Social Sciences and Education. Washington, DC: National Academy Press.

New York State Department of Health. (1999). *Clinical practice guideline. Report of the recommendations: Autism/pervasive developmental disorders, assessment and intervention for young children (age 0–3 years).* New York: Author.

NICHD Early Child Care Research Network. (2001). Nonmaternal care and family factors in early development: An overview of the NICHD Study of Early Child Care. *Applied Developmental Psychology, 22*, 457–492.

Osofsky, J.D. (1995). The effects of violence exposure on young children. *American Psychologist, 50*, 782–788.

Park, J., Turnbull, A.P., & Turnbull, H.R. (2002). Impacts of poverty on quality of life in families of children with disabilities. *Exceptional Children, 68*, 151–170.

Pianta, R.C., & Cox, M.J. (Eds.). (1999). *The transition to kindergarten.* Baltimore: Paul H. Brookes Publishing Co.

Pianta, R.C., Marvin, R.S., Britner, P.A., & Borowitz, K.C. (1996). Mothers' resolution of their children's diagnosis: Organized patterns of caregiving representations. *Journal of Infant Mental Health, 17*, 239–256.

Roach, M.A., Orsmond, G.I., & Barratt, M.S. (1999). Mothers and fathers of children with Down syndrome: Parental stress and involvement in childcare. *American Journal on Mental Retardation, 104*, 422–436.

Rule, S., Losardo, A., Dinnebeil, L.A., Kaiser, A., & Rowland, C. (1998). Research challenges in naturalistic intervention. *Journal of Early Intervention, 21*, 283–293.

Sainato, D.M., & Morrison, R.S. (2001). Transition to inclusive environments for young children with disabilities: Toward a seamless system of service delivery. In M.J. Guralnick (Ed.), *Early childhood inclusion: Focus on change* (pp. 293–306). Baltimore: Paul H. Brookes Publishing Co.

Sameroff, A.J., & Fiese, B.H. (2000). Models of development and developmental risk. In C.H. Zeanah, Jr. (Ed.), *Handbook of infant mental health* (pp. 3–19). New York: The Guilford Press.

Sameroff, A.J., Seifer, R., Barocas, R., Zax, M., & Greenspan, S. (1987). Intelligence quotient scores of 4-year-old children: Social-environmental risk factors. *Pediatrics, 79*, 343–350.

Sandall, S., McLean, M., & Smith, B. (2000). *DEC recommended practices in intervention/early childhood special education.* Longmont, CO: Sopris West.

Smith, B.J., & McKenna, P. (1994). Early intervention public policy: Past, present, and future. In L.J. Johnson, R.J. Gallagher, M.J. LaMontagne, J.B. Jordan, J.J. Gallagher, P.L. Hutinger, & M.B. Karnes (Eds.), *Meeting early intervention challenges: Issues from birth to three* (pp. 251–264). Baltimore: Paul H. Brookes Publishing Co.

Spiker, D., Hebbeler, K., Wagner, M., Cameto, R., & McKenna, P. (2000). A framework for describing variations in state early intervention systems. *Topics in Early Childhood Special Education, 20*, 195–207.

Taylor, L., Zuckerman, B., Harik, V., & Groves, B.M. (1994). Witnessing violence by young children and their mothers. *Journal of Developmental and Behavioral Pediatrics, 15*, 120–123.

Trahms, C.M., Leavitt, A., Heffernan, J., & Garretson, J. (2000). An infant with phenylketonuria. In M.J. Guralnick (Ed.), *Interdisciplinary clinical assessment for young children with developmental disabilities* (pp. 269–280). Baltimore: Paul H. Brookes Publishing Co.

U.S. Department of Education. (2001). *Twenty-third annual report to Congress on the implementation of the Individuals with Disabilities Education Act.* Washington, DC: U.S. Government Printing Office.

CHAPTER 2

SERVICE COORDINATION AND INTEGRATION IN A DEVELOPMENTAL SYSTEMS APPROACH TO EARLY INTERVENTION

MARY BETH BRUDER

My son, Jason, woke up vomiting again, but at least he only woke up once during the night. Jason was born 2 months premature and has struggled since his birth. Jason currently has seven different specialists (not all in the same cities), as well as our Birth to Three providers that include two evaluators, a physical therapist, an occupational therapist, and a special education teacher. I change the set-up for Jason's feeding pump while I try to clean him up. After another load of laundry, I am able to get him to drink an ounce and a half of formula. As I am congratulating him for his accomplishment, I remember that the occupational therapist is coming to work on his feeding skills. I hope she comes prepared to do something else because Jason won't be hungry when she gets here, and I hope she understands that I don't want to sit and watch anymore. I need to learn ways to incorporate these skills and techniques into our everyday lives if Jason is ever going to improve.

There are not enough hours in the day to work on all the different things that the providers and physicians tell me are so important. Each specialist has a different focus and agenda. I want to be a good mom, but it is impossible for me to do all of the prescribed activities every day. And why can't they ever meet together? At least they could then talk to each other.

At 8 A.M. I get a telephone call from the nursing agency telling me my nurse is sick (this is the second Tuesday in a row) and they do not have a

---

The author expresses gratitude to the investigators at the Research and Training Center on Service Coordination: Gloria Harbin, Ph.D., Kathleen Whitbread, Ph.D., Michael Conn-Powers, Ph.D., Carl Dunst, Ph.D., Richard Roberts, Ph.D., and Melissa Van Buren, Ph.D.

replacement for her. I can't get anyone else, so I call work to tell them I won't be in again. I have been trying so hard to find a back-up child care arrangement. The good news is that Jason won't have to miss swimming because I will be home to drive him. We get charged for the pool time whether we use it or not. It's ironic that my insurance pays for a physical therapist appointment, but we do not get any help to pay for swimming, even though he does more there than he does with the physical therapist. I check our schedule board at home and realize Jason has a nephrology appointment tomorrow at 4 P.M. I had planned to take part of the day off, but because I will miss work today, I will have to see if my husband can take him to that appointment. Keeping track of Jason's appointments is time consuming, and having to make choices based on 10 differing opinions and trying to prioritize these choices is exhausting. I can't even attempt to integrate them into the type of life I want for my family.

SERVICE INTEGRATION IN EARLY INTERVENTION

Through Part C of the Individuals with Disabilities Education Act (IDEA) Amendments of 1997 (PL 105-17), Congress identified an "urgent and substantial" need to enhance the development of infants and toddlers with disabilities, as well as enhance the capacity of families to meet the special needs of their infants and toddlers with disabilities. The attention on families in this law was a welcome provision that acknowledged the important role of parents in the development of their child. As a result, early intervention programs have tried to provide enrolled families with a sense of confidence and competence about their children's current and future learning and development (Bailey et al., 1998; Dunst, 2000; Turnbull & Turnbull, 1997). One of the ways this can happen is through the development of early intervention systems that are coordinated around a family's priorities, most important as they relate to meeting the special needs of their child.

A core principle of the developmental systems approach of early intervention is the coordination and integration of agencies, services, and personnel within the key components of service delivery as outlined in Chapter 1 (see also Guralnick, 2001). This principle has been a cornerstone of early intervention for as many years as there have been formalized systems of service delivery (Elder & Magrab, 1980; Swan & Morgan, 1993). In addition, and more important, service integration has been a component of service delivery from as far back as the colonial period, and it has been a hallmark of social services availability (Kagan & Neville, 1993).

This is not surprising as there are obvious benefits to integrated, collaborative service delivery models, the most important being an improvement in service delivery to the target population. This occurs as a result of more efficient and effective use of services, providers, and funding streams across agencies (Dinnebeil, Hale, & Rule, 1999; Roberts, Innocenti, & Goetze, 1999; Summers et al., 2001), and reduction in service duplication (Bruder & Bologna, 1993). In addition, collaborative efforts enable parents and service providers to efficiently locate and manage the varied resources, supports, and services required by a family (Dunst & Bruder, 2002). Unfortunately, in analyzing the long history surrounding the concept of service integration, one is struck by its nobility of intent, its tenacity of purpose, and its ineffectiveness in implementation (Kagan & Neville, 1993).

No one in the field of early intervention would argue that infants and toddlers with disabilities, or those at risk for disability, often require the combined expertise of numerous personnel, services, and agencies (Bruder & Bologna, 1993). For example, personnel having medical expertise, therapeutic expertise, and educational/developmental and social services expertise traditionally have been involved in the provision of services to infants and young children with disabilities and their families (Stayton & Bruder, 1999). However, the coordination and integration of these entities are frequently overwhelming. Each of these service providers may represent a different professional discipline, be employed by a different agency, and practice under conflicting philosophical models of service delivery. In fact, at the service level, coordination can be fraught with tension because of the inherent structure of personnel preparation programs and subsequent discipline-specific practices (Bruder & Dunst, in preparation; Kilgo & Bruder, 1997). Each discipline has its own training sequence (some require undergraduate degrees), licensing and/or certification requirements (most of which do not require age specialization for young children), and treatment modality (e.g., occupational therapists may focus on sensory integration techniques; Bruder, 2000; McCollum, 2000). Equally problematic are those issues confronting the agencies that employ early intervention personnel (see Table 2.1). Whether at the agency, service, or personnel level, such issues add to the perception that child development and family support are the products of independent domains, rather than an interdependent interaction across processes (Guralnick, 2001).

The purpose of this chapter is to address the issues related to service coordination and integration within the developmental systems approach to early intervention: in particular for infants and young children who are eligible for Part C services under IDEA. Although the majority of this population must have an established disability or delay to qualify for services, infants and toddlers at risk for disability also are eligible for services

Table 2.1.   Issues in interagency collaboration

Competitiveness between agencies
  Turf issues
  Lack of information about other agencies' functions
  Political issues
Lack of organizational structure for coordination
  Differing philosophies
  Independent goals
  Haphazard team process
  Lack of a facilitator
  Lack of monitoring and evaluation process
  Lack of planning
  Lack of power and authority to make and implement decisions
Technical factors
  Resources: staff, time, budget
  Logistics: distance, geography
Personnel
  Parochial interests
  Resistance to change
  Poor staff attitudes
  Lack of commitment to community needs
  Questionable administrative support
  Discipline-specific jargon and perspectives

in seven states; thus the impact of the federal legislation in these states reaches a wider range of children and families in need of early intervention. The primary reason for the focus on Part C is because of the collaborative nature of both the spirit and letter of the law, thus laying a foundation for coordination and integration across and within all levels of service delivery. However, the intent of this emphasis is not to negate the effectiveness of practices demonstrated by case management or care coordination conducted under the auspices of other early intervention programs serving specific populations (Kagan & Neuman, 2000; Nickel, Cooley, McAllister, & Samson-Fang, 2003; Roberts, Behl, & Akers, 1996b; Rosman & Knitzer, 2001; Smith, Gabard, Dale, & Drucker, 1994; Summers et al., 2001) but rather to view service coordination and integration within the most cohesive service delivery frame available. In doing so, the chapter will rely on a definition of service integration that has evolved from the work of Kagan and Neville (1993) and Kagan, Goffin, Golub, and Pritchard (1995). Service integration is the realization of a truly collaborative model of early intervention that involves all supports and services that a family uses, regardless of whether the supports and services are related to a child's disability.

SERVICE COORDINATION AND
INTEGRATION IN PART C OF IDEA

In 1986, Part H of the Education of the Handicapped Act Amendments (now Part C of IDEA) created an early intervention program with much promise. Inherent in this program was the concept of a statewide system of family-centered, culturally competent, coordinated, comprehensive, multidisciplinary, interagency early intervention services for infants and toddlers with disabilities and their families (Hanson & Bruder, 2001). This concept required a commitment by all service agencies and providers to cooperatively and collaboratively plan, implement, and evaluate services that enhance the development of an eligible child and the capacity of the family to meet the special needs of the child. To do this, the law required coordination and collaboration at both the state and local level. For example, specific requirements included and still include

1. **The establishment of statewide interagency coordinating councils (ICCs) composed of parents and representatives from relevant state agencies and service providers.** These councils must consist of between 15 and 25 members, and the chair must not be from the lead agency. Councils may vary in how many agencies are represented, and at least 20% of the membership must be parents.

2. **The maintenance of a lead agency for general administration, supervision, and monitoring of programs and activities, including responsibility for carrying out the entry into formal interagency agreements and the resolution of disputes.** Approximately 15 states have chosen the Department of Health as their lead agency; 16 others have the Department of Health and another agency; 13 have the Department of Education; and 12 have other agencies as lead.

3. **The development of interagency and multidisciplinary models of service delivery for eligible infants, toddlers, and their families as specified in the individualized family service plan (IFSP), which is directed by the family.** *Multidisciplinary* has been further defined by the U.S. Department of Education to mean efforts involving people representing at least two disciplines. The IFSP is required to have integrated goals and objectives for each child and family.

4. **The appointment of a service coordinator to facilitate and ensure the implementation of the IFSP.** The service coordinator is responsible for the implementation of the IFSP and for ongoing coordination with other agencies and individuals to ensure the timely and effective delivery of services.

Collectively, these components provide a framework to describe the collaborative foundation of early intervention under Part C, and individually they contribute to the development of comprehensive systems of early intervention. Yet, data collected by the Research and Training Center on Service Coordination (2004), as well as others (Campbell & Halbert, 2002; Dinnebeil, Hale, & Rule, 1996; Roberts, Akers, & Behl, 1996a, 1996b; Wesley, Buysse, & Tyndall, 1997), suggested difficulty implementing true service integration: the result being that agencies, services, and personnel operate as independent entities when interfacing with families. The promises of early intervention service integration have yet to be realized, as demonstrated by Jason's mother at the beginning of the chapter.

STATE MODELS OF SERVICE COORDINATION

Although IDEA requires the provision of service coordination, it does not specify how it should be implemented at the state level. Research (Dinnebeil et al., 1999; Dunst, Trivette, Gordon, & Starnes, 1993; Harbin, 1996; Jung & Baird, 2003; Park & Turnbull, 2003; Summers et al., 2001) and practice recommendations (Bruder & Bologna, 1993; Harbin, McWilliam, & Gallagher, 2000; Roberts, Rule, & Innocenti, 1998; Rosin, Whitehead, et al., 1996; Swan & Morgan, 1993; Thurman, Cornwell, & Gottwald, 1997) have produced a plethora of recommendations on how to design and implement collaborative service models. However, there is a lack of comprehensive, developmental system examples from which to glean evidence on effective early intervention coordination and integration practices that lead to positive system, family, and child outcomes (Dunst & Bruder, 2002). Much of this is because of the complexities demonstrated by agencies, services, and providers as they attempt to individualize services and supports for families in a collaborative manner (Bruder & Bologna, 1993).

As previously stated, state policy makers are free to decide which model of service coordination to use in their states. Five such models have been identified: 1) independent and dedicated—the role of the service coordinator is dedicated to service coordination only, and the agency providing service coordination is independent from service provision; 2) independent but not dedicated—the agency providing service coordination is independent from service provision, but the service coordinator performs other responsibilities (such as system entry tasks) in addition to service coordination; 3) dedicated but not independent—the service coordinator provides service coordination only in an agency that also provides intervention services; 4) blended—the service coordinator also provides developmental intervention; and 5) multilevel blended and dedicated—children and families with the most complex service coordination needs are assigned a dedicated service coordinator, while intervention service providers carry out service coordination tasks in addition to providing intervention for children and families with less complex needs (Harbin & West, 1998).

In an attempt to identify and understand the service coordination models currently in place across the country, the Research and Training Center on Service Coordination (Harbin et al., 2004) conducted a survey in all 50 states and 7 territories. Findings suggest that each of the entities administers early intervention and service coordination differently, according to the unique political and contextual variables of their locale. When asked about specific state models, 47% reported variability across all of the previously described models, 27% reported using a dedicated model (a person dedicated to only providing service coordination), and the remainder of the respondents reported models divided among the others mentioned previously. It is no surprise that the National Early Intervention Longitudinal Study has also identified service coordination as one of the more difficult aspects of early intervention service delivery to describe (Hebbeler, Simeonsson, & Scarborough, 2000, p. 204). As a result of these variations, the literature on service coordination and integration is replete with the barriers that impede service integration (Friend & Cook, 1996; Johnson, Ruiz, LaMontagne, & George, 1998; Pugach & Johnson, 1995; Stegelin & Jones, 1991) and the complexity and variation of state practices (Hebbeler et al., 2000). A conclusion is that a state model may or may not contribute to the facilitation of early intervention service coordination and integration, or provide enough clarity and specificity to enable a service coordinator to fulfill his or her job responsibilities.

THE ROLE OF SERVICE COORDINATION

According to Part C of IDEA, *service coordination* is defined as the activities carried out by a service coordinator to assist and enable the eligible child and his or her family to receive the rights, procedural safeguards, and services that are authorized to be provided under the state's early intervention program. This includes coordinating all services across agency lines and serving as the single point of contact to help families obtain the services and assistance they need. In order to do accomplish these tasks, service coordinators must demonstrate knowledge and understanding about eligible infants and toddlers, Part C of IDEA and its regulations, the nature and scope of services available under the state's early intervention system, and the payment system as well as other pertinent information. Table 2.2 contains the qualifications, responsibilities, tasks, and outcomes of service coordination under the law.

Table 2.2. Service coordinator expectations under Part C of IDEA '97

Qualifications →	Responsibilities →	Tasks →	Outcome
Knowledge and understanding about • Infants and toddlers who are eligible under Part C of IDEA • Part C of IDEA and the regulations of this part • The nature and scope of services available under the state's early intervention program, the system of payments for services in the state, and other pertinent information	Assisting parents of eligible children in gaining access to the early intervention services and other services identified in the individualized family service plan (IFSP) Coordinating the provision of early intervention services and other services (e.g., medical services for other than diagnostic and evaluation purposes) so that the child's needs are being met Facilitating the timely delivery of available services Continuously seeking the appropriate services and situations necessary to benefit the development of each child being served for the duration of the child's eligibility	Coordinating the performance of evaluations and assessments Facilitating and participating in the development, review, and evaluation of IFSPs Assisting families in identifying available service providers Coordinating and monitoring the delivery of available services Informing families of the availability of advocacy services Coordinating with medical and health providers Facilitating the development of a transition plan to preschool services, if appropriate	Children and families receive appropriate supports and services that meet their individual needs

Though straightforward as described by law, the service coordinator is ultimately responsible for the coordination, maintenance, and evaluation of services and supports delivered to a family and child. However, the complexities of tasks across the multiple levels of early intervention (family, service providers, and system administrators) are growing every day. Underlying each of these levels are fiscal challenges facing both families of children with multiple needs and state and local systems of care that are trying to coordinate multiple (shrinking), confusing, and diverse funding streams for service delivery (Akers & Roberts, 1999; McCollum, 2000;

Striffler, Perry, & Kates, 1997). This is occurring simultaneously with expanding system reforms across systems such as welfare (Janko-Summers & Joseph, 1998; Ohlson, 1998; Rosman & Knitzer, 2001), child care (Kagan, 1996; Spencer, Blumenthal, & Richards, 1995), health care (Braddock & Hemp, 1996; Lobach, 1995), and mental health (Knitzer, 2000; Knitzer & Page, 1998).

A FRAMEWORK FOR SERVICE COORDINATION AND INTEGRATION

Elder and Magrab (1980) first described a hierarchy for an integrated early intervention service model. The first level of such a hierarchy would consist of cooperation wherein people and agencies cooperate for a common goal. The second is a more active attempt whereby the people and entities coordinate activities in order to reach a goal. The last level is a collaborative relationship in that the entities work together throughout the achievement of a goal (Melaville & Blank, 1994). Though helpful, this hierarchy has proven inadequate to describe the depth and levels of collaboration needed to achieve the service coordination and integration necessitated in current systems of early intervention (Bruder & Bologna, 1993; Hanson & Bruder, 2001).

A more relevant framework for the complexity of service integration in early intervention today is based on the ecological framework of Bronfenbrenner (1993), as applied to the Developmental Systems Model (Guralnick, 2001) illustrated in this volume. This orientation requires attention be given to the multiple characteristics of a service system, suggesting that child and family outcomes of service coordination and integration are influenced by the individuals, organizations, agencies, cultures, communities, and states involved in service delivery and system administration. In addition, the child and family exist within a series of complex contexts such as their history, values, culture, ethnicity, structure, home routines and community activities, child disability, child age, economic status, and geographic location. Likewise, service providers and coordinators possess attitudes, values, knowledge (of resources and recommended practices), previous experiences, training, and skills that they bring to the service implementation endeavor. These characteristics of both the family and service provider also influence the multiple elements of service coordination. Finally, service coordination is also influenced by the existing system infrastructure. The infrastructure is made up of multiple organizations, agencies, and programs that can facilitate or hinder effective service coordination. Although funding is an important piece of the infrastructure, other aspects of the infrastructure are equally important (e.g., personnel development, service coordination caseload). Families, service providers, and service system infrastructure are embedded within community contexts, all combining to influence not only the nature of service coordination but also the consequent outcomes as well.

SERVICE COORDINATION AND INTEGRATION

Over the last decade, work in early intervention service delivery has focused on the identification of factors that facilitate service coordination and integration. In particular, work by Harbin and colleagues (Harbin, 1996; Harbin et al., 2000; Harbin & West, 1998) has consistently broadened the view of system issues to include seemingly intangible, yet essential, qualities that lead to successful service integration models. In particular, Harbin and colleagues (2000) identified seven broad interactive variables that facilitate service integration: 1) state and community context, 2) state policy, 3) service delivery model, 4) leadership, 5) service provider skills and characteristics, 6) family characteristics, and 7) service provider/family relationships. Other researchers reinforced their findings and also have examined the interrelationship of variables that contribute to effective collaborative early intervention models (Johnson, Zorn, Tam, LaMontagne, & Johnson, 2003; Park & Turnbull, 2003; Summers et al., 2001). Categories of practice such as the management and delivery of services, the approach for teaming, the program philosophy and climate, and the personal characteristics of providers (including months of experience and attendance in training) have been identified by both parents and service coordinators as facilitating collaboration (Dinnebeil et al., 1999; Jung & Baird, 2003). Although it is no surprise that service delivery and management (e.g., caseload, funding) have been consistently identified as critical facilitators to coordinated service delivery (Dinnebeil et al., 1996; Harbin & West, 1998; Hebbeler, 1997), the personal characteristics of those involved (e.g., willingness to work together, leadership, common vision, trust) have also been increasingly acknowledged as a key to successful service integration (Dunst et al., 1993; Harbin et al., 2000; Johnson et al., 2003; McWilliam, Tocci, & Harbin, 1998; Park & Turnbull, 2003). In fact, it has been concluded that effective service integration is built on the foundation of partnerships between the people who comprise agencies, services, and families (Summers et al., 2001). Under Part C of IDEA, the person designated as the service coordinator has the ultimate responsibility to build and nurture these partnerships.

DEVELOPMENTAL SYSTEMS APPROACH

In an attempt to provide guidance to the service coordination and integration process, the components of the early intervention developmental systems approach have been compared with the tasks of a service coordinator under Part C of IDEA (see Table 2.3). The parallels are easy to see and for this reason, the developmental systems approach will be used to define service coordination and integration strategies that have been used successfully in early intervention. These components will be described in regard to practices within each that facilitate coordinated and integrated early intervention service delivery systems. The intent is not to provide information that is more comprehensively described in the following chapters but to briefly illustrate examples of practices that support the principles of service coordination and integration in early intervention. Table 2.3 contains the components and sample practices.

Screening, Referral, and Access

A lack of a coordinated, comprehensive screening, referral, and access process for children and families in need of further assessment is not only

Table 2.3. Comparison of developmental systems approach components and service coordination tasks

Developmental systems approach	Service coordination tasks
Screening, referral, and access	

Comprehensive interdisciplinary assessment
    Eligibility and program entry
    Family assessment
	Coordinating the performance of evaluations and assessments

Development and implementation of a comprehensive program	Facilitating and participating in the development, review, and evaluation of individualized family service plans
	Assisting families in identifying eligible service providers
	Coordinating with medical and health providers
Monitoring and outcome evaluations	Coordinating and monitoring the delivery of available services
	Informing families of the availability of advocacy services
Transition planning	Facilitating the development of a transition plan to preschool services, if appropriate

inefficient but also results in additional stress for families, service providers, and agencies. As described in Chapter 5, a single point of access into the early intervention service system is predicated on a collaborative approach to screening and referral for all children. Early identification of children in need of services is a national issue. For example, there are multiple models for developmental and medical screening programs (McLean, 2003); however, the coordination of the screening programs across populations of children and service sectors is usually absent. An example of a problem that can occur when there is a lack of such coordination is when children may not have access to a medical home (Nickel et al., 2003) and, therefore, are not provided with the medical and developmental screens that may be required by law (Dworkin, 2000). Most recently, this concern was identified in relation to children who are screened as newborns for hearing and are referred for further evaluation by pediatricians but do not show up for further assessment. Likewise, a concern also has been expressed about children who pass a newborn hearing screen but do not receive another hearing screening until school entry (American Academy of Pediatrics, 2003; Widen, Bull, & Folsom, 2003).

Although screening, referral, and access are considered early intervention systems issues and are not required under the service coordination provision of Part C of IDEA, a national survey found that 15 states do assign a service coordinator to a family on system entry because of either an automatic eligibility to service or referral for assessment after screening (Harbin et al., 2004). This assistance into the system should be helpful across all levels, and perhaps other state systems could follow this lead and assign service coordinators to assist families during this time. To ensure a smooth progression from screening, referral, and subsequent assessment if needed, an additional outcome of this practice would be the coordination of social, medical, and developmental background by the service coordinator prior to system entry.

Another coordination and integration practice for screening, referral, and access is the move by states to implement birth defect surveillance programs. As of 2004, 33 states have surveillance programs, and of these, 13 have implemented an identification and referral system into early intervention (Farel, Meyer, Hicken, & Edmonds, 2003). Although many issues need to be resolved with this practice (e.g., confidentiality), states have reported success on many levels. Not surprisingly, a survey of parents reported satisfaction with the use of a birth defects registry to track and refer (as appropriate) children to early intervention (Farel, Meyer, & Hicken, 2001), thus assisting in system entry in a timely manner.

Comprehensive Interdisciplinary Assessment

Inherent in the comprehensive interdisciplinary assessment component of early intervention is the determination of eligibility through a multidisciplinary evaluation and the administration of further assessments, including family assessments, after eligibility is determined. A service coordinator in Part C of IDEA has the responsibility to coordinate the performance of evaluation and assessments. This coordination encompasses both the people who administer the assessment and the tools and processes used during the assessment.

Assessment is the process of gathering information in order to make a decision. Assessment is an important component of the developmental systems approach of early intervention, yet traditional assessment models (e.g., discipline specific, in a novel setting with contrived activities, conducted by strangers) prove inadequate when working with infants and toddlers with disabilities (Meisels & Fenichel, 1996). Effective early childhood assessment protocols must rely on a sensitivity to the age of the child, the nature of his or her delay or disability, the family context, and the integration of a child's behaviors across developmental domains.

In order to qualify for services, most children will require an assessment to determine eligibility. This assessment can serve a diagnostic function and create an accurate portrayal of the child's needs across the medical, educational, and social systems perspectives. It should be noted that an eligibility assessment is not needed for children who may qualify for early intervention because they have received a diagnosis of a medical condition that qualifies as an established condition for early intervention. Recommendations in regard to diagnostic assessment include a focus on the process as opposed to just the product of assessment (Vig & Kaminer, 2003). This supports the strongly held belief that it is nonproductive to assess a very young child on developmental skills assigned by domain, as these domains are interdependent (McLean, 2003). This does not mean that professionals with discipline-specific expertise are not an important component of the assessment protocol, but rather, they collaborate as a team on the assessment process and integrated assessment report so that the child is seen as a whole rather than domain by domain.

The service coordinator must ensure that a team process occurs prior to (planning), during (process), and after (reporting) an assessment. The first challenge is to identify team members who are competent in both their discipline and in early development. Part of this task can occur through the assurance that team members have met discipline-specific standards. The more difficult challenge is to assess a team member's competencies in early development (Bruder, 2000). At this time, it is the latter task that is most problematic, as most training programs do not provide training in cross-disciplinary skills or early developmental processes (Kilgo & Bruder, 1997).

Second, the service coordinator must ensure that the team members are competent in team process and collaborative consultation. Although these competencies have been advocated for many years in regard to early intervention (Bruder, 1996; Rapport, McWilliam, & Smith, 2004), comprehensive research on team functioning and collaborative consultation is sparse in regard to the assessment process. Nonetheless, Part C of IDEA requires the use of multidisciplinary teams in evaluation and assessment. The composition of these teams is then dictated by the unique needs of the child and family in relation to the purpose of assessment. For example, a diagnostic assessment may require more in-depth involvement from numerous professionals in a variety of specialized disciplines. The service coordinator must identify the team members for the assessment process and must develop a collaborative climate in which all can work as a team on this component of early intervention. Larson and LaFasto (1989) highlighted a number of features characteristic of successful collaborative teams including 1) clear roles and accountability, 2) the monitoring of individual performance and the provision of feedback, 3) fact-based judgments, and 4) an effective communication system. This last feature can be immeasurably enhanced through the use of collaborative consultation strategies.

Collaborative consultation is an interactive process that enables people with diverse expertise to generate creative solutions to mutually defined problems. The process encompasses a number of interpersonal competencies that cross discipline boundaries. These include written and oral communication skills; personal characteristics, such as the ability to be caring, respectful, empathic, congruent, and open; and collaborative problem-solving skills (West & Cannon, 1988). The last attribute is critical to the development of a relationship of parity between both (or among all, if there are more than two) individuals involved in the consultation. However, the use of collaborative problem solving does not override the need for the consultant to use his or her specialized and discipline-specific skills to meet the consultee's needs (Bruder, 1996).

Finally, the team should develop an integrated assessment report for both an eligibility evaluation and comprehensive assessment for program planning, and this should be coordinated by the service coordinator. Assessment information must be summarized from the recorded observations, interviews, checklists, and scales. The purpose of the assessment report is to provide a picture of the child and his or her family to help create objectives and intervention adaptations, supports, and strategies. The report should be representative of the total process and report on strengths as well as needs (Wolery, 2003).

Of special note is the family assessment that also occurs in this component. The service coordinator needs to make sure that the family assessment is culturally sensitive, family centered, and representative of the family's values, concerns, and priorities. The service coordinator must ensure that this assessment is coordinated and integrated with the total assessment protocol.

Develop and Implement a Comprehensive Program

An early intervention program of supports and services for a child and family under Part C of IDEA is coordinated through an IFSP. It is the service coordinator's responsibility to ensure that this is developed, reviewed, and evaluated periodically. The plan must represent a family's priorities, concerns, and resources; the child's developmental needs; and other needs identified by the family. The IFSP must be comprehensive and collaborative if it is going to result in positive outcomes for a child and family. The collaborative components include a plan with integrated outcomes and objectives that cross agency boundaries as needed (including coordination of social, medical, and health needs). In addition, service providers (who meet the state's highest personnel standards) must be identified to implement the plan's integrated outcomes and objectives. The subsequent program of services must be implemented within a child's natural environment.

The service coordinator can assist in this component of the systems model by coordinating and monitoring the delivery of services through an interagency service plan (see Salisbury, Crawford, Marlowe, & Husband, 2003). Salisbury and colleagues (2003) demonstrated the use of such a plan that allows for agency (as well as cross-disciplinary) collaboration and integration. The plan is the tool used to integrate services and supports. The data supplied by Salisbury contrast with previous data collected on IFSP development (Boone, McBride, Swann, Moore, & Drew, 1998; Bruder & Staff, 1998; McWilliam, Ferguson, et al., 1998). A difference may be that the interagency plan relies more on a collaborative process than conforming to the requirements of a product. In addition to an interagency process, the plan must represent a valid and cohesive model of intervention if it is to have a positive impact on families, providers, and systems. An early intervention framework that provides a model for IFSP development is the use of family-identified activity settings as the context of learning and the use of a primary provider to provide the services needed. These learning contexts support a variety of subcontexts that can be used to describe the experiences and learning opportunities given to children as part of daily living. They include child and family routines, family rituals, family and community celebrations, and family traditions. Termed *activity settings* (Gallimore, Goldenberg, & Weisner, 1993; Galli-more, Weisner, Bernheimer, Guthrie, & Nihira, 1993), these units are important features of any planned interventions for children and their families (Roberts, 1999).

Surveys and case studies have documented the abundant sources of activity settings in children's lives (Bruder & Dunst, 2000; Dunst & Bruder, 2002). Most children, regardless of their disability or severity of delay, experience multiple kinds of learning opportunities regardless of where they live. For example, findings indicate that young children experience learning opportunities, on average, in about 15 different home locations and 23 different community locations. These locations, in turn, support an average of 87 home and 76 community activity settings, respectively. These learning environments, in turn, result in an average of 113 learning opportunities in the child's home and 106 in the community. Consequently, an individual child could be expected to experience some 200 or more learning opportunities in the context of his or her family and community life beyond those provided as part of a child's involvement in an early intervention or preschool program.

The emphasis on learning through everyday learning opportunities has repercussions for the personnel serving children in early intervention, as well as the service coordinator. Not only do personnel have to understand learning theory, but also they have to understand basic principles such as the integration of development across domains (Bruder, 1997), an effective team process (Bruder, 1996), family-centered strategies (Bruder, 2000), collaborative consultation models (Hanft & Pilkington, 2000; Palsha & Wesley, 1998; Stayton & Bruder, 1999), and the integration of expertise across professionals into a primary provider (Harbin et al., 2000; McWil-liam, 2003). The prime requirement of providing early intervention through a model that promotes learning through family-identified oppor-tunities and experiences is the replacement for the model of service delivery that uses discipline-specific people focusing on one developmental domain.

Monitoring and Outcome Evaluations

A comprehensive program can only be effective if data are collected regu-larly on child and family service implementation, learning opportunities, intervention strategies, and developmental and behavioral outcomes. A service coordinator is responsible for the coordination and monitoring of such services and informing families of the availability of advocacy services, especially if the family wants different/more/fewer services than agencies are able to provide (Brown, 2003). As with other components, this responsibility requires a philosophy of coordination and integration, as services and outcomes should only be measured within a collaborative framework (Roberts et al., 1999).

A practice to facilitate this component of the developmental systems model is ongoing team meetings in which professionals meet with the service coordinator and family to review and monitor a child and family's progress through the early intervention service plan. Unfortunately, the reason these meetings do not occur with regularity is because of a lack of infrastructure supports such as a funding for meeting time (McCollum, 2000; Roberts et al., 1999). In those systems in which such meetings occur, however, both satisfaction and progress are reported (Salisbury et al., 2003), and many individuals have recommended the use of such meetings to ensure quality collaborations (Campbell & Halbert, 2002; Johnson et al., 2003).

In regard to system monitoring of outcomes, statewide data sets have been advocated as a mechanism to coordinate information and integrate reporting requirements across agencies, programs, and personnel (Buysse, Bernier, & McWilliam, 2002; Roberts et al., 1999). Unfortunately, at this time, states organize their Part C database specific to their state needs, and rarely are these data sets coordinated with other state data sets either within or across states. States should avail themselves of the opportunity to design data requirements for federal and state needs in such a way as to facilitate the monitoring of family and child outcomes as well as system (both local and state needs) outcomes across levels of service (Gilliam & Leiter, 2003; Spiker, Hebbeler, Wagner, Cameto, & McKenna, 2000). Inherent in this strategy is a common vision of the measurement of indicators most important for inclusion on a statewide data base (Carta, 2002; Hauser-Cram, Warfield, Upshur, & Weisner, 2000; Wolery & Bailey, 2002).

Transition Planning

The importance of transition has been addressed in state and federal legislation, federal funding initiatives, and professional literature (Hanson et al., 2000; Rosenkoetter, Whaley, Hains, & Pierce, 2001; Rous, Hemmeter, & Schuster, 1999; Wischnowski, Fowler, & McCollum, 2000). A successful transition is a series of well-planned steps to facilitate the movement of the child and family into another setting (Bruder & Chandler,

1996). Successful transition is a major component of the developmental systems approach. Under Part C of IDEA, the service coordinator has the responsibility of coordinating transitions. Needless to say, the type of planning and practices that are employed can influence the success of transition and satisfaction with the transition process.

Within the field of early intervention, *transition* is defined as "the process of moving from one program to another or from one service delivery mode to another" (Chandler, 1992, p. 246). Others have emphasized the dynamic process of transition, as children with disabilities and their families will move among different service providers, programs, and agencies as the child ages (Rosenkoetter et al., 2001). Although formal transition for young children with disabilities typically occurs at the age of 3 (into preschool), transition between services, providers, and programs also can occur throughout these early years. Part C of IDEA increases the potential number of transitions. For example, transition can begin for some children at the moment of birth if professionals determine that their health status requires transfer to a special care nursery and subsequent developmental interventions (Bruder & Walker, 1990).

According to Wolery (1989), transition should fulfill four goals: 1) ensure continuity of services, 2) minimize disruptions to the family system by facilitating adaptations to change, 3) ensure that children are prepared to function in the receiving program, and 4) fulfill the legal requirements of the Education of the Handicapped Act Amendments of 1986 (PL 99-457). In order to achieve these goals, it is necessary to plan for transition. The responsibility for transition planning should be shared across the sending and receiving program and should involve families (Bruder & Chandler, 1996). Transition procedures should assist families and their children and promote collaboration between the service providers, service coordinators, and families who comprise the transition team.

The two practices associated with successful transitions focus on collaboration. One practice is the formation and maintenance of a team consisting of those involved in the child's services, and the second is an actual document that is used to guide the process. Both have facilitated a seamless move between and among services for families and providers (Rous et al., 1999). The transition plan should address the roles and responsibilities of both the sending program/service and receiving program/ service and their staffs. Most important are the provisions of appropriate and adequate information, education, and support to families throughout the process and the use of a transition document to formalize and record the outcomes expected for an individual child's transition (Wischnowski et al., 2000).

FUTURE DIRECTIONS

Service coordination and integration can result in many benefits to families, service providers, and systems. A number of issues need to be resolved, however, if professionals are to overcome the many barriers inherent in current service systems that discourage, and in some instances prohibit, actual service integration. Two of these issues are described in an effort to illuminate these challenges to be overcome if we are to realize a comprehensive, integrated, early intervention service system.

Clarify the Intention of
Service Coordination and Integration

In many instances, the concept is used interchangeably as both an outcome and as a practice. Although this may indeed be the status of service integration and coordination, the field would benefit from clarification as individual service programs are designed for families. Traditionally, service coordination under Part C of IDEA has been thought of as an outcome for those participating in early intervention: That is, if an individual is eligible and chooses to receive services, he or she is assigned a service coordinator. Many individuals view the receipt of the service itself (and other services under Part C of IDEA) as the outcome of importance. However, recommendations for early intervention research have called attention to the need to better articulate child and family outcomes within and across the many variables associated with service delivery (Carta, 2002; Dunst & Bruder, 2002; Guralnick, 2002; Roberts, 1999; Shonkoff, 2002; Wolery & Bailey, 2002). This recommendation follows the federal emphasis on outcomes that has resulted in the federally funded Early Childhood Outcomes Center, which is charged with designing a system that measures child and family outcomes as a result of participation in various dimensions of Part C of IDEA or preschool special education under IDEA.

A series of studies have begun to identify outcomes related to service coordination under Part C of IDEA. The Research and Training Center on Service Coordination conducted a series of national studies that have identified a core group of outcomes for both systems and families as a result of receiving Part C early intervention. Focus groups (26), surveys (5), and family and service coordinator interviews (125) have included families, service providers, service coordinators, and system administrators. Through both quantitative and qualitative methodology, data were summarized and reduced across all of the studies, and an expert advisory board approved a final listing of outcomes (see http://www.uconnucedd.org to see these studies). Figure 2.1 contains these outcomes as included in a logic model framework (see Gilliam & Leiter, 2003; W.K. Kellogg Foundation, 2001).

These outcomes are but one model that can be used to measure the effectiveness of service coordination; furthermore, studies are needed to explicitly test the model in regard to various system components as represented by service coordination tasks (Dunst & Bruder, 2002; Guralnick, 2002). These studies can then support the developmental systems approach of early intervention and contribute to an understanding of the interrelationship of state models, local practices (including service coordination), and family characteristics that interact to produce positive outcomes for all.

Address the Training Needs of Those Involved in Service Coordination

There have been many articles (e.g., Bruder, 1998; Bruder, Lippman, & Bologna, 1994; McCollum, 2000; Stayton & Bruder, 1999; Thorp & McCollum, 1994) and books (e.g., Winton, 2000; Winton, McCollum, & Catlett, 1997) written on early intervention personnel preparation; yet, statewide systems of early intervention continue to struggle with providing effective and appropriate training to service coordinators (Romer & Umbreit, 1998). System variables including a lack of funding affect both the scope and delivery of training, and inadequate implementation of service coordination models (e.g., high caseloads) can override the positive outcomes of training that does occur (Trivette, 1998; Winton, 1998). In fact, various curricula (Edelman, Greenland, & Mills, 1992; Rosin, Green, Hecht, Tuchman, & Robbins, 1996; Zipper, Hinton, Weil, & Rounds, 1993) are available and a number of content areas (Roberts et al., 1998) are recommended for service coordinators; yet, a lack of training continues to be a barrier to effective service coordination and integration.

The Research and Training Center on Service Coordination conducted a survey of training opportunities and curricula for service coordinators in each of the 57 states and territories. The final sample consisted of 49 states and 4 territories. Twenty-six of the respondents reported separate job standards and requirements for service coordinators including seven states that required a 4-year degree and eight states that required competencies that demonstrated that the service coordinator had the skills and the knowledge required by law. A total of 37 states provided training for service coordinators, and 20 of these mandated that service coordinators attend the training. Fifteen of the respondents reported that the length of training was variable, and the remaining 22 stated the average length

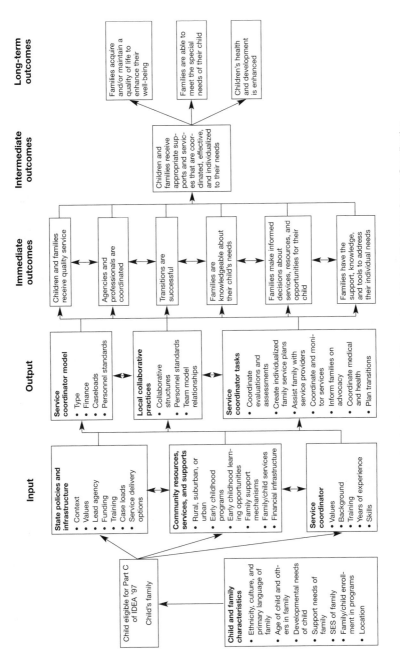

Figure 2.1. Final listing of outcomes from a series of national studies by the Research and Training Center on Service Coordination.

49

of training was 2.9 days. Seventeen of these states provided some type of follow-up to initial service coordination training. Twenty-nine of the states that had training provided curricula and training materials that were analyzed for content (see http://www.uconnucedd.org for the complete training report).

It seems reasonable to suggest that training for service coordinators must be addressed as a system support if we are to expect service integration to occur for families. Although many of the tasks assigned to service coordinators seem perfunctory, many would agree that the quality with which they occur ensures positive outcomes. Training, follow-up, and ongoing evaluation must occur in a systematic manner if we are to expect quality. The service coordinator's job is challenging and varies on a day-to-day basis depending on the interactions of systems, families, and needs. Service coordinators need tools to address these needs, and they must be able to provide service using family-centered practices, including a focus on relationships (McWilliam, Tocci, et al., 1998). These practices include treating families with dignity and respect; being culturally and socioeconomically sensitive to family diversity; providing choices to families in relation to their priorities and concerns; fully disclosing information to families so they can make decisions; focusing on a range of informal, community resources as sources of parenting and family supports; and employing practices that are empowering and competency-enhancing, including the provision of parent-to-parent models (Dunst, 1999; Santelli, Turnbull, Marquis, & Lerner, 2000). Considerable literature has been amassed on the individual and collective use of these practices, as they add value to early intervention by contributing to improved family and child outcomes (Dunst, 2000; Dunst, Brookfield, & Epstein, 1998; Dunst, Trivette, Boyd, & Hamby, 1996; Mahoney & Bella, 1998; McWilliam, Tocci, et al., 1998; Thompson et al., 1997; Trivette & Dunst, 1998). Service coordination delivered in this way forms the foundation for the tasks that must be accomplished within the components of the developmental systems approach of early intervention philosophy and practice.

CONCLUSION

Effective service coordination and integration are expected to result in better outcomes for everyone involved. Within the developmental systems approach for early intervention, this principle is predicated on the availability of a universal system of supports and services to facilitate positive outcomes for all children and families. However, challenges to collaborative service integration will remain as long as people, services, and agencies continue to deliver early intervention idiosyncratically. Kagan (1996) proposed a structure of service integration that is multidimensional and includes a focus on infrastructure reform, direct services reform, and improved outcomes for families. This structure has been used in this chapter to describe service coordination and integration efforts for those families and children eligible for Part C of IDEA. This framework provides a basis for continued research in this area, as does the developmental systems approach of early intervention. The opportunity is upon us to incorporate the values, philosophy, and outcomes inherent in a collaborative model as we address the comprehensive needs of the children and families whose quality of life we are trying to improve.

REFERENCES

Akers, A.L., & Roberts, R.N. (1999). The use of blended and flexible funding in Part C programs at the community level. *Infants and Young Children, 11*(4), 46–52.

American Academy of Pediatrics. (2003). Hearing assessment in infants and children: Recommendations beyond neonatal screening. *Pediatrics, 111*(2), 436–440.

Bailey, D.B., Jr., McWilliam, R.A., Darkes, L.A., Hebbeler, K., Simeonsson, R.J., Spiker, D., & Wagner, M. (1998). Family outcomes in early intervention: A framework for program evaluation and efficacy research. *Exceptional Children, 64*(3), 313–328.

Boone, H.A., McBride, S.L., Swann, D., Moore, S., & Drew, B.S. (1998). IFSP practices in two states: Implications for practice. *Infants and Young Children, 10*(4), 36–45.

Braddock, D., & Hemp, R. (1996). Medicaid spending reductions and developmental disabilities. *Journal of Disability Policy Studies, 7*, 2–31.

Bronfenbrenner, U. (1993). The ecology of cognitive development: Research models and fugitive findings. In R.H. Wozniak & K.W. Fischer (Eds.), *Development in context: Acting and thinking in specific environments* (pp. 3–44). Mahwah, NJ: Lawrence Erlbaum Associates.

Brown, S.E. (2003). Advocacy for young children under IDEA: What does it mean for early childhood educators? *Infants and Young Children, 16*(3), 227–237.

Bruder, M.B. (1996). Interdisciplinary collaboration in service delivery. In R.A. McWilliam (Ed.), *Rethinking pull-out services in early intervention: A professional resource* (pp. 27–48). Baltimore: Paul H. Brookes Publishing Co.

Bruder, M.B. (1997). The effectiveness of specific educational/developmental curricula for children with established disabilities. In M.J. Guralnick (Ed.), *The effectiveness of early intervention* (pp. 523–548). Baltimore: Paul H. Brookes Publishing Co.

Bruder, M.B. (1998). A collaborative model to increase the capacity of childcare providers to include young children with disabilities. *Journal of Early Intervention, 21*(2), 177–186.

Bruder, M.B. (2000). Family centered early intervention: Clarifying our values for the new millennium. *Topics in Early Childhood Special Education, 20*(2), 105–115.

Bruder, M.B., & Bologna, T.M. (1993). Collaboration and service coordination for effective early intervention. In W. Brown, S.K. Thurman, & L. Pearl

(Eds.), *Family-centered early intervention with infants and toddlers: Innovative cross-disciplinary approaches* (pp. 103–127). Baltimore: Paul H. Brookes Publishing Co.

Bruder, M.B., & Chandler, L. (1996). Transition. In S. Odom & M. McLean (Eds.), *Early intervention/early childhood special education: Recommended practices* (pp. 287–307). Austin, TX: PRO-ED.

Bruder, M.B., & Dunst, C.J. (2000). Expanding learning opportunities for infants and toddlers in natural environments: A chance to reconceptualize early intervention. *Zero to Three, 20*(3), 34–36.

Bruder, M.B., & Dunst, C.J. (in preparation). *Personnel preparation in recommended early intervention practices: Degree of emphasis across disciplines.*

Bruder, M.B., Lippman, C., & Bologna, T.M. (1994). Personnel preparation in early intervention: Building capacity for program expansion within institutions of higher education. *Journal of Early Intervention, 18*(1), 103–110.

Bruder, M.B., & Staff, I. (1998). A comparison of the effects of type of classroom and service characteristics on toddlers with disabilities. *Topics in Early Childhood Special Education, 18*(1), 26–37.

Bruder, M.B., & Walker, L. (1990). Discharge planning: Hospital to home transitions for infants. *Topics in Early Childhood Special Education, 9*(4), 26–42.

Buysse, V., Bernier, K.Y., & McWilliam, R.A. (2002). A statewide profile of early intervention services using the Part C data system. *Journal of Early Intervention, 25*(1), 15–26.

Campbell, P.H., & Halbert, J. (2002). Between research and practice: Provider perspectives on early intervention. *Topics in Early Childhood Special Education, 22*(4), 213–224.

Carta, J.J. (2002). An early childhood special education research agenda in a culture of accountability for results. *Journal of Early Intervention, 25*(2), 102–104.

Chandler, L.K. (1992). Promoting young children's social competence as a strategy for transition to mainstreamed kindergarten program. In S.L. Odom, S.R. McConnell, & M.A. McEvoy (Eds.), *Social competence of young children with disabilities* (pp. 245–276). Baltimore: Paul H. Brookes Publishing Co.

Dinnebeil, L.A., Hale, L.M., & Rule, S. (1996). A qualitative analysis of parents' and service coordinators' descriptions of variables that influence collaborative relationships. *Topics in Early Childhood Special Education, 16*(3), 322–347.

Dinnebeil, L.A., Hale, L.M., & Rule, S. (1999). Early intervention program practices that support collaboration. *Topics in Early Childhood Special Education, 19*(4), 225–235.

Dunst, C.J. (1999). Placing parent education in conceptual and empirical context. *Topics in Early Childhood Special Education, 19*(3), 141–146.

Dunst, C.J. (2000). Revisiting "rethinking early intervention." *Topics in Early Childhood Special Education, 20*, 95–104.

Dunst, C.J., Brookfield, J., & Epstein, J. (1998). *Family-centered early intervention and child, parent and family benefits.* (Final report). Washington, DC: U.S. Department of Education, Office of Special Education Programs.

Dunst, C.J., & Bruder, M.B. (2002). Valued outcomes of service coordination, early intervention and natural environments. *Exceptional Children, 68*(3), 361–375.

Dunst, C.J., Trivette, C.M., Boyd, K., & Hamby, D. (1996). Family-oriented program models, helpgiving practices, and parental control appraisals. *Exceptional Children, 62*, 237–248.

Dunst, C.J., Trivette, C.M., Gordon, N.J., & Starnes, A.L. (1993). Family-centered case management practices: Characteristics and consequences. In G.H.S. Singer & L.E. Powers (Eds.), *Families, disability, and empowerment: Activating coping skills and strategies for family interventions* (pp. 89–119). Baltimore: Paul H. Brookes Publishing Co.

Dworkin, P.H. (2000). Preventive health care and anticipatory guidance. In J.P. Shonkoff & S.J. Meisels (Eds.), *Handbook of early intervention* (2nd ed., pp. 327–338). New York: Cambridge University Press.

Edelman, L., Greenland, B., & Mills, B.L. (1992). *Building parent/professional collaboration*. St. Paul, MN: Pathfinder Resources.

Education of the Handicapped Act Amendments of 1986, PL 99-457, 20 U.S.C. §§ 1400 *et seq.*

Elder, J., & Magrab, P. (1980). *Coordinating services to handicapped children: A handbook for interagency collaboration*. Baltimore: Paul H. Brookes Publishing Co.

Farel, A.M., Meyer, R.E., & Hicken, M. (2001). *Report to March of Dimes Birth Defects Foundation*. Chapel Hill: Western Chapter, University of North Carolina at Chapel Hill.

Farel, A.M., Meyer, R.E., Hicken, M., & Edmonds, L. (2003). Registry to referral: A promising means for identifying and referring infants and toddlers for early intervention services. *Infants and Young Children, 16*(2), 99–105.

Friend, M., & Cook, L. (1996). *Interactions: Collaborative skills for school professionals* (2nd ed.). White Plains, NY: Longman.

Gallimore, R., Goldenberg, C.N., & Weisner, T.S. (1993). The social construction and subjective reality of activity settings: Implications for community psychology. *American Journal of Community Psychology, 21*, 537–559.

Gallimore, R., Weisner, T.S., Bernheimer, L.P., Guthrie, D., & Nihira, K. (1993). Family responses to young children with developmental delays: Accommodation activity in ecological and cultural context. *American Journal on Mental Retardation, 98*, 185–206.

Gilliam, W.S., & Leiter, V. (2003). Evaluating early childhood programs: Improving quality and informing policy. *Zero to Three, 23*(6), 6–13.

Guralnick, M.J. (2001). A developmental systems model for early intervention. *Infants and Young Children, 14*(2), 1–18.

Guralnick, M.J. (2002). Model service systems as research priorities in early intervention. *Journal of Early Intervention, 25*(2), 100–101.

Hanft, B.E., & Pilkington, K.O. (2000). Therapy in natural environments: The means or end goal for early intervention? *Infants and Young Children, 12*(4), 1–13.

Hanson, M.J., Beckman, P.J., Horn, E., Marquart, J., Sandall, S.R., Greig, D., & Brennan, E. (2000). Entering preschool: Family and professional experiences in this transition process. *Journal of Early Intervention, 23*(4), 279–293.

Hanson, M.J., & Bruder, M.B. (2001). Early intervention: Promises to keep. *Infants and Young Children, 13*(3), 47–58.

Harbin, G.L. (1996). The challenge of coordination. *Infants and Young Children, 8*(3), 68–76.

Harbin, G.L., Bruder, M.B., Reynolds, C., Mazzarella, C., Gabbard, G., & Staff, I. (2004). Early intervention service coordination policies and models: National status. *Topics in Early Childhood Special Education, 24*(2), 89–97.

Harbin, G.L., McWilliam, R.A., & Gallagher, J.J. (2000). Services for young children with disabilities and their families. In J.P. Shonkoff & S.J. Meisels (Eds.), *Handbook of early childhood intervention* (2nd ed., pp. 387–415). New York: Cambridge University Press.

Harbin, G.L., & West, T. (1998). *Early intervention service delivery models and their impact on children and families*. Chapel Hill: Early Childhood Research Institute on Service Utilization, Frank Porter Graham Child Development Center, University of North Carolina at Chapel Hill.

Hauser-Cram, P., Warfield, M.E., Upshur, C.C., & Weisner, T.S. (2000). An expanded view of program evaluation in early childhood intervention. In J.P. Shonkoff & S.J. Meisels (Eds.), *Handbook of early childhood intervention* (2nd ed., pp. 487–509). New York: Cambridge University Press.

Hebbeler, K., Simeonsson, R.J., & Scarborough, A. (2000). *Describing disability in young children: A national study of early intervention eligibility.* Paper presented at Conference on Research Innovations in Early Intervention (CRIEI), San Diego.

Hebbeler, K.M. (1997). A system in a system: Sociopolitical factors and early intervention. In S.K. Thurman, J.R. Cornwell, & S.R. Gottwald (Eds.), *Contexts of early intervention: Systems and settings* (pp. 19–38). Baltimore: Paul H. Brookes Publishing Co.

Individuals with Disabilities Education Act Amendments of 1997, PL 105-17, 20 U.S.C. §§ 1400 *et seq.*

Janko-Summers, S., & Joseph, G. (1998). Making sense of early intervention in the context of welfare to work. *Journal of Early Intervention, 21*(3), 207–210.

Johnson, L.J., Ruiz, D.M., LaMontagne, M.J., & George, E. (1998). The history of collaboration: Its importance to blending early childhood special education. In L.J. Johnson, M.J. LaMontagne, P.M. Elgas, & A.M. Bauer (Eds.), *Early childhood education: Blending theory, blending practice* (pp. 1–18). Baltimore: Paul H. Brookes Publishing Co.

Johnson, L.J., Zorn, D., Tam, B.K.Y., LaMontagne, M., & Johnson, S.A. (2003). Stakeholders' views of factors that impact successful interagency collaboration. *Exceptional Children, 69*(2), 195–209.

Jung, L.A., & Baird, S.M. (2003). Effects of service coordinator variables on individualized family service plans. *Journal of Early Intervention, 25*(3), 206–218.

Kagan, S.L. (1996). Looking backward-looking forward: The state of early childhood policy. *Dimensions of Early Childhood, 24,* 3–4.

Kagan, S.L., Goffin, S.G., Golub, S.A., & Pritchard, E. (1995). *Toward systemic reform: Service integration for young children and their families.* Falls Church, VA: National Center for Service Integration.

Kagan, S.L., & Neuman, M.J. (2000). Early care and education: Current issues and future strategies. In J.P. Shonkoff & S.J. Meisels (Eds.), *Handbook of early childhood intervention* (2nd ed., pp. 339–360). New York: Cambridge University Press.

Kagan, S.L., & Neville, P.R. (1993). *Integrating services for children and families: Understanding the past to shape the future.* New Haven, CT: Yale University Press.

Kilgo, J., & Bruder, M.B. (1997). Creating new visions in institutions of higher education: Interdisciplinary approaches to personnel preparation in early intervention. In P.J. Winton, J. McCollum, & C. Catlett (Eds.), *Reforming personnel preparation in early intervention: Issues, models, and practical strategies* (pp. 81–102). Baltimore: Paul H. Brookes Publishing Co.

Knitzer, J. (2000). Early childhood mental health services: A policy and systems development perspective. In J.P. Shonkoff & S.J. Meisels (Eds.), *Handbook of early childhood intervention* (2nd ed., pp. 416–438). New York: Cambridge University Press.

Knitzer, J., & Page, S. (1998). *Map and track: State initiatives for young children and families.* New York: National Center for Children in Poverty, Columbia School of Public Health.

Larson, C.E., & LaFasto, F.M.J. (1989). *Teamwork: What must go right/what can go wrong.* Newbury Park, CA: Sage Publications.

Lobach, K.S. (1995). Health policy in the Family Support Act of 1988. In P.L. Chase-Lansdale & J. Brooks-Gunn (Eds.), *Escape from poverty: What makes a difference for children?* (pp. 159–169). New York: Cambridge University Press.

Mahoney, G., & Bella, J.M. (1998). An examination of the effects of family-centered early intervention on child and family outcomes. *Topics in Early Childhood Special Education, 18*(2), 83–94.

McCollum, J.A. (2000). Taking the past along: Reflecting on our identity as a discipline. *Topics in Early Childhood Special Education, 20*(2), 79–86.

McLean, M. (2003). Assessment and its importance in early intervention/early childhood special education. In M. McLean, M. Wolery, & D. Bailey (Eds.), *Assessing infants and preschoolers with special needs* (3rd ed., pp. 1–21). Upper Saddle River, NJ: Merrill/Prentice Hall.

McWilliam, R.A. (2003). The primary-service provider model for home- and community-based services. *Psicologia, XVII*(1), 115–135.

McWilliam, R.A., Ferguson, A., Harbin, G.L., Porter, P., Munn, D., & Vandiviere, P. (1998). The family-centeredness of individualized family service plans. *Topics in Early Childhood Special Education, 18*(2), 69–82.

McWilliam, R.A., Tocci, L., & Harbin, G.L. (1998). Family-centered services: Service providers' discourse and behavior. *Topics in Early Childhood Special Education, 18*(4), 206–221.

Meisels, S.J., & Fenichel, E. (Eds.). (1996). *New visions for the developmental assessment of infants and young children.* Washington, DC: ZERO TO THREE.

Melaville, A.I., & Blank, M.J. (1993). *Together we can: A guide for crafting a pro-family system of education and human services.* Washington, DC: U.S. Department of Education.

Melaville, A.I., & Blank, M. (1994). *What it takes: Structuring interagency partnerships to connect children and families with comprehensive services.* Washington, DC: Education and Human Services Consortium.

Nickel, R.E., Cooley, W.C., McAllister, J.W., & Samson-Fang, L. (2003). Building medical homes for children with special health care needs. *Infants and Young Children, 16*(4), 331–341.

Ohlson, C. (1998). Welfare reform: Implications for young children with disabilities, their families, and service providers. *Journal of Early Intervention, 21*(3), 191–206.

Palsha, S.A., & Wesley, P.W. (1998). Improving quality in early childhood environments through on-site consultation. *Topics in Early Childhood Special Education, 18*(4), 243–253.

Park, J., & Turnbull, A.P. (2003). Service integration in early intervention: Determining interpersonal and structural factors for its success. *Infants and Young Children, 16*(1), 48–58.

Pugach, M.C., & Johnson, L.J. (1995). *Collaborative practitioners, collaborative schools.* Denver, CO: Love.

Rapport, M.J.K., McWilliam, R.A., & Smith, B.J. (2004). Practices across disciplines in early intervention: The research base. *Infants and Young Children, 17*(1), 32–44.

Research and Training Center on Service Coordination. (2004). *RTC newsletter.* Farmington: University of Connecticut, A.J. Pappanikou Center for Excellence in Developmental Disabilities Education, Research, and Service. Reports available online at http://www.uconnucedd.org.

Roberts, R.N. (1999). Supporting families where children live: Community principles in action. In R.N. Roberts & P.R. Magrab (Eds.), *Where children live: Solutions for serving young children and their families* (pp. 31–72). Stamford, CT: Ablex.

Roberts, R.N., Akers, A.L., & Behl, D.D. (1996a). Family-level service coordination within home visiting programs. *Topics in Early Childhood Special Education, 16*(3), 279–301.

Roberts, R.N., Behl, D.D., & Akers, A.L. (1996b). Community-level service integration within home visiting programs. *Topics in Early Childhood Special Education, 16*(3), 302–321.

Roberts, R.N., Innocenti, M.S., & Goetze, L.D. (1999). Emerging issues from state level evaluations of early intervention programs. *Journal of Early Intervention, 22*(2), 152–163.

Roberts, R.N., Rule, S., & Innocenti, M.S. (1998). *Strengthening the family–professional partnership in services for young children.* Baltimore: Paul H. Brookes Publishing Co.

Romer, E.F., & Umbreit, J. (1998). The effects of family-centered service coordination: A social validity study. *Journal of Early Intervention, 21*(2), 95–110.

Rosenkoetter, S.E., Whaley, K.T., Hains, A.H., & Pierce, L. (2001). The evolution of transition policy for young children with special needs and their families: Past, present, and future. *Topics in Early Childhood Special Education, 21*(1), 3–14.

Rosin, P., Green, M., Hecht, L., Tuchman, L., & Robbins, S. (1996). *Pathways: A training and resource guide for enhancing skills in early intervention service coordination.* Madison, WI: Waisman Center.

Rosin, P., Whitehead, A.D., Tuchman, L.I., Jesien, G.S., Begun, A.L., & Irwin, L. (1996). *Partnerships in family-centered care: A guide to collaborative early intervention.* Baltimore: Paul H. Brookes Publishing Co.

Rosman, E.A., & Knitzer, J. (2001). Welfare reform: The special case of young children with disabilities and their families. *Infants and Young Children, 13*(3), 25–35.

Rous, B., Hemmeter, M.L., & Schuster, J. (1999). Evaluating the impact of the STEPS model on development of community-wide transition systems. *Journal of Early Intervention, 22*(1), 38–50.

Salisbury, C.L., Crawford, W., Marlowe, D., & Husband, P. (2003). Integrating education and human service plans: The interagency planning and support project. *Journal of Early Intervention, 26*(1), 59–75.

Santelli, B., Turnbull, A., Marquis, J., & Lerner, E. (2000). Statewide parent-to-parent programs: Partners in early intervention. *Infants and Young Children, 13*(1), 74–86.

Shonkoff, J.P. (2002). A call to pour new wine into old bottles. *Journal of Early Intervention, 25*(2), 105–107.

Smith, K., Gabard, D., Dale, D., & Drucker, A. (1994). Parental opinions about attending parent support groups. *Children's Health Care, 32*(2), 127–136.

Spencer, M.B., Blumenthal, J.B., & Richards, E. (1995). Child care and children of color. In P.L. Chase-Lansdale & J. Brooks-Gunn (Eds.), *Escape from poverty: What makes a difference for children?* (pp. 138–158). New York: Cambridge University Press.

Spiker, D., Hebbeler, K., Wagner, M., Cameto, R., & McKenna, P. (2000). A framework for describing variations in state early intervention systems. *Topics in Early Childhood Special Education, 20*(4), 195–207.

Stayton, V., & Bruder, M.B. (1999). Early intervention personnel preparation for the new millennium: Early childhood special education. *Infants and Young Children, 12*(1), 59–69.

Stegelin, D.A., & Jones, S.D. (1991). Components of early childhood interagency collaboration: Results of a statewide study. *Early Education and Development, 2*(1), 54–67.

Striffler, N., Perry, D.F., & Kates, D.A. (1997). Planning and implementing a finance system for early intervention systems. *Infants and Young Children, 10*(2), 57–65.

Summers, J.A., Steeples, T., Peterson, C., Naig, L., McBride, S., Wall, S., Leibow, H., Swanson, M., & Stowtischek, J. (2001). Policy and management supports for effective service integration in Early Head Start and Part C programs. *Topics in Early Childhood Special Education, 21*(1), 16–30.

Swan, W., & Morgan, J. (1993). *Collaborating for comprehensive services for young children and their families: The local interagency coordinating council.* Baltimore: Paul H. Brookes Publishing Co.

Thompson, L., Lobb, C., Elling, R., Herman, S., Jurkiewicz, T., & Hulleza, C. (1997). Pathways to family empowerment: Effects of family-centered delivery of early intervention services. *Exceptional Children, 64*(1), 81–98.

Thorp, E.K., & McCollum, J.A. (1994). Personnel in early intervention programs: Areas of needed competence. In L.J. Johnson, R.J. Gallagher, M.J. LaMontagne, J.B. Jordan, J.J. Gallagher, P.L. Hutinger, & M.B. Karnes (Eds.), *Meeting early intervention challenges: Issues from birth to three* (pp. 167–184). Baltimore: Paul H. Brookes Publishing Co.

Thurman, S.K., Cornwell, J.R., & Gottwald, S.R. (1997). *Contexts of early intervention: Systems and settings.* Baltimore: Paul H. Brookes Publishing Co.

Trivette, C.M. (1998). How much is enough: Training issues regarding family-centered practices. *Journal of Early Intervention, 21*(2), 111–113.

Trivette, C.M., & Dunst, C.J. (1998). *Family-centered helpgiving practices.* Paper presented at the 14th Annual Division for Early Childhood International Conference on Children with Special Needs, Chicago.

Turnbull, A., & Turnbull, H. (1997). *Families, professionals and exceptionality: A special partnership* (3rd ed.). Upper Saddle River, NJ: Prentice Hall.

Vig, S., & Kaminer, R. (2003). Comprehensive interdisciplinary evaluation as intervention for young children. *Infants and Young Children, 16*(4), 342–353.

Wesley, P.W., Buysse, V., & Tyndall, S. (1997). Family and professional perspective on early intervention: An exploration using focus groups. *Topics in Early Childhood Special Education, 17*(4), 435–456.

West, J.F., & Cannon, G.S. (1988). Essential collaborative consultation competencies for regular and special educators. *Journal of Learning Disabilities, 21,* 56–63.

Widen, J.E., Bull, W., & Folsom, R.C. (2003). Newborn hearing screening: What it means for providers of early intervention services. *Infants and Young Children, 16*(3), 249–257.

Winton, P. (1998). Socially valid but difficult to implement: Creative solutions needed. *Journal of Early Intervention, 21*(2), 114–116.

Winton, P.J. (2000). Early childhood intervention personnel preparation: Backward mapping for future planning. *Topics in Early Childhood Special Education, 20*(2), 87–94.

Winton, P.J., McCollum, J.A., & Catlett, C. (Eds.). (1997). *Reforming personnel preparation in early intervention: Issues, models, and practical strategies.* Baltimore: Paul H. Brookes Publishing Co.

Wischnowski, M.W., Fowler, S.A., & McCollum, J.A. (2000). Supports and barriers to writing an interagency agreement on the preschool transition. *Journal of Early Intervention, 23*(4), 294–307.

W.K. Kellogg Foundation. (2001). *Using logic models to bring together planning, evaluation, and action: Logic model development guide.* Battle Creek, MI: Author.

Wolery, M. (1989). Transition in early childhood special education: Issues and procedures. *Focus on Exceptional Children, 22,* 1–16.

Wolery, M. (2003). Using assessment information to plan intervention programs. In M. McLean, M. Wolery, & D. Bailey (Eds.), *Assessing infants and preschoolers with special needs* (3rd ed., pp. 517–544). Upper Saddle River, NJ: Merrill/Prentice Hall.

Wolery, M., & Bailey, D.B. (2002). Early childhood special education research. *Journal of Early Intervention, 25*(2), 88–99.

Zipper, I.N., Hinton, C., Weil, M., & Rounds, K. (1993). *Service coordination for early intervention: Parents and professionals.* Cambridge, MA: Brookline Books.

CHAPTER 3

INCLUSION AS A CORE PRINCIPLE IN THE EARLY INTERVENTION SYSTEM

MICHAEL J. GURALNICK

In the context of the Developmental Systems Model of early intervention, the principle of inclusion represents all efforts to maximize the participation of children and families in typical home and community activities (Guralnick, 2001a). Although inclusion is often thought of in the context of encouraging interactions between children with and without disabilities, it is conceptualized in the broadest possible manner as a core principle in the Developmental Systems Model. The ideological and philosophical rationales for a principle that encourages full participation of all children in community life are important in their own right, but failure to translate this principle into practice within the early intervention system will likely have numerous adverse consequences on children's development, including limiting the full range of stimulation that children can experience, restricting social and educational learning opportunities, and perhaps creating low expectations for achievement (Guralnick, 2001b).

More specifically, inclusion emphasizes full involvement of the child in family routines and in social activities with relatives and friends, as well as taking advantage of the entire array of educational and recreational opportunities that communities have to offer (see Bruder, 2001; Dunst, 2001). Of importance, this principle has legal status with respect to the delivery of early intervention services. The Education for All Handicapped Children Act of 1975 (PL 99-142; now known as the Individuals with Disabilities Education Act [IDEA]), along with subsequent amendments, reauthorizations, and related legislation (PL 101-476, PL 102-119, and PL 105-17), sought to ensure that children with disabilities remained in as normal settings as possible while services and supports were being provided. For infants and toddlers, participation in natural environments was mandated (i.e., interventions should occur in places where one would usually find typically developing children; Walsh, Rous, & Lutzer, 2000).

59

For preschool-age children, the law required that every effort be made to ensure that children with developmental delays fully participate with their typically developing peers in early childhood programs. But again, inclusion as a core principle in a developmental systems framework has broader implications (see Guralnick, 2001a).

Unfortunately, powerful forces continue to exert pressure toward isolation and separation when a child has a disability. Despite considerable progress over the years, negative attitudes at all levels of the community still surround children with disabilities (Stoneman, 2001), and state-administered early intervention programs have failed to meet most reasonable contemporary goals for inclusion (Guralnick, 2001b). But, it is also the case that family patterns of interaction involving a child with a disability can increase the risk of isolation from peers and from community activities and limit a child's participation in the life of his or her own family. For example, families of children with disabilities (see Chapter 1; Guralnick, 1998) often need information with respect to reading their child's cues or adjusting to their child's limited expressive language to achieve the proper development-enhancing balance in their relationship. In the absence of that information, the quality of parent–child transactions can be compromised, affecting the quality of the relationship between a child and other family members during daily family routines (Fiese, 2002; Gallimore, Weisner, Bernheimer, Guthrie, & Nihira, 1993). As a consequence, children's participation in those routines may become less productive from a developmental perspective, even distressing to those involved, and will ultimately occur less frequently. Similarly, parents' confidence in their ability to manage their child's behavior or perhaps interpersonal or family distress in family or community activities stemming from their child's "disability status" can further limit children's experiences that would normally be initiated and organized by family members. These circumstances may even lead families to select unnecessarily restrictive early intervention alternatives such as a segregated preschool educational program.

Accordingly, as these examples illustrate, stressors created by a child's characteristics can affect family patterns of interaction (e.g., parent–child transactions, community experiences organized by parents) that influence a child's inclusion in home and community life and may adversely influence a child's development as well. A similar process operates for stressors on family patterns of interaction whose origins are linked to the characteristics of the families themselves. For example, families experiencing mental health problems or who have limited financial resources or social supports are far more likely to lack the ability to negotiate community life in a manner that orchestrates appropriately stimulating experiences for their child or the ability to engage in parent–child transactions during family routines that are enjoyable and developmentally enhancing (see Burchinal,

Roberts, Hooper, & Zeisel, 2000; Sameroff, Seifer, Barocas, Zax, & Greenspan, 1987).

Clearly, then, for children with established disabilities or those at risk for developmental problems, these and related threats to inclusion must be addressed when families and children are involved in the early intervention system. Indeed, virtually every component of the early intervention system is relevant to inclusive practices. Accordingly, the purpose of this chapter is to suggest strategies designed to maximize inclusion in home and community life for children and families encountering the early intervention system as presented in the Developmental Systems Model. This discussion will be organized in accordance with the separate structural components of the model: screening program or referral, surveillance, point of access, comprehensive interdisciplinary assessment, entry into a preventive intervention program, entry into an early intervention program, assessment of stressors, developing and implementing a comprehensive program, monitoring and outcome evaluations, and transition planning. See Chapter 1 or Guralnick (2001a) for more detailed descriptions of each component.

SCREENING PROGRAM OR REFERRAL

People seeking services who encounter any service system, including one focusing on early intervention, risk being stigmatized. Stigmatization can, of course, occur in any component of the system, but initial contacts with a system can create long-lasting effects. As such, special care must be taken to thoughtfully discuss the meaning and implications of any screening results or reasons for referral (i.e., risk factors). Families are likely to have numerous questions about the implications of routine screening for their child's short- and long-term development. Therefore, a frank, professional discussion about the results, as well as recognizing the limitations of the screening process and the inherent variability in developmental rates, is in order. Similarly, expressing as much optimism as is reasonable and appropriate and ensuring that discussions remain firmly within a developmental framework should be essential features of these initial encounters with children and families.

SURVEILLANCE

If screening fails to result in a referral but concerns remain, then the surveillance or monitoring programs that are arranged should follow a similar approach outlined previously for screening. Questions by parents are likely to arise at each monitoring point but especially if concerns or risks are sufficient to result in a referral. Continuing to emphasize the value of full participation for children and families in home and community activities should be an integral part of the monitoring phase.

POINT OF ACCESS

Identified concerns or clear risks to a child's development that result in a referral (self or otherwise) generally initiate contact with what is best referred to as a point of access in the early intervention system. Inclusion would certainly be maximized if the point of access were part of a broader system of community-based child development supports and services to which all children had access. There are many advantages for such a comprehensive point of access beyond communicating that all children, irrespective of risk or disability, are part of the same community (see Harbin, McWilliam, & Gallagher, 2000). Nevertheless, most points of access are organized in accordance with risk and disability conditions and are quite diverse from community to community and state to state (Harbin et al., 2000; Spiker, Hebbeler, Wagner, Cameto, & McKenna, 2000). Given this situation, it is vital that special efforts be taken to avoid stigmatizing families as they make contact with what is usually a formal system and that information is gathered for future use for program planning and administrative purposes.

Minimizing the use of labels, stressing how this particular point of contact operates in the context of the larger community, providing a warm and inviting setting for families, and ensuring the confidentiality of information all can help in this regard. These strategies are especially important if points of contact are large agencies serving a fairly substantial community (usually established for reasons of efficiency) or if the agency is one that is highly specialized or disorder-focused (e.g., clinics specializing in metabolic disorders or autism spectrum disorders).

COMPREHENSIVE INTERDISCIPLINARY ASSESSMENT

Based on information collected and organized at the point of access, many children for whom there are concerns about their development in the form of a delay or disability participate with their families in a comprehensive interdisciplinary assessment (Farrell & Pimentel, 1995; Guralnick, 2000b; Thyer & Kropf, 1995). As a result of this process, a child's developmental profile is generated, information with respect to diagnostic/etiologic decisions is gathered, and general recommendations about next steps (e.g., referrals to early intervention programs or other specialists) are provided

(Guralnick, 2000c). This encounter with an interdisciplinary team of specialists can be very intimidating to families and frequently occurs in highly specialized medical or evaluation centers.

Once again, the way in which complex information is communicated to families can substantially influence their orientation in terms of inclusion. First, diagnostic information must be presented in a way that helps families work through and resolve any issues surrounding acceptance and understanding of the diagnosis. Failure to do so increases the likelihood that families will have difficulty forming attachments with their child and adversely affect parent–child transactions (Pianta, Marvin, Britner, & Borowitz, 1996). As a consequence, full involvement of the child in family activities may be compromised. Second, maintaining a developmental perspective is critical in conveying information to families regarding their child's developmental profile. Variations and even atypical forms of behavior and development can and should be presented as part of a larger developmental framework pointing not only to similarities in their child's developmental trajectory and to the organization of their child's development common to all children but also to the important influences on development shared by all. Finally, even general recommendations for supports and services should focus on as many inclusive options as possible. Families should be encouraged to seek out services in their local communities and, to the extent possible, participate with their child's peer group of children without disabilities. Providing lists of local community agencies, such as child care programs, that can effectively accommodate children with disabilities is an example of a strategy that communicates an inclusive philosophy to families.

PREVENTIVE INTERVENTION PROGRAM

Those children who do not have an identified delay or disability but who are judged to be at sufficient risk for developmental problems are referred to a preventive intervention program. The reason for referral could be related to child characteristics (i.e., premature birth, low birth weight), but many children entering preventive intervention programs exhibit family characteristics (e.g., maternal mental health problems, limited financial resources, absence of social supports) that can stress family patterns of interaction, leading to social isolation and a general lack of involvement for families and their child in numerous activities. For families entering this component of the system, professional staff should give special attention toward establishing positive personal relationships and building trust and confidence (Berlin, O'Neal, & Brooks-Gunn, 1998). This relationship is an essential bridge to community involvement of the child and family and, if properly established, will likely yield a more valuable assessment of stressors that will form the basis for preventive intervention approaches.

EARLY INTERVENTION PROGRAM

Children for whom a delay or disability is highly likely or has been firmly established will now begin an ongoing relationship with a range of providers of early intervention services and supports. Establishing a positive relationship between parents and professionals is critical for families, even in the absence of family characteristics that would create additional risk factors. The way in which a preliminary intervention program is carried out when families enter the early intervention program, and the extent to which conscious decisions are made to promote community participation while developing a partnership with families, can clearly have a major effect both now and in the future on all aspects of inclusion.

Establishing that services and supports, even in the context of a preliminary intervention program, will be coordinated effectively constitutes another important potential influence on inclusion for families. Highly coordinated and integrated services and supports reduce parental anxiety and allow parents more time to pursue community activities with their child and foster their child's involvement in family routines. Additional child care demands alone can drain the energy of many families—further responsibilities for coordinating often disparate services can dramatically restrict a child's full participation in home and community life. Also, good parent–professional relationships and efficient service coordination can facilitate the ongoing assessment of stressors needed to develop and implement well-designed and effective comprehensive intervention programs, including components relevant to inclusion.

ASSESSMENT OF STRESSORS

For children with disabilities, information needs, interpersonal and family distress, resource needs, and confidence threats to parenting frequently arise as a consequence of a child's characteristics. This can lead to stress on family interaction patterns, which can adversely affect the child's development (Guralnick, 1998). Similarly, as noted previously, certain family characteristics or environmental risk factors can stress family patterns of interaction in a number of ways and contribute to a child's developmental delays. Assessing these potential child- and family-generated influences is one of the most critical components of the Developmental Systems Model (Guralnick, 2001a), and much of the information gathered in the course of this assessment is relevant to inclusion. Perhaps of most importance, the assessment should include considerable information about family routines and community activity patterns that families find important and satisfying. The ultimate goal is to work with families to try to maintain those patterns and include children with disabilities or those who are at risk. Increased attention has been given to strategies for gathering information on family routines and community activities and for determining family needs in connection with sustaining and enhancing these routines and activities in the context of early intervention (Bernheimer & Keogh, 1995; Bruder, 2001; Dunst, 2001; Dunst, Hamby, Trivette, Raab, & Bruder, 2000). In addition, a discussion with respect to a child's involvement with his or her peers should be initiated as this frequently is an area of concern for young children with disabilities (Guralnick, 1997). Parents' roles in organizing playgroups or arranging playdates should be part of the assessment. In this way, parental needs designed to help support a child's involvement with peers at home and in the community can be identified. Finally, families are unlikely to have sufficient information about the formal service system principles and options with respect to natural environments or inclusive educational programs under IDEA. Introducing that topic and probing the family's level of understanding of the issues will allow more thoughtful decisions to be made during the development and implementation of a comprehensive program phase of the early intervention system.

DEVELOPING AND IMPLEMENTING A COMPREHENSIVE PROGRAM

The provision of resource supports, social supports, and information and services to families (i.e., early intervention services and supports) in order to support full participation of a child with a disability or a child at risk in home and community activities occurs in this component of the model. It is hopeful that families' contacts with the early intervention system all along have emphasized a community orientation and a developmental framework, and that assessments have focused on topics related to family routines and community activities. Having reached this point in the early intervention system, the decisions that families and professionals make about specific intervention programs should reflect that inclusive orientation. Indeed, the development of intervention plans should reference maximum participation as a goal. Specific family routines and community contexts should be considered to be central as well, with intervention plans embedded within those contexts (see Dunst, Trivette, Humphries, Raab, & Roper, 2001). Without question, services chosen by families of children with disabilities should be considered in the framework of natural environments or inclusive early childhood programs. For families who are participating in preventive intervention programs, especially for those children at high environmental risk, the design and implementation of a comprehensive program should reflect similar efforts to support family routines and enhance developmental opportunities as part of community involvement. If intervention-oriented child care is part of the preventive intervention plan, then every effort should be made for inclusion (Guralnick, 2000a).

Access to various forms of inclusive programs is, unfortunately, not universally available. Similarly, there is a concern about the quality of many of these programs because they have difficulty appropriately accommodating to and meeting the individualized needs of all children in the setting (see Guralnick, 2001b). Yet, in well-designed inclusive programs, children do at least as well developmentally and socially in comparison with their participation in noninclusive programs (see Guralnick, 2001b). Consequently, for the development and implementation component of the early intervention system, those involved may be required to become advocates for more available and higher quality inclusive programs in order to maximize inclusion. Accordingly, discussions during the individualized planning processes that normally take place should focus on both of these issues. Admittedly, these are frequently difficult discussions, often pitting prospects to meet child and family needs against prospects for real change in the quality of programs.

MONITORING AND OUTCOME EVALUATIONS

To ensure that the core principle of inclusion is embedded in all components of the early intervention system, specific qualitative and quantitative assessments should be developed to evaluate both the extent to which that has occurred and how effectively efforts to support inclusion have been implemented. Straightforward self-report checklists for professionals involved in various components of the early intervention system asking about activities that occur in support of inclusion serve not only an evaluative function but also as a reminder about strategies that may be useful. Periodic interviews with families focusing on how their experiences with various components of the system influenced their decisions about inclusive services and supports or helped guide their goals for their child provide a complementary perspective (see Bailey et al., 1998).

TRANSITION PLANNING

As children make transitions to other programs in the early intervention system, inclusive options should be a strong consideration. This is especially critical when children make the shift from the infant-toddler program to preschool educational programs. During the planning process, visits to the range of inclusive programs available should be encouraged along with frank discussions of the advantages and disadvantages of each option.

For transitions to appropriate inclusive settings to occur, the system needs to have a well-developed coordinating capacity among the various agencies involved and parents must, of course, be well informed about all options. Continuing efforts to prepare professionals properly to support children in inclusive settings and to prepare children to master the techniques to maximize their effective participation in inclusive environments must occur (see Sainato & Morrison, 2001).

CONCLUSION

In this chapter, strategies designed to maximize the inclusion of children and families in home and community activities are discussed in the context of the Developmental Systems Model for early intervention. Strategies are described for each of the model's major components which, taken together, provide a clear message for families (i.e., that full participation of the child and family in home and community life is possible despite circumstances of child risk and disability). The justification for this approach is based on philosophical, legal, developmental, and empirical grounds (see Guralnick, 2001b) and is clearly consistent with research and conceptualizations on the value of working within family routines to sustain interventions (Gallimore, Keogh, & Bernheimer, 1999) and findings indicating that families prefer interventions embedded in activities within community settings (Bruder, 2001; Dunst, 2001). A sensitive application of the strategies discussed in this chapter, as well as others to be developed, are critical for the success of the Developmental Systems Model for early intervention to incorporate in both letter and spirit the core principle of inclusion.

REFERENCES

Bailey, D.B., Jr., McWilliam, R.A., Darkes, L.A., Hebbeler, K., Simeonsson, R.J., Spiker, D., & Wagner, M. (1998). Family outcomes in early intervention: A framework for program evaluation and efficacy research. *Exceptional Children, 64*, 313–328.

Berlin, L.J., O'Neal, C.R., & Brooks-Gunn, J. (1998). What makes early intervention programs work? The program, its participants, and their interaction. *Zero to Three, 18*, 4–15.

Bernheimer, L.P., & Keogh, B.K. (1995). Weaving interventions into the fabric of everyday life: An approach to family assessment. *Topics in Early Childhood Special Education, 15*, 415–433.

Bruder, M.B. (2001). Inclusion of infants and toddlers: Outcomes and ecology. In M.J. Guralnick (Ed.), *Early childhood inclusion: Focus on change* (pp. 203–228). Baltimore: Paul H. Brookes Publishing Co.

Burchinal, M.R., Roberts, J.E., Hooper, S., & Zeisel, S.A. (2000). Cumulative risk and early cognitive development: A comparison of statistical risk models. *Developmental Psychology, 36,* 793–807.

Dunst, C.J. (2001). Participation of young children with disabilities in community learning activities. In M.J. Guralnick (Ed.), *Early childhood inclusion: Focus on change* (pp. 307–333). Baltimore: Paul H. Brookes Publishing Co.

Dunst, C.J., Hamby, D., Trivette, C.M., Raab, M., & Bruder, M.B. (2000). Every-day family and community life and children's naturally occurring learning opportunities. *Journal of Early Intervention, 23,* 151–164.

Dunst, C.J., Trivette, C.M., Humphries, T., Raab, M., & Roper, N. (2001). Contrasting approaches to natural learning environment interventions. *Infants and Young Children, 14*(2), 48–63.

Education for All Handicapped Children Act of 1975, PL 94-142, 20 U.S.C. §§ 1400 *et seq.*

Farrell, S.E., & Pimentel, A.E. (1995). Interdisciplinary team process in developmental disabilities. In A.J. Capute & P.J. Accardo (Eds.), *Developmental disabilities in infancy and childhood: Vol. I. The spectrum of developmental disabilities* (2nd ed., pp. 431–441). Baltimore: Paul H. Brookes Publishing Co.

Fiese, B.H. (2002). Routines of daily living and rituals in family life: A glimpse at stability and change during the early child-raising years. *Zero to Three, 22*(4), 10–13.

Gallimore, R., Keogh, B.K., & Bernheimer, L.P. (1999). The nature and long-term implications of early developmental delays: A summary of evidence from two longitudinal studies. In L.M. Glidden (Vol. Ed.), *International review of research in mental retardation* (Vol. 22, pp. 105–135). San Diego: Academic Press.

Gallimore, R., Weisner, T.S., Bernheimer, L.P., Guthrie, D., & Nihira, K. (1993). Family responses to young children with developmental delays: Accommodation activity in ecological and cultural context. *American Journal on Mental Retardation, 98,* 185–206.

Guralnick, M.J. (1997). The peer social networks of young boys with developmental delays. *American Journal on Mental Retardation, 101,* 595–612.

Guralnick, M.J. (1998). The effectiveness of early intervention for vulnerable children: A developmental perspective. *American Journal on Mental Retardation, 102,* 319–345.

Guralnick, M.J. (2000a). The early intervention system and out-of-home child care. In D. Cryer & T. Harms (Eds.), *Infants and toddlers in out-of-home care* (pp. 207–234). Baltimore: Paul H. Brookes Publishing Co.

Guralnick, M.J. (Ed.). (2000b). *Interdisciplinary clinical assessment for young children with developmental disabilities.* Baltimore: Paul H. Brookes Publishing Co.

Guralnick, M.J. (2000c). Interdisciplinary team assessment for young children: Purposes and processes. In M.J. Guralnick (Ed.), *Interdisciplinary clinical assessment for young children with developmental disabilities* (pp. 3–15). Baltimore: Paul H. Brookes Publishing Co.

Guralnick, M.J. (2001a). A developmental systems model for early intervention. *Infants and Young Children, 14*(2), 1–18.

Guralnick, M.J. (2001b). A framework for change in early childhood inclusion. In M.J. Guralnick (Ed.), *Early childhood inclusion: Focus on change* (pp. 3–35). Baltimore: Paul H. Brookes Publishing Co.

Harbin, G.L., McWilliam, R.A., & Gallagher, J.G. (2000). Services for young children with disabilities and their families. In J.P. Shonkoff & S.J. Meisels

(Eds.), *Handbook of early childhood intervention* (2nd ed., pp. 387–415). Cambridge: Cambridge University Press.

Individuals with Disabilities Education Act (IDEA) Amendments of 1991, PL 102-119, 20 U.S.C. §§ 1400 *et seq.*

Individuals with Disabilities Education Act (IDEA) Amendments of 1997, PL 105-17, 20 U.S.C. §§ 1400 *et seq.*

Individuals with Disabilities Education Act (IDEA) of 1990, PL 101-476, 20, U.S.C. §§ 1400 *et seq.*

Pianta, R.C., Marvin, R.S., Britner, P.A., & Borowitz, K.C. (1996). Mothers' resolution of their children's diagnosis: Organized patterns of caregiving representations. *Journal of Infant Mental Health, 17,* 239–256.

Sainato, D.M., & Morrison, R.S. (2001). Transition to inclusive environments for young children with disabilities: Toward a seamless system of service delivery. In M.J. Guralnick (Ed.), *Early childhood inclusion: Focus on change* (pp. 293–306). Baltimore: Paul H. Brookes Publishing Co.

Sameroff, A.J., Seifer, R., Barocas, R., Zax, M., & Greenspan, S. (1987). Intelligence quotient scores of 4-year-old children: Social-environmental risk factors. *Pediatrics, 79,* 343–350.

Spiker, D., Hebbeler, K., Wagner, M., Cameto, R., & McKenna, P. (2000). A framework for describing variations in state early intervention systems. *Topics in Early Childhood Special Education, 20,* 195–207.

Stoneman, Z. (2001). Attitudes and beliefs of parents of typically developing children: Effects on early childhood inclusion. In M.J. Guralnick (Ed.), *Early childhood inclusion: Focus on change* (pp. 101–126). Baltimore: Paul H. Brookes Publishing Co.

Thyer, B.A., & Kropf, N.P. (Eds.). (1995). *Developmental disabilities: A handbook for interdisciplinary practice.* Cambridge, MA: Brookline Books.

Walsh, S., Rous, B., & Lutzer, C. (2000). The federal IDEA natural environments provisions: Making it work [Monograph Series No. 2]. In S. Sandall & M. Ostrosky (Eds.), *Young exceptional children: Natural environments and inclusion* (pp. 3–15). Longmont, CO: Division of Early Childhood/Sopris West.

PRACTICES: NATIONAL PERSPECTIVES

CHAPTER 4

SCREENING AND SURVEILLANCE IN EARLY INTERVENTION SYSTEMS

WALTER S. GILLIAM, SAMUEL J. MEISELS, AND LINDA C. MAYES

Developmental screening is a deceptively simple method for identifying young children who may be at risk for problems in their health, development, or other areas of functioning. It is simple because developmental screenings are brief, inexpensive, do not take long to learn how to administer, and can be re-administered after relatively short intervals. It is deceptive because sound developmental screening requires careful selection of content, thoughtful consideration given to the use of the screening data, and assiduous attention to psychometric principles.

When these characteristics are realized, it becomes clear that developmental screening is not something to take for granted or to consider as an afterthought. Developmental screening is fundamentally a preventive process that identifies problems in young children before they become serious or acute. Accordingly, it deserves a great deal of attention because screening programs help reduce morbidity and disability and may contribute to children's opportunities to live full and meaningful lives.

Screening is a deliberate and methodical process by which data are collected to identify which children are most likely to need intervention services. The methods of screening that are used can include assessment of individual children's development, either by direct assessment of the child or by report of parents and other caregivers, and the utilization of various risk and protective indices that predict developmental delays (Meisels, 1996; Sameroff, Seifer, Barocas, Zax, & Greenspan, 1987; Werner, 2000). Developmental surveillance, another method for quickly learning about a child's status, is largely based on clinical impressions formed on the basis of brief observation and parental report (Dworkin, 2000). Developmental surveillance techniques are most frequently used in pediatric and other health care settings in which children's development may not always be the primary presenting concern and in which the amount of contact with individual children and families may be limited. Although this method may have some limited utility in detecting delays, concerns regarding social-emotional growth and the development of independence are not accurately detected by relying on expressed parental concern (Glascoe, Altemeier, & MacLean, 1989). Developmental surveillance may include formal screening for developmental delays, but objective instruments are not utilized in the majority of instances (Dobos, Dworkin, & Bernstein, 1994).

THE RATIONALE FOR EARLY IDENTIFICATION

The rationale for effective systems of early screening and identification is based on three assumptions. First, intervention services for young children can help reduce developmental delays and prevent or attenuate the adverse developmental effects of biological and environmental risk factors. Second, intervention is more effective when begun early in the life of a child or as soon as possible after the onset of those factors that place children's development at risk. Third, effective early screening and assessment systems can result in earlier provision of intervention and remediation services. Considerable evidence exists to support the first two of the assumptions as described next. The third assumption, though logical in its assertion, remains an area in need of further research.

A considerable amount of evidence accumulated since the 1980s from an array of methodologically sound studies demonstrates the effectiveness of early intervention and early childhood education programs for children in the first 5 years of life (Guralnick, 1997; Shonkoff & Meisels, 2000). The intervention programs include those serving children with specific developmental disorders (e.g., autism, genetically based mental retardation), children with developmental delays, and children from families living in poverty. The delivery models include those focused primarily on direct services to young children; those targeting enhanced parental efficacy; and those that take a two-generation approach, serving both parents and their offspring. Some are primarily home based, whereas others are center based; some consist of well-defined interventions, whereas others have a wide focus. Although a close consideration of these studies may suggest that some models may be more effective than others and some disabilities more amenable to intervention, the bulk of the literature supports early intervention (Farran, 2000).

Several examples support the position that intervening as early as possible maximizes positive impacts and decreases the continuing adverse impact of certain disabling conditions (Shonkoff & Phillips, 2000; Shore, 1997). In the Abecedarian Study (Campbell & Ramey, 1995), children who were at risk were randomly assigned to treatment groups receiving early intervention services during different periods of early childhood (e.g., birth to 3 years, 3 years to 5 years). Benefits in the areas of reading, math, and reduced grade retention were most clearly observed in the groups that received intervention the earliest. In addition, very early intervention during infancy has been shown to reduce or ameliorate the developmental impact of hearing loss, prematurity, and metabolic disorders such as phenylketonuria (PKU; National Institutes of Health, 2000), indicating the clear importance of early intervention.

Of course, early intervention relies on early identification, and therein rests the importance of effective and efficient systems of screening, assessment, and referral. Early preventive interventions are aimed at reducing the developmental effects of certain risk factors (e.g., poverty, domestic violence, biological disorders) or providing developmental remediation for children who already present with developmental delays. In any case, valid and efficient systems for identifying young children with these risk factors or conditions as early as possible are a prerequisite to providing the earliest possible interventions.

An examination of the Michigan service rates for early intervention and special education found that the service rates did not reach the expected epidemiological prevalence rate of about 12% until children were 8 years or older, despite the fact that most developmental delays are observable by infancy or toddlerhood (Meisels & Wasik, 1990). In fact, assuming a 12% prevalence rate for developmental disorders, not until children are 6 years old are even half of the children with special needs identified and provided services. The rates for children 3 and 4 years old are only about 15% and 27% of the expected prevalence, and for children birth through 2 years old, the rate is less than 6%. Simple math suggests that our current methods of screening can miss as many as 73%–85% of 3- and 4-year-olds and as many as 94% of infants and toddlers who could be eligible for developmental services.

PRINCIPLES OF EFFECTIVE SCREENING SYSTEMS

Several hallmarks of effective community-level screening for children at developmental risk or for those manifesting delays can be described, as screening and surveillance are critical aspects of the community-oriented Developmental Systems Model (Guralnick, 2001). First, screening should be both periodic and available as needed. Because the primary goal of screening is to identify children in need of services as early as possible, screening methods should target children at various ages throughout the first years of life. All infants born in United States hospitals are provided at least some rudimentary screening at birth for various genetic, structural, metabolic, and infectious disorders. The presence of toxins (e.g., from possible exposure to alcohol or other drugs in utero) and prematurity or low birth weight also are identified; however, not all children who will demonstrate developmental delays and disabilities later in life screen positive for these biological conditions at the time of birth. Once children reach the age at which they may be participating in federally or state-funded preschool services—typically by age 3 or 4—identification may result from developmental screening that sometimes occurs as part of these program requirements or through referral by the program staff. However, children are left unidentified from birth to age 3 or 4.

Second, effective systems of screening must focus on all areas of children's development. Many screening instruments are limited only to the areas of language, cognitive, or motor development, missing important dimensions of development in the areas of social and emotional functioning, emerging independence, motivation to learn, behavior, and articulation. Because expressed parental concern often lacks desired sensitivity to these latter issues (Glascoe et al., 1989), the absence of these dimensions from many screening systems complicates early identification.

Third, young children often behave differently in different contexts, and formal assessment procedures at this age level often yield an incomplete picture of a young child's developmental status (Greenspan & Meisels, 1996). Therefore, effective screening procedures should employ a variety of methods and informants. For example, a screening system might include both a developmental rating scale completed by the parents or other caregivers, such as the child's child care provider, and a brief, individually administered screening test. Referral for a more complete diagnostic or service eligibility assessment would be made on the basis of either or both of these measures.

Fourth, screening measures should have adequate psychometric properties. In order to fulfill their goal of accurately identifying children who may require further diagnostic or service eligibility assessment, screening tests should yield scores that are predictive of performance on more comprehensive diagnostic assessments but require substantially less time to administer and score. The goal of all screening tests is to identify correctly those children who would likely score poorly on a more comprehensive assessment and to reduce two possible sources of error: false positives and false negatives. The ability of a screening instrument to reduce rates of false negative identifications is referred to as the test's *sensitivity*, or its ability to accurately detect children with delays or disabilities. Conversely, the ability of a screening tool to reduce rates of false positives is referred to as its *specificity*, or its ability to avoid identifying a child as having delays or a disability when in fact that child does not. Although it is desirable to reduce the percentage of both types of error, sensitivity may be more important than specificity with screening tests because it is assumed that follow-up assessment will correct any false positives. Meisels (1989) recommended that developmental screening instruments possess both sensitivity and specificity levels of at least 80%. Unfortunately, many tools do not provide these data or do not meet this criterion.

Fifth, measures used in systems of developmental screening should be efficient. Because the purpose of screening is to identify children for which comprehensive assessments are warranted, screening itself should not be as costly an endeavor as assessment. At least four aspects of efficiency can be identified. These pertain to requirement of material costs, time, personnel, and accuracy. Efficient screening measures should not cost providers much in terms of purchasing the materials or the professional time needed to administer them. As contrasted to diagnostic assessment tools, most instruments designed for use in screening may be administered by trained paraprofessionals, although even in these circumstances, astute observation and synthesis of both objective and clinical data are required (Gilliam & Mayes, 2004). If the screening instrument is to be used by professionals whose time is more costly, then the instrument should be very brief to administer, score, and interpret. Brevity, however, is often at odds with accuracy, and no screening system can be considered cost efficient if it often yields inaccurate results (Johnson, Ashford, Byrne, & Glascoe, 1992).

Sixth, in order to be effective tools for early identification, screening systems must have a clear mechanism of delivery and articulation to subsequent assessment and intervention. The personnel responsible for administering the screening and the funding methods should understand fully their roles and be in agreement with the relevance and accuracy of the screening tool. Similarly, the mechanisms by which children that screen positive are referred for further diagnostic assessment and intervention should be clearly articulated. Therefore, appropriate receiving agencies and professionals (most typically, early intervention services, special education preschool programs, and community professionals) who are able to manage the volume of referrals must be identified, and clear guidelines for referral criteria must be negotiated.

DEVELOPMENTAL SCREENING AND DEVELOPMENTAL SURVEILLANCE

Despite these clear principles of developmental screening, for some years pediatricians and other health professionals have sought to institute a brief form of screening known as *developmental surveillance, opportunistic*

surveillance, or *developmental monitoring*. Although these terms are not necessarily equivalent, practices related to them have grown in popularity
within primary care pediatric practice (see Meisels & Atkins-Burnett, 2000,
from which this section is adapted, for a more complete discussion of
these issues).

According to Dworkin, developmental monitoring refers to "the process of closely watching children's development, without implying any
specific process or technique. Monitoring may be periodic or continuous,
systematic or informal, and may or may not involve such processes as
screening, surveillance, or assessment" (1989, p. 1001). First introduced in
Britain, the rationale for developmental monitoring is tied to the purported
limited validity of developmental screening instruments and the amount
of time, effort, and money required to conduct such screenings, especially
in the primary care medical setting (cf. Bain, 1989; Houston & Davis,
1985; Hutchison & Nicoll, 1988; Sturner, Funk, & Green, 1994). When
explored more closely, however, these arguments are fairly weak. For
example, the cost–benefit argument is not very convincing. Several studies
have examined the relative cost effectiveness of various approaches to early
detection of developmental disabilities (Glascoe, Foster, & Wolraich, 1997;
Squires, 1996). Not surprisingly, these studies found that costs decreased
as screening instruments increased in sensitivity and specificity. Overall,
the studies support the economic value of early detection and intervention
when sound screening methods and instruments are used.

From another perspective, the expense associated with developmental
screening can be viewed within a preventive framework of costs and benefits. Developmental screening can represent a secondary level of prevention. It consists of actions taken to prevent developmental delays from
occurring at all or becoming more severe, or actions intended to halt the
progress of a condition before it becomes debilitating (Meisels, 1988).
Although only 5%–7% of an unselected preschool population is actually
at risk for future delays, the savings to society of identifying these children
is very significant in terms of avoiding special education and rehabilitation;
pursuing productive livelihoods and contributing to society; and supporting
children and families, thus avoiding other costs that would otherwise have
to be borne by public funds.

In terms of accuracy, evidence has been mounting for some time that
screening can take place with substantial precision. Published reports of
a variety of developmental screening instruments demonstrate sensitivity
and specificity that is highly acceptable (see Meisels, Liaw, Henderson,
Browning, & Ten Have, 1993; Meisels, Marsden, Wiske, & Henderson,
1997; Squires, 1996; Squires & Bricker, 1991; Squires, Nickel, & Bricker,

1990), although the use of some screening instruments is still highly questionable (see, e.g., Glascoe, Byrne, Ashford, Johnson, & Chang's [1992] analysis of the Denver II). The lack of valid and reliable screening instruments is no longer a barrier to engaging in this type of data gathering with young children.

But the crux of the argument for developmental surveillance is closely connected to the issue of personnel in assessments. It assumes that most pediatricians can make accurate, informal evaluations of children's development. Unfortunately, the evidence in support of this statement is not strong. Various studies (e.g., Costello et al., 1987; Sharp, Pantell, Murphy, & Lewis, 1992) demonstrate that pediatricians in private or clinical practice miss a high proportion of the problems in the children they see for routine care. One group of authors who reviewed videotapes provided by 34 pediatric and family medicine residents of child health visits for 34 children ages 5–12 years found that physicians responded with information, reassurance, guidance, or referral in only 40% of the cases. "Of interest, experienced board-certified pediatricians in private practice and a prepaid clinic responded to fewer than half the psychological concerns of mothers during audiotape-recorded well-child visits" (Sharp et al., 1992, p. 622). These authors suggested that this type of unresponsiveness contributes to the advent of "an unheeded new morbidity" in which a large proportion of learning, behavioral, and emotional problems are not detected at an early age. Primarily what the data show is a high rate of under-referral on the part of the pediatricians, particularly when the problem is emotional/behavioral in origin.

The clear view from the field about personnel in assessment is that no single professional preparation is ideally suited or unsuited for the tasks of evaluation and identification. Rather, multiple perspectives from parents (see Diamond & Squires, 1993; Henderson & Meisels, 1994; Sexton, Thompson, Perez, & Rheams, 1990) and from other professionals (Ireton, 1996; Meisels & Provence, 1989) contribute to reasonable and responsible views of children's emerging skills, abilities, and difficulties. Despite the practical problems of trying to perform developmental screening in a busy pediatric practice, developmental surveillance may not be a solution to the challenge of early identification. Because of the risk of its over-reliance on a single professional perspective, as well as its setting (a busy clinic or pediatric facility), timing (children who are ill or who are anxious because of visiting a physician and the brevity of the visit), and the absence of a standardized protocol (see Kemper, Osborn, Hansen, & Pascoe, 1994), it is likely that developmental surveillance may result in large numbers of errors of over- and under-identification. Developmental monitoring and surveillance can play an important role in early assessment when it is used only as a *supplement*, rather than a *replacement*, for other personnel, perspectives, and methods.

SYSTEMS AND SETTINGS IN WHICH SCREENING CAN BE EMBEDDED

Federally Mandated Screening and Child-Find Systems

The need for effective methods of developmental screening for young children has been acknowledged in federal legislation governing both Medicaid services for low-income families and mandated early intervention and preschool special education services. Children from low-income families participating in the federal Medicaid program also are entitled to health and developmental screening through Medicaid's Early and Periodic Screening, Diagnosis and Treatment (EPSDT) program. This system relies heavily on developmental screening and referrals provided by pediatricians. Unfortunately, this program of developmental surveillance has been largely a failure in providing children from low-income families access to either health or developmental services. According to a study by the United States General Accounting Office (USGAO, 2001), about 60% of children participating in managed care Medicaid did not receive any of the EPSDT screenings to which they were entitled. Furthermore, since 1995, legal suits have been filed against at least 28 states for their failure to provide these mandated screening and referral services (USGAO, 2001).

In 1986, federal special education laws were revised to mandate special education services for children 3–5 years old and to allow states to offer early intervention services to children from birth to 3 years old. Currently, all 50 states provide special education services throughout the birth through 5-year-old age range. Infants and toddlers qualify for these intervention services if they have documented developmental delays in motor (gross or fine), communication (receptive or expressive), cognitive, social, or self-help skills or by having an environmental or biological condition that is likely to lead to a significant developmental delay in one or more of the previous areas. By law, assessments must draw from information from multiple sources (e.g., both direct assessment and caregiver report), and an individualized intervention plan must be developed based on the unique needs and strengths of the child and family. Furthermore, states must create a system for identifying eligible children, often referred to as a *child-find system*, using various methods of recruitment and developmental screening.

Mandated systems of screening and referral, such as Medicaid and special education, rely on the cooperation and agency agreements between systems such as pediatricians and family practice physicians and other health, education, and social services providers, as well as parent referrals to a hotline. Of course, the effectiveness of these provider agreements will depend largely on the quality of the developmental surveillance and screening being accomplished by the providers, and the effectiveness of any hotline rests on the quality of the public service announcements designed to elicit calls and the efficiency and responsiveness of the system. As previously noted, caregivers often are accurate reporters of their children's developmental concerns but are markedly less so in the developmental areas of social, emotional, and emerging independence and self-sufficiency.

Public-Funded Early Childhood Education and Care Settings

Programs that specialize in serving children and families of low income are logical settings for screening procedures. First, these settings often have the necessary infrastructure to deliver screening (e.g., facilities and support staff that can be trained to administer the instruments) and frequently have collaborative arrangements with early intervention and special education staff. Second, by virtue of the low-income population these programs serve, participating children and families already have demonstrated developmental risk factors, reducing the incidence of unnecessary screening. Third, many of these programs are aimed at developing social services plans for children and families, and developmental screening could be integrated into the overall services and referral package.

Program standards for the federal Head Start and Early Head Start programs (which annually serve more than 900,000 children from birth to 5 years old who are from low-income families; Head Start Bureau, 2003) stipulate that local providers must provide developmental screening (including the areas of sensory, behavioral, motor, language, social, cognitive, perceptual, and emotional functioning) for all participating children within 45 days of each child's start of participation and must utilize multiple informants and assessment methods (Head Start Bureau, 2002). In addition, state-funded prekindergarten systems currently operating in 40 states serve more than 911,000 3- to 5-year-olds, and screening for physical health, mental health, vision, and hearing are mandated in about 60% of these systems (Gilliam & Ripple, 2004, as revised by unpublished data from an ongoing study by Gilliam). As several of these state-funded prekindergarten systems have scaled up to universal access, and several more are making moves in this direction, these programs offer an ideal setting for developmental screening and referral for children in the 3- to 5-year-old range.

Unfortunately, an examination of the types of developmental assessments typically used in the programs suggests that many are of poor or unknown validity for young children (Gilliam & Zigler, 2000).

Because most of these publicly funded preschool programs have collaborative agreements with public school special education preschool programs, it should be possible to design appropriate connections between screening and service delivery in these settings. In many cases, preschool special education personnel regularly interact with these programs in order to provide services in a naturalistic setting and to deliver their services through a classroom-based consultation model. The bigger challenge is likely to be faced by the three quarters of these programs that, although fiscally collaborative with the public schools, are offered in a variety of other settings through contracted service agreements, such as for-profit child care programs, faith-affiliated centers, and other nonprofit agencies. In these cases, collaboration with special education staff and community providers may be limited. Speculation about the future roles of Head Start and state-funded prekindergarten systems is complicated by considerable uncertainty regarding future service mandates as the nation debates increased coordination between these two systems (Koppelman, 2003).

Screening services could be mandated as part of the nation's public-funded child care system. However, collaborative arrangements with providers and staff necessary to administer the screening would be even scarcer, given the general lack of programmatic standards in these settings (Young, Marsland, & Zigler, 1997). Additional public-funded programs that could serve as settings for developmental screening and referral include child protective services, family support services, and programs for low-income families, such as the Supplemental Nutrition Program for Women, Infants, and Children (WIC).

A SELECTIVE REVIEW OF SCREENING MEASURES

Several of the more common instruments used in screening systems are presented in Table 4.1. All screening tests presented use direct assessment or observation of the child, unless otherwise stated. Most also allow for caregiver report of information in order to gain additional data about behaviors that may be difficult to elicit in the brief assessment period. Some, however, are based solely on caregiver report (e.g., Developmental Profile–II, Alpern, Boll, & Shearer, 1986; Developmental Observation Checklist System, Hresko, Miguel, Sherbenou, & Burton, 1994). Others are observational or multigate screening systems designed for classroom or child care center application. A few of the most noteworthy and recommended screening instruments are described more fully next.

Table 4.1. Developmental screening tests

Screening test	Age span	Domains[a]	Norm sample	Reliability/validity	Comment
Battelle Developmental Inventory Screening Test (BDI; Newborg, Stock, Wnek, Guidubaldi, & Svinicki, 1984)	6 months–7 years	PS; Ad; GM; FM; EC; RC; Cg	Representative, but small for 6 months to 7 years (N = 800)	Correlation with the full BDI	Suffers from significant psychometric limitations inherent on the full BDI
Bayley Infant Neurodevelopmental Screen (Aylward, 1995)	3–24 months	N; RC; EC/M; Cg			
Birth to Three Developmental Scale (Bangs & Dodson, 1979)	Birth–36 months	EC/RC; Cg; PS; M	Small (N = 357), questionable representation	Strong interrater reliability, but little evidence of validity	
Denver Developmental Screening Test II (Frankenburg et al., 1990)	Birth–6 years	GM; FM/Cg; PS; EC/RC	2,096, all from Colorado	Significant concerns with validity (may overidentify as many as 72% of children)	
Developmental Activities Screening Inventory–II (Fewell & Langley, 1984)	Birth–60 months	15 areas assess sensory and problem solving	More than 200 children with multiple disabilities	Little evidence of reliability; ample validity with children who have severe delays	Can be used with children who have language and/or visual impairments
Developmental Assessment for the Severely Handicapped (Dykes, 1980)	Birth–6 years	EC/RC; SM; SE; Ad; AS	Not normed	Strong internal reliability, but little additional data	Specifically for children with severe developmental delays, but lacks adaptive instructions
Developmental Indicators for the Assessment of Learning–Revised (Mardell-Czudnowski & Goldenberg, 1990)	2 years–6 years	M; AS; EC/RC; B	2,447; nationally representative	Acceptable reliability and validity	

(continued)

83

Table 4.1. *(continued)*

Screening test	Age span	Domains[a]	Norm sample	Reliability/validity	Comment
Developmental Profile-II (Alpern, Boll, & Shearer, 1986)	Birth–9.5 years	M; Ad; PS; AS; EC/RC	3,008	Adequate reliability and validity	1. Parent report only 2. May be useful for educational planning for children with severe delays
Diagnostic Inventory for Screening Children-4 (Amdur, Mainland, & Parker, 1996)	Birth–60 months	FM; GM; RC; EC; AM; VM; Ad; PS	573 in Southwest Ontario, Canada	Excellent reliability; limited evidence of validity	
Early Screening Inventory–Revised (Meisels, Marsden, Wiske, & Henderson, 1997)	3 years–6 years	VM/Ad; L/Cg; GM	ESI-K: 5,034 across 10 states; ESI-P: 977 across five states	Strong reliability and predictive ability; strong sensitivity and acceptable specificity	One of the best validated screening measures available
Early Screening Profiles (Harrison, 1990)	2 years–6 years	Cg; EC/RC; M; Ad/PS; Ar	1,149; nationally representative	Good reliability overall, but Motor is marginal; exceptional validity	One of the best validated screening measures available
Kent Infant Development Scales (Reuter & Bickett, 1985)	Birth–12 months	Cg; M; EC/RC; Ad; PS	480 from Northeast Ohio	Adequate test–retest reliability and validity	Primarily parent report
Learning Accomplishment Profile–Diagnostic Edition (LeMay, Griffin, & Sanford, 1978)	Birth–6 years	FM; GM; EC/RC; Cg; Ad	Not normed	Strong reliability; validity unknown	May be useful in educational planning

Instrument	Age range	Domains[a]	Standardization	Reliability/Validity	Comments
Minnesota Child Development Inventory (Ireton, 1996)	1 year–6 years	GM; FM; EC; RC; Ad; PS; GD	796 in Minneapolis (all middle-class)	Limited information on reliability and validity; concern with interpretation of "percent below age level" scores	Parent report only
Perceptions of Developmental Status (PODS; Bagnato & Neisworth, 1989)	12–72 months	EC/RC; SM; M; SE; Cg; PS	Not normed	Acceptable reliability and validity	1. Useful in educational planning 2. Informant report only
Project Memphis Comprehensive Developmental Scale (Quick & Campbell, 1987)	Birth–5 years	GM; FM; PS; EC/RC; Cg	No information	No information	1. May be useful in educational planning 2. Ceiling at 5 years old
Reynell-Zinkin Developmental Scales (Reynell & Zinkin, 1979)	Birth–60 months	7 tactile and auditory skills domains	109 children with visual impairments	No information	Designed specifically for educational planning of children with visual impairments
Rockford Infant Developmental Evaluation Scales (Project RHISE, 1979)	Birth–4 years	PS/Ad; FM/Cg; RC; EC; GM	Not normed; field tested on 92 children	No information	1. Informal assessment for educational planning 2. Teacher report only

[a] Ad = Adaptive, Self-Help, or Daily Living; AM = Auditory Attention and Memory; Ar = Articulation; AS = Academic or Pre-academic Skills; B = Behavior; Cg = Cognitive or Problem Solving; EC = Expressive Communication/Language; FM = Fine Motor; GD = General Development; GM = Gross Motor; L = Language; M = Motor or Physical; N = Neurological Intactness; PS = Personal-Social; RC = Receptive Communication/Language; SE = Social-Emotional or Self-Regulation; SM = Sensorimotor; VM = Visual Attention and Memory.

Note: A slash mark (/) indicates that multiple domains are assessed in the same scale or subtest.

Early Screening Inventory–Revised

The Early Screening Inventory–Revised (ESI-R; Meisels et al., 1997) is a brief developmental screening instrument that is individually administered to children from 3 to 6 years of age. It is designed to identify children who may need special educational services in order to perform successfully in school. The ESI-R contains two forms: the preschool version (ESI-P) for children 36–54 months old and the kindergarten version (ESI-K) for children 54–72 months old. Both forms take approximately 15–20 minutes to administer and are easy to learn, highly accurate, inexpensive, and accompanied by a parent questionnaire. The ESI-R assesses performance in three areas of development: Visual-Motor/Adaptive, Language and Cognition, and Gross Motor, with screening recommendations based solely on the total score. Poor performance on the ESI-R (i.e., a score in the "Refer" range) suggests not merely a lack of general knowledge but the possibility of a delay or disorder in the child's *potential* for acquiring knowledge. Children whose scores are in the "Rescreen" range and who remain in that range after rescreening also may benefit from specialized services or individualized classroom instruction.

The ESI-R has strong psychometric properties, especially for a screening instrument. Both the preschool and kindergarten versions show strong interrater and test–retest reliability, and studies with more than 350 children show that the ESI-R is also highly valid for predicting later developmental status. Psychometric hallmarks of efficient screening instruments are their ability to avoid two possible sources of error: false positives and false negatives. As noted, the ability of a screener to reduce false negative rates is referred to as the test's *sensitivity*, its ability to accurately detect children with delays or disabilities. Conversely, the ability of a screener to reduce false positives is referred to as the test's *specificity*, its ability to avoid mislabeling a child as delayed or disabled when in fact that child is developmentally normal. Although it is desirable to reduce the percentage of both types of error, sensitivity is more important than specificity with tests designed to be used for screening purposes because, as mentioned previously, it is assumed that follow-up assessment will correct false positives. Both versions of the ESI-R show strong sensitivity (ESI-P = .92; ESI-K = .93) and acceptable specificity (both = .80).

Early Screening Profiles

The Early Screening Profiles (ESP; Harrison, 1990) is applicable for children 2 through 6 years of age. It screens for cognitive, language, speech, physical, and social disabilities or delays that may interfere with a child's learning and warrant further diagnostic assessment. Children complete three different subtests: Cognitive/Language (assessing children's visual discrimination, logical reasoning, verbal concepts, basic school readiness skills), Motor (assessing both fine and gross motor skills), and Speech Articulation. Total testing time per child is only 15–30 minutes, depending on the child's age. In addition, the person who administers the test completes a 2- to 3-minute Behavior Survey documenting the child's behaviors during the assessment (e.g., activity level, attention span, cooperativeness, independence). Caregivers, or sometimes teachers, complete three different rating forms: the Self-Help/Social Profile (which provides a rating of the child's adaptive behaviors), the Home Survey (regarding the caregiver's perception of the child's home environment and caregiver–child interaction), and the Health History Survey (which provides information regarding immunizations, health problems, and prenatal health and delivery). Each of these rating forms can be completed in about 5 minutes. The ESP provides a wide variety of scores for all domains and subdomains, including age equivalents, standard scores, percentile ranks, and easy-to-use 6-point screening categories. Internal consistency and test–retest reliability across all ages exceeds .80 for all but the motor domain, where reliability is marginal. Sensitivity and specificity for the ESP were measured in terms of its ability to correctly identify children who were later identified as needing special education services. Results indicated marginal sensitivity (.67) and acceptable specificity (.88). Cut-off points can be set at several different levels in order to manipulate the false-positive to false-negative ratio.

Other Models of Screening Instruments

In addition to these screening instruments that focus on several areas or dimensions of development and utilize individual assessment of children's responses to a formal test administration, there are other models that are either observational, rely on caregiver report, or focus specifically on social-emotional or behavioral functioning. Depending on the purposes of the screening and context in which screening procedures may be administered, these relatively less utilized models can be useful. With infants and toddlers, the Infant Developmental Assessment (IDA) has proven to be very useful as a screening instrument regarding developmental status and health and family supports. Information is collected largely from observation of the infant and caregiver interview. The Infant-Toddler Social-Emotional Assessment (ITSEA) is also quite useful as a caregiver-informant measure of social, emotional, and behavioral functioning. Because most developmental screening instruments ignore social, emotional, and behavioral areas, the addition of the ITSEA or a similar instrument would help round out screening efforts. Finally, a few observational measures are designed for classroom-based use in child care and preschool settings to identify children at risk for social, emotional, or behavioral challenges. The Early Screening Project and the Devereaux Social-Emotional Scale for Preschool Classrooms are excellent examples of relatively easy-to-use scales that can be used to identify children who are at risk largely through classroom observation and with relatively few demands on teachers.

RECOMMENDATIONS FOR EFFECTIVE COMMUNITY-BASED SCREENING

Rather than rely on a single source of referrals, effective systems for identifying young children who might benefit from special developmental services should utilize data from multiple sources throughout the early childhood years. An efficient and cost-effective multiple gate model of screening might employ methods of referral that are based both on universal (or near universal) screening at certain time intervals and on formal screening of targeted populations who are at risk. Multiple gate methods of screening utilize low-cost methods of initial identification, followed by more formal screening of children who are identified as being at risk during initial screening and diagnostic assessment of children who screen positive. Of course, any system of screening needs to have standardized methods of administration, identified professionals or agencies responsible for administration and referral, and a feasible method of finance and mandate.

Figure 4.1 provides a model for how a large-scale system of screening might be implemented, taking advantage of widely available systems of care and education for young children and a host of mechanisms for identifying children who are at risk for developmental delays and would most likely benefit from screening. Nontargeted (or universal) methods of screening include the use of prenatal and birth risk registries in all hospitals and developmental and social-emotional screening of all children participating in licensed child care settings (birth to 5 years old) and prekindergarten programs (3–5 years old). Targeted methods take advantage of selection methods for other social services to help identify those children most at risk. Both of these strategies are reflected in Figure 4.1, which provides a schema of screening that could be adopted in tandem with current efforts through both EPSDT and special education mandated child-find systems.

Hospital-Based Prenatal and Birth Screening

As previously discussed, all U.S. hospitals provide at least some level of screening for complications during the prenatal to neonatal period.

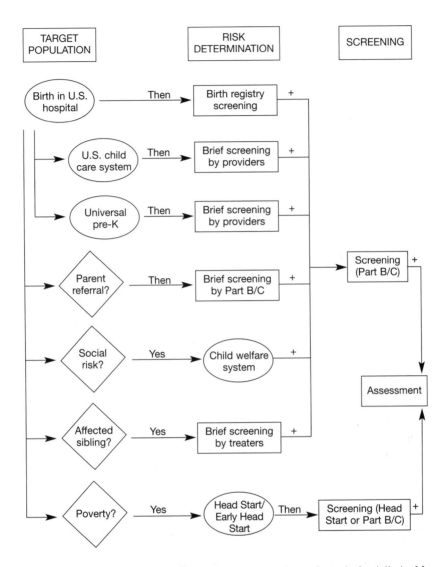

Figure 4.1. A model communitywide system for developmental screening and referral. (A plus [+] sign is used to show that if the condition is true, then the following condition should apply.)

However, there are currently no clear federal guidelines for how complications should trigger further screening, follow-up, or early intervention. Clear guidelines regarding prenatal and birth conditions that would trigger developmental screening and follow-up should be articulated in the federal Part C legislation that mandates early intervention services for children birth to 3 years old. At present, there is a mandate that infants with conditions that place them at risk for developmental delay or disability must be provided early intervention services. States, however, are given great discretion as to which conditions can trigger referral.

Hospital staff can easily identify many known risk factors for developmental delay and disability. These risk factors include prematurity and/or low birth weight (or any of the medical complications that sometimes accompany premature delivery—e.g., bronchopulmonary dysplasia, intestinal dysmotility, intraventricular hemorrhages), genetic anomalies with known developmental sequela, inborn errors of metabolism, anoxic episodes during delivery, exposure to infection during gestation or birth, in utero exposure to recreational drugs or significant amounts of alcohol, or poor overall health condition at birth (as reflected by low 10-minute Apgar scores or extended hospital stay prior to discharge to home). In addition to these medical issues regarding the infant, various social indicators of risk that are routinely collected or easily obtained by hospital staff can be utilized to identify infants with an elevated likelihood of developmental delay (e.g., low parental education, single-parent household, history of social services or court involvement, family history of developmental or learning disabilities). Together, these medical and social risk factors can be utilized in an inventory for identifying infants who are at risk for developmental disabilities. Identification through such hospital-based procedures should trigger an automatic referral to the Part C early intervention system in the family's home area, necessitating an immediate determination of whether the infant satisfies state criteria for developmental risk and is therefore entitled to services. If the infant referred is not found to be eligible, then developmental screening by the Part C system should be initiated when the infant is 6–12 months old and again when the infant is 18–24 months old (or earlier if recommended during initial screening or if a different event triggers a screening). Positive screening results at either stage would result in an immediate diagnostic developmental assessment and subsequent service recommendations.

Child Care, Prekindergarten, and Head Start Systems

High-quality child care provides an underutilized opportunity for supporting educational service delivery and should serve as a hub for linking children and families to necessary services, such as early intervention and preschool special education (Lombardi, 2003). With about 5 million of the nation's 11 million infants and toddlers from all socioeconomic strata spending 25 hours or more each week in out-of-home care (Larner, Behrman, Young, & Reich, 2001), child care provides an excellent setting for near universal application of screening. Unfortunately, current state child care licensure laws do not support child care functioning as a reliable source of identification and referral for young children with developmental disabilities.

There are at least three mechanisms by which screening systems might be embedded in child care: state licensure, federal quality set-asides, and the influence of state prekindergarten systems. Child care licensure laws vary by state and are typically concerned with mandating minimal standards by which to ensure children's general health and safety, rather than focused on promoting educational and intervention goals. Nonetheless, it may be possible for child care licensure laws to embrace the need for adequate methods of screening for delays or disabilities in much the same way that some states have embraced the need for licensed child care settings to have clear guidelines regarding the administration of medications. In addition, states have access to a 4% federal set-aside for quality enhancement through the Child Care Development Fund (CCDF), which is funded at a combined federal and state total of more than $5 billion annually (Committee on Ways and Means, 2000). These funds could be tapped for the development and funding of statewide developmental screening systems embedded in child care programs that accept CCDF money to serve children from low-income families up to 85% of their respective state's median family income.

Increasingly, state prekindergarten systems have provided a way for state educational objectives to be embedded in child care systems. Most state prekindergarten systems target children from low-income families, but nontargeted applications of prekindergarten are becoming more prevalent. When early care and education settings participate in these statewide systems, they generally must agree to provide certain levels of quality in classroom and support services. Although developmental screening is rarely required by state prekindergarten agencies, its provision could be incorporated into state mandates. The federally funded Head Start (serving children 3–5 years old) and Early Head Start (serving children birth to 3 years) have performance mandates to provide regular developmental screening and to target services to children with disabilities. As Congress considers the reauthorization of Head Start and the possibility of greater state control of this program, the future of developmental screening as a part of this program is uncertain. If the importance of screening is embraced, then the potential increase in the number of children served through a state-coordinated Head Start could make developmental screening accessible to an even larger number of children.

In order for developmental screening to be incorporated in child care and state prekindergarten settings, at least two main challenges must be addressed: availability of trained staff and the need for better collaborative partnerships between child care, public schools, and Part C systems. Facilitating an adequate level of teacher training and compensation has long been recognized as the major barrier to ensuring quality in early childhood care and education settings. Although state prekindergarten systems on the whole require a higher overall level of staff credential than child care licensure or Head Start mandates, only about half of all states require lead prekindergarten teachers to hold a bachelor's degree and fewer than half require a minimum amount of annual in-service training (Gilliam & Ripple, 2004). Frequently low levels of teacher training along with low teacher–child ratios and spotty access to support professions conspire to undermine an infrastructure conducive to thoughtful screening and referral. In addition, many child care settings that have not been incorporated into state prekindergarten systems may have no real relationship with local Part B and C systems, which are necessary for ensuring sound referral systems and supportive transitions. Clearly, much work would be needed on supporting the quality and infrastructure in child care systems before child care could be a feasible setting for reliable screening efforts.

Utilizing Risk Status and Program Eligibility as a Form of Prescreening

In addition to the universal screening method possible in hospitals and the quasi-universal methods possible in the early care and education systems, children can be prescreened for developmental delays or disabilities solely on the basis of their eligibility for certain risk-determined social services. Such services might include identification by child welfare services, programs for homeless families or for children with an incarcerated parent, or programs for low-income families (e.g., Food Stamp Program, Special Supplemental Nutrition Program for Women, Infants, and Children). Children and families that are eligible for support from these programs are likely to have a host of risk factors for developmental delay and disability (e.g., poverty, hunger, teen pregnancy, poor health care and prenatal care). Given the evident risk of these children, their identification for these supports serves as a form of prescreening for developmental delay and should trigger a formal screening that would be provided with funds either from the referring service, Part B or C, or through private insurance or the public-supported State Children's Health Insurance Program (SCHIP).

Annually, more than 150,000 children birth to 5 are placed in foster care due to abuse, neglect, or other circumstances that render parents unable to care for their children, and many additional cases come to the attention of child protective services that do not result immediately with placement in the foster care system (Knitzer, 2001). As a routine part of child protective services investigations, these children, by virtue of their observable risk status, should be provided formal developmental and social-emotional screening in order to provide the best possible recommendations for their support.

Similarly, siblings of children with certain types of developmental delays or genetic conditions that might lead to such delays are at elevated risk for developmental delays and disorders themselves. These siblings of affected children are in a special category of risk and should be provided access to periodic developmental screening that can be provided through the clinic services that are treating the affected sibling (financed by private or public insurance or through Part B or C mechanisms).

Utilizing Risk Factors to Create a System of Graduated Follow-Up

The various ideas outlined in this chapter and presented in Figure 4.1 provide a schema for how a comprehensive system of early detection for developmental concerns could be created using extant social services systems and widely documented risk factors. All of the risk factors described have been associated with developmental delays or disabilities, and the social services discussed have eligibility requirements that are based on certain distal risk factors, such as poverty, homelessness, or history of abuse or neglect. The utilization of these risk factors and social services eligibility criteria in the development of a comprehensive system of early detection relies on a complex matrix of risk factors, with each risk factor either leading to continued informal monitoring, increased monitoring through various social services, access to formal developmental screening, or immediate early intervention. Of course, which of these risk factors lead to what type of follow-up should depend on a variety of factors, such as the relative predictive power of each risk factor in isolation or in combination and the availability and quality of the social services systems through which follow-up screening and assessment would be provided.

Certain risk factors should lead immediately to early intervention, with regular assessment for the purposes of intervention planning and monitoring effects. These risk factors are those for which some level of developmental delay or disability is highly likely and primarily include factors that are either apparent at birth or usually shortly thereafter. These include certain genetic, metabolic, and endocrinologic disorders and conditions with known development sequela (e.g., Down syndrome, various fatty acid disorders). Also, certain birth conditions can be highly associated with developmental delays, such as significant prematurity and/or low birth weight, especially when accompanied by certain medical conditions that may arise from premature birth (e.g., intraventricular hemorrhages, severe respiratory and digestive problems). Given the difficulties of early identification for social, emotional, and behavioral disabilities, various social risk factors that are highly predictive of later disorders in these areas should be considered as indicators for the need for follow-up intervention. These might include a history of abuse or severe neglect that has resulted in child protective services involvement, homelessness, and parental substance abuse or incarceration. Each of these risk factors is predictive enough to warrant immediate assessment and continued services, and each is also highly concomitant with other significant risk factors.

Some risk factors, by their very nature, tend to be associated with other risk factors. These include risk factors such as in utero exposure to alcohol or other drugs, low parental education, sibling or close familial history of developmental disabilities, and a family history of significant social services or court involvement. Often, these risk factors tend to cluster, and poverty may be a common underlying factor. Although many children with these risk factors may never exhibit a significant developmental delay or disability, the increased risk associated with each of these conditions warrants formal developmental screening and appropriate follow-up, either referral for a complete developmental assessment or close monitoring.

The success of early intervention rests in the ability of early screening mechanisms to identify those children most in need of services as early and as reliably as possible. Given the complex and often disjointed array of existing social services, a method of state or federal screening that utilizes extant methods of identifying children at risk and embeds itself in more universal systems of care and education may provide the best compromise between adequate coverage versus financial and logistic feasibility. The success of such a system is dependent on our ability to coordinate efforts across agencies and to envision a broad goal for our current systems of caring for young children. There will never be a time when our nation, states, or communities will be wealthy enough to warrant failing to invest in the success of our children through well-conceptualized methods of early identification and intervention. Likewise, there will never be a time when the United States will be so cash poor as to warrant failing to maximize the social capital of its numerous extant systems of early care and support through better coordination of services and a greater shared vision of comprehensive service access.

REFERENCES

Alpern, G.D., Boll, T.J., & Shearer, M. (1986). *Developmental profile-II.* Aspen, CO: Psychological Development Publications.

Amdur, J.R., Mainland, M.K., & Parker, K.C.H. (1996). *Diagnostic inventory for screening children (DISC) manual* (4th ed.). Kitchner, Ontario, Canada: Kitchner-Waterloo Hospital.

Aylward, G.P. (1995). *Bayley Infant Neurodevelopmental Screen.* San Antonio, TX: Psychological Corporation.

Bagnato, S.J., & Neisworth, J.T. (1989). *Perceptions of developmental status (PODS).* Circle Pines, MN: American Guidance Service.

Bain, J. (1989). Developmental screening for pre-school children: Is it worthwhile? *Journal of the Royal College of General Practitioners, 39*, 133–137.

Bangs, T.E., & Dodson, S. (1979). *Birth to three developmental scale.* Allen, TX: DLM Teaching Resources.

Campbell, F.A., & Ramey, C.T. (1995). Cognitive and school outcomes for high-risk African-American students at middle adolescents: Positive effects of early intervention. *American Educational Research Journal, 32*, 743–772.

Committee on Ways and Means, U.S. House of Representatives. (2000). *2000 green book: Background material and data on programs within the jurisdiction of the Committee on Ways and Means.* Washington, DC: U.S. Government Printing Office.

Costello, E.J., Edelbrock, C., Costello, A.J., Dulcan, M.K., Burns, B.J., & Brent, D. (1987). Psychopathology in pediatric primary care: The new hidden morbidity. *Pediatrics, 82*, 415–424.

Diamond, K.E., & Squires, J. (1993). The role of parental report in the screening and assessment of young children. *Journal of Early Intervention, 17*(2), 107–115.

Dobos, A., Dworkin, P., & Bernstein, B. (1994). Pediatricians' approaches to developmental problems: Has the gap been narrowed? *Journal of Developmental and Behavioral Pediatrics, 15*, 34–38.

Dworkin, P.H. (1989). British and American recommendations for developmental monitoring: The role of surveillance. *Pediatrics, 84*, 1000–1010.

Dworkin, P.H. (2000). Preventive health care and anticipatory guidance. In J.P. Shonkoff & S.J. Meisels (Eds.), *Handbook of early childhood intervention* (2nd ed., pp. 327–338). New York: Cambridge University Press.

Dykes, M.K. (1980). *Developmental assessment of the severely handicapped.* Austin, TX: Exceptional Resources.

Farran, D.C. (2000). Another decade of intervention for children who are low income or disabled: What do we know now? In J.P Shonkoff & S.J. Meisels (Eds.), *Handbook of early childhood intervention* (2nd ed., pp. 510–548). New York: Cambridge University Press.

Fewell, R.R., & Langley, M.B. (1984). *Developmental Activities Screening Inventory-II.* Austin, TX: PRO-ED.

Frankenburg, W.K., Dodds, J., Archer, P., Bresnick, B., Maschka, P., Edelman, N., & Shapiro, H. (1990). *Denver II: Technical manual.* Denver, CO: Denver Developmental Materials.

Gilliam, W.S., & Mayes, L.C. (2004). Integrating clinical and psychometric approaches: Developmental assessment and the infant mental health evaluation. In R. DelCarmen-Wiggins & A. Carter (Eds.), *Handbook of infant, toddler, and preschool mental health assessment* (pp. 185–203). New York: Oxford University Press.

Gilliam, W.S., & Ripple, C.H. (2004). What can be learned from state-funded prekindergarten initiatives? A data-based approach to the Head Start devolution debate. In E. Zigler & S.J. Styfco (Eds.), *The Head Start debates* (pp. 477–497). Baltimore: Paul H. Brookes Publishing Co.

Gilliam, W.S., & Zigler, E.F. (2000). A critical meta-analysis of all evaluations of state-funded preschool from 1977 to 1998: Implications for policy, service delivery and program evaluation. *Early Childhood Research Quarterly, 15*, 441–473.

Glascoe, F., Altemeier, W., & MacLean, E. (1989). The importance of parents' concerns about their children's development. *American Journal of Diseases of Children, 143*, 855–858.

Glascoe, F.P., Byrne, K.E., Ashford, L.G., Johnson, L.L., Chang, B. (1992). Accuracy of the Denver-II in developmental screening. *Pediatrics, 89*, 1221–1225.

Glascoe, F.P., Foster, M., & Wolraich, M.L. (1997). An economic analysis of developmental detection methods. *Pediatrics, 99,* 830–837.

Greenspan, S.I., & Meisels, S.J. (1996). Toward a new vision for the developmental assessment of infants and young children. In S.J. Meisels & E. Fenichel (Eds.), *New visions for the developmental assessment of infants and young children* (pp. 11–26). Washington, DC: ZERO TO THREE: National Center for Infants, Toddlers, and Families.

Guralnick, M.J. (Ed.). (1997). *The effectiveness of early intervention.* Baltimore: Paul H. Brookes Publishing Co.

Guralnick, M.J. (2001). A developmental systems model for early intervention. *Infants and Young Children, 14*(2), 1–18.

Harrison, P.L. (1990). *Early screening profiles (ESP): Manual.* Circle Pines, MN: American Guidance Service.

Head Start Bureau. (2002). *Head Start program regulations and program guidance.* Retrieved January 28, 2003, from http://www.acf.hhs.gov/programs/hsb/performance/index.htm

Head Start Bureau. (2003). *2003 Head Start fact sheet.* Retrieved January 28, 2003, from http://www2.acf.dhhs.gov/programs/hsb/research/03_hsfs.htm.

Henderson, L.W., & Meisels, S.J. (1994). Parental involvement in the developmental screening of their young children: A multiple source perspective. *Journal of Early Intervention, 18,* 141–154.

Houston, H.L.A., & Davis, R.H. (1985). Opportunistic surveillance of child development in primary care: Is it feasible? *Journal of the Royal College of General Practitioners, 35,* 77–79.

Hresko, W., Miguel, S., Sherbenou, R., & Burton, S. (1994). *Developmental Observation Checklist System* (DOCS). Austin, TX: PRO-ED.

Hutchison, T., & Nicoll, A. (1988). Developmental screening and surveillance. *British Journal of Hospital Medicine, 39,* 22–29.

Ireton, H. (1996). The child development review: Monitoring children's development using parents' and pediatricians' observations. *Infants and Young Children, 9,* 42–52.

Johnson, K.L., Ashford, L.G., Byrne, K.E., & Glascoe, F.P. (1992). Does Denver II produce meaningful results? *Pediatrics, 90,* 477–479.

Kemper, K.J., Osborn, L.M., Hansen, D.F., & Pascoe, J.M. (1994). Family psychosocial screening: Should we focus on high-risk settings? *Developmental and Behavioral Pediatrics, 15,* 336–341.

Knitzer, J. (2001). Federal and state efforts to improve care for infants and toddlers. *The Future of Children, 11*(1), 79–97.

Koppelman, J. (2003, April 11). *Reauthorizing Head Start: The future federal role in preschool programs for the poor* [NHPF Issue Brief, No. 789]. Washington, DC: National Health Policy Forum, The George Washington University.

Larner, M., Behrman, R.E., Young, M., & Reich, K. (2001). Caring for infants and toddlers: Analysis and recommendations. *The Future of Children, 11*(1), 7–19.

LeMay, D., Griffin, P.M., & Sanford, A. (1978). *Learning Accomplishment Profile-Diagnostic Edition (LAP-D).* Lewisville, NC: Kaplan School Supply.

Lombardi, J. (2003). *Time to care: Redesigning child care to promote education, support families, and build communities.* Philadelphia: Temple University Press.

Mardell-Czudnowski, C.D., & Goldenberg, D. (1990). *DIAL-R (Developmental Indicators for the Assessment of Learning-Revised).* Edison, NJ: Childcraft Education.

Meisels, S.J. (1988). Developmental screening in early childhood: The interaction of research and social policy. In L. Breslow, J.E. Fielding, & L.B. Lave (Eds.), *Annual review of public health* (pp. 527–550). Palo Alto, CA: Annual Reviews, Inc.

Meisels, S.J. (1989). Can developmental screening tests identify children who are developmentally at risk? *Pediatrics, 83,* 578–585.

Meisels, S.J. (1996). Charting the continuum of assessment and intervention. In S.J. Meisels & E. Fenichel (Eds.), *New visions for the developmental assessment of infants and young children* (pp. 27–52). Washington, DC: ZERO TO THREE: National Center for Infants, Toddlers, and Families.

Meisels, S.J., & Atkins-Burnett, S. (2000). The elements of early childhood assessment. In J.P. Shonkoff & S.J. Meisels (Eds.), *Handbook of early childhood intervention* (2nd ed., pp. 231–257). New York: Cambridge University Press.

Meisels, S.J., Liaw, F., Henderson, L.W., Browning, K., & Ten Have, T. (1993). New evidence for the effectiveness of the Early Screening Inventory. *Early Childhood Research Quarterly, 8,* 327–346.

Meisels, S.J., Marsden, D.B., Wiske, M.S., & Henderson, L.W. (1997). *The Early Screening Inventory Revised (ESI-R).* New York: Pearson Early Learning.

Meisels, S.J., & Provence, S. (1989). *Screening and assessment: Guidelines for identifying young disabled and developmentally vulnerable children and their families.* Washington, DC: National Center for Clinical Infant Programs.

Meisels, S.J., & Wasik, B.A. (1990). Who should be served? Identifying children in need of early intervention. In S.J. Meisels & J.P. Shonkoff (Eds.), *Handbook of early childhood intervention* (pp. 605–632). New York: Cambridge University Press.

National Institutes of Health. (2000, October). *Phenylketonuria (PKU): Screening and management. NIH consensus statement, 17*(3), 1–33.

Newborg, J., Stock, J., Wnek, L., Guidubaldi, J., & Svinicki, J.S. (1984). *Battelle Developmental Inventory (BDI).* Allen, TX: DLM/Teaching Resources.

Project RHISE. (1979). *Rockford Infant Developmental Scales (RIDES).* Bensenville, IL: Scholastic Testing Service.

Quick, A.D., & Campbell, A.A. (1987). *Project Memphis Comprehensive Developmental Scale.* Memphis, TN: Memphis State University.

Reuter, J., & Bickett, L. (1985). *Kent Infant Development Scale (KIDS).* Kent, OH: Developmental Metrics.

Reynell, J., & Zinkin, K. (1979). *Reynell-Zinkin Developmental Scales for Young Visually Handicapped Children.* Chicago: Stoelting.

Sameroff, A.J., Seifer, R., Barocas, R., Zax, M., & Greenspan, S. (1987). Intelligence quotient scores of 4-year-old children: Social-emotional risk factors. *Pediatrics, 79,* 343–350.

Sexton, D., Thompson, B., Perez, J., & Rheams, T. (1990). Maternal versus professional estimates of developmental status for young children with handicaps: An ecological approach. *Topics in Early Childhood Special Education, 10,* 80–95.

Sharp, L., Pantell, R.H., Murphy, L.O., & Lewis, C.C. (1992). Psychosocial problems during child health supervision visits: Eliciting, then what? *Pediatrics, 89,* 619–623.

Shonkoff, J.P., & Meisels, S.J. (Eds.). (2000). *Handbook of early childhood intervention* (2nd ed.). New York: Cambridge University Press.

Shonkoff, J.P., & Phillips, D.A. (Eds.). (2000). *From neurons to neighborhoods: The science of early childhood development.* Washington, DC: National Academy Press.

Shore, R. (1997). *Rethinking the brain: New insights into early development.* New York: Families and Work Institute.

Squires, J. (1996). Parent-completed developmental questionnaires: A low-cost strategy for child-find and screening. *Infants and Young Children, 9,* 16–28.

Squires, J., & Bricker, D. (1991). Impact of completing infant developmental questionnaires on at-risk mothers. *Journal of Early Intervention, 15*(2), 162–172.

Squires, J., Nickel, R., & Bricker, D. (1990). Use of parent-completed developmental questionnaires for child-find and screening. *Infants and Young Children, 3*(2), 46–57.

Sturner, R.A., Funk, S.G., & Green, J.A. (1994). Simultaneous technique for acuity and readiness testing (START): Further concurrent validation of an aid for developmental surveillance. *Pediatrics, 93,* 82–88.

U.S. General Accounting Office (USGAO). (2001, July). *Medicaid: Stronger efforts needed to ensure children's access to health screening services* [GAO-01-749]. Washington, DC: Author.

Werner, E.E. (2000). Protective factors and individual resilience. In J.P. Shonkoff & S.J. Meisels (Eds.), *Handbook of early childhood intervention* (2nd ed., pp. 115–132). New York: Cambridge University Press.

Young, K.T., Marsland, K.W., & Zigler, E. (1997). Regulatory status of center-based infant and toddler child care. *American Journal of Orthopsychiatry, 67,* 535–544.

Chapter 5

Designing an Integrated Point of Access in the Early Intervention System

Gloria L. Harbin

BACKGROUND

Sara is a low birth weight infant, born to a teenage mother who lives in poverty, and was identified as needing services by the hospital in which she was born.

Marques has a rare medical condition and both parents work, yet they manage to barely squeak by financially. They have no insurance but found their way to the local health department.

Carmen's grandmother is worried because Carmen is not developing at the same rate as other children and mentioned this to the family's social worker.

Rashad's mother and his child care provider want some help because Rashad has been resistant to being potty trained.

Jason is the center of concern at Child Protective Services (CPS) because an investigation indicated that he had been abused and neglected.

Brian's birth was uneventful and he appeared to be developing typically. However, now Brian's mother is frantic and exhausted because he sleeps very little, is active, is destructive, does not pay attention, and does not seem to have any emotional connection with anyone in the family. Brian's physician advised her to find a "special" program.

Karen's parents suspect she isn't hearing everything.

These seven children and their families are diverse in many ways: 1) the child's age, condition, functioning, and behavior; 2) the age of the parents;

3) the family's racial and ethnic background; 4) the socioeconomic status of the families; 5) the skills, education level, and amount of social support possessed by the families; and 6) the sector of the community that helped to identify their need. Yet, all of the children present concerns that need to be examined and addressed by an exemplary point of access (POA) to the service system. It is impossible for any single program, agency, or provider to adequately assess or meet the array of needs of these diverse children and families. In fact, many children with risks and disabilities are eligible for services from multiple programs. Yet, the federal and state governments have established "categorical" programs, each with its own eligibility criteria and funds only to be used for children or families who meet the specific eligibility criteria. Although each of the various agencies cares about the missions and services of the other agencies, each agency has its own mission and responsibilities and hires staff with special expertise to carry out the activities needed to accomplish the mission of the agency (Harbin, 1996). For example, many of the individuals hired by the health department have knowledge, skills, and experience in some area related to the health of the child (e.g., physicians, nurses, nutritionists); however, individuals hired by the public schools as teachers, therapists (occupational, physical, speech-language), and school psychologists are trained to understand the educational and developmental needs of children. Consequently, as the result of categorical and fragmented services, one of the most frequent complaints of parents is the difficulty they experience in their efforts to gain access to needed services (Harbin, McWilliam, & Gallagher, 2000; Turnbull, Turbiville, & Turnbull, 2000; Turnbull & Turnbull, 1986). Indeed, in interviews with numerous families from diverse backgrounds, states, and communities conducted by the author over the course of 15 years, one of the most frequently requested solutions by families was a single point or place to gain access to services provided by all agencies in the community.

As a result of parents' complaints, the legislation and regulations for many federal programs require a coordinated system of services, with linkages to the activities of other agencies and programs. For example, federal legislation for Parts B and C of the Individuals with Disabilities Education Act (IDEA) of 1997, funded by the Office of Special Education Programs (OSEP) in the U.S. Department of Education, as well as Head Start, which is funded by the Administration for Children, Youth, and Families (ACYF) in the U.S. Department of Health and Human Services, requires coordination with the screening, public awareness, and child-find activities of other agencies in order to ensure easier access to all needed services for children and their families.

Despite the *practical need* articulated by numerous families and the *legal requirement* for coordinated access and referrals across agencies and programs, most programs continue to have autonomous points of access. Similarly, each agency runs autonomous public awareness, child-find, and screening initiatives. Further complicating the situation is the lack of sufficient organizational linkages between many programs that results in a lack of referrals of children and their families to all relevant agencies and programs. Staff from each program primarily focus their questions on identifying the child and family needs that can be addressed within their own agency's area of emphasis. Consequently, families complain that they have to be "found" by each relevant program, or families have had to actively search for each relevant program on their own. Parents have described access to services as a mysterious undertaking and as both labor and time intensive. The current approach to autonomous public awareness, child-find, and system points of access has resulted in four interrelated and serious system access problems. First, there is a lack of *early identification*. Despite a strong body of literature to support the value of early identification (Meisels & Shonkoff, 1990; Shonkoff & Meisels, 2000), many children are not identified as early as possible because of fragmented and confusing system entry procedures. This often results in the loss of precious intervention time. The data from the U.S. Department of Education's 2003 report to Congress revealed that the infant-toddler program (Part C of IDEA '97) served 2.24% of the total population, whereas the preschool special education program (Section 619 of Part B of IDEA '97) served 5.56%, and the school-age population served was 11.31%. More effort must be made to find children with disabilities earlier. It is equally important to find and serve children with risk factors as early as possible in order to prevent them from developing delays or prevent their circumstances from worsening (Guralnick, 2001a).

The second system entry problem is the lack of *easy access*. This problem contributes to the previous problem because it delays the initiation of services. As described, many families have a difficult time finding and gaining access to the service system because they do not know where to go or whom to contact. Third, there is a lack of *timely access* to services for some children and families. As previously mentioned, finding and gaining access to services from a fragmented system is time consuming for families and leads to delays in gaining access to all needed and relevant services in a timely manner. Part C of IDEA '97 tried to address this problem by requiring a 45-day timeline from referral to development of an individualized family service plan (IFSP). Unfortunately, in many states and communities, lead agencies enter children and families into services within the 45-day time frame but they are *not always* linked to relevant services provided by other agencies and programs. Fourth, there is a lack of *full access*. Even after the 45-day time frame and well into service delivery, children and families frequently are not linked to the full array of resources to meet their individual needs. They will have access to services and resources from a single program but are not referred or linked to services provided by other agencies for which they are eligible. For example, local social services programs often neglect to refer or link potentially eligible children to the Part C program for infants and toddlers with delays and disabilities.

DESIGNING AN INTEGRATED POINT OF ACCESS

One approach is to consider an integrated and coordinated POA. This is certainly one of the options within the Developmental Systems Model (Guralnick, 2001a). This approach is innovative in four important ways: 1) the manner in which tasks are viewed and how those important tasks are performed, 2) the meaningful participation of the family and other important caregivers, 3) the breadth of the needs addressed, and 4) the staffing and organization of the POA.

This section contains the dimensions to be addressed by state and local planners as they seek to develop an exemplary POA. The concept of *integration* is woven through the elements of the POA. The model is concerned with recognizing and facilitating the integrated nature of the child's development and views the child as integrated into the life of the family. The exemplary POA includes the integration of diverse disciplines and agencies. Finally, the integration of multiorganizational activities (e.g., child-find) provides a foundation for integration.

The section begins with a description of the purposes or goals to be accomplished by an effective POA. The goals are followed by the tasks needed to accomplish the goals, the delineation of the values that guide the manner in which POA staff perform the tasks, and a description of the staff competencies needed to effectively accomplish POA tasks. The section concludes with a description of the key features of the infrastructure needed to support an exemplary POA, including an effective organizational structure. Figure 5.1 presents the conceptual framework for an exemplary integrated POA.

Purposes and Goals of the Point of Access

Once a concern about a child's development has been identified, families need to be referred, or refer themselves, to a specific place that can begin the process of examining this concern. The POA needs to be equipped to welcome children and families who are diverse and facilitate their journey in opening doors to possibilities and opportunities. Families' experiences within the POA set the stage and lay the foundation for their future

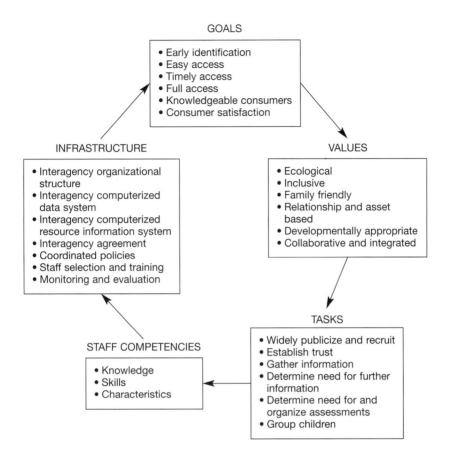

GOALS

- Early identification
- Easy access
- Timely access
- Full access
- Knowledgeable consumers
- Consumer satisfaction

INFRASTRUCTURE

- Interagency organizational structure
- Interagency computerized data system
- Interagency computerized resource information system
- Interagency agreement
- Coordinated policies
- Staff selection and training
- Monitoring and evaluation

VALUES

- Ecological
- Inclusive
- Family friendly
- Relationship and asset based
- Developmentally appropriate
- Collaborative and integrated

STAFF COMPETENCIES

- Knowledge
- Skills
- Characteristics

TASKS

- Widely publicize and recruit
- Establish trust
- Gather information
- Determine need for further information
- Determine need for and organize assessments
- Group children

Figure 5.1. Coordinated point of access.

expectations about their role and participation in subsequent stages in the process (e.g., interdisciplinary assessment, development of service plans, selection of relevant services and resources). The experiences also influence the families' expectations about the breadth of services, resources, and opportunities available to them.

The four service access problems described previously in this chapter must be addressed in order to ensure effective and smooth entry into the service system. All too often, programs design the POA with little thought about the desired outcomes of this important component of the Developmental Systems Model. One of the first important steps in creating an effective POA is to consciously *set goals* for effective evaluation.

Seven groups of diverse early intervention (EI) stakeholders were asked to participate in a Delphi study to identify desired outcomes for children, their families, and the service system (Harbin, Pelosi, Kameny, McWilliam, Kitsul, Fox, & Rodriguez, 2004). The stakeholders consisted of national experts, state policy makers from diverse agencies (e.g., health, developmental disabilities, education, mental health), state personnel development staff (both in-service and preservice), national technical assistance staff, local program administrators from multiple agencies, service providers from multiple agencies, and families of children with a wide array of disabilities. These diverse stakeholders identified system entry outcomes as some of the most important service system outcomes to be addressed and evaluated. The stakeholders identified six system level outcomes that are relevant to the POA. These include

1. Early identification—identify children and families as early as possible.

2. Easy access—provide information and supports so that parents and professionals can easily gain access to the service system.

3. Timely entry—conduct POA activities within a short time frame, ensuring quick access to resources and thus reducing parents' frustration while simultaneously increasing the likelihood of child progress.

4. Full access—link children and their families to the full array of resources for which they are eligible and that will meet their individual educational, health, and human resource needs.

5. Knowledgeable consumers—increase families' knowledge about how to navigate the service system and gain access to available services, resources, and opportunities.

6. Consumer (family) satisfaction—increase families' satisfaction and reduce frustrations.

Tasks

To accomplish these important goals, professionals will need to successfully undertake a set of broad tasks that include 1) creating public awareness about how to contact the POA, 2) developing trusting relationships with families in order to obtain useful information, 3) gathering essential information, and 4) dividing children into broad groups to facilitate decisions about appropriate next steps to enhance their development.

Create Public Awareness

Both early identification and easy access depend on a strong and active public awareness campaign. The more visible, well known, and accepted the POA is by everyone in the community, the higher the likelihood that families will have easy and early access to the service system. Administrators of the POA need to use a variety of strategies to advertise the availability of services, as well as provide information about how to contact or visit the POA. Focusing on a broad population will allow *all* families, including those who have children with risks and disabilities, to find out that the POA is a welcoming place they can turn to for assistance with their concerns (Harbin, Herrmann, Wasik, Dobbins, & Lam, 2004).

Unfortunately, each categorical service program has developed its own approach to finding children and families (Harbin et al., 2004). Each program has its own telephone number, brochure, logo, public awareness activities, and screening methods, which result in confusion for families. For example, families are confused when the health department may use the Denver Developmental Screening Test (Frankenburg & Dodds, 1968), while the Part C program and the public schools each use a different screening measure. Some programs do not use a formal screening measure but use a program-developed measure or procedure, which is even more confusing to families.

A single, well-publicized telephone number for families who have *any* type of questions or concerns is more likely to result in easier access to the system by families of children with risks and disabilities. Use of a catchy title and logo, along with colorful and attractive materials in multiple languages, are more likely to entice families and other concerned adults to contact the POA. Similarly, unlike brochures for individual programs that advertise the availability of a narrow range of services, the materials for the POA should advertise access to community resources in the 13 categories delineated later in this chapter. This integrated approach to public awareness requires all relevant agencies to come together and collaboratively develop materials. Collaborative presentations to diverse groups (such as local and county businesses and governmental officials) increase visibility and support. These joint agency presentations provide the additional benefit of increasing the recognition that programs have come together to support families and make their journey into the service system smooth and less frustrating. All parents and child care providers should know how to gain access to the POA. Religious, civic, and cultural leaders also are important individuals to involve in an effective public awareness campaign. These key community leaders have the trust of some individuals who may be hesitant to seek out help from traditional agencies out of fear or as a result of previous adverse experiences. It is advantageous to advertise the POA as a friendly and resourceful organization that links families to a broad array of services, resources, and opportunities.

It also will be natural for parents to seek out specialized programs to meet the needs of their children with low-incidence disabilities (e.g., visual impairments, hearing impairments, motor impairments; Guralnick, 2001a).

Furthermore, families may be receiving services from one of the other human services agencies. Therefore, personnel from all human services agencies (e.g., health, social services, public schools), as well as private providers such as physicians, need to understand the importance of and process for referring *all* children with or at risk of disabilities to the integrated POA. For example, in an integrated POA, the health department might be serving a child through the Children With Special Health Care Needs (CSHCN) program. However, if the health department staff suspect the child has a disability, or if the child has a medical condition such as Down syndrome that makes the child eligible for Part C services under IDEA '97, then the CSHCN program should automatically refer the child and family to the integrated POA. The health department continues to meet the medical needs of the child but refers the child to the POA so that the child and his or her family can be linked to a wider array of specialized and natural resources, services, supports, and opportunities to meet their needs.

Finally, POA administrators need to establish linkages with existing developmental screening programs and initiatives, including a variety of newborn screening programs such as newborn hearing screening that is being conducted in some states. Similarly, linkages with high-risk registries, such as those that contain children with biological risk factors and conditions, are equally important.

Develop Trusting Relationships

Once children and families are referred to, or refer themselves to, the integrated POA, one of the most important tasks is to develop a positive and trusting relationship with the families. McWilliam, Tocci, and Harbin (1998) discovered that caring about and establishing a relationship with the child lays the foundation for the ability to develop a trusting relationship with the family and the child's other caregivers. A trusting relationship is essential for families to feel comfortable talking about a variety of needs (Atkins-Burnett & Allen-Meares, 2000). Trivette, Dunst, and Hamby (1996) described the help-giving style and skills most associated with parents' feelings of control over service provision. It is clear that particular skills are needed to develop trusting and empowering relationships with families. Much of the literature describes use of these skills during interdisciplinary assessments and service delivery. Consequently, all too frequently, most professionals use a personable but distant approach in undertaking the traditional "intake" tasks performed at the POA. However, in an exemplary POA, staff members understand the importance of using the type of help-giving skills described by Trivette, Dunst, and Deal (1996), which leads to trusting and empowering relationships with families. Three clusters of factors appear to contribute to effective helping (Trivette, Dunst, & Deal, 1996): 1) prehelping attitudes and beliefs (e.g., have positive view of help-seekers, build on strengths), 2) help-giving behaviors (e.g., use active and reflective listening, build problem-solving skills, develop partnerships), and 3) posthelping responses and consequences (e.g., accept and support help-seekers' decisions, minimize sense of indebtedness).

Although many programs contend that developing a trusting relationship is an important goal of their traditional "intake" activities, their procedures and questions often feel bureaucratic to many families. This is because staff focus on the completion of the required steps and forms. What is needed is a "paradigm shift" away from a bureaucratic focus and toward a more relationship-based focus. This can be accomplished by creating a welcoming and friendly climate and by changing *how* information is collected from families.

One important step to building trusting relationships is to eliminate the use of the word *intake*. This term sounds bureaucratic, creating walls and distance between the family and staff of the POA. Conversely, an exemplary POA creates a climate that *welcomes* all families to begin their journey in building on existing strengths and gaining access to new services, supports, and resources. It is more family centered to use the terms *welcome* or *getting to know you* visit. These terms are likely to evoke positive images and feelings. The POA can begin to develop trusting relationships through the use of family-friendly terminology.

Gather Essential Information

One of the most important tasks to be accomplished by the POA is to gather the necessary information to create a picture of the child and family. This information can be used to guide decisions about grouping the children (described more fully later in this chapter); in organizing relevant assessments; and in initial identification of resources, programs, or services for which the child and family might be eligible. Four types of information need to be gathered. First, most communities currently have multiple screening initiatives (see Chapter 4). Ideally, screening initiatives would be integrated, with states and communities designing *universal* screening programs and conducting screening on all children based on the American Academy of Pediatrics schedule (Kochanek, 1989; Meisels & Provence, 1989). Unfortunately, most screening initiatives are autonomous and uncoordinated. Currently, in some situations, the child is referred to the POA as a result of screening, but the screening assessment results are not automatically forwarded to the POA. In this instance, the POA staff needs to do some detective work to hunt down developmental screening information if it exists.

The second type of information that needs to be gathered is from the referral source. Instead of asking the referral source to complete a form, it is better to simply ask why the child and the family were referred. The referral source is then more likely to provide richer and clearer information than would be included on a form. In a relationship-based approach, the staff ask questions and complete the necessary paperwork instead of asking the individual from the referral source or the family to do so.

Third, the POA staff need to gather useful demographic information about the child and family, which can be used to contact the family and identify possible eligibility for other programs. For example, eligibility for many other programs is based on the family's financial status (e.g., Early Periodic Screening, Diagnosis and Treatment; Supplemental Nutrition Program for Women, Infants, and Children [WIC]; Temporary Assistance for Needy Families [TANF]; Head Start; Early Head Start) as well as the child's medical condition or the parents' education. The reader can find an example of a family-friendly demographic questionnaire titled *Getting to Know Me and My Family* at http://www.fpg.unc.edu/~beacons/forms/demographic.pdf. Instead of having the family complete the form independently, POA staff should use the form as a discussion vehicle. Parents are then not only writing their answers but also talking about them. This interactive discussion is more likely to build rapport with the family rather than having the family complete the form on their own, which often sets a mechanical and distant tone. This form should be entered into an integrated database that other agencies can have access to.

All too frequently, "intake" procedures and forms obtain information about factors that are not directly related to determining eligibility or identifying needed services. An example of this type of information is asking the mother if she smoked during her pregnancy. Professionals sometimes use questions such as this to make negative judgments about the parents. Therefore, it is best to avoid judgmental questions that will not enhance understanding the child's service delivery needs.

The fourth and final type of information relates to the child's functioning, family concerns, and successes. In a relationship-based approach, a POA staff member asks the family to "tell their story." Staff in the integrated or coordinated POA should have a "conversation" with the family using three tools to assist in gathering information. These tools include 1) the demographic questionnaire referred to previously (Getting to Know Me and My Family); 2) an abbreviated form of the Routines-Based Interview (RBI; McWilliam, 1992), which can be found immediately following the demographic form; and 3) the Family Needs Survey (Bailey & Simeonsson, 1990; see Chapter 7).

McWilliam (see Chapter 9) suggests that the RBI be conducted once eligibility has been determined and prior to the development of the IFSP or the individualized education program (IEP). Use of an *abbreviated* RBI by the POA staff, however, would meaningfully include families in this important first step of the service delivery process. As mentioned previously, the RBI is a family-centered, family-friendly, relationship-based, and natural approach to obtaining important information. Asking families these questions as part of the POA process also stimulates families' thinking so that if they are asked to complete this form at a later time, they will have had time to think about these questions.

Children with disabilities or at risk are a diverse group, and broad demographic factors (e.g., race, socioeconomic status) are not good predictors of the individual needs of families. The Family Needs Survey (Bailey & Simeonsson, 1990) is a useful tool to obtain information in seven areas: 1) child growth and development, 2) playing with the child, 3) teaching the child, 4) challenging behaviors, 5) child's condition or disability, 6) available services, and 7) future services the child might need. The Family Needs Survey also sends a message to families about the breadth of opportunities and resources available to them. Use of both the abbreviated RBI and the Family Needs Survey can stimulate the families' thinking about their strengths and concerns across a wide range of areas. Families should feel hopeful and supported after the information-gathering procedures of the POA (demographic form, abbreviated RBI, and Family Needs Survey). POA staff should then use the information gathered from these three tools to develop an *ecomap* of child and family involvement with agencies, programs, groups, and key individuals (McWilliam, 1992).

This combination of information will be extremely useful in making decisions about grouping the children. The information also will be valuable to other programs and services that eventually are chosen to provide services to children and their families. As mentioned previously, families only have to provide this information once. Future assessors and service providers can build on this information by asking more in-depth questions. In the case of children at risk (biologic and environmental), information gathered through the three suggested approaches will provide information about the kind of *preventative* intervention programs for children, as well as services and supports needed by their families to help reduce or eliminate the child's risk status. The information also will be useful to those planning a truly individualized, multidisciplinary assessment for children who are suspected of having delays and disabilities.

Divide Children into Broad Groups

The POA will receive children and families who need to follow different service paths. POA staff will need to gather sufficient information (through the tasks described previously) that can guide them as they determine which of the three service paths is best suited to a child and his or her family. This grouping is not an official eligibility determination for Part C or preschool special education services but facilitates the steps needed to design an appropriate intervention program and to begin identifying programs for which the child and family are eligible.

Group 1 consists of children with the probability of delays or disabilities. This group includes children who have medical conditions, such as Down syndrome, that make them automatically eligible for Part C services. Most states have a list of conditions that can be used in determining whether the child has a particular medical condition that meets this eligibility criterion. Group 1 also includes children who have obvious developmental delays, as well as those children who are *suspected* of having a delay. Finally, in some states, children with certain risk factors or a combination of risk factors are eligible for Part C services. States that include children with risk conditions in their Part C eligibility have developed a list of risk factors to be used in determining whether the child belongs in Group 1. Once information has been gathered using the tools described previously, children in this group should receive a comprehensive interdisciplinary assessment.

Group 2 consists of children and families at risk who are likely to not be eligible for Part C services. Children and families in Group 2 have one or more biologic and/or environmental risk factors (Guralnick, 2001a; Tjossem, 1976). This group contains those children with risk factors who, based on adequate developmental screening, are not currently exhibiting developmental delays nor do they meet eligibility criteria for those states that include children with particular risk conditions in their eligibility criteria for Part C services. Information gathered should be used to identify early, preventative intervention programs for the child (e.g., Early Head Start, Head Start, Even Start, high quality child care and education). In addition, the information can be used to effectively identify the resources needed by families (e.g., job training, general educational development, literacy, transportation, housing, recreation, mental health) that will help to reduce or eliminate risks. If the child has not received a developmental screening prior to arriving at the POA, then the POA should obtain a screening assessment.

Group 3 consists of all other children and families who find their way to the POA. Because the public awareness campaign has made the POA a visible and respected resource in the community, it will likely receive calls from families and child care providers with a range of requests for information about a variety of *temporary* concerns. For example, a family may telephone to ask about available dentists or child care providers or to obtain advice from a professional about a particular issue, such as how to get their child to sleep through the night or how to handle temper tantrums more effectively. This is perhaps the easiest of the three groups because once the request for information has been addressed, nothing more needs to be done for children and families in this group. However, it would be beneficial for the POA to determine if the child in this group is part of a periodic screening initiative and if not, help link the family to a screening program.

Values

The values underlying the POA certainly will influence how the tasks described previously will be completed. An interrelated set of values is needed to successfully accomplish the goals of an exemplary, integrated POA.

Ecological

It is widely accepted that the child's environment significantly influences his or her interactions within the family (Bronfenbrenner, 1975, 1979, 1992; Sameroff & Chandler, 1975; Sameroff & Fiese, 1990). Therefore, the integrated POA needs to look beyond the child and his or her characteristics. Currently, many Part C programs, as well as programs for children at risk, primarily focus on the educational needs of the child. A holistic and ecological approach, however, would suggest designing procedures that recognize the diverse needs of not only the children but also their families. Trivette, Dunst, and Deal (1996) delineated broad categories in which children and/or their families may have needs. Only one of these categories addresses the child's education or developmental skills (e.g., cognitive, motor, language). Harbin and her colleagues (2004) modified the categories developed by Trivette and her colleagues (1996), producing the resources presented in Table 5.1. The ecological approach will require

Table 5.1. Ecological service resources and supports

Child development, education, and specialized therapies
Child care
Child protection and safety
Medical, dental, and nutrition
Food and clothing
Housing
Mental health and support
Transportation
Adult education, training, and information
Cultural, social, and religious
Economic
Legal
Recreation

gaining a broader view of the child and family than merely how the child performed on a developmental screening instrument. When asking the family to tell their story, including areas of strengths and concerns, having these 13 categories in mind is useful so that a fuller picture of the child in his or her context can be developed. This can be shared with the child's assessment team or can be used to identify possible needs and resources for which the child and family are eligible. When the POA staff use the demographic questionnaire, abbreviated RBI, Family Needs Survey, and the construction of an ecomap, they will obtain information that supports an ecological approach. Use of ecological values and an ecological approach will help to accomplish the POA goal of full access.

Inclusion

An exemplary POA is based on the concept that children with disabilities or at risk are best served in programs, activities, and environments that include children without disabilities (Guralnick, 2001b). Complementary to the value of inclusive services is the viewpoint that encourages the development of early intervention and early childhood programs for *all* children, instead of segregating children with disabilities and children with risks (e.g., low birth weight, environmental poverty) into separate and isolated programs. Using the broadest concept of the inclusion philosophy, the POA would be an inclusive organization, dedicated to being a resource to all children and families within the community. As mentioned in the section on public awareness, the broader or more inclusive the population targeted by the POA, the higher the likelihood that earlier and easier access to services will occur. In addition, having an inclusive POA will set the stage, or lay the foundation, for inclusive service delivery. An inclusive POA will reduce stigma for children with risks and disabilities and will create greater visibility in, as well as support from, the broader community (see Chapter 7 for a more in-depth explanation of this philosophy).

Family Friendly

The POA needs to be a pleasant and inviting place in which diverse families feel welcome. Families are more comfortable and feel safer sharing their thoughts and feelings in a more informal and friendly environment than in a more formal, structured, or bureaucratic environment. First encounters form initial impressions, set the stage for future encounters, and influence the quality of the relationships developed with families. Families from diverse cultures and economic status need to feel heard and assisted. Therefore, the physical space and environment of the POA needs to be conducive to conversations. Although staff need office space with desks, computers, and telephones, the POA needs to have "conversation space" for meeting with families. Families naturally have conversations while sitting on the couch in the living room or around a kitchen or dining room table. Creating more comfortable and natural settings is more likely to put families at ease than using offices, therapy rooms, or conference rooms. The POA also should consider going to the families' homes to complete the information-gathering tasks because it is likely to be more convenient and comfortable for families and to provide important contextual and environmental information.

Relationship-Based

There is robust literature on the importance of service providers developing an *empowering* relationship with the families of children with risks and disabilities (Dunst, Johansen, Trivette, & Hamby, 1991; Dunst, Trivette, & Deal, 1988, 1994; McWilliam, 1992; Turnbull, Turbiville, & Turnbull, 2000; Turnbull & Turnbull, 1986). Empowering relationships are based on valuing the family's knowledge of their child and respecting their values, beliefs, and opinions. In developing empowering relationships, the service provider recognizes and builds on the strengths of the child and the family (Dunst, Trivette, & Deal, 1994). To foster family independence and competence, service providers need to act as coaches who provide information and support to families, encouraging families to be informed decision makers and consumers (McWilliam, Ferguson, et al., 1998). In addition, McWilliam and his colleagues found that a caring relationship between the professional and the child was necessary to "opening the door" in developing an empowering relationship with the family.

Developmentally Appropriate

The procedures used by the POA need to reflect knowledge of child development in order to ensure adequate understanding and interpretation of the information provided through referrals, screenings, and interviews. National professional organizations, as well as the literature, delineate the importance of using developmentally appropriate interventions (Sandall, McLean, & Smith, 2000). The POA can set the stage for the use of developmentally appropriate interventions by asking questions about the child and family's routines and activities. As mentioned earlier, an abbreviation of the RBI can be used effectively by staff at the POA to gather developmentally appropriate information about the child's function in natural routines and settings.

Collaboration, Partnerships, and Integration

Collaborative partnerships rely on a relationship-based approach. In order to obtain the needed information about the child, staff at the integrated

POA need to develop collaborative relationships with families. In addition, in order to identify individuals who could contribute to the assessment and assist in better understanding the child and family, staff at the POA need to develop collaborative relationships with individuals within the POA and with others outside of the POA.

A high level of collaboration among staff (McGonigel, Woodruff, & Roszmann-Millican, 1994) from a wide array of disciplines is needed to understand diverse children and families; to plan assessments; and to integrate services to children with risks and delays, as well as to their families (Bagnato & Neisworth, 1991; Bruder, 1993; Garland, McGonigel, Frank, & Buck, 1989; Guralnick, 2001a; Linder, 1990; McGonigel & Garland, 1988; McWilliam, 2000; Woodruff, Hanson, McGonigel, & Sterzin, 1990). The diversity of needs requires individuals who understand the medical, health, nutrition, educational, and emotional needs of the child, as well as individuals who are knowledgeable about meeting basic needs, parent education, support, and training. In short, the POA team needs to be comprised of individuals who are knowledgeable about the resource categories.

The POA team "needs to transcend the confines of individual disciplines, forming a team that crosses and recrosses disciplinary boundaries to maximize communication, interaction, and cooperation among the members" (McGonigel, Woodruff, & Roszmann-Millican, 1994, p. 103). In accordance with the developmentally appropriate approach, the POA team views children's development as integrated and interactive. Therefore, instead of developing separate goals, solutions, and plans for future assessments and services based on their own disciplines, the professionals (in partnership with the family) integrate their knowledge and collaboratively develop next steps to be taken. Family participation is integral to the collaborative team approach (Bruder & Bologna, 1993).

Upon referral to the integrated POA, each child and family is assigned a service or POA coordinator who has primary responsibility for managing and carrying out the activities within the POA by coordinating with and obtaining information from individuals from other relevant disciplines and agencies. The POA coordinator should also gather the needed information. It would be advantageous for this person to continue as the service coordinator during the succeeding steps in the Developmental Systems Model (interdisciplinary assessment, development of IFSP or IEP, and service delivery). At the very least, however, the POA service coordinator will need to communicate information to future assessment personnel and service providers so that families do not have to repeat information. Retaining the same coordinator across all phases will facilitate continuity for the family and enhance the development of an empowering and trusting relationship. If families are continually assigned new service coordinators, then it is less likely that they will be willing to make the investments needed for a trusting and collaborative relationship.

Staff Competencies

A great deal has been written about the staff competencies needed to perform adequate assessments (Bagnato & Neisworth, 1991; Bailey & Wolery, 1992; Meisels & Provence, 1989; Neisworth & Bagnato, 2000), conduct effective interventions with children (Farran, 1990, 2000; McWilliam, 1992; Meisels & Shonkoff, 1990; Odom & McLean, 1996; Sandall, McLean, & Smith, 2000; Shonkoff & Phillips, 2000; Wolery, 2000), and establish supportive and empowering relationships with families (Dunst, Trivette, Starnes, Hamby, & Gordon, 1993; Simeonsson & Bailey, 1990; Turnbull & Turnbull, 1986). Despite the importance of the "first contacts" with families, however, which typically occur during the "intake," surprisingly little has been written about the competencies needed by POA staff. One exception to this is the First Contacts section of the Brass Tacks: Evaluation Version (McWilliam & McWilliam, 1993). This lack of information is interesting because POA staff are responsible for setting the stage in establishing important relationships with families, as well as setting the tone and expectations for the remaining steps in service delivery. In accomplishing the tasks discussed previously, staff of the POA are called on to play multiple roles—coordinator, advocate, coach, team member, and resource accessor. This section discusses the knowledge, training, skills, and characteristics needed by these important individuals who play multiple roles during completion of POA tasks. The competencies and characteristics reflect the nature of the tasks described earlier, as well as the values that guide the performance of these tasks.

Knowledge

Staff at the POA need to be knowledgeable about many areas in order to adequately and effectively establish relationships with the child and family, gather relevant information, and determine the nature of the next steps in service delivery. Knowledge of child development is essential in recognizing the possibility of delays, as well as in differentiating between a significant delay and a behavior that is within the normal developmental range. Equally important is the presence of a group of staff members who are knowledgeable about a variety of medical conditions, environmental risk factors, and diverse disabilities. This multidisciplinary knowledge is essential in gaining an accurate picture of the child and family, in guiding future assessments, and in laying the foundation for identifying and selecting appropriate services and resources. The diverse abilities and needs of children and families require staff with knowledge of relevant laws and the eligibility requirements of diverse programs (e.g., IDEA, CSHCN, TANF, Medicaid).

Training

No single discipline is equipped to address the diverse array of child and family needs and characteristics. The expertise of individuals representing medicine, nursing, nutrition, special education, therapies, psychology, family support, adult education, and social work is required. It is rare that a single program contains staff with this wide range of expertise. As mentioned previously, it is not sufficient to merely have staff representing these disciplines—they must be able to work as a collaborative team, integrating their knowledge and skills. It also is prudent to consider including family members because their experiences can be helpful to other families, and their perspective and perceptions can be useful to professionals employed by the POA.

Skills

Relationship-building is foremost among the skills needed by the POA staff. As mentioned previously, staff members need to establish collaborative relationships with a wide array of individuals: families, children, other staff members at the POA, and individuals representing diverse community resources. Consistent with the family-centered approach (Dunst, Trivette & Deal, 1988, 1994; McGonigel, Woodruff, & Roszmann-Millican, 1994), staff will need the interpersonal skills required to build relationships with, as well as to enhance the capacities of, families from diverse cultural and linguistic backgrounds. The POA staff need skills in gathering information using multiple approaches including conducting sensitive interviews, giving careful analysis of existing documents, and interpreting screening results, if available. POA tasks require interpersonal skills for developing collaborative relationships with other professionals and the consultation skills needed to enhance the capacities of others. Finally, the POA staff should have the skills needed to adequately complete forms and use resources (e.g., policies, computerized eligibility program, computerized directory) to determine eligibility for all relevant programs and services, regardless of which agency or program provides them.

Characteristics

The effective execution of POA activities requires a special combination of characteristics. In a qualitative study of exemplary service providers, researchers identified five crucial interpersonal characteristics: being positive, being responsive, orientating to the entire family (not just the child), being friendly, and having sensitivity (McWilliam, Tocci, & Harbin, 1998). In addition, all staff need to be engaging, supportive, and respectful of diverse families. Families also have identified the importance of service providers who were hopeful, optimistic, and resourceful (Harbin, Gardener, Rodriguez, & Kleckner, 2003). The infrastructure, described more fully in the next section, can enhance the response of the POA staff by having a fund for family emergencies, as well as ordinary supplies needed by families (e.g., diapers, milk, baby food). Civic organizations often are willing to contribute funds to purchase these necessities so they are readily available when needed by families.

Infrastructure

Traditionally, the separate points of access to autonomous programs have resulted in barriers to easy access to multiple programs or services by many families and the professionals who try to assist them. Therefore, to achieve early, easy, and timely access to a full array of resources, the question of what kind of infrastructure is best suited to the situation needs to be considered. Clearly, the practice of separate and poorly coordinated points of access to autonomous services and resources has been ineffective, resulting in children and families who are inadequately served. This section describes the elements of the infrastructure needed for a coordinated and integrated POA. These elements include an interagency organizational structure; integrated, interagency data system; computerized, broad-based resource directory; interagency agreements; coordinated policies; staff selection and development; and monitoring and evaluation.

Interagency Organizational Structure

Collaboration among professionals from different disciplines and programs requires an organizational structure and mechanisms that support collaborative decision making and activities. The co-location of staff has served as an effective strategy in many communities. Co-location refers to the practice of locating staff from many programs in one location (Alamprese, 1996; Dwyer, 1995). As previously mentioned, there are many agencies containing programs that help to meet the needs of children with or at risk for disabilities and their families. Co-location has been found to improve family accessibility, particularly when time constraints and transportation are seen as obstacles. If the POA houses staff from different disciplines and agencies (e.g., health department, social services, child care resource and referral, Part C, public schools), then all relevant areas of child and family need likely will be identified and assessed.

Despite the success of the co-location of staff from different agencies, no state Part C lead agencies have selected this approach. Currently, some states have established a separate agency charged with conducting *system entry tasks* for infants and toddlers with disabilities (Harbin et al., 2002). This organizational design is derived from the medical model in which the focus of system entry is a traditional multidisciplinary assessment that takes place in "testing" rooms. This model is descended from university-based developmental evaluation "clinics" instituted in the 1960s. These models have been criticized for their lack of family-centeredness and their inability to prepare useful assessment reports and functional IFSPs and IEPs. In some of these states, the staff is employed by the lead agency for Part C services. Consequently, staff members often are most knowledgeable about, and focus on, the *educational* and *therapeutic* services provided by the lead agency, resulting in a lack of service options.

Other states with a separate *system entry* agency have attempted to provide access to a wider array of resources and have designed their POAs to be impartial brokers, selecting among an array of *private providers* once an assessment is conducted. In this organizational model, the lead agency is not seen as the primary provider of developmental and therapeutic intervention. Therefore, the emphasis of this current organizational model is the objective selection of service providers. Current criticism of this latter model, which is referred to as the *private provider approach*, is the mechanical nature of the performance of entry tasks, the selection of unqualified providers, the lack of teamwork among separate providers, and the use of providers who do not use family-centered practices. In the remaining group of states, those individuals who conduct assessments and provide services usually conduct POA and system entry. In these states, there often is confusion between what level of information is needed by the POA step in the process and the level and type needed for a comprehensive and individualized interdisciplinary assessment. Consequently, professionals using a medical model collect more information than is needed for screening but less than is needed for an adequate assessment. Assessments often are mechanical and extremely similar from child to child, focusing on the child's educational and therapeutic needs. The same criticisms often are made about assessments conducted by the public schools.

Regardless of which of the three previous approaches are being used by Part C programs, they share one characteristic in common—POA activities usually are carried out with a focus on Part C eligibility and the child's functioning in the traditional developmental areas (e.g., cognitive, language). At most, the other primary area of focus is the child's health status, but that is not always the case.

To gain access to the diverse knowledge base and linkages to a wide array of health, educational, and social services, an interagency or transagency organization is needed to meet a broad range of needs for both children and families. The integrated and coordinated POA would offer an organizational home that is "neutral," belonging to and representing all resources within the community or region of the state. Different programs or agencies would contribute staff, but all would be housed in one location to collaborate and share information. All POA staff, regardless of their funding agency, would share a common mission: to help diverse children and families gain access to a broad array of specialized and natural resources to adequately meet their individual needs. This is made possible because staff members possess diverse areas of expertise with linkages to a comprehensive array of programs and resources listed in Table 5.1.

Each staff member serves as a liaison to programs in one of the 13 resource categories (see Table 5.1). If families contact a particular program, such as the health department, because they are concerned about the child's medical problems, however, then the program that was first contacted by the family should assist them in linking to the POA to receive access to a fuller array of services. The original program that was contacted (e.g., health department) can participate as a team member by gathering some initial information for the POA. In this example, the health department would serve as a liaison with the POA, as well as assist the family in identifying and providing future health services.

To understand the organizational functioning of the exemplary POA, one needs to make a distinction between a *single* portal of entry and an *integrated and coordinated* portal of entry. The former usually implies that a single agency is designed to provide access to resources from multiple agencies. Efforts to develop and implement a single portal of entry have been hampered by the lack of linkages between the single portal agency and other service provision agencies.

In an exemplary POA, all agencies, programs, private providers, and community members are seen as providing *multiple paths* to a *coordinated* POA. The use of staff from different agencies, who serve as liaisons with key agencies, enhances the communication between the POA and other agencies while simultaneously addressing the traditional problem regarding lack of sufficient linkages between the POA and other human services agencies. In addition, the exemplary POA is designed to coordinate information through a common or integrated data system that meets the needs of all agencies. The exemplary POA also addresses another limitation of the traditional single portal of entry by using an integrated, computerized resource directory. The combination of agency liaisons (mentioned previously), an integrated data system, and a computerized directory are organizational strengths of an exemplary POA. The latter two elements are described more fully later in the chapter. Figure 5.2 depicts the multiple paths leading to the integrated POA, as well as the bi-directional or interactive relationship between these referral paths and the integrated POA.

Currently, many programs have resource, referral, and "intake" responsibilities, such as child care resource and referral programs; Part C of IDEA '97; preschool special education programs located in public schools;

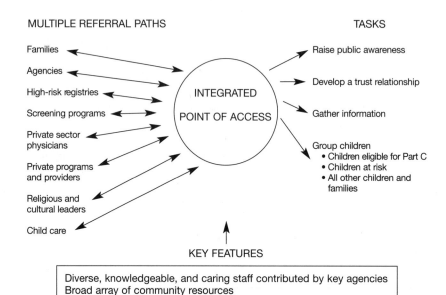

Figure 5.2. Operation of integrated point of access.

CSHCN and Early Periodic Screening, Diagnosis and Treatment (EPSDT) services, both of which are located in the health department; CPS and TANF, which are located in the social services agency; and WIC, which is sometimes located in the health department and other times in social services. Other programs that offer their own POA include Head Start, Early Head Start, Even Start, and other literacy programs, as well as programs that serve children with specific disabilities (e.g., cerebral palsy, autism, hearing and vision impairments, Down syndrome). The POA function takes place within individual programs, which duplicates the effort and results in fewer resources identified and fewer needs met for children and families (Harbin, McWilliam, & Gallagher, 2000). An integrated POA reduces duplication of program efforts and reduces the number of times parents are asked to provide the same information.

There are existing entities in each community that could be broadened into this more comprehensive and integrated POA. Some communities have a child care resource and referral agency or a family resource center. The broader the target population of the POA, the broader the appeal to all families in the community, reducing families' fear of stigmatization and reluctance to make an inquiry.

The Part C lead agencies in some states have established POAs to be responsible only for children with disabilities. Consequently, in many of the states with separate system entry or POAs, children with biological and/or environmental risks are not eligible for services. Child-find initiatives and system entry for these children are conducted by another agency, and in most instances, multiple agencies. Therefore, in most states, the development of a POA that encompasses both children with disabilities and those with risks requires some type of organizational collaboration and union among multiple agencies.

The separate entities established by some states for Part C system entry could establish an integrated and comprehensive POA by housing staff from other agencies, resulting in a more comprehensive system entry and POA for children with risks, delays, and disabilities. If the Part C lead agency is unable to get other agencies to agree to contribute staff, then the lead agency can *hire* staff that represent diverse disciplines. These staff members could serve as the liaison between the POA and other agencies.

The number of locations for the POA could vary, depending on the size of the community. There could be a single POA for a group of counties in a rural area or for a small town. There could be several POAs in a metropolitan area to ensure that all neighborhoods are being served.

A comprehensive POA representing a wide array of agencies and programs needs an interagency group, including several family representatives, to oversee the effectiveness and efficiency of its activities and to determine whether the previously described goals are being achieved. An existing group, such as a local interagency coordinating council, likely can be broadened to represent additional agencies and segments of the community resource system. Collaboratively, the POA and each agency are responsible for ensuring implementation of all relevant federal laws such as Part C of IDEA '97 and its reauthorization.

Integrated, Interagency Data System

Families are frequently required to provide the same demographic and background information to several agencies. Agencies often mistakenly think that confidentiality requirements prevent sharing information with other agencies. In most instances, however, an agency only needs to obtain family consent to share demographic information. Most families gladly provide consent if it means reduced work and frustration for them. Furthermore, currently no formal mechanisms or tools facilitate communication between agencies and service providers who rely solely on informal, verbal communication between professionals to coordinate services. With an integrated data system, families only have to provide demographic and background information once. The POA, or an interagency task force, can use the forms from various agencies and programs to create a common cross-agency computer form (Garland, personal communication, October 12, 2002).

Policy makers also have recognized the need for an integrated data system. Many state legislators want a single count of children and families served as well as a portrait of services provided. An integrated data system would provide that information as well as other useful information, such as the number of children and families served by multiple agencies, including the various combinations of agencies. An integrated data system could monitor and track steps in the service delivery process (from intake through assessment and service delivery) for each child and family, easily communicating this management information to all relevant staff and interested agencies. This data system could be designed to produce a daily "to-do" list for POA staff, including service or access coordination. In addition, the data system could provide a staff management chart for administrators to use in examining the length of time dedicated to each child and family during each step of the process. This would provide a better understanding of the workload of each staff member and the amount of effort needed to assist families with different characteristics and circumstances at different stages of the process.

The integrated data system would be even more useful if it contained eligibility criteria for diverse services or programs. The sheer number of categorical programs across health, education, and social welfare makes it difficult for every service provider to know the eligibility criteria for all of these programs. Policy changes and staff turnover make this even more problematic. However, use of a computer program containing all relevant eligibility criteria for programs across the 13 resource categories in Table 5.1 would significantly reduce the barriers to access resulting from a lack of staff knowledge. For example, after an individual enters the child and family's demographic information, the computer program could determine whether the child or the family is eligible for a child care subsidy, EPSDT, or WIC, in addition to Part C services. If the child and family is not eligible for federal or state programs, then the database should contain alternate resources that could be used to meet the identified need (e.g., state insurance, child care scholarship, food bank, Lion's Club, Habitat for Humanity). If all programs contribute information to the eligibility portion of the integrated database, then staff will be able to identify a wider array of resources. Use of an integrated data system would be more likely to identify children who are eligible for more than one federal program. All too frequently, children who are eligible for multiple programs fail to be referred to all programs for which they or their families are eligible.

The integrated data system also could be linked to the monitoring program that systematically tracks the development of children with biological and environmental risk factors. In addition, this integrated data system could be used to track child and family progress and outcomes as a result of service delivery. Finally, the integrated data system is essential to facilitating adequate communication and coordination across agencies that is required for collaborative and integrated activities.

Computerized, Broad-Based Resource Directory

Many programs have created their own resource directory, which often is a paper document, making the directory difficult, time-consuming, and expensive to update and reproduce. Most of these directories are organized by descriptions of programs containing a list of multiple services, making it difficult and time-consuming to identify all providers of a particular type or category of service. For example, the Even Start program provides multiple services, including literacy training and parenting skills to parents of young children, as well as some intervention to their children as well. If a staff member is trying to identify adult literacy services, he or she typically would have to read entire program descriptions to identify those providing adult literacy.

To be valuable and useful, the computerized directory should be organized using the broad categories presented in Table 5.1. These larger categories can be subdivided into more specific categories. Part C of IDEA '97 requires states to create and maintain a central directory of services. However, many states have developed a service directory that focuses primarily on the educational, therapeutic, and health needs of the child. States and communities could build on and extend this required directory by using existing service directories from other programs to produce a more comprehensive list.

Interagency Agreements

A collaborative or integrated approach to POA tasks requires meaningful interagency agreements that contain sufficient specificity and detail (Harbin et al., 2004; Harbin & McNulty, 1990; Rogers & Farrow, 1983). The interagency agreement is the single policy that is recognized by all relevant participating agencies. Therefore, the more specific the contents of the interagency agreement, the more guidance it provides to individuals representing diverse agencies who are trying to work collaboratively with staff from other agencies. It is helpful if the agreement contains the *binding authority* or legal basis (i.e., law or regulation) that permits each agency's participation and serves as the basis for complying with the contents of the agreement. In addition, the agreement should include 1) the *purposes* of the integrated POA; 2) the underlying *values* that guide professionals' practice; 3) the *tasks and responsibilities* of each participating agency, program, or individual provider; and 4) the *contributions* of each participant (e.g., fiscal, facilities, staff, materials, staff development; Harbin & Van Horn, 1990).

The interagency agreement needs to address the tasks and responsibilities to be performed by staff from multiple agencies for the public awareness and child-find components. In addition, the agreement should address the roles and responsibilities of the agencies related to the integrated data system, including confidentiality procedures, password-protected access, and steps to be taken when there are disputes between agencies.

Coordinated Policies

A meaningful interagency agreement does much to lay a policy foundation for an integrated POA. The policies of each of the agencies were created to support separate and autonomous programs, each with its own set of services and accompanying regulations (Flynn & Harbin, 1987). To facilitate optimum coordination and integration of POA activities across programs and agencies, agencies need to review their policies and revise them to be in concert with the values and activities agreed on in the interagency agreement. This will result in policies that are more complementary with regard to procedures and definitions (Bronheim, Cohen, & Magrab, 1985; Harbin & McNulty, 1990; Steiner, 1976).

Staff Selection and Development

As mentioned previously, staff should be selected to represent diverse disciplines and areas of expertise. Frequently, state agencies set forth qualifications for direct services providers, including the type of degree required. For a POA to be effective, staff provided by diverse agencies must have the values, knowledge, skills, and characteristics outlined in this chapter and represent the cultural and linguistic background of children and families visiting the POA. A collaborative interview process, in which candidates are asked how to handle "real-life" scenarios and dilemmas, will be more likely to result in identifying and hiring staff with the needed competencies. The use of the collaborative approach requires that team members engage in an ongoing collaborative process of teaching others and learning from one another. In addition, POA staff would benefit from ongoing training designed to improve their knowledge and skills. Frequently, most of the training provided by state agencies focuses on skills and knowledge needed to conduct assessments, develop individualized intervention plans, provide effective interventions with children, and work effectively with families. Although this information is useful to staff of the POA, state and local administrators would be wise to provide training that is designed to specifically enhance activities conducted by the POA, including service coordination.

Monitoring and Evaluation

POA administrators must engage in systematic evaluation of effectiveness in order to ensure that the purposes of the POA are achieved (e.g., early, easy, timely, accessible) and that they are achieved in the desired manner (e.g., family centered, culturally sensitive). To that end, administrators can make use of data that are collected and entered into the integrated data system. In addition, an interagency policy group that includes families should provide oversight. Administrators need to make a special effort to evaluate the extremely important tasks conducted by the POA that lay the foundation for the subsequent tasks in service delivery.

CONCLUSIONS AND IMPLICATIONS

Although families have articulated the need for integrated service delivery, and there are legal requirements for coordinated referrals and access across agencies and programs, Congress has done little to eliminate categorical programs. Thus, administrators and service providers are severely hampered by the categorical nature of these important federal programs. Further complicating the situation is the current lack of sufficient organizational linkages between and among categorical programs at the federal, state, and local levels. Consequently, the current multiple autonomous public awareness and child-find activities, as well as POAs to services, have resulted in four interrelated problems: lack of early identification of children, lack of easy access, lack of access to the full array of resources needed by the child and family, and lack of timely access to services.

The Developmental Systems Model described by Guralnick (2001a) is designed to improve all phases of service delivery to a diverse array of children with risks (biological and environmental), disabilities, and disabling conditions (e.g., Down syndrome). This group of children comprises a sizable segment of the population; therefore, this chapter recommends the use of an integrated and coordinated POA to address the breadth of the population and the scope of needed agencies, resources, services, and supports. The exemplary POA described in this chapter is designed to ensure early, easy, timely, and full access to resources. The organizational structure, climate, and activities will be family-friendly, family-centered, and culturally sensitive. This requires major changes in 1) how the POA tasks currently are performed, 2) the role and inclusion of families as meaningful participants, and 3) the organization and staffing of the POA.

These changes require a paradigm shift away from a bureaucratic and de-personalized approach, traditionally referred to as "intake," to an empowering and empathetic "welcoming" of children and families in a caring manner in more natural contexts. The effective use of this innovative approach to the POA also requires an organizational shift from a single agency with a narrow array of resources, to an approach that coordinates and takes advantage of a wide array of resources and supports made available by a diverse group of providers. The final paradigm shift pertains to the organization and use of technology. This requires a shift from simplistic use of technology, which limits the capabilities of the POA, to a more complex use of technology to increase the capabilities of the POA in identifying and coordinating a broad array of child and family resources.

Coordinating the POA for resources provided by multiple agencies is more efficient and less frustrating for families because they only have to answer questions once. It is also a more efficient use of public resources by individual programs because it reduces staff time spent on duplicative tasks. In addition, the coordinated and integrated POA is more effective because it uses procedures to gather information that are more functional and relevant to families.

Professionals must address four broad challenges if they are to make significant progress in the development of a coordinated and integrated POA. First, some evidence shows that creating a system of opportunities and resources for all children and families results in improved outcomes for children with disabilities and their families (Harbin, McWilliam, & Gallagher, 2000). A universal service system would likely reduce or eliminate the stigma sometimes associated with programs for those who are at an economic disadvantage and have disabilities and would likely result in wider acceptance of, and support for, services for young children.

Second, the quality of the POA is dependent on the nature of the leadership provided by its administrators as well as the administrators of relevant programs in various agencies (Garland & Linder, 1994; Harbin, McWilliam, & Gallagher, 2000; Kagan & Bowman, 1997). Special efforts need to be undertaken to develop a cadre of leaders with skills in multi-agency systems development, including both specialized and naturally occurring community resources (Harbin, McWilliam, & Gallagher, 2000; Trivette et al., 1996). These leaders must have a collaborative vision of a comprehensive system as well as the process and political skills needed to gain consensus from all stakeholders. Only with this type of leadership can professionals make progress in understanding and developing interagency organizational structures (Garland & Linder, 1994; Harbin et al., 2004).

Third, much progress has been made in the area of technology. In large part, however, human services have lagged behind business in making effective use of technology. Human services agencies can be more responsive to families and serve families more effectively by using technology in a more sophisticated manner. Integrated data management programs take time to develop but yield substantial benefits. The North Carolina legislature recognized the importance of this type of endeavor by funding a pilot project to develop an integrated data system across all service agencies for children birth through age 5 (North Carolina House of Representatives, 1999).

The fourth challenge is adequate pre- and in-service training of personnel across disciplines and agencies. Gaining acceptance from families, therapists, and physicians for the collaborative and integrated approach is going to be a significant undertaking. In order to achieve early, easy, timely, and full access to resources for children and families, however, it is incumbent on individuals to put aside what is "comfortable and easy" and begin the difficult work needed to collaboratively develop a coordinated and integrated POA.

REFERENCES

Alamprese, J. (1996). Integrated services, cross-agency collaboration, and family literacy. In L. Benjamin & J. Lord (Eds.), *Family literacy: Directions in research and implications for practice* (pp. 17–23). Washington, DC: U.S. Department of Education.

Atkins-Burnett, S., & Allen-Meares, P. (2000). Infants and toddlers with disabilities: Relationship-based approaches. *Social Work, 45,* 371–379.

Bagnato, S.J., & Neisworth, J.T. (1991). *Assessment for early intervention: Best practices for professionals.* New York: Guilford Press.

Bailey, D., & Simeonsson, R. (1990). *Family Needs Survey.* Chapel Hill: Frank Porter Graham Child Development Institute, University of North Carolina.

Bailey, D.B., & Wolery, M. (1992). *Teaching infants and preschoolers with disabilities.* Columbus, OH: Macmillan.

Bronfenbrenner, U. (1975). *Influences on human development.* Hinsdale, IL: Dryden Press.

Bronfenbrenner, U. (1979). Ecology of the family as a context for human development: Research perspectives. *Developmental Psychology, 22*(6), 723–742.

Bronfenbrenner, U. (1992). Ecological systems theory. In R. Vasta (Ed.), *Six theories of child development: Revised formulations and current issues* (pp. 187–249). Philadelphia: Kingsley.

Bronheim, S., Cohen, P.D., & Magrab, P.R. (1985). *Evaluating community collaboration: A guide to self-study.* Washington, DC: Georgetown University Child Development Center.

Bruder, M.B. (1993). The provision of early intervention and early childhood special education within community early childhood programs: Characteristics of effective service delivery. *Topics in Early Childhood Special Education, 13*(1), 19–37.

Bruder, M.B., & Bologna, T.M. (1993). Collaboration and service coordination for effective early intervention. In W. Brown, S.K. Thurman, & L.F. Pearl (Eds.), *Family-centered early intervention with infants and toddlers: Innovative cross-disciplinary approaches* (pp. 103–127). Baltimore: Paul H. Brookes Publishing Co.

Dunst, C., Johansen, C., Trivette, C., & Hamby, D. (1991). Family-oriented early intervention policies or practices: Family-centered or not? *Exceptional Children, 58*, 115–126.

Dunst, C., Trivette, C., & Deal, A. (1988). *Enabling and empowering families: Principles and guidelines for practice.* Cambridge, MA: Brookline Books.

Dunst, C.J., Trivette, C.M., & Deal, A.G. (Eds.). (1994). *Supporting and strengthening families: Methods, strategies, and practices* (Vol. 1). Cambridge, MA: Brookline Books.

Dunst, C.J., Trivette, C.M., Starnes, A.L., Hamby, D.W., & Gordon, N.J. (1993). *Building and evaluating family support initiatives: A national study of programs for persons with developmental disabilities.* Baltimore: Paul H. Brookes Publishing Co.

Dwyer, C. (1995). *Guide to quality: Even Start family literacy programs.* Portsmouth, NH: RMC Research Corporation.

Farran, D. (1990). Effects of intervention with disadvantaged and disabled children: A decade review. In S.J. Meisels & J.P. Shonkoff (Eds.), *Handbook of early childhood intervention* (pp. 501–539). New York: Cambridge University Press.

Farran, D. (2000). Another decade of intervention for children who are low income or disabled: What do we do now? In J.P. Shonkoff & S.J. Meisels (Eds.), *Handbook of early childhood intervention* (2nd ed., pp. 510–548). New York: Cambridge University Press.

Flynn, C., & Harbin, G.L. (1987). Evaluating interagency coordination efforts using a multidimensional, interactional, developmental paradigm. *Remedial and Special Education, 8*(3), 35–44.

Frankenburg, W., & Dodds, J. (1968). *Denver Developmental Screening Test.* Denver: University of Colorado Medical Center.

Garland, C.W., & Linder, T.W. (1994). Administrative challenges in early intervention. In L.J. Johnson, R.J. Gallagher, M.J. LaMontagne, J.B. Jordan, J.J. Gallagher, P.L. Hutinger, & M.B. Karnes (Eds.), *Meeting early intervention challenges: Issues from birth to three* (pp. 133–163). Baltimore: Paul H. Brookes Publishing Co.

Garland, C.W., McGonigel, M.J., Frank, A., & Buck, D. (1989). *The transdisciplinary model of service delivery.* Lightfoot, VA: Child Development Resources.

Guralnick, M.J. (2001a). A developmental systems model for early intervention. *Infants and Young Children, 14*(2), 1–18.

Guralnick, M.J. (Ed.). (2001b). *Early childhood inclusion: Focus on change.* Baltimore: Paul H. Brookes Publishing Co.

Harbin, G. (1996). The challenge of coordination. *Infants and Young Children, 8*(3), 68–76.

Harbin, G., Bruder, M.B., Reynolds, C., Mazzarella, C., Gabbard, G., & Staff, I. (2002). *Service coordination policies and models: National status.* Chapel Hill: Frank Porter Graham Child Development Institute, University of North Carolina.

Harbin, G., Gardener, L., Rodriguez, I., & Kleckner, M. (2003). *Beacons of excellence: Case studies three early intervention systems.* Chapel Hill: Frank Porter Graham Child Development Institute, University of North Carolina.

Harbin, G., Herrmann, S., Wasik, B., Dobbins, D., & Lam, W. (2004). Integrating services for family literacy. In B. Wasik (Ed.), *Handbook for family literacy* (pp. 373–397). York, PA: Tech Books.

Harbin, G., & McNulty, B.A. (1990). Policy implementation: Prescriptives on service coordination and interagency cooperation. In J.P. Shonkoff & S.J. Meisels (Eds.), *Handbook of early childhood intervention* (pp. 700–721). New York: Cambridge University Press.

Harbin, G., McWilliam, R.A., & Gallagher, J.J. (2000). Services for young children with disabilities and their families. In J.P. Shonkoff & S.J. Meisels (Eds.), *Handbook of early childhood intervention* (2nd ed., pp. 387–415). New York: Cambridge University Press.

Harbin, G.L., Pelosi, J., Kameny, R., McWilliam, R., Kitsul, Y., Fox, E., & Rodriguez, I. (2004). *Identifying and predicting successful outcomes of coordinated service delivery.* Chapel Hill, NC: FPG Child Development Institute, The University of North Carolina at Chapel Hill.

Harbin, G.L., & Van Horn, J. (1990). *Interagency coordinating council roles and responsibilities.* Chapel Hill: Carolina Policy Studies Program, Frank Porter Graham Child Development Center, University of North Carolina.

Individuals with Disabilities Education Act (IDEA) Amendments of 1997, PL 105-17, 20 U.S.C. §§ 1400 *et seq.*

Kagan, S.L., & Bowman, B.T. (Eds.). (1997). *Leadership in early care and education.* Washington, DC: National Association for the Education of Young Children.

Kochanek, T.T. (1989). A serial, multivariate screening and assessment model. In S. Meisels & S. Provence (Eds.), *Identifying and assessing young disabled and developmentally vulnerable children and their families: Recommended guidelines.* Washington, DC: ZERO TO THREE: National Center for Infants, Toddlers, and Families.

Linder, T.W. (1990). *Transdisciplinary play-based assessment: A functional approach to working with young children.* Baltimore: Paul H. Brookes Publishing Co.

McGonigel, M.J., & Garland, C.W. (1988). The individualized family service plan and the early intervention team: Team and family issues and recommended practices. *Infants and Young Children, 1*(1), 10–21.

McGonigel, M.J., Woodruff, G., & Roszmann-Millican, M. (1994). The transdisciplinary team: A model for family-centered early intervention. In L.J. Johnson, R.J. Gallagher, M.J. LaMontagne, J.B. Jordan, J.J. Gallagher, P.L. Hutinger, & M.B. Karnes (Eds.), *Meeting early intervention challenges: Issues from birth to three* (2nd ed., pp. 95–131). Baltimore: Paul H. Brookes Publishing Co.

McWilliam, P.J., & McWilliam, R.A. (1993). *Brass Tacks: Evaluation Version.* Chapel Hill: Frank Porter Graham Child Development Center, University of North Carolina.

McWilliam, R.A. (1992). *Family-centered intervention planning: A routines-based approach.* Tucson, AZ: Communication Skill Builders.

McWilliam, R.A. (2000). Recommended practices in interdisciplinary models. In S. Sandall, M.E. McLean, & B.J. Smith (Eds.), *DEC recommended practices in early intervention/early childhood special education* (pp. 47–54). Longmont, CO: Sopris West.

McWilliam, R.A., Ferguson, A., Harbin, G.L., Porter, P., Munn, D., & Vandiviere, P. (1998). The family-centeredness of individualized family service plans. *Topics in Early Childhood Special Education, 18*(2), 69–82.

McWilliam, R.A., Tocci, L., & Harbin, G.L. (1998). *Family-centered services: Lessons from early intervention service providers.* Chapel Hill, NC: Early Childhood Research Institute on Service Utilization.

Meisels, S., & Provence, S. (1989). *Screening and assessment: Guidelines for identifying young disabled and developmentally vulnerable children and their families.* Washington, DC: National Center for Clinical Infant Programs.

Meisels, S.J., & Shonkoff, J.P. (Eds.). (1990). *Handbook of early childhood intervention.* New York: Cambridge University Press.

Neisworth, J., & Bagnato, S. (2000). Recommended practices in assessment. In S. Sandall, M. McLean, & B. Smith (Eds.), *DEC recommended practices.* Longmont, CO: Sopris West.

North Carolina House of Representatives. (1999). House Bill 1840: Early Intervention Services. North Carolina General Assembly. S.L. 1999-237, Section 11.42

Odom, S.L., & McLean, M.E. (1996). *Early intervention/early childhood special education: Recommended practices.* Austin, TX: PRO-ED.

Rogers, C., & Farrow, F. (1983). *Effective state strategies to promote interagency collaboration: A report of the handicapped public policy analysis project.* Washington, DC: Center for the Study of Social Policy.

Sameroff, A., & Chandler, M. (1975). Reproductive risk and the continuum of caretaking causality. *Review of Child Development Research, 4,* 187–244.

Sameroff, S., & Fiese, B. (1990). Transactional regulation and early intervention. In S.J. Meisels & J.P. Shonkoff (Eds.), *Handbook of early childhood intervention* (pp. 3–32). New York: Cambridge University Press.

Sandall, S., McLean, M.E., & Smith, B.J. (2000). *DEC recommended practices in early intervention/early childhood special education.* Longmont, CO: Sopris West.

Shonkoff, J.P., & Meisels, S.J. (2000). *Handbook of early childhood intervention* (2nd ed). New York: Cambridge University Press.

Shonkoff, J., & Phillips, D. (2000). *From neurons to neighborhoods: The science of early childhood development.* Washington, DC: National Academy Press.

Simeonsson, R., & Bailey, D. (1990). Family dimensions in early intervention. In S.J. Meisels & J.P. Shonkoff (Eds.), *Handbook of early childhood intervention* (pp. 428–444). New York: Cambridge University Press.

Steiner, G. (1976). *The children's cause.* Washington, DC: Brookings Institute.

Tjossem, T. (1976). *Intervention strategies for high risk infants and young children.* Baltimore: University Park Press.

Trivette, C.M., Dunst, C.J., & Deal, A.G. (1996). Resource-based early intervention practices. In S.K. Thurman, J.R. Cornwell, & S.R. Gottwald (Eds.), *The contexts of early intervention, systems and settings* (pp. 73–92). Baltimore: Paul H. Brookes Publishing Co.

Trivette, C., Dunst, C., & Hamby, D. (1996). Factors associated with perceived control appraisals in a family-centered early intervention program. *Journal of Early Intervention, 20,* 165–178.

Turnbull, A.P., Turbiville, V., & Turnbull, H.R. (2000). Evolution of family-professional partnerships: Collective empowerment as the model for the early 21st century. In J.P. Shonkoff & S.L. Meisels (Eds.), *Handbook of early childhood intervention.* (2nd ed., pp. 630–650). New York: Cambridge University Press.

Turnbull, A., & Turnbull, H. (1986). *Parents speak out: Views from the other side of the two-way mirror.* Columbus, OH: Merrill.

U.S. Department of Education. (2003). *Twenty-fourth annual report to Congress on the implementation of the Individuals with Disabilities Education Act.* Washington, DC: Author.

Wolery, M. (2000). Recommended practices in child-focused intervention. In S. Sandall, M.E. McLean, & B.J. Smith (Eds.), *DEC recommended practices in early intervention/early childhood special education* (pp. 29–38). Longmont, CO: Sopris West.

Woodruff, G., Hanson, C.R., McGonigel, M., & Sterzin, E.D. (1990). *Community-based services for children with HIV infection and their families: A manual for planners, service providers, families, and advocates.* Brighton, MA: South Shore Mental Health Center.

CHAPTER 6

The Role of Comprehensive Interdisciplinary Assessments in the Early Intervention System

MARK L. WOLRAICH, ROBIN H. GURWITCH,
MARY BETH BRUDER, AND LAURA A. KNIGHT

INTERDISCIPLINARY APPROACH

Although infants and young children with disabilities may require the combined expertise of numerous professionals providing specialized services, the coordination of both people and services is frequently overwhelming. For example, personnel having medical, therapeutic, educational/developmental, and social services expertise traditionally have been involved in the provision of services to infants and young children with disabilities and their families (Stayton & Bruder, 1999). Each of these service providers may represent a different professional discipline and a different philosophical model of service delivery. In fact, each discipline has its own training sequence (some require undergraduate degrees, whereas others require graduate degrees), licensing and/or certification requirements (most of which do not require age specialization for young children), and treatment modality (e.g., occupational therapists may focus on sensory integration techniques).

In order to improve the efficiency of the individuals providing early intervention, a team approach has been suggested for all facets of service delivery, beginning with assessment. A group of people become a team when their purpose and function are derived from a common philosophy with shared goals (Maddux, 1988). The types of teams that typically function for young children with disabilities have been identified as multidisciplinary, interdisciplinary, or cross/transdisciplinary. The commonality of each is the need for collaborative expertise from people with different disciplinary backgrounds (see Guralnick, 2000).

The interdisciplinary approach originally was conceived as a framework for professionals to share important information and skills with primary caregivers. This approach integrates a child's developmental needs across the major developmental areas identified by professionals who have expertise in these areas. To be successful, the interdisciplinary approach involves collaboration from all team members and, for this reason, may be difficult to implement. The primary purpose of the approach is to pool and integrate the expertise of team members so that more efficient and comprehensive assessment and intervention services may be provided to a child and family. The communication style in this type of team involves continuous give and take between all members (especially the parents) on a regular, planned basis. Professionals from different disciplines teach, learn, and work together to accomplish assessment protocols and intervention goals for a child and his or her family. Designated members of the team carry out assessment, intervention, and evaluation jointly. *Multidisciplinary* refers to multiple evaluations without the extensive collaboration and communication, and *cross/transdisciplinary* refers to shared roles in which clinicians from one discipline can take on the activities for several disciplines (Linder, 1990).

Although collaborative, interdisciplinary early intervention teams appear simple in concept, implementation of this strategy can be difficult because of the differences between it and the more familiar, structured, discipline-specific intervention structures (Bruder, 1995). In particular, the time commitment required to implement a collaborative team model effectively across all individuals may be difficult for some early intervention assessment or early intervention programs (Bruder, 1994).

The benefits of interdisciplinary services extend beyond those immediate to the individual child. The integration of assessment procedures between disciplines reduces the need for repeated assessments, often conducted without reference to each other, which may be a source of irritation for families (McConachie, 1999). Furthermore, interdisciplinary service provision reduces other areas of reported parental dissatisfaction with regard to a child's services: overlap between services, a lack of communication between the professionals providing services, and no identified person responsible for overall monitoring of the child (Howard, 1994). Interdisciplinary teams provide both a comprehensive and coordinated approach to assessment and often are a more efficient and cost-effective means of accomplishing this task than traditional single-discipline assessments (American Academy of Pediatrics, 1994).

Having an interdisciplinary team based in a child development center extends the benefits to team members by having physical space for the team to meet, facilitating team building and communication, and providing a base for in-service training. The center may also serve as a community resource for children and their families (McConachie, Salt, Chadury, McLachlan, & Logan, 1999). However, the evaluation does not necessarily need to be conducted in the center. Some environments that are more familiar to the child, such as home or child care, may allow for a more optimal observation.

Interdisciplinary service provision is not without its obstacles. Interdisciplinary reports are more difficult to compile and, thus, take longer to be sent to relevant parties (McConachie, 1999). Moreover, Perrin (1999) advised that intrinsic differences in the training and theoretical foundations of professionals from different disciplines may make collaborating challenging. Different underlying paradigms and expectations about the appropriate pace, scope, and scheduling of care may lead to conflict among team members. For a collaborative practice to work, the participants must value each other's expertise and understand the added value of the collaboration. Team members must define responsibilities clearly, identify difficulties, get information from each other, and communicate regularly.

Families of children with disabilities are faced not only with the difficult task of accepting the child's condition but also with sorting out conflicting advice from multiple sources of information. Assessment of a child in an interdisciplinary setting ensures that the child receives the complete and coordinated service best suited to his or her individual needs (Howard, 1994) and helps to provide families with a clear strategic framework so that they can be supported in working toward specific, attainable goals (Cass, Price, Reilly, Wisbeach, & McConachie, 1999). Whereas families may once have relied solely on their pediatrician for their child's physical and developmental needs, families are now more likely than ever to have access to a variety of service providers, thus benefiting both the child and the family.

The comprehensive interdisciplinary assessment is a key component in the Developmental Systems Model (Guralnick, 2001) with many important goals (see the next section). In this chapter, the authors present an overview of the process in connection with some key disciplines (see also Guralnick, 2000) and outline the types of assessment information that should be gathered. Ideally, such a process would be available to all (or most) children. However, for a variety of reasons, this is not often possible. In the last section of this chapter, the authors suggest how key features of the process can be implemented in communities with varying resources.

ASSESSMENT

Providing early intervention services to children with special needs must begin with their assessment. The assessment provides several important functions. First, it determines if a child meets the criteria required for him or her to be eligible for the program. Although the ideal situation would be to provide services to all children, most early intervention programs place some limits on how many children they can serve. They need to set their limits based on a balance between the extent of their funding, the needs of the children, and where they are likely to have the most impact. Therefore, it is critical for programs to determine each child's condition including both diagnosis and severity. This component of the assessment focuses on determining the extent of delay, the presence of a medical diagnosis, or the presence of environmental threats placing the child at risk for having or developing a developmental disability.

The first level of this model is arriving at a diagnosis of the child's disability or disorder. Parents' most basic expectation of the interdisciplinary team is that they should have a diagnosis of their child's disorder and its cause. Next, identification of a diagnosis may help the team predict the range of neurological or other related disabilities (e.g., sensory, cognitive, motor, language) that may be expected. For example, underdiagnosis of sensory impairment appears to be common, and these impairments may have a profound effect on a wide range of higher functions (e.g., attainment of motor or cognitive milestones, general level of alertness and motivation; Cooper, Majnemer, Rosenblatt, & Birnbaum, 1995; Thompson, 1982). A team can work with the family to address these concerns and the impact of one aspect of a child's status on other aspects of development.

To illustrate ways in which unresolved problems in one area of functioning may prevent effective management of problems in other areas, Cass et al. (1999) described the case history of a boy with spastic quadriplegia who was referred to the neurodisability clinic of a London children's hospital for his lack of progress in active communication. A thorough multidisciplinary assessment revealed that the boy's physical discomfort, malnutrition, general poor health, and lack of motivation for communication stemmed from severe feeding problems and aspiration that had gone undiagnosed. The team determined that strategies aimed at developing communication and improving the boy's use of electronic equipment were unlikely to be successful until these problems were rectified. Six months after treatment, the boy was in good general health and was consistently more alert, interested, and responsive, thus indicating an appropriate time to consider interventions to increase communication.

Assessment is the process of gathering information in order to make a decision. Assessment is an important component of early intervention, yet traditional assessment models (e.g., discipline-specific, in a novel setting with contrived activities, conducted by a stranger) prove inadequate when working with infants and toddlers with disabilities (Meisels & Fenichel, 1996). Effective early childhood assessment protocols must rely on sensitivity to the age of the child, the nature of his or her delay or disability, and the family context.

Assessment instruments include a variety of standardized and criterion-referenced instruments that provide information across the traditional areas of development including cognition, fine and gross motor, receptive and expressive communication, social-emotional, and self-help. Professionals representing different professional disciplines may utilize assessments that focus on specific developmental areas. It is most important that the instruments that are used match the intended outcomes of the assessment purpose.

As noted previously, an important component of assessment is identifying any diagnosable conditions. These diagnosable conditions will help identify possible causes for the children's delays. The causes may be biological, such as a known syndrome (e.g., Down syndrome), or environmental (e.g., limited stimulation from a mother with depression.) In most cases, both biological and environmental factors are likely to be contributing to the children's delays. The evaluation process helps identify needs for interventions that go beyond the services of developmental stimulation and education that are usually provided. In the example of maternal depression, it is important to identify services for the mother to treat her depression as a component of the intervention plan. The diagnosis also can provide prognostic information; for example, the child's condition may be progressive (e.g., Tay-Sachs disease).

Second, the initial assessment is important to determine the level of functioning of the child and to identify any delays and unusual patterns in his or her development, language, personal-social, gross motor, and fine motor skills. The process of assessing the children's levels of functioning in the various domains also provides an opportunity to determine both their strengths and their weaknesses. This process helps those providing the services to include a strengths-based approach to the interventions, and it provides the information that clinicians can utilize to develop an individualized family service plan (IFSP).

Third, the assessment provides baseline information that can be used to determine the effectiveness of the program. It is important for all programs to be accountable both to the families they serve and to the agencies that are funding their program. The evaluation system needs to provide information on the individual progress of each child to help parents monitor the progress of their children as well as aggregated information to help determine the overall benefit of the program. The initial assessment can provide needed baseline information. If it is possible for the periodic assessments to be performed independent of the staff providing the services, then the assessments provide independent and less biased information.

The optimal assessments entail an interdisciplinary process in which the various aspects of the children and their environments can be assessed. A comprehensive assessment requires input from a number of professional disciplines that may include medicine, psychology, early childhood education, speech and language pathology, physical and occupational therapy, nutrition, audiology, social work, and nursing (see Guralnick, 2000). Because of expense and time, most teams do not require and are not able to provide all of the disciplines. For illustrative purposes, the disciplines of medicine, psychology, and education are presented to provide examples of the approaches utilized in the interdisciplinary assessment of young children. To develop a plan that will be meaningful to the children and their families, the different disciplines need to coordinate their efforts so that they develop a comprehensive picture that addresses each child and his or her family individually and not just as a sum of different disciplinary evaluations. The assessments themselves need to be integrated and combined so children and their families are not overtaxed by the process and useful information and recommendations are provided. Frequently, multiple clinicians will perform the evaluations simultaneously in order to keep the assessment times realistic for the age of the child and to obtain optimal performance. Observations in the home and videotapes of the child can provide further information because optimal performance may not occur during formal evaluations.

Medical Assessment

As part of the medical evaluation, physicians will use what has been referred to as the *medical model*. The medical model refers to a process in which information is gathered in order to establish a diagnosis. By establishing a diagnosis, the physician may be able to 1) determine an etiology for the delays, if possible; 2) identify possible treatments that may cure, but more frequently improve, a child's condition or at least prevent further deterioration; 3) identify whether the child is at increased risk for secondary conditions; and 4) provide prognostic information about future functioning. Parents typically react to their child's problem by asking "why" it has happened. Although this question is frequently unanswerable, understanding what causes the condition and providing a name is helpful to parents as they adjust to their child's condition.

The diagnosis also may be helpful to the parents in family planning. Knowing the condition may make it possible to inform the parents about the risks of having another child with the same condition. For example, if professionals determine that a child has Down syndrome, they can determine if the condition was caused by an error in how the chromosomes separated or by an extra chromosome attaching to another chromosome (nondisjunction). In the latter case, there is a considerably higher risk of the parents having another child with Down syndrome.

Identifying and treating some conditions can prevent most of the developmental problems that can occur. The identification of phenylketonuria (PKU) or congenital hypothyroidism in the newborn period and placing an infant on a special diet low in phenylalanine, an amino acid, in the case of PKU and thyroid hormone replacement in the case of congenital hypothyroidism can prevent mental retardation from occurring in both conditions. About a dozen conditions now can be screened in the newborn period. For other conditions, early identification and treatment can reduce the effects. Early identification of autism and the provision of intensive behavioral therapy can reduce the extent of the disability (Ruble & Brown, 2003).

In addition, the diagnosis can help the clinicians monitor their clients for possible secondary conditions. For example, if it is known that a child has Down syndrome, the clinicians and family will know that the child's ears and hearing have to be monitored closely because frequent ear infections and hearing loss are common (McBrien, 2003). They also will know that the child is at greater risk for other problems such as congenital heart disease, infections, and leukemia and that the cervical spines in his or her neck will need to be evaluated before participation in contact sports.

Physicians use three components of the diagnostic process to establish a diagnosis—the child's medical history, a physical examination, and other tests including laboratory and imaging studies. The history usually begins by identifying the caregiver's concerns. The clinician then usually collects information specifically pertinent to the possible condition. This information includes identifying when the caregivers first noticed any problems, how long the problems have lasted, and what the parents already have done regarding the problems. The physician may further pursue certain possibilities that he or she may suspect by asking specific questions that will help to rule in or out conditions suggestive from the history that he or she obtains. In addition to the history of the current condition, the physician also will ask questions to assess the child's overall health and environmental situation. This information will include the prenatal and birth history to help identify possible teratogens that the fetus may have been exposed to, such as alcohol or nicotine; difficulties during the pregnancy or during the birth process, such as gestational diabetes or fetal distress at delivery; or postnatal complications, such as infection or jaundice. Last, the clinician will assess the child's overall health by checking about possible allergies, hospitalizations, surgeries, significant injuries, medications, and any other symptoms.

The physician also will perform a physical and neurological examination. In addition to the routine physical examination, the clinician will be careful about measuring the child's height, weight, and head circumference to detect less than expected growth and also greater than expected growth. A head circumference that is too large may be an indication of hydrocephalus, and a larger than normal growth in all areas can be seen in Sotos syndrome (Jones, 1997). The physician also will look for any physical features that appear out of the ordinary. Chromosomal abnormalities, resulting in conditions such as Down syndrome (McBrien, 2003), and environmental teratogens, causing conditions such as fetal alcohol syndrome (FAS; Clarren, 2003), cause specific changes in the facial appearance of children. Careful physical examination is important because many syndromes affect other organs, such as the heart. The neurological examination will help to identify abnormal tone, which can be found with cerebral palsy, or balance problems, which can be found with ataxia. The physician also will ascertain the child's developmental level in a more or less formal manner depending on his or her training and to the extent that his or her evaluation is part of an interdisciplinary process in which professionals in other disciplines will be providing that component of the assessment.

On the basis of the results of the history and physical examination, the physician can then decide if any further tests are required in establishing the diagnosis. Much progress has been made since the 1990s in imaging internal organs such as the brain and in identifying specific genetic disorders. In the past, trying to view the brain in living individuals was limited because the brain is encapsulated in bone. X-rays only provided limited information, and obtaining a better image required invasive procedures such as injecting air into the brain ventricles (spaces in the middle of the brain containing spinal fluid) through a spinal tap in a procedure called a pneumoencephalogram. Great strides have been made in imaging the brain to examine localized brain activity. These advances started with computerized X-rays, called computerized axial tomography (CAT), which could image soft tissues such as the brain even through bone and could provide images of different sections. This technology has been followed by magnetic resonance imaging (MRI), which is even more detailed in its imaging and does not require radiation. The advances in technology have allowed clinicians to examine the shape of different parts of the brain to find evidence of damage without painful or risky procedures.

One step beyond examining the structure of the brain has been the ability to examine brain activity. Most of these assessments have remained primarily experimental for studying children because of their recent development or because they necessitate exposure to radiation. Positron emission tomography (PET) scans entail injecting glucose (a sugar found in blood and used by the brain for energy) or a neurotransmitter with added positrons to the bloodstream and then examining the emissions from the brain that are increased with brain activity. A similar process that does not use radiation is called functional magnetic resonance imaging; however, this procedure requires children to sit still for a more extended time and is still quite costly. Computerized electroencephalograms (EEGs) provide better localization of brain activity than regular EEGs but are not able to localize the activity to specific sections of the brain as well.

Tests to detect genetic and chromosomal abnormalities also have greatly improved. In addition to detecting major changes such as the extra chromosome in Down syndrome, it is now possible to detect specific gene abnormalities such as the repeated duplication of base pairs in a specific gene associated with fragile X syndrome (Hagerman, 2003) or the deletion of base pairs in specific genes associated with Prader-Willi (Thompson & Butler, 2003) or Williams (Wang & Blum, 2003) syndromes. To detect these abnormalities, tests such as the Southern blot or the fluorescent *in-situ* hybridization are employed. Tests for biochemical abnormalities in cases of inborn errors of metabolism such as PKU or maple syrup urine disease may be obtained if these are part of the differential diagnosis.

The medical evaluation then needs to be integrated with other evaluations. Information from the other evaluations may help in the diagnosis process, and likewise, information about the diagnosis may provide useful information to other therapists in their plan of services. Most important, the information presented to the parents should be integrated with those of the rest of the team, and the information should ensure that the family's concerns have been adequately addressed.

Psychological Assessment

Psychologists have gained recognition as important members of interdisciplinary teams because the cognitive, emotional, and social development of children, as well as the risk factors that may impair that development, are increasingly viewed as critical to comprehensive care (Perrin, 1999). For example, although an estimated 11%–20% of children seen in primary care settings have significant mental health problems (American Academy of Pediatrics, 1978), most physicians do not address these problems (Sharp, Pantell, Murphy, & Lewis, 1992). This signals a need to include mental health services as part of a comprehensive treatment plan.

The psychologist on an interdisciplinary team can play many roles. One unique aspect of training for psychologists involves a comprehensive understanding of psychological testing instruments. As such, a psychologist is able to choose the state-of-the-art instruments to be used in evaluating cognitive/intellectual functioning as well as social-emotional issues. Furthermore, psychologists serving on interdisciplinary teams generally have knowledge related to assessment of other areas of development. The psychologist can integrate information that is gleaned about the child's abilities by the entire team to produce a comprehensive treatment plan.

In addition to developmental questions about their child, families often present with behavioral concerns. A second role of the psychologist on the interdisciplinary team is to identify and define problematic behaviors that may interfere with the child's overall developmental progress (Miller et al., 2001). The psychologist can identify antecedents to these problem behaviors and the consequences that shape and maintain these behaviors. From this information, a treatment plan can be formulated to address current problems and prevent future ones. Evaluating family issues, such as parental stress and potential violence, can be incorporated into the social-emotional assessment of the child (Perrin, 1999).

The increase in the number of older children being treated for serious emotional and behavioral problems suggests a decrease in early identification and intervention for preschool children (Schroeder, 1999). The inclusion of psychologists on early intervention teams will help to correct this. Family factors such as low family cohesion, negative life events, and maternal negative affect have demonstrated some predictive utility for later-emerging problems, and assessment of these factors should be part of early intervention screenings (Lavigne et al., 1999).

The psychologist with training in interpersonal relations, as well as developmental disabilities, can take a leading role in providing feedback to families at the conclusion of the evaluation. This feedback is often difficult for families to process because it affects them on both an emotional and cognitive level. The psychologist can provide emotional support and can lead a team discussion with the family about the child's recommended course of treatment. The psychologist can help translate often difficult and technical information into terms that a family can understand and feel empowered to address.

The importance of the inclusion of a psychologist in an interdisciplinary evaluation is clearly shown in the following case study. A preschool child referred for a developmental evaluation to a child study center was first seen by an interdisciplinary team. Because the child had a history of prenatal exposure to alcohol and other drugs, concerns were raised about the affect of the substances on his development as well as his behavior. The psychological evaluation revealed mild delays in cognitive development.

Furthermore, parent reports indicated significant levels of parental stress as well as behavior difficulties that included aggressive behaviors, noncompliance, and defiance. The speech-language pathologist found mild delays in expressive and receptive language. Although no motor delays were indicated, concerns regarding sensory integration issues were raised. Finally, the medical evaluation indicated several features consistent with prenatal exposure to alcohol. In a treatment planning session with team members and the family, the affect of substances on overall development and behavioral functioning was discussed. The child and family were referred for an evaluation to assess FAS. The child also was referred to special education services to include speech-language therapy through the local public school system, and a complementary program for the child's foster family also was recommended. Finally, a specialized behavior management program available at the study center was offered to the family. In this context, the effect of developmental delays and negative behaviors on family stress was explored.

Clearly, had this child only been seen for developmental concerns, the behavior problems that may impede interventions directed at increasing developmental progress might not have been addressed. Furthermore, continued stress and frustration by everyone working with the child would be predicted. With the program and family working as a team, the child's full potential could be realized. A follow-up interdisciplinary evaluation found significant improvements in behavior and a similar decrease in the level of parental stress. Although delays continued, the school program was addressing these with the child and family. An alcohol-related disorder was clearly evident, and this information was shared with the family, along with implications for the child's future learning potential and anticipated behavioral concerns. This team evaluation allowed for integrated and coordinated services for the child and family as well as providing the family with a single point of contact for ongoing concerns.

Special Education Assessment

The early childhood special educator is responsible for at least four areas of emphasis within an assessment protocol for a young child. The first area is the family *context, background, and priorities for the child.* Parents are most knowledgeable about their children, and children are most comfortable with their parents. A comprehensive assessment process includes gathering information about a wide range of a child's abilities, and parents know the most about areas such as motivation, interactive abilities, learning style, and tolerance for learning. If assessment is viewed as an integral part of intervention, then parent participation in assessment introduces the parent as an equal partner in facilitating his or her child's development.

The family can provide invaluable information about the child's developmental history and current behavioral repertoire in the home and community such as the child's current developmental achievements or new behaviors the parent has noticed. Discussions with family members are an integral part of any assessment. The family's priorities and concerns for their child should guide the development of the assessment protocol, including, but not limited to, family priorities, preferred language, and cultural orientation. It is important to remember that the family knows the child best and can usually provide detailed information about the child's ability to participate in daily routines and activities (e.g., eating, dressing, going to bed, playing with friends). The family also can share information about ways they have tried to support their child's participation and learning. The conversations should also explore the family's interests, the things the family would like the child to be able to do, and the concerns the family has about the child's ability to learn.

Discussions with the family should occur before, during, and after any formal assessments are conducted with the child. For example, prior to an assessment, family members can describe how they expect their child to behave in the situations being observed and how the behaviors may differ from the child's home and family environment. These initial family discussions can assist the assessment process in three ways: 1) the early childhood special educator gains a sense of what to expect when observing the child; 2) the early childhood special educator begins to understand the family's perceptions of their child and their understanding of child development in general; and 3) the family begins to think about ways to assist the child to participate in a variety of learning opportunities.

During the assessment, the early childhood special educator should continue the discussion with the family by encouraging their observations, thoughts, and reactions to their child's performance. At this time, the family can confirm if the child's behavior is an accurate portrayal of what he or she can typically do. Before attempting an adaptation that enables a child to be successful in performing a skill, the early childhood special educator can ask the family whether they have tried the adaptation already and how well it worked or whether they have used other adaptations. Discussions during the assessment also provide valuable information about family interests as the family may focus on a certain aspect of the assessment that has the most relevance to their concerns. Families should be integrally involved in the assessment protocol as much as possible.

After the assessment, discussions can center on what the family observed and their interpretations of their child's performance. Again, discussions help to measure the family's perception of their child and will assist in developing and talking families through the assessment findings as well as the subsequent recommendations for interventions. This also provides another opportunity to ask the family how the child's performance differs from his or her behavior in other situations and to brainstorm about possible environmental differences that affect the child's behaviors.

A second area of concentration for the early childhood special educator is an *assessment of the areas of development that impinge on a child's learning*. This includes not only focusing on a child's cognition but also assessing how the cognitive area (which includes such constructs as mastery motivation, coping and problem solving, and social competence and engagement) affects, or is affected by, a child's performance across all areas of development. The child's background and family information can assist the educator to ensure that the most appropriate developmental tools are used to assess the child's strengths and needs.

An effective assessment is comprehensive so that a broad range of the child's strengths and needs over all developmental areas can be identified. Although the goal of assessment and subsequent intervention is a holistic picture of the child (integrated across areas), certain specific developmental areas should be included: cognition, physical development (including vision and hearing), communication, social or emotional development, and adaptive development. This would require that both general development assessments and domain-specific tools will be used, according to a child's individual profile, and will be integrated with and complement formal assessments by specialists in the disciplines of medicine and psychology.

There are multiple methods to collect development information about a child. The most traditional is through the use of an assessment tool. In a diagnostic or eligibility assessment, the most commonly used assessment tools are norm-referenced tools. A standardized norm-referenced assessment tool is an instrument that uses standard materials, is administered in a specific manner, and usually provides scores that are reflective of developmental levels demonstrated by typically developing children. Standardized instruments allow a comparison of a child's performance to the performance of other children the same age. Standardized assessment tools often are used as one method for determining eligibility for early intervention services or to present a picture of the child's developmental level to support a diagnosis.

In addition to norm-referenced assessment tools, checklists and developmental scales also may be used to guide the early childhood educator through an assessment. Commercially available scales address developmental milestones in general or specific developmental processes, such as parent–child interaction, social competence (Guralnick, 1992), and coping (Zeitlin, Williamson, & Szczepanski, 1988). Depending on the scale, items may be scored by either the presence or absence of a behavior or by a rating system for how well the child performs a behavior. The latter clearly provides more of an opportunity to determine behavior quality.

Checklists are another kind of tool that can be used to record and organize behaviors. The advantage to a checklist is that the assessor can tailor it to the family's interests and child's abilities. Behavior quality, behavior components, and environmental observations also can be included. For example, in order for an infant to sit without support, he or she needs sufficient head and neck control, trunk control, and balance as well as the ability to turn his or her legs outward and bend at the knees. These steps—as well as the quality of the child's behavior and the social and physical environment before, during, and after the child's behavior—all can be included on a checklist.

A third area of emphasis for the early childhood special educator is an *assessment of the functional application of the child's skills.* The process of assessment is as important as the actual scores on tools; therefore, it is important that the educator take the lead in ensuring that the child's performance across developmental domains is observed in relation to his or her performance of the functions that are required for full participation in his or her family and community context, in particular the everyday activities identified as important by the family. These activity settings provide opportunities for gathering assessment information and subsequent intervention recommendations.

Most often, observation is used as the method to assess how a child uses his or her skills in natural, everyday activity settings. Observations also provide an opportunity to obtain information about useful skills that are often difficult to test (e.g., ability to initiate social interactions, engagement with problem solving). Collecting information through such observation has many advantages, including 1) the opportunity to see the range of a child's behavior; 2) the opportunity to collect information about behaviors that occur in everyday routines and activities; and 3) the opportunity to use more flexibility in collecting information about the child's behaviors.

In addition, developmental skills and abilities are mastered in three phases: first, acquisition, or the child's ability to perform the skill; second, fluency and maintenance, or the child's ability to perform the skill frequently over time; and last, generalization, or the child's ability to perform the skill across time and activity settings with different people and materials. A functional assessment will address the child's abilities within these phases across activity settings. A functional assessment also facilitates the identification of those activity settings that are of most interest to the child and, as such, can promote a higher level of learning and mastery. For example, the child may show a higher level of problem solving at mealtime than at a structured tabletop activity because eating may provide more opportunities to be reinforced naturally.

The functional assessment should address both the level of child involvement to determine how to increase participation and the type of behaviors that are used by the child to participate in order to determine the next developmental skills. During the functional assessment, the early childhood special educator also may identify minor changes to the environment that can promote child participation and learning, such as changing the child's positioning, which can help him or her more fully engage in an activity rather than struggle with body stability. These simple adaptations can be tried during a functional observation. The success of the adaptation can be included in the assessment findings, providing further evidence of the child's functioning, which can be used in diagnosis or recommendations for intervention.

The last area for the early childhood special educator is another shared responsibility with other team members—*developing an integrated, accurate, and comprehensive assessment report* that is clearly written and understandable to the family. Assessment information should be summarized from all recorded observations, interviews, checklists, and scales. The purpose of an assessment report is to provide a picture of the child and his or her activity settings that will help create objectives and intervention adaptations, supports, and strategies. Although the structure of the report might vary, every report should describe child performance in a detailed and objective manner from a strengths-based perspective. The report should be worded according to what the child did versus what the child did not do, as well as the quality of the behaviors using age-appropriate expectations. It also should describe what the child could do independently and with help, defining the level of help provided. Words used should be behaviorally descriptive so the reader can "see" the child performing the behaviors. For example, phrases such as "using his whole hand" or "looked at her mother and smiled after throwing the stick in the lake" create a picture of the child. Unclear words and phrases such as "appropriate," "difficulty," and "did a good job" should be avoided. Second, child performance should be related to the child's underlying developmental processes. The report should describe the developmental processes that were exemplified by the child's behavior. For example, the statement, "The child smiled and looked at the completed puzzle, *demonstrating* an understanding of goal completion," implies that the assessor is confident the child's behavior indicates the underlying process. Third, behaviors should be described within the context of the functional assessment. As previously discussed, the social and physical environment will influence the child's participation and learning. Similar behaviors across different environments should be described within the report, identifying the characteristics in each environment that may have promoted the behaviors. For example, a report might state, "The child communicated what he wanted to do by looking at his mother, then looking at something in the environment, then back to his mother. He communicated this way when he was swimming (looked to the edge of the pool to get out) and when he was at the playground (looked at the swing)." This description illustrates the important finding that the child had a consistent communication mode he used with his mother. Differences in behaviors across environments also should be reported to determine if there are environmental variations that change child behaviors. Last, jargon-free and sensitive language should be used throughout the reports. All reports are shared with family members and should be written sensitively. Sensitive reports are nonjudgmental and state the child's behaviors and interests positively. People from a variety of disciplines and backgrounds, including family members and community providers, use assessment reports. Reports written in clear, jargon-free language will facilitate communication among all team members.

PLACE IN THE DEVELOPMENTAL SYSTEMS MODEL

The development of an interdisciplinary assessment team is a community-wide responsibility. The organization of the team will vary greatly from community to community based on the resources. Key community entities such as governmental early intervention programs; health departments; and institutions of higher learning, particularly medical schools and psychology and education departments, are important resources that can shape the composition and structure of the teams. Governmental and nongovernmental financial sources also will significantly affect the organization and composition of initial assessments. Essential to all of the programs is communication between team members and programs. Communication is a time-consuming and rarely compensated activity. Yet, it is one, if not the most, important element.

For some conditions such as PKU or autism, professionals with specific expertise in these areas are required. Lower prevalence rates may make it too costly for a team with such specific expertise to be available in each local area. Regional programs such as those at medical centers can provide the added expertise to provide initial assessments and monitor progress. It is critical, however, that these programs develop adequate communication with local teams. The recommendations from more distant programs need to take into account the local resources in order to develop a meaningful program, again making communication a key element.

In smaller communities, particularly, it may not be feasible to develop comprehensive teams as suggested in the ideal model. However, it is possible for a core team to work with a regional interdisciplinary team or to bring in local consultants as needed. The core team should consist of at least a primary care clinician capable of providing a medical home; an early childhood educator; and a professional from psychology or the allied health fields of physical, occupational, or speech therapy, depending on the needs of the child and his or her family. In families with multiple stressors, social work and case coordination also may be essential elements.

CONCLUSION

The comprehensive interdisciplinary assessment of children entering the early intervention system is the foundation required in the formulation of a meaningful and successful program. The process requires input from multiple disciplines in order to generate a development profile, provide diagnostic/etiologic information, and make general recommendations for early intervention. Communication is key to the success of this complex but vital process.

REFERENCES

American Academy of Pediatrics. (1994). Health care of children in foster care. *Pediatrics, 93,* 335–338.

American Academy of Pediatrics, Task Force on Pediatric Education. (1978). *The future of pediatric education.* Evanston, IL: Author.

Bruder, M.B. (1994). Working with members of other disciplines: Collaboration for success. In M. Wolery & J.S. Wilbers (Eds.), *Including children with special needs in early childhood programs* (pp. 45–70). Washington, DC: National Association for the Education of Young Children.

Bruder, M.B. (1995). Early intervention. In J.W. Wood & A.M. Lazzari (Eds.), *Exceeding the boundaries: Understanding exceptional lives* (pp. 534–569). Fort Worth, TX: Harcourt Brace & Company.

Cass, H., Price, K., Reilly, S., Wisbeach, A., & McConachie, H. (1999). A model for the assessment and management of children with multiple disabilities. *Child: Care, Health, and Development, 25,* 191–211.

Clarren, S. (2003). Fetal alcohol syndrome. In M. Wolraich (Ed.), *Disorders of development and learning* (3rd ed., pp. 235–248). Hamilton, Ontario, Canada: BC Decker.

Cooper, J., Majnemer, A., Rosenblatt, B., & Birnbaum, R. (1995). The determination of sensory deficits in children with hemiplegic cerebral palsy. *Journal of Child Neurology, 10,* 300–309.

Guralnick, M.J. (1992). *Assessment of peer relations.* Seattle: University of Washington, Child Development and Mental Retardation Center.

Guralnick, M.J. (Ed). (2000). *Interdisciplinary clinical assessment for young children with developmental disabilities.* Baltimore: Paul H. Brookes Publishing Co.

Guralnick, M.J. (2001). A developmental systems model for early intervention. *Infants and Young Children, 14,* 1–18.

Hagerman, R.J. (2003). Disorders of mental development: Fragile X syndrome. In M. Wolraich (Ed.), *Disorders of development and learning* (3rd ed., pp. 225–234). Hamilton, Ontario, Canada: BC Decker.

Howard, L.M. (1994). Multidisciplinary quality assessment: The case of a child development team, part 1. *British Journal of Occupational Therapy, 57,* 345–348.

Jones, K. (1997). *Smith's recognizable patterns of human malformation.* Philadelphia: W.B. Saunders Company.

Lavigne, J.V., Gibbons, R.D., Arend, R., Rosenbaum, D., Binns, H.J., & Christoffel, K.K. (1999). Rational service planning in pediatric primary care: Continuity and change in psychopathology among children enrolled in pediatric practices. *Journal of Pediatric Psychology, 24,* 393–403.

Linder, T.W. (1990). *Transdisciplinary Play-Based Assessment.* Baltimore: Paul H. Brookes Publishing Co.

Maddux, R.B. (1988). *Team building: An exercise in leadership.* Los Altos, CA: Crisp Publications.

McBrien, D. (2003). Disorders of mental development: Down syndrome. In M. Wolraich (Ed.), *Disorders of development and learning* (3rd ed., pp. 207–224). Hamilton, Ontario, Canada: BC Decker.

McConachie, H.R. (1999). Conceptual frameworks in evaluation of multidisciplinary services for children with disabilities. *Child: Care, Health, and Development, 25,* 101–113.

McConachie, H.R., Salt, A., Chadury, Y., McLachlan, A., & Logan, S. (1999). How do child development teams work? Findings from a UK national survey. *Child: Care, Health, and Development, 25,* 157–168.

Meisels, S.J., & Fenichel, E. (1996). *New visions for the developmental assessment of infants and young children.* Washington, DC: ZERO TO THREE: National Center for Infants, Toddlers, and Families.

Miller, C.K., Burklow, K.A., Santoro, K., Kirby, E., Mason, D., & Rudolph, C.D. (2001). An interdisciplinary team approach to the management of pediatric feeding and swallowing disorders. *Children's Health Care, 30*(3), 201–218.

Perrin, E.C. (1999). Commentary: Collaboration in pediatric primary care: A pediatrician's view. *Journal of Pediatric Psychology, 24,* 453–458.

Ruble, L., & Brown, S. (2003). Pervasive developmental disorders: Autism. In M. Wolraich (Ed.), *Disorders of development and learning* (3rd ed., pp. 249–266). Hamilton, Ontario, Canada: BC Decker.

Schroeder, C.S. (1999). Commentary: A view from the past and a look to the future. *Journal of Pediatric Psychology, 24,* 447–452.

Sharp, L., Pantell, R.H., Murphy, L.O., & Lewis, C.C. (1992). Psychosocial problems during child health supervision visits: Eliciting, then what? *Pediatrics, 89,* 619–623.

Stayton, V., & Bruder, M.B. (1999). Early intervention personnel preparation for the new millennium: Early childhood special education. *Infants and Young Children, 12*(1), 59–69.

Thompson, R.J. (1982). Multidimensional problems and findings in developmentally disabled children. *Developmental and Behavioral Pediatrics, 3,* 153–158.

Thompson, T., & Butler, M. (2003). Prader-Willi syndrome: Clinical, behavioral and genetic findings. In M. Wolraich (Ed.), *Disorders of development and learning* (3rd ed., pp. 267–282). Hamilton, Ontario, Canada: BC Decker.

Wang, P., & Blum, N. (2003). Williams syndrome. In M. Wolraich (Ed.), *Disorders of development and learning* (3rd ed., pp. 283–298). Hamilton, Ontario, Canada: BC Decker.

Zeitlin, S., Williamson, G.G., & Szczepanski, M. (1988). *Early Coping Inventory.* Bensenville, IL: Scholastic Testing Service.

CHAPTER 7

ASSESSING THE INFORMATION NEEDS OF FAMILIES IN EARLY INTERVENTION

DONALD B. BAILEY, JR., AND TRACI POWELL

INTRODUCTION

When working with young children, families and family support are viewed as central to the process. Since being formalized through federal legislation in 1984, early intervention and preschool programs in the United States have had a dual focus—serving children with disabilities and providing support for their families. Drawing on such diverse perspectives as ecological theory, family systems theory, attachment theory, research on stress and coping, and empowerment theory, overwhelming evidence of the important roles that families play in shaping their child's development, growing recognition of the role of culture in the lives of children and families, and the experiences of families told time and again in case studies, books, movies, and compelling testimonials have produced a collective argument that having a child with a disability has profound implications for families, and, thus, early intervention must attend to family issues and concerns (Bailey et al., 1999; Dunst, 2002; Krauss, 2000; Krauss & Selzer, 1998; Marsh, 1992; Minnes, 1998; Myers, 1996; Shapiro, Blacher, & Lopez, 1998; Turnbull et al., 1993).

Working with families encompasses a wide range of activities guided by models and assumptions about family dynamics and by both explicit and implied goals for early intervention. Following the Developmental Systems Model (Guralnick, 2001), this chapter focuses on one specific dimension of family support—the *information needs of families*. The chapter begins with a brief overview of goals and philosophies of working with

The authors express their appreciation to Dr. Debra Skinner for her comments on an earlier draft of this chapter.

families, showing how the need for information fits within these broader frameworks. Then, drawing on an instrument developed by the first author more than 15 years ago to assess family needs, we review a set of studies describing and documenting the types of information needs that families most frequently report. In order to provide a practical example, we conclude by describing a newly emerging area of family needs for information—information about genetics and genetic disorders. The rapid proliferation of genetic discoveries and the significant increase in the number of known genetic causes of developmental disabilities has added a new dimension of complicated information that both parents and early intervention professionals need and want to understand. We give examples of the types of information related to genetics and genetic disorders that families might want, identify ways that parents currently get this information (ranging from the popular media to the professional genetics counselor), and discuss implications for early childhood intervention professionals.

FAMILIES AND EARLY INTERVENTION

Many theories have been suggested for why working with families is so important in early intervention, but from a practical perspective two factors are central. *First, the family environment influences the development and behavior of children with disabilities.* Successful adaptation is largely dependent on the child's physical and social environment. For young children, the family is the most proximal and generally the most powerful environmental influence. Families provide the context within which development occurs, and they mediate other environmental factors. Family environments can range in the extent to which they are effective in promoting development and emotional regulation. Childhood disability often presents unique challenges to knowing how to promote development, and, thus, some families may feel frustrated in their parenting roles. As a result, when parents need and want support for fostering their child's development, early intervention professionals should work with families to help them identify and learn ways to interact with their children or structure the home environment to match the developmental and behavioral needs of their children (Kaiser & Hancock, 2003). *Second, the experience of having a child with a disability often has a significant impact on the family.* Families of children with disabilities face numerous challenges. They must cope with the sadness that almost inevitably accompanies the discovery that their child has a major disability. This discovery can cause personal distress, guilt, or depression, which in turn can affect family relations and marital adjustment. Families also must seek out and interact with a wide range of professionals and specialized service providers. These interactions sometimes can be frustrating and expensive, and families often feel that their children are not receiving the services needed to maximize their development. Families who experience frustration and failure with the service system may experience a loss of control and feelings of inadequacy. As a result, early intervention professionals often are encouraged to interact with families in ways that are supportive and empowering and to assist families in identifying and using informal supports (Dunst, 2000).

In addition to these two general statements about families, however, two other points are equally important. *Families are complicated systems involving multiple members with varying relationships, experiences, and perceptions that are mutually constituted and change over time.* Relationships among family members and environmental influences on families are rarely one-directional, single events but rather a transactional series of interactions in which each participant constantly responds to and shapes the behavior of the others over time (Bronfenbrenner, 1979; Sameroff & Fiese, 2000). In fact, family life might be best characterized as a series of evolving accommodations and adaptations to a range of life experiences (Gallimore, Coots, Wiesner, Garner, & Guthrie, 1996). Professionals need to recognize the fluid and constantly changing nature of family needs and resources and adopt practices that are flexible and responsive to these changes.

Families vary widely in the ways in which they respond to disability. Although it is possible to make generalizations about families, even more remarkable is the enormous range of variability in family adaptation to disability. Some families provide highly facilitative environments for their children; others do not. Some are virtually devastated by the disability; others find strength and a sense of purpose that transforms their lives in positive ways. Many factors have been studied to try to predict how different families will respond to disability, including the severity and nature of the child's disability, the child's temperament and behavioral style, gender (of both child and parent), socioeconomic status, access to formal and informal support systems, spouse support, cognitive coping and appraisal strategies, religion and religiosity, cultural belief systems, and maternal IQ. All have been shown to be related to family functioning but in different ways and at different times. Perhaps the single most important lesson from research is that applying general knowledge about families to an individual family's situation is virtually impossible. This means that professionals need to individualize their work with families and engage in formal and informal assessment strategies to understand how one family differs from another and what services each needs.

A special consideration in this process is a recognition that families exist in cultural and socio-political contexts that influence their beliefs, perceptions, and practices. Ethnic and cultural groups may vary considerably in their beliefs about disability, the nature of family and community supports, caregiving roles of parents and siblings, the use of professional services, and what constitutes appropriate treatment (Bailey, Skinner, Correa, et al., 1999; Gartner, Lipsky, & Turnbull, 1991; Harry, 1992; Ingstad & Whyte, 1995). These variations shape a family's responses and adaptations to disability. Ethnicity and culture can influence access to services, sometimes as a result of discriminatory practices and sometimes as a result of cultural beliefs regarding what course of treatment is desirable, or the appropriateness of relying on others for help. In addition to ethnic variations, larger communities and the socio-political and cultural worlds within which disability occurs also influence families. Families may find that these larger worlds provide resources that help them meet their family's needs, or they may find a lack of resources and support in programs and policies. Families may enter new communities as a result of disability, communities that can be supportive but that can also change perceptions and practices, as in the case of parent groups advocating particular philosophies about the causes or treatments of particular disabilities. Professionals need to be aware of the powerful role of these various cultural worlds in the lives of families and be able to adapt their styles of interacting and providing services accordingly.

Family Support in the Context of Goals for Early Intervention

Accepting the assumption that family support is a primary aspect of early intervention naturally leads to practical issues of implementation and discussions about the relative importance of various goals for early intervention. Differing goals and philosophies have direct implications both for the types of services that should be provided and the ways in which professionals should interact with children and families.

Early Intervention Goals

Why has so much money been invested in a national system of services for children with disabilities and their families, and what desired outcomes or results of these services are expected? For children, this question is relatively easy to answer. Major goals would be to maximize developmental trajectories; promote social competence and adaptive behavior; assure full participation in the least restrictive environment; and prevent or reduce the likelihood of behavior problems, health problems, or other conditions secondary to any disabling condition (Bailey & Wolery, 1992).

With regard to outcomes for families, the issue is more complicated and has evolved over time. Federal legislation in the 1980s focused on the family as the child's natural home. As a result, a primary goal was to reduce institutionalization and other out-of-home placements for children with disabilities. From a professional perspective, early models viewed parents primarily as instruments of change, serving as at-home extensions of professionals. Thus, the reason for working with families was to help them be better teachers to their children under the assumption that by maximizing the quality of the home environment and parental efficacy, professionals would have a better chance of achieving the major goals set for children. However, as research shed light on the experiences and challenges faced by families of children with disabilities, and families themselves became more involved in advocating for the types of services they wanted, new models for working with families began to emerge. These models focused on reconceptualizing both the goals for working with families and the nature of interactions needed to achieve those goals. Dunst (2002) integrated much of what is now considered recommended practice in a *family-centered approach* to early intervention. This approach is characterized by

> Beliefs and practices that treat families with dignity and respect; individualized, flexible, and responsive practices; information sharing so that families can make informed decisions; family choice regarding any number of aspects of program practices and intervention options; parent-professional collaboration and partnerships . . . ; and the provision and mobilization of resources and supports necessary for families to care for and rear their children in ways that produce optimal child, parent, and family outcomes. (p. 139)

Adopting a family-centered approach has direct implications for how programs and professionals go about their work. A central tenet is to individualize family services in accordance with family resources, priorities, and concerns. This requires both a general understanding of family needs and specific strategies for determining what an individual family needs to achieve the outcomes it desires.

Operationalizing Family Goals

Other than the goal to reduce institutionalization, federal legislation has not been very helpful because it has focused more on the process of working with families rather than on the outcomes of this process. For example, programs serving infants and toddlers with disabilities are required to 1) include families as a part of the team that develops an individualized family service plan (IFSP); 2) use a family-directed assessment of family resources, priorities, and concerns; 3) develop and provide ways to address both child and family needs according to family preference; 4) fully explain the IFSP, family rights, and procedural safeguards; and 5) assign a service coordinator responsible for implementing the plan and coordinating with other agencies and people.

Several publications have attempted to address more specifically the outcomes that might be expected as a result of working with families (e.g., Bailey, 2001; Bailey et al., 1998; Dunst, 2000; Early Childhood Research Institute on Measuring Growth and Development, 1998; Roberts, Innocenti, & Goetze, 1999; Turnbull, Turbiville, & Turnbull, 2000). Although each of these publications articulates family goals in different ways, a number of common themes have emerged. All agree that as a result of early intervention families ought to 1) feel competent in their efforts to raise a child with a disability; 2) have a clear understanding of their rights and responsibilities according to state and federal law; 3) be capable of effectively navigating the service system and advocating for services; 4) be satisfied with the services they receive and have a positive view of professionals, the service system, and the way they have been treated; 5) experience hope and optimism about the future and their ability to handle future challenges; and 6) experience a positive quality of life for themselves and for their child.

Identifying expected outcomes of early intervention for families has been a challenging process because in reality each family has its own individualized set of needs and perspectives on what they want from the early intervention system. Incorporating these broad goals into a system that increasingly holds programs accountable for achieving specific outcomes will require much additional work (Bailey, 2001).

Information and Empowerment

Underlying almost all discussions about the role of early intervention vis-à-vis families is the fundamental concept that families should be considered as competent and key participants in the decision-making process about goals and services. In order to fill this role adequately, however, many parents feel that they are at a disadvantage relative to professionals. In part, this perceived disadvantage is lack of experience with the early intervention and special education bureaucracy. But more important is the perceived discrepancy between the information held by *professionals* versus the information held by *parents*. Thus, a central task of early intervention is to help families gain access to the information they need as they seek to fulfill their roles as participants in both the formal decision-making process as well as informal day-to-day decisions (Gowen, Christy, & Sparling, 1993; Sontag & Schacht, 1994).

Rooted in much of the writing about working with families is the concept of *empowerment*. Based on early work by Rappaport (1981) and originally articulated by Dunst (1985) as a primary goal of early intervention, empowerment generally refers to having the knowledge and confidence needed to make decisions and advocate effectively. Subsequently,

Dunst and his colleagues have written extensively about professional practices likely to enable and empower families (e.g., Dunst, 2000; Dunst, Trivette, & Deal, 1988; Dunst, Trivette, & LaPointe, 1992).

Turnbull, Turbiville, and Turnbull (2000) argued that a historical challenge in relationships between parents and professionals has centered on power—particularly power as it relates to gaining access to resources and decision-making authority with regard to services. They argued for a collective empowerment model of early intervention in which power is shared equally by families and professionals. However, the authors acknowledged that for this model to work, "participants must be knowledgeable about the resources that would make the most substantial difference to them in gaining a sense of control in their lives" (p. 642).

Thus, helping families gain access to information is important for the utility of the information itself but also has broader symbolic implications. Being informed is an important part of having and exercising power (Kahn, 1997; Lieberman, Forbes, Uttaro, & Sarkis, 1996). Without information, power in decision making is limited to legalistic or bureaucratic power. In special education, for example, parents have explicitly delegated power in terms of certain rights with regard to approval or disapproval of the individualized plans that are developed and with regard to due process if they are dissatisfied with plans or services. Information has the potential to change the power dynamics so that the decision-making process is based as much as possible on fully informed logic and rational decision making involving equally well-informed participants, as opposed to a process in which power is based on who owns the resources or who has the right to sign or not sign a document. Thus, how and to what extent information is made available to families becomes a critical component of early intervention.

Assessing Family Needs

In the early 1980s, the first author of this chapter began working with a team of colleagues on several projects to better understand the needs of families of young children with disabilities and the skills and perspectives of the professionals who worked with those families. In the process of developing a rudimentary model for how to approach families, Bailey and colleagues (1986) focused heavily on the assessment domain. How could professionals get information from and about families that could help them be more responsive to family needs and priorities? The authors realized that many of the measures available at that time for assessing families had been developed for clinical (e.g., psychotherapy) or research purposes and thus were often not directly applicable to early intervention practice (Bailey & Henderson, 1993). In fact, a number of the measures focused on domains such as marital interactions or parenting stress in ways that families felt were intrusive and professionals perceived to be of little practical help in providing early intervention services.

In an attempt to provide one format for family assessment, Bailey and Simeonsson (1988) developed an instrument: the Family Needs Survey. The intent was to create an instrument that was not diagnostic or clinical but rather functional—a tool that could make it easier for professionals to learn about a family's needs for information and services and for parents to share that information. At that time, many professionals were making assumptions about family needs and providing services based entirely on those assumptions. For example, early research on parenting a child with a disability described how parents sometimes altered their styles of communicating or playing with their children. This led to intervention programs that assumed this would be a problem in all families and focused on teaching play and communication skills to all parents. Bailey and Simeonsson felt that a more appropriate approach would be to first ask parents to identify domains in which they felt they needed assistance themselves. Based on this information, individualized services could be provided, potentially avoiding problems that occurred when parents felt they were provided services they did not want or need.

Bailey and Simeonsson (1988) began by reviewing the literature on families of children with and without disabilities (e.g., Sparling & Lowman, 1983) and by reflecting on their own experiences in early intervention. The literature suggested at least six potential areas of family needs. *Information needs*, the domain most directly relevant to this chapter, are those needs for knowledge that could help parents make informed decisions and might include learning about their child's condition, gaining access to available services, teaching their child, or dealing with a developmental or behavioral issue. *Support needs* reflects needs for functional or emotional support from friends, family members, or from other community professionals. *Explaining to others* addresses a frequent challenge experienced by families, namely how to respond when friends, neighbors, strangers, or extended family members ask about their child's condition. *Community service needs* addresses needs for services such as child care, medical care, or dental care. The availability of these services is usually taken for granted by most parents, but families of children with disabilities often experience challenges in finding a child care program or health care professional willing and able to care for a child with special health or developmental needs. *Financial needs* covers a range of needs for assistance, including paying for basic living expenses as well as for the unique costs inherent in raising a child with a disability (e.g., specialized equipment, therapy, transportation, medication). Finally, *family functioning* addresses needs for help in family problem solving, internal support systems, family roles, and family recreational activities.

Bailey and Simeonsson (1988) generated a large pool of items that tapped each of these domains and then met with a group of early intervention professionals to review and comment on the pool of items. An initial instrument based on 35 items distributed across the six areas of need was developed and prepared for pilot testing. Bailey and Simeonsson decided on a simple 3-point response format consisting of 1 (I definitely do not need help with this), 2 (Not sure), and 3 (I definitely need help with this). However, they were not so focused on a score per se, as the measure was primarily designed as a tool to facilitate interactions between parents and professionals.

In reflecting back on this process, clearly family members should have been involved in instrument development from the beginning. This would have almost certainly made the instrument more valid and would have reflected a family-centered approach. Despite this failing, Bailey and Simeonsson quickly moved into a series of studies to determine its utility with families, including a study directly intended to assess family perspectives on the instrument itself and the process by which it is used.

Since the instrument was developed, at least 11 studies have been published in which a total of 1,368 families have completed the scale. These studies, summarized in Table 7.1, have drawn on a diverse set of families to determine the utility of the scale and the distribution of needs reported by families. They represent Caucasian, Latino, and African American families living throughout the United States as well as in Australia, Sweden, Canada, and China. They represent families of young children with disabilities, families of older children with disabilities, and parents of children diagnosed with cancer or other chronic health conditions. Two additional studies have been published describing parents' ratings of the usefulness of the measure. A number of conclusions can be drawn from our initial work in developing the measure and from data collected in these studies.

Families Find the Measure Both Acceptable and Useful

Many of the published studies reported anecdotally that family members willingly completed the measure and felt that it was an acceptable and useful way of reporting family needs. Two studies directly assessed parents' perspectives on the survey. Bailey and Blasco (1990) asked 229 parents living in 10 different states to 1) rate how helpful they thought the scale would be for them in sharing their needs with professionals, 2) rate how helpful they thought the scale would be for professionals in planning

Table 7.1. Summary of studies reporting data using the Family Needs Survey (Bailey & Simeonsson, 1988)

Reference	Study participants	N	Location	Ethnic distribution	Information needs[1]	All other needs[2]
Bailey, Blasco, and Simeonsson (1992)	Parents of young children with disabilities	422	Multiple states throughout the U.S.	54% European American 46% Other minority	50%	17%
Bailey, Skinner, Correa, et al. (1999)	Parents of young children with disabilities	200	Multiple states throughout the U.S.	50% Mexican American 50% Puerto Rican	75%	47%
Chen and Simeonsson (1994)	Parents of children with disabilities	101	People's Republic of China	100% Chinese	68%	40%
Cooper and Allred (1992)	Parents of young children with disabilities	171	Illinois	83% European American 17% Other minority	29%	14%
Ellis et al. (2002)	Parents of children with disabilities	91	Massachusetts	Not reported	47%	25%
Garshelis and McConnell (1993)	Parents of young children with disabilities	43	Minnesota	Not reported	42%	17%
Graves and Hayes (1996)	Parents of children with chronic conditions	38	Canada	Not reported	1.9[3]	1.5[3]

Linfoot (1997)	Parents of young children with disabilities	29	New South Wales, Australia	Not reported	67%	44%
Roll-Pettersson (1992)	Parents of young children with disabilities	143	Sweden	Not reported	37%	15%
Sexton, Burrell, and Thompson (1992)	Parents of young children with disabilities	53	Louisiana	52% European American 48% African American	51%	23%
Shields et al. (1995)	Parents of children with cancer	77	Ohio	Not reported	49%	31%

Note: Figures here represent mean item scores by domain.

[1]Mean percentage of parents who indicated a definite need for help on each item in the Information subscale of the Family Needs Survey.

[2]Mean percentage of parents who indicated a definite need for help on each item in all other subscales combined on the Family Needs Survey.

[3]In this study, the authors reported findings by the 3-point rating scale for each item (1 = I definitely do not need help with this; 2 = not sure; 3 = I definitely need help with this).

services, 3) tell how comfortable they felt responding to items on the survey, 4) choose whether they would prefer using a written format or more conversational format for sharing needs, and 5) make recommendations for changes. Most parents were very positive about the measure. More than two thirds felt that it would be helpful or very helpful in describing their format and half a conversational format. African American and Latino parents, as well as low-income parents, were at least as positive as European American respondents and middle- or upper-income respondents in their reactions to the instrument and were even more positive on a number of items.

A number of additional items were suggested by only one or two parents, reflecting highly specialized needs or very unique circumstances. Also, several changes in wording were suggested—the strongest recommendation was to change the response format away from "I need help." In 1990, Bailey and Simeonsson revised the scale (see Figure 7.1). This revision incorporated several wording changes in the items, added an open-ended item to give families the opportunity to mention unique needs not reflected on the scale, and changed the response format to "Would you like to discuss this topic with a staff person from our program?"

In a second study of parent perspectives, Sexton, Snyder, Rheams, Barron-Sharp and Perez (1991) asked 48 mothers and 25 professionals to rate and compare three different family needs surveys. Surprisingly, parents rated the surveys as more useful, usable, and appropriate than did professionals. All surveys were rated positively, but the Family Needs Survey (Bailey & Simeonsson, 1990) received the highest mean scores.

The first lesson learned from this research is that the scale reflects a set of needs common to many families and that parents have a positive perception about being asked about a wide range of needs. Research shows that families from many different countries and cultures willingly complete the scale, which is consistent with findings using other measures (e.g., Lieberman et al., 1996; Sexton et al., 1991). When asked, most individuals perceive a written survey such as the Family Needs Survey to be of great potential usefulness but only if the information is then used. In our survey of parent perceptions, the one negative comment frequently expressed concerned situations in which professionals asked personal information of families but then never used it for any practical or supportive purposes.

Factor analyses suggest that the scale taps distinct domains, one of which is informational needs. In our first major study of the instrument, Bailey, Blasco, and Simeonsson (1992) conducted a factor analysis to determine if the items clustered in the six areas originally hypothesized when the scale was developed. The factor analysis yielded six clusters of items,

Family Needs Survey

Child's name: _____ Date completed: _____

Person completing survey: _____ Relationship to child: _____

Dear Parent:

Many families of young children have needs for information or support. If you wish, our staff is very willing to discuss these needs with you and work with you to identify resources that might be helpful.

Listed below are some needs commonly expressed by families. It would be helpful to us if you would check in the columns on the right any topics you would like to discuss. At the end, there is a place for you to describe other topics not included in the list.

If you choose to complete this form, the information you provide will be kept confidential. If you would prefer not to complete the survey at this time, you may keep it for your records.

Would you like to discuss this topic with a staff person from our program?

TOPICS	NO	NOT SURE	YES
Information			
1. How children grow and develop			
2. How to play or talk with my child			
3. How to teach my child			
4. How to handle my child's behavior			
5. Information about any condition or disability my child might have			
6. Information about services that are presently available for my child			
7. Information about the services my child might receive in the future			
Family and Social Support			
1. Talking with someone in my family about concerns			
2. Having friends to talk to			
3. Finding more time for myself			
4. Helping my spouse accept any condition our child might have			
5. Helping our family discuss problems and reach solutions			
6. Helping support each other during difficult times			
7. Deciding who will do household chores, child care, and other family tasks			
8. Deciding on and doing family recreational activities			
Financial			
1. Paying for expenses such as food, housing, medical care, clothing, or transportation			
2. Getting any special equipment my child needs			
3. Paying for therapy, day care, or other services my child needs			
4. Counseling or help in getting a job			

Figure 7.1. Family Needs Survey. (Developed by Donald B. Bailey, Jr., & Rune J. Simeonsson. [1990]. FPG Child Development Institute, The University of North Carolina at Chapel Hill.)

(continued)

Figure 7.1.   *(continued)*

Would you like to discuss
this topic with a staff
person from our program?

TOPICS	NO	NOT SURE	YES
5. Paying for babysitting or respite care			
6. Paying for toys that my child needs			
Explaining to Others			
1. Explaining my child's condition to my parents or my spouse's parents			
2. Explaining my child's condition to his or her siblings			
3. Knowing how to respond when friends, neighbors, or strangers ask questions about my child			
4. Explaining my child's condition to other children			
5. Finding reading material about other families who have a child like mine			
Child Care			
1. Locating babysitter or respite care providers who are willing and able to care for my child			
2. Locating a day care program or preschool for my child			
3. Getting appropriate care for my child in a church or synagogue during religious services			
Professional Support			
1. Meeting with a minister, priest, or rabbi			
2. Meeting with a counselor (psychologist, social worker, psychiatrist)			
3. More time to talk to my child's teacher or therapist			
Community Services			
1. Meeting and talking with other parents who have a child like mine			
2. Locating a doctor who understands me and my child's needs			
3. Locating a dentist who will see my child			

Other: Please list other topics or provide any other information that you would like to discuss.

_____

_____

_____

Is there a particular person with whom you would prefer to meet?

_____

_____

_____

Thank you for your time.
We hope this form will be helpful to you in identifying the services that you feel are important.

generally reinforcing the original grouping of items. However, a number of scales were reorganized, and three items related to child care and three related to professional support emerged as separate clusters. Three items did not fit statistically into any factor cluster but have been retained and combined to form a Community Services cluster because of their practical usefulness. In a 1999 study of 200 Latino parents, the original factor structure was upheld (Bailey, Skinner, Correa, et al., 1999).

For the purpose of this chapter, it is worth noting that informational needs consistently stand out as a strong factor in which the items are closely interrelated, even though they tap different types of needs. When we developed the scale, seven areas seemed important and questions were generated for each area.

1. *How children grow and develop.* This item was based on the assumption that some families need basic information about normal developmental processes. This is true for all families, but families of children with disabilities, especially if this is their first child, may have difficulty sorting out normal developmental and behavioral challenges from those associated with disability.

2. *How to play or talk with my child.* Much of what happens between parents and children during the early years revolves around play and informal communication. Some children with disabilities may exhibit atypical patterns of development or behavior that make normal play and communication patterns more challenging for parents. Thus, some parents may want support in how to read their child's cues or how to use or adapt normal interaction patterns to meet their child's needs.

3. *How to teach my child.* All parents teach their children, using both direct and intentional instructional techniques (e.g., guiding the child, providing information, giving feedback) as well as indirectly (e.g., by arranging the physical environment in certain ways, by providing a narrow or expanded range of opportunities to explore new environments or meet new people, by the values and culture expressed in living every day). Some parents of children with disabilities may experience frustration in their roles as teachers, especially if their child has severe developmental or behavioral problems. These parents may want information and support that will help them structure the physical environment or their own style of interaction in ways that maximize their child's ability to learn or to generalize skills learned in other contexts (e.g., in speech therapy).

4. *How to handle my child's behavior.* Some children with disabilities display unique or problematic behaviors. These could range from a lack of social initiative to more serious problems such as failure to thrive,

repetitive self-stimulation, aggression, self-injury, tantrums, or acting out in other ways that interfere with learning and the development of social relations with others. Research has shown that behaviors such as these often are particularly troubling to parents and are more likely to lead to parental stress and depression than the delayed development alone (Hauser-Cram, Warfield, Shonkoff, & Krauss, 2001). Parents of children with behaviors such as these often want information about the cause, nature, and treatment of problem behaviors. Sometimes, treatments involve medication or therapy that families are not familiar with, and thus they may want information not only about what they can do but also about how to evaluate and integrate various recommendations made by health care, education, psychology, and allied health professionals.

5. *Information about any condition or disability my child may have.* Children enter early intervention because of a wide range of disabilities or conditions that could lead to a disability (Scarborough et al., in press). Most families initially want to know as much as they can about the condition their child might have. They search for a cause and many are not satisfied until a definitive diagnosis is made. Once a condition is identified, parents usually want as much information about that condition as possible. New information about most conditions and disorders is constantly being generated through research, so the need for this type of information usually remains at a high level.

6. *Information about the services that are presently available for my child.* Once a child has been identified as having a disability or a condition that leads to a disability, most families want services to help assure that their child's specialized needs are addressed. This remains a life-long need for families, but professionals in early intervention have both a special opportunity and a special obligation in this regard because they usually meet parents who are going through this experience for the first time. Most did not expect to have a child with a disability and are not familiar with the range of professions, agencies, rules and regulations, laws, or their rights for services.

7. *Information about the services my child might receive in the future.* Although current services typically are the primary focus of parents' concerns, very quickly they begin to think about the future. A diagnosis of a disability is usually unexpected, and parents often find themselves worrying about what the future will be like for their child. Will she be able to finish school? Will he have friends? Will she be able to live independently? Who will take care of him when we are no longer able to do so? These questions lead many parents to seek information not

only about the normal developmental course of their child's condition but also about the types of programs and services that might be available throughout their child's life span. Early intervention professionals may not be aware of all of these services, but they need to be able to help families gain access to other professionals or information sources that could provide some answers.

Although our research suggests a clear domain of family needs for information, as evidenced by items that cluster statistically to comprise an information subscale, note that the items in each of the other domains likely have informational components as well. For example, a family may indicate a need for help in "locating a child care program or preschool for my child," an item in the Child Care subscale. Addressing this need may require informational services such as access to a directory of child care programs in the community, data on the willingness of each program to serve children with disabilities and the expertise of available staff in the program, ways in which special education and allied health professionals could provide support to child care teachers, and guidelines for evaluating quality of child care. Thus, the scale is only the first step in the assessment process. It can be used as a tool to facilitate understanding but must be followed up by discussions with families.

Informational Needs Are Consistently Reported to Be the Highest Among Families

In all 11 studies, the need for information was rated substantially higher than any of the other domains. On an average item in the information domain, 52% of the respondents indicated a definite desire for help, whereas on an average item in the other domains, 28% of respondents indicated a definite desire for help. These data show a clear and consistent pattern—parents from a wide range of countries, ethnicities, and age groups view the need for information as paramount, which is consistent with other research (e.g., Gowen et al., 1993; Santelli, Turnbull, Sergeant, Lerner, & Marquis, 1996; Sontag & Schacht, 1994). Furthermore, this need does not appear to diminish as the child ages because no studies have shown a significant relationship between the age of the child and the number or distribution of needs expressed. Thus, it is an enduring need and one for which professionals working with parents of children of all ages will need to be prepared.

Some Needs for Information Are More Frequently Expressed than Others

Table 7.2 displays the distribution of responses for the 11 studies across the seven items in the Information domain. On all items, at least 38% of

Table 7.2. Expressed needs for information (in percentages)

Reference	How children grow and develop	How to play or talk with my child	How to teach my child	How to handle my child's behavior	My child's condition or disability	Presently available services	Services available in the future
Bailey, Blasco, and Simeonsson (1992)[1]	39	31	59	38	50	60	72
Bailey, Skinner, Correa, et al. (1999)	65	58	72	69	74	89	97
Chen and Simeonsson (1994)	67	52	70	61	85	70	70
Cooper and Allred (1992)	23	21	39	20	22	34	47
Ellis et al. (2002)	NA[2]	NA[2]	56	55	NA[2]	63	79
Garshelis and McConnell (1993)	36	NA[2]	NA[2]	NA[2]	33	38	62
Graves and Hayes (1996)	1.7[3]	1.4[3]	1.9[3]	1.8[3]	2.0[3]	2.7[3]	1.9[3]
Linfoot (1997)	59	48	66	62	72	79	79
Roll-Pettersson (1992)	22	26	51	31	28	40	62
Sexton, Burrell, and Thompson (1992)	38	30	62	34	51	68	76
Shields et al. (1995)	31	36	39	39	58	60	81
Mean for item[4]	**42**	**38**	**57**	**45**	**53**	**60**	**73**

Note: Figures here represent mean item scores on this scale.

[1] Mean percentage of parents who indicated a definite need for help on each item in the Information subscale of the Family Needs Survey.

[2] This item was not included in this study.

[3] In this study, the authors reported findings by the 3-point rating scale for each item (1 = definitely need help; 2 = not sure; 3 = definitely need help).

[4] Mean percentage of parents across all studies who indicated a definite need for help for the item in question. Includes only those studies for which data on the particular item were collected and not the Graves and Hayes (1996) study.

parents indicated a need for help but for some the percentage was much greater. The items for which there is most consistently and frequently a need for help are the two items about current ($M = 60\%$) and future ($M = 73\%$) services, a finding reinforced by other studies (e.g., Sontag & Schacht, 1994). This reflects parents' ongoing concerns about the nature, intensity, and quality of services and a frequently reported concern regarding what will happen to their child in the future, both the near future (the next year or two) as well as the distant future (when the child becomes an adult or when the parents die or are too old to care for the child).

Predicting Individual Parent and Family Needs Is Virtually Impossible Based on Demographic Characteristics

One of the most important lessons gleaned from this research is how difficult it is to predict who will express what needs based on demographic variables that one would think might make a difference. In our studies, for example, we have examined variables such as ethnicity, country of origin, maternal education, child's age, child's gender, birth order, severity of delay, and family economic resources. None of these variables turned out to be reliable predictors of expressed needs. This finding reinforces the importance of individualized assessment of needs for information and other sources of support and suggests that designing a "packaged program" with a specific set of services will not meet the needs of all families served by an early intervention program.

Family's Needs for Information About Genetics

Information needs are shaped in part by the historical contexts in which families live. For example, in the 1950s, most individuals with disabilities were institutionalized, so strategies to support families who kept their children at home were virtually nonexistent. Today, few children are institutionalized and, thus, a primary focus of early intervention is to help assure that families have the supports they need to care for their children adequately at home. And, in the 1970s, little attention was paid to the challenges that families experienced in seeking child care for their young children with disabilities because few mothers worked and children with disabilities were rarely placed in regular child care settings. Today, employment for mothers of young children is the norm, and numerous models have been developed and are being implemented around the country in an effort to help families find high-quality child care and to provide the training and support that child care providers need to be able to appropriately care for children with disabilities.

In a similar vein, in the 1970s, the consequences of genetic disorders for families were not a major concern because few such disorders were known. Today, the psychological and social impact on families of genetic and inherited disorders, and the confusing and complicated information about each disorder, brings a special set of implications for families as well as for early intervention professionals. As more inherited and genetic causes of disability are identified, families will increasingly have access to information about their own genetic makeup and risk. They will be faced with the challenge of learning about the genetic nature of their child's condition, a complicated enough task in single gene or chromosomal disorders such as fragile X syndrome or Down syndrome, but one that becomes much more difficult in disorders such as autism, which are likely associated with multiple genes and may carry an uncertain risk for expression or transmission. The full ramifications for families of this knowledge are as yet relatively unexplored but have implications for an individual's identity or self-concept, the meaning and significance of family and kin, and moral and ethical decisions. With the expansion of testing for genetic abnormalities, families will increasingly be involved in debates on testing for reproductive planning, on who should be allowed to know their genetic makeup, and on how much detail is desirable. These discussions will have direct implications for families and will likely have an impact on them psychologically and socially in ways we have only just begun to understand (Alper et al., 2002; Collins, 1999; Collins & McKusick, 2001).

The rapid emergence of genetic knowledge is a concrete example of the many facets of information needed by both families and practitioners. In the remainder of this chapter, we explore the ramifications of expanding genetic knowledge and make suggestions for how early intervention professionals can respond to this rapidly changing need for information.

Recent Trends in Genetics

During the 1950s, building on the knowledge generated by a number of other researchers, Nobel prize winners James Watson and Francis Crick discovered that DNA, the basic code for all genetic information, was arranged in a double helix with certain properties regarding how the two strands bonded together. This discovery ushered in a new era of *genomics* and an explosion of knowledge about genetics that is still ongoing today (Watson, 2003). The Human Genome Project, an international effort to map and sequence the entire human genome, has advanced understanding of basic genetic processes at the molecular level (Emilien, Ponchon, Caldas, Isacson, & Maloteaux, 2000; Falcon de Vargas, 2002) and has led to the discovery of the genetic basis for thousands of diseases, disorders, and traits. The first step, "mapping" the entire genome, is now nearly complete and has led to new lines of research such as *proteomics* (studying the proteins for which genes encode), *transcriptomics* (learning where and when genes are expressed), *gene therapy* (attempts to correct genetic flaws through altering disrupted genetic codes), and *pharmacogenetics* (developing new medicines that are specifically targeted to individual genetic profiles; Watson, 2003). In addition to creating basic knowledge about genetic processes, a primary goal of this research is to develop more effective strategies for prevention and treatment of diseases and disorders (Mowat, 2002).

Unlike other basic research, which usually is not reported in the public media, rarely does a week go by without at least one headline related to newly emerging genetic information or the controversies engendered by such information (Conrad, 2002). Stories such as the rush to win the race to map the human genome, the discovery of genes that could underlie personality traits or suggest risk for diseases such as breast cancer or Alzheimer's disease, animal or human cloning, genetic alteration of crops, genetic privacy, and genetic differences among races or between humans and animals have captured the public's attention. Although polls suggest that the public does not always understand this information, they generally have a positive view of genetic research and its implications (Singer, Corning, & Lamias 1998) primarily because most media stories portray this research as triumphs of medicine and science (Petersen, 2001).

Implications of Emerging Genetic Knowledge

Families of children with disabilities already are being affected by genetic discoveries in obvious ways and in ways we can only imagine right now. The following examples outline some of the implications of this rapid expansion of genetic knowledge for families and practitioners.

There Will Be Many More Known Genetic Causes of Disability, Many of Them Rare

Until the 1990s, early intervention professionals worked with little knowledge or interest in genetic advances. Even now, no genetic causes are known for most children with disabilities in early intervention programs. But this situation is rapidly changing. Currently, more than 750 genetic disorders associated with mental retardation and developmental disabilities have been identified (Opitz, 1996). However, many of these disorders are rare. Most professionals have heard of Down syndrome or fragile X syndrome, but beyond a list of 10 or so of the most common disorders, many disorders are unfamiliar to the majority of practitioners in the field. When parents receive one of these diagnoses, often it is for a disorder they have never heard of. This scenario presents a daunting challenge to professionals and to parents. How can professionals possibly keep up with the rapid expansion of knowledge, and how can they know about each individual disorder? Of course, this is an impossible expectation, so professionals need strategies by which they can gain access to this information and help families gain access to and evaluate information from a variety of sources.

Parents and Professionals Will Need Comprehensible Information About Genetics in General and Specific Disorders in Particular

Most parents and professionals have heard of genes and chromosomes but beyond that are unfamiliar with genetic principles and concepts. When confronted with a specific diagnosis, understanding the disorder itself will first require an understanding of basic genetic facts and mechanisms of inheritance. Then, information is needed regarding how these processes are disrupted by a particular disorder.

To illustrate the complex information that families and professionals will face, consider the case of Fragile X syndrome, the most common inherited cause of mental retardation. Fragile X syndrome is a trinucleotide repeat expansion disorder. This means that a nucleotide triplet (CGG: cytosine–guanine–guanine) in the DNA at a particular point on the X chromosome (Xq27.3) expands far beyond the usual number of CGG,CGG repetitions. If the number of repeats is greater than 59, then the individual is considered to have premutation fragile X syndrome and be an unaffected carrier of the disorder. If the number of repeats is 200 or more, then the individual is considered to have full mutation fragile X syndrome and will experience a number of developmental and behavioral problems, including mental retardation, autistic behavior, anxiety, and language delays. These problems occur because a protein considered essential for normal brain development (FMRP) is no longer produced or is produced in much lower quantities than normal.

The story of fragile X syndrome may seem complicated already, but this is only the beginning. Researchers are working hard to understand the precise role of FMRP and its effects on messenger RNA as well as brain morphology and function (including synaptic connections and dendritic expression). They have recently learned that although fragile X syndrome is considered a single gene disorder, the fragile X gene may actually play an important role in regulating the function of many other genes (Zalfa & Bagni, 2004). And there is a complicated inheritance pattern involving carrier status and varying levels of risk of expansion from premutation to full mutation.

As evidenced in the previous two paragraphs, a disorder considered to be a relatively simple one from a genetic perspective turns out to be very complicated. The paragraphs are laced with terminology not familiar to the general public or most early intervention professionals—clear evidence that both families and professionals will need access to comprehensible information about particular disorders. Of course, parents desperately want as much information about their child's condition as possible. They expect professionals to be knowledgeable about their child's disorder and especially about potential treatments. But such an expectation is impossible to fulfill except in the most common disorders.

To prepare themselves for this information challenge, professionals will need new knowledge and must be able to speak the basic language of genetics. All early intervention professionals ought to know 1) basic genetic processes and terms (e.g., DNA, genes, chromosomes, carrier); 2) basic laws of inheritance; and 3) the genetic basis of at least four to five major disorders, such as Down syndrome, fragile X syndrome, Williams syndrome, and Prader-Willi syndrome. This information will provide a foundation on which information about new disorders can be built as professionals encounter families who have children with other conditions. Early intervention professionals also should be aware of major web sites and other reliable sources for easy access to information about other disorders.

The Inherited Nature of Many Disorders Will Cause Challenges for Many Families

Down syndrome is a genetic disorder but is not inherited. In other words, it is not typically passed down from generation to generation and only in rare cases is someone considered to be a "carrier" for Down syndrome. However, other disorders are inherited, and they create unique needs and consequences for families. Again, fragile X syndrome provides a good example of these issues. Gender is determined by the sex chromosomes known as X and Y. Males have one X chromosome and one Y chromosome, whereas females have two X chromosomes. Because fragile X syndrome is carried on the X chromosome, both males and females can be affected by the disorder or be carriers. A boy (XY) with the disorder necessarily inherits it from his mother, as he would have received a Y chromosome from his father. The chance of inheriting the fragile X gene from a carrier mother is 50%, and the chances that it will "expand" into the full mutation (thus resulting in developmental disabilities) increases with each generation. Girls (XX instead of XY in boys) can inherit the gene from either parent. Daughters of carrier mothers have a 50% chance of inheriting the fragile X gene (because the mother has two Xs but transmits only one) and could inherit it in its carrier state or as a full mutation. All daughters of carrier fathers will inherit the gene (because the father has only one X to transmit), but for some reason, fathers transmit the gene only in its carrier state. Therefore, daughters of carrier fathers always are carriers and never have the full mutation themselves.

Most parents of children diagnosed with fragile X syndrome did not know that they were carriers of the disorder. Once their child has been identified, many must assume the responsibility of informing their own parents or siblings, a process that can be very difficult (Bailey, Skinner, & Sparkman, 2003). Parents, and especially mothers, bear the burden of having transmitted (albeit usually unknowingly) a disorder to their child and have associated feelings of responsibility or guilt. Once their own genetic risk is known, parents must make decisions about whether to have future children and, if so, whether and how to use genetic information and genetic testing in reproductive planning. Exacerbating the situation is that some carrier mothers may experience subtle genetic effects (Hagerman & Hagerman, 2002), and mothers who themselves have the full mutation may experience cognitive and emotional challenges.

Thus, for inherited disorders, parents have additional needs for information and support. What are the odds that another child will have this disorder? Who else in my family might be at risk for being a carrier? Whose responsibility is it to tell them? Are there options for reproductive planning that do not involve abortion or not having children? Who can tell me what my risks will be? Obviously, early intervention professionals should not be the people providing definitive answers to these questions. A medical geneticist or genetic counselor should be the primary source of information and support for families about inherited disorders and reproductive options (Green, 1999). However, early intervention professionals should be aware of the issues that face families of children with inherited disorders and should know where the nearest resource for genetic counseling is located. Unfortunately, most smaller communities do not have these professionals, and families must travel to meet with specialists. Ideally, the early intervention team should meet with the nearest medical geneticist or genetic counselor to learn more about available resources, accessibility, and so forth so that they can better serve as referral sources for information for families. When families get genetic information from specialists, early intervention professionals should learn about and seek to understand this information. Research shows that a family's recall of information regarding their genetic disorder may vary (Michie, French, Allanson, Bobrow, & Martinea, 1997). Thus, an important role for early interventionists may be working with individual families to make sure they understand the information given to them so they can then make informed decisions.

Families Will Focus Much Energy on the Unique Needs and Alternative Treatments Associated with Their Child's Particular Disorder

Professionals in early intervention and preschool programs focus much of their training on general principles of working with young children with disabilities. However, for parents (and for many professionals), once the etiology or cause of the child's condition is known, questions arise about the specific intervention needs unique to this particular disability. This reflects a larger discussion in the field of developmental disability with regard to the role of knowledge about a diagnosed condition in planning early intervention services. Individualized assessment will continue to be a central component for all intervention planning, but the unique needs of each diagnosed condition are being recognized (Hodapp, DesJardin, & Ricci, 2003). Many families will seek out and argue for etiology-specific treatment approaches. Early intervention professionals will need to have information about various treatment options and help families gain access to objective information that can lead to informed decision making. When efficacy data are not available, professionals often will be in the position of helping families sort through uncertain information to make their best guess about reasonable treatment alternatives.

Etiology-specific information can be crucial to understanding the needs of a child with a particular condition. For example, almost all boys with the full mutation fragile X syndrome have mental retardation. Many also exhibit a high level of anxiety and arousal that can interfere with learning and environmental adaptation, much more so than is evident in other disorders. This anxiety and arousal can lead to autistic behavior, self-injury, tantrums, or other acting-out behaviors. Knowing about characteristics such as these could be very useful in planning interventions for a child with fragile X syndrome. But not all children with fragile X syndrome exhibit these behaviors. Thus, with any disorder, the extent to which general characteristics of the disorder apply to a particular child should not be assumed and only should be determined through individualized assessment.

Genetic research is opening the possibility for more targeted and unique treatments than have been available to date. Although pharmacological approaches have been used with children with disabilities for many years, genetic research and a new field called *pharmacogenetics* create an opportunity for more targeted drug treatments based on genetic profiles and knowledge about the condition. In fragile X syndrome, three major classes of medication are currently being used. Stimulant medications are prescribed for many children to control attention and hyperactivity. Other medications are prescribed for anxiety or arousal, and now a third class of drugs known as "cognitive enhancers" are being tested. Unfortunately, very little empirical data are available that assess the efficacy of these medications for children with particular genetic syndromes. Therefore, families try to sort through as much information as possible and often must trust their physician to make the best decision. Early intervention professionals can help families evaluate the efficacy of medications so that they can determine more clearly whether medications are having a real effect on their child's behavior.

Increasingly, the known genetic nature of a disorder brings hope that ultimately it could be cured through a technique such as gene therapy. In fragile X syndrome, for example, the single-gene nature of the disorder has led some to speculate that it may be a relatively easy candidate for an ultimate cure as a result of gene therapy, creating both optimism and frustration as parents hope and push for research that would make such a cure a reality. Unfortunately, it will be years and perhaps decades before such treatments could be made available. Professionals will need to be able to support families in striving to reach a balance between maintaining optimism for a cure and realizing how difficult and long-term that task will be.

Finally, it seems that once a particular diagnosis is made, the door opens for the emergence of alternative or sometimes controversial treatments (Nickel, 1996). These may include dietary treatments or behavioral/environmental interventions that are inconsistent or at odds with standard medical or behavioral practices. Parents may hear about these treatments from any number of sources and, in their efforts not to overlook anything that could possibly help their child, may try them, often at great expense to themselves and their family. Because these treatments are often expensive or are inconsistent with professional practice, professionals may be put in an awkward position with families. Professionals need to be aware of a range of standard and nonstandard treatments and be able to help families gain objective information about the rationale for and evidence in support of (or refuting the efficacy of) these treatments (Nickel, 1996).

Families Will Seek Out and Get to Know Other Families Who Have a Child with a Condition Similar to Their Child's

Parent support groups and parent-to-parent programs can be very supportive for families, both in terms of informational support as well as emotional support (Frank, Newcomb, & Beckman, 1996; Santelli, Turnbull, Marquis, & Lerner, 2000). Historically, two types of support groups have emerged. One type focuses on children with disabilities as a group, as in the case of statewide or local parent-to-parent programs. However, the identification of the specific nature of their child's disorder can provide the entrée for many families into a broader community of parents and professionals whose lives are focused on a particular disorder. The nature and proximity of the latter type of group will vary considerably as a function of the disorder. For example, larger communities may have a support program for families of children with mental retardation, autism, or Down syndrome. In the fragile X syndrome community, support groups are more likely to be at a state or regional level.

National organizations and advocacy groups also provide important support for families (Stockdale & Terry, 2002). For example, the National Fragile X Association maintains an active and frequently updated web site providing information to families about the disorder and about what is known about its treatment. The Internet has made such web sites common, and with the advent of Listserv and other electronic mailing lists, the concept of parent support groups has rapidly expanded in some cases to include a worldwide network of "virtual" support.

Professionals need to be aware of the important roles that these support groups and organizations play in the lives of families. They need to know how to gain access to information about support groups and to help families sort out legitimate from questionable information. The Internet has been a tremendous boon to the information collecting processing but has also provided indiscriminate and often inaccurate information. Parents may need support in how to evaluate the legitimacy of various web sites or of specific information provided from these sources.

Families Will Be Especially Concerned About Genetic Privacy and Genetic Discrimination

How will genetic information be used and protected? Genetic privacy will be an increasingly important concern of families. Even though the benefits of DNA technology in medicine are immeasurable, one of the major risks of genetic information can be discrimination at many levels. Healthy individuals who have been identified as carriers of a disease causing genetic mutation may be refused life or medical insurance (Falcon de Vargas, 2002). These individuals also may be at risk for loss of employment if their employers have any reason to suspect future disabling conditions.

In fragile X syndrome, these issues are coming into focus around the possibility of newborn screening. Soon it will be technically possible to screen a newborn for fragile X syndrome immediately after birth. This could provide early entrée into early intervention programs and provide parents with important information about future reproductive risk. However, a number of issues about confidentiality and desirability of newborn screening are being discussed (e.g., Bailey, in press; Wald & Morris, 2003). One of the fundamental issues is whether it would be desirable to screen for carrier status. Concerns have been raised that carrier status bears no immediate risk for the child, but disclosure of carrier status may result in social discrimination or loss of insurability. Also of concern is the likelihood that newborn screening would necessarily implicate grandparents or other relatives with regard to carrier status, even though they did not themselves give permission for genetic testing.

Families need to be well versed in the details of the benefits and risks of genetic information before they make any decisions. Confidentiality and autonomy concerning genetic information will be important to families. Professionals need to be aware of the major controversies in this arena and provide families with whatever information and assurances are available.

Genetic Information Has the Potential to Affect Many Other Aspects of Family or Parent Well-Being

For example, following a diagnosis, parents (and perhaps other family members as well) may begin to define or explain various aspects of their lives in the context of their child's genetic condition or of their own carrier status. For some, realizing the genetic nature of their child's condition raises important and unique philosophical and religious questions about the meaning of life events, whether those events are random or planned, and the relative influence of biology and environment on development and behavior. Professionals will need to be able to provide families with information about counselors and others who can help them wrestle with these issues.

CONCLUSION

In this chapter we have argued that helping families gain access to information is a key part of a family-centered approach to early intervention. Information provides parents with both the "ammunition" they need to participate effectively in decisions about services for their child as well as the security and confidence needed to reassure parents that the decisions for which they are advocating are indeed appropriate. Thus, information has the potential to empower families to be and feel more effective as advocates for their children.

Professionals play many different and important roles in facilitating and supporting parents' access to and interpretation of information. Decisions about professional roles should be individualized based on family needs and preferences; *although information can be empowering, the way in which professionals handle information and share it with families may or may not be empowering.* For example, a professional could 1) directly provide information or 2) show parents where information can be obtained. Likewise, a professional could 1) evaluate the quality of available information or 2) help families evaluate the quality of information for themselves. Some families may want a professional's clear opinion on an issue, whereas others may want facts and then make their own conclusions based on the data.

We showed that an instrument such as the Family Needs Survey can be a useful tool in helping to ascertain a family's need for information. Applications of the measure in research studies highlighted the importance of informational needs and reinforced the need for individualized assessment before providing services. A survey such as this rarely provides sufficient information for decision making, however, and it is mainly through conversations with parents that professionals can determine whether and what kinds of informational needs are expressed by families and how best to meet those needs.

Finally, we used emerging genetic information and technology as a case in point to demonstrate that information is increasingly becoming more complex and can rapidly change. In some ways, we have moved from a paucity of information to information overload. A key role for early interventionists will be to develop personal strategies for rapidly gaining access to and evaluating information and to help families develop these strategies as well.

REFERENCES

Alper, J.S., Ard, C., Asch, A., Beckwith, J., Conrad, P., & Geller, L.N. (Eds.). (2002). *The double-edged helix: Social implications of genetics in a diverse society.* Baltimore: Johns Hopkins University Press.

Bailey, D.B. (2001). Evaluating parent involvement and family support in early intervention and preschool programs. *Journal of Early Intervention, 24,* 1–14.

Bailey, D.B. (in press). Newborn screening for fragile X syndrome. *Mental Retardation and Developmental Disabilities Research Reviews.*

Bailey, D.B., Aytch, L.S., Odom, S.L., Symons, F., & Wolery, M. (1999). Early intervention as we know it. *Mental Retardation and Developmental Disabilities Research Reviews, 5,* 11–20.

Bailey, D.B., & Blasco, P.M. (1990). Parents' perspectives on a written survey of family needs. *Journal of Early Intervention, 14,* 196–203.

Bailey, D.B., Blasco, P.M., & Simeonsson, R.J. (1992). Needs expressed by mothers and fathers of young children with disabilities. *American Journal on Mental Retardation, 97,* 1–10.

Bailey, D.B., & Henderson, L.W. (1993). Traditions in family assessment: Toward an inquiry-oriented, reflective model. In D.M. Bryant & M.A. Graham (Eds.),

Implementing early intervention: From research to effective practice (pp. 124–147). New York: Guilford Press.

Bailey, D.B., McWilliam, R.A., Darkes, L.A., Hebbler, K., Simeonsson, R.J., Spiker, D., & Wagner, M. (1998). Family outcomes in early intervention: A framework for program evaluation and efficacy research. *Exceptional Children, 64,* 313–328.

Bailey, D.B., Jr., & Simeonsson, R.J. (1988). Assessing needs of families with handicapped infants. *Journal of Special Education, 22,* 117–127.

Bailey, D.B., & Simeonsson, R.J. (1990). *Family Needs Survey.* Chapel Hill: FPG Child Development Institute, The University of North Carolina at Chapel Hill.

Bailey, D.B., Simeonsson, R.J., Winton, P.J., Huntington, G.S., Comfort, M., Isbell, P., O'Donnell, K.J., & Helm, J.M. (1986). Family-focused intervention: A functional model for planning, implementing and evaluating individualized family services in early intervention. *Journal of the Division for Early Childhood, 10,* 156–171.

Bailey, D.B., Skinner, D., Correa, V., Arcia, E., Reyes-Blanes, M.E., Rodriguez, P., Vázques-Montilla, E., & Skinner, M. (1999). Needs and supports reported by Latino families of young children with developmental disabilities. *American Journal on Mental Retardation, 104,* 437–451.

Bailey, D.B., Skinner, D., Rodriguez, P., Gut, D., & Correa, V. (1999). Awareness, use, and satisfaction with services for Latino parents of young children with disabilities. *Exceptional Children, 65,* 367–381.

Bailey, D.B., Skinner, D., & Sparkman, K. (2003). Discovering fragile X syndrome: Family experiences and perceptions. *Pediatrics, 111,* 407–416.

Bailey, D.B., & Wolery, M. (1992). *Teaching infants and preschoolers with disabilities* (2nd ed.). Englewood Cliffs, NJ: Merrill.

Bronfenbrenner, U. (1979). *The ecology of human development: Experiments by nature and design.* Cambridge, MA: Harvard University Press.

Chen, J., & Simeonsson, R.J. (1994). Child disability and family needs in the People's Republic of China. *International Journal of Rehabilitation Research, 17,* 25–37.

Collins, F.S. (1999). Medical and societal consequences of the Human Genome Project. *New England Journal of Medicine, 341,* 28–37.

Collins, F.S., & McKusick, V.A. (2001). Implications of the Human Genome Project for medical sciences. *Journal of the American Medical Association, 285,* 540–544.

Conrad, P. (2002). Genetics and behavior in the news: Dilemmas of a rising paradigm. In J.S. Alper, C. Ard, A. Asch, J. Beckwith, P. Conrad, & L.N. Geller (Eds.), *The double-edged helix: Social implications of genetics in a diverse society* (pp. 58–79). Baltimore: Johns Hopkins University Press.

Cooper, C.S., & Allred, K.W. (1992). A comparison of mothers' versus fathers' needs for support in caring for a young child with special needs. *Infant-Toddler Intervention, 2,* 205–221.

Dunst, C.J. (1985). Rethinking early intervention. *Analysis and Intervention in Developmental Disabilities, 5,* 165–201.

Dunst, C.J. (2000). Revisiting "rethinking early intervention." *Topics in Early Childhood Special Education, 20,* 95–104.

Dunst, C.J. (2002). Family-centered practices: Birth through high school. *Journal of Special Education, 36,* 139–147.

Dunst, C.J., Trivette, C.M., & Deal, A. (1988). *Enabling and empowering families: Principles and guidelines for practice.* Cambridge, MA: Brookline Books.

Dunst, C.J., Trivette, C.M., & LaPointe, N. (1992). Toward clarification of the meaning and key elements of empowerment. *Family Science Review, 5*, 111–130.

Early Childhood Research Institute on Measuring Growth and Development. (1998). *Family outcomes in a growth and development model* (Tech. Rep. No. 7). Minneapolis, MN: University of Minnesota, Center for Early Education and Development.

Ellis, J.T., Luiselli, J.K., Amirault, D., Byrne, S., O'Malley-Cannon, B., Taras, M., Wolongevicz, J., & Sisson, R.W. (2002). Families of children with developmental disabilities: Assessment and comparison of self-reported needs in relation to situational variables. *Journal of Developmental and Physical Disabilities, 14*, 191–202.

Emilien, G., Ponchon, M., Caldas, C., Isacson, O., & Maloteaux, J.M. (2000). Impact of genomics on drug discovery and clinical medicine. *Quarterly Journal of Medicine, 93*, 391–423.

Falcon de Vargas, A. (2002). The Human Genome Project and its importance in clinical medicine. *International Congress Series, 1237*, 2–13.

Frank, N., Newcomb, S., & Beckman, P.J. (1996). Developing and implementing support groups for families. In P.J. Beckman (Ed.), *Strategies for working with families of young children with disabilities* (pp. 127–150). Baltimore: Paul H. Brookes Publishing Co.

Gallimore, R., Coots, J., Wiesner, T., Garner, H., & Guthrie, D. (1996). Family responses to children with early developmental delays II: Accommodation intensity and activity in early and middle childhood. *American Journal on Mental Retardation, 101*, 215–232.

Garshelis, J.A., & McConnell, S.R. (1993). Comparison of family needs assessed by mothers, individual professionals, and interdisciplinary teams. *Journal of Early Intervention, 16*, 36–49.

Gartner, A., Lipsky, D., & Turnbull, A. (1991). *Supporting families with a child with a disability*. Baltimore: Paul H. Brookes Publishing Co.

Gowen, J.W., Christy, D.S., & Sparling, J. (1993). Informational needs of parents of young children with special needs. *Journal of Early Intervention, 17*, 194–210.

Graves, C., & Hayes, V.E. (1996). Do nurses and parents of children with chronic conditions agree on parental needs? *Journal of Pediatric Nursing, 11*, 288–299.

Green, R.B. (1999). Genetic medicine and the conflict of moral principles. *Families, Systems, and Health, 17*, 63–74.

Guralnick, M.J. (2001). A developmental systems model for early intervention. *Infants and Young Children, 14*(2), 1–18.

Hagerman, R.J., & Hagerman, P.J. (2002). The fragile X premutation: Into the phenotypic fold. *Current Opinion in Genetics and Development, 12*, 278–283.

Harry, B. (1992). *Cultural diversity, families, and the special education system: Communication and empowerment*. New York: Teachers College Press.

Hauser-Cram, P., Warfield, M.E., Shonkoff, J.P., & Krauss, M.W. (2001). Children with disabilities: A longitudinal study of child development and parental well-being. *Monographs of the Society for Research in Child Development, 66* (3, Serial No. 266).

Hodapp, R.M., DesJardin, J.L., & Ricci, L.A. (2003). Genetic syndromes of mental retardation: Should they matter for the early interventionist? *Infants and Young Children, 16*, 152–160.

Ingstad, B., & Whyte, S. (Eds.). (1995). *Disability and culture*. Berkeley: University of California Press.

Kahn, G. (1997). Digital interactive media and the health care balance of power. In R.L. Street, W.R. Gold, & T. Manning (Eds.), *Health promotion and interactive technology: Theoretical applications and future directions* (pp. 187–208). Mahwah, NJ: Lawrence Erlbaum Associates.

Kaiser, A.P., & Hancock, T.B. (2003). Teaching parents new skills to support their young children's development. *Infants and Young Children, 16*, 9–21.

Krauss, M.W. (2000). Family assessment within early intervention programs. In J.P. Shonkoff & S.J. Meisels (Eds.), *Handbook of early childhood intervention* (2nd ed., pp. 290–308). Cambridge, UK: Cambridge University Press.

Krauss, M.W., & Selzer, M.M. (1998). Life course perspectives in mental retardation research: The case of family caregiving. In J.A. Burack, R.M. Hodapp, & E. Zigler (Eds.), *Handbook of mental retardation and development* (pp. 504–520). Cambridge, UK: Cambridge University Press.

Lieberman, H., Forbes, J., Uttaro, T., & Sarkis, L. (1996). Using needs surveys to foster consumer and family empowerment. *Administration and Policy in Mental Health, 23*, 357–360.

Linfoot, K. (1997). *Access to early intervention for families of children with disabilities in rural areas of New South Wales.* Nepean, Australia: University of Western Sydney.

Marsh, D.T. (1992). *Families and mental retardation: New directions in professional practice.* New York: Praeger.

Michie, S., French, D., Allanson, A., Bobrow, M., & Martinea, T.M. (1997). Information recall in genetic counseling: A pilot study of its assessment. *Patient Education and Counseling, 32*, 93–100.

Minnes, P. (1998). Mental retardation: The impact upon the family. In J.A. Burack, R.M. Hodapp, & E. Zigler (Eds.), *Handbook of mental retardation and development* (pp. 693–712). Cambridge, UK: Cambridge University Press.

Mowat, D. (2002). Ethical, legal, and social issues surrounding the Human Genome Project. *Internal Medicine Journal, 32*, 89–90.

Myers, B.A. (1996). Coping with developmental disabilities. In A.J. Capute & P.J. Accardo (Eds.), *Developmental disabilities in infancy and childhood: Vol. I. Neurodevelopmental diagnosis and treatment* (pp. 473–484). Baltimore: Paul H. Brookes Publishing Co.

Nickel, R.E. (1996). Controversial therapies for young children with developmental disabilities. *Infants and Young Children, 8*(4), 29–40.

Opitz, J. (1996). *Historiography of the causal analysis of mental retardation.* Speech to the 29th Annual Gatlinburg Conference on Research and Theory in Mental Retardation, Gatlinburg, TN.

Petersen, A. (2001). Biofantasies: Genetics and medicine in the print news. *Social Science and Medicine, 52*, 1255–1268.

Rappaport, J. (1981). In praise of paradox: A social policy of empowerment over prevention. *American Journal of Community Psychology, 9*, 1–25.

Roberts, R.N., Innocenti, M.S., & Goetze, L.D. (1999). Emerging issues from state level evaluations of early intervention programs. *Journal of Early Intervention, 22*, 152–163.

Roll-Pettersson, L.R. (1992). *The child's disability: Family needs.* Stockholm: Stiftelsen ALA.

Sameroff, A.J., & Fiese, B.H. (2000). Transactional regulation: The developmental ecology of early intervention. In J.P. Shonkoff & S.J. Meisels (Eds.), *Handbook of early childhood intervention* (2nd ed., pp. 135–159). Cambridge, UK: Cambridge University Press.

Santelli, B., Turnbull, A., Marquis, J., & Lerner, E. (2000). Statewide parent-to-parent programs: Partners in early intervention. *Infants and Young Children, 13*(1), 74–88.

Santelli, B., Turnbull, A., Sergeant, J., Lerner, E.P., & Marquis, J.G. (1996). Parent to parent programs: Parent preferences for supports. *Infants and Young Children, 9*(1), 53–62.

Scarborough, A.A., Spiker, D., Mallik, S., Hebbeler, K.M., Bailey, D.B., & Simeonsson, R.J. (in press). A national picture of children and families entering early intervention. *Exceptional Children.*

Sexton, D., Burrell, B., & Thompson, B. (1992). Measurement integrity of the Family Needs Survey. *Journal of Early Intervention, 16,* 343–352.

Sexton, D., Snyder, P., Rheams, T., Barron-Sharp, B., & Perez, J. (1991). Considerations in using written surveys to identify family strengths and needs during the IFSP process. *Topics in Early Childhood Special Education, 11,* 81–91.

Shapiro, J., Blacher, J., & Lopez, S.R. (1998). Maternal reactions to children with mental retardation. In J.A. Burack, R.M. Hodapp, & E. Zigler (Eds.), *Handbook of mental retardation and development* (pp. 606–636). Cambridge, UK: Cambridge University Press.

Shields, G., Schondel, C., Barnhart, L., Fitzpatrick, V., Sidell, N., Adams, P., Fertig, B., & Gomez, S. (1995). Social work in pediatric oncology: A family needs assessment. *Social Work in Health Care, 21,* 39–54.

Singer, E., Corning, A., & Lamias, M. (1998). The polls-trends: Genetic testing, engineering, and therapy: Awareness and attitudes. *Public Opinion Quarterly, 62,* 1–23.

Sontag, J.C., & Schacht, R. (1994). An ethnic comparison of parent participation and information needs in early intervention. *Exceptional Children, 60,* 422–433.

Sparling, J., & Lowman, B. (1983). Parent information needs as revealed through interests, problems, attitudes, and preferences. In R. Haskins (Ed.), *Parent education and public policy* (pp. 304–323). Norwood, NJ: Ablex.

Stockdale, A., & Terry, S.F. (2002). Advocacy groups and the new genetics. In J.S. Alper, C. Ard, A. Asch, J. Beckwith, P. Conrad, & L.N. Geller (Eds.), *The double-edged helix: Social implications of genetics in a diverse society* (pp. 80–101). Baltimore: Johns Hopkins University Press.

Turnbull, A.P., Patterson, J.M., Behr, S.K., Murphy, D.L., Marquis, J.G., & Blue-Banning, M.J. (1993). *Cognitive coping, families, and disability.* Baltimore: Paul H. Brookes Publishing Co.

Turnbull, A.P., Turbiville, V., & Turnbull, H.R. (2000). Evolution of family-professional partnerships: Collective empowerment as the model for the early twenty-first century. In J.P. Shonkoff & S.J. Meisels (Eds.), *Handbook of early childhood intervention* (2nd ed., pp. 630–650). Cambridge, UK: Cambridge University Press.

Wald, N.J., & Morris, J.K. (2003). A new approach to antenatal screening for fragile X syndrome. *Prenatal Diagnosis, 23,* 345–351.

Watson, J.D. (2003). *DNA: The secret of life.* New York: Alfred A. Knopf.

Zalfa, F., & Bagni, C. (2004). Molecular insights into mental retardation: Multiple functions for the fragile X mental retardation protein? *Current Issues in Molecular Biology, 6*(2), 73–88.

CHAPTER 8

ASSESSING INTERPERSONAL AND FAMILY DISTRESS AND THREATS TO CONFIDENT PARENTING IN THE CONTEXT OF EARLY INTERVENTION

GAEL I. ORSMOND

The multidisciplinary early intervention assessment process typically focuses on the development of the infant or toddler while it acknowledges the critical role of the family. Although a variety of validated systems for the multidisciplinary assessment of the child's development have been developed and are commonly used (Guralnick, 2000), an equally thorough assessment of the family's contributions, strengths, and needs is rarely conducted. This chapter focuses on the assessment of interpersonal and family distress and threats to confident parenting in families of children at biological risk or those with established disabilities. This specific and narrow focus of parent and family assessment reflects a developmental systems approach to family assessment in the context of community-based early intervention services and supports (see Guralnick, 2001). Areas of potential parental stress, including interpersonal and family distress, are seen as influencing family patterns of interaction, which in turn have the potential to affect child outcomes. Thus, addressing interpersonal and family distress and threats to confident parenting within the context of early intervention will potentially influence family interaction patterns, with the eventual goal of promoting optimal child and family outcomes. The question then becomes, "What information is needed to help maximize family patterns of interaction?" (Guralnick, 2001, p. 11). By considering family assessment within this realm, we realize the utter importance and helpfulness of conducting such an assessment.

The first part of this chapter focuses on what is known about important aspects of parent and family development during early childhood and how a child with an established disability or at biological risk for disability may influence these aspects of parental well-being. That is, what does the literature tell us about what needs to be assessed with respect to interpersonal and family distress and threats to confident parenting? This research is reviewed with a specific focus on the early childhood years. Then, some common measures that assess these areas of parental and family well-being are reviewed. Finally, the ultimate goal of this chapter is to provide early intervention professionals with some specific recommendations for evaluating interpersonal and family distress and threats to confident parenting during the assessment process. Thus, the recommendations made are derived from the needs and areas of concern cited in the literature and are therefore, in a sense, evidence based. But, they also attempt to be sensitive to the viewpoints of families and realistic within the context of early intervention programs.

FAMILY ASSESSMENT IN EARLY INTERVENTION

Several notable researchers have previously discussed assessing families during the early intervention process (e.g., Bailey & Henderson, 1993; Bailey & Simeonsson, 1984; Bailey & Simeonsson, 1988; Beckman & Bristol, 1991; Krauss, 2000; Krauss & Jacobs, 1990; Winton & Bailey, 1988). These authors outlined some of the theoretical considerations, as well as some of the issues and pitfalls, of conducting family assessment. Identifying the strengths and needs of the family is acknowledged to be an important component of the individualized family service plan (IFSP; Beckman & Bristol, 1991). Typically, this type of assessment of the family during early intervention includes basic demographic information collected during the intake process and clinical impressions based on observations made during home visits (Krauss & Jacobs, 1990). Formal or standardized assessment of families is rarely conducted, partly because of the partnership model emphasized in early intervention and partly because early intervention professionals are trained in child development rather than family issues.

Some concerns about nonstandardized family assessment include questions about the validity of such informal measurements; the potential for cultural and class bias in observation (although this is also problematic in standardized assessments); and the need for standardized service outcomes, particularly with respect to family adaptation (Bailey et al., 1998; Krauss & Jacobs, 1990; Mott et al., 1986). In contrast, the concerns over more formal assessment center on conducting family assessment in a thoughtful and sensitive way that does not judge families but rather empowers them and helps establish partnerships with professionals (Guralnick, 2001; Krauss & Jacobs, 1990). A family typically enters an early intervention program because of concerns about their child's development, not because of difficulty within the family. Many of the standardized measures developed for family research purposes may not be appropriate in clinical settings (Beckman & Bristol, 1991; Slentz & Bricker, 1992). Although some researchers and professionals have expressed strong concerns over the appropriateness and necessity of assessing families (Beckman & Bristol, 1991; Slentz & Bricker, 1992), others have emphasized the need for some standardization to the process and for family outcome measures (Whitehead, Deiner, & Toccafondi, 1990). The view expressed in this chapter is that family assessment can be done in a sensitive and respectful manner and that we have much to gain by using a common set of procedures and measures for family assessment across early intervention programs.

Thus, the goal of this chapter is to expand on the issues outlined in the literature and to take the process one step further by making specific recommendations to early intervention professionals. The scope of assessment in this chapter is fairly narrow because it is focused on interpersonal and family distress and threats to confident parenting, rather than more broad assessments of family functioning. Finally, an attempt is made to include both mother and father perspectives with respect to stress and confident parenting because prior research has shown that the effects of stress are not uniform to mothers and fathers (e.g., Roach, Orsmond, & Barratt, 1999). Furthermore, because mothers and fathers have been shown to differ in their report of perceived benefits from early intervention services, their perspectives must be assessed independently as well as conjointly (Upshur, 1991).

DOMAINS OF ASSESSMENT

Considerable research has documented the fact that parenting a young child with a disability or at biological risk for disability can be stressful (e.g., Beckman & Pokorni, 1988; Button, Pianta, & Marvin, 2001; Dyson, 1993; Roach et al., 1999). Furthermore, high levels of parental stress can contribute to poor mother–child interaction (Barnard, Morisset, & Spieker, 1993; Magill-Evans & Harrison, 2001) and consequently have adverse effects on child outcomes in families of children with disabilities (Friedrich, Greenberg, & Crnic, 1983). Moreover, parenting a child with a disability or at biological risk can affect attitudes and beliefs about one's own parenting (Donenberg & Baker, 1993; Johnston & Mash, 1989; Rodrigue, Morgan, & Geffken, 1992), especially as parents experience stigma associated with disability (Goffman, 1963). The areas of family stress most commonly researched include parenting stress, parental depression, marital stress, social isolation, and family cohesion.

Parenting and Family Distress

Distress related to parenting a child with a disability or at biological risk has most commonly been assessed within the framework of the Parenting Stress Index (PSI; Abidin, 1995), a measure that examines child-related parenting stress (stress emanating from child characteristics) and parent-related parenting stress (stress emanating from parent characteristics).

Parenting Stress in Parents of Children with Established Disabilities

Considerable research, most commonly using the PSI, has indicated that parents of young children with disabilities have reported greater stress related to their child's characteristics than parents of children who are typically developing (Beckman, 1991; Britner, Morog, Pianta, & Marvin, 2003; Roach et al., 1999), especially with respect to feeling that their child was less adaptable; more distractible, demanding, and active; and not measuring up to their expectations. Parent-related stress also has been observed to be greater among parents of young children with disabilities, including Down syndrome and autism (Dumas, Wolf, Fisman, & Culligan, 1991; Fisman & Wolf, 1991; Roach et al., 1999), compared with parents of typically developing children. Specifically, parents of children with Down syndrome and other developmental disabilities have reported feeling less competent as parents and have reported greater problems with their health, greater social isolation, less support from their spouse, feeling as if their family roles are restricted, and greater symptoms of depression (all domains within the PSI's parenting-related stress) than parents of typically developing children (Beckman, 1991; Roach et al., 1999). Similar to other studies, however, the Roach et al. study reported that only a handful of parents reported excessive levels of parental stress.

Moreover, the research suggests that parenting a child with an autism spectrum disorder may produce greater stress in parents than parenting children with other types of disabilities (Dumas et al., 1991; Fisman & Wolf, 1991; Holroyd & McArthur, 1976; Kasari & Sigman, 1997; Tobing & Glenwick, 2002; Wolf, Noh, Fisman, & Speechley, 1989). More specifically, these researchers have reported that mothers of children with autism are most stressed by thoughts of their child's continued dependence on people (Holroyd & McArthur, 1976; Koegel et al., 1992) and other characteristics such as the child's inability to adjust to changes in the environment (Fisman & Wolf, 1991).

Parenting stress appears to remain relatively stable through the early childhood years for parents of children with identified disabilities. For example, Dyson (1993) found that parental stress was relatively stable in parents of children with disabilities (primarily mental retardation and physical impairments) through the early childhood years and remained elevated compared with stress in parents of children without disabilities. Similarly, others have reported that levels of stress do not appear to vary over time for parents whose children are in early intervention programs (Hanson & Hanline, 1990). In contrast, researchers have found that the severity or type of disability in the child, rather than the age, affects parental stress (Boyce, Behl, Mortensen, & Akers, 1991; Hanson & Hanline, 1990).

Parenting Stress in Parents of Children at Biological Risk for Disability

The research on how parents adapt to the birth of a preterm infant, and particularly the subsequent caring demands beyond hospital discharge, is surprisingly sparse compared with that of children with established disabilities. Up until recently, few studies documented parental adaptation with this population, despite the societal concerns of this increasing population (Singer et al., 1999). The available research on parenting stress in parents who have children at biological risk for disability (e.g., preterm infants) indicates that stress tends to diminish over time (Beckman & Pokorni, 1988) but is dependent on the health and risk status of the child (Halpern, Brand, & Malone, 2001). Parents of preterm infants with low risks, such as those without respiratory and other health complications, generally show high levels of stress that diminish over time to levels that are comparable to those of parents of healthy full-term infants (Crnic, Greenberg, & Slough, 1986; Halpern & MacLean, 1997; Halpern et al., 2001; Singer, Davillier, Breuning, Hawkins, & Yamashita, 1996; Singer et al., 1999; Trause & Kramer, 1983). Initially, parents of high-risk preterm infants tend to report that their children are more distractible, hyperactive, and demanding than parents of low-risk preterm or healthy full-term infants (Singer et al., 1999).

Parenting Stress in Parents of Children in Early Intervention

Parenting stress rarely has been assessed in the context of early intervention, with the exception of Whitehead and colleagues (1990), who reported on their model demonstration project, and Boyce and colleagues (e.g., Boyce et al., 1991; Innocenti, Huh, & Boyce, 1992), who assessed parenting stress in the context of a series of large-scale longitudinal studies of early intervention. Whitehead et al. reported that more than half of their families scored in the "normal" range of parenting stress compared with parents of children without disabilities. Boyce and colleagues also compared scores with their participants to published norms. Parents of children in early intervention programs reported greater child-related stress, whereas parent-related stress was only somewhat elevated. Of note, McDowell, Saylor, Taylor, Boyce, and Stokes (1995) found that parenting stress increased slightly for the first 3 years for a diverse group of parents of preterm children with intraventricular hemorrhage in early intervention. Moreover, a non–Caucasian group of these parents reported higher levels of parenting stress than the Caucasian sample; a greater increase in child-related parenting stress was associated with lower income levels (McDowell et al., 1995).

Differences in Parenting Stress in Mothers and Fathers

In general, the research indicates that mothers report greater stress than fathers, with many fathers of children with disabilities not reporting greater parenting stress than fathers of children without disabilities. For example, several researchers (Factor, Perry, & Freeman, 1990; Freeman, Perry, & Factor, 1991; Konstantareas & Homatidis, 1989) found that fathers tended to report lower levels of stress than mothers of children with autism. Noh, Dumas, Wolf, and Fisman (1989) found that mothers of children with autism or Down syndrome reported greater parenting stress than mothers of typically developing children, but fathers in the three groups did not differ. Rodrigue et al. (1992) also did not find that fathers of school-age children with autism reported more stress than fathers of children with Down syndrome.

In particular, mothers and fathers appear to differ with respect to parent-related rather than child-related stress. With respect to child-related parenting stress, several researchers have found that mothers and fathers do not differ in their appraisals of the effect of their child's developmental disability on the family (Beckman, 1991; Konstantareas & Homatidis, 1989; Roach et al., 1999; Trute & Hiebert-Murphy, 2002; Wolf et al., 1989) or on social isolation (Beckman, 1991). Moreover, Whitehead et al. (1990) found that mothers and fathers reported similar levels of child-related parenting stress in their early intervention program. In the Beckman (1991) study, however, fathers reported greater difficulty with attachment.

With respect to parent-related parenting stress, Beckman (1991) found that fathers reported less parent-related stress than mothers, specifically in the areas of depression, restrictiveness of the parental role, sense of competence, relationship with spouse, and health. Dumas et al. (1991) and Fisman and Wolf (1991) also found that mothers of children with autism or Down syndrome were at greater risk of parent-related stress compared with mothers of typically developing children, whereas fathers were not at greater risk for parent-related stress.

Other researchers have measured the effect of the child's disability on the mother and father along slightly different dimensions (e.g., Baker, Blacher, Crnic, & Edelbrock, 2002; Donenberg & Baker, 1993; Rodrigue et al., 1992). Donenberg and Baker found that both mothers and fathers of children with developmental delays reported greater negative impact of the child on the family than did parents of typically developing children. Similar to other research (e.g., Freeman et al., 1991; Kostantareas & Homatidis, 1989), Baker et al. found that parental stress was related to child behavior problems rather than cognitive delay.

Mothers and fathers of preterm infants also appear to experience stress differently. Hughes and McCollum (1994) examined mothers' and fathers' reports of stress associated with the birth and subsequent adjustment of a preterm infant. They found that mothers and fathers differed in their number (fathers reported fewer) and types of stresses reported. However, the most important stressors for both were related to the infant's health status and physical separation from the infant due to hospitalization. Mothers frequently reported feelings of guilt regarding the preterm birth of the infant, whereas fathers mentioned medical causes of the preterm birth and did not express feelings of guilt. Trause and Kramer (1983) also found that mothers expressed greater distress following the birth of preterm infant than did fathers.

In addition, examining the predictors of stress for mothers and fathers separately has yielded important findings. For example, Roach et al. (1999) found that parental stress was predicted by different factors for mothers and for fathers. For mothers, the factors did not differ according to whether they had a child with Down syndrome or a child who was typically developing. In general, parental stress in mothers was associated with having an older child (still younger than the age of 5), a greater number of caregiving demands and child care responsibilities, working more hours per week, and reporting of parental stress by fathers. In contrast, fathers of children with Down syndrome reported greater parental stress than fathers of typically developing children, but if fathers were more involved in child care and worked fewer hours, then they reported less parental stress. Mothers' stress also reciprocally affected fathers' reports of stress. Similarly, Upshur (1991) compared mothers' and fathers' reports of the perceived benefits of early intervention services and found differences in their reported experiences. Thus, evaluating the unique needs and experiences of mothers and fathers separately is important in order to gain an accurate picture of family functioning and adaptation.

Family Distress

Although aspects of family distress have been studied less frequently with families of young children with disabilities, family cohesiveness (closeness) has been found to be an important protective factor (Hauser-Cram, 1993; Hauser-Cram et al., 1999; Mink, Nihira, & Meyers, 1983). Parenting stress has been reported to be lower in families in which there are cohesive and supportive relationships with little conflict (Dyson, 1993). Furthermore, cohesive and harmonious family functioning has been observed to predict greater acquisition of new skills in children (Frey, Fewell, & Vadasy, 1989). Hauser-Cram (1993) observed that children with Down syndrome from families with higher levels of cohesiveness had better cognitive and social outcomes.

Families of young children with disabilities, however, do not appear to have particular difficulty with family flexibility and cohesion. Whitehead et al. (1990) reported that family flexibility and closeness in families of children in their early intervention program were similar to published norms. Similarly, Dyson (1993) found that parents of children with disabilities (primarily mental retardation and physical impairments) did not differ from parents of children without disabilities in terms of family functioning. Crowley and Taylor (1994) found that mothers and fathers of children in early intervention did not differ on their perceptions of flexibility and closeness in their families. Furthermore, family functioning has been observed to be relatively stable through infancy and the preschool years (Dyson, 1993).

Marital Distress

Marital stress has been shown to be an important predictor of parenting stress (Britner et al., 2003; Trute & Hiebert-Murphy, 2002), especially for mothers. The research on whether marital relationships are adversely affected by the presence of a child with a disability presents contradictory findings (Fisman & Wolf, 1991). Dunst, Trivette, and Deal (1988) reported a negative effect of disability on the marital relationship; Fisman and Wolf (1991) found that mothers of children with autism reported less marital intimacy than mothers of typically developing children; and Bristol, Schopler, and Gallagher (1988) found that mothers and fathers of children with developmental disabilities reported more marital adjustment problems than did parents of typically developing children. Trute and Hauch (1988), however, found that mothers of children with disabilities did not report marriage quality to be different than mothers of children without disabilities. Similarly, Donenberg and Baker (1993) and Koegel et al. (1983) found that mothers of children with autism reported similar levels of marital satisfaction to a normative group of happily married mothers. Rodrigue et al. (1992) also found no difference in marital satisfaction between fathers of children with autism or Down syndrome and fathers of typically developing children.

Emotional Distress

Some research indicates that mothers of children with developmental disabilities, particularly autism, have higher levels of depression and anxiety than parents of typically developing children (Hastings & Brown, 2002;

Miller, Gordon, Daniele, & Diller, 1992). Few parents, however, report extreme problems in their emotional well-being. In a series of studies, Wolf and colleagues (Dumas et al., 1991; Fisman & Wolf, 1991; Wolf et al., 1989) found that mothers of children with autism scored significantly higher than mothers of typically developing children on depressive symptoms, with mothers of children with Down syndrome in between and not significantly different from either. Fathers of children with autism and Down syndrome did not report significantly more depressive symptoms (Dumas et al., 1991; Wolf et al., 1989).

Other researchers have found little evidence of elevated depressive symptoms in parents of children with disabilities. Bristol et al. (1988) and Donenberg and Baker (1993) found that parents of children with autism did not report significantly greater depressive symptoms than a control group. Bristol et al. (1988) observed that 61% of mothers and 80% of fathers of children with developmental disabilities were *not* at risk for depression. Scott, Atkinson, Minton, and Bowman (1997) found that mothers and fathers of infants with Down syndrome reported only slightly higher depressive symptoms, and few individuals reported extreme depression; 80% of the parents showed no or minimal signs of depression. Similarly, Frey, Greenberg, et al. (1989) found that parents of young children with disabilities scored comparable to norms published for a group of adults in the general population. Gowen, Johnson-Martin, Goldman, and Applebaum (1989) found that feelings of depression were noted specifically when the child with disabilities was reported to be difficult to care for but that the mean level of reported depressive symptoms was not elevated for parents of children with disabilities compared with parents of typically developing children.

The research on parents of children at biological risk for disability indicates that mothers of high-risk preterm infants may have elevated symptoms of anxiety and depression up to 2 years following the birth of their child (Singer et al., 1999). But, by age 3, these mental health symptoms seem to return to normative levels (Singer et al., 1999).

Depression has been shown to differ between mothers and fathers, regardless of the presence of a child with a disability (e.g., Bristol et al., 1988; Scott et al., 1997). Consistently, mothers report more depressive symptoms than fathers (Bristol et al., 1988; Scott et al., 1997; Wolf et al., 1989). Krauss (1993), however, found no differences in depression between mothers and fathers of toddlers with disabilities.

Coping Skills

Some studies report altered coping strategies in parents of young children with disabilities, whereas other studies find no differences. Margalit, Raviv, and Ankonina (1992) found that parents of children with disabilities (e.g., learning disorders, mental retardation, emotional/behavior disorders) reported greater use of avoidant coping strategies than parents of children without disabilities. Sviberg (2002) reported that mothers and fathers of children with autism tended to use more nonconstructive coping strategies than parents of typically developing children.

Miller et al. (1992), however, found that mothers of children with disabilities did not differ in their types of coping strategies from mothers of young children without disabilities. Frey, Greenberg, et al. (1989) and Miller et al. (1992) did find that greater use of problem-focused coping was associated with less psychological distress for mothers of young children with disabilities. Bristol (1987) observed that active coping strategies were more important in predicting parenting quality than social support for mothers of children with autism.

Mothers of preterm infants do not appear to have altered coping patterns compared with mothers of full-term infants (Singer et al., 1999), although the research is limited. All parents in the Singer et al. study endorsed similarly positive feelings of accomplishment and mastery with respect to parenting.

Some fathers also appear to adjust the ways in which they cope with parenting when they have a child with a disability. Rodrigue et al. (1992) found that fathers of children with Down syndrome and fathers of children with autism used different coping strategies than fathers of typically developing children. Frey, Greenberg, et al. (1989) found that mothers and fathers differ in the ways they cope with the stresses associated with parenting a child with disabilities; cognitive coping strategies were more important to the adjustment of fathers than mothers.

Social Isolation

Several studies have indicated that having a child with a disability can erode social relationships. Social support is important because it has been shown to predict parental adjustment (Frey, Fewell, et al., 1989; Frey, Greenberg, et al., 1989; McDowell et al., 1995) and may buffer the negative effects of stress on depression for mothers (Fisman & Wolf, 1991; Gill & Harris, 1991). Sviberg (2002) found that parents of children with autism reported less social support than parents of typically developing children. Other researchers (e.g., Erickson & Upshur, 1989), however, found that mothers of infants *without* disabilities were less satisfied with their social support than mothers of infants with disabilities. The families of children with disabilities in this study, though, were all enrolled in early intervention services, which may have increased their perceptions of support.

Kazak and Wilcox (1984) also found that the social networks of families of children with spina bifida were smaller than a comparison group of families, but they noted that network size may not reflect quality of support received. Accordingly, using several different measures, Margalit et al. (1992) found that satisfaction with family network support was high for mothers of children with disabilities, although the actual size of the networks was small. Similarly, Frey, Fewell, et al. (1989) found that satisfaction with support, rather than amount of support, was important in predicting parental adjustment.

Research on parents of preterm infants has not found differing levels of social support from parents of full-term infants (Singer et al., 1996). In one study, greater informal social support was associated with decreased stress, whereas formal support was not related to reports of stress in mothers of preterm infants (Beckman & Pokorni, 1988). Furthermore, social support was relatively stable and did not change over the first 2 years of life.

Differences in social support between mothers and fathers also have been noted. Crowley and Taylor (1994) found that mothers reported receiving more support from parents, relatives, friends, parent groups, and professionals, whereas fathers reported receiving more spousal support.

Threats to Confident Parenting

Parental attitudes toward child rearing have been shown to play an important role with respect to child developmental outcomes (Sameroff & Seifer, 1983). Having a child who is difficult to care for can negatively influence feelings of parenting competence (Gowen et al., 1989). Gowen and colleagues, however, found that overall, parents of children with disabilities did not feel less competent as parents than parents of typically developing children. Similarly, Rodrigue et al. (1992) found that fathers of children with Down syndrome or autism reported similar feelings of parenting competence to fathers of typically developing children, and Singer et al. (1996) found that parents of preterm infants did not differ from parents of full-term infants in terms of feelings of parenting competence.

Parental feelings of self-efficacy also are related to parenting stress in both parents of typically developing children (Coleman & Karraker, 1998) and parents of children with disabilities (Frey, Greenberg, et al., 1989; Hastings & Brown, 2002). For example, Hastings and Brown found that self-efficacy mediated the relationship between child behavior problems and parental anxiety and depression for mothers of school-age children with autism. For fathers, self-efficacy moderated (rather than mediated) the relationship between child behavior problems and anxiety. Fathers with high self-efficacy reported less anxiety than those with low self-efficacy when their child had a high level of behavior problems.

Research shows that maternal perceptions of stigmatization (that individuals with disabilities are devalued and discriminated against) may increase maternal distress, specifically subjective caregiving burdens (Green, 2003). Researchers have argued that family members of individuals with disabilities experience "courtesy stigma" (Goffman, 1963); that is, stigma because of their affiliation with an individual with a disability, rather than because of any characteristics of their own (Gray, 1993). Dudley (1997) noted that individuals with developmental disabilities (and their families) in postindustrialized Western societies, such as the United States, likely experience stigma because of the value placed on intelligence, attractiveness, and self-sufficiency.

Gray (1993) suggested that parents of children with autism may experience greater stigma because of their child's typical physical appearance combined with the public's poor understanding of autism and intolerance of socially inappropriate behaviors. He contrasted this with Down syndrome, which is a relatively well-known disability with distinctive physical features. In his study, Gray found that mothers felt more stigmatized than fathers, which he interprets in light of the mother's greater tendency to take responsibility for the public presentation of the family and possible feelings of guilt regarding their child's disability. Gray also found that parents of younger children with autism or those who had more severe symptoms reported greater stigmatization. He noted that parents of younger children may have more recently experienced accusations of incompetent parenting for their child who has not yet received a diagnosis.

Because of fear of stigma, parents may actually avoid the services, such as support groups, that may provide them with support in their parenting role (Birenbaum, 1970). Moreover, families may avoid public encounters because this is where parental competence may be judged by others and is threatened, leading to further social isolation (Gray, 1993; Voysey, 1972).

POTENTIAL MEASURES AND RECOMMENDATIONS

Considerations and Issues in Conducting Family Assessment

Approaching families about assessment in a way that informs them about the importance of making sure all family members are able to contribute to the intervention process will allow them to see the assessment process in a positive way. When family members have been asked what type of assessment process they have appreciated most, they typically have stated that they prefer open-ended conversations and informal approaches to more structured interview procedures (Summers et al., 1990). Whitehead et al. (1990) recommended beginning with a general open-ended interview that helps families focus on their unique strengths and needs. Bailey and Henderson (1993) also recommended asking open-ended rather than closed-ended questions and asking about family routines so that the family members tell stories. Using open-ended questions functions as a means to build trust and rapport (Winton & Bailey, 1988).

Choices can also be provided to the family members as to whether they prefer written or conversational formats (Bailey & Henderson, 1993). In one study, mothers reported primarily preferring sharing information during an interpersonal discussion, whereas fathers reported that they would rather complete a written survey (Bailey & Simeonsson, 1984).

With respect to the actual assessment, Whitehead et al. (1990) recommended a menu-driven approach in which family members receive only the measures that are necessary and appropriate. Similarly, Slentz and Bricker (1992) recommended a brief needs assessment during the initial interview, followed by additional assessment as needed. Winton and Bailey (1988, 1990) suggested a moderate degree of structure whereby interviewers identify specific topics to cover during the interview and use a guide with questions and objectives but have choice in the order and manner in which questions are asked. This allows unanticipated areas of concern to emerge. Additional guidelines for competently assessing families in the early intervention context can be found in Bailey and Henderson (1993), Whitehead et al. (1990), and Winton and Bailey (1988, 1990).

Taken together, the consensus about family assessment appears to be a brief screening in the major areas of concern, prior to more in-depth assessment. Accordingly, the process recommended here is a two-tiered approach, beginning with open-ended (and some closed-ended) questions to elicit areas of concern for further assessment, followed by formal assessment in areas of concern, whereby additional information would be gathered to help the early intervention professional or team develop family goals or make appropriate referrals as necessary. Table 8.1 presents a set of recommended screening questions and standardized measures in the domains of focus in this chapter. A review of potential measures leading to these suggestions is provided next.

Measures of Parenting and Family Distress

By far, the most frequently used measure of parenting stress in the research literature is the PSI (Abidin, 1995), which was designed to assess parent perceptions of stress in the parent–child system. The PSI has been used in early intervention programs (Boyce et al., 1991; Innocenti et al., 1992; McDowell et al., 1995; Sexton, Burrell, Thompson, & Sharpton, 1992; Warfield, Krauss, Hauser-Cram, Upshur, & Shonkoff, 1999; Whitehead

Table 8.1. Recommended screening questions and follow-up assessment measures for assessing interpersonal and family distress and threats to confident parenting

Domain	Screening questions	Recommended standardized measures
Parenting Stress	1. Have you been feeling stressed lately, either in your parenting role or in your personal life?	Parenting Stress Index (PSI), full or short form (Abidin, 1995)
	2. How does your child adjust to his or her environment when things change? (PSI Adaptability domain)	
	3. What does your child do when you do something special for him or her? (PSI Reinforces domain)	
	4. Do you feel your child places excessive demands on you, given his or her skills and age? (PSI Demandingness domain)	
	5. Is your child different from how you expected a child of yours to be? (PSI Acceptability domain)	
	6. How emotionally close do you feel with your child? (PSI Attachment domain)	
	7. How much control do you feel you have with respect to how you do things at home? (PSI Role Restriction domain)	
Family Distress	1. What types of activities do you enjoy doing together as a family?	FACES III (Olson, 1986)
	2. Do you feel that communication between family members is clear and helpful?	
	3. Do you feel close as a family?	
	4. What happens in your family when there is a crisis?	
Marital Distress	1. Do you feel your spouse supports you in working with and caring for your child?	Dyadic Adjustment Scale (DAS; Spanier, 1976)
	2. Do you have any concerns about your marriage that you think would affect your child or family's treatment here?	Also covered in the PSI (Spouse domain)
Emotional Distress	1. How has your mood been lately?	Beck Depression Inventory-Short Form (BDI; Beck & Beck, 1972)
	2. Have you felt sad or discouraged at all?	
	3. Do you have any other mental health concerns you would like to share with me?	Brief Symptom Inventory (BSI; Derogatis, 1977)
		Also covered in the PSI (Depression domain)
Coping	1. How do you tend to cope with stressful situations?	Ways of Coping Scale (WCS; Folkman & Lazarus, 1988)

Social Support	1.	Who are the people who provide support to you when you need it?	Family Support Scale (FSS; Dunst et al., 1984)
	2.	In general, do you feel adequately supported, or do you wish others would do more?	Also covered in the PSI (Isolation domain)
Parenting Competence	1.	What do you do when your child does something wrong? (PSI)	Parenting Sense of Competence Scale (PSCS; Johnston & Mash, 1989)
	2.	How do you feel when your child does something wrong? (PSI)	
	3.	How do you feel about your competence as a parent? (Bailey & Henderson, 1993)	Also covered in the PSI (Competence domain)
	4.	How do other people seem to treat you when they are around you and your child?	

et al., 1990) and in studies of parents of young children with a variety of disabilities (Beckman, 1991; Button et al., 2001; Hanson & Hanline, 1990; Smith, Oliver, & Innocenti, 2001), parents of children with autism (Donenberg & Baker, 1993; Dumas et al., 1991; Fisman & Wolf, 1991; Freeman et al., 1991; Kasari & Sigman, 1997; Noh et al., 1989; Tobing & Glenwick, 2002), parents of children with Down syndrome (Fisman & Wolf, 1991; Noh et al., 1989; Roach et al., 1999), parents of toddlers with cerebral palsy (Britner et al., 2003), and parents of preterm infants (Halpern et al., 2001; Magill-Evans & Harrison, 2001; Singer et al., 1996, 1999). Furthermore, Reitman, Currier, and Stickle (2002) used the short form with primarily low-income African American mothers of children in Head Start and concluded that the use of the PSI with this population is appropriate and supported. Hutcheson and Black (1996) also examined the psychometric properties of the PSI with a sample of low-income African American mothers of infants and toddlers and determined that the PSI was a reliable and valid measure with this population.

Additional measures of parenting stress include the Family Impact Questionnaire (FIQ; Donenberg & Baker, 1993) and the Impact on Family Scale (IFS; Stein & Jessop, 2003), which were designed to assess the impact of a child with a disability on the family. The FIQ was first used by Donenberg and Baker with parents of preschool-age children with behavior problems or autism and later used by Baker et al. (2002) with parents of preschool-age children with developmental delays. The IFS is a similar scale that includes the areas of impact of financial and personal strains; disruption of family, social, and sibling relations; and coping abilities. The IFS was used by Singer et al. (1999) and Lee, Penner, and Cox (1991) with parents of preterm infants and by Rodrigue et al. (1992) with fathers of school-age children with Down syndrome or autism.

Measures that target family distress (i.e., lack of cohesion and adaptability) that have been used with parents of young children with disabilities include the Questionnaire on Resources and Stress (QRS; Holroyd, 1974), the Family Environment Scale (FES; Moos & Moos, 1981), the Family Adaptability and Cohesion Evaluation Scale (FACES III; Olson, 1986), the Family Functioning domain of the Family Needs Survey (Bailey & Simeonsson, 1988), and the Family Issues and Concerns portion of the Infant-Toddler and Family Instrument (ITFI; Apfel & Provence, 2001).

The QRS was developed to specifically assess the impact of a family member with a disability on other family members and has been used with parents of children in early intervention (Dunst, Jenkins, & Trivette, 1984; Sexton et al., 1992) and children with autism (Bristol, 1987; Factor et al., 1990; Freeman et al., 1991; Holroyd & McArthur, 1976; Koegel et al., 1992; Konstantareas, Homatidis, & Plowright, 1992), Down syndrome, and other forms of mental retardation (Dyson, 1993; Holroyd & McArthur, 1976; Konstantareas et al., 1992); preterm infants (Beckman & Pokorni, 1988); and children with a variety of disabilities, such as physical impairments, cerebral palsy, and other health conditions (Dyson, 1993; Frey, Fewell, et al., 1989; Frey, Greenberg, et al., 1989).

The FES (Moos & Moos, 1981) assesses family structure, functioning, and communication. The domain of Family Relationships has been most often used and includes subscales measuring cohesion, expressiveness, and conflict. The FES was used by Dyson (1993), Frey and colleagues (Frey, Fewell, et al., 1989; Frey, Greenberg, et al., 1989), and Margalit et al. (1992) with parents of young children with a variety of disabilities and by Bristol (1987) and Henderson and Vandenberg (1992) with mothers of children with autism.

The FACES III (Olson, 1986) also has been used fairly frequently in research and measures flexibility and emotional closeness among family members. Family members are asked for their current perception about their family and how they would ideally like their family to be. Several researchers of early intervention programs (Boyce et al., 1991; Crowley & Taylor, 1994; Hauser-Cram et al., 1999; Whitehead et al., 1990) have used the FACES III, and Rodrigue et al. (1992) used the measure in their research with fathers of school-age children with autism or Down syndrome.

The Family Needs Survey (Bailey & Simeonsson, 1988) primarily addresses family needs such as information, support, and financial needs but includes two domains that are relevant to the scope of this chapter: Support and Family Functioning. Family members have reported feeling comfortable sharing the information on this form (Bailey & Blasco, 1990).

The ITFI (Apfel & Provence, 2001) was developed to be used by a wide variety of family service providers, including those who do not have professional training or degrees, to help create a plan for family support and services. Resulting information includes a summary of the family's strengths and vulnerabilities, child characteristics and stressors, and how well caregivers are meeting their child's basic needs. The caregiver interview includes three parts: Home and Family Life (including family and friend support), Child Health and Safety, and Family Issues and Concerns. The third part of this measure includes questions about family discord and mental health concerns of the caregivers.

Finally, the Family Quality of Life Scale (Poston et al., 2003) has not been used with families of young children with disabilities but appears highly appropriate, although a few questions may not apply well to families of young children. Its suggested uses include research and outcome assessment, and the authors emphasized that the concept of family quality of life is consistent with a service delivery model that requires individualized and appropriate interventions and services for children with disabilities and their families. Ten domains are outlined in the measure: Family Interaction, Daily Life, Parenting, Financial Well-Being, Emotional Well-Being, Health, Physical Environment, Productivity, Social Well-Being, and Advocacy. Items are rated in terms of importance and satisfaction and grouped in the survey according to Family Interaction, Parenting, Health and Safety, Family Resources, and Support for Persons with Disabilities.

Recommendation

Questions that parallel the domains of the PSI are outlined in Table 8.1. If further assessment is warranted, then the PSI (either the full or short form) is recommended. There is good support for convergent and discriminate validity of the PSI (Bigras, LaFreniere, & Dumas, 1996). The short form (36 items) is regarded as an appropriate and less time-consuming form and correlates highly (.94) with the full PSI (Abidin, 1995). The short form, however, only results in three factor scores (Parental Distress, Parent–Child Dysfunctional Interaction, and Difficult Child subscales) as well as a Total Stress score. Therefore, it is less comprehensive and does not assess some other areas of interpersonal and family distress outlined in Table 8.1. Thus, practitioners might want to choose either the short form or the long form, depending on how many additional areas of interpersonal and family distress they anticipate assessing. The screening questions outlined on Table 8.1 within the parenting stress area have been derived to tap the domains on the PSI that are most relevant to the scope of this chapter.

The screening questions in Table 8.1 in the Family Distress domain are adapted from Dunst et al. (1988). Dunst et al. provided additional guidelines and suggestions for assessing family functioning style and social support for readers who desire more information. As a measure of whole family functioning, the FACES III is recommended. It is a simple and reliable measure and has been used considerably with this population.

Marital Distress

The two primary measures of marital adjustment are the Dyadic Adjustment Scale (DAS; Spanier, 1976) and the Marital Adjustment Scale (MAS; Locke & Wallace, 1959). The DAS was used by Trute and colleagues (Trute & Hauch, 1988; Trute & Hiebert-Murphy, 2002) with parents of children with developmental disabilities, by Magill-Evans and Harrison (2001) with parents of preterm infants, by Britner et al. (2003) with parents of toddlers with cerebral palsy, and by Donenberg and Baker (1993) and Koegel et al. (1992) with mothers of children with autism. Similarly, the MAS has been used with parents of school-age children with autism (Bristol, 1987; Rodrigue et al., 1992). Both of these measures are widely used in other areas of research as well.

Recommendation

Each parent should be asked, separately, to describe the support he or she receives from his or her spouse. Example questions are outlined in Table 8.1. If at least one parent expresses concern regarding spousal support, then the DAS could be administered separately to each parent to prompt further discussion, establish goals, or arrange for a referral. Although either the DAS or the MAS are appropriate, the DAS has been used more frequently with this population and thus appears to be more appropriate in the context of early intervention.

Emotional Distress

Measures used for emotional distress include a variety of screening measures for mental health concerns, such as the Brief Symptom Index (BSI; Derogatis, 1992; Derogatis & Nelisaratos, 1983) and the Symptoms Checklist 90–Revised (SCL-90–R; Derogatis, 1977). In addition, measures that focus on depression include the Center for Epidemiological Studies Depression Scales (CES-D; Radloff, 1977) and the Beck Depression Inventory (BDI; Beck & Beck, 1972).

The BSI (Derogatis, 1992; Derogatis & Nelisaratos, 1983) is a short form of the SCL-90–R (Derogatis, 1977). Both measure overall psychological distress and also provide scores in domains such as Depression, Somatic Complaints, Interpersonal Sensitivity, Anxiety, and Psychoticism. The BSI was used in research by Singer and colleagues (Singer et al., 1996, 1999) with parents of preterm infants, by Reitman et al. (2002) with mothers of children attending Head Start programs, and by Miller et al. (1992) with mothers of young children with a variety of disabilities. The SCL-90–R was used by Thompson et al. (1994) and Meyer et al. (1995) with mothers of infants who were preterm and had low birth weights.

The BDI was used in research with parents of children with a variety of developmental disabilities (Frey, Fewell, et al., 1989; Trute & Hauch, 1988; Trute & Hiebert-Murphy, 2002), with parents of infants and young children with Down syndrome (Donenberg & Baker, 1993; Dumas et al., 1991; Fisman & Wolf, 1991; Scott et al., 1997; Wolf et al., 1989), and with parents of children with autism (Donenberg & Baker, 1993; Dumas et al., 1991; Fisman & Wolf, 1991; Gill & Harris, 1991; Wolf et al., 1989). The CES-D has been used less frequently with parents of young children with disabilities. Gowen et al. (1989) used the measure with mothers of infants with various impairments as did Bristol in her research with parents of children with autism or communication disorders (Bristol, 1987; Bristol, Gallagher, & Holt, 1993; Bristol et al., 1988).

Recommendation

A thorough evaluation of emotional distress is typically not necessary, although the literature does suggest that parents may experience either transient or more lasting feelings of depression. Thus, a brief query of depressive symptoms and any other emotional concerns is suggested (see Table 8.1). If a parent describes feeling depressed, anxious, or has other worrisome emotional reactions, then the BDI or the BSI can be administered. The BDI has been used more frequently with this population than the CES-D and is the most prominent and frequently cited self-report measure of depression (Shaver & Brennan, 1991). Construct validity is reported to be excellent, and additional information on reliability and validity are provided by Shaver and Brennan (1991). Various forms are available for different populations, cultures, and age groups. The short form contains 13 items (Beck & Beck, 1972) and can be administered quickly. If further evaluation of mental health concerns appears advisable, then the BSI can be administered. The BSI correlates highly with the SCL-90–R (Derogatis, 1977).

Coping Strategies

Measures of coping include those developed for use in the general population as well as those developed for use with families in special circumstances. As a general measure of coping style, the Ways of Coping Scale (WCS; Folkman & Lazarus, 1988) has been used by Miller et al. (1992) with mothers of young children with a variety of disabilities, by Rodrigue et al. (1992) with fathers of school-age children with autism or Down syndrome, and by Sviberg (2002) with mothers and fathers of children and adolescents with autism.

McCubbin has developed several measures for use with families of children with disabilities and health concerns, including the Family Coping Strategies Scale (F-COPES; McCubbin & Patterson, 1981), which was used by Trute and Hiebert-Murphy (2002) with parents of children with developmental disabilities, and the Coping Health Inventory for Parents (CHIP; McCubbin & Patterson, 1981), used by Bristol (1987) with mothers of children with autism or communication impairments. The F-COPES focuses on problem-solving attitudes and behaviors of families and individual and intrafamilial coping strategies.

Recommendation

If the parent describes maladaptive responses such as avoiding the situation or becoming overemotional, then a more thorough evaluation of coping may be appropriate. The WCS has been used most consistently in this population and is a widely used and revered measure. It could be used to help parents learn about the ways they cope and whether those coping strategies seem to be working. Eight scales are derived that tap into the areas of confrontive coping, distancing, self-controlling, seeking social support, accepting responsibility, escape-avoidance, planful problem-solving, and positive reappraisal. Although the F-COPES is also appropriate with this population, it is focused specifically on coping in the context of having a family member with a disability, and a more broad-based coping measure may provide more rounded information. The F-COPES does have reported reliability, is easy to administer and score, and provides norms, but all of the items are positively keyed (Olson, 1986), which may press the respondent for socially desirable responses.

Social Support

Social support has been measured in a variety of ways, including tallying the number of people listed as being members of parents' social support network, as well as measures that ask respondents to rate members in their social support network along a number of dimensions such as availability and satisfaction. The measure most frequently used with this population is the Family Support Scale (FSS; Dunst et al., 1984), which has been used in research on early intervention programs (Boyce et al., 1991; Crowley & Taylor, 1994; Dunst et al., 1984; McDowell et al., 1995; Whitehead et al., 1990) and in research with parents of young children with disabilities such as Down syndrome, cerebral palsy, and other health conditions (Britner et al., 2003; Button et al., 2001; Erickson & Upshur, 1989; Frey, Fewell, et al., 1989; Frey, Greenberg, et al., 1989; Miller et al., 1992).

The other most frequently used social support measure is the Carolina Parent Social Support Scale (Bristol & DeVellis, 1981), which is similar to the FSS. It was used by Gowen et al. (1989) and Beckman and Pokorni (1988) with mothers of preterm infants, by Bristol (1987) with mothers of children with autism or communication impairments, and by Beckman (1991) with parents of young children with a variety of disabilities.

Recommendation

The research suggests that quality, rather than quantity, may be more important to parental well-being. If the parent lists few sources of support or expresses feelings of social isolation, then the FSS could be administered. Given its history of use with this population, the FSS is an appropriate follow-up standardized measure. The FSS includes 18 items that measure the availability of 18 possible sources of social support, as well as the family's judgment of the helpfulness of each type of support. Each item is rated on a 5-point Likert scale. The measure includes subscales assessing support in family, spouse, social groups, and professional service providers. Reliability and validity of the FSS have been established (Dunst et al., 1984).

Threats to Confident Parenting

Assessment of parents' feelings of competence in their roles and their experiences of stigma have been relatively infrequent. Potential measures to include in this domain are the Parenting Sense of Competence Scale (PSCS; Johnston & Mash, 1989) or the Parenting Attitudes Towards Childrearing Questionnaire (Easterbrooks & Goldberg, 1984). The PSCS was used by Rodrigue et al. (1992) with fathers of school-age children with Down syndrome or autism and by Donenberg and Baker (1993) with parents of children with autism or behavior problems. It assesses parents' feelings in two areas of parenting self-esteem: parenting efficacy (the perceived skills and knowledge about being a parent) and satisfaction (the value and comfort attached to the parenting role). Halpern and colleagues (Halpern et al., 2001) used the Parenting Attitudes Towards Childrearing Questionnaire with parents of very low birth weight infants. Finally, Green (2003) modified the Devaluation-Discrimination scale (Link, Cullen, & Streuning, 1989) for use with parents of children with a variety of disabilities. This measure sums items so that higher scores represent greater perceptions of stigma, but the measure was initially designed for people with mental disorders and may be less appropriate with families of children in early intervention.

Recommendation

Several questions are suggested in Table 8.1 to assess parental feelings of competency in the parenting role and perceptions of stigma that may affect their feelings of parenting competence. If parents appear to blame themselves or express other feelings of inadequacy in their parenting role, then the PSCS could be administered as a measure of parenting competence. Seventeen items are rated on a 5-point Likert scale. Alternately, if the full PSI is being administered, the Competency scale could be examined and there would likely be no need for an additional measure. Given the limited research on stigma in this population, no formal measure is recommended at this time, although professionals may be interested in examining the Devaluation-Discrimination scale.

CONCLUSION

This chapter has synthesized the research available on interpersonal and family distress and threats to confident parenting as relevant to families participating in early intervention. Through this review of what is known, the author identified measures that appear to be the best options for standardized assessment. These measures are not perfect, as they were not developed specifically for use in early intervention programs. But, they enjoy a history of research in the areas relevant to early intervention.

Prior to administering such standardized assessments, however, a set of open-ended and guiding questions were suggested to assist early intervention specialists in their systematic evaluation of parenting and family distress in families entering early intervention programs. The domains and questions outlined in Table 8.1 provide a framework so that early intervention professionals can be assured that they have covered the factors that research suggests are important for families of young children with disabilities or at biologic risk for disability. These screening questions are suggested as a starting point, to be followed by discussion with parents about their responses to determine whether additional assessment would be useful. These open-ended probes can be followed by more formal measures at a later visit addressing the areas of expressed family concerns. Further assessment should not be conducted unless the information is going to be used in a way that the family sees as useful, such as in setting a family goal or making an appropriate referral.

Throughout this chapter, differences in mothers' and fathers' responses to having a child with a disability or at risk for a disability are highlighted. Although the research has begun to include fathers' perspectives, the truth is that mothers are typically the primary respondent in the clinical setting. Theoretical and research considerations, however, suggest that both parents' views should be assessed, sometimes even separately, as in the example of marital satisfaction. Thus, this chapter serves as a call for early intervention specialists to make a greater effort to include fathers, as well as other family members such as siblings, in the early intervention assessment and treatment process.

Thus, this chapter provides a useful framework for professionals to organize their inquiry into assessing interpersonal and family distress and threats to confident parenting. By outlining the research within each of these domains, early intervention professionals will realize the importance of these variables in their work with the family. It is also helpful to remember that every interaction with the family is an assessment (Bailey & Henderson, 1993), and thus the process continues long after the initial assessment phase is viewed as complete.

REFERENCES

Abidin, R.R. (1995). *Parenting Stress Index* (3rd ed.). Odessa, FL: Psychological Assessment Resources.

Apfel, N.H., & Provence, S. (2001). *Manual for the Infant-Toddler and Family Instrument (ITFI)*. Baltimore: Paul H. Brookes Publishing Co.

Bailey, D.B., & Blasco, P.M. (1990). Parents' perspectives on a written survey of family needs. *Journal of Early Intervention, 14*, 196–203.

Bailey, D.B., & Henderson, L.W. (1993). Traditions in family assessment: Toward an inquiry-oriented, reflective model. In D.M. Bryant & M.A. Graham (Eds.), *Implementing early intervention: From research to effective practice*. (pp. 124–147). New York: Guilford Press.

Bailey, D.B., McWilliam, R.A., Darkes, L.A., Hebbeler, K., Simeonsson, R.J., Spiker, D., & Wagner, M. (1998). Family outcomes in early intervention: A framework for program evaluation and efficacy research. *Exceptional Children, 64*, 313–328.

Bailey, D.B., & Simeonsson, R.J. (1984). Critical issues underlying research and intervention with families of young handicapped children. *Journal of the Division for Early Childhood, 9*, 38–48.

Bailey, D.B., & Simeonsson, R.J. (1988). *Family assessment in early intervention*. New York: Merrill.

Baker, B.L., Blacher, J., Crnic, K.A., & Edelbrock, C. (2002). Behavior problems and parenting stress in families of three-year-old children with and without developmental delays. *American Journal on Mental Retardation, 107*, 433–444.

Barnard, K.E., Morisset, C.E., & Spieker, S. (1993). Preventive interventions: Enhancing parent-infant relationships. In C.H. Zeanah, Jr. (Ed.), *Handbook of infant mental health* (pp. 386–401). New York: Guilford Press.

Beck, A.T., & Beck, R.W. (December, 1972). Screening depressed patients in family practice. A rapid technique. *Postgraduate Medicine, 52*, 81–85.

Beckman, P. (1991). Comparison of mothers' and fathers' perceptions of the effect of young children with and without disabilities. *American Journal on Mental Retardation, 95*, 585–595.

Beckman, P.J., & Bristol, M.M. (1991). Issues in developing the IFSP: A framework for establishing family outcomes. *Topics in Early Childhood Special Education, 11,* 19–31.

Beckman, P.J., & Pokorni, J.L. (1988). A longitudinal study of families of preterm infants: Changes in stress and support over the first two years. *The Journal of Special Education, 22,* 55–65.

Bigras, M., LaFreniere, P.J., & Dumas, J.E. (1996). Discriminant validity of the parent and child scales of the Parenting Stress Index. *Early Education and Development, 7,* 167–178.

Birenbaum, A. (1970). On managing a courtesy stigma. *Journal of Health & Social Behavior, 11,* 196–206.

Boyce, G.C., Behl, D., Mortensen, L., & Akers, J. (1991). Child characteristics, family demographics and family processes: Their effects on the stress experienced by families of children with disabilities. *Counseling Psychology Quarterly, 4,* 273–288.

Bristol, M.M. (1987). Mothers of children with autism or communication disorders: Successful adaptation and the double ABCX model. *Journal of Autism and Developmental Disorders, 17,* 469–486.

Bristol, M.M., & DeVellis, R. (1981). *The Definition Scale: Parental attributions about their special child.* Unpublished instrument. Chapel Hill: University of North Carolina.

Bristol, M.M. (1987). Mothers of children with autism or communication disorders: Successful adaptation and the double ABCX model. *Journal of Autism and Developmental Disorders, 17,* 469–486.

Bristol, M.M., Gallagher, J.J., & Holt, K.D. (1993). Maternal depressive symptoms in autism: Response to psychoeducational intervention. *Rehabilitation Psychology, 38,* 3–10.

Bristol, M.M., Schopler, E., & Gallagher, J.J. (1988). Mothers and fathers of young developmentally disabled and nondisabled boys: Adaptation and spousal support. *Developmental Psychology, 24,* 441–451.

Britner, P.A., Morog, M.D., Pianta, R.C., & Marvin, R.S. (2003). Stress and coping: A comparison of self-report measures of functioning in families of young children with cerebral palsy or no medical diagnosis. *Journal of Child and Family Studies, 12,* 335–348.

Button, S., Pianta, R.C., & Marvin, R.S. (2001). Partner support and maternal stress in families raising young children with cerebral palsy. *Journal of Developmental and Physical Disabilities, 13,* 61–81.

Coleman, P.K., & Karraker, K.H. (1998). Self-efficacy and parenting quality: Findings and future applications. *Developmental Review, 18,* 47–85.

Crnic, K.A., Greenberg, M.T., & Slough, N.M. (1986). Early stress and social support influences on mothers' and high-risk infants' functioning in late infancy. *Infant Mental Health Journal, 7,* 19–33.

Crowley, S.L., & Taylor, M.J. (1994). Mothers' and fathers' perceptions of family functioning in families having children with disabilities. *Early Education and Development, 5,* 213–225.

Derogatis, L.R. (1977). *SCL-90: Administration, scoring, & procedures manual for the revised version.* Baltimore: Clinical Psychometric Research.

Derogatis, L.R. (1992). *The Brief Symptom Inventory manual.* Baltimore: Clinical Psychometric Research.

Derogatis, L.R., & Nelisaratos, N. (1983). The Brief Symptom Inventory: An introductory report. *Psychological Medicine, 13,* 595–605.

Donenberg, G., & Baker, B.L. (1993). The impact of young children with externalizing behaviors on their families. *Journal of Abnormal Child Psychology, 21,* 179–198.

Dudley, J.R. (1997). *Confronting the stigma in their lives: Helping people with a mental retardation label.* Springfield, IL: Charles C Thomas.

Dumas, J.E., Wolf, L.C., Fisman, S.N., & Culligan, A. (1991). Parenting stress, child behavior problems, and dysphoria in parents of children with autism, Down syndrome, behavior disorders, and normal development. *Exceptionality, 2,* 97–110.

Dunst, C.J., Jenkins, V., & Trivette, C.M. (1984). The Family Support Scales: Reliability and validity. *Wellness Perspectives, 1,* 45–52.

Dunst, C.J., Trivette, C.M., & Deal, A.G. (1988). *Enabling and empowering families: Principles and guidelines for practice.* Cambridge, MA: Brookline Books.

Dyson, L.L. (1993). Response to the presence of a child with disabilities: Parental stress and family functioning over time. *American Journal on Mental Retardation, 98,* 207–218.

Easterbrooks, M.A., & Goldberg, W.A. (1984). Toddler development in the family: Impact of father involvement and parenting characteristics. *Child Development, 55,* 740–752.

Erickson, M., & Upshur, C.C. (1989). Caretaking burden and social support: Comparison of mothers of infants with and without disabilities. *American Journal on Mental Retardation, 94,* 250–258.

Factor, D.C., Perry, A., & Freeman, N. (1990). Brief report: Stress, social support, and respite care use in families with autistic children. *Journal of Autism and Developmental Disorders, 20,* 139–146.

Fisman, S., & Wolf, L. (1991). The handicapped child: Psychological effects of parental, marital, and sibling relationships. *Psychiatric Clinics of North America, 14,* 199–217.

Folkman, S., & Lazarus, R.S. (1988). *Manual for the Ways of Coping Questionnaire: Research edition.* Palo Alto, CA: Consulting Psychologists Press.

Freeman, N.L., Perry, A., & Factor, D.C. (1991). Child behaviours as stressors: Replicating and extending the use of the CARS as a measure of stress: A research note. *Journal of Child Psychology and Psychiatry, 32,* 1025–1030.

Frey, K.S., Fewell, R.R., & Vadasy, P.F. (1989). Parental adjustment and changes in child outcomes among families of young handicapped children. *Topics in Early Childhood Special Education, 8,* 38–57.

Frey, K.S., Greenberg, M.T., & Fewell, R.R. (1989). Stress and coping among parents of handicapped children: A multidimensional approach. *American Journal on Mental Retardation, 94,* 240–249.

Friedrich, W.N., Greenberg, M.T., & Crnic, K. (1983). A short-form of the Questionnaire on Resources and Stress. *American Journal of Mental Deficiency, 88,* 41–48.

Gill, M.J., & Harris, S.L. (1991). Hardiness and social support as predictors of psychological discomfort in mothers of children with autism. *Journal of Autism and Developmental Disorders, 21,* 407–416.

Goffman, E. (1963). *Stigma: Notes on the management of spoiled identity.* Upper Saddle River, NJ: Prentice Hall.

Gowen, J.W., Johnson-Martin, N., Goldman, B.D., & Appelbaum, M. (1989). Feelings of depression and parenting competence of mothers of handicapped and nonhandicapped infants: A longitudinal study. *American Journal on Mental Retardation, 94*, 259–271.

Gray, D.E. (1993). Perceptions of stigma: The parents of autistic children. *Sociology of Health and Illness, 15*, 102–120.

Green, S. (2003). "What do you mean 'What's wrong with her?' ": Stigma and the lives of families of children with disabilities. *Social Science and Medicine, 57*, 1361–1374.

Guralnick, M.J. (Ed.). (2000). *Interdisciplinary clinical assessment of young children with developmental disabilities.* Baltimore: Paul H. Brookes Publishing Co.

Guralnick, M.J. (2001). A developmental systems model for early intervention. *Infants and Young Children, 14*, 1–18.

Halpern, L.F., Brand, K.L., & Malone, A.F. (2001). Parenting stress in mothers of very-low-birth-weight (VLBW) and full-term infants: A function of infant behavioral characteristics and child-rearing attitudes. *Journal of Pediatric Psychology, 26*, 93–104.

Halpern, L.F., & MacLean, W.E., Jr. (1997). "Hey mom, look at me!" *Infant Behavior and Development, 20*, 515–529.

Hanson, M.J., & Hanline, M.F. (1990). Parenting a child with a disability: A longitudinal study of parental stress and adaptation. *Journal of Early Intervention, 14*, 234–248.

Hastings, R.P., & Brown, T. (2002). Behavior problems of children with autism, parental self-efficacy, and mental health. *American Journal on Mental Retardation, 107*, 222–232.

Hauser-Cram, P. (1993). Mastery motivation in three-year-old children with Down syndrome. In D.J. Messer (Ed.), *Mastery motivation: Children's investigation, persistence, and development* (pp. 230–250). London: Routledge.

Hauser-Cram, P., Warfield, M.E., Shonkoff, J.P., Krauss, M.W., Upshur, C.C., & Sayer, A. (1999). Family influences on adaptive development in young children with Down syndrome. *Child Development, 70*, 979–989.

Henderson, D., & Vandenberg, B. (1992). Factors influencing adjustment in the families of autistic children. *Psychological Reports, 71*, 167–171.

Holroyd, J. (1974). The Questionnaire on Resources and Stress: An instrument to measure family response to a handicapped family member. *Journal of Community Psychology, 2*, 92–94.

Holroyd, J., & McArthur, D. (1976). Mental retardation and stress on the parents: A contrast between Down's syndrome and childhood autism. *American Journal of Mental Deficiency, 80*, 431–436.

Hughes, M.A., & McCollum, J. (1994). Neonatal intensive care: Mothers' and fathers' perceptions of what is stressful. *Journal of Early Intervention, 18*, 258–268.

Hutcheson, J.J., & Black, M.M. (1996). Psychometric properties of the Parenting Stress Index in a sample of low-income African-American mothers of infants and toddlers. *Early Education and Development, 7*, 381–400.

Innocenti, M.S., Huh, K., & Boyce, G.C. (1992). Families of children with disabilities: Normative data and other considerations on parenting stress. *Topics in Early Childhood Special Education, 12*, 403–427.

Johnston, C., & Mash, E.J. (1989). A measure of parenting satisfaction and efficacy. *Journal of Clinical Child Psychology, 18*, 167–175.

Kasari, C., & Sigman, M. (1997). Linking parental perceptions to interactions in young children with autism. *Journal of Autism and Developmental Disorders, 27*, 39–57.

Kazak, A.E., & Wilcox, B.L. (1984). The structure and function of social support networks in families with handicapped children. *American Journal of Community Psychology, 12*, 645–661.

Koegel, R.L., Schreiman, L., Loos, L.M., Dirlich-Wilhelm, H., Dunlap, G., Robbins, F.R., & Plienis, A.J. (1992). Consistent stress profiles in mothers of children with autism. *Journal of Autism and Developmental Disorders, 22*, 205–216.

Koegel, R.L., Schreiman, L., O'Neill, R.E., & Burke, J.C. (1983). The personality and family-interaction characteristics of parents of autistic children. *Journal of Consulting and Clinical Psychology, 51*, 683–692.

Konstantareas, M.M., & Homatidis, S. (1989). Assessing child symptom severity and stress in parents of autistic children. *Journal of Child Psychology and Psychiatry and Allied Disciplines, 30*, 459–470.

Konstantareas, M.M., Homatidis, S., & Plowright, C.M.S. (1992). Assessing resources and stress in parents of severely dysfunctional children through the Clarke modification of Holroyd's Questionnaire on Resources and Stress. *Journal of Autism and Developmental Disorders, 22*, 217–234.

Krauss, M.W. (1993). Child-related and parenting stress: Similarities and differences between mothers and father of children with disabilities. *American Journal on Mental Retardation, 97*, 393–404.

Krauss, M.W. (2000). Family assessment within early intervention programs. In J.P. Shonkoff & S.J. Meisels (Eds.), *Handbook of early childhood intervention* (2nd ed., pp. 290–308). New York: Cambridge University Press.

Krauss, M.W., & Jacobs, F. (1990). Family assessment: Purposes and techniques. In S.J. Meisels & J.P. Shonkoff (Eds.), *Handbook of early childhood intervention* (pp. 303–325). Cambridge, UK: Cambridge University Press.

Lee, S.K., Penner, P.L., & Cox, M. (1991). Impact of very low birth weight infants on the family and its relationship to parental attitudes. *Pediatrics, 88*, 105–109.

Link, B.G., Cullen, F.T., & Streuning, E.L. (1989). A modified labeling theory approach to mental disorders: An empirical assessment. *American Sociological Review, 54*, 400–423.

Locke, H.J., & Wallace, K.M. (1959). Short marital-adjustment and prediction tests: Their reliability and validity. *Marriage and Family Living, 8*, 251–255.

Magill-Evans, J., & Harrison, M.J. (2001). Parent-child interactions, parenting stress, and developmental outcomes at 4 years. *Children's Health Care, 30*, 135–150.

Margalit, M., Raviv, A., & Ankonina, D.B. (1992). Coping and coherence among parents with disabled children. *Journal of Clinical Child Psychology, 21*, 202–209.

McCubbin, H.I., & Patterson, J.M. (1981). *Systematic assessment of family stress, resources, and coping: Tools for research, education and clinical intervention.* St. Paul, MN: Family Social Science.

McDowell, A.D., Saylor, C.F., Taylor, M.J., Boyce, G.C., & Stokes, S.J. (1995). Ethnicity and parenting stress change during early intervention. *Early Child Development and Care, 111*, 131–140.

Meyer, E.C., Coll, C.T.G., Seifer, R., Ramos, A., Kilis, E., & Oh, W. (1995). Psychological distress in mothers of preterm infants. *Developmental and Behavioral Pediatrics, 16*, 412–417.

Miller, A.C., Gordon, R.M., Daniele, R.J., & Diller, L. (1992). Stress, appraisal, and coping in mothers of disabled and nondisabled children. *Journal of Pediatric Psychology, 17*, 587–605.

Mink, I.T., Nihira, K., & Meyers, C.E. (1983). Taxonomy of family life styles: I. Homes with TMR children. *American Journal of Mental Deficiency, 87*, 484–497.

Moos, R.H., & Moos, B.S. (1981). *Family Environment Scale manual* (2nd ed.). Palo Alto, CA: Consulting Psychologists Press.

Mott, S.E., Fewell, R.F., Lewis, M., Meisels, S.J., Shonkoff, J.P., & Simeonsson, R.J. (1986). Methods for assessing child and family outcomes in early childhood special education programs: Some views from the field. *Topics in Early Childhood Special Education, 6*, 1–15.

Noh, S., Dumas, J.E., Wolf, L.C., & Fisman, S.N. (1989). Delineating sources of stress in parents of exceptional children. *Family Relations, 38*, 456–461.

Olson, D.H. (1986). Circumplex model VII: Validation studies and FACES III. *Family Process, 25*, 337–351.

Poston, D., Turnbull, A., Park, J., Mannan, H., Marquis, J., & Wang, M. (2003). Family Quality of Life: A qualitative inquiry. *Mental Retardation, 41*, 313–328.

Radloff, L. (1977). The CES-D scale: A self-report depression scale for research in the general population. *Applied Psychological Measurement, 1*, 385–401.

Reitman, D., Currier, R.O., & Stickle, T.R. (2002). A critical examination of the Parenting Stress Index-Short Form (PSI-SF) in a Head Start population. *Journal of Clinical Child and Adolescent Psychology, 31*, 384–392.

Roach, M.A., Orsmond, G.I., & Barratt, M.S. (1999). Mothers and fathers of children with Down syndrome: Parental stress and involvement in childcare. *American Journal on Mental Retardation, 104*, 422–436.

Rodrigue, J.R., Morgan, S.B., & Geffken, G.R. (1992). Psychosocial adaptation of fathers of children with autism, Down syndrome, and normal development. *Journal of Autism and Developmental Disorders, 22*, 249–263.

Sameroff, A.J., & Seifer, R. (1983). Familial risk and child competence. *Child Development, 54*, 1254–1268.

Scott, B.S., Atkinson, L., Minton, H.L., & Bowman, T. (1997). Psychological distress of parents of infants with Down syndrome. *American Journal on Mental Retardation, 102*, 161–171.

Sexton, D., Burrell, B., Thompson, B., & Sharpton, W.R. (1992). Measuring stress in families of children with disabilities. *Early Education and Development, 3*, 60–66.

Shaver, P.R., & Brennan, K.A. (1991). Measures of depression and loneliness. In J.P. Robinson & P.R. Shaver (Eds.), *Measures of personality and social psychological attitudes* (pp. 195–289). San Diego: Academic Press.

Singer, L.T., Davillier, M., Bruening, P., Hawkins, S., & Yamashita, T.S. (1996). Social support, psychological distress, and parenting strains in mothers of very low birth weight infants. *Family Relations, 45*, 343–350.

Singer, L.T., Salvator, A., Guo, S., Collin, M., Lilien, L., & Baley, J. (1999). Maternal psychological distress and parenting stress after the birth of a very low-birth-weight infant. *Journal of the American Medical Association, 281*, 799–805.

Slentz, K.L., & Bricker, D. (1992). Family-guided assessment for IFSP development: Jumping off the family assessment bandwagon. *Journal of Early Intervention, 16*, 11–19.

Smith, T.B., Oliver, M.N.I., & Innocenti, M.S. (2001). Parenting stress in families of children with disabilities. *American Journal of Orthopsychiatry, 71*, 257–261.

Spanier, G.B. (1976). Measuring dyadic adjustment: New scales for assessing the quality of marriage and similar dyads. *Journal of Marriage and the Family, 38*, 15–28.

Stein, R.E.K., & Jessop, D.J. (2003). The Impact on Family Scale revisited: Further psychometric data. *Journal of Developmental and Behavioral Pediatrics, 24*, 9–16.

Summers, J.A., Dell'Oliver, C., Turnbull, A.P., Benson, H.A., Santelli, E., Campbell, M., & Siegel-Causey, E. (1990). Examining the Individualized Family Service Plan process: What are family and practitioner preferences? *Topics in Early Childhood Special Education, 10*, 78–99.

Sviberg, B. (2002). Family system and coping behaviors. *Autism, 6*, 397–409.

Thompson, R.J., Goldstein, R.F., Oehler, J.M., Gustafson, K.E., Catlett, A.T., & Brazy, J.E. (1994). Developmental outcome of very low birth weight infants as a function of biological risk and psychosocial risk. *Developmental and Behavioral Pediatrics, 15*, 232–238.

Tobing, L.E., & Glenwick, D.S. (2002). Relation of the Childhood Autism Rating Scale-Parent version to diagnosis, stress, and age. *Research in Developmental Disabilities, 23*, 211–223.

Trause, M.A., & Kramer, L.I. (1983). The effects of premature birth on parents and their relationships. *Developmental Medicine and Child Neurology, 25*, 459–465.

Trute, B., & Hauch, C. (1988). Building on family strength: A study of families with positive adjustment to the birth of a developmentally disabled child. *Journal of Marital and Family Therapy, 13*, 185–193.

Trute, B., & Hiebert-Murphy, D. (2002). Family adjustment to childhood developmental disability: A measure of parent appraisal of family impacts. *Journal of Pediatric Psychology, 27*, 271–280.

Upshur, C.C. (1991). Mothers' and fathers' ratings of the benefits of early intervention services. *Journal of Early Intervention, 15*, 345–357.

Voysey, M. (1972). *A constant burden.* London: Routledge & Kegan Paul.

Warfield, M.E., Krauss, M.W., Hauser-Cram, P., Upshur, C.C., & Shonkoff, J.P. (1999). Adaptation during early childhood among mothers of children with disabilities. *Journal of Developmental and Behavioral Pediatrics, 20*, 9–16.

Whitehead, L.C., Deiner, P.L., & Toccafondi, S. (1990). Family assessment: Parent and professional evaluation. *Topics in Early Childhood Special Education, 10*, 63–77.

Winton, P.J., & Bailey, D.B. (1988). The family-focused interview: A collaborative mechanism for family assessment and goal-setting. *Journal of the Division for Early Childhood, 12*, 195–207.

Winton, P.J., & Bailey, D.B. (1990). Early intervention training related to family interviewing. *Topics in Early Childhood Special Education, 10*, 50–62.

Wolf, L.C., Noh, S., Fisman, S.N., & Speechley, M. (1989). Brief report: Psychological effects of parenting stress on parents of autistic children. *Journal of Autism and Developmental Disorders, 19*, 157–166.

CHAPTER 9

ASSESSING THE RESOURCE NEEDS OF FAMILIES IN THE CONTEXT OF EARLY INTERVENTION

R.A. McWILLIAM

Henry Miller wrote, "Life is constantly providing us with new funds, new resources, even when we are reduced to immobility. In life's ledger there is no such thing as frozen assets" (1956, p. 33). As soon as families are enrolled in early intervention, someone needs to figure out what resources families need in order to accomplish their priorities. This chapter discusses families' resource needs and provides a specific method for determining the needs.

Guralnick (1997, 1998) has proposed a model of factors influencing children's developmental outcomes and applied that model to the design on early intervention systems (the Developmental Systems Model; Guralnick, 2001). These outcomes are most proximally affected by family patterns, which in turn are affected by family characteristics and potential stressors to these family patterns created by the child's disability or biological risk. Those stressors are information needs, interpersonal and family distress, resource needs, and confidence threats. Although these stressors to family patterns of interaction cannot easily be separated, this chapter focuses on resource needs.

RESOURCE NEEDS

Resources covers much territory and has been used in early intervention to include the assets families have (Dunst, 2001; Part C of the Individuals with Disabilities Education Act [IDEA] Amendments of 1997 [PL 105-17]); material support, such as financial assistance and equipment (McWilliam & Scott, 2001); and potential places, activities, and settings in which intervention can occur (Trivette, Dunst, & Deal, 1997). The importance of the definition of resources is revealed by the widespread description of early intervention as a set of *services*, which is too narrow. A *resource*-based approach is preferred (Trivette et al., 1997) because it can encompass but go beyond services, especially to include community activities, places, and events (Schwartz & Rodriguez, 2001). Outside of the United States, this approach has been tried at the community level: One Portuguese city explicitly designed community-based early intervention to use existing community resources, along with health care, education, and social services (Boavida, Espe-Sherwindt, & Borges, 2000). Approaching early intervention with a focus on resources entails a comprehensive set of professional activities.

Professionals' and families' focusing on resource assessment and intervention has had direct and indirect consequences for families. For example, one of the rationales for this approach in social work is that obtaining resources might be a vehicle for establishing a positive relationship with the family (Atkins-Burnett & Allen-Meares, 2000). Therefore, resources are both an end and a means.

Resources discussed here are heavily concentrated on *external* resources compared with intra-individual characteristics that would be considered *internal* resources. Internal resources are, however, important, as seen in research on out-of-home placement in which the extent of external resource use was found to be related to plans to maintain the child at home until age 21, over and above child-related stressors and family resources (Cole & Meyer, 1989). Yet families with high levels of internal resources were more apt to report plans for keeping the child at home indefinitely. Another internal resource is parents' locus of control. In a study of family-centered early intervention programs, families' indications that they had control over services, resources, and supports were considered a positive outcome (Trivette, Dunst, & Hamby, 1996). Judge (1997) found that professionals' appropriate help-giving practices were associated with families feeling in control; therefore, assessing resource needs appropriately requires a process that addresses both external and internal resource needs.

FAMILY NEEDS

Families need emotional support, material support, and informational support. *Emotional support* from early intervention providers consists of behaviors and attitudes such as being positive with and about children and parents, being responsive, showing interest in the whole family, being friendly, and being sensitive (McWilliam, Tocci, & Harbin, 1998). In a study of multicultural infants and toddlers who were deaf and hard of hearing, one of the most helpful resources for the families was "service with heart" (Wu, 2002, p. 42).

Material support consists of access to financial resources, equipment, and other objects that help families achieve their tasks (McWilliam & Scott, 2001). One potential material support need of families is related to employment. In a British study of parenting and employment decisions of parents with a preschool child with a disability, a disproportionate number of mothers were employed only part time, compared with mothers of children with typically developing children (Cuskelly, Pulman, & Hayes, 1998). The mothers of children with disabilities reported that the medical needs of the child were the reason for their employment situation. If a family needs material support, then it is significant because it is likely to have an impact on their ability to carry out interventions (Maslow, 1943).

Informational support is the third type of support or resource that families are likely to need. They often need information about their child's disability, resources about services, typical child development, and what to do with the child (McWilliam & Scott, 2001). Informational support is the crux of early intervention and is what home-based therapy and special instruction should consist of (McWilliam, in press). Early intervention programs have been found to provide higher levels of family services related to informational support (i.e., child information, family instructional activities, systems engagement) compared with material support (i.e., personal and resource assistance; Mahoney & Filer, 1996).

When considering families' needs, it might be worth exploring fathers' needs individually. In a British survey of 189 fathers of children with developmental disabilities, the fathers' top priorities were informational support, specifically information about their child, and materials support, specifically available resources (Hadadian & Merbler, 1995). American fathers have reported, however, that they prefer activities that are not separate from the rest of the family (Turbiville & Marquis, 2001). Therefore, families tend to need various types of support—emotional, material, and informational. The last two are commonly considered "resources."

ROUTINES-BASED ASSESSMENT

A practical approach to assessing families' resource needs is a routines-based assessment, which is an exploration into the daily functioning needs of families and children, organized by times of the day and frequently occurring events. This section defines *routines* and presents the conceptual framework for this kind of assessment. The central feature of the assessment is explained, and implications for intervention planning and service delivery are discussed.

Definition of Routines

Routines are defined as the events and activities of family life that occur with some regularity. They are not established times of the day, although, within one family, they often happen in a predictable order (e.g., waking up is followed by a diaper change, which is followed by breakfast). Some routines are daily and others less frequent. For example, going to preschool 3 days per week, going to church weekly, going to a doctor monthly, and so forth all can be considered routines. Sometimes families discuss family interactions that have become rituals (see Schuck & Bucy, 1997), so they would be included. Typically, however, routines are commonplace activities or events.

Conceptual Framework

Four traditions in early intervention come together to form the conceptual framework for this method of assessing needs. First, the use of routines or niches as an organizing framework for child and family functioning has been useful for assessment and intervention (Bernheimer & Keogh, 1995; Weisner, Bausano, & Kornfein, 1983). Second, a support paradigm has been used to explain variation in early intervention outcomes (Bronfenbrenner, 1979; Cohen & Wills, 1985; Dunst, 1985) and to systematize home visiting practices (McBride & Peterson, 1994). Third, a functional concept of child behavior, rather than a test-domain concept, has been articulated in a routines-based approach to intervention planning (McWilliam, 1992). The functional categories of behavior are engagement, independence, and social relationships. Fourth, quality of life has been identified as a worthy family and child goal of early intervention (Mitchell, 1993). This is indicated, in this framework, as satisfaction with routines.

Within the context of routines, support enhances child functioning in that 1) emotional support provides encouragement; 2) material support provides the necessary resources both for children to be able to do things independently (e.g., equipment) and for families to be able to meet basic needs (e.g., financial resources); and 3) informational support leads to intervention. In turn, if the child is functioning through engagement, independence, and social relationships, then the family's quality of life is likely to be enhanced. Children will participate, do things on their own, get along well with others, and be able to communicate. Family satisfaction with routines is proposed as an indicator of the family's quality of life. Not only does support have an impact on quality of life when mediated by child functioning but also it is theorized to have a direct effect. Thus, the extent to which families receive emotional, material, and informational support is considered to have an impact on families' satisfaction with routines. Eventually, these direct and mediating effects need to be tested empirically. Theoretically, however, this is the conceptual framework for the routines-based approach to assessment of resources.

Routines-Based Interview

One proven way to determine families' past and current resources is to interview them (Winton & Bailey, 1988; Wu, 2002). The routines-based interview (RBI; see Figure 9.1) process described here was published previously in a book on family-centered intervention planning (McWilliam, 1992). Since then, hundreds of practitioners have been trained, and the RBI has been institutionalized in a number of states (e.g., Colorado, Nevada, and New Mexico have incorporated it into their Part C system). The RBI requires preparation, which includes making decisions about settings and people. The interview itself concludes with the family's making decisions about intervention.

Preparation

Giving families an opportunity to prepare is respectful. For the initial development of an intervention plan (i.e., individualized family service plan [IFSP] or individualized education program [IEP]), the interviewer typically will have basic demographic information, assessment results, and the family's main concerns, which are usually discussed during the intake process. If a plan is being developed for a child already in an intervention program, then the interviewer might have had contact with the child and family if he or she is a member of the child's intervention team.

The family is asked to consider what goes on during different routines, how the child manages, and whether the family would like to change anything about the routines. The interviewer can devise a simple form for families to write out their routines and any changes they would like to make (see McWilliam, 1992; only available through http://www.Vanderbilt ChildDevelopment.us).

Options for Settings and People

The interview can take place anywhere. For children in birth to 3 programs, it often will be appropriate for the interview to occur in the home; for older children, it might take place where other administrative and assessment activities take place, such as in an office, conference room, or empty classroom.

Who should be present at the interview? Inform the family about how the RBI will be conducted so that they can decide whom they would like to participate. Minimally, one parent (the primary caregiver) needs to

Routines-Based Interview (RBI)
Report Form

Directions:

This form is designed to be used to report the findings from the McWilliam model of conducting a routines-based interview. A second person (e.g., someone assisting the lead interviewer) can use the form to summarize the discussion during the interview, or it can be filled out at the end of the interview.

1. Complete the information below.
2. For each routine, write a short phrase defining the routine (e.g., waking up, breakfast, hanging out, circle, snack, centers).
3. Write brief descriptions about the child's engagement in the Engagement box (e.g., participates with breakfast routine, bangs spoon on the high chair, pays attention to the teacher, names songs when asked, often leaves circle before it has ended).
4. If the interview revealed no information about one of the three domains, circle No information in that domain for that routine.
5. Write brief descriptions about the child's independence in the Independence box (e.g., feeds herself with a spoon, drinks from a cup but spills a lot, sings all of the songs with the group but needs prompting to speak loudly enough).
6. Write brief descriptions about the child's communication and social competence in the Social Relationships box (e.g., looks parent in the eye when pointing to things in the kitchen, pays attention to the teacher at circle but can't stand touching other children).

Child's Name
Date of birth
Who is being interviewed
Interviewer
Date of interview

Routine		No information
Engagement		No information
Independence		No information
Social Relationships		No information

Home: Satisfaction with routine (circle one)	*Classroom:* Fit of routine and child (circle one)
1. Not at all satisfied	1. Poor goodness of fit
2.	2.
3. Satisfied	3. Average goodness of fit
4.	4.
5. Very satisfied	5. Excellent goodness of fit

Domains addressed (circle all that apply):

   Physical   Cognitive   Communication   Social or emotional   Adaptive

Routine		No information
Engagement		No information
Independence		No information
Social Relationships		No information

Home: Satisfaction with routine (circle one)	*Classroom:* Fit of routine and child (circle one)
6. Not at all satisfied	6. Poor goodness of fit
7.	7.
8. Satisfied	8. Average goodness of fit
9.	9.
10. Very satisfied	10. Excellent goodness of fit

Domains addressed (circle all that apply):

   Physical   Cognitive   Communication   Social or emotional   Adaptive

Figure 9.1   Routines-Based Interview (RBI) Report Form. (McWilliam, R.A. [1992]. *Family-centered intervention planning: A routines-based approach.* Tucson, AZ: Communication Skill Builders. Reprinted by permission.)

be present; the family itself can decide how many other family members should participate. Families also should have the choice of anyone else they would like. They should know, however, that the discussion would be centered around everyday routines, so that might have some bearing on whom they would like to participate.

When Does the Routines-Based Interview Take Place?

The RBI typically occurs just before the completion of the IFSP or IEP. The following process is what typically occurs in infant-toddler services. It begins with a referral and an intake contact. At the intake contact, among other activities, the professionals ask the family about their major concerns and seek permission to evaluate the child. The person doing the intake will find out whether the child is referred because he or she has an established condition or is suspected of having a delay. The RBI plays a slightly different role with each of these methods of entry to the system. When the child has an established condition, a multidisciplinary evaluation is required but *testing* is not. In fact, many states and local programs still test children as their method of conducting a multidisciplinary evaluation. In many states, the RBI can be used as the method of assessment because, if conducted right, it produces descriptive information about all five domains required in IDEA '97: cognitive development, physical development, communication development, social or emotional development, and adaptive development. If two or more professionals were involved in the RBI, then it can be considered a multidisciplinary evaluation. The term *multidisciplinary* should not be confused with a philosophy and method of service delivery (e.g., interdisciplinary, transdisciplinary). It simply refers to the number of professionals. Technically, a multidisciplinary evaluation, as defined in the law, could be conducted in a transdisciplinary fashion (see Linder, 1990).

When the child is suspected of having a delay, testing is necessary in most states. Professionals conduct a norm- or criterion-referenced test to determine whether the child's scores meet eligibility criteria. Results of the testing determine whether the child can proceed in receiving services. The RBI can still be used to gather a description of the child's functioning because completing test items clearly does not indicate functional needs for intervention. There is still a need for a process to identify meaningful outcomes for children who are eligible for services based on their tested delay.

The RBI can be the single point at which functional needs are assessed and families make their outcome choices. With eligibility no longer in question, it is worth the investment of professional time to conduct a lengthy interview to obtain a description of the child's current level of functioning; determine the family's choice of outcomes; and determine their concerns, priorities, and resources (described later in the chapter).

Family Preparation Form

The Family Preparation Form (McWilliam, 1992) was designed to help parents sort through relevant information before the RBI. The rationale was that professionals, who know how the process works, go to IFSP or IEP meetings with the confidence that they have enough information (e.g., assessment reports, an intake report, medical records) to participate meaningfully. Families, however, might not know how to prepare to participate meaningfully, especially if it is their first planning meeting. The Family Preparation Form provides them with an opportunity to list their major concerns and identify their routines. For each routine, the family is asked to consider what everyone in the family does at that time, what the child does, and whether they are satisfied with the routine.

Who Should Conduct the Interview?

Conducting an RBI is ostensibly simple but operationally complex. The skillful interviewer keeps the tone conversational, is positive and affirming, asks relevant questions, and above all is friendly and informal. The structure will be described in the next section, but the appropriate people for interviewing the family need to be considered early on. Programs can consider the following options: 1) everyone who works with families; 2) professionals who have an affinity for this type of clinical activity; 3) members of an evaluation team; 4) dedicated service coordinators; 5) members of a certain profession, such as social workers or psychologists; 6) those who are most likely to be providing ongoing services to the family; 7) those who have something in common with the family, such as neighbors or those who speak the same language; and 8) those who have expertise in the disability of the child.

In 20 years experience with the RBI, none of the options has proven to be the sole answer, and many programs have chosen various combinations of the options. The three characteristics most important for successful use of the RBI are 1) conveying acceptance with no implication of passing judgment; 2) being informal and friendly; and 3) knowing child development, family functioning, and disabilities. It is unfair to lump three large bodies of knowledge into one characteristic (Item 3), but this is information that professionals can learn.

How Many People Are Involved?

Often, two people are involved in the RBI. If it is used for the multidisciplinary evaluation, then representatives of two disciplines or professions must be involved. When professionals are first using the RBI, it often is helpful to have a second person to ask additional questions, take notes, or handle interruptions. Ultimately, programs need to make a decision based on how many people are legally required and what is expedient for the program.

The Interview

The interview has two distinct stages. First, the interviewer explains why he or she will be asking about child and family functioning during everyday routines: to get relevant information to be able to make wise recommendations and to provide a framework for the family to decide what they want to work on. Second, the interviewer begins with the beginning of the respondent's day and asks five questions for each routine: 1) What does everyone do at this time? 2) How does the child participate (engagement)? 3) What is the child's independence like? 4) What are the child's social relationships like? 5) How satisfied is the parent with this routine? This is the bulk of the interview and can last more than an hour.

The RBI form (available from http://www.IndividualizingInclusion .us) provides a structure for the interviewer or his or her partner to document the family member's answers. It is used to write short descriptions of the child's engagement, independence, and social relationships during each routine. It also provides a scale from 1 to 5 for the interviewer to ask the family how satisfied they are with the routine. Finally, the form lists the five domains on IFSPs, so the team can see what routines provide descriptive information for documenting the child's current level of functioning in those domains. The form serves both as a prompt and a place for documentation but should never be used in a structured-interview manner.

The interviewer reads aloud notes of particular concerns and strengths that arose during the discussion of routines and asks the respondents to decide which of them to work on. This usually generates six to ten "outcomes" or goals. The interviewer asks the family to put the outcomes in order of priority and tells the family what will happen next. Although the steps are important, they are not part of the actual interview. The interviewer alerts the family that the next steps will involve the decisions to be made by the team, resources needed to accomplish goals, and strategies or actions needed to accomplish goals. Other team members also will provide suggestions once early intervention services are begun.

Implications for Intervention Planning and Service Delivery

Weekly home visits have become a default method for delivering early intervention services, and some experts believe that it is appropriate (see Blackman, 1996). The RBI tends to have the following effects on IFSP or IEP development and the provision of services: 1) the family talks more than professionals do during the meeting; 2) the intervention plan has more specific outcomes than those developed without an RBI; 3) the outcomes are clearly functional for the child and family; 4) the plan is worded in ordinary language with a minimum or lack of jargon; 5) outcomes are not overtly discipline specific, which implies that a generalist or a primary service provider from any discipline could provide support to the family *on the whole plan;* and 6) fewer discrete ongoing service providers are needed; a "consultative," "transdisciplinary," or "primary service provider" model is more feasible. In general, the RBI has important effects on the delivery of early intervention beyond simply asking families what their days are like.

EXAMPLES OF RESOURCE NEEDS DETECTED THROUGH A ROUTINES-BASED INTERVIEW

Two examples of using the RBI to detect families' needs, desires, and priorities are provided next. They show how the process can be applied to assess needs associated with maintaining family routines.

HIGH-COMPLEXITY EXAMPLE

Valerie lived in a homeless shelter while waiting for her boyfriend to get out of jail. She had three children, all with different fathers. Two of the children were enrolled simultaneously in the early intervention system after a referral by the social services agency. Valerie believed she had little choice but to participate in the program because she thought she would lose custody of her children.

I (Interviewer):   Valerie, if it's okay by you, I'd like to ask you about your day—how the day goes, what you and the children do, and so on. That way, I'll be able to make sensible suggestions that fit into your daily life. You don't have to tell me anything you don't want to. Is that okay?

V (Valerie):   Whatever.

I: When you're done talking about your day, I'll ask you what you want the intervention team to help you with. That way, it will be your decision. Is that okay?

V: Okay.

I: Before we get started, what are your main worries, if any, about Jonquil's development?

V: I don't have any. She's doing great.

I: I know she was tested a week ago. Did that raise any red flags for you?

V: Not really. I can't really remember what they said—I think they said she's behind.

I: Behind in what areas?

V: I don't rightly remember.

I: When they told you those results, were you worried about anything?

V: Not really.

I: Did they say she was different from other children in the way she moves or what her muscle tone is like?

V: They said she's behind in moving because she has several (sic) palsy.

I: They actually mentioned cerebral palsy to you.

V: Yes.

I: Okay, so right now you don't have any major worries about how Jonquil is developing but you have heard she's behind in her moving.

V: Right.

I: All right. As we talk about your daily routines, we'll see whether that makes a difference. So, how does your day start?

V: With one of these young-uns screaming to get out of bed.

I: So you're awakened by kids screaming to get up?

V: Right.

I: Do you have your own room for the four of you at the shelter?

V: Yes, but it don't have no door on it.

I: So the kids' screaming could bother other people.

V: I don't care about them. It's me it bothers.

I: Right. Now, is Jonquil one of the ones screaming?

V: Sometimes.

I: When she's upset, can you tell what it is she wants?

V: Like I said, she wants to get out of the crib. She has to share it with the next one.

The interview proceeded through some early morning routines. The following discussion was about breakfast.

I: What happens next?

V: We get our breakfast.

I: How does that work?

V: Most people go through a line, but we get to sit down at a table and someone brings us our breakfast.

I: Jonquil doesn't sit in a chair, does she?

V: No, of course not. I have her on my lap.

I: Does she sit there okay?

V: No, she gets all stiff and about slides off on to the floor.

I: She gets stiff where?

V: Like her back gets stiff and her legs go straight.

I: Why is that, do you know?

V: 'Cause of the several (sic) palsy.

I: How has cerebral palsy been explained to you?

V: They tried explaining it to me, but I couldn't take it all in.

I: So do you still need some information about cerebral palsy?

V: I reckon.

Later, Valerie said she tried to get out of the shelter for as much of the day as possible.

I: You don't like it in there?

V: Them people are mean.

I: Do you mean the other people staying there or the people who work there?

V: The other ones that stay there.

I: So, in the mornings, after breakfast, you go out with the kids. How does that work for you?

V: It's a pain, dragging three young-uns all over the place.

I: How do you manage it? Do you have a stroller or anything?

V: I've got a halfway broken down old stroller, but that only takes one of the kids. Sometimes I squish two in but then it doesn't roll so good.

I: It sounds like you're always with the kids, in the shelter, out of the shelter, everywhere. Right?

V: Yes. What else am I going to do with them?

I: Do you ever get any time away from them?

V: Sometimes one of the other women will watch them for me while I have a cigarette outside the back door, but I can't be gone for too long.

I: Are you ever able to go out without them?

V: Are you kidding?

I: If we were able to find a way, would that be helpful to you?

V: That would be great, but I don't trust anyone with my kids, so I don't think it's realistic.

As the interview went on, the interviewer had more questions about the housing situation.

I: How long will you stay at the shelter?

V: I don't know. When my boyfriend gets out, we want to find some place to live.

I: Do you have any leads?

V: I don't and I doubt he does. I don't know what we're going to do.

Toward the end of the interview, a new twist came into the story.

I: After the kids are asleep, then what do you do?

V: Hang out with some of the other people.

I: Where? I guess you can't in your room, really.

V: We stand outside, where we can smoke. I can hear the kids or someone comes to tell me if they can hear them.

I: Is this a good time of the day for you, when you get to hang out with some adults?

V: Not really. They drink. They're not supposed to, but they do.

I: And you don't drink?

V: I'm an alcoholic, so I try not to touch the stuff.

I: Are you getting any help with that, or are you doing it on your own?

V: I'm pretty much on my own. My social worker checks up on me but that's mostly to warn me that if I get drunk she'll take away my kids.

I: She actually says that?

V: Pretty much.

I: So do they have programs at the shelter or help you get into an AA group or anything?

V: No, not really.

I: Is that something that might be helpful to you?

V: Yeah, especially if I have to hang around a bunch of drunks.

I: Well, with any luck, you won't have to after a while, but I'll mark it down as an area you might be interested in. Okay?

At the end of the RBI, Valerie chose the following among her priorities:

1. Babysitting

2. Information on cerebral palsy

3. Housing

4. Staying sober

APPARENTLY LOW-COMPLEXITY EXAMPLE

Todd and Marissa were interviewed to help them determine intervention priorities for their 4-year-old son who has significant functional limitations related to his autism. These excerpts came from the latter part of the interview.

I (Interviewer): What happens when Todd comes home?

T (Todd): I used to roughhouse with Preston (age 4) and Rachael (age 2) until I got a hernia. Now, I still play with them but in a quieter way.

I (to T): Is that going well?

T: Okay, I guess.

I: What do you do as a group? You had mentioned that you aren't as active right now as you used to be.

T: I still play with them a lot.

I: So, when you get home, do you take the children right away and do something with them?

Todd and Marissa look at each other.

M (Marissa): Well, eventually.

T: Sometimes it takes a while to unload my stuff and such, but the kids come running up to me right away.

I: Okay, so you have the kids, Todd. Marissa, is this finally a break for you, or is it that you now have a third person to attend to?

M: It's that I have a third person.

I: Okay, I'll come back to that. Todd, what do you and the kids do?

T: We go out in the yard, maybe read a book if the weather is not good. But they like to do more active stuff than that. So, it's kind of hard not being able to rough around with them.

I: So, right now it's hard to keep them entertained as well as you used to because you're recovering from the hernia operation?

T: Right.

I: When you play with the kids at this time, what does Preston do? How does he play with you?

T: He'll jump on my back or push me and then run away, wanting me to chase him.

I: Does he use any words when he does this?

T: Not really. Even though he knows how to say a lot of words, when we ask him, "What's this?" he doesn't use them when he's playing with me like this.

I: Okay, and what about his movements? Is he coordinated, clumsy? How would you describe the way he moves around?

T: He's completely coordinated—at least as much as I'd expect out of a 4-year-old.

I: So he jumps around, pushes, runs, and so on?

T: Right.

I: When you do something with Rachael, what does he do?

T: Sometimes, he acts jealous, like he pushes me or pulls on my shirt or my hand. Sometimes, he just skips off and wanders around the room ignoring us.

I: Does he ever join the two of you?

T: Sometimes it's all three of us rolling around on the floor.

I: Okay, so he will join in at times, perhaps when he's sort of tricked by the momentum of the game?

T: Yeah, that's it. If I try to get him involved in some activity with Rachael, like reading a book, he'll resist.

Because this gave a reasonable picture of Preston's engagement, independence, and social relationships during this play time with Dad, the interviewer moved to the satisfaction question.

I: Is this a good time of day for you?

T: Yeah, it's pretty good. The kids are usually in a good mood.

I: But it's just *pretty* good.

T: It's not exactly like it's my down time after I've been going hard at work. It's not like I can walk in the door and put my feet up.

I: That would be nice, wouldn't it?

T: Yeah, but totally unrealistic.

I: Marissa, what are you doing while Todd's playing with the children?

M: He's not always playing with the children. Sometimes he needs to tell me something about his day at work, or I need to tell him something about my day or the kids. We try to wait until later, but....

I: Okay, so sometimes you two have some catching up to do. What are the kids doing in the meantime?

M: Going nuts, trying to play with Daddy. It's not like we can really have good conversations at this time.

I: So, it sounds as though this transition time, when Todd comes home in the evening, isn't exactly satisfactory for either one of you.

M: True.

T: True.

The first discussion about Preston at mealtime came up when discussing dinner because during the week Preston eats both breakfast and lunch at preschool.

I: How does dinnertime go?

M: We eat in shifts—the kids first and us later.

I: Is that how you want to do it or is that just the only way you've been able to manage to do it?

M: That's the only way we really can do it, so it's how we want to do it.

I: Fair enough. So Preston and Rachael eat first. Do they eat the same thing at the same time?

M: Well, there's a problem there. Preston will eat only Italian—spaghetti, lasagna, ravioli.

I: Can you get him to eat anything with those—any vegetables, for example?

M: Not really. Sometimes, if I actually cook those things instead of getting them out of a can, I can cook in some vegetables, but that isn't too often.

I: You said this was a problem. What is the problem?

M: It's just not enough variety.

I: Do you mean for his diet or because it's just weird not to eat a greater variety?

T: It's weird.

M: Yeah, weird.

I: What happens when you do try to get him to eat something else?

M: He refuses and he will get mad and throw a fit if we try to get pushy.

T: But we don't want meals to become a battleground.

I: Very wise, but I am correct, am I not, that you would like Preston to take in a greater variety of foods?

M: That's correct.

I: Who have you talked to about this so far?

M: No one. I've talked to the teachers about it. At school, he'll eat cereal in the morning and nothing but Italian at lunch. I have to send cans for them to keep there.

I: What about the pediatrician or any other health care person? Anyone talked to you about this?

M: No.

I: A nutritionist?

M: No, do you think he needs to see one?

I: I don't know yet. Let's see what we end up with as your plan of action and then see what professionals would be necessary to get that plan accomplished.

M: Okay.

Later in the interview, the interviewer asked what happens after the children go to bed.

M: That's when he and I have our dinner.

I: So is this a time where you can catch up with each other if you couldn't talk earlier?

M: Right.

I: Do you have other opportunities for just the two of you?

M: No, not really.

I: Is that okay?

M: I would like to be able to go out.

I: Do you mean by yourself or with Todd?

M: Both.

I: Todd, how about you?

T: I have my time to myself at work, but I'd like to be able to go out with Marissa.

I: What about her going out by herself, without the kids?

T: That would be good for her. She doesn't have any time to herself.

I: So, why doesn't this happen right now?

M: There's no one to keep the kids—well, Preston. Todd's father and step-mother are in town, but they're no good with Preston.

I: Do you know any babysitters, neighborhood kids, or whomever?

M: No, none who would understand how to deal with Preston.

I: Has anyone mentioned respite to you?

M: No, what's that?

During the recapitulation of the interview, the interviewer included reminders that Marissa and Todd had talked about the need for down time for one or both of them during the hours from hell, about their desire to know more about Preston's diet, and about their desires to go out. Other goals were established, but at the end of the RBI, Marissa and Todd chose the following among their priorities:

1. Parents will go out together without children.

2. Marissa will have 2 hours to herself every week.

3. Preston will eat greater variety of foods than Italian—and his parents will get information on nutrition.

4. Todd will have one down time after work per week, and Marissa will have one down time during the day per week.

CONCLUSION

Discovering a family's assets, including family routines, has become a critical part of the early intervention enterprise. Professionals have many ways to gain this information, ranging from informal conversations, to semi-structured or structured interviews, to questionnaires. This chapter provides a model for integrating the assessment of family routines into the overall assessment and intervention planning process. Even though legislation has been used, principally through the IFSP, to prompt professionals to determine families' concerns, priorities, and resources, too often this information is simply assessed and listed, with little connection to the rest of the early intervention activities. By assessing resources in the context of daily routines, the information is likely to be used. Indeed, the RBI always ends with a list of family-directed outcomes or goals. The connection from resource assessment to intervention is tangible. The resources that families need to accomplish their priorities by maintaining or enhancing their routines can be directly derived from the interview. Most important, the resources are being applied to the attainment of meaningful goals.

The first scenario gives a somewhat extreme example of the importance of assessing resource needs in the family's context. It also shows the importance of using a personal approach to the assessment. If Valerie had been handed a form to complete, then it is possible she would not have completed it or would not have been truthful. Her list of resource needs is all about information, but three of the needs—babysitting, housing, and staying sober—are likely to require considerable follow-through.

The second scenario shows 1) how important it is to establish a relationship with the family while assessing resources related to routines, 2) how specific services are not identified until after outcomes are decided (i.e., the nutritionist), and 3) the blending of parent and child needs into the single intervention plan. An important note about the difference between resources and services needs to be made. When Preston's family asked about a nutritionist, the interviewer correctly deferred the recommendation until the outcomes were decided. If a family goes into the assessment process with a view to obtain a specific service (e.g., physical therapy) but without a clear idea of why, then the team should gently refocus the discussion to the desired outcome (i.e., goal) first. Finally, the interview with Preston's family shows how an RBI can produce meaningful family outcomes. Early interventionists are effective in determining child-level outcomes but less so in determining family-level ones; this process can help balance the outcomes. This balance is important as soon as one understands the reciprocal relationship between family and child needs.

Assessing families' resource needs is, therefore, vital, not only because the resources might be important for the child's and family's development but also because the process of identifying the needs and implementing them can be the platform for a family-centered approach to early intervention. The more we help families with their resources and their routines, the more we help families in general.

REFERENCES

Atkins-Burnett, S., & Allen-Meares, P. (2000). Infants and toddlers with disabilities: Relationship-based approaches. *Social Work, 45*, 371–379.

Bernheimer, L.P., & Keogh, B.K. (1995). Weaving interventions into the fabric of everyday life: An approach to family assessment. *Topics in Early Childhood Special Education, 15*, 415–533.

Blackman, J.A. (1996). Social policy solutions to social problems. *Journal of Early Intervention, 20*, 296–297.

Boavida, J., Espe-Sherwindt, M., & Borges, L. (2000). Community-based early intervention: The Coimbra Project (Portugal). *Child: Care, Health and Development, 26*, 343–353.

Bronfenbrenner, U. (1979). *The ecology of human development: Experiments by nature and design.* Cambridge, MA: Harvard University Press.

Cohen, S., & Wills, T.A. (1985). Stress, social support, and the buffering hypothesis. *Psychological Bulletin, 98*, 310–357.

Cole, D.A., & Meyer, L.H. (1989). Impact of needs and resources on family plans to seek out-of-home placement. *American Journal on Mental Retardation, 93*, 380–387.

Cuskelly, M., Pulman, L., & Hayes, A. (1998). Parenting and employment decisions of parents with a preschool child with a disability. *Journal of Intellectual and Developmental Disability, 23*, 319–332.

Dunst, C.J. (1985). Rethinking early intervention. *Analysis and Intervention in Developmental Disabilities, 5*, 165–201.

Dunst, C.J. (2001). Participation in community learning activities. In M.J. Guralnick (Ed.), *Early childhood inclusion: Focus on change* (pp. 307–336). Baltimore: Paul H. Brookes Publishing Co.

Guralnick, M.J. (1997). Second-generation research in the field of early intervention. In M.J. Guralnick (Ed.), *The effectiveness of early intervention* (pp. 3–22). Baltimore: Paul H. Brookes Publishing Co.

Guralnick, M.J. (1998). The effectiveness of early intervention for vulnerable children: A developmental perspective. *American Journal on Mental Retardation, 102*, 319–345.

Guralnick, M.J. (2001). A developmental systems model for early intervention. *Infants and Young Children, 14*(2), 1–18.

Hadadian, A., & Merbler, J. (1995). Parents of infants and toddlers with special needs: Sharing views of desired services. *Infant Toddler Intervention, 5*, 141–152.

Individuals with Disabilities Education Act (IDEA) Amendments of 1997, PL 105-17, 20 U.S.C. §§ 1400 et seq.

Judge, S.L. (1997). Parental perceptions of help-giving practices and control appraisals in early intervention programs. *Topics in Early Childhood Special Education, 17,* 457–476.

Linder, T.W. (1990). *Transdisciplinary play-based assessment: A functional approach to working with young children.* Baltimore: Paul H. Brookes Publishing Co.

Mahoney, G., & Filer, J. (1996). How responsive is early intervention to the priorities and needs of families? *Topics in Early Childhood Special Education, 16,* 437–457.

Maslow, A.H. (1943). A theory of human motivation. *Psychological Review, 50,* 370–396.

McBride, S.L., & Peterson, C. (1994, December). *Home-based intervention: Who is doing what?* Paper presented at the National Center for Clinical Infant Programs conference, Dallas, TX.

McWilliam, R.A. (1992). *Family-centered intervention planning: A routines-based approach.* Tucson, AZ: Communication Skill Builders.

McWilliam, R.A. (in press). Home-based services. In M. Wolery, R.A. McWilliam, & D.B. Bailey, Jr., (Eds.), *Teaching infants and preschoolers with disabilities* (3rd ed.). Columbus, OH: Charles E. Merrill.

McWilliam, R.A., & Scott, S. (2001). A support approach to early intervention: A three-part framework. *Infants and Young Children, 13*(4), 55–66.

McWilliam, R.A., Tocci, L., & Harbin, G.L. (1998). Family-centered services: Service providers' discourse and behavior. *Topics in Early Childhood Special Education, 18,* 206–221.

Miller, H. (1956). *Quiet days in Clichy.* Berkeley, CA: Grove Press.

Mitchell, D. (1993). Quality of life for infants and toddlers. *Australia and New Zealand Journal of Developmental Disabilities, 18,* 229–234.

Schuck, L.A., & Bucy, J.E. (1997). Family rituals: Implications for early intervention. *Topics in Early Childhood Special Education, 17,* 477–493.

Schwartz, I.S., & Rodriguez, P.B. (2001). A few issues to consider: The who, what, and where of family support. *Journal of Early Intervention, 24,* 19–21.

Trivette, C.M, Dunst, C.J., & Deal, A. (1997). Resource-based early intervention practices. In S.K. Thurman, J.R. Cornwell, & S.R. Gottwald (Eds.), *The contexts of early intervention: Systems and settings* (pp. 73–92). Baltimore: Paul H. Brookes Publishing Co.

Trivette, C.M., Dunst, C.J., & Hamby, D.W. (1996). Factors associated with perceived control appraisals in a family-centered early intervention program. *Journal of Early Intervention, 20,* 165–178.

Turbiville, V.P., & Marquis, J.G. (2001). Father participation in early education programs. *Topics in Early Childhood Special Education, 21,* 223–231.

Weisner, T.S., Bausano, M., & Kornfein, M. (1983). Putting family ideas into practice: Pronaturalism in conventional and non-conventional California families. *Ethos, 11,* 278–304.

Winton, P.J., & Bailey, D.B. (1988). The family-focused interview: A collaborative mechanism for family assessment and goal-setting. *Journal of the Division for Early Childhood, 12,* 195–207.

Wu, C.L. (2002). Resource-based early intervention with multicultural deaf/hard of hearing infants, toddlers and their families. *Dissertation Abstracts International: Section B: The Sciences and Engineering, 62,* 42.

CHAPTER 10

ASSESSING FAMILY CHARACTERISTICS RELEVANT TO EARLY INTERVENTION

JEAN F. KELLY,
CATHRYN BOOTH-LAFORCE, AND SUSAN J. SPIEKER

INTRODUCTION

It has long been recognized that the family is the principal context in which child development takes place and that the development of children is not biologically fixed but is affected in large part by environment (Bronfenbrenner, 1986, 1992). Research accumulated since the 1980s shows that the extent of a family's well-being, including both psychosocial and economic factors, has important consequences for a child's social-emotional and cognitive growth (Hauser-Cram, Warfield, Shonkoff, & Krauss, 2001; National Research Council and Institute of Medicine, 2000). Guralnick (2001) pointed out that unprecedented numbers of families are confronting a vast array of risk factors that threaten family well-being. In order for early intervention to critically affect child outcomes, it is necessary to identify and address family characteristics that support or stress the family system.

Family support movements that began in the 1960s and have flourished since then recognize the wisdom of providing "services to families that empower and strengthen adults in their roles as parents, nurturers, and providers" (Weissbourd & Kagan, 1989, p. 21). Programs such as Part C of the Individuals with Disabilities Education Act of 1990 (PL 101-476) and its amendments, which serve young children with special needs, and Early Head Start, a program for low-income families, include goals to enhance the capacity of parents to perform their caregiving roles (U.S. House of Representatives Report 99-860; Early Head Start National Resource Center @ Zero to Three, 2003). Despite the clear mandate for supporting the family in the best interests of the child, there is no easy system for assessing and relieving family stressors that may interfere with family functioning. First, there is reluctance on the part of providers to intrude into areas of family life that providers feel are personal and beyond their ability to affect. Second, parents may be reluctant to reveal family characteristics that they feel are beyond the scope of the intervention program. Finally, pre- and postservice training efforts are just now starting to prepare providers to address these areas in appropriate and sensitive ways. This chapter addresses two primary questions relevant to these issues: What are the family characteristics that affect parenting and that providers need to assess in order to confidently support families, and how can providers learn about individual family characteristics in a sensitive way in order to plan effective intervention efforts tailored to the family's strengths and needs?

THEORETICAL CONSTRUCTS AS THE BACKGROUND FOR ASSESSING FAMILY CHARACTERISTICS

Before discussing specific family characteristics that mediate child development, it is important to examine the theoretical bases for including assessment of family characteristics in intervention programs. Several researchers have proposed complementary models for looking at determinants of effective parenting. Guralnick stated that, "In many ways, family characteristics frame the entire [intervention] process—we gain access to family strengths but also become aware of constraints that can have widespread effects on family patterns of interaction" (2001, p. 12). He proposed that child developmental outcomes are governed by three patterns of family interactions: the quality of parent–child transactions, family-orchestrated child experiences, and provisions for the child's health and safety. Guralnick went on to identify a set of family characteristics that can function as stressors and disrupt the three patterns of family interaction. Personal characteristics of parents, such as mental health, intellectual ability, and child-rearing attitudes; financial resources; social supports including the marital relationship, family/friend/community networks; and child temperament mediate patterns of family interaction, which in turn affect child development outcomes. He cautioned that the important question to keep in mind is "What information is needed to help maximize family patterns of interaction?" (p. 11). That is, how can we better understand the effects of stressors in order to attempt to strengthen a family's abilities to interact most effectively with their child, to orchestrate community experiences that will maximize their child's development, and to ensure that their child's health and safety are protected?

Belsky (1984) developed a model focused on factors affecting parental behavior and the means by which such factors affect caregiving, which in turn affects child outcomes. From his review of the literature, Belsky concluded that parenting is determined by multiple characteristics of the parent, the child, and social support systems. Although all three of these sets of characteristics are important, they are not equally influential in determining parenting. Personal history and personality shape parenting indirectly, by first influencing the broader context in which parent–child relationships exist (i.e., marital relationships, social networks, educational and work experience).

Belsky (1984) further stated that parental personality and psychological well-being are the most influential determinants in supporting good parenting and that social support is greater than the influence of child characteristics on parental functioning. He concluded that child risk characteristics are easier to overcome if either one of the other two determinants (parental characteristics and social support) is adequate. No particular attention is given to the importance of the family's financial resources.

McCubbin and Patterson revisited Hill's ABCX family crisis model (1949, 1958) and Burr's (1973) synthesis of family stress research and concluded "family outcomes following the impact of a stressor and a crisis are the byproduct of multiple factors in interaction with each other" (1983, p. 7). In McCubbin and Patterson's model, the following factors taken together influence the family's ability to prevent the stressor event from creating a crisis: the stressor event, the family's resources for dealing with the stressor, the definition the family makes of the situation, and the resulting stress. In looking at the resources the family has for meeting demands and needs, adaptive resources appear to be of two general types: existing resources and expanded family resources. Both of these types of resources seem relevant to our discussion of assessing family characteristics to identify relevant family support interventions. Existing resources are already part of the family's repertoire and minimize the effect of the stress and reduce the probability that the family will enter crisis. Examples of existing resources are the ability to engage in occupational activities; family resources of togetherness, shared values, and expressiveness; and community resources such as friendships and religious involvement. Expanded resources are those new resources strengthened or developed in response to the demands emerging out of the crisis situation. Examples of expanded resources include new personal development, new community resources, and increased involvement of extended family members. One of the most important resources for reducing the affect of a stressor is *social support*, defined as information that the family is cared for and loved, is esteemed and valued, and belongs to a network of mutual obligation and understanding (Cobb, 1976).

Pearlin, Mullan, Semple, and Skaff (1990) adapted the previous model to study the experiences of family caregivers of individuals with Alzheimer's disease. In their research, they found that caregiving stress is mediated by two primary characteristics: coping ability and social support. In their research, the mediators usually are called on to explain differences in outcomes for caregivers. That is, caregivers who have effective coping strategies or strong social support systems are more likely to be more successful in dealing with the stresses of caregiving situations than those who have ineffective coping and support systems.

Crnic, Friedrich, and Greenberg (1983) proposed a model to account for 1) the range of family adaptation involving the impact of perceived stress to having a child with mental retardation (considered a stressful life event) and 2) the family's coping resources and ecological environments as interactive systems that serve to mediate the family's response to the stressful event. They introduced their model with the position that the relationships and influences between children with mental retardation and their families are reciprocal and circular. Families are affected by the presence of their children, and the children are affected by their families' responses to them. There is some evidence that the satisfactory emotional development of children with mental retardation may be more dependent on the families' responses to them than to the disability itself (Bentovim, 1972).

In the previous model, the affect of the stressful event on the family is related to the family members' appraisal of the situation and the family's coping resources that include broad categories of health/energy/morale (includes physical and emotional well-being prior to and during the course of a stressful event), problem-solving skills, social networks, utilitarian resources (includes socioeconomic status and income), and general and specific beliefs (includes feelings of self-efficacy, greater internal locus of control, and belief in some higher purposes). The family's coping resources and functioning are mediated by the ecological systems within which they interact and are acted on. The use of this model accounts for individual variations in family adaptation, critical in designing early childhood intervention programs based on individual family strengths and needs.

The research described previously gives us important information about which characteristics to consider in planning appropriate and individualized intervention activities. In summary, in addition to looking at more fixed family characteristics, such as family socioeconomic status, it is important to consider additional psychosocial factors that mediate family and child outcomes, such as family emotional environment, coping skills, social support, and parenting attitudes toward child rearing.

RELATION BETWEEN FAMILY CHARACTERISTICS AND CHILD AND FAMILY OUTCOMES

In this section, we review the relation between child and family outcomes and the following family characteristics: depression, coping skills/problem solving, social support, parenting attitudes toward child rearing, and socioeconomic status. Our discussion touches on families with children who are typically developing, children with special needs, and children at risk due to environmental circumstances.

Depression

Numerous research studies have found an association between parental mental health issues—particularly in mothers who suffer from depression—and poorer child adjustment (Ehrle & Moore, 1999; Moore, Chalk, Scarpa, & Vandivere, 2002). Maternal depression is widespread with estimates that 12% of mothers who have recently given birth are affected (O'Hara, 1986) and approximately 8% of mothers are clinically depressed at any given time (Downey & Coyne, 1990; Weissman, Leaf, & Bruce, 1987). Because of the high prevalence of depression, it is important to consider how depression affects children, both short and long term.

Children of parents who are depressed are at increased risk for social, educational, behavioral, and vocational difficulties (Downey & Coyne, 1990). Familial risk is in part genetically transmitted, but other pathways also exist. The developing fetus is exposed to maternal neuroendocrine dysfunction associated with maternal depression during pregnancy (Kofman, 2002; Lundy et al., 1999). Similarly, the child is exposed to increased family conflict and distress associated with the presence of a parent who is depressed (Downey & Walker, 1992) and to disturbances in the affective, interactive, and cognitive capacities of the parent who is depressed (Lovejoy, Graczyk, O'Hare, & Neuman, 2000).

The results of Petterson and Albers (2001) research suggest that in some cases affluence buffers the negative effect of moderate maternal depression on child development outcomes, whereas children from impoverished families show poorer outcomes when mothers report moderate maternal depression. In another study, Lyons-Ruth, Connell, Grunebaum, and Botein (1990) examined the benefits of a home visiting program for 31 infants at high social risk (risk factors included poverty, maternal depression, and caregiving inadequacy). A significant interaction between the treatment group and depression suggested that infants of mothers who were depressed in the treatment group showed higher mental development than infants of mothers who were depressed in the nontreatment group. Infants from low socioeconomic status families whose mothers were not depressed showed the highest levels of mental development scores, which were comparable with national norms. In their discussion, the authors made the point that the infants at greatest risk were those who had a combination of low socioeconomic status, maternal depression, and other high risk factors and that low socioeconomic status alone was not necessarily related to poor outcomes.

Kobe and Hammer (1994) found the association between maternal depression and child depression also to be true for children with special needs. In a study of 29 children with developmental delays, the total score on the Children's Depression Inventory (Kovacs, 1992) was related to higher scores on the Parenting Stress Index (Abidin, 1983), especially the parent subdomains of maternal depression, sense of parenting competence, parent health, attachment, and relationship with spouse. Gowen, Johnson-Martin, Goldman, and Appelbaum (1989) studied 21 infants with special needs and 20 typically developing infants and examined how child characteristics (sociability, irritability, caregiving difficulty, and level of functioning) and social support measures were related to maternal reports of depression and parenting competence at multiple time points. At 11 months, greater child sociability, more helpful social supports, and more positive perceptions of family relations were related to lower levels of depression among mothers of infants with special needs. For typically developing infants, greater infant irritability was related to greater maternal depression, and more positive family relations and helpfulness of social supports were related to lower levels of maternal depression. In these studies, the mother was reporting both on her own symptoms as well as on the child's symptoms. To more reliably assess the family's and child's strengths, direct observations also are needed.

Coping Skills/Problem Solving

Another parent characteristic that affects a family's sense of well-being is a parent's style of coping or problem solving, and research suggests that a family's style of coping is a major factor in the relation between stress and outcomes. Depending on the type of coping strategy used and the availability of resources, ways of coping can be considered as risk or protective factors, and, further, they may lead to either resilience or vulnerability in the face of adverse events (Rutter & Garmezy, 1983). Lazarus and Folkman (1984) described a model for understanding stressful situations and how people cope with them. They suggested that coping is a result of the cognitive and behavioral efforts made to manage stress and discussed specific coping strategies that people use to manage stress. In problem-focused coping, active problem solving, seeking social support, and active efforts to alter the situation are used. In contrast, emotion-focused coping strategies include wishful thinking, denial, or avoidance. Research on the efficacy of various coping strategies suggests that problem-focused coping results in reduced distress (Aldwin & Revenson, 1987; Folkman, Lazarus, Dunkel-Schetter, DeLongis, & Gruen, 1986), whereas emotion-focused coping is positively related to depressed moods (Bolger, 1990; Folkman et al., 1986; Quinn, Fontana, & Reznikoff, 1987). Vitaliano, DeWolfe, Maiuro, Russo, and Katon (1990) discussed the importance of matching the appraisal of the event with the coping strategy. For example, when problem-focused coping is used in a situation appraised as changeable, lower depression levels are found. However, when emotion-focused coping is used in a situation judged to be changeable, increased depression levels are found.

The research examining stress related to parenting young children with disabilities illustrates Lazarus and Folkman's (1984) model. In their study of 132 children (69 with special needs and 63 typically developing) between birth and 7 years, Miller, Gordon, Daniele, and Diller (1992) found that emotion-focused coping (especially strategies related to self-control over emotions, escape-avoidance, and responsibility) was related to greater psychological distress for mothers of children with disabilities; and problem-focused coping (especially problem solving) was related to less psychological distress in the mothers, even after controlling for the type of stressor. Judge (1998), in a study with 69 parents of children with disabilities between birth and 5 years who were involved in early intervention, found that parental reports of ways of coping significantly predicted parents' reports of family strengths (commitment, confidence, challenge, and control) above and beyond family demographics. In particular, seeking social support as a way of coping uniquely predicted greater family strength, whereas coping strategies involving self-blame, bottled-up feelings, and wishful thinking were related to lower levels of perceived family strengths. Scorgie, Wilgosh, and McDonald (1998) examined 25 studies of stress and coping in families of children with a variety of disabling conditions and ages. They concluded that families that cope effectively reported higher family cohesion than families that demonstrate distress. The high-cohesion families also perceived themselves as capable of meeting family needs and engaged in creative problem solving in reaction to stress, and reported healthy marital relationships. Strong families showed acceptance of their child with disabilities, displayed realistic expectations of the child's abilities, and were committed to creating an environment that contributed to the growth of all family members. Finally, high-coping families were able to gain access to resources that ameliorated stress.

Social Support

The ability to depend on relationships for support is one of the most important buffers to stress in families. Several kinds of relationships in the social network affect stress: relationships with spouse/partner, family, friends, and community members.

The effects of marital conflict on parenting and child development are well documented. Cummings and Davies (2002) summarized the first generation research that has demonstrated increased probability for children's disorders associated with marital discord, including cognitive, social, academic, and psychobiological effects (Ellis & Garber, 2000; Fergusson & Horwood, 1998). In addition to having child effects, marital conflict negatively affects parenting (Cox, Paley, & Harter, 2001, Krishnakumar & Buehler, 2000) and sibling relationships (Dunn & Davies, 2001; Noller, Feeney, Sheehan, & Peterson, 2000). In addition, marital conflict has been related to the impact of divorce on children (Amato & Keith, 1991; Buchanan & Heiges, 2001), parental depression (Cummings & Davies, 1992), alcoholism (El-Sheikh & Cummings, 1998), and physical and sexual abuse (Appel & Holden, 1998; Howes, Cicchetti, Toth, & Rogosch, 2000). Cummings and Davies (2002) reviewed research that concentrates on a process-level understanding of these effects. They argued that the key to explaining the effects of marital conflict on children is an understanding of the processes underlying the relationship between marital conflict and child outcomes. In order to understand these processes, it is necessary to consider several levels of analysis that yield expanded perspectives, including perspectives on coping responses, coping strategies, and higher-order coping styles. For example, in examining children's coping responses, Grych and Fincham (1990) placed special emphasis on the effects of marital conflict on children's cognitive processes and the role of children's cognitive processes in affecting children's emotions and behaviors. Evidence supports the notion that self-blame may be especially elevated in girls and perceived that threat-to-self increased in boys, although gender differences are not entirely consistent across studies (Cummings, Davies, & Simpson, 1994; Grych, 1998). Furthermore, perceived threat-to-self and self-blame have been shown to act as mediators or moderators of the effects of marital conflict on children's internalizing disorders (Dadds, Atkinson, Turner, Blums, & Lendich, 1999; Kerig, 1998). This review illustrates the importance of exploring multiple pathways of effect associated with family characteristics. If we are to recognize and plan interventions related to family characteristics in an effort to improve outcomes for children, then it is important to more clearly understand the complexity of these processes.

Turning to a specific segment of the population, the research involving families of children with special needs also shows a relation between the marital relationship and parenting outcomes. In their study of children between the ages of 2 and 6, Bristol, Gallagher, and Schopler (1988) found that a spouse's expressive support was the best predictor of observations of parenting in the home for both mothers and fathers of boys with disabilities. In his study of 88 families with a child with a disability (birth to 8 years), Trute (1990) examined child characteristics, parental and family characteristics, and marital characteristics as predictors of family functions and found that dyadic cohesion and consensus in the marital relationship each made unique contributions to the prediction of family functions. His results indicated the importance of the marital system for families with young children with disabilities.

Current research points to the importance of the emotional climate in families as an important factor for child functioning. In their book *Meta-emotion: How Families Communicate Emotionally*, Gottman, Katz, and Hooven (1996) defined *meta-emotion* as an organized set of feelings and thoughts about one's own emotions and the emotions of one's children. They found that meta-emotion has been shown to inhibit parental negative affect; facilitate positive parenting; affect children's regulatory physiology and their capacity to regulate emotions; and influence a variety of children's behavioral, cognitive, and emotional responses. Parents who understand their own thoughts and feelings can "coach" their children by helping them understand and regulate their own emotions. Parents who use an "emotion coaching" parenting style show empathy and acceptance for their children's feelings, set appropriate limits for behavior, and teach problem-solving strategies for handling strong feelings. Children who are raised with an "emotion coaching" parenting style do better in school, are more self-confident, have fewer behavioral problems, get along better with friends and others, have fewer infections and illnesses, and can weather their parents' conflicts better.

In addition to family relationships, extended family, friends, and other community contacts are important parts of the social network. Cochran and Niegro (1995) examined the links between social network influences and parents in their caregiving roles and summarized research relating different social supports to parental behavior. For example, Crockenberg (1988) identified particular processes by which benefits of social support might be conveyed to parents. A provision of instrumental support such as babysitting, financial assistance, or child-rearing advice can reduce the number of stressful events. Second, emotional support from social contacts may serve as a buffer, preventing the parent from being adversely affected by a stressful event. Third, social supports may help parents construct active coping strategies that result in better child-rearing skills or other positive initiatives that benefit the child. Finally, drawing on the work of Crittenden (1985), emotional support may affirm a parent's own feelings as a person deserving of care and capable of caring for someone else. This encourages the individual's inclination to be nurturing to others.

Cochran and Niegro (1995) then discussed the constraints on parents' access to network membership and reviewed the evidence that network resources available to parents vary substantially depending on parents' educational experience, income, occupation, the number of parents in the household, race, and even the culture in which they live. Fischer (1982) was the first sociologist to provide empirical evidence for the relationships between dimensions of social class and network ties. In a cross section of 1,000 people representing diversity in education, occupation, economic situation, gender, and life-cycle characteristics, Fischer found that educational level had the most consistent effect on personal networks. Other things being equal, the more educational credentials respondents had, the more broad, deep, and rich the social network. Fischer also found that people with more income included more non-kin in their networks and were more likely to report adequate amounts of companionship and practical support than people with less income. He also found that children restricted the social involvement of their parents, especially of their mothers. Cochran and Niegro (1995) concluded their chapter with a recommendation that early intervention, early childhood, or family support programs should include network change as a possible outcome and encouraged evaluators to include measures of network-related consequences as part of their overall assessment strategy.

Dunst, Trivette, and Jodry (1997) reviewed the literature on social support in families of children with disabilities after the passage of the Education of the Handicapped Act Amendments of 1986 (PL 99-457). They suggested that informal support—from a partner, friends, kin, and other personal network members—is related to greater personal functioning of the parent, more positive perceptions of the child's behavior, better family functioning, more positive parenting behavior, and more positive and less negative child affect. They suggested a mediational model wherein social support has an indirect affect on child outcomes through a positive affect on the recipient's health and well-being, family functioning, and parent–child interactions.

Dunst, Trivette, and Deal (1988) broadly defined *intervention* as the provision of support (i.e., resources provided by others) by members of a family's informal and formal social network that either directly or indirectly influences child, parent, and family functioning. Considered this way, effective intervention should become part of the family's social support system that empowers and strengthens the family in its caregiving role, instead of merely the provision of a specific educational or therapeutic treatment. The point that Dunst et al. (1988) made has major implications for assessment and intervention practices. In order to become part of an empowering support system, providers need to establish a long-term relationship with the family based on trust, empathic and sensitive responses, and a mutual understanding of the family's strengths and needs. These aspects will be discussed later in this chapter.

Parenting Attitudes Toward Child Rearing

Holden and Buck (1995) provided a summary of some of the representative findings about parental child-rearing attitudes and their role in child development. For example, Easterbrooks and Goldberg (1984) discovered that maternal attitudes of strictness and paternal attitudes of aggravation with the child were related to less secure attachment in 20-month-old boys. Egeland and Farber (1984) also found an attitude-attachment link in which mothers of insecurely attached children were less likely to accept the emotional complexity of child rearing than were mothers of securely attached children. Deal, Halverson, and Wampler (1989) revealed positive effects for parents who share similar child-rearing attitudes. Spouses with high levels of agreement were characterized as having higher marital satisfaction, using more positive parenting skills, and generally having healthier families. Other studies have found that positive relations exist between mothers' attitudes toward democratic child rearing and IQ scores of toddlers (Ramey, Farran, & Campbell, 1979) and preschoolers (Radin & Glasser, 1972). Holden concluded that child-rearing attitudes represent a powerful construct for understanding, predicting, and changing parental behavior. However, in order to build an accurate understanding of the role that child-rearing attitudes play in both children's and their parents' functioning and development, we have to move beyond first-stage research to more evolved conceptualization and greater methodological sophistication.

Examples of second-stage research are the studies conducted by Pinderhughes, Dodge, Bates, Petit, and Zelli (2000) and Daggett, O'Brien, Zanolli, and Peyton (2000). Pinderhughes et al. examined two models of the direct and mediated effects of relations between 1) socioeconomic status and parental discipline and 2) ethnicity and parental discipline. Parental beliefs was identified as one pathway linking socioeconomic status and parenting practices and ethnicity and parental discipline. Pinderhughes and colleagues found support for the notion that parental beliefs (e.g., valued spanking) mediated the association between low socioeconomic status and more harsh parental discipline. Daggett et al. (2000) examined relations among parents' perceptions of their childhood, attitudes about life, expectations for child behavior, attitudes about their child's behavior, and the child-rearing environment that parents provide. Mothers who reported harsh parenting as children, negative attitudes about life, and unrealistic developmental expectations had negative attitudes about their own child. These attitudes were related to provision of lower quality home environments. Results support a constructivist approach to understanding parental social cognitions and behavior.

Socioeconomic Status: Maternal IQ Score, Financial Resources, and Educational Level/Occupation

Considerable evidence exists that children of mothers with cognitive challenges are at risk for developmental delay, psychosocial mental retardation, and behavior disorders (Feldman, Case, Towns, & Betel, 1985). Although affecting maternal education and IQ is usually outside the realm of intervention efforts, it is important to apply knowledge regarding this characteristic in the design of an early intervention program. In their article on low maternal intelligence as a risk factor for children's intellectual development, Kelly, Morisset, Barnard, and Patterson (1996) pointed out that carefully planned interventions could enhance a mother's ability to provide a supportive learning environment for her young child. Although some research indicates that responsive caregiving is associated with children's outcomes simply because responsive caregiving shares a relationship with mother's intelligence (Longstreth et al., 1981; Scarr, 1985), research with socioeconomically disadvantaged mothers with low IQ scores indicates that there is an increasing effect of the quality of the home environment and mother–child interaction on children's IQ scores over time. The quality of mother–child interaction continued to predict child outcomes even after controlling for maternal IQ scores (Kelly, Morisset, Barnard, Hammond, & Booth, 1996; Yeates, MacPhee, Campbell, & Ramey, 1983). This latter research shows the importance of considering low maternal IQ as a risk factor and designing interventions tailored to support the mother's ability to provide sensitive and responsive caregiving that, in turn, affects child outcomes.

Family financial resources also appear to affect child outcomes. Duncan, Brooks-Gunn, and Klebanov (1994) examined data from the Infant Health and Development Program targeting low birth weight infants. In their study, family income made unique contributions to child IQ scores and behavior problems as measured by the Child Behavior Profile (CBP; Achenbach & Edelbrock, 1984). This was true above and beyond family demographics, such as the sex of the child, ethnicity, birth weight, mothers' education, and household structure. More proximal home and parenting measures, such as the Home Observation for Measurement of the Environment (HOME; Caldwell & Bradley, 1984), social support, depression, and coping accounted for one third to one half of the effect of family income on child outcomes. More specifically, the home learning environment partially mediated the effect of income on IQ scores, and maternal depression and coping mediated the effect of income on behavior problems.

Yeung, Linver, and Brooks-Gunn (2002) examined data from 753 typically developing children (3–5 years old) and their families. They found that positive family structuring of the home environment and provision of cognitively stimulating materials and activities mediated associations between family income and children's cognitive outcomes. The negative association between family income and child externalizing behavior was mediated by maternal depressed mood and parenting practices. In their study of 153 children with special needs and their mothers, Wallander, Varni, Babani, Banis, and Wilcox (1989) found that both utilitarian resources (family income and maternal education) and psychological resources (family cohesion and environment) made significant contributions to predicting child adjustment as measured by the Child Behavior Checklist (CBCL; Achenbach & Edelbrock, 1983). This line of research strongly indicates that family income affects child outcomes, but it also shows that other family characteristics, more easily ameliorated by effective intervention, moderate the deleterious effects of low income.

Hoff-Ginsberg and Tardif (1995) summarized the research on socioeconomic status and parenting and made specific recommendations for future research directions. They stated that the literature on parenting makes it clear that parents in different social strata parent differently, and the biggest gap in our current knowledge is in establishing the paths of influence from the conditions and experiences that define socioeconomic status to the parenting outcomes associated with socioeconomic status. For example, both occupation and education are adult experiences that may have socializing effects, thus influencing parenting behavior. Kohn and Schooler (1982) showed that job conditions affect personality dimensions such as intellectual flexibility that might, in turn, affect parenting. Crouter and McHale (1993) provided evidence that the communicative style parents experience in the workplace affects the style that parents use with their children at home. Greenberger, O'Neil, and Nagel (1994) found within a middle-class sample that more challenging work was associated with less harsh discipline, even after controlling for education. Hoff-Ginsberg and Tardif (1995) concluded that some external influences, such as poverty and crowded living conditions, operate to influence parenting directly. Then, some external influences, such as education and occupation, operate to influence parenting indirectly. "Clearly more work is needed to identify the causal variables and causal processes that underlie the associations between SES and parenting" (Hoff-Ginsberg & Tardif, 1995, p. 182).

ASSESSING FAMILY CHARACTERISTICS RELEVANT TO EARLY INTERVENTION

There is no prescribed method for assessing family characteristics in early intervention. Legislative guidelines do state that it is necessary to identify the family's strengths and needs, as identified by the family, and to give parents a primary role in identifying the specific types of services and supports best suited to their individual family lifestyle and desires (Krauss, 1990). These guidelines give us important information about the methods and reasons for assessing family characteristics. First, sensitive assessments require parents to be in control of how and what they share with providers; and second, assessments should match family strengths and needs with available intervention services that seem appropriate and valuable to the family.

Sensitive Assessment

With respect to parents being in control of their sharing, Krauss pointed out that

> Assessment is not something done 'to' or 'on' the family; it is something that takes place with the family. Assessment is not a process for exposing the family's deficiencies; it is a process for identifying the family's goals. . . . It helps to create an understanding between early interventionists and the family about what types of assistance are desired (if any), as determined by the family. (2000, p. 298)

If service providers expect to be trusted with a family's perceptions of strengths and needs around such issues as mental health, coping styles, family emotional environment, and amount and quality of social support, a true understanding will take place over the course of many interactions. Family assessment and its resulting goals is an ongoing process that requires time and sensitivity.

Kelly, Zuckerman, Sandoval, and Buehlman (2003) proposed that the service provider's sensitive approach with parents as they share information about their child and family is the foundation for any early intervention. In order to establish this foundation, providers need to successfully join— that is, create—an emotional connection with parents that allows them to support the family appropriately. Kelly et al. (2003) described basic elements in the joining process: recognizing and respecting the uniqueness of each family, responding sensitively to parents as they share information, empathizing with parents about feelings and stories that are shared, and repairing the interactions when the relationship is moving in the wrong direction. They emphasized that joining is a process in which providers engage in these types of interactions over many visits. As trust in the relationship is established, parents can begin to see providers as safe havens to share their successes, strengths, frustrations, and disappointments. Most of all, parents need to sense that providers care first about their well-being and have a sense of connectedness with them based on genuine caring.

The study authors suggested conversations with the family that take place over time, determined by the comfort level and desire of the family.

Matching Needs with Services

A basic requirement of family assessment is connecting family needs and priorities to areas in which early intervention programs have something to offer (Krauss, 2000). Assessment methods should yield information that has prescriptive utility (Bailey et al., 1998). Early intervention programs must be clear about their program goals and the types of services they are able to offer. For example, the ability to provide therapeutic treatment to resolve marital conflicts, problems with family dynamics, financial difficulties, and mental health problems may fall outside the expertise of the professional and the scope of an intervention program. As mentioned in Kelly and Barnard (2000), however, this does not mean the assessment should not include discussion of these issues; rather, when the treatment identified by the assessment process cannot be offered by the program, an available list of resources and financial costs should be available for referral, and the professional, if appropriate, can help the parent in making the initial contacts and arranging follow-up assistance.

Structuring a Relationship-Focused Assessment

In order to focus on family strengths and needs in ways that feel guided by the family, the conversations should be informal and open ended. Providers need to give caregivers opportunity and time to share their stories, concerns, feelings, and histories. It is appropriate to begin the conversation with questions directly related to the way the parent views the child and his or her parenting of the child. These questions are central to early intervention goals that support the parenting role and focus on why interventionists are beginning their relationship with the family. Stepanek, Newcomb, and Kettler (1996) suggested that the conversation focus initially on the child and then turn to issues affecting the family. As the family gets to know the provider over time and begins to trust the relationship, other questions can help providers more fully understand the family's strengths and needs. By focusing on daily routines, parenting issues, and parenting support, family concerns will surface naturally.

Shevrin and Shechtman (1973) explained that the goal of family assessment is to form a personal relationship through which the assessor can elicit information from the family and observe a range of psychological functioning so the problem can be understood and a plan can be made together to address it. The formation of a personal relationship with the family involves creating a safe and caring environment so that parents feel free to share important information. Developing a connection with the parents is similar to developing a meaningful connection with a child:

> When a child is held in mind, the child feels it, and knows it. There is a sense of safety, of containment, and, most important, existence in that other, which has always seemed to me vital. . . . It seems to me that one of life's greatest privileges is just that—the experience of being held in someone's mind. (Hirshberg, 1996, p. 85)

Hirshberg then described the essential process of conducting an interview with parents in a way that lets the parents know that the interventionist will engage in the same act of connection, offering to hold the parents and the infant in his or her own mind as fully and completely as possible. He explained that information is better learned through the parents' account of the baby and the family rather than as a result of a list of routine questions in different areas.

The type of questions (see the next section) and the discussion of how to carry on a relationship-focused conversation (from Kelly et al., 2003) can help providers begin and continue the joining process with parents and identify family strengths and needs that are important for supporting parents in their roles as nurturing caregivers.

Questions for Discussion

1. Can you describe a typical day for you and your child, starting when he or she gets up to when he or she goes to bed?

    Prompts: When does he or she get up, sleep during the day, eat meals, play, and so forth?

2. How would you describe your child?

    Prompts: Has his or her personality or style changed since he or she was born? How does your child react to new experiences, new people, and changes in routine? Is it easy to soothe your child when he or she becomes upset? How is your child's health?

3. How would you describe your relationship with your child?

    Prompts: What four words could you use to describe your relationship? What recent experiences have you had with your child that illustrate these words?

4. Does someone else take care of your child sometimes? If yes, who? How do you feel about this child care situation?

    Prompts: How do you feel when you leave? What does your child do when you say good-bye and leave? If your child becomes upset, how do you think he or she is feeling when you leave? How does he or she behave when you are gone? (Does he or she settle down or stay upset?)

5. What do you like about being a parent?

    Prompts: Could you describe a recent experience with your child that was especially enjoyable? How did the experience make you feel? How did your child feel?

6. What are your concerns about your child, if any?

7. Are there any challenges that you want to talk about that you feel affect your parenting?

    Prompts: Are there times you feel overwhelmed? Can you describe how you feel? Is there anyone you can turn to when you feel this way? How do these challenges affect your family life (if concerns are expressed)? Do you talk about these concerns with your partner/ family? How do you feel after you talk about these concerns? Do you feel you have the help you need to handle these concerns?

8. Do you get support in your role as parent?

    Prompts: Who gives you support? Do you get as much support as you feel you need? If no, what kind of support do you need?

9. Do you feel like you have enough time in your day for all that you want to do?

    Prompts: Do you have time for yourself? What do you do to relax? Do you have time to spend with other members of your family? Friends?

If the child has a special need, then questions 10–15 are relevant.

10. When did you first realize that your child had a special need?[1]

    Prompts: Was the realization gradual or sudden?

11. What were your feelings at the time of this realization?

12. Have your feelings changed over time?

13. If the child already has a diagnosis: Tell me what happened when you learned of your child's diagnosis?

    Prompts: Where were you? Who else was there? What were you feeling and thinking at that moment?

---

[1]Questions 10–13 were adapted from Pianta, R.C., & Marvin, R.S. (1993). *Manual for classification of the reaction to diagnosis interview*. Unpublished manuscript, University of Virginia.

14. How are you feeling now?

15. How are the other members of your family feeling? If concerns are expressed: How is this affecting your family right now? Are you able to talk about it? If yes, do you feel better after talking about it?

16. Is there anything you would like to talk about that we have not discussed?

Relationship-Focused Discussions

It is important for the interviewer to consider the parent–provider conversation as a dynamic process. The discussion is guided by the information and cues parents give in sharing the details of their and their child's personal lives. During visits with parents, it is helpful for the interviewer to observe his or her own behaviors and their effect on caregivers. For example, if some parents tire after a few questions, then questions need to be spaced over many visits. Initially, some parents will respond better to questions that require brief answers than to questions that require more in-depth answers. Asking open-ended questions allows the parent to control the discussion and to give cues about the level of comfort of the discussion. Here are some questions providers can ask themselves as they have discussions with parents: *Am I comfortable giving control to parents during our conversations? Am I looking carefully for parent cues that guide our interactions? Is the material I want to cover guiding the pace of the interactions, or are parent cues and desires determining the pace and content?*

Sometimes parents' cues may be difficult to read, and the interviews may need to use additional relationship-focused techniques. For example, using an open-ended question or reflecting on what the parent says can create a pause and help the provider to gather more information before proceeding. Open-ended questions allow others to express what is most important or relevant to them. Reflective comments incorporate what the parent has said and felt while feeding back key information in the style the parent has initiated. For example, if a parent shares without clear emotion that she has recently been told by her mother that "she is spending too much time trying to teach Amy and that she should relax and just play with Amy," then the provider may want to know if the parent is feeling blamed, angry, worried, informed, or relieved. The provider may ask an open-ended question such as, "How did you feel about this?" or reflect back in a neutral tone, "Your mother feels that you and Amy should relax and play more together." Open-ended questions and reflections can lead to more input from the parent so the provider is better able to understand the meaning of what the parent has said and how the parent feels about it. Open-ended questions and reflections avoid labels, professional jargon, and personal evaluations of what others share or have shared. They also can help providers avoid giving their own meaning to what has been said when the meaning is not clear, telling how or what others feel or should feel, or supplying feelings to others that have not been shared.

Providers also need to pay attention to their own uncomfortable feelings because they can give cues about the success or failure of the joining attempts. If the parent expresses uncomfortable feelings such as shame, anger, doubt, or fear, then it is important for providers to respond empathetically and to pause and listen. Providers should avoid the temptation to think that they can make uncomfortable feelings go away or fix the problem that causes these feelings. It probably is not in a provider's power to do either of these things. However, accepting and listening are powerful tools in establishing a relationship and validating the importance of these issues for both the parent and child. (See Hirshberg, 1996, for more discussion of transference and response to parental anxiety.)

Sometimes parents are anxious for immediate information from the service provider and are not comfortable with the joining process or the information-gathering period. It is important for the service provider to give feedback when asked for information but to make sure the feedback is based on enough information to be valid and helpful. If the provider can give accurate information in response to a question, then information should not be withheld because the usual "getting acquainted" period has not occurred. However, if the provider does not have enough information to respond appropriately, then he or she needs to be honest and say, "We need to have more time together to learn about that." This might be a good time to reinforce with the parent that he or she is the best source of information about the child and to make comments that let the parent know that conversations with him or her about the child and the family will help provide needed information for jointly developing intervention plans.

Finally, it is worth mentioning that nonverbal behaviors are powerful messages for confirming what the parent has said and felt and for letting the parent know that the provider is interested in forming a relationship, not just gathering information. Nodding, smiling, showing looks of concern, having eye contact, avoiding constant note taking, and so forth let the parent know that what he or she is saying is important to the provider and to the intervention process.

Even after an initial discussion, the provider should be able to focus on several strengths and needs that families may have. After many visits, the provider should have a clearer picture of the family's strengths and needs as perceived and willingly shared by the family.

FOCUSED MEASURES OF FAMILY CHARACTERISTICS

Because family–provider conversations uncover specific areas of strength and need, service providers and parents may want to focus more intensively on some areas relating to family characteristics in order to better structure intervention services: socioeconomic and psychosocial.

Socioeconomic

When parents express socioeconomic concerns, the early intervention program can refer the parent to community resources that are available and appropriate and assist in making initial and follow-up contacts. If the family identifies financial issues and wants to discuss their concerns in greater detail, then the provider can use questions from The Family Resource Scale (Dunst & Leet, 1987) to guide a focused discussion about financial concerns or have the parent complete the scale in questionnaire form. The Family Resource Scale assesses adequacy of both physical and human resources (e.g., food, shelter, transportation, time to be with family and friends, health care, money to pay bills, child care) on a 5-point scale from "not at all adequate" to "almost always adequate." In studies using the scale, Dunst, Trivette, and Deal (1994) reported that personal and family needs form a hierarchy that generally conforms to the sequence of needs and resources proposed by Hartman and Laird (1983), ranging from nutritional needs to planning for and contributing to the future. Dunst et al. further found that mothers who reported inadequacies in family resources were less likely to see child-level educational and therapeutic needs as immediately important. They pointed out that if basic needs are not being met, the probability that parents can commit to child-level interventions is diminished, and efforts should be made to mediate provisions of support in order to provide the types of resources necessary for healthy family functioning.

Parents may differ in their attitudes and comfort in completing interviews and questionnaires. Sexton, Snyder, Rheams, Barron-Sharp, and Perez (1991, as reported in Krauss, 2000) examined the opinions of 48 mothers of children in early intervention and 25 service providers regarding their preferences for personal interviews versus questionnaires. About half of the mothers preferred the use of written surveys and the other half preferred personal interviews. It may be that some parents prefer the anonymity afforded by standardized questionnaires and a sense of control over responses in contrast to the personal sharing required in interviews and the lack of control over possible probing by the interviewer.

Psychosocial

Many early intervention programs now employ mental health specialists who are prepared to address parents' psychosocial concerns. If therapeutic concerns fall outside of the expertise of the intervention program, then the program should help parents identify and contact appropriate community resources.

Several measures address specific family psychosocial characteristics such as family functioning, family coping, family environment, social support, and parental attitudes. If parents are more comfortable with a less personal assessment related to their identified need and prefer completing written assessments, then professionals can remain family focused by letting the families decide if and when to fill out forms and by remaining nonjudgmental in problem-solving efforts. If parents are comfortable sharing information in personal interviews, then it is not advisable to administer measures in questionnaire form; however, familiarization with the measures can help professionals better recognize areas of strength and need as parents discuss and describe their family routines, parenting joys, challenges, feelings, and needs. Reviews of several of these measures follow.

McMaster Family Assessment Device

Epstein, Baldwin, and Bishop (1983) developed the McMaster Family Assessment Device as a 53-item screening measure based on the McMaster Model of Family Functioning, a clinically oriented conceptualization of family functioning. The model identifies six dimensions of family functioning: 1) problem solving (the family's ability to resolve problems that threaten the functional capacity of the family); 2) communication (the exchange of information among family members and whether verbal messages are clear); 3) roles (whether the family has established patterns of behavior for handling a variety of family functions ([e.g., provision of resources, nurturance and support]); 4) affective responsiveness (the extent to which members are able to experience appropriate affect over a range of stimuli); 5) affective involvement (the extent to which family members are interested in and place value on each other's activities and concerns); and 6) behavior control (that is, the way in which a family expresses and maintains standards for behavior). The scales show good to high internal consistency. An examination of validity revealed that the scales discriminated between clinical families and nonclinical families in a sample of 503 study participants.

Family Functioning Style Scale

The Family Functioning Style Scale (FFSS; Deal, Trivette, & Dunst, 1988) yields information about strengths and capabilities from the family's perspective and allows the interventionist to build on the positive and unique aspects of a family's functioning style. Twenty-six items, rated on a 5-point scale, assess three domains: 1) family identity (commitment, appreciation, allocation of time, sense of purpose, congruence); 2) information sharing (communication, rules, values); and 3) coping/resource mobilization (coping strategies, problem-solving abilities, positivism, flexibility/adaptability, balance). Trivette, Dunst, Deal, Hamby, and Sexton (1994) described reliability and validity data on the FFSS. They reported high internal consistency among the full scale's 26 items and found that a principal components factor analysis produced five interpretable factors: family interactional patterns, family values, coping strategies, family commitment, and resource mobilization. Criterion validity was demonstrated through associations with the Family Hardiness Index. FFSS scores also were associated with parental reports of fewer family-related health problems, less negative affect, and greater overall psychological well-being, providing evidence of predictive validity.

Family Adaptability and Cohesion Evaluation Scales

The Family Adaptability and Cohesion Evaluation Scales (FACES III; Olson, Portner, & Lavee, 1985) assess the degree of family adaptability (ability of the marital or family system to change in response to situational and developmental stress) and family cohesiveness (the emotional bonding among family members). The 20-item scale is designed to measure both perceived and ideal descriptions of the marital and family system. The self-report measure is completed twice, once for perceived and once for ideal descriptions of the family. The perceived–ideal discrepancy is an indirect measure of family satisfaction. The greater the perceived–ideal discrepancy, the less the family satisfaction (Olson, 1986). The measure has adequate internal consistency for the subscales and the total score and good test-retest reliability (4–5 weeks). The authors also cited very good evidence for face and content validity, as well as discrimination between groups.

Family Environment Scale

The Family Environment Scale (Moos & Moos, 1986), a 90-item self-report measure with a dichotomous response format (true/false), was developed as a family-based screening procedure. It is intended for use in clinical settings to facilitate family counseling and teach clinicians and program evaluators about family systems, and in program evaluation. Moos (2002) listed multiple uses for the scale: diagnosis of problems, program monitoring, program improvement, parenting improvement, strengthening the family unit, describing program impact, and risk identification. The 90 items are grouped into 10 subscales with three dimensions: 1) relationship (cohesion, expressiveness, conflict); 2) personal growth (independence, achievement orientation, intellectual–cultural orientation, active–recreational orientation, moral–religious emphasis); and 3) system maintenance (organization, control). Moos (1990) reported studies that showed good short-term and long-term test-retest reliability and construct validity (e.g., cohesiveness subscale related to marital adjustment, conflict to family arguments, organization to regular family routines), as well as concurrent and predicative validity (scores were related to adjustment during family transitions and children's social and cognitive development).

Family Support Scale

The Family Support Scale (Dunst, Jenkins, & Trivette, 1988) is an 18-item self-report measure designed to assess the degree to which potential sources of support have been helpful to young children. Dunst, Trivette, and Hamby (1994) defined *social support* as the emotional, psychological, physical, informational, instrumental, and material aid and assistance provided by others that influence the recipient's behavior. A previous study of reliability and validity among 139 parents of children at risk or with disabilities showed good internal consistency among items and test-retest reliability at 1 and 18 months. A principal components factor analysis yielded a 5-factor solution: informal kinship, social organizations, formal kinship, immediate family, and specialized professional services. The total scale score was related to parental well-being and family functioning, indicating criterion validity. Dunst, Trivette, and Hamby (1994) also reported that greater social support measured with the Family Support Scale was related to fewer personal and family problems. They maintained that the scale is a sensitive instrument for discriminating among individuals who are experiencing differing levels of stress and coping, and their studies support the contention that social support is related to physical and emotional well-being.

Parental Attitude Research Instrument

The Parental Attitude Research Instrument (PARI; Schaefer & Bell, 1958) is one of the most popular scales used to assess parental attitudes. The scale comprises 115 items and uses a 4-point response format with a range from "strongly agree" to "strongly disagree." Twenty-three subscales are measured, each being evaluated by five items. The subscales cover such areas as encouraging verbalization, fostering dependency, seclusion of the mother, fear of harming the baby, marital conflict, strictness, intrusiveness, and so forth. Several authors have adapted the PARI, which has resulted in independent factor analyses and factor structures. Three major factors have been identified: 1) authoritarianism–control, 2) hostility–rejection, and 3) democracy or egalitarianism (Radin & Glasser, 1972; Zuckerman,

Oltean, & Monashkin, 1958). Other popular scales include the Child Rearing Practices Report (CRPR; Block, 1965) and the Maternal Attitude Scale (MAS; Cohler, Weiss, & Grunebaum, 1970).

This summary of selected measures is not intended to be exhaustive but rather to provide examples of available measures that can help professionals become more familiar with existing research and questions regarding the assessment of family characteristics in early intervention.

CONCLUSION

In order to identify family characteristics that support the caregiving role, it is important for professionals to have a firm knowledge of the importance of family characteristics to family and child functioning and the ways in which family characteristics contribute to functioning. Research over the past few decades informs us that psychosocial characteristics, such as parental mental health, family functioning and coping styles, family environment, social support, and parenting attitudes, all contribute to family and child outcomes and are important to consider in early intervention efforts. Other family characteristics such as resources related to family socioeconomic status may affect the type of intervention services that families want and desire.

In addition to knowledge about these characteristics, it is equally important to become skilled at exploring family strengths and needs with parents. This requires the ability to converse sensitively with parents in ways that promote parents' strengths and enable change that meets family needs. With sensitivity and care, professionals can join with parents around their shared stories and accounts and develop a relationship based on trust and caring. In the context of this relationship, parents can allow professionals to become safe havens to share successes, frustrations, strengths, disappointments, and challenges. This relationship is central to the development of an intervention program tailored to individual family characteristics.

If expressed areas of family need fall outside the expertise of the intervention program, then together with parents, professionals can identify and contact appropriate community resources. Knowledge of the research and development of standardized assessments can enable professionals to better assess family strengths and needs. In all intervention efforts, it is important to keep in mind that family characteristics frame the intervention process, and the parent–provider relationship is the context for successful assessment and intervention practice.

REFERENCES

Abidin, R.R. (1983). *Parenting Stress Index–Manual.* Charlottesville, VA: University of Virginia Press.

Achenbach, T.M., & Edelbrock, C.S. (1983). *Manual for the Child Behavior Checklist and Revised Behavior Profile.* Burlington: University of Vermont.

Achenbach, T.M., & Edelbrock, C.S. (1984). Psychopathology of childhood. *Annual Review of Psychology, 35,* 227–256.

Aldwin, C., & Revenson, T.A. (1987). Does coping help? A re-examination of the relation between coping and mental health. *Journal of Personality and Social Psychology, 53*(2), 337–348.

Amato, P.R., & Keith, B. (1991). Consequences of parental divorce for children's well-being: A meta-analysis. *Psychological Bulletin, 110,* 26–46.

Appel, A.E., & Holden, G.W. (1998). The co-occurrence of spouse and physical child abuse: A review and appraisal. *Journal of Family Psychology, 12,* 578–599.

Bailey, D.B., McWilliam, R.A., Darkes, L.A., Hebbeler, K., Simeonsson, R.J., Spiker, D., & Wagner, M. (1998). Family outcomes in early intervention: A framework for program evaluation and efficacy research. *Exceptional Children, 64,* 313–328.

Belsky, J. (1984). The determinants of parenting: A process model. *Child Development, 55,* 83–96.

Bentovim, A. (1972). Emotional disturbances of handicapped pre-school children and their families: Attitudes to the child. *British Medical Journal, 3,* 579–581.

Block, J.H. (1965). *The child-rearing practice report: A set of Q items for the description of parental socialization attitudes and values.* Berkeley: University of California, Institute of Human Development.

Bolger, N. (1990). Coping as a personality process: A prospective study. *Journal of Personality and Social Psychology, 59,* 525–537.

Bristol, M.M., Gallagher, J.J., & Schopler, E. (1988). Mothers and fathers of young developmentally disabled boys: Adaptation and spousal support. *Developmental Psychology, 24,* 441–451.

Bronfenbrenner, U. (1986). Ecology of the family as a context for human development: Research perspectives. *Developmental Psychology, 22,* 723–742.

Bronfenbrenner, U. (1992). Ecological systems theory. In R. Vasta (Ed.), *Annals of child development. Six theories of child development: Revised formulations and current issues* (pp. 187–249). London: Jessica Kingsley.

Buchanan, C.M., & Heiges, K.L. (2001). When conflict continues after the marriage ends: Effects of post-divorce conflict on children. In J. Crych & F. Fincham (Eds.), *Child development and interparental conflict* (pp. 337–362). New York: Cambridge University Press.

Burr, W.F. (1973). *Theory construction and the sociology of the family.* New York: John Wiley & Sons.

Caldwell, B., & Bradley, R. (1984). *Home Observation for Measurement of the Environment.* Little Rock, AR: University of Little Rock.

Cobb, S. (1976). Social support as a moderator of life stress. *Psychosomatic Medicine, 38,* 300–314.

Cohler, B.J., Weiss, J.L., & Grunebaum, H.U. (1970). Child care attitudes and emotional disturbance among mothers of young children. *Genetic Psychology Monographs, 82,* 3–47.

Cochran, M., & Niegro, S. (1995). Parenting and social networks. In M.H. Bornstein (Ed.), *Handbook of parenting: Vol. 3. Status and social conditions of parenting* (pp. 393–418). Mahwah, NJ: Lawrence Erlbaum Associates.

Cox, M.J., Paley, B., & Harter, K. (2001). Interparental conflict and parent-child relationships. In J. Grych & F. Fincham (Eds.), *Child development and interparental conflict* (pp. 249–272). New York: Cambridge University Press.

Crittenden, P.M. (1985). Social networks, quality of child-rearing, and child development. *Child Development, 56,* 1299–1313.

Crnic, K.A., Friedrich, W.N., & Greenberg, M.T. (1983). Adaptation of families with mentally retarded children: A model of stress, coping, and family ecology. *American Journal of Mental Deficiency, 88*(2), 125–138.

Crockenberg, S. (1988). Social support and parenting. In H. Fitzgerald, B. Lester, & M. Yogman (Eds.), *Theory and research in behavioral pediatrics* (Vol. 4, pp. 141–174). New York: Plenum.

Crouter, A.C., & McHale, S.M. (1993) The long arm of the job: Influences of parental work on childrearing. In T. Luster & L. Okagaki (Eds.), *Parenting: An ecological perspective* (pp. 179–202). Mahwah, NJ: Lawrence Erlbaum Associates.

Cummings, E.M., Davies, P., & Simpson, K. (1994). Marital conflict, gender, and children's appraisal and coping efficacy as mediators of child adjustment. *Journal of Family Psychology, 8,* 141–149.

Cummings, E.M., & Davies, P.T. (1992). Parental depression, family functioning, and child adjustment: Risk factors, process, and pathways. In D. Cicchetti & S. Toth (Eds.), *Rochester symposium on developmental psychopathology: A developmental approach to the affective disorders* (Vol. 4, pp. 283–322). Rochester, NY: University of Rochester Press.

Cummings, E.M., & Davies, P.T. (2002). Effects of marital conflict on children: Recent advances and emerging themes in process-oriented research. *Journal of Child Psychology and Psychiatry, 43*(1), 31–63.

Dadds, M.R., Atkinson, E., Turner, C., Blums, G.J., & Lendich, B. (1999). Family conflict and child adjustment: Evidence for a cognitive-contextual model of intergenerational transmission. *Journal of Family Psychology, 13,* 194–208.

Daggett, J., O'Brien, M., Zanolli, K., & Peyton, V. (2000). Parents' attitudes about children: Association with parental life histories and child rearing quality. *Journal of Family Psychology, 14,* 187–199.

Deal, A.G., Trivette, C.M., & Dunst, C.J. (1988). Family Functioning Style Scale. In C.J. Dunst, C.M. Trivette, & A.G. Deal (Eds.), *Enabling and empowering families: Principles and guidelines for practice* (pp. 179–184). Cambridge, MA: Brookline Books.

Deal, J.E., Halverson, C.F., Jr., & Wampler, K.S. (1989). Parental agreement on child-rearing orientations: Relations to parental, marital, family, and child characteristics. *Child Development, 60,* 1025–1034.

Downey, G., & Coyne, J.C. (1990). Children of depressed parents: An integrative review. *Psychological Bulletin, 108*(1), 50–76.

Downey, G., & Walker, E. (1992). Distinguishing family-level and child-level influences on the development of depression and aggression in children at risk. *Development and Psychopathology, 4,* 81–95.

Duncan, G.J., Brooks-Gunn, J., & Klebanov, P.K. (1994). Economic deprivation and early childhood development. *Child Development, 65,* 296–318.

Dunn, J., & Davies, L. (2001). Sibling relationships and interparental conflict. In J. Grych & F. Fincham (Eds.), *Child development and interparental conflict* (pp. 273–290). New York: Cambridge University Press.

Dunst, C.J., Jenkins, V., & Trivette, C.M. (1988). Family Support Scale. In C.J. Dunst, C.M. Trivette, & A.G. Deal (Eds.), *Enabling and empowering families: Principles and guidelines for practice.* Cambridge, MA: Brookline Books.

Dunst, C.J., & Leet, H.E. (1987). Measuring the adequacy of resources in households with young children. *Child: Care, Health and Development, 13,* 111–125.

Dunst, C.J., Trivette, C.M., & Deal, A.G. (1988). *Enabling and empowering families: Principles and guidelines for practice.* Cambridge, MA: Brookline Books.

Dunst, C.J., Trivette, C.M., & Deal, A.G. (Eds.). (1994). *Supporting and strengthening families: Methods, strategies, and practices* (Vol. 1). Cambridge, MA: Brookline Books.

Dunst, C.J., Trivette, C.M., & Hamby, D.W. (1994). Measuring social support in families with young children with disabilities. In C.J. Dunst, C.M. Trivette, & A.G. Deal (Eds.), *Supporting and strengthening families: Methods, strategies, and practices* (Vol. 1, pp. 152–159). Cambridge, MA: Brookline Books.

Dunst, C.J., Trivette, C.M., & Jodry, W. (1997). Influences of social support on children with disabilities and their families. In M.J. Guralnick (Ed.), *The effectiveness of early intervention* (pp. 499–522). Baltimore: Paul H. Brookes Publishing Co.

Early Head Start National Resource Center @ Zero to Three. (2003). *What is Early Head Start?* Retrieved from http://www.ehsnrc.org/AboutUs/ehs.htm

Easterbrooks, M.A., & Goldberg, W.A. (1984). Toddler development in the family: Impact of father involvement and parenting characteristics. *Child Development, 55,* 740–752.

Education of the Handicapped Act Amendments of 1986, PL 99-457, 20 U.S.C. §§ 1400 *et seq.*

Egeland, B., & Farber, E.A. (1984). Infant-mother attachment: Factors related to its development and changes over time. *Child Development, 55,* 740–752.

Ehrle, J.L., & Moore, K.A. (1999). *1997 NSAF benchmarking measures of child and family well-being* (Report No. 6). Washington, DC: Urban Institute.

Ellis, B.J., & Garber, J. (2000). Psychosocial antecedents of variation in girls' pubertal timing: Maternal depression, stepfather presence, and martial and family stress. *Child Development, 71,* 485–501.

El-Sheikh, M., & Cummings, E.M. (1998). Marital conflict, emotional regulation, and the adjustment of children of alcoholics. In K.C. Barrett (Ed.), *The communication of emotion: Current research from diverse perspectives. New directions for child development* (No. 77, pp. 25–44). San Francisco: Jossey-Bass.

Epstein, N.B., Baldwin, L.M., & Bishop, D.S. (1983). The McMaster family assessment device. *Journal of Marital and Family Therapy, 9*(2), 171–180.

Feldman, M.A., Case, L., Towns, F., & Betel, J. (1985). Parent education project I: The development and nurturance of children of mentally retarded parents. *American Journal of Mental Deficiency, 90,* 253–258.

Fergusson, D.M., & Horwood, L.J. (1998). Exposure to interparental violence in childhood and psychosocial adjustment in young adulthood. *Child Abuse and Neglect, 22,* 339–357.

Fischer, C.L. (1982). *To dwell among friends: Personal networks in town and city.* Chicago: University of Chicago Press.

Folkman, S., Lazarus, R.S., Dunkel-Schetter, C., DeLongis, A., & Gruen, R.J. (1986). Dynamics of a stressful encounter: Cognitive appraisal, coping, and encounter outcomes. *Journal of Personality and Social Psychology, 50,* 992–1003.

Folkman, S., Lazarus, R.S., Gruen, R.J., & DeLongis, A. (1986). Appraisal, coping, health status, and psychological symptoms. *Journal of Personality and Social Psychology, 50,* 571–579.

Gottman, J.M., Katz, I.F., & Hooven, C. (1996). *Meta-emotion: How families communicate emotionally.* Mahwah, NJ: Lawrence Erlbaum Associates.

Gowen, J.W., Johnson-Martin, N., Goldman, B.D., & Appelbaum, M. (1989). Feelings of depression and parenting competence of mothers of handicapped and nonhandicapped infants: A longitudinal study. *American Journal on Mental Retardation, 94*(3), 259–271.

Greenberger, E., O'Neil, R., & Nagel, S.K. (1994). Linking workplace and homeplace: Relations between the nature of adults' work and their parenting behaviors. *Developmental Psychology, 30*, 990–1002.

Grych, J.H. (1998). Children's appraisal of interparental conflict: Situational and contextual influences. *Journal of Family Psychology, 12*, 437–453.

Grych, J.H., & Fincham, F.D. (1990). Marital conflict and children's adjustment: A cognitive-contextual framework. *Psychological Bulletin, 108*, 267–290.

Guralnick, M.J. (2001). A developmental systems model for early intervention. *Infants and Young Children, 14*(2), 1–18.

Hartman, A., & Laird, J. (1983). *Family-centered social work practice.* New York: Free Press.

Hauser-Cram, P., Warfield, M.E., Shonkoff, J.P., & Krauss, M.W. (2001). Children with disabilities: A longitudinal study of child development and parent well-being. *Monographs of the Society for Research in Child Development, 66* (3, Serial No. 266).

Hauser-Cram, P., Warfield, M.E., Shonkoff, J.P., Krauss, M.W., Upshur, C.C., & Sayer, A. (1999). Family influences on adaptive development in young children with Down syndrome. *Child Development, 70*, 979–989.

Hill, R. (1949). *Families under stress.* New York: Harper & Row.

Hill, R. (1958). Generic features of families under stress. *Social Casework, 49*, 139–150.

Hirshberg, L.M. (1996). History-making, not history-taking: Clinical interviews with infants and their families. In S.J. Meisels & E. Fenichel (Eds.), *New visions for the developmental assessment of infants and young children* (pp. 85–124). Washington, DC: ZERO TO THREE: National Center for Infants, Toddlers, and Families.

Hoff-Ginsberg, E., & Tardif, T. (1995). Socioeconomic status and parenting. In M.H. Bornstein (Ed.), *Handbook of parenting* (Vol. 2, pp. 161–199). Mahwah, NJ: Lawrence Erlbaum Associates.

Holden, G.W., & Buck, M.J. (1995). Parental attitudes toward childrearing. In M.H. Bornstein (Ed.), *Handbook of parenting* (Vol. 3, pp. 359–392). Mahwah, NJ: Lawrence Erlbaum Associates.

Howes, P.W., Cicchetti, D., Toth, S.L., & Rogosch, F.A. (2000). Affective, organizational, and rational characteristics of maltreating families: A system perspective. *Journal of Family Psychology, 14*, 95–110.

Individuals with Disabilities Education Act (IDEA) of 1990, PL 101-476, 20 U.S.C. §§1400 *et seq.*

Judge, S.L. (1998). Parental coping strategies and strengths in families of young children with disabilities. *Family Relations, 47*(3), 263–268.

Kelly, J.F., & Barnard, K.E. (2000). Assessment of parent-child interactions: Implications for early intervention. In J.P. Shonkoff & S.J. Meisels (Eds.), *The handbook of early intervention* (2nd ed., pp. 278–302). New York: Cambridge University Press.

Kelly, J.F., Morisset, C.E., Barnard, K.E., Hammond, M.A., & Booth, K.L. (1996). The influence of early mother-child interaction on preschool cognitive/linguistic outcomes in a high social risk group. *Infant Mental Health Journal, 17*(4), 310–321.

Kelly, J.F., Morisset, C.E., Barnard, K.E., & Patterson, D.L. (1996). Risky beginnings: Low maternal intelligence as a risk factor for children's intellectual development. *Infants and Young Children, 8*(3), 11–23.

Kelly, J.F., Zuckerman, T.G., Sandoval, D., & Buehlman, K. (2003). *Promoting first relationships: A curriculum for service providers to help parents and other caregivers meet the social and emotional needs of young children.* Seattle, WA: NCAST-AVENUW Publications.

Kerig, P. (1998). Gender and appraisals as mediators of adjustment in children exposed to interparental violence. *Journal of Emotional Abuse, 15*, 87–105.

Kobe, F.H., & Hammer, D. (1994). Parenting stress and depression in children with mental retardation and developmental disabilities. *Research in Developmental Disabilities, 15*(3), 209–221.

Kofman, O. (2002). The role of prenatal stress in the etiology of developmental behavioral disorders. *Neuroscience and Biobehavioral Review, 26*, 457–470.

Kohn, M.L., & Schooler, C. (1982). Job conditions and personality: A longitudinal assessment of their reciprocal effects. *American Journal of Sociology, 87*, 1257–1283.

Kovacs, M. (1992). *Children's Depression Inventory* (CDI). Los Angeles: Western Psychological Services.

Krauss, M.W. (1990). New precedent in family policy: The individualized family service plan. *Exceptional Children, 56*, 388–395.

Krauss, M.W. (2000). Family assessment within early intervention programs. In J.P. Shonkoff & S.J. Meisels (Eds.), *Handbook of early childhood intervention* (2nd ed., pp. 290–308). New York: Cambridge University Press.

Krishnakumar, A., & Buehler, C. (2000). Interparental conflict and parenting behaviors: A meta-analytic review. *Family Relations, 49*, 25–44.

Lazarus, R.S., & Folkman, S. (1984). *Stress, appraisal, and coping.* New York: Springer.

Longstreth, L.E., Davis, B., Carter, L., Flint, D., Owen, J., Rickert, M., & Taylor, E. (1981). Separation of home intellectual environment and maternal IQ as determinants of child IQ. *Developmental Psychology, 17*(5), 532–541.

Lovejoy, C., Graczyk, P., O'Hare, E., Neuman, G. (2000). Maternal depression and parenting behavior: A meta-analytic review. *Clinical Psychology Review, 20*, 561–592.

Lundy, B., Jones, N., Field, T., Nearing, G., Davalos, M., Pietro, P., Schanberg, S., & Kuhn, C. (1999). Prenatal depression effects on neonates. *Infant Behavior and Development, 22*, 119–129.

Lyons-Ruth, K., Connell, D.B., Grunebaum, H.U., & Botein, S. (1990). Infants at social risk: Maternal depression and family support services as mediators of infant development and security of attachment. *Child Development, 61*, 85–98.

McCubbin, H.I., & Patterson, J.M. (1983). The family stress process: The double ABCX model of adjustment and adaptation. *Marriage and Family Review, 6*, 7–37.

Miller, A.C., Gordon, R.M., Daniele, R.J., & Diller, L. (1992). Stress, appraisal, and coping in mothers of disabled and nondisabled children. *Journal of Pediatric Psychology, 17*(5), 587–605.

Moore, K.A., Chalk, R., Scarpa, J., & Vandivere, S. (2002, August). Family strengths: Often overlooked, but real. *Child Trends Research Brief*, 1–8.

Moos, R.H. (1990). Conceptual and empirical approaches to developing family-based assessment procedures: Resolving the case of the Family Environment Scale. *Family Process, 29*, 199–208.

Moos, R.H. (2002). *The Family Environment Scale*. Retrieved November, 2002, from http://www.mindgarden.com/Assessments/Info/FESINFO.htm.

Moos, R.H., & Moos, B. (1986). *Family Environment Scale manual* (2nd ed.). Palo Alto, CA: Consulting Psychologists Press.

National Research Council and Institute of Medicine. (2000). *From neurons to neighborhoods: The science of early childhood development.* Committee on Integrating the Science of Early Childhood Development. Washington, DC: National Academy Press.

Noller, P., Feeney, J.A., Sheehan, G., & Peterson, C. (2000). Marital conflict patterns: Links with family conflict and family member's perceptions of one another. *Personal Relationships, 7*, 79–94.

O'Hara, M. (1986). Social support, life events, and depression during pregnancy and the puererium. *Archives of General Psychiatry, 43*, 569–573.

Olson, D.H. (1986). Circumplex model VII: Validation studies and FACES III. *Family Process, 25*, 337–351.

Olson, D.H., Portner, J., & Lavee, Y. (1985). *FACES III.* St. Paul: Family Social Science, University of Minnesota.

Pearlin, L., Mullan, J., Semple, S., & Skaff, M. (1990). Caregiving and the stress process: An overview of concepts and their measures. *The Gerontologist, 30*, 583–594.

Petterson, S.M., & Albers, A.B. (2001). Effects of poverty and maternal depression on early child development. *Child Development, 72*, 1794–1813.

Pianta, R.C., & Marvin, R.S. (1993). *Manual for classification of the reaction to diagnosis interview.* Unpublished manuscript, University of Virginia.

Pinderhughes, E.E., Dodge, K.A., Bates, J.E., Petit, G.S., & Zelli, A. (2000). Discipline responses: Influences of parents' socioeconomic status, ethnicity, beliefs about parenting, stress, and cognitive-emotional process. *Journal of Family Psychology, 14*, 380–400.

Quinn, M.E., Fontana, A.F., & Rezinkoff, M. (1987). Psychological distress in reaction to lung cancers as a function of spousal support and coping strategy. *Journal of Psychosocial Oncology, 4*, 79–90.

Radin, N., & Glasser, P. (1972). The utility of Parental Attitude Research Instrument for intervention programs with low-income families. *Journal of Marriage and the Family, 34*, 448–458.

Ramey, C.T., Farran, D.C., & Campbell, F.A. (1979). Predicting IQ from mother–infant interactions. *Child Development, 50*, 804–814.

Rutter, M., & Garmezy, N. (1983). Developmental psychology. In E.M. Hetherington (Ed.), *Socialization, personality, and social development* (pp. 775–911). New York: John Wiley & Sons.

Scarr, S. (1985). Constructing psychology: Making facts and fables for our times. *American Psychology, 40*, 499–512.

Schaefer, E.S., & Bell, R.Q. (1958). Development of parental attitude research instrument. *Child Development, 29*, 339–361.

Scorgie, K., Wilgosh, L., & McDonald, L. (1998). Stress and coping in families of children with disabilities: An examination of recent literature. *Developmental Disabilities Bulletin, 26*(1), 22–42.

Sexton, D., Snyder, P., Rheams, T., Barron-Sharp, B., & Perez, J. (1991). Considerations in using written surveys to identify family strengths and needs during the IFSP process. *Topics in Early Childhood Special Education, 11,* 81–91.

Shevrin, H., & Shechtman, F. (1973). The diagnostic process in psychiatric evaluation. *Bulletin of the Menninger Clinic, 35,* 451–494.

Stepanek, J.S., Newcomb, S., & Kettler, K. (1996). Coordinating services and identifying family priorities, resources, and concerns. In P. Beckman (Ed.), *Strategies for working with families of young children with disabilities* (pp. 69–90). Baltimore: Paul H. Brookes Publishing Co.

Trivette, C.M., Dunst, C.J., Deal, A.G., Hamby, D.W., & Sexton, D. (1994). Assessing family strengths and capabilities. In C.J. Dunst, C.M. Trivette, & A.G. Deal (Eds.), *Supporting and strengthening families: Methods, strategies and practices* (Vol. 1, pp. 132–139). Cambridge, MA: Brookline Books.

Trute, B. (1990). Child and parent predictors of family adjustment in households containing young developmentally disabled children. *Family Relations, 39,* 292–297.

Vitaliano, P.P., DeWolfe, D.J., Maiuro, R.D., Russo, J., & Katon, W. (1990). Appraised changeability of a stressor as a modifier of the relationship between coping and depression: A test of the hypothesis of fit. *Journal of Personality and Social Psychology, 59,* 582–592.

United States House of Representatives 99th Congress, 2nd session. Report 99-860. *Report accompanying the Education of the Handicapped Act Amendments of 1986.*

Wallander, J.L., Varni, J.W., Babani, L., Banis, H.T., & Wilcox, K.T. (1989). Family resources as resistance factors for psychological maladjustment in chronically ill and handicapped children. *Journal of Pediatric Psychology, 14*(2), 157–173.

Weissbourd, B., & Kagan, S.L. (1989). Family support programs: Catalyst for change. *American Journal of Orthopsychiatry, 59,* 20–31.

Weissman, M., Leaf, P., & Bruce, M.L. (1987). Single parent women. *Social Psychiatry, 22,* 29–36.

Yeates, K.O., MacPhee, D., Campbell, F.A., & Ramey, C.T. (1983). Maternal IQ and home environment as determinants of early childhood intellectual competence: A developmental analysis. *Developmental Psychology, 19*(5), 731–739.

Yeung, W.J., Linver, M.R., & Brooks-Gunn, J. (2002). How money matters for young children's development: Parental investment and family processes. *Child Development, 73*(6), 1861–1879.

Zuckerman, M., Oltean, M., & Monashkin, I. (1958). The parental attitudes of mothers of schizophrenics. *Journal of Consulting Psychology, 22,* 307–310.

CHAPTER 11

DEVELOPING AND IMPLEMENTING PREVENTIVE INTERVENTION PROGRAMS FOR CHILDREN AT RISK

Poverty as a Case in Point

DALE CLARK FARRAN

INTRODUCTION

A causal link between educational status and poverty has been assumed since the 1960s, when President Johnson began the "war on poverty." The notion that poverty produced an early educational disadvantage that then persisted throughout the school years led to the creation of Head Start in 1964—with its curriculum focused on school readiness skills—and eventually culminated in Goal 1 of the National Education Goals Panel (NEGP): "By the year 2000, all children in America will start school ready to learn" (NEGP, n.d.). Thus, we have had 40 years of experience creating interventions prior to formal school entry for children whose families live in poverty. This chapter describes the continuing need for this effort, the results of the efforts so far, and suggestions for what communities can do for their children at risk due to poverty. Poverty, of course, constitutes only one aspect of a complex set of stressors or risk factors for families who live in disadvantaged circumstances. As such, a comprehensive array of health, social, and educational/developmental programs are needed. However, this chapter emphasizes preventive interventions that are educational/developmental in their focus. The suggestions presented are based on evaluation and developmental research as well as the author's personal experiences of working more than 30 years in this field. Moreover, these suggestions can be integrated into more comprehensive models for preventive interventions as part of a larger systems approach for early intervention programs (see Guralnick, 2001).

SCHOOL ACHIEVEMENT AND POVERTY: A CONTINUING PROBLEM

The Nature and Extent of Poverty in the United States

The face of poverty has changed considerably in the United States since the late 1950s when the age group with the largest percentage of impoverished people was composed of individuals 65 years and older (U.S. Bureau of the Census, 2002). In the mid-1970s, children younger than age 18 became the group with the highest rate of poverty—a status that children have maintained since that time. Although the percentage of children who are impoverished has steadily decreased from a high of 22% in 1993 to a rate of 15.8% in 2001, the absolute number of children who are impoverished has continued to rise. In 2001, there were almost 3 million *more* children living in families who met the criteria for poverty than in 1993, a figure that has grave implications for services.

Not only do rates of poverty in the United States differ by age but also by ethnicity. The U.S. Bureau of the Census (2002) provided data comparing four ethnic groups: white non-Hispanic, black, Hispanic, and Asian and Pacific Islander. The percentage of children younger than age 18 living in poverty who are black or Hispanic is three times the rate for white non-Hispanic children (27%–30% compared with 9%), and the rate for Asian and Pacific islanders is slightly higher than whites.

Moreover, it is important to realize that current estimates of poverty in the United States are likely to be highly underestimated, given that the official United States poverty rate was developed in the 1960s and is based on the cost of a single item in the family's budget—food (Pearce & Brooks, 2002). It has only been updated since then to reflect inflation and does not account for such important differences among families as geographic region (housing and utility costs are just a few of the things that differ by region), age of children (e.g., the need for child care), or the demographic characteristics of the family (whether one or both parents are working). This is a crucial point when one considers the many services that become less available to families once they cross the thresholds set by the current poverty guidelines—housing, child care, food stamps, and health coverage, just to name a few.

There are other reasons why impoverished people in the United States today are more impoverished than they were in the 1970s (Harris, 1998).

By the late 1990s, the federal government was investing about 40% less in education and job training than it had in the 1970s. The minimum wage adjusted for inflation actually buys less today than it did in the 1970s. These reductions in federal spending disproportionately affect young families with children; these are the people most likely to be in minimum wage jobs and to need access to education and job training as a way to advance beyond minimum wage jobs. Maintaining closer equality among the various income strata in a country (by means of job training and income transfer approaches such as food stamps and child support) is important not only to the health of the impoverished but also to the health of the nation as a whole (Hertzman, 1999). In countries with similar levels of wealth, those who have more income equity have higher life expectancy rates as well as higher rates of academic achievement than those with greater inequality in income. As Hertzman pointed out, "those countries with relatively equal income distributions are healthier than those with relatively unequal distributions" (1999, p. 23). It appears to be in everyone's interest for the society as a whole to be responsible for its most impoverished members, and children are the most vulnerable of the impoverished. The following section provides evidence of the pernicious effect of poverty on children's academic achievement and school completion rates.

Academic Achievement of Children from Impoverished Families

Academic Skills

Children from economically disadvantaged homes are likely to begin school with significantly poorer academic skills than their more affluent peers and are at a much greater risk for school failure (e.g., Alexander & Entwisle, 1988; St. Pierre & Layzer, 1998; Stipek & Ryan, 1997; U.S. Department of Education [USDOE], National Center for Education Statistics [NCES], 2001). Even when they begin school with similar readiness levels, over time African American children fall behind their Caucasian counterparts in elementary school, particularly in reading (Phillips, 2000). By fourth grade, impoverished and minority children have begun to fall farther and farther behind middle-class Caucasian (majority) children in test scores and on other indices of school performance and affiliation. As impoverished and minority children move from elementary to high school, their school grades become lower and absences greater than those of children from lower risk backgrounds (Gutman, Sameroff, & Cole, 2003). Despite progress in achievement for both minority and majority children, the achievement gap between the two groups has remained unchanged since 1990

(USDOE, Institute of Education Sciences [IES], NCES, National Assessment of Educational Progress [NAEP], 2000). This escalating gap results in an estimated loss of 18–23 SAT points for minority children by the end of high school (Phillips, 2000). The effects of poverty on achievement are so significant that, in their studies of heritability, Turkheimer, Haley, Waldron, D'Onofrio, and Gottesman (2003) concluded that the developmental forces at work in poor environments were qualitatively different from those in adequate environments.

It is clear that elementary schools should be examined for their effectiveness in educating the impoverished, because even when children at risk have participated in early intervention programs, those advanced skills evident when the children entered school disappeared by the end of second grade (Farran, 1990, 2000; Lazar & Darlington, 1983). This may be due in part to a quantum leap in the difficulty of the academic subject matter between late second grade and early fourth grade. Chall, Jacobs, and Baldwin (1990) discovered that impoverished children who were reading at grade level in second grade lost ground rapidly after this period to fall 2–3 years below grade level (Chall, Jacobs, & Baldwin, 1990); they referred to this phenomenon as the "fourth-grade slump." According to Armbruster et al. (1991), content reading in fourth grade requires completely different skills involving independent and exploratory thinking and task persistence to a much greater degree than earlier material. Thus, school "readiness" must be defined as being ready to participate successfully in learning at least through the middle grades.

Grade Retention and Referral to Special Education

Preventing school failure is extremely important because the result of school failure is often placement in special education programs and/or retention practices that have been determined to be ineffective and sometimes harmful (Meisels & Liaw, 1993; Powell, 1995). Moreover, these practices target some groups of children more than others. The risk of repeating grades is at least twice as high for children from low-income families (Duncan & Magnuson, 2003). Data from national, regional, and local districts identify several characteristics of the groups who are more likely to be retained. Meisels and Liaw (1993) examined data from the 1988 National Education Longitudinal Study and found that minority students were being retained in significantly higher proportions; among retainees, boys significantly outnumbered girls; and 33.9% of the repeaters were from the lowest socioeconomic quartile, compared with 8.6% from the highest quartile. Thus, the typical profile of a child retained in early elementary school is male, African American, and from a family with fewer resources and less educated parents (Dauber, Alexander, & Entwisle, 1993; Land & Legters, 2002; McDermott, 1995).

Special education placements show the same effects. A review by Farran and Shonkoff (1994) concluded that over the course of the school years, 20% of the population will at some time receive a diagnosis as having special needs and that early referrals are related to gender, ethnicity, and social class. Special education referrals show a dramatic and sustained increase from third through the sixth grade (North Carolina Department of Public Instruction, 1999). Coincidentally, during this period the school curriculum changes dramatically.

School Completion Rates

High school dropout rates are related to poverty, to parental education, and, even when both are held constant, to ethnicity as well (Land & Legters, 2002). Although about 7% of all Caucasians are likely to drop out of high school, the rate for African Americans is nearly twice as high, and the rate for Hispanics is four times higher. High school completion rates are in large part predicted by early test scores. Unfortunately, test scores are predicted by poverty, which has its most negative effects on young children and especially if poverty is persistent when children are young (Duncan & Brooks-Gunn, 1998). Whatever the causal factors, the cost of dropping out of high school has risen dramatically over the past several years because of the large decrease in the number of unskilled jobs available (Land & Legters, 2002). Keeping children engaged and attending high school is important because each year that a student remains in school leads to a 7% increase in adult income (Ceci & Williams, 1997). High school dropout rates also are significant for communities as a whole (Alspaugh, 1998); in counties with high dropout rates, there is much higher unemployment, higher crime rates, and lower family income levels.

The Additional Effect of Gender

Finally, it should be noted that risks for lower achievement, grade retention, and dropping out of high school are uniformly higher for boys than they are for girls. There is some evidence that boys have begun entering kindergarten with less developed reading readiness skills than girls (USDOE, NCES, 2001) and that girls in Head Start programs enter kindergarten with higher reading achievement (Kreisman, 2003). In the NCES national study, kindergarten teachers rated girls as more eager to learn than boys, as paying attention better, and as being more persistent in tasks. The NCES data have not been reported for gender within socioeconomic status, but one would suspect that poverty is an independent risk factor, meaning that boys from impoverished families would be even more at risk and in need of special attention. Kreisman found that the Head Start boys did not start catching up to girls until the third grade. The gender gap among children from low-income families gains more credence when one notes that almost all of the longitudinal studies of preschool intervention for impoverished children have found that the effects were more positive for females than for males (e.g., Campbell, Ramey, Pungello, Sparling, & Miller-Johnson, 2002; Schweinhart & Weikart, 1997). The following section reviews current and past efforts to improve the educational achievement for children whose families are impoverished.

EARLY INTERVENTION FOR IMPOVERISHED CHILDREN: WHAT WE KNOW FROM WHERE WE HAVE BEEN

Summary of Results

Attempts to intervene early with children in poverty have a 40-year history, and the results have not been totally encouraging (Farran, 1990, 2000). The tested developmental performance of the children involved in individual programs, especially programs created in university settings, was improved immediately and was especially high at age 3, in which early intervention seems to produce an inflated, but unsustainable, test score. In the elementary grades, the tested performance of children from intervention programs did not continue to show significant effects after the first 1–3 years of public school experience. Children in the control group tested significantly behind the children in the experimental group beginning in the middle of the second year of life for programs that began in infancy (Brooks-Gunn, Liaw, & Klebanov, 1992; Ramey & Campbell, 1984) and almost immediately for those programs that began in preschool (Gray, Ramsey, & Klaus, 1982; Schweinhart, Barnes, & Weikart, 1993). The test scores of children in the control group gradually "caught up" to those of children in the experimental group so that by the second, third, or fourth grades, the differences between them were usually neither statistically nor educationally significant.

In the most scientifically sound, longitudinal study of early intervention, researchers with the Abecedarian Project located almost all of the adults who had been enrolled in the project during their preschool years. High school achievement data demonstrated small but significant positive effects for the intervention on reading and math calculation test scores, as well as a significant 4-point advantage for the intervention on IQ scores tested in adulthood (Campbell, Pungello, Miller-Johnson, Burchinal, & Ramey, 2001). Females who had been in the intervention program had attained significantly more years of education and more of them were still in school (Campbell et al., 2002). These findings suggest that lasting achievement gains can occur in a very well-run, small, university-based program that maintains continuing contact with the participants over many years. Moreover, these gains may translate into adult behaviors that are more socially desirable in a community.

Difficulty of Large-Scale Implementation

There have been difficulties, however, with using programs such as the Abecedarian Project as a base for expanding and offering programs on a broader scale.

Head Start, Title I, and State-Funded Prekindergartens

In the United States, the two most heavily funded federal intervention projects for the prevention of school failure among impoverished children are Head Start and Title I preschool education (U.S. General Accounting Office [USGAO], 2000a). Both have been criticized for not providing enough evaluative information on how well they prepare children for school (USGAO, 1997, 2000a, 2000b). Head Start, housed in the Administration for Children and Families, a division of the U.S. Department of Health and Human Services, is the oldest universal program in the United States for low-income children. Head Start primarily serves 3- and 4-year-olds in full- or half-day preschool classrooms that can be administered by a variety of local agencies. Title I of the U.S. Department of Education is the single largest federal investment in elementary and secondary education. Its primary purpose is "to help local education agencies and schools improve the teaching and learning of children who are failing or are most at risk of failing to meet challenging academic standards" (USGAO, 2000b, pp. 4–5). In 1986, Title I funds were approved to establish prekindergarten classrooms. In its survey, the GAO found that 90% of school districts in the United States received Title I funds, and 17% had chosen to use some of the funds to serve preschool children (USGAO, 2000b).

In addition to prekindergarten classrooms supported by Title I funds, a large number of states are investing state money in preschool education, and, often, those classrooms are associated with the public schools. Gilliam and Zigler (2001) presented a summary of evaluations of state-funded preschools through 2000. They concluded that the evaluations were, for the most part, poorly done. Most did not use a comparison group to measure differential outcomes. For those few that did, the findings were similar to ones for smaller programs—immediate positive effects for participating followed by no lasting effects beyond first grade when the comparison children caught up to the achievement levels of those who had the prekindergarten experience. Georgia is one of the few states that has begun to collect systematic data on the effectiveness of this large investment in preschool education for its 4-year-olds, especially those in poverty (Henry et al., 2003). Comparing its state-supported prekindergarten program with private preschools and Head Start, Henry and colleagues concluded that, after controlling for family characteristics, children from Georgia's program caught up with the skills of those children in the private preschools and outscored those children who had been in Head Start classrooms. The gains were related to the quality of the prekindergarten program.

Even Start and the Infant Health and Development Program

Two other large-scale programs have been implemented widely and evaluated thoroughly in the past 10–15 years—Even Start and the Infant Health and Development Program (IHDP). The findings are worth reviewing from their evaluations because they suggest the difficulties that communities face in taking a project "to scale"—attempting to implement a successful program from a limited and narrow setting to using it more broadly.

In 1991, the Even Start authorization (Title I, Part B) of the Elementary and Secondary Education Act of 1965 (PL 89-10), as amended by the Hawkins-Stafford Elementary and Secondary School Improvement Amendments of 1988 (PL 100-297), was amended by Congress to require the program to combine early childhood education and adult education for parents as a collaborative project among agencies in the community (St. Pierre, Swartz, Murray, & Deck, 1996). The Even Start program combines early childhood education, adult literacy, and parenting education. To be eligible to participate, a family must have an adult who is eligible for adult education (typically without a high school education and in need of the GED), have a child younger than 8 years old, and live in a Chapter 1, Title I, elementary school attendance area.

Abt Associates conducted a major evaluation of the Even Start programs. Initially, Even Start child participants gained more than the children in the control group (St. Pierre et al., 1996), but those advantages were lost 18 months later as the control group caught up with the participating children on both the Peabody Picture Vocabulary Test (PPVT; Dunn & Dunn, 1981) and the Preschool Inventory, a measure of school readiness developed by Abt Associates (1991). There were no effects from participating in Even Start on such measures as the quality of the home environment, parent–child interaction during book reading, parental expectations for their children, or employment or income. Moreover, 46% of Even Start mothers were classified as having high levels of depressive symptoms at the outset, and those symptoms were not affected by participation in Even Start.

Again, as with other programs with marginal or disappearing effects, explaining why the effect dissipated is crucial. In general, St. Pierre and colleagues (1996) found that all three programmatic elements were ill-defined. Local sites had control over the early childhood education component because the funder specified no structure or content (St. Pierre & Swartz, 1996). About one third of the programs chose to use the High/Scope curriculum. The adult education component was also unspecified and not systematically implemented across sites. At least 14% of the families left Even Start in the first year of their enrollment because of a "general lack of interest" (St. Pierre & Swartz, 1996, p. 25).

The Abecedarian Project and Project Care together served as the "prototype for the IHDP intervention program" according to Ramey, Bryant, Wasik, Sparling, Fendt, & LaVange (1992, p. 460). Unlike previous intervention efforts, IHDP was conceived as a "randomized clinical trial" (Spiker, Kraemer, Scott, & Gross, 1991) in which the same specified intervention would be delivered in eight monitored sites simultaneously. The IHDP targeted low birth weight infants, a large percentage of whom came from disadvantaged circumstances. The Abecedarian curriculum was developed in an intervention program for children in poverty. Applying it to low birth weight infants was using the curriculum with a new type of sample.

Because this was a randomized control trial in which the exact intervention was to be delivered at each site, careful monitoring of adherence to the program was undertaken. IHDP children have been followed through age 8 with major publications emerging from the assessments at age 5 (Brooks-Gunn et al., 1994) and age 8 (McCarton et al., 1997). At the age 5 assessment, the investigators retained 82% of the sample. The 9.4 IQ score difference obtained between the intervention and control children at age 3 had reduced to a difference of 0.02 points on the Wechsler Preschool and Primary Scale of Intelligence (WPPSI; Wechsler, 1967) at age 5. The scores of the intervention group decreased by about 2 points, but the control group's score of 7 points higher erased most of the early difference found between the groups. At age 8, no significant differences favored the experimental group on any measure. The pattern obtained in smaller studies was again demonstrated in this larger, well-controlled study; early positive effects were very difficult to maintain.

Hill, Brooks-Gunn, and Waldfogel (2003) re-analyzed the IHDP in a sophisticated exploration of the effects of greater participation in an intervention program. In every program, some families, for various reasons, do not receive the intervention as much as others—children do not attend the center, families move, crises prevent the family from keeping appointments, or the intervention has a lower priority than other events in the family's life. In a large-scale implementation, loss of families is even more likely to occur than in the smaller, more intense university-related studies. Hill et al. compared high participators with families in the control group who had similar characteristics at the beginning of the implementation. They concluded that there had indeed been a positive effect for those who had attended most regularly, and the effects persisted through age 8. Communities implementing services can learn two lessons from the IHDP: 1) the importance of supporting families' participation and 2) not assuming an approach will not work until the level of actual participation has been taken into account.

The following section provides more specific recommendations for the organization and content of services for young children from impoverished families.

Guiding Principles

The first part of this section deals with general guiding principles to be used as a framework for thinking about what intervention services to provide (and to whom). The second section deals with the general framework of a system of intervention, whereas the subsequent sections deal with the content with a special focus on preschool and the transition to elementary school.

General Developmental Processes

Although children's development is a complex and multifaceted process, six general developmental processes could be used as the foundation for a community's plans for children at risk because of poverty.

1. *Development appears to proceed in bursts rather than in a steadily linear fashion.* Even physical growth from infancy through puberty is marked by mini-growth spurts followed by periods of stasis (Hermanussen, 1998). Frequent measurements have shown that children's leg bone lengths do not change for days and weeks at a time but then show sharp growth spurts overnight (Hermanussen, Geiger-Benoit, Burmeister, & Sippell, 1988). "Human growth over short periods is therefore a discontinuous, irregular, and unpredictable process" (Thalange, Foster, Gill, Price, & Clayton, 1996, p. 427). What is true for physical growth is likely to be true for other areas of development. For example, cognitive development is marked by periods of great change followed by latency periods. The age period from 5 to 7 years is marked by major transitions in children's mental and social development, as is the period from age 12 to 14 (McCall, Appelbaum, & Hogarty, 1973; White, 1965). Given the irregularity of human growth, changes during these periods can be sudden and variable (e.g., the child who seems to learn to read overnight). This principle argues

against premature labeling of children as well as against separating young children from gaining access to environments that facilitate development.

2. *In development, many paths lead to the same outcome and no particular pathway is more desirable than another.* This is the concept of "equipotentiality," or the idea that children can arrive at the same outcome even though they start from many different places (Thelen & Smith, 1994). Development appears uniform and predictable only from a distance if one smoothes over the great irregularities among individuals. The closer one observes individual progress, the less predictable and less similar to others it becomes. The intervention environments provided for children, therefore, should be substantive and also responsive. Rigid developmental checklists and highly didactic, predetermined curricula are unlikely to be effective and may stifle the development of many children by forcing them into trajectories that are not appropriate. Creating responsive educational environments requires informed, intelligent, and caring educators, something difficult to achieve in a political climate in which child care is one of the poorest paid professions.

3. *Human beings are extremely social, and individual characteristics can be modified greatly by the surrounding social group.* Even children who are aggressive and come from dysfunctional families moderate their behaviors if they attend schools that are stable and where the majority of children are not aggressive (Rutter & Quinton, 1977). Intervention typically focuses on changing characteristics of individuals; little attention has focused on changing the characteristics of the groups to which the individual belongs (the classroom and the school). In fact, children with behavioral or learning problems often are placed in groups with other children who have similar problems—a situation that exacerbates the individual characteristics. Unfortunately, early childhood teachers are seldom knowledgeable about how to create working classroom environments and learning communities. Programs are typically funded for specific groups of children, which tends to isolate children into groups with similar backgrounds and/or presenting problems. Universal programs serving a variety of children would enable teachers to use social referencing and peer role models more effectively to create more facilitative environments. To do this effectively, however, teachers must have the right training.

4. *All major changes produce a period of disorganization followed by reorganization.* Younger children may take longer to reorganize following a change (e.g., a new classroom, a new school), and the disorganization may be more pervasive because they have fewer alternative behaviors in their repertoire. Some change is normative and therefore unavoidable (e.g., puberty); other change is non-normative and imposed by society (e.g., the age at which children enter high school, the number of different classes children attend in a day). The simultaneous accumulation of normative and non-normative

changes creates stress and reduces academic achievement and also causes increases in behavioral difficulties (Simmons, Burgeson, Carlton-Ford, & Blyth, 1987), especially for males. Communities have control over the degree of additional stress they place on children and families. Avoiding non-normative stress is a principle that communities could adopt when planning a system of programs for children. Current policies frequently and thoughtlessly disrupt care for children by changing eligibility requirements at specific ages (e.g., 3 years) or with specific circumstances of the family (e.g., income). Preschool planning should occur at the community level so that families are aware of the options, transitions, and placements that are available.

5. *It is important to remember that development remains malleable well into adulthood if appropriate alternative options are available.* Although intervention in early childhood is desirable and likely to have the most cost-effective results, it is not the only time individuals can make changes in their lives (Bruer, 1997; Farran, 2002). In Werner's longitudinal study of those who had developed in very high-risk situations, remarkable changes in life course trajectories occurred when individuals were in their late 20s and 30s—when there were positive options open to them (Werner & Smith, 1992). Yet, closing off options and removing children's "future orientation," especially in adolescence, increases the possibility of negative outcomes (Trommsdorff, 1983).

6. *Children process information differently during different age spans.* These differences have been termed *stages* by theorists such as Piaget and Freud or *modes of functioning* by Donaldson (1992). Most theorists agree that the age from birth through the early grades of school is one broad developmental stage with certain characteristics important for intervention. One could term this first period as *rule generation.* Up until the shift in development that occurs between the ages of 5 and 7 years, children actively and continuously construct rules about how the particular cultural and physical world they inhabit works. The rules concern everything—the physical properties of objects, the structure of language, and the methods of social interaction, among others. Children construct the rules from incomplete and messy data. Good examples of rule generation come from the study of language development. Research shows that 8-month-old infants develop rules for word boundaries after hearing 2 minutes of organized nonsense words (Saffran, Aslin, & Newport, 1996). The rules children construct can only reflect the material to which they have been exposed, an important consideration for educators as children from diverse backgrounds first enter school.

Although children generate rules from messy data, it is very likely that stimulation can be too fragmented or experiences too isolated and nonrepeating to allow children to derive the general principles. Intervention for children with fragmented and disconnected early experiences must be organized and structured with parameters that children can grasp and depend on. Teachers must understand the necessity of creating enriched experiences that follow predictable patterns.

Developmental Goals for Intervention

In addition to the developmental principles outlined previously, it is important to focus on what the goals of intervention should be to achieve long-term favorable outcomes for children. "Children who do well [in unfavorable environments] have adults who care for them, brains that are developing normally, and, as they grow older, the ability to manage their own attention, emotions, and behavior" (Masten & Coatsworth, 1998, p. 215). The issue for communities is which systems can be put into place to help ensure these outcomes. The suggestions that follow will be based on the framework provided by Masten and Coatsworth, who described competencies needed across the age spans, starting with infancy. They argued that very young children need to be with caring adults, ones to whom the children can form an enduring attachment relationship. During that same developmental period, children need to develop attention regulation in multiple domains; they need to be able to focus their attention, to regulate negative reactions, to comply with rules, and to interact competently with peers. As children enter school, they must be able to get along with groups of children, engage in socially appropriate conduct, and have enough individual resources to respond effectively to instruction. Masten and Coatsworth also discussed the resources that children need in order to succeed. These include schools in which high-quality instruction occurs; families are involved in the child's education; and there is access to extracurricular enrichment activities, especially in middle and high school. Research on the effects of specific programs tends to support the areas highlighted by Masten and Coatsworth.

Levels of Intervention

Another dimension that communities must consider in attempting to address the needs of young children from low-income families is the level at which intervention will take place. Offord et al. (1999) proposed three levels of possible intervention and the advantages and disadvantages of each. The clinical level is the one most acceptable to the public and politicians. This level of intervention targets children after they have exhibited a problem. For the problem of school failure among impoverished children, this level of intervention is found in programs such as Reading

Recovery (Clay, 1996)—individual treatment that begins at the end of first or second grade when children have been identified as not reading at grade level. The least positive application of this level of intervention is grade retention; children who fail a grade are identified, retained, and forced to repeat it. Offord et al. asserted that these types of interventions are most helpful when the population affected by the disorder is relatively small, when the characteristics and prognosis for a condition are clear, and when effective treatments exist. School failure of children in poverty does not fit those requirements.

The next level of intervention Offord et al. (1999) proposed is targeted intervention. Children are identified for intervention because they have a high risk of developing a problem. They can be identified by characteristics such as family income, which is the model that Head Start and many state-funded prekindergarten programs follow, or because the children live in a catchment area that feeds into a Title I school, which is how some Title I prekindergarten programs operate. Children also can be identified because they have some characteristics that suggest they are already at risk themselves for the problem. Many Title I prekindergarten programs, for example, enroll 4-year-old children only after a screening assessment indicates they are educationally behind. The advantage of this approach is that intervention is possible before the problem becomes well established and thus prevent its occurrence. These programs are more expensive and harder to sell to the public. Moreover, the programs carry with them the implicit assumption that the problem resides within the individual (rather than the community), and they can divert attention away from focusing on communitywide mechanisms for change (e.g., more funding for elementary schools in high poverty areas).

Finally, Offord et al. (1999) talked about universal programs. When communities adopt universal programs, the programs are made available to everyone. Universal programs avoid the labeling and stigmatization that can occur with both clinical and targeted interventions. The prekindergarten program in the state of Georgia is an example of a universal program; it is available to all and, as Offord et al. asserted, it therefore has the support of middle-class parents, and the quality is higher. These programs are expensive, however, so they can be difficult to sell to the public. Most of the children receiving the program may not be in any danger of developing school achievement problems and thus may not actually need the program.

Offord et al. (1999) recommended that policy makers consider creating services within their communities that are a mix of all three levels of intervention. The strategies recommended in the remainder of this chapter will consist of a mixture of the three levels. The focus of the recommendations is facilitating the development of the positive characteristics that

Masten and Coatsworth (1998) described in order to prevent the school-related problems so prevalent in impoverished neighborhoods. The first section is an overview of the components of a community system that need to be in place and interrelated. Following that is a more developed description for how preschools should be organized and what their educational focus should be. Finally, the importance of the transition to school and systems that can make that process more successful for impoverished children are discussed.

COMPONENTS OF A COMMUNITY SYSTEM

The following proposals take into account the principles laid out in the preceding section to create a system that would begin in infancy and continue through the early grades of elementary school. The goal is to keep children connected and engaged—with their families, their teachers, and their schools—and to provide both support and wide latitude for development. School success ultimately means not only graduating but also the possibility of attaining enough credits to be minimally qualified to apply for college. Each component of the system is described followed by a summary of what communities can do to implement the component.

Home Visits by Public Health Nurses

Although home visiting programs targeted to impoverished families have not generally proven to be effective (Gomby, Culross, & Behrman, 1999), visits provided by public health nurses have had long-term, continued positive effects. In studies of these programs, home visits by nurses typically began either during pregnancy or when the infant was 6 weeks old and continued through the first 6–24 months of the child's life (e.g., Olds, Henderson, Tatelbaum, & Chamberlin, 1986). The positive results obtained by Olds and colleagues in Vermont have been replicated in other parts of the United States (Kitzman et al., 1997) as well as in Australia (Armstrong, Fraser, Dadds, & Morris, 2000) and Ireland (Johnson, Howell, & Molloy, 1993).

The results from all of the studies are roughly similar, with some variation. Children who are visited by public health nurses are healthier (with fewer illnesses and more immunizations) and have fewer injuries and fewer days hospitalized for injuries and ingestions of foreign substances. The latter may indicate increased parental diligence. In some studies, parents receiving intervention report feeling closer to their children and more competent as parents. There is evidence that rates of parental depression can also be lowered through these nurse home visits, and the visits achieve an increase in spacing between pregnancies. There is evidence to suggest that this early intervention may have persistent effects on at least a few adolescent outcomes (e.g., running away, number of sexual partners; Olds et al., 1998). However, an overview of nurse home visit programs suggests the effects are much stronger in the first 2 years of the child's life and do not maintain themselves in long-term follow-up with no further intervention (Kendrick et al., 2000).

Implications for Communities

Identify low-income families during pregnancy—or at least immediately following birth—and institute a home visiting program by public health nurses. The minimum length of the visits should be during the first 6 months of the child's life. Visits should occur every 2 weeks. The focus of the program should be on children's health, the parent–child relationship, and family planning for the mother.[1] The expense of this program means that it would likely be provided as a targeted intervention, not a universal one (although all families might benefit).

Universally Available Care Through Age 2

The most difficult age for a community to plan for is the infant/toddler period. Some evidence suggests that children's extensive group-care experience is linked with later social and behavioral problems, especially for children from low-income families (Haskins, 1985; National Institute for Child Health and Human Development [NICHD] Early Child Care Research Network, 2003). Although this finding is controversial (Love et al., 2003), the connection between group care and problematic behavior has been made so often that attention to its cause is important. By definition, "extensive" group-care experiences will have begun in the infant/toddler period. One possible contributor to later social difficulties is the fact that toddlers experience physiologically measurable stress when they are near multiple peers all the same age (Watamura, Donzella, Alwin, & Gunnar, 2003).

Therefore, the decision for how to support low-income families and their children's development when the children are younger than 3 years is not straightforward or simple. There are conflicting needs. Families are assisted best when the care situation is available, is established early in the child's life, is continuous and does not have to be re-established—especially because of a crisis—and is of such high quality that children are actually

---

[1]If communities wish to follow the successful program developed by David Olds and his colleagues in Vermont, then details of that program are available (Olds, 1988).

receiving compensatory experiences in the child care setting. Achieving all of these goals, however, is almost impossible.

In the United States, there is no organized system of care for young children. Family child care homes and other such arrangements that are smaller and less institutional tend to fall apart often and precipitously. Although the NICHD (2003) study did not find long-term effects for children due to repeated changes in child care, it is very stressful for families to suddenly lose child care and to have to find a new arrangement. Low-income families who have sometimes just entered the labor force are most often employed in situations that do not allow much flexibility.

Yet, group care in child care centers is far more stable. Although individual teachers turn over at a remarkably high rate, the centers themselves tend to be stable. Someone at the center will cover another teacher's absence, and a central office finds replacements for teachers who leave. Stability makes child care centers attractive, but the quality of care typically found is low. National studies rate an astounding 70% or more of infant/toddler care as being of minimal quality (Peisner-Feinberg & Burchinal, 1997). Low-quality care makes center-based care a poor choice for children who need compensatory high-quality care because of the poverty, low education, and stress in their families.

Part of the difficulty in providing quality child care for infants and toddlers involves the education and training of the staff and the economics of improving both of them. When child care ratios are 1:4 for infants and 1:10 for toddlers, as national associations prescribe, infant/toddler care is extremely expensive. In order to afford care for infants and toddlers, many programs end up cutting teacher salaries. Yet, requiring teachers to have more education would require higher rates of pay. In Wisconsin, a state with a long history of proactive support for child care, the rate of pay for child care teachers in 2003 was $7.50 per hour, and annual incomes of child care teachers ranged from $13,000 to $15,000 (McGurk, 2003). These are not salaries that will attract those with professional training in caring for children.

The T.E.A.C.H. program in North Carolina represents an attempt to create an early child care statewide system that would improve both the stability of child care workers and their level of training (Child Care Services Association, 2003). Through state and foundation funds, T.E.A.C.H. offers child care workers the possibility of enrolling in school (at whatever level they are ready to begin), covering their tuition and books. Child care centers agree at the outset to release the teachers for part of the day and to increase their salaries when they complete the educational degree. In addition, T.E.A.C.H. offers health insurance, a state-administered group health plan open to child care centers whose teachers are participating in the educational benefit as well as to centers whose staff all have 2- or 4-year degrees. Health insurance helps to ensure staff stability. The program has already shown important effects on the North Carolina child care work force. Turnover among participants has been reduced from a North Carolina average of 32% per year to 11%. Most important, the quality of the classrooms of the participating teachers has significantly improved in both infant/toddler and preschool classrooms (Cassidy, Buell, Pugh-Hoese, & Russell, 1995). The North Carolina comprehensive approach is being adopted by other states (e.g., Washington, Wisconsin).

Although child care is not precisely intervention, attending to its quality is important because poor quality experiences can actually increase children's developmental difficulties. With many more women who have young children entering the labor market because of 1996 welfare reform (Chase-Lansdale et al., 2003), it is important for communities to determine how they will support impoverished families in caring for their very young children.

Implications for Communities

A coordinated system for referral and quality assurance for programs can be created to serve children under age 3. The funds of charitable agencies and local and state agencies to subsidize the training and salaries of teachers who care for young children can be coordinated. A group health care system can be created so that child care centers can provide adequate coverage for their workers, and the help can be tied to the enhancement of quality in the child care provided. According to Offord et al. (1999), these recommendations must be for a universal program because it focuses on the centers and not just the targeted families. These infant/toddler centers would serve children from a variety of income backgrounds. In order to reach low-income families, communities must also provide an outreach system that will apprise impoverished families of their choices, starting with the birth of their child. Centers must be placed in low-income neighborhoods and near transportation options so that low-income families can gain access to them easily.

Prekindergarten Programs for 3- and 4-Year-Olds

Many different and unrelated sources of support for preschool educational programs for children from low-income families include Head Start, Title I funds that support prekindergarten classrooms (USGAO, 2000a), charitable agency support (e.g., United Way), and state funds.[2] A few states, notably Georgia, provide "universal" prekindergarten programs (Henry et al., 2003), whereas others, such as North Carolina, have several different initiatives to support preschools. Many state initiatives are focused solely on 4-year-olds, whereas Head Start serves 3- and 4-year-olds in all states.

Besides the different ages served, there are other difficulties in coordinating prekindergarten programs. First, the funding comes from different agencies that have different eligibility and program requirements. Head Start funding is through the Administration for Children and Families of the U.S. Department of Health and Human Services. Title I funds come through the Elementary and Secondary Education Act of the U.S. Department of Education. State funds are most often administered by their state departments of education, but states may decide to allow programs to be housed in both public and private agencies providing child care (see Denton, n.d.). Second, administrative staff for the programs at the local level may have no history of working together and, in many cases, may not know each other. Third, the programs come under different local regulatory requirements. Head Start and community nonprofit centers (e.g., United Way) must meet state child care licensing requirements. In many states, the education agencies have successfully lobbied to be exempt from such oversight. Fourth, over the years, suspicion and contempt have been allowed to fester so that groups with the same goals refuse to coordinate their efforts (as one education official said, "We are not *day care!*"). As more attention is paid to providing more educational experiences to children from impoverished families before they attend formal school, it is no longer defensible for agencies not to work together in a local community.

In Guilford County, North Carolina, the Guilford County Schools and the United Child Development Services agency that administered Head Start began to work together to serve all children from low-income families in the county prior to formal school entry. Much of this effort came about because of the dogged determination of Dot Kearns, a tireless advocate for children who had served as a county commissioner and school board member, and with the support of Jerry Weast, then Superintendent of Schools (Superintendent of the Montgomery County Public Schools in Maryland at the time this book was published). It is important to mention this because it illustrates what leadership at the local level can accomplish. Ms. Kearns pushed the school system and Head Start to develop preschools

---

[2]This list does not include other preschool programs such as Even Start, funded by the U.S. Department of Education; Even Start Family Literacy Program; and the Preschool Grants Program of the U.S. Department of Education, Office of Special Education.

in catchment areas throughout the county that complemented each other rather than competed. For example, she oversaw the development of a coordinated screening system. Using the same screening instruments, the school system and Head Start collaboratively determined for which program each child was eligible and assigned children to classrooms accordingly. With the subsequent participation of Robin Britt, who became Executive Director of United Child Development Services in the mid-1990s, the two agencies have developed a standard curriculum to be used in all classrooms and are working toward having the same licensure requirements for teachers. Guilford County is an example of what can be done at the local level despite obstacles presented by the lack of central coordination of preschool programs at the national level.

Implications for Communities

An administrative structure at the local level can be developed to be responsible for a coordinated system of prekindergarten classrooms for 3- and 4-year-old children from impoverished families. In addition, communities can gain access to all of the funds available for school readiness initiatives but funnel them through a central oversight group (some have created formal staff housed in the mayor's office). This group can be responsible for shared planning of facilities, shared screening, and shared curricular and teacher licensure requirements, with the goal that wherever a child is served, the educational experiences will be equivalent. Unless there is a change in the policies of several agencies, this will have to be a targeted initiative.

THE EDUCATIONAL FOCUS OF PREKINDERGARTEN PROGRAMS

The Search for an Early Childhood Education Curriculum

With the components outlined previously in place, the next important question is to decide what the focus of the prekindergarten programs should be. The search for the best curriculum model for young children in general has a history that is intertwined with intervention efforts (Goffin, 1994). In the 1960s, there was an explosion of early childhood curriculum models; the curriculum developers, however, provided much of the information about their own curricular effectiveness, and few independent evaluations were conducted. In the 1970s, Miller, an evaluation specialist, and her colleagues (Miller & Dyer, 1975) mounted an extensive investigation of four preschool programs (Bereiter-Englemann, Darcee [Susan Gray's program], Montessori, and what they termed *traditional nursery school*).

Classrooms were randomly assigned to conditions, and children were followed through high school (Miller & Bizzell, 1983, 1984). In the high school assessment, Miller and Bizzell obtained a differential treatment effect related to gender: high school boys who had been in Montessori preschools were achieving significantly better than boys from other programs, whereas high school girls who had been in the Darcee model were outperforming other girls. Thus, more than 2 decades ago, a randomized design investigating the longitudinal effects of different preschool curricula determined that different types of preschool experiences were important for males and females from low-income families. Neither curricula with the long-term positive effects is currently available for adoption. Darcee no longer exists, and Montessori requires teacher training that is out of the mainstream of teacher preparation.

In the 1970s and 1980s, curriculum models were all but forgotten as a huge number of children entered child care programs when women joined the labor force in dramatic fashion (Goffin, 1994). Hot debates about the long-term effects of various curriculum models from the 1960s continued, however, among the developers of competing models that were still available (e.g., Engelmann, 1999; Schweinhart, Weikart, & Larner, 1986). In addition, the National Association for the Education of Young Children (NAEYC) issued a revised position statement in 1997 on what it termed *developmentally appropriate practice* (DAP) (Bredekamp & Copple, 1997). DAP is less a curriculum than it is a prescribed set of general teacher behaviors (do's and don'ts).

Thus, we are in the position in which many of the general child development curriculum models from the 1960s and 1970s are recommended to school districts and states as they implement prekindergarten programs (see Lunenberg, 2000; see Dodge, Colker, & Heroman, 2002, for a well-developed example of a general child development approach). At the same time, newer curriculum models reflect an orientation toward more focused educational goals such as literacy (see Pellin & Edmonds, 2001). Neither the developmental nor the educational model has sufficient or rigorous enough research to support its adoption. States and communities that prescribe a set of acceptable curricula for their prekindergarten classrooms include both types.

Deciding on the focus of prekindergarten instruction is important because historically the transition to school from all types of preschools has been difficult, and the early gains are seldom sustained (e.g., Whitehurst et al., 1999). The lack of sustainability may be due to an inappropriate instructional focus (Farran & Lipsey, 2003). Programs based in child development theory may be diffuse and without stated goals to guide the teacher's instruction. Yet, the worry about some of the more focused educational programs is that classrooms will become didactic and harsh, forcing children prematurely into anxiety about learning (Stipek, Feiler, Daniels, & Milburn, 1995). It seems clear that young children who are delayed in such basic areas as vocabulary and mathematics knowledge need an environment rich with immediate learning possibilities. The trick is to find out how to provide those in a manner that engages children naturally.

Literacy Emphasis

Children growing up in poverty generally have poorly developed language skills (Hart & Risley, 1995). Poor language skills are thus a significant part of the reason children from disadvantaged families are at risk for school failure. Moreover, given the centrality of reading and verbal ability to school performance, there is little doubt that early language-related skills have causal influence on later school success. Longitudinal studies have consistently found such variables to be among the strongest predictors of academic outcomes during the early school years. Kurdek and Sinclair (2000) found that verbal readiness at kindergarten entry was the strongest predictor of first- through fifth-grade standardized test scores and grades in math and reading. In Torgesen et al. (1999), the strongest kindergarten predictors of second-grade reading comprehension included rapid naming and general verbal ability. Pianta and McCoy (1997) demonstrated that language skills at kindergarten entry differentiated children who were retained in a grade, placed in special education, and scored low on achievement tests in the second grade. Other longitudinal studies have produced similar findings.

A small body of research has assessed preschool programs with instruction on specific language-related skills and shows effects that endure beyond preschool. For example, Whitehurst et al. (1999) evaluated a literacy program added to the regular Head Start curriculum that consisted of sound- and letter-awareness activities with interactive reading at home and in the classroom. Positive effects were found at the end of the preschool year on emergent literacy skills and vocabulary that lasted through kindergarten but not through the first and second grades. Similarly, Blachman, Tangel, Ball, Black, and McGraw (1999) assessed an intervention to develop phonological awareness and word recognition skills for kindergarten children from low-income families. At the end of first grade, children who received treatment outperformed the control group on phonological awareness, letter name and sound knowledge, and word recognition, and they were still superior on word recognition at the end of the second grade.

A focus on specific literacy-related skills, such as phonemic awareness, represents a relatively narrow approach to literacy. Reading is a complex process made up of multiple components that should be promoted together

(Byrnes, 2001). Students must first learn to decode and for that, phonemic awareness and rapid naming are strong predictors (Rayner, Foorman, Perfetti, Pesetsky, & Seidenberg, 2002). Those skills by themselves, however, do not show much relationship to reading comprehension, a skill that is critical for children's progress in school (Schatschneider, Carlson, Francis, Foorman, & Fletcher, 2002; Torgesen et al., 1999).

The language variable that does predict reading comprehension is vocabulary (Snow, Burns, & Griffin, 1998). Dickinson and Tabors (2001) and colleagues' longitudinal study of young children's exposure to language in their homes and child care settings found that reading comprehension in the fourth and seventh grades was predicted by measures of receptive vocabulary and oral language taken at kindergarten (Tabors, Snow, & Dickinson, 2001). Snow et al. (1998) also reported that focused instruction to improve vocabulary has been shown to increase children's reading comprehension. Interestingly, the type of instruction effective for this purpose was not drill and practice but involved providing children with conceptual understanding of the words. This finding parallels work on vocabulary acquisition by young children (Booth & Waxman, 2002; Waxman & Booth, 2001), indicating that children as young as 3 years old acquire and retain vocabulary based on conceptual information and connections, something they term a "dramatic and uniquely human process" (Booth & Waxman, 2002, p. B20). In contrast to focusing on specific emergent literacy skills, the preschool literacy program that might have stronger and more lasting effects on educational achievement is one emphasizing vocabulary growth and language in a way that connects concepts to children's experiences.

Literacy Is Not Enough

As the earlier work by Miller and her colleagues indicated, there may be a gender difference in what young children are most receptive to during the preschool years, a difference that is linked generally to long-term school achievement (Miller & Bizzell, 1983, 1984). A strictly literacy focus therefore could be disproportionately suitable for girls, whose language development at this age tends to be ahead of that of boys. What is most important, however, is that children from low-income backgrounds enter elementary school with far less extensive mathematical knowledge than children from middle-income families (Denton & West, 2002; Griffin, Case, & Siegler, 1994; Jordan, Huttenlocher, & Levine, 1992). Moreover, current preschool programs have minimal effects on mathematics skills (Farran, Lange, & Boyles, 2003; Zill et al., 2001). Although including mathematics is not the only additional emphasis to suggest, it is one for which there is a demonstrable need and on which current work is being done so that teachers have curricular activities from which to choose

(Clements & Sarama, 2003; Griffin, Case, & Capodilupo, 1995; Griffin et al., 1994; Starkey, Klein, & Wakeley, in press).

Mathematics is a content area that appears to be particularly vulnerable to instruction. In 1996, Coleman asserted that science and math achievement were highly dependent on school instruction (as opposed to family background). In a review of work done in the 1970s in six countries, he concluded that "mathematics is the subject . . . for which school makes the most difference, science is next, and verbal skills, writing, and civics are the subjects for which school makes the least difference" (Coleman, 1996, p. 214). Children from low-income and minority backgrounds continue to achieve far less in mathematics than children from higher income, majority families (USDOE, IES, NCES, NAEP, 2000). In a large study of children who differed by socioeconomic status as well as the presence or absence of mild disabilities, Cawley, Parmar, Foley, Salmon, and Roy (2001) concluded that socioeconomic status was a greater risk factor to mathematics achievement than disability status. Although one could speculate why this is so, it does appear as if something about poverty environments is having a particularly negative effect on children's mathematical understandings. Thus, it is essential to help prekindergarten teachers understand and provide instruction in mathematics more effectively for children from low-income backgrounds.

Classrooms and schools in which children from low-income families test higher tend to spend more time on task and have teachers who make greater demands for achievement (Snow et al., 1998). Both cognitively challenging activities (Kontos & Keyes, 1999; Kontos & Wilcox-Herzog, 1997) and cognitively challenging talk (Smith & Dickinson, 1994) are associated with increases in cognitive skills.

Teaching Format Is Crucial

The danger of including more "academic" material in prekindergarten is that teachers will teach in an instructional format that is unsuited for learning by young children. Preschool curricula with an educational focus may unwisely present the material in a whole-group teaching format in which 20 or more 4-year-olds are supposed to attend to the teacher for 20–40 minutes at a time. For example, in *Bright Beginnings* (Pellin & Edmonds, 2001), the whole-group format is mandated to occur four times a day, albeit recommended for shorter times than 40 minutes. Studying preschool classrooms, Smith (2001) found two characteristics to be consistently and strongly predictive of later vocabulary and emergent literacy: how much time children were in small-group instruction and the quality of the writing program in the classroom (having a writing center and eliciting ideas for writing from children). Neither time in free play nor scores on a general child development environmental measure were related to later *literacy* outcomes. (The study did not have measures of other outcomes such as mathematics achievement or self-regulation.)

The use of small-group instruction as the primary vehicle for learning interactions between teachers and children in preschool has not received the concentrated attention it deserves. Small-group instruction involves the teacher and four to six children interacting over material typically prescribed by the teacher. Small groups are more likely to meet the first requirement for learning, which is joint attention between the learner and the instructor, or what is termed *intersubjectivity*. Joint attention is difficult to establish in larger groups given the developmental characteristics of young children described earlier—they have a hard time directing and sustaining their attention on command. Children from low-income backgrounds have particular difficulty with distractibility (Howse, Lange, Farran, & Boyles, 2003), and in a large group, teachers simply cannot determine when to adapt instruction developmentally up or down (P. Starkey & A. Klein, February 3, 2004, personal communication). The Kamehameha Early Education Program (KEEP), one of the few culturally responsive intervention programs with sustained effects, had as its central tenant teacher-led instruction in small groups (Au, 1997; Tharp & Gallimore, 1988).

Whole-group instruction is important for establishing a sense of community and for interactive finger plays and songs that are noisy and therefore only possible with the entire class participating. These group times can be short and fun and bear no real instructional burden. When teachers use whole-group activities, it is important that they manage them well. In his study of preschool classrooms, Dickinson (2001) created a composite variable, Extended Teacher Discourse, made up primarily of linguistic and behavioral teaching strategies used by teachers during whole-group instruction. Language-related strategies included "cognitive extending" by the teacher for conversational topics (e.g., talking about past, future, and the hypothetical) and analyzing the text during book reading. The behavioral strategy included in this composite was "group focusing," which related to the teachers' management and control of behavior during large-group instruction. This composite variable was significantly predictive of both ends of kindergarten receptive vocabulary and emergent literacy. These findings suggest that when teachers instruct the entire group, they need to be very conscious of the strategies they use and the type of content they provide for children.

Independent, center-based activities are important for a separate set of reasons. Moving from center to center and choosing which activities to be involved in and for how long allows children to develop focused concentration. Independent, center-based activities also provide children a chance to talk to each other and to engage in more complex play behavior (Farran & Son-Yarbrough, 2001). In a Montessori curriculum, children are given "lessons" in how to use materials before they are allowed free access to them. (Montessori also advocates private use of materials without a great deal of peer interaction, something not being advocated here.) But, if possible, children should know how to use the materials available to them in the centers, and this may require "lessons" from the teacher. There are just too many beautifully stocked preschool classrooms, especially newly established, state-funded preschools, in which the children clearly have no idea how to use unfamiliar materials. The presence of good materials with no one using them will create very few gains in any subject area.

Well-Prepared Licensed Teachers

Another robust finding in education research is the effect of teacher education on classroom quality child outcomes (Kontos & Wilcox-Herzog, 1997). The number one recommendation from the National Academy of Sciences panel on preschool education is that every group of children should have a teacher who has a bachelor's degree with specialized education in early childhood development (Bowman, Donovan, & Burns, 2000). As states implement their own preschool programs, it is essential that teacher licensing (or at least 4-year degrees) be preserved. In a survey of state actions in this area, Gilliam and Zigler (2001) determined that not all states required teachers to be licensed; some had no requirements for teacher qualifications at all. Although it is true that the provision of licensed teachers drives up the costs, this is such a critical element that it would be better for states to start with fewer programs, staffed adequately and expanding slowly, rather than reduce requirements for teachers (Ferguson & Brown, 2000).

Implications for Communities

After setting up the prekindergarten system in the community, attention must be paid to both the content and mode of instruction in the classrooms. A joint education committee should be established to help teachers with their curriculum approach. Instruction should be language rich, with multiple opportunities to learn about books, as well as the alphabet and the sounds of language and, most important, to develop vocabulary that has depth and breadth. Vocabulary should be part of an approach to literacy that involves genuine meaning for children. Moreover, children should have multiple opportunities to learn mathematical reasoning (not just counting) and in-depth conceptual understanding of the physical and social world. Instruction should take place in small groups, carefully created by teachers; but a mixture of whole-group, small-group, and center-based, independent activities should comprise the day.

Connections Between
Preschool Programs and Kindergarten

Finally, even with excellent prekindergarten programs, preschool gains may not be sustained because of the classrooms into which children transition (Lee & Loeb, 1995). The children most likely to suffer fade-out effects are those who attend the worst-quality schools after leaving preschool (Currie & Thomas, 2000). Lee and Loeb found that the elementary school achievement of children who had attended Head Start was related to the average achievement level of the elementary school and the density of low achieving children in the classrooms in which they were placed. Within classrooms, children from public preschool programs are more likely to be assigned to lower achieving-ability groups that tend to receive fewer challenging tasks and less attention from the teacher (Entwisle, 1995). At the same time, children from low-income backgrounds are likely to spend a larger percentage of their day on academic subjects and less on enrichment activities than children from middle-income families (Roth, Brooks-Gunn, Linver, & Hofferth, 2002), which suggests that school immediately becomes a less than satisfying experience for impoverished children.

The importance of these early grades was demonstrated by La Paro and Pianta (2000) who summarized 70 studies of children's transition to school and determined that individual differences in children's achievement just before and after entering school accounted for a moderate portion of the variance in similar outcomes measured 1–2 years later. Their data suggested that the early grades could be a major influence on the individual variability in educational success. Phillips (2000) also argued that the early grades represent the most malleable time in the educational life of children and that achievement trajectories become much harder to affect in middle school and beyond.

The goal for elementary schools should be to foster a sense of connection between the children and the school. Children's early relationships with the teacher and the other children in their kindergarten classrooms are an important determinant of their adjustment to the transition and predictors of later achievement. Pianta, Steinberg, and Rollins (1995) found that children with warm, close, communicative relationships with their teachers were better adjusted and had greater later achievement. Skinner, Bryant, Coffman, and Campbell (1998) reported that the teaching style that worked best for former Head Start children involved holding high expectations, focusing on what the child could do rather than what he or she could not do, and using praise and gentle redirection for classroom management. Children taught this way liked school better, and children who like school better are more likely to participate in classroom activities (Ladd, Buhs, & Seid, 2000). Peer relationships also influence classroom participation. Ladd, Birch, and Buhs (1999) showed that children who were rejected by their peers (often for aggressive behavior) were less likely to participate in cooperative classroom activities. Participation in classroom activities, in turn, was a significant predictor of achievement.

Another way to maintain children's connections to school is for them to feel successful in learning. Before kindergarten, children from disadvantaged backgrounds show the same levels of self-confidence and positive attitudes about school as children from more advantaged families (Howse et al., 2003; Stipek & Ryan, 1997). Over the first few years of elementary school, however, the motivation of the children from low-income families drops off rapidly (Covington, 2000; Eccles & Wigfield, 2002; Entwisle, 1995). This undermines children's participation in classroom activities and their initiative in taking advantage of learning opportunities, which is a significant predictor of subsequent academic achievement.

Finally, class size is one of the more robust predictors of both quality and outcomes in education (Finn & Achilles, 1999; Nye, Hedges, & Konstantopoulos, 2002). These studies showed that to be effective for children from low-income families, classrooms from kindergarten through third grade should average 13–17 children. Children in these smaller classes had superior academic performance when compared with children in classes of 22 to 26, even when the teacher had an aide. A small school size is equally as important as a small class size. Larger schools have more curriculum diversity, but they have higher dropout rates and poorer school climates (Alspaugh, 1998; Land & Legters, 2002).

Implications for Communities

The early primary grades are critical for establishing the trajectory for children from low-income families. The overarching goal of the primary grades is for the child and the family to feel connected to the school and for the child to feel successful. Small class sizes in smaller schools in which the emphasis is on both instruction and enrichment, in which children have positive relationships with their teachers and peers, and in which teachers know how to provide an orderly classroom focused on instruction will help preserve the gains achieved in preschool.

CONCLUSION

Poverty in the United States continues to be an important problem, increasing in its significance as the country moves rapidly toward becoming a nation of have's and have not's. Children are most vulnerable to the effects of poverty, and their school achievement is the area most affected. Maintaining children's connections to school through high school graduation is critical, especially because manufacturing and other jobs that used to be available to those without a high school degree have all but disappeared. This chapter suggests a system of support for young children and their families that communities could institute during pregnancy or shortly after the birth of the child. It involves early home visits by public health nurses, a coordinated referral system and supervision of care for infants and toddlers, and a publicly supported set of prekindergarten programs for children when they are 3 and 4 years old. The chapter advocates that prekindergarten programs are instructed by licensed (or at least degreed) teachers, one to a group, with instructional opportunities carefully provided during small-group interactions. The content of the instruction should involve at least literacy (reading for meaning) and general mathematical knowledge. In addition to the small-group instruction in their prekindergarten classes, children would also spend some limited time in whole groups, primarily to develop group cohesion, and a lot of time in independent activities introduced to them by their teachers. Prekindergarten programs must be tied into the public schools so that schools understand the importance of the transition to elementary school and work collaboratively to assure children's early feelings of belonging and success. Good relationships with teachers who are instructional leaders and who know how to foster positive social interactions among children in the class are critical. These seem most likely to be achieved in small classes housed in small schools. Only when communities are seriously concerned for their youngest and most vulnerable and take positive steps on their behalf will they make a difference to the future of the children and the community.

REFERENCES

Abt Associates. (1991). *Preschool Inventory (PSI)*. Cambridge, MA: Abt Associates.

Alexander, K., & Entwisle, D. (1988). Achievement in the first 2 years of school: Patterns and processes. *Monographs of the Society for Research in Child Development*, 53 (2, Serial No. 218).

Alspaugh, J.W. (1998). The relationship of school and community characteristics to high school drop-out rates. *The Clearing House*, 71(3), 184–188.

Armbruster, B.B., Anderson. T.H., Armstrong, J.O., Wise, M.A., Janisch, C., & Meyer, L.A. (1991). Reading and questioning in content area lessons. *Journal of Reading Behavior*, 23, 35–59.

Armstrong, K., Fraser, J., Dadds, M., & Morris, J. (2000). Promoting secure attachment, maternal mood and child health in a vulnerable population: A randomized control trial. *Journal of Pediatrics and Child Health*, 36, 555–562.

Au, K. (1997). A sociocultural model of reading instruction: The Kamehameha Elementary Education Program. In S. Stahl & D. Hayes (Eds.), *Instructional models in reading* (pp. 181–202). Mahwah, NJ: Lawrence Erlbaum Associates.

Blachman, B.A., Tangel, D.M., Ball, E.W., Black, R., & McGraw, C.K. (1999). Developing phonological awareness and word recognition skills: A two-year intervention with low-income, inner-city children. *Reading and Writing: An Interdisciplinary Journal, 11,* 239–273.

Booth, A., & Waxman, S. (2002). Word learning is 'smart': Evidence that conceptual information affects preschoolers' extension of novel words. *Cognition, 84,* B11–B22.

Bowman, B.T., Donovan, M.S., & Burns, M.S. (Eds.). (2000). *Eager to learn: Educating our preschoolers.* Washington, DC: National Academy Press.

Bredekamp, S., & Copple, C. (Eds.). (1997). *Developmentally appropriate practice in early childhood programs* (Rev. ed.). Washington, DC: National Association for the Education of Young Children.

Brooks-Gunn, J., Liaw, F., & Klebanov, P. (1992). Effects of early intervention on cognitive function of low birth weight preterm infants. *The Journal of Pediatrics, 120,* 350–359.

Brooks-Gunn, J., McCarton, C., Casey, P., McCormick, M., Bauer, C., Bernbaum, J., Tyson, J., Swanson, M., Bennett, F.C., Scott, D., Tonascia, J., & Meinert, C. (1994). Early intervention in low birth-weight premature infants. *Journal of the American Medical Association, 272,* 1257–1262.

Bruer, J. (1997). *The myth of the first three years.* New York: Basic Books.

Byrnes, J. (2001). *Minds, brains, and learning.* New York: The Guilford Press.

Campbell, F., Pungello, E., Miller-Johnson, S., Burchinal, M., & Ramey, C. (2001). The development of cognitive and academic abilities: Growth curves from an early childhood educational experiment. *Developmental Psychology, 37,* 231–242.

Campbell, F., Ramey, C., Pungello, E., Sparling, J., & Miller-Johnson, S. (2002). Early childhood education: Young adult outcomes from the Abecedarian project. *Applied Developmental Science, 6,* 42–57.

Cassidy, D., Buell, M., Pugh-Hoese, S., & Russell, S. (1995). The effect of education on child care teachers' beliefs and classroom quality: Year one evaluation of the TEACH early childhood associate degree scholarship program. *Early Childhood Research Quarterly, 10,* 171–183.

Cawley, J., Parmar, R., Foley, T., Salmon, S., & Roy, S. (2001). Arithmetic performance of students: Implications for standards and programming. *Exceptional Children, 67,* 311–328.

Ceci, S., & Williams, W. (1997). Schooling, intelligence and income. *American Psychologist, 52,* 1051–1058.

Chall, J.S. (1983). *Stages of reading development.* New York: McGraw-Hill.

Chall, J.S., Jacobs, V.A., & Baldwin, L. (1990). *The reading crisis: Why poor children fall behind.* Cambridge, MA: Harvard University Press.

Chase-Lansdale, P.L., Moffitt, R., Lohman, B., Cherlin, A., Coley, R., Pittman, L., Roff, J., & Votruba-Drzal, E. (2003). Mothers' transitions from welfare to work and the well-being of preschoolers and adolescents. *Science, 299,* 1548–1552.

Child Care Services Association. (2003). *T.E.A.C.H. early childhood project.* Retrieved February 5, 2004, from http://childcareservices.org/TEACH/TEACH_Project.html

Clay, M. (1996). Accommodating diversity in early literacy learning. In D. Olson & N. Torrance (Eds.), *Education and human development: New models of learning, teaching and schooling* (pp. 202–224). Cambridge, MA: Blackwell Publishers.

Clements, D., & Sarama, J. (2003). *DLM express math resource package.* Columbus, OH: SRA/McGraw-Hill.

Coleman, J. (1996). What is learned in school and what is learned outside? In C. Benbow & D. Lubinski (Eds.), *Intellectual talent* (pp. 211–215). Baltimore: Johns Hopkins University Press.

Covington, M.V. (2000). Goal theory, motivation, and school achievement: An integrative review. *Annual Review of Psychology, 51*, 171–200.

Currie, J., & Thomas, D. (2000). School quality and the longer-term effectiveness of Head Start. *Journal of Human Resources, 35*, 755–774.

Dauber, S.L., Alexander, K.L., & Entwisle, D.R. (1993). Characteristics of retainees and early precursors of retention in grade: Who is held back? *Merrill-Palmer Quarterly, 39*, 326–343.

Denton, D. (n.d.). *Prekindergarten and parent support programs.* Retrieved February 4, 2003, from http://www.sreb.org/program/srr/pubs/PreK/PreK_parentsupport .asp.

Denton, K., & West, J. (2002). *Children's reading and mathematics achievement in kindergarten and first grade.* Washington, DC: National Center for Education Statistics. Available at http://nces.ed.gov/pubsearch/pubsinfo.asp?pubid= 2002125

Dickinson, D.K. (2001). Putting the pieces together: Impact of preschool on children's language and literacy development in kindergarten. In D.K. Dickinson & P.O. Tabors (Eds.), *Beginning literacy with language: Young children learning at home and school* (pp. 257–287). Baltimore: Paul H. Brookes Publishing Co.

Dickinson, D.K., & Tabors, P.O. (Eds.). (2001). *Beginning literacy with language: Young children learning at home and school.* Baltimore: Paul H. Brookes Publishing Co.

Dodge, D., Colker, L., & Heroman, C. (2002). *The creative curriculum for preschool* (4th ed.). Washington, DC: Teaching Strategies.

Donaldson, M. (1992). *Human minds: An exploration.* London: Allen Lane/Penguin Press.

Duncan, G., & Brooks-Gunn, J. (1998). Urban poverty, welfare reform, and child development. In F. Harris & L. Curtis (Eds.), *Locked in the poorhouse: Child, race, and poverty in the United States* (pp. 21–32). Lanham, MD: Rowman & Littlefield.

Duncan, G., & Magnuson, K. (2003). Off with Hollingshead: Socioeconomic resources, parenting, and child development. In M.H. Bornstein & R. Bradley (Eds.), *Socioeconomic status, parenting, and child development* (pp. 83–106). Mahwah, NJ: Lawrence Erlbaum Associates.

Dunn, L.M., & Dunn, L.M. (1981). *Peabody Picture Vocabulary Test–Revised.* Circle Pines, MN: American Guidance Service.

Eccles, J.S., & Wigfield, A. (2002). Motivational beliefs, values and goals. *Annual Review of Psychology, 53*, 109–132.

Elementary and Secondary Education Act of 1965 (PL 89-10) 20 U.S.C. §§ 241 *et seq.*

Engelmann, S. (1999). How sound is High/Scope research? *Educational Leadership, 56*, 83–84.

Entwisle, D.R. (1995). The role of schools in sustaining early childhood program benefits. *The Future of Children, 5*(3), 133–144

Farran, D.C. (1990). Effects of intervention with disadvantaged and disabled children: A decade review. In S. Meisels & J. Shonkoff (Eds.), *Handbook of early intervention* (pp. 501–539). New York: Cambridge University Press.

Farran, D.C. (2000). Another decade of intervention for disadvantaged and disabled children: What do we know now? In J.P. Shonkoff & S.J. Meisels (Eds.), *Handbook of early childhood intervention* (2nd ed., pp. 510–548). New York: Cambridge University Press.

Farran, D.C. (2002). The importance of experience for the human brain: Why intervention is so important in risk situations. *Childrenz Issues, 6*, 7–11.

Farran, D.C., Lange, G., & Boyles, C. (2003, April). *Predicting standardized tests scores for low-income children.* Roundtable discussion at the annual meeting of the American Educational Research Association, Chicago, IL.

Farran, D.C., & Lipsey, M. (2003, April). *Conceptual, theoretical and analytic issues related to evaluating preschool curricula.* Paper presented at the biannual meeting of the Society for Research in Child Development, Tampa, FL.

Farran, D.C., & Shonkoff, J. (1994). Developmental disabilities and the concept of school readiness. *Early Education and Development, 5,* 141–151.

Farran, D.C., & Son-Yarbrough, W. (2001). Title I funded preschools as a developmental context for children's play and verbal behaviors. *Early Childhood Research Quarterly, 16,* 245–262.

Ferguson, R.F., & Brown, J. (2000). Certification test scores, teacher quality, and student achievement. In D.W. Grissmer & J.M. Ross (Eds.), *Analytic issues in the assessment of student achievement* (pp. 133–156). Washington, DC: U.S. Department of Education.

Finn, J.D., & Achilles, C.M. (1999). Tennessee's class size study: Findings, implications, misconceptions. *Educational Evaluation and Policy Analysis, 21,* 97–109.

Gilliam, W., & Zigler, E. (2001). A critical meta-analysis of all evaluations of state-funded preschool from 1977 to 1998: Implications for policy, service delivery and program evaluation. *Early Childhood Research Quarterly, 15,* 441–473.

Goffin, S. (1994). *Curriculum models and early childhood education.* New York: Merrill.

Gomby, D., Culross, P., & Behrman, R. (1999). Home visiting: Recent program evaluations—analysis and recommendations. *The Future of Children, 9,* 4–26.

Gray, C.W., Ramsey, B., & Klaus, R. (1982). *From 3 to 20: The early training project.* Baltimore: University Park Press.

Griffin, S., Case, R., & Capodilupo, A. (1995). Teaching for understanding: The importance of the central conceptual structures in the elementary mathematics curriculum. In A. McKeough, J. Lupart, & A. Marini (Eds.), *Teaching for transfer: Fostering generalization in learning* (pp. 123–151). Mahwah, NJ: Lawrence Erlbaum Associates.

Griffin, S., Case, R., & Siegler, R. (1994). Rightstart: Providing the central conceptual prerequisites for first formal learning of arithmetic to students at risk for school failure. In K. McGilly (Ed.), *Classroom lessons: Integrating cognitive theory and classroom practice* (pp. 25–49). Cambridge, MA: MIT Press.

Guralnick, M.J. (2001). A developmental systems model for early intervention. *Infants and Young Children, 14*(2), 1–18.

Gutman, L., Sameroff, A., & Cole, R. (2003). Academic growth curve trajectories from 1st grade to 12th grade: Effects of multiple social risk factors and preschool child factors. *Developmental Psychology, 39,* 770–790.

Harris, F. (1998). The Kerner Report thirty years later. In F. Harris & L. Curtis (Eds.), *Locked in the poorhouse: Child, race, and poverty in the United States* (pp. 7–19). Lanham, MD: Rowman & Littlefield.

Hart, B., & Risley, T.R. (1995). *Meaningful differences in the everyday experience of young American children.* Baltimore: Paul H. Brookes Publishing Co.

Haskins, R. (1985). Public school aggression among children with varying daycare experience. *Child Development, 56,* 689–703.

Henry, G., Henderson, L., Ponder, B., Gordon, C., Mashburn, A., & Rickman, D. (2003). *Report of the fundings from the early childhood study: 2001–02.* Unpublished paper available from Dr. Gary T. Henry, Georgia State University, 140 Decatur Street, Urban Life Building, Suite 1030, Atlanta, GA, 30303.

Hermanussen, M. (1988). Knemometry, a new tool for the investigation of growth: A review. *European Journal of Pediatrics, 147*(4), 350–355.

Hermanussen, M. (1998). The analysis of short-term growth. *Hormone Research*, *49*(2), 53–64.

Hermanussen, M., Geiger-Benoit, K., Burmeister, J., & Sippell, W.G. (1988). Periodical changes of short term growth velocity ('mini growth spurts') in human growth. *Annals of Human Biology*, *15*(2), 103–109.

Hertzman, C. (1999). Population health and human development. In D. Keating & C. Hertzman (Eds.), *Developmental health and the wealth of nations* (pp. 21–40). New York: The Guilford Press.

Hill, J., Brooks-Gunn, J., & Waldfogel, J. (2003). Sustained effects of high participation in an early intervention for low-birth-weight premature infants. *Developmental Psychology*, *39*, 730–744.

Howse, R., Lange, G., Farran, D.C., & Boyles, C. (2003). Motivation and self regulation as predictors of achievement in economically disadvantaged young children. *Journal of Experimental Education*, *71*, 151–174.

Johnson, Z., Howell, F., & Molloy, B. (1993). Community mothers programme: Randomised controlled trial of non-professional intervention in parenting. *British Medical Journal*, *306*, 1449–1452.

Jordan, N., Huttenlocher, J., & Levine, S. (1992). Differential calculation abilities in young children from middle- and low-income families. *Developmental Psychology*, *28*, 644–653.

Kendrick, D., Elkan, R., Hewitt, M., Dewey, M., Blair, M., Robinson, J., Williams, D., & Brummell, K. (2000). Does home visiting improve parenting and the quality of the home environment? A systematic review and meta analysis. *Archives of Disease in Childhood*, *82*, 443–451.

Kitzman, H., Olds, D., Henderson, C., Hanks, C., Cole, R., Tatelbaum, R., McConnochie, K., Sidora, K., Luckey, D., Shaver, D., Engelhardt, K., James, D., & Barnard, K. (1997). Effect of prenatal and infancy home visitation by nurses on pregnancy outcomes, childhood injuries, and repeated childbearing: A randomized controlled trial. *Journal of the American Medical Association*, *278*, 644–652.

Kontos, S., & Keyes, L. (1999). An ecobehavioral analysis of early childhood classrooms. *Early Childhood Research Quarterly*, *14*, 35–50.

Kontos, S., & Wilcox-Herzog, A. (1997). Influences on children's competence in early childhood classrooms. *Early Childhood Research Quarterly*, *12*, 247–262.

Kreisman, M. (2003). Evaluating academic outcomes of Head Start: An application of general growth mixture modeling. *Early Childhood Research Quarterly*, *18*, 238–254.

Kurdek, L., & Sinclair, R. (2000). Psychological, family, and peer predictors of academic outcomes in first through fifth-grade children. *Journal of Educational Psychology*, *92*, 449–457.

Ladd, G., Birch, S., & Buhs, E. (1999). Children's social and scholastic lives in kindergarten: Related spheres of influence? *Child Development*, *70*, 1373–1400.

Ladd, G.W., Buhs, E.S., & Seid, M. (2000). Children's initial sentiments about kindergarten: Is school liking an antecedent of early classroom participation and achievement? *Merrill-Palmer Quarterly*, *46*, 255–279.

Land, D., & Legters, N. (2002). The extent and consequences of risk in U.S. education. In S. Stringfield & D. Land (Eds.), *Educating at-risk students: One hundred-first yearbook of the National Society for the Study of Education* (pp. 1–28). Chicago: The University of Chicago Press.

La Paro, K., & Pianta, R. (2000). Predicting children's competence in the early school years: A meta-analytic review. *Review of Educational Research, 70,* 443–484.

Lazar I., & Darlington, R. (1983). *As the twig is bent.* Mahwah, NJ: Lawrence Erlbaum Associates.

Lee, V., & Loeb, S. (1995). Where do Head Start attendees end up? One reason why preschool effects fade out. *Educational Evaluation and Policy Analysis, 17,* 62–82.

Love, J., Harrison, L., Sagi-Schwartz, A., van Ijzendoorn, M., Ross, C., Ungerer, J., Raikes, H., Brady-Smith, C., Boller, K., Brooks-Gunn, J., Constantine, J., Kisker, E., Paulsell, D., & Chazan-Cohen, R. (2003). Child care quality matters: How conclusions may vary with context. *Child Development, 74,* 1021–1033.

Lunenberg, F. (2000). Early childhood education programs can make a difference in academic, economic, and social arenas. *Education, 120,* 519–528.

Masten, A., & Coatsworth, J.D. (1998). The development of competence in favorable and unfavorable environments. *American Psychologist, 53,* 205–220.

McCall, R., Appelbaum, M., & Hogarty, P. (1973). Developmental changes in mental performance. *Monographs of the Society for Research in Child Development, 38*(3, Serial No. 150).

McCarton, C., Brooks-Gunn, J., Wallace, I., Bauer, C., Bennett, F., Bernbaum, J., Broyles, S., Casey, P., McCormick, M., Scott, D., Tyson, J., Tonascia, J., & Meinert, C. (1997). Results at age 8 years of early intervention for low-birth weight premature infants. *Journal of the American Medical Association, 277,* 126–132.

McDermott, P.A. (1995). Sex, race, class and other demographics as explanations for children's ability and adjustment: A national appraisal. *Journal of School Psychology, 33,* 75–91.

McGurk, K. (2003). *R.E.W.A.R.D. Wisconsin.* Retrieved February 5, 2004, from http://www.state.wi.us/dws/programs/childcare/teach/reward.htm

Meisels, S.J., & Liaw, F.R. (1993). Failure in grade: Do retained students catch up? *Journal of Educational Research, 87,* 69–77.

Miller, L., & Bizzell, R. (1983). Long-term effects of four preschool programs: Sixth, seventh, and eighth grades. *Child Development, 54,* 727–741.

Miller, L., & Bizzell, R. (1984). Long term effects of four preschool programs: Ninth and tenth grade results. *Child Development, 55,* 1570–1587.

Miller, L., & Dyer, J. (1975). Four preschool programs: Their dimensions and effects. *Monographs of the Society for Research in Child Development, 40*(5–6, Serial No. 162).

National Education Goals Panel. (n.d.). *History, 1989 to present.* Retrieved January 13, 2004, from http://www.negp.gov/index.htm.

National Institute for Child Health and Human Development Early Child Care Research Network. (2003). Does amount of time spent in child care predict socioemotional adjustment during the transition to kindergarten? *Child Development, 74,* 976–1005.

North Carolina Department of Public Instruction. (1999). *North Carolina IDEA headcount for special education.* Raleigh: North Carolina Department of Public Instruction.

Nye, B., Hedges, L.V., & Konstantopoulos, S. (2002). Do low-achieving students benefit more from small classes? Evidence from the Tennessee class size experiment. *Educational Evaluation and Policy Analysis, 24,* 201–217.

Offord, D., Kraemer, H., Kazdin, A., Jensen, P., Harrington, R., & Gardner, J. (1999). Lowering the burden of suffering: Monitoring the benefits of clinical, targeted, and universal approaches. In D. Keating & C. Hertzman (Eds.), *Developmental health and the wealth of nations* (pp. 293–310). New York: The Guilford Press.

Olds, D. (1988). The Prenatal/Early Infancy project. In R. Price, E. Cowen, R. Lorion, & J. Ramos-McKay (Eds.), *Fourteen ounces of prevention: A case book of practitioners* (pp. 9–23). Washington, DC: American Psychological Association.

Olds, D., Henderson, C., Cole, R., Eckenrode, J., Kitzman, H., Luckey, D., Pettitt, L., Sidora, K., Morris, P., & Powers, J. (1998). Long-term effects of nurse home visitation on children's criminal and antisocial behavior: 15-year follow up of a randomized controlled trial. *The Journal of the American Medical Association, 280*, 1238–1244.

Olds, D., Henderson, C., Tatelbaum, R., & Chamberlin, R. (1986). Improving the delivery of prenatal care and outcomes of pregnancy: A randomized trial of nurse home visitation. *Pediatrics, 78*, 16–28.

Pearce, D., & Brooks, J. (2002). *The self sufficiency standard for Tennessee.* Retrieved November 15, 2003, from http://www.tennesseeallianceforprogress.org.

Peisner-Feinberg, E., & Burchinal, M. (1997). Concurrent relations between child care quality and child outcomes: The study of cost, quality, and outcomes in child care centers. *Merrill-Palmer Quarterly, 43*, 451–477.

Pellin, B., & Edmonds, E. (2001). *Charlotte-Mecklenburg Schools Bright Beginnings Pre-Kindergarten Program.* Retrieved on February 1, 2001, from http://www.cms.k12.nc.us/k12/curricul/prek/index.htm

Phillips, M. (2000). Understanding ethnic differences in academic achievement: Empirical lessons from national data. In D.W. Grissmer & J.M. Ross (Eds.), *Analytic issues in the assessment of student achievement* (pp. 103–132). Washington, DC: U.S. Department of Education.

Pianta, R.C., & McCoy, S.J. (1997). The first day of school: The predictive validity of early school screening. *Journal of Applied Developmental Psychology, 18*, 1–22.

Pianta, R.C, Steinberg, M.S., & Rollins, K.B. (1995). The first two years of school: Teacher-child relationships and deflections in children's classroom adjustment. *Development and Psychopathology, 7*, 225–230.

Powell, D.R. (1995). *Enabling young children to succeed in school.* Washington, DC: American Educational Research Association.

Ramey, C., Bryant, D., Wasik, B., Sparling, J., Fendt, K., & LaVange, L. (1992). Infant Health and Development Program for low birth weight, premature infants: Program elements, family participation, and child intelligence. *Pediatrics, 3*, 454–465.

Ramey, C., & Campbell, F. (1984). Preventive education for high-risk children: Cognitive consequences of the Carolina Abecedarian Project. *American Journal of Mental Deficiency, 88*, 515–523.

Rayner, K., Foorman, B., Perfetti, C., Pesetsky, D., & Seidenberg, M. (2002). How should reading be taught? *Scientific American, 286*, 84–91.

Roth, J., Brooks-Gunn, J., Linver, M., & Hofferth, S. (2002). *What happens during the school day? Time diaries from a national sample of elementary school teachers.* Retrieved January 7, 2003, from http://www.tcrecord.org

Rutter, M., & Quinton, D. (1977). Psychiatric disorder: Ecological factors and concepts of causation. In H. McGurk (Ed.), *Ecological factors in human development* (pp. 173–188). Amsterdam: North-Holland Publishing Company.

Saffran, J., Aslin, R., & Newport, E. (1996). Statistical learning by 8-month old infants. *Science, 274*, 1926–1928.

Schatschneider, C., Carlson, C., Francis, D., Foorman, B., & Fletcher, J. (2002). Relationship of rapid automized naming and phonological awareness in early reading development: Implications for the double-deficit hypothesis. *Journal of Learning Disabilities, 35,* 245–256.

Schweinhart, L., Barnes, H., & Weikart, D. (1993). *Significant benefits: The High/Scope Perry Preschool study through age 27.* Ypsilanti, MI: The High/Scope Press.

Schweinhart, L., & Weikart, D. (1997). The High/Scope preschool curriculum comparison study through age 23. *Early Childhood Research Quarterly, 12,* 117–144.

Schweinhart, L., Weikart, D., & Larner, M. (1986). Consequences of three curriculum models through age 15. *Early Childhood Research Quarterly, 1,* 15–45.

Simmons, R., Burgeson, R., Carlton-Ford, S., & Blyth, D. (1987). The impact of cumulative change in early adolescence. *Child Development, 58,* 1220–1234.

Skinner, D., Bryant, D., Coffman, J., & Campbell, F. (1998). Creating risk and promise: Children's and teacher's discourse and practice in the cultural world of kindergarten. *Elementary School Journal, 98,* 297–310.

Smith, M. (2001). Children's experiences in preschool. In D.K. Dickinson & P.O. Tabors (Eds.), *Beginning literacy with language: Young children learning at home and school* (pp. 149–174). Baltimore: Paul H. Brookes Publishing Co.

Smith, M., & Dickinson, D. (1994). Describing oral language opportunities and environments in Head Start and other preschool classrooms. *Early Childhood Research Quarterly, 9,* 345–366.

Snow, C., Burns, S., & Griffin, P. (Eds.). (1998). *Preventing reading difficulties in young children.* Washington, DC: National Academy Press.

Spiker, D., Kraemer, H., Scott, D., & Gross, R. (1991). Design issues in a randomized clinical trial of a behavioral intervention: Insights from the Infant Health and Development Program. *Developmental and Behavioral Pediatrics, 12,* 386–393.

St. Pierre, R.G., & Layzer, J.I. (1998). Improving the life chances of children in poverty: Assumptions and what we have learned. *Social Policy Report: Society for Research in Child Development, 12*(4).

St. Pierre, R.G., & Swartz, J. (1996). *The Even Start family literacy program: Early implementation.* Cambridge, MA: Abt Associates.

St. Pierre, R.G., Swartz, J., Murray, S., & Deck, D. (1996). *Improving family literacy: Findings from the national Even Start evaluation.* Cambridge, MA: Abt Associates.

Starkey, P., Klein, A., & Wakeley, A. (in press). Enhancing young children's mathematical knowledge through a pre-kindergarten mathematics intervention. *Early Childhood Research Quarterly.*

Stipek, D., Feiler, R., Daniels, D., & Milburn, S. (1995). Effects of different instructional approaches on young children's achievement and motivation. *Child Development, 66,* 209–223.

Stipek, D.J., & Ryan, R.H. (1997). Economically disadvantaged preschoolers: Ready to learn but further to go. *Developmental Psychology, 33,* 711–723.

Tabors, P., Snow, C., & Dickinson, D. (2001). Homes and schools together: Supporting language and literacy development. In D.K. Dickinson & P.O. Tabors (Eds.), *Beginning literacy with language: Young children learning at home and school* (pp. 313–334). Baltimore: Paul H. Brookes Publishing Co.

Thalange, N.K., Foster, P.J., Gill, M.S., Price, D.A., & Clayton, P.E. (1996). Model of normal prepubertal growth. *Archives of Disease in Childhood, 75*(5), 427–431.

Tharp, R., & Gallimore, R. (1988). *Rousing minds to life.* Cambridge, UK: Cambridge University Press.

Thelen, E., & Smith, L. (1994). *A dynamic systems approach to the development of cognition and action.* Cambridge, MA: The MIT Press.

Torgesen, J., Wagner, R., Rashotte, C., Rose, E., Lindamood, P., Conway, T., & Garvan, C. (1999). Preventing reading failure in young children with phonological processing disabilities: Group and individual responses to instruction. *Journal of Educational Psychology, 91*, 579–593.

Trommsdorff, G. (1983). Future orientation and socialization. *International Journal of Psychology, 18*, 381–407.

Turkheimer, E., Haley, A., Waldron, M., D'Onofrio, B., & Gottesman, I. (2003). Socioeconomic status modifies heritability of IQ in young children. *Psychological Science, 14*, 623–628.

U.S. Bureau of the Census. (2002). *Poverty status of people, by age, race, and Hispanic origin: 1959 to 2002.* Retrieved on January 13, 2004, from http://www.census.gov/hhes/poverty/histpov/hstpov3.html

U.S. Department of Education, Institute of Education Sciences, National Center for Education Statistics, National Assessment of Educational Progress (NAEP). (2000). *The nation's report card: Mathematics 2000.* Washington, DC: National Center for Education Statistics.

U.S. Department of Education, National Center for Education Statistics. (2001). *Entering kindergarten: A portrait of American children when they begin school: Findings from The Condition of Education, 2000.* Washington, DC: U.S. Government Printing Office.

U.S. Department of Education, National Center for Education Statistics. (2003). *The condition of education 2003 in brief.* Washington, DC: U.S. Department of Education.

U.S. General Accounting Office. (1997). *Head Start: Research provides little information on impact of current program.* Report to the Chairman, Committee on the Budget, House of Representatives (GAO/HEHS-97-59). Washington, DC: Author.

U.S. General Accounting Office. (2000a, February). *Early childhood programs: Characteristics affect the availability of school readiness information.* Report to the Chairman, Subcommittee on Oversight of Government Management, Restructuring and the District of Columbia, Committee on Governmental Affairs, U.S. Senate (GAO/HEHS-00-38). Washington, DC: Author.

U.S. General Accounting Office. (2000b, September). *Title I preschool education: More children served but gauging effect on school readiness difficult.* Report to the Chairman, Subcommittee on Oversight of Government Management, Restructuring and the District of Columbia, Committee on Governmental Affairs, U.S. Senate (GAO/HEHS-00-171). Washington, DC: Author.

Watamura, S., Donzella, B., Alwin, J., & Gunnar, M. (2003). Morning-to-afternoon increases in cortisol concentrations for infants and toddlers at child care: Age differences and behavioral correlates. *Child Development, 74*, 1006–1020.

Waxman, S., & Booth, A. (2001). On the insufficiency of evidence for a domain-general account of word learning. *Cognition, 78*, 277–279.

Wechsler, D. (1967). *Manual for the Wechsler Preschool and Primary Scale of Intelligence.* New York: The Psychological Corporation.

Werner, E., & Smith, S. (1992). *Overcoming the odds: High risk children from birth to adulthood.* Ithaca, NY: Cornell University Press.

White, S.H. (1965). Evidence for a hierarchical arrangement of learning processes. In L.P. Lipsitt & C.C. Spiker (Eds.), *Advances in child development and behavior* (Vol. 2, pp. 187–220). New York: Academic Press.

Whitehurst, G., Zevenbergen, A., Crone, D., Schultz, M., Velting, O., & Fishchel, J. (1999). Outcomes of an emergent literacy intervention from Head Start through second grade. *Journal of Educational Psychology, 91*, 261–272.

Zill, N., Resnick, G., Kwang, K., McKey, R.H., Clark, C., Pai-Samant, S., Connell, D., Vaden-Kiernan, M., O'Brien, R., & D'Elio, M. (2001). *Head Start FACES: Longitudinal findings on program performance, Third progress report.* Washington, DC: U.S. Government Printing Office.

CHAPTER 12

DEVELOPING AND IMPLEMENTING EARLY INTERVENTION PROGRAMS FOR CHILDREN WITH ESTABLISHED DISABILITIES

DONNA SPIKER,
KATHLEEN HEBBELER, AND SANGEETA MALLIK

The context, research base, and expectations for providing services to young children with disabilities and their families have evolved dramatically since the 1970s and 1980s. A substantial research base exists about early developmental processes, family functioning, and early intervention program models and practices (Guralnick, 1997; Shonkoff & Meisels, 2000; Zeanah, 2000). The research base provides essential information for developing a comprehensive early intervention system of services and supports for children with established disabilities and their families. Although best practices have been repeatedly identified (Bredekamp & Copple, 1997; Sandall, McLean, & Smith, 2000; Smith et al., 2002), the actual realization of a comprehensive system that meets the needs of children and families remains an ambitious but elusive goal (Bruder, 2000; Shonkoff, Phillips, & Keilty, 2000). At the same time, the number of children served continues to grow. In 2001, 803,531 children with disabilities between birth and 5 years of age received special services—an increase of 47% over the number of children served a decade earlier (U.S. Department of Education, 2002).

Designing a comprehensive system of early intervention services and supports for infants, toddlers, and preschoolers with established disabilities needs to begin with recognition of the intended goals of the system. The federal legislation governing the provision of services to infants and toddlers with disabilities—Part C of the Individuals with Disabilities Education Act (IDEA) Amendments of 1997 (PL 105-17)—provides a set of goals that are as meaningful today as they were when the legislation (originally called Part H) was passed in 1986. The Congress of the United States believed that services to young children and their families were needed to enhance the development of infants and toddlers with disabilities, to minimize the potential for developmental delay, and to enhance the capacity of families to meet the special needs of their infants and toddlers with disabilities. Most families would agree with these goals and might also add that they want their children with disabilities to be able to participate in family and community activities to the maximal extent possible. During the early years of life, families want their children to grow and learn to their maximum potential, to take part fully in typical daily activities and family routines, to develop positive peer relationships and friendships, to participate with peers in settings and activities, and to develop the early competencies that will allow them to be as successful as possible when they reach school.

In this chapter, the Developmental Systems Model proposed by Guralnick (2001a) is used to frame a description of what a model comprehensive early intervention system would look like. This developmental framework espouses an approach that is family centered and aims to address stressors generated by the child or family or both. The ultimate goal is to strengthen the family's capacity to interact effectively with the child, to orchestrate community experiences that will maximize the child's development and well-being, and to ensure that the child's health and safety are adequately protected. Stressors that can disrupt these family patterns include information needs of the family (e.g., implications of a diagnosis), interpersonal and family distress, resource needs (e.g., housing), and confidence threats (e.g., ability to effectively carry out parenting role). The Developmental Systems Model posits that early intervention programs capable of assessing these stressors and providing families the necessary supports, information, and services to promote optimal family patterns of interaction will ultimately enhance children's development.

Three core principles of the Developmental Systems Model provide the foundation for a system of early intervention programs for children with established disabilities and developmental delays (see Chapter 1). This chapter describes how the three core principles—a developmental framework, integration of services, and inclusion of young children with disabilities within the community—would be reflected in this model system of services. The system as proposed is based on what is known about who is receiving services in early intervention and preschool special education as well as what is known and recommended about effective intervention.

The chapter begins with some general comments about the context of early intervention services in the United States today. This is followed by an elaboration of core tenets of a developmental framework and their general implications for services provision. The next three sections elaborate on what must be provided to families in effective programs: resource supports, social supports, and information and services. Concepts related to the developmental framework, integration of services, and inclusion are woven into each section. Barriers to implementation also are addressed. The chapter ends with general conclusions about a comprehensive system and the challenges that need to be addressed to make this vision a reality.

The chapter addresses programs for children with established disabilities and encompasses those with diagnosed conditions (e.g., Down syndrome, blindness) and those with developmental delays with no known etiology. IDEA uses the phrase *early intervention* to describe services for children from birth to 3 years old and *preschool special education* to describe services for children from 3 through 5 years old. For ease of communication, *early intervention* is used in this chapter to describe services for the entire age spectrum of children with disabilities and delays who are younger than school age.

Throughout the chapter, data from the National Early Intervention Longitudinal Study (NEILS; see http://www.sri.com/neils) is included when these data can inform the discussion. NEILS is the first study of a nationally representative sample of children and families receiving early intervention services under Part C of IDEA. This study provides the national estimates of characteristics of children and families receiving early intervention services and the services they received.[1] Because the NEILS data are national estimates, they provide important information about the early intervention services as they are currently delivered. Comparable information on services for 3- through 5-year-olds is not available.

CONTEXT OF EARLY INTERVENTION

A comprehensive developmental approach to early intervention that calls for coordinating and integrating programs, services, and supports for young children with disabilities must take into account some of the significant developments taking place in the early childhood policy arena. Many states are engaging in important efforts to encourage early care and education, including universal preschool efforts and initiatives to improve the availability and quality of early child care, and to promote young children's school readiness (Dwyer, Chait, & McKee, 2000; Gilliam & Zigler, 2000;

---

[1]The NEILS participants were enrolled into the study as they were entering early intervention at the time of the development of the family's first individualized family service plan (IFSP). All participants were recruited between September 1997 and November 1998. See http://www.sri.com/neils for more information.

Saluja, Scott-Little, & Clifford, 2000). In addition, there is widespread recognition of the need for the various programs and agencies to work together to provide a more coordinated approach to serving children and families (Dinnebeil, Hale, & Rule, 1999). The importance of incorporating the needs of young children with disabilities in the planning and implementation of these broader policy efforts is also acknowledged (Rosman, Yoshikawa, & Knitzer, 2002). Thus, it is important to remember that young children with disabilities and their families are not just participants in the early intervention system for children with disabilities. These children and their families also are likely to be receiving services and supports from federal, state, and local programs that can include

- Health care services, including routine well-child pediatric care and hospital-based and clinic-based services

- Child care programs (family- and center-based)

- State-funded prekindergarten, Early Head Start, and Head Start programs

- Social services, including the child welfare system

- Mental health services

- Public assistance programs such as Temporary Assistance for Needy Families (TANF) and Medicaid

- Community-based programs and services for young children and families (e.g., recreation and library programs, parenting classes, family support programs)

Secular trends that influence the overall well-being of families with young children also will have implications for the families of young children with disabilities (Demo & Cox, 2000; Fujiura & Yamaki, 2000). These trends will affect the needs of families and will influence how an early intervention system should be designed. Many contextual factors will influence families' quality of life, their ability to participate in programs and services offered, and their individual needs vis-à-vis their young child with a disability. Factors such as poverty, single parenthood, employment status, and parental mental and physical health are important considerations when planning for a comprehensive system of services and supports for families with a young child with a disability.

The NEILS data indicate that there is no such thing as a typical child or family receiving early intervention services (Bailey, Scarborough, & Hebbeler, 2003; Hebbeler et al., 2001; Hebbeler, Spiker, Mallik, Scarborough, & Simeonsson, 2003; Scarborough et al., in press; Spiker et al., 2004). For instance, at entry into early intervention services,

- Most of the children receiving early intervention services (62%) had one or more developmental delays, another 22% had an established disability, and another 17% were receiving services for a risk condition (e.g., low birth weight)

- Of children who were eligible for early intervention because of a diagnosed condition, 44% entered early intervention in their first 6 months of life

- The first individualized family service plan (IFSP) for a child with a diagnosed condition was developed on average when the child was 11 months old compared with an average age of 21 months for children with developmental delays

- Nearly one third (32%) of all infants and toddlers receiving early intervention were born with low birth weights (fewer than 2,500 grams)

- A sizeable proportion of children in early intervention are in poor health: 16% of children receiving early intervention were reported to have fair or poor health compared with only 2% of the general population of children younger than 3 years of age

- Many children in early intervention have other significant health risks and problems: 38% spent some time in a neonatal intensive care unit (NICU) after birth; 26% regularly used medications; and 16% used some type of medical device (e.g., apnea monitor, nebulizer)

- Many children in early intervention are living in poverty: 43% were in families with household incomes of less than $25,000 per year, and 27% were in families with incomes of less than $15,000 per year

- Some mothers of young children with disabilities have limited education; 17% did not finish high school

- Family structure also has implications for the design of a service delivery system: 16% of the children in early intervention were living in households with only one adult, only 63% were living with their biological fathers, and 20% were living in a household with another child with special needs

- A disproportionate number of young children with disabilities are in foster care: 7% of the children in early intervention were in foster care, a rate 10 times that of the general population

- Minority children with disabilities are more likely than Caucasian children to have multiple environmental risks (e.g., living in poverty, limited maternal education): 38% of the children in early intervention had three or more environmental risks

- Those children with the poorest health were significantly more likely to also have substantial environmental risks

Two points are clear: First, there is much variability within the population of children receiving services in early intervention programs. Second, a sizeable proportion of children who are at risk for poor development due to a diagnosed condition or developmental delay also have significant environmental risk factors. These children are at especially high risk for poor development. A system of services to address the stressors related to the child's disability must also address the stressors related to the life circumstances of the family if the goal of optimized child development is to be realized (see Chapter 10).

CORE TENETS OF A DEVELOPMENTAL SYSTEMS MODEL

Before describing the supports and services for children with disabilities and their families, some core tenets of a developmental framework are identified. A number of major developmental themes form the basis for how early intervention efforts should be designed. They also suggest the kinds of services and supports needed by children and families and the approaches and issues that should be considered when designing and implementing interventions.

Intervening as Early as Possible and with Sufficient Intensity Is Critical to Achieving Optimal Outcomes for Some Conditions

A National Academy of Science panel convened to review the science of early childhood development and concluded that early intervention is better for some conditions and that intensity needs to be carefully considered in light of the expected benefits (Shonkoff & Phillips, 2000). The panel specifically noted the importance of intervening earlier with premature newborns and for children with hearing loss. The need for early and intensive interventions to achieve the best outcomes for children with disabilities has been argued repeatedly (Guralnick, 1997; Harris & Handleman, 2000; Oser & Cohen, 2003). This issue has been particularly salient with children who have autism, for which there is strong advocacy for intensive applied behavior analysis approaches (Lovaas & Smith, 2003). For children with autism, the benefits of starting early, having many hours of intervention (intensity), and continuing for a long period of time (duration) have received some empirical support (National Research Council,

2001). For instance, treatment length predicted outcomes for young children with autism (Luiselli, Cannon, Ellis, & Sisson, 2000).

The primary reason for the emphasis on earlier and more intensive interventions is the hope that interventions in the first 5 years of life can lead to higher levels of functioning later and a higher probability for better functional outcomes such as improved school performance and later independence. Therefore, for young children with disabilities, there is a strong belief that identification of the disability or delay early in life and starting interventions as early as possible ultimately can lead to better outcomes. Failing to start interventions as early as possible is seen as missing an important opportunity for learning and favorably influencing early brain development.

A holistic understanding of child development is necessary because the skills, behaviors, and conditions necessary for optimal development are interrelated. Child development research since the 1970s and 1980s has contributed more complete and detailed information about how infants and young children learn and develop, demonstrating that cognitive, social, emotional, motor, and language development are interconnected. It is now well appreciated how the social relationships of infants and young children with adults and peers provide the critical context for learning and how social interaction, emotional development, communication, and exploration are interrelated (Zigler, Finn-Stevenson, & Hall, 2002). There is now a better understanding of the interconnectedness of social and communication development and of early developmental sequences of prelinguistic communication and pragmatic and play skills. Much more is now known about the subskills and developmental sequences within different developmental domains and the ways they affect how children explore and engage in both physical and social environments. By assessing children's subskills from both a developmental and functional perspective, interventionists and parents can identify the skills that should be taught and targeted.

From a holistic perspective, there also is an appreciation of how the child's temperamental characteristics, sensory capabilities, motor abilities, and emotional regulation influence social interaction patterns and learning styles. A thorough understanding of early development, including the sequences of skills within developmental domains and the interconnections across domains, is essential knowledge for early interventionists who are designing and implementing programs and services for young children and families. Such knowledge is necessary for providers and professionals regardless of their discipline or role.

If the initial assessment process has been done well, then information about the child's behaviors, skills, and difficulties across different developmental domains (social, emotional, fine and gross motor, communication, self-help, cognitive) will be sufficiently detailed so it can be used for planning appropriate services. Although many children with established disabilities have significant learning difficulties or even mental retardation, communication and social skill deficits as well as behavior problems can become the predominant factors that limit the child's access to inclusive environments (Roberts, Mazzucchelli, Taylor, & Reid, 2003; Sigafoos, 2000). For this reason, early interventionists must take a holistic view in designing services for young children and attend explicitly to social and behavioral skill acquisition.

Parenting Behaviors, Interactions, and Attitudes in the Early Years of Life Are Important Influences on Children's Development

The child development research field has had a long-standing interest in the role of the home environment, parent–child interactions, and parenting attitudes and beliefs on children's development. Highly stimulating and responsive home environments have been consistently found to predict children's optimal early development and subsequent school performance (Bradley, Corwyn, Burchinal, McAdoo, & Coll, 2001). A large body of research about parent–child interaction styles indicates that responsive and nurturing patterns are associated with optimal development, including young children with disabilities (Spiker, Boyce, & Boyce, 2002). Many studies have identified critical qualities of optimal interaction styles that include warmth and a positive affective tone combined with attentiveness to the child's signals and interests. The parent will respond contingently to the child's cues, follow the child's lead, and provide input and suggestions that build on the child's focus of attention and activity (Spiker et al., 2002). Learning activities and language input that are well matched to the child's developmental level and for which the child is an active participant are the most beneficial for development (Bornstein, 1989).

The complex, interactive process by which development unfolds has been well articulated in the transactional model of development posited by Sameroff and Fiese (2000). Simply put, this model suggests that development occurs in a dynamic process that is continuously changing over time. The behavior of the individual child evolves and changes in response to interactions with parents and caregivers, who, in turn, evolve and change as a result of those interactions. Young children's interactions with peers also follow this kind of transactional process of mutual influence and change.

Because infants and young children initially are learning via social interaction with parents and caregivers and then with peers, social interaction should be a primary intervention context. More information is now known about prelinguistic communication, social interaction, play, joint attention, and parent–child interaction styles. Some of the most important research in early intervention has focused on early prelinguistic communication. This interest is because communication and language is an area of developmental concern across most disabilities and risk conditions. Furthermore, long-term outcomes for children with disabilities and mental retardation are strongly related to their social and communication skills and abilities (Burack, Hodapp, & Zigler, 1998).

In a review of the mother–child interaction literature with young children with disabilities, Spiker et al. (2002) argued that research evidence supports the importance of responsive parent–child interactions for the optimal development of young children with disabilities. This review summarized research that highlighted ways that infants and young children with disabilities may be difficult social partners. Across a number of disabilities, many young children may provide less readable cues, be less responsive, or respond in ways that may less predictable. These differences are in emotional expressiveness, joint attention and social referencing skills, initiation of social interactions, and responsiveness to social cues, as well as in the exhibition of some atypical behaviors (e.g., repetitive behaviors, passivity). A rather large body of research has shown how infants and young children with disabilities may have difficulties regulating arousal, attention, and other important functions that come into play in social interactions. Within a transactional model that recognizes that early social interactions are bi-directional, such child differences can set the stage for difficulties in parent–child interactions. Parents may inadvertently adopt a highly directive or intrusive style of interaction, which a number of research studies have identified as less than optimal for supporting the young child's development. For instance, research about infants with Down syndrome has shown that many infants may have a passivity that may provoke parents to interact with them in somewhat intrusive ways (Linn, Goodman, & Lender, 2000). Other studies show how children with Down syndrome have differences in mastery motivation (Niccols, Atkinson, & Pepler, 2003).

Early intervention providers, regardless of professional discipline, need to be aware of this research base about early social interactions. This awareness will be reflected in how they assist parents and caregivers to engage in the most reciprocal, mutually gratifying interactions with their children possible—that is, in how they minimize stressors to parent–child transactions (Guralnick, 2001a; see Chapter 1). Interventionists need to have an awareness of the specific behavioral patterns and difficulties of children in terms of attention, arousal, sensory awareness, and emotion expression because these behavior patterns help define a child's learning style. They need to be taken into account when designing intervention plans and activities, structuring learning environments, and targeting particular interventions.

Healthy Development of Young Children Depends on the Complex Interaction of Biological and Social-Environmental Factors

The theoretical models and empirical literature about early childhood development document how children's biological and constitutional capacities and their family contexts interact to affect how they develop and learn. The idea that interaction of biological and social factors in promoting optimal child development has been around since the 1970s and 1980s (Escalona, 1982), but with the surge of research about early brain development, has renewed appreciation for the role of the environment in promoting or hindering the development of brain structure and function (Nelson & Bloom, 1997).

On the biological side, difficulties in a child's birth history, especially low birth weight or significant neonatal medical complications, is a significant risk factor for developmental difficulties and later school problems, both academically and behaviorally (e.g., Botting, Powls, Cooke, & Marlow, 1998; Gross, Spiker, & Haynes, 1997; McCormick, McCarton, Brooks-Gunn, Belt, & Gross, 1998; Taylor, Klein, Schatschneider, & Hack, 1998). These studies indicated that these difficulties begin early and are persistent. Other assaults early in life, such as maternal alcohol or drug use during pregnancy, child abuse, accidents, or poor nutrition, can have serious and long-lasting, damaging effects on the central nervous system (Shonkoff & Marshall, 2000).

On the environmental side, a number of social-environmental risk factors are associated with a greater likelihood of less-than-optimal development as well as early school difficulties. These include, for instance, family poverty, single parent family status, low maternal education levels, significant marital discord, family history of psychological or psychiatric problems, substance abuse, legal problems, and lack of social support (Christian, Morrison, & Bryant, 1998; Greenberg, Lengua, Coie, & Pinderhughes, 1999; Sameroff & Fiese, 2000). The more risk factors that are present, the greater the likelihood that a child will experience behavioral, psychological, cognitive, and academic difficulties (Sameroff, Seifer, Baldwin, & Baldwin, 1993).

Of particular importance is the role of poverty (see Chapter 11). Research on the effects of poverty on child development has consistently documented its detrimental effects on children, with early and persistent poverty having the most long-lasting and detrimental impacts (McLoyd, 1998). The large empirical literature about the role of poverty has focused on understanding the characteristics of children who are living in poverty and how poverty puts them at risk for poor outcomes (Aber, Jones, & Cohen, 2000; Duncan & Brooks-Gunn, 1997). Three interrelated characteristics of parents are powerful predictors of whether young children live in poverty: marital status, education, and employment (Aber et al., 2000). Young children who live with single mothers were more likely to be living in poverty, as were those whose most educated parent did not finish high school. Moreover, no matter what a parent's education level, nearly three fourths of children with neither parent working were living in poverty (Aber et al., 2000). Not surprisingly, many poor children enter school at a developmental disadvantage compared with children not living in poverty (Case, Griffin, & Kelly, 2001; Wertheimer, 2003; Zill & West, 2001).

The interaction of biological and environmental factors applies to the development of children with disabilities. For example, Crombie and Gunn (1998) reported that social disadvantage was a key predictor of the long-term effects of early intervention in children with Down syndrome. Similarly, research has shown that many of the very sickest and tiniest low birth weight infants are at high risk to develop significant disabilities, including cerebral palsy (Covey, 1997). Low birth weight infants who have severe neonatal problems, particularly those with intraventricular hemorrhage (IVH), tend to have the poorest developmental outcomes. For example, in an 8-year follow-up of low birth weight infants with severe neonatal complications, Boyce, Smith, and Casto (1999) found that 62% of the infants had cerebral palsy and many of these had visual and attentional and other behavior problems. The grade of the IVH and the length of time spent in an NICU after birth predicted the outcomes. A number of other studies have shown that the chances of poorer outcomes are significantly increased in the presence of high social-environmental risk (Hack et al., 2002). As reported previously, data from NEILS indicate that a high proportion of young children receiving Part C services have multiple environmental risk factors in addition to a disability or developmental delay. The co-occurrence of disability and environmental risk has important implications for how early intervention programs must be designed if they are to sufficiently address the needs and stressors of these families (see Guralnick, 1998).

Early Child Development Is a Result of the Complex Interactions of Child-, Family-, Neighborhood-, and Community-Level Factors

Increasingly, research has suggested the need for a comprehensive and ecological model for thinking about early child development. This ecological perspective posits that child development takes place in the context of processes, events, and relationships that occur in interactions between the child and his or her immediate social environment, which in turn interacts with the larger social systems that make up our neighborhoods and communities (Bronfenbrenner, 1979; Garbarino & Ganzel, 2000). Representations of ecological models acknowledge the mutual and bi-directional influences across levels from child to family to neighborhood to larger community contexts.

The presence or absence of supports and opportunities in the community can enhance the family's sense of well-being or, alternately, act as a stressor. Communities with high rates of unemployment, violent crime, and lack of high quality child care will make parenting a young child with a disability more challenging. Families' capacity to meet basic needs for food, housing, and transportation are somewhat dependent on where they live. The extent to which the community provides supports for general family functioning will affect the development of all young children in the community but could be especially important for the development of young children with disabilities. Intervention programs will need to see families in the context of their communities and assist families in finding the supports they need to effectively promote the development of their child.

The nature and availability of community services and programs become especially important when including young children with disabilities with typically developing peers. In communities without high quality early childhood and child care programs, families of young children with disabilities have no options for how their son or daughter can be included on a regular basis with their typically developing preschoolers. Similarly, communities without recreation or library programs for young children that are readily accessible and affordable provide limited opportunities for enrichment for all young children, including those with disabilities. The nature of the resources in the community will have a substantial impact on the nature of the experiences that families can provide for the child outside of the home as well as on the family's ability to address the child's health and safety needs. Building a model system of early intervention services could entail helping communities examine how they support or impede families in parenting their children.

SERVICE PROVISION IN A DEVELOPMENTAL SYSTEMS FRAMEWORK

For most children with established disabilities and their families, the appropriate intervention plan should involve a combination of services and supports. The constellation of services and supports might include

- Information about the child's disability

- Ongoing health monitoring to meet both routine and specialized medical needs

- Individualized one-to-one services or therapies targeted to promote specific skill acquisition or improvements in functioning

- Parent education and training that focuses on optimal responsivity to promote the child's learning and participation in daily activities and routines

- Opportunities for interactions with peers in group settings

In the next sections, the principles of a developmental systems approach are applied to the design of early intervention programs for children with disabilities that address family stressors through resource supports, social supports, and information and services (Guralnick, 2001a). The three core principles—the developmental framework tenets just described, the integration of services across agencies, and the inclusion of children with disabilities in the community—constitute the foundation for building a delivery system that will support families in their caregiving role and ultimately result in optimal development for their children. Resources, supports, and services and information are discussed separately but they really should be seen as a coordinated and integrated system of services and supports. This vision of a comprehensive system should involve a constellation of services and supports that

- Involve families in all decisions and choices of goals and preferred participation

- Focus on key functions and developmental processes that can support the child's active engagement and participation in daily activities and routines

- Use assessment information about key developmental functions that identify developmental levels to use in planning interventions to promote the child's emerging skills

- Use meaningful activities that occur in natural contexts to the greatest extent possible

The discussion is based on the assumptions that families of young children with disabilities can encounter one or more different categories of stressors to optimal family patterns of interactions and each has different implications for the kinds of resources and supports that an early intervention system must be able to provide. The resources and services can be conceptualized as a hierarchy ranging from general to specific. The needs of families of young children with disabilities could be addressed through resources and services that are

- General (i.e., support all families raising young children; e.g., good health care, safe streets, recreation opportunities)

- Specific to the needs of all children and families with disabilities (e.g., pediatricians trained to recognize delays and who are able to connect families to Part C services, preschool special education services, and high quality inclusive preschools; an adequate supply of personnel trained to work with young children with disabilities and their families)

- Specific to the needs of children and families with particular kinds of disabilities (e.g., support groups for parents of children with autism, information about the development of children with Down syndrome, access to specialized medical knowledge or therapists with a particular kind of expertise)

- Specific to the needs of certain families but not related to the child's disability (e.g., services and supports for maternal depression, substance abuse, economic support, domestic violence)

Families facing these special challenges will need additional supports, such as job training, counseling programs, drug rehabilitation programs, accessible and affordable mental health services, and domestic violence shelters, to be able to provide a good caregiving environment for the child.

Of the four categories of family needs, only the second and third are traditionally considered part of the system of services for young children with disabilities and their families. A comprehensive system of resources and services based on a Developmental Systems Model, however, will need to assist families in addressing needs across all four categories. The assessment carried out to identify the extent of a family's needs should result in identifying the kinds of services and supports needed within each of the four categories.

Early intervention programs vary in the extent to which they view services that extend beyond traditional disability services as part of early intervention. Harbin and West (1998) identified six qualitatively different models of early intervention service delivery. These included a single program model that consisted entirely of services for children with disabilities with weak links to other programs in the community; a multiple program model with programs for children with disabilities that were linked to other programs in the community that addressed the health and welfare needs of children and families in addition to needs related to disability; and a multiple program model in which programs for children with disabilities were thoroughly integrated into a broader network of programs serving children and families in the community. In this last model, the linking of programs produced a comprehensive array of specialized and natural community programs and resources that shared common values and were intentionally designed to work together to form a cohesive whole. The last model is most consistent with a developmental systems framework in that it provides the fullest array of services and supports for families and thus by design acknowledges the diversity of stressors faced by families of young children with disabilities (see Chapter 5). By integrating these services at an agency or programmatic level (as opposed to requiring service coordination to weave services together individually for each family), this model that is labeled as "comprehensive services for all" increases the likelihood that the early intervention system will be able to successfully link families of young children with disabilities with the full range of services and supports they need including those that extend beyond disability-related services.

Resource Supports

Resources refer to the possible types of community assistance that could be used to meet the needs of young children with disabilities. National data on families entering early intervention indicate that early intervention programs are providing families with some kinds of resources more frequently than others (see Figure 12.1). Most families were provided with information about child development and their legal rights, but fewer than one third were offered information about recreation and only 12% were given help with meeting basic needs for food or clothing (unpublished NEILS data). Interestingly, many families indicated they did not need the category of help that was not offered to them, although there were some exceptions. Among those families not offered help, half wanted information about child development and how to play and talk with their child. Other categories of help needed by those who did not get it were legal rights, help with other agencies that might help their child, help with special toys or equipment, and finding out about recreation for their child. These data could indicate that the kinds of help being provided to early intervention are tailored to family's needs, but they also can be seen as an indication of which resources early intervention programs currently see as within their scope of responsibility and which ones they see as falling outside of it.

A resource-based approach to early intervention has been extensively discussed and researched by Dunst, Trivette, and colleagues (Dunst, 2000; Dunst, Leet, & Trivette, 1988; Trivette, Dunst, & Deal, 1997). They contrasted services-based approaches to early intervention with resources-based approaches, with *service* being defined as a "specific or particular activity employed by a professional or professional agency to assist an

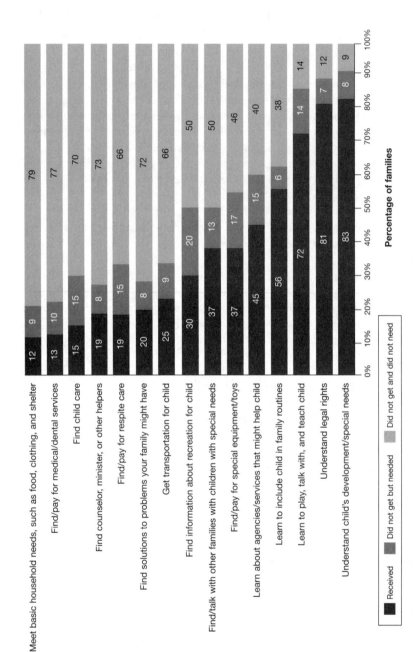

Figure 12.1.   Families' report of receipt of various kinds of assistance from their early intervention program.

individual or group" (Trivette et al., 1997, p. 75). Resources-based approaches are characterized by solutions for families that focus on a range of community resources incorporating both formal and informal supports and focusing on building capacity rather than correcting weaknesses.

Resources that can be used to promote optimal family interactions encompass a vast array of people, groups, organizations, and programs in communities that can be used by parents of young children to provide experiences that can positively influence parent and child behavior. Most of these resources are general community-based resources in the sense that they are available to all families in the community, not just to parents of children with disabilities. Trivette et al. (1997) identified the following 13 resource categories: economic, physical and environmental, food and clothing, medical and dental, employment and vocational, transportation and communication, adult education and enrichment, child education and intervention, child care, recreational, emotional, cultural, and social. Their conceptualization of resources is broad and includes the total array of community assets that are available to families in promoting the development of their children. For purposes of designing an early intervention program based on a Developmental Systems Model, social support and services and information will be discussed.

Although most of the resources available to families of young children with disabilities are general resources designed for all families, some communities may also offer specialized resources (e.g., a Special Olympics program).

The availability of resources to meet basic needs becomes especially important in supporting parents, given the large number of young children with disabilities living in low-income households (Hebbeler et al., 2003). Adequate employment or job training activities, health insurance, affordable housing, and good public transportation are examples of resources that could make a critical difference in the lives of these families. Financial support programs that augment family income or alleviate family expenses, such as TANF, public health insurance, food stamps, and subsidized child care also are important resources designed to meet the needs of the subset of families of young children with disabilities who have limited incomes. Unless families of young children with disabilities have ways to address their need for financial assistance, the specialized disability services may be of little value. Needs for financial resources could be addressed in a Developmental Systems Model through coordination provided by the early intervention system or through links to other community agencies that can connect families to the resources they need.

One example of a financial resource designed specifically for families of children with disabilities is Supplemental Security Income (SSI). SSI is a program administered by the Social Security Administration that provides financial support to children who are blind or have other disabilities and who are living in homes with limited income and resources. To qualify for SSI, the family must have a child with a physical or mental condition (or a combination of conditions) that can be medically proven and that causes "marked and severe" functional limitations. The condition(s) must have lasted or be expected to last at least a year or end in death. In December 2003, the average monthly SSI payment from all sources (federal and state supplementation) for people younger than the age of 18 was about $500.

Implementing a resource-based approach requires identifying the resources in the community (referred to as resource mapping), and working to build the capacity of communities to add additional resources or improve resources that are available (Trivette et al., 1997). Although it is true that communities have many untapped and unrecognized resources (Krietzmann & McKnight, 1993), it is also true that communities vary tremendously in the resources they have available to assist families of young children in supporting their children's development. Safe parks and playgrounds, indoor recreation areas for inclement weather, swim programs, accessible libraries, zoos, and museums are community resources that not all families have available to them because they do not exist in all communities. Communities also vary in the specialized resources that might be needed by families of young children with disabilities. Rural communities, in particular, often lack the specialized health care and assessment services that young children with rare conditions need (Lishner, Richardson, Levine, & Patrick, 1996).

A number of changes would need to occur for early intervention to move from being the set of specialized services that it is today to a Developmental Systems Model that would also assist families in gaining access to a range of community resources. Early intervention systems would need to begin by mapping the resources available to families in their community. A community map provides a visual picture of resources available in the community, how they are connected to one another, and what is considered within and outside of the Part C system of services. Community maps also are useful in identifying resources that the community needs to build. Roberts and Akers (2002) provided an example of a community map that was developed as part of a project designed to help a community improve how they were serving young children with disabilities. In this community, the mapping process itself served as a means of improving the early intervention system in that previously unidentified resources were discovered.

Strong interagency and inter-program linkages are needed to ensure that community resources work together to serve the needs of all families in the community. A focus on resources also requires changing how professionals see themselves. Early intervention professionals will need to see their roles not just as providers of service or even consultants to other providers but also as helpers that link families to community resources. A natural extension of the service coordinator's current role could be to serve as the source of information about the full range of community resources and linkages to those resources. Other providers will work to assist families in how to use those resources as learning opportunities (a topic discussed in more detail next).

Social Supports

Numerous studies have documented the unique emotional and physical demands that raising a child with a chronic medical condition or disability places on a parent (Bruce, Schultz, Smyrnios, & Schultz, 1994; Florian & Findler, 2001; Hauser-Cram, Warfield, Shonkoff, & Krauss, 2001; Law, 2000; Shonkoff, Hauser-Cram, Krauss, & Upshur, 1992; Wade, Taylor, Drotar, Stancin, & Yeates, 1996; Warfield, Krauss, Hauser-Cram, Upshur, & Shonkoff, 1999). Parents have to cope with the many uncertainties about their child's health and prognosis, frequent medical appointments and procedures, and the additional workload of looking after a child with special needs. Stressors associated with having a child with a disability can detract from parent well-being, the quality of family relationships, and parenting skills (Barnett, Clements, Kaplan-Estrin, & Fialka, 2003). It is not surprising that several studies have found increased symptoms of depression among parents of children with medical conditions (Blacher, Lopez, Shapiro, & Fusco, 1997; McKinney & Peterson, 1987). Interestingly enough, these families are less likely to rely on prior social supports because the sources often are unsure of how to help (Powers, 1993; Speltz, Armsden, & Clarren, 1990).

The evidence is strong that support from spouses, friends, and families has a positive effect on healthy adaptation among families of a child with a disability (Barakat & Linney, 1992; Crnic, Greenberg, Ragozin, Robinson, & Basham, 1983; Florian & Findler, 2001). Several factors have been shown to predict lower stress associated with parenting a child with a diagnosed condition including the size of the family's support system (Hodapp, Fidler, & Smith, 1998), spousal support (Bristol, Gallagher, & Schopler, 1988), and parental perceptions of their ability to positively influence child outcomes (Affleck, Tennen, & Gershman, 1985). Furthermore, parental coping and perceptions of control and stress also have been found to buffer parenting sensitivity to the stressors of having a child with a disability (Atkinson et al., 1995).

The provision of social support is seen as one way to help parents cope with the challenges of caring for a child, and the need for such support could be even greater for parents of a child with a disability. Such support can increase the likelihood of optimal family patterns of interaction. Social support is a multidimensional construct derived from several theoretical traditions. Social support encompasses both formal and informal connections in the community. Informal sources of social support include immediate family, friends, and extended family as well as social groups such as churches, social clubs, and peer support groups. Professionals provide formal sources of support (Crnic & Stormshak, 1997; Dunst, Trivette, & Jodry, 1997). The importance of social support in promoting developmental competence is based on an ecological perspective that maintains that factors that support or impede the parents' well-being influence their ability to care for their child, which can affect the child's development (Bronfenbrenner, 1979). Social support can indirectly influence the child's development through its effect on parents or directly influence development through the range of people who provide both formal and informal support to the child (Cochran & Brassard, 1979). Parenting support networks affect parenting behavior by influencing specific parenting attitudes and behaviors and by providing models and opportunities to learn alternative parent–child interaction styles (Cochran, 1990).

Research has shown that social support, especially informal social support, can be a positive influence on how mothers interact with their children, maternal parenting satisfaction, and maternal life satisfaction (Crnic & Stormshak, 1997). The positive impact of support on parenting behaviors extends beyond naturally occurring support and also includes support that is intentionally provided, which is important if social support is to be construed as an intervention. Social support provided intentionally and in response to a need can exert a positive influence on the behavior of families of children with disabilities. However, this is not true of social support that is not provided in response to a family's needs or life circumstances (Dunst et al., 1997). This underscores the importance of accurately identifying each family's needs through the assessment process and individualizing the resources and supports.

Early intervention programs that strengthen parental perceptions of control, support, and coping are likely to be successful at helping parents provide the types of behaviors that will support healthy development in their children. Barnett et al. (2003) suggested that parent groups can provide social support to families by doing the following:

- Identifying and validating a range of feelings and parental strengths

- Encouraging mutual support and sharing of information among group members

- Increasing perceptions of support available and received as well as quality of important relationships

- Improving skills at seeking information, support, and resources regarding child medical diagnoses and services for children and families

- Promoting parenting sensitivity and effective parenting skills

Provision of social support must be a key component of an early intervention program in a developmental systems framework. Social support can address the stressors faced by families of young children with disabilities. The myriad individuals and social networks to which the family is linked provide social support. Informal social support can be provided through family, friendships, neighborhoods, and churches; and professionals can provide formal support. For social support to be effective as an intervention, it must reflect the needs of the individual family and must be delivered in a way that more closely resembles the characteristics of informal support.

Information and Services

The information and services component in a Developmental Systems Model refers to services provided by professionals. It includes specialized services for children with disabilities as well as services needed by all children in the community, such as health care and high-quality preschools. The specialized services are the early intervention services provided to infants and toddlers under Part C and preschool special education and related services that are provided for 3- through 5-year-olds through school systems. These services are generally provided to the child, the family, or both. They are aimed at promoting and supporting the child's development, daily functioning, and quality of life. They are delivered in a variety of settings, most commonly the child's home or in an early childhood center or school, and include specialized instruction and therapies. Provision of information is a type of service valued by families of children with disabilities. Parents need information about the child's disability, about how to best support the child's development, and about what kinds of services to expect.

Information

When a child has a disability, parents have immediate and continuing needs for information about the condition. Children with an established diagnosis often receive the diagnosis (e.g., Down syndrome) at birth or during the first 2 years of life. Other conditions emerge gradually over the first several years of life, with symptomatic delays or difficulties in development and behavior preceding any formal diagnosis (e.g., cerebral palsy, fragile X syndrome, autism). Whether parents have been given a formal diagnosis or they have concerns about delays or behavioral symptoms without a formal label, they initially face a challenge of learning about the specific diagnosis. Interviews with parents of young children with disabilities revealed that families wanted information that is comprehensive and organized. They wanted information about specialized and nonspecialized resources available to them, and they wanted a family-friendly directory of resources (Harbin, McWilliam, & Gallagher, 2000).

The search for information often begins with medical professionals, but parents can now gain access to a vast amount and variety of information on the Internet. An Internet search using the term *Down syndrome* yielded more than 2.5 million hits; a search for *autism* resulted in 1.8 million hits, a search for *blindness* yielded 1.2 million hits, and a search for *cerebral palsy* resulted in 401,000 hits. One challenge for parents is how to identify and evaluate the accuracy and value of information available to them. Besides information about specific disabilities and treatments, the Internet can also serve as a source of social support through sites that allow families with children with specific disabilities to connect with each other and share experiences.

When parents have a child with a specific diagnosed condition, they will naturally seek out information specific to that disability, such as medical information and possible treatments. Because established disabilities often are initially diagnosed by medical professionals or within medical settings, parents may first seek medical information and look for medical therapeutic treatments, perhaps assuming that there are treatments specific to the child's particular disability. One interesting byproduct of the information explosion is that it has supported parents in becoming strong advocates for particular types and the intensity of services. For example, there has been a great deal of litigation about provision of early intervention services for young children with autism (Mulick & Butter, 2002), which shows how consumers have driven service models for this particular disability (Jacobson, 2000).

The need to assist parents in either identifying the sources of information they need and then evaluating the accuracy of the information available suggests that one member of the intervention team might be assigned the role of information broker. This team member would be responsible for compiling and organizing the types of questions and information needs that a family has and then determining how best to gather and disseminate information to the family and to other team members. This individual would not need to have all of the expertise to address all of the information needs but would serve in a coordination function. The current service coordinator role could be well situated to perform the information broker role. This would require, however, a reconceptualization of the role because service coordinators are more likely to be seen as service brokers than as information brokers. Medical care providers also could serve in this role, but financial and time constraints, among other possible obstacles, may prevent them from filling such a role.

Services

IDEA (PL 105-17), the federal legislation governing the provision of services for children with disabilities, identifies the kinds of specialized service to be provided to these children and their families. Part C, the section governing the services to infants and toddlers, refers to these services as "early intervention services," whereas Part B, the section governing service provision for children 3 years and older, uses the phrase "special education and related services." Special education is specially designed instruction to meet the unique needs of a child with a disability. Related services are the developmental, corrective, and other supportive services to assist a child with a disability to benefit from special education. Services identified in IDEA for each age group are listed in Table 12.1.

Services for young children with disabilities can be characterized across a number of dimensions. A common descriptor is the location of the services: home- or center-based (Harbin et al., 2000). Another way to characterize the service is by the provider (e.g., special educator, speech-language pathologist).

Another common descriptor is the amount of service or time in service (Bailey, 2000; Shonkoff et al., 2000; Smith & McKenna, 1994). Despite popular media stories reporting about young children with disabilities,

Table 12.1.   Specialized services for young children with disabilities

Part C early intervention services (birth to 3)	Part B special education and related services (ages 3–5)
Assistive technology services	Audiology
Audiology	Counseling services
Family training, counseling, and support	Speech-language pathology
Health services	Medical services for diagnostic and evaluation purposes
Medical services for diagnosis and evaluation	Occupational therapy
Nursing services	Orientation and mobility services
Nutrition services	Physical therapy
Occupational therapy	Psychological services
Physical therapy	Recreation, including therapeutic recreation
Psychological services	Social work services
Service coordination services	Special education
Special instruction for the child	Transportation
Speech-language pathology	
Transportation	
Vision services	

particularly those with autism, receiving many hours of intervention per week, the actual number of hours per week of services typically received by children and families participating in early intervention is fewer than 2 (Kochanek & Buka, 1998). NEILS found that 63% of the children in early intervention were scheduled to receive 2 hours or less of service per week, and one third were scheduled to receive 1 hour or less (Mallik & Hebbeler, 2002). Considerably more research needs to be done to address how much early intervention services children and families should be receiving, especially because the amount of service is so closely linked to the cost of service. Although it should not always be assumed that more is better, it is almost certainly true that there is a minimum amount of service necessary for most interventions to be effective. Effective services might have a lower boundary below which the services will not have an impact. There might also be an upper bound above which no additional benefit is accrued from more service or more service results in negative impacts on the child or family.

Specialized Instruction

Instructional services are a major component of early intervention services. According to NEILS data, 43% of infants and toddlers received specialized instructional services during their first 6 months in early intervention. Nearly one third (32%) worked with a child development or infant specialist, and 28% worked with a special educator (Mallik & Hebbeler, 2002).

Learning in Early Childhood Programs

Children's learning occurs in a variety of settings throughout the day. Young children's learning, in particular, is heavily influenced by the environment and experiences provided to them by their caregivers across settings. Early intervention has incorporated this developmental principle in different ways. A traditional mainstay of early intervention programming, especially for toddlers and preschoolers, has been the center-based program. This is a program attended by children, most or all with delays and disabilities, and staffed by a special educator and some combination of therapists. Children attend for several hours a day, several days a week. Wolery (2000) noted four effects that disability is likely to have on children's learning and development and why children with disabilities require more than typical child-rearing practices: 1) children's disabilities make them dependent on others; 2) disabilities often result in developmental delays that become greater as children get older; 3) children's disabilities often interfere with how well they can learn from typical environmental structures and interactions; and 4) without intervention, children's disabilities often lead to the emergence of additional or secondary disabilities. To offset these predictable effects, early intervention works to enhance the child's learning environment to increase the likelihood of improving development. The instructional content of early intervention programs is based on one or more curricula, and specific interventions may be woven into the program to address the needs of individual children (Sandall, McLean, & Smith, 2000; Sandall & Schwartz, 2002). Bruder (1997) noted that curricula for children with disabilities tend to be eclectic, incorporating a variety of theoretical approaches such as a developmental approach or a functional approach.

The emerging recognition of the importance of including even young children with disabilities in the activities of typically developing children in their communities has resulted in changing the service setting for early intervention. Settings that serve only young children with disabilities have become increasingly recognized as inconsistent with the goal of inclusion, one of the principles of a developmental systems framework (see Chapter 3). Instead, young children with disabilities are to receive instructional services and supports in natural environments alongside typically developing peers (e.g., child care programs, preschools, Head Start Programs; see Guralnick, 2001b). Early intervention programs now must work with these community-based programs to weave specialized services and supports into the program's curriculum.

The goal of serving young children with disabilities in inclusive settings, although supported as a laudable one by researchers, practitioners, parents, and policy makers, still remains elusive. Guralnick (2001c) argued that the notion of providing services and supports to young children with disabilities with their typically developing peers is perhaps the most "radical component" of the IDEA legislation. Guralnick and others (e.g., Bricker, 2000; Guralnick, 2001c; Harbin et al., 2000; Kontos, Moore, & Giorgetti, 1998) have reviewed some of the challenges and have noted that progress has been slow in integrating young children with disabilities and their families in many programs and activities that are readily available to typically developing children and their families. The best examples of successful inclusion are from demonstration and research-oriented projects (Bricker, 2000). A review of state policies revealed that the availability of inclusive high-quality child care is scarce, and many families with children with disabilities may not be eligible for certain child care funded services (Mezey, Neas, & Irish, 2003).

The empirical base for inclusion is still relatively limited; attitudes and beliefs are commonly cited obstacles to access; and far-reaching changes are needed in both preservice and in-service personnel training. Nevertheless, parents have increasingly become advocates for inclusion for several reasons. First, they simply need to be able to have their children attending child care and preschool programs with other children when they are working. Second, they want their child with a disability to be able to participate in the typical activities available to their siblings and peers without disabilities (e.g., preschool programs, playgroups, recreational programs, church activities). Third, they believe that the social interactions with typical peers can benefit the child's social, language, and cognitive skill acquisition and learning because of the typical peer models available in inclusive settings. This belief is supported by a growing body of research that is demonstrating that positive behavioral and developmental outcomes can be achieved with individualized, developmentally oriented instructional techniques and curricula (Guralnick, 2001b; McConnell, 2002; Odom, 2000).

Much is now known about what constitutes high-quality practices to achieve successful inclusion, which includes a combination of developmentally appropriate practices with individualization based on the child's unique characteristics (Buysse, Skinner, & Grant, 2001). Furthermore, research about the play of young children with developmental delays can inform practice by helping interventionists understand what kinds of impairments the young children have that can interfere with their full inclusion. For instance, Guralnick, Hammond, and Connor (2003) investigated the nonsocial play of young children with and without developmental delays in a playgroup setting. By understanding specific peer interaction patterns that can limit a child's full participation in group settings, focused teacher behaviors or environmental manipulations can be strategically applied.

The importance of play as the context for intervention activities has been argued repeatedly because it is a primary context in which young children naturally learn and practice emerging skills (Casby, 2003; Morrison, Sainato, Benchaaban, & Endo, 2002). Play provides the context in which the young child's integrated social, emotional, communicative, and behavioral competencies come together. Although cognitive, speech, and language delays often seem to be the most salient concerns for many parents with young children with established disabilities, deficits and delays in social skills are increasingly becoming a critical focus of interventions. For example, some available models of intervention are devoted to social skills training such as the LEAP model for preschoolers with autism (Strain & Hoyson, 2000). Other work has demonstrated how discrete trial methods can be integrated in ongoing classroom activities to promote child engagement (McBride & Schwartz, 2003). An analysis of the current status and future areas of development relative to fostering children's peer-related social competence has been provided by Guralnick (2001d).

One major challenge to inclusion is how to effectively train child care providers and preschool teachers. One of the most promising developments in the early childhood special education field is the development of naturalistic teaching approaches such as activity-based intervention (Bricker, 1998). Hemmeter (2000) and others have argued convincingly that these naturalistic teaching approaches, which can be done during ongoing classroom activities, can make the goal of inclusion more likely. Managing behavior also can be a challenge for early childhood professionals. Both social skill deficits and behavioral difficulties make it hard for children to participate successfully in preschool and child care programs with their typical peers. Nevertheless, research-based strategies to promote social and communication skills in group settings with peers (Garfinkle & Schwartz, 2002; Hancock & Kaiser, 2002) and social skills training interventions for young children with limited skill repertoires or sensory and behavioral difficulties are increasingly being developed (Brown, Odom, & Conroy, 2001).

Some of the most promising approaches to inclusion involve embedded instruction whereby children with disabilities receive extra support in inclusive early childhood programs so they can participate and benefit from the naturally occurring classroom activities and acquire new skills (Horn, Lieber, Li, Sandall, & Schwartz, 2000). This approach requires that the child's goals are meaningful and functional and are relevant to the classroom activities and routines in order for teachers or caregivers to understand and implement the approach. A variety of terms such as naturalistic instruction, embedded instruction, activity-based intervention, and milieu teaching have been used to describe an approach to instruction in which the teacher "embeds the learning opportunity in the ongoing classroom activities, builds on child interest, and provides necessary support for child successes" (Odom, 2000, p. 23). A review of the empirical support for naturalistic teaching approaches that summarized annotated research articles and resources for activity-based intervention shows that this is an exciting new development in early intervention instruction (Pretti-Frontczak, Barr, Macy, & Carter, 2003).

Learning at Home and in the Community

Not all children receive their specialized instruction in an early childhood program. NEILS data indicate that 76% of infants and toddlers with disabilities receive services in the home (Mallik & Hebbeler, 2002). Little is known about the nature of what is transpiring during these home visits, however. Suggested practice is that the interventionist should support the child's caregivers in assisting the child in the areas of development previously identified by the team as the focus of intervention. The child's parents and caregivers spend far more time with the child than intervention professionals and therefore can have a greater effect on the child's development. Suggestions from professionals should be practical, simple to implement, and compatible with the caregivers' resources and desires (McWilliam, 2000).

The alternative to the interventionist working with the family is for the interventionist to work with the child. This is a much more traditional model of service delivery, and literature on best practice suggests that this approach has been set aside for a more family-centered approach. Working with the child is still a part of early intervention service delivery, which suggests that little is known about the actual delivery of early intervention services. Providers reported that in 44% of families receiving early intervention home visits, the focus was on the child rather than the child and the family (Hebbeler & Spiker, 2004). Harbin et al. (2000) cited several of their studies that provide support for the conclusion that early intervention continues to be child focused. Their research suggested that professionals set the stage for a child-centered approach by focusing all of the initial program activities and questions on the child. Interventionists need to "open the door" to a more family-centered approach by shifting the focus of early interactions with families by routinely and effectively identifying the kinds of assistance that families want and need. This suggests that the family assessment in a developmental systems approach plays a critical role in how families will come to view what early intervention is and how it can support them. It also suggests that professional orientation and training will play a crucial role in how early intervention is defined for families.

What kinds of specialized services can early intervention provide to support families in nurturing the development of a child with a disability? Some have argued for an increased emphasis on parent education in early intervention, defined as "the process of providing parents and other caregivers with specific knowledge and childrearing skills with the goal of promoting the development and competence of their children" (Mahoney et al., 1999, p. 131). Three major goals of parent education are 1) to teach parents strategies to assist the child to achieve developmental skills, 2) to help parents to manage the child's behavior in daily routines, and 3) to promote the parents' skills to engage the child in social interaction and play. These goals fit well with what is known about the critical role of social interaction and play in early development, and they also match family goals to promote the child's participation and engagement in daily routines and activities.

Recognizing the strong support for models that provide early intervention in collaboration with parents, Mahoney et al. (1999) also argued that parent education strategies can be developed and implemented in ways that are consistent with parent-centered best practices. The developmental and parent–child interaction research has provided the basis for interventions to teach parents more optimal interaction strategies that are responsive to child signals and encouraging of the child's active social participation, which can result in important developmental and functional skills. For instance, McCathern, Yoder, and Warren (1995) described three types of directives and their relationship to language development in children with Down syndrome. Follow-in directives (e.g., directives that followed the child's lead and were related to the child's immediate interest and focus of attention) were found to be the most effective for promoting language development. Redirectives, which initiate a new topic, and introductions, which are directives given to an unengaged child, were less effective. Follow-in directives may, however, be difficult to use with some children whose interest and attention are fleeting and hard to connect with and sustain.

These studies have contributed to a growing body of research demonstrating the benefits of teaching parents responsive interaction strategies (Kaiser et al., 1996). For example, Mahoney and Perales (2003) described a relationship-focused model of early intervention for young children with autism. The emphasis is on responsive interactive strategies in daily routine interactions, with the goal of promoting social-emotional development and communication. There are other examples about how to engage and involve parents effectively with children with cerebral palsy (Ketelaar, Vermeer, Helders, & Hart, 1998). Still, other researchers have been identifying how prelinguistic communication and social interaction should be a primary focus area for early intervention activities for children with a variety of disabilities (Hwang & Hughes, 2000; Pinder & Olswang, 1995; Warren, 2000).

Dunst and colleagues (Bruder, 2000; Bruder & Dunst, 1999; Dunst & Bruder, 2002; Dunst, Hamby, Trivette, Raab, & Bruder, 2000) have advocated an approach to intervention that uses the learning opportunities that exist in children's natural environments. These can be family or community settings in which activities take place that children participate in and learn from. These include family routines, play and entertainment activities, family rituals and celebrations, outings, church or religious activities, and so forth. This model requires the interventionist to inventory the child's activity settings and categorize the learning activities that can take place in them. In this approach, early intervention can be happening throughout the child's entire waking day, in all of the settings in which the child is present. The role of the early intervention providers is to provide parents and the child's other caregivers with information and assistance to help the family make it possible for the child to learn in everyday environments. Professionals are to use their specialized knowledge and techniques to help the family support the child's learning. This approach is closely linked with the use of a variety of resources in the community as learning opportunities. By using naturally occurring learning opportunities, the skills and behaviors being supported are functional and meaningful for the child and the family.

Helping families use naturally occurring learning opportunities fits well with a focus on working with children and families to achieve desired functional outcomes. This fits well because the kinds of functional outcomes that families have for their children frequently involve increasing the child's ability to participate in typical family routines and other activities engaged in by their siblings and peers without disabilities (Moes & Frea, 2002). This approach also fits well with several other key issues. First, active, child-initiated learning experiences, which are contingently responsive, lead to optimal learning. Second, models about family outcomes have been emphasizing conceptualizations that more explicitly delineate what families want and expect from the early intervention system. For instance, families should expect the system to help them to improve their quality of life and that of their child, to assist them concretely in their daily lives in caring for their child, and to seek their input about their goals for their child and their participation (Bailey et al., 1998).

One of the significant challenges for the early intervention field, however, is how to effectively translate this kind of research information into practice for providers and parents to use on a daily basis (Hemmeter, 2000). Although the research field has touted transdisciplinary models, relationship-based service models, use of naturally occurring learning opportunities, embedded instruction, and parent–professional empowerment philosophies, the widespread implementation of such models and practices is still not a reality (Pilkington & Malinowski, 2002). Because much of early intervention takes place in homes, much more attention needs to be paid to understanding what actually goes on in early intervention home visits, how parents understand the goals of the home visits, and the relationships between the individuals visiting the home and the parents (Brady, Peters, Gamel-McCormick, & Venuto, 2004; Hebbeler & Gerlach-Downie, 2002; Klass, 1997).

Specialized Therapies

Individual one-to-one therapy or instructional services may be one component of a comprehensive set of services and supports for some children and families receiving early intervention. As shown in Table 12.1, early intervention services include a number of different therapy services. For many infants and young children with established disabilities, physical, occupational, or speech therapy can help to teach or target specific skills or provide specific techniques or activities to support skill acquisition. For instance, occupational and physical therapy can identify and help parents and caregivers with techniques and activities to promote movement and reduce sensory difficulties, which can help with activities of daily living (feeding, dressing, toileting), lead to improved self-regulation, and allow the child to more fully participate in play and family routines. One-to-one play interventions may be used to target the acquisition of specific subskills that can enhance social interaction or communicative competencies (e.g., joint attention skills). The purpose of such individual therapy or instruction is to provide intensive intervention on specific skills or behaviors. The goal would be to increase those skills or behaviors that are needed for social interaction, to reduce those that are interfering with social interaction, and to enhance the child's ability to be as independent as possible. Achieving those goals should in turn promote the child's ability to be a more competent social partner, to participate in play, and to reduce caregiving burdens. Thus, these individual, child-focused interventions are not ends in themselves; rather, they are targeted and strategic interventions aimed at moving the child toward greater participation in everyday activities and routines.

Therapies are a key component of early intervention service provision. Data from NEILS indicate that during the first 6 months of early intervention, 52% of infants and toddlers receive speech therapy, 39% receive occupational therapy, and 37% receive physical therapy. The predominance of these therapies raises significant challenges for early intervention service provision in light of current and future shortages of these professionals (Hebbeler, 1994; Yoder & Coleman, 1990). Concerns also have been raised about providing individualized therapies in isolation from other early intervention services (McWilliam, 1996). Current thinking in the field suggests that therapy services should be provided through a transdisciplinary model in which team members, including the family, plan and work together to provide integrated services. This approach addresses the personnel shortage by alleviating the need for face-to-face time with a series of therapists and is also considered a more effective approach to service delivery. Harbin et al. (2000) noted that for therapies to be effective, they must be integrated into the child's natural activities and routines. This means the therapists need to work outside of the traditional therapeutic environment and change the way therapy is delivered. Therapists need to assist other providers who work with the child and family on a regular basis to help them integrate therapy goals into the family's normal routines.

This model of therapy services supports a developmental systems framework because it provides families with information and support that allows them to better orchestrate their child's daily experiences.

Respite Services

Many infants and young children with established disabilities have significant health problems, developmental delays, and behavioral difficulties that make daily caregiving extremely burdensome. Respite services can be a critical need for many families and should be regularly assessed. In discussing the need for respite care for families with young children with disabilities, Jimenez (1999) argued for early intervention programs to maintain a list of respite care providers and information about schedules and fees; develop relationships with private, volunteer agencies that can provide respite care; and have clear guidelines for the provision of respite care as part of the IFSP.

Health Care and Medical Services

Special health care needs also make it essential that the pediatrician or other primary medical care providers be active members of the family's early intervention team. Spiker and Hebbeler (1999) argued for the critical importance of the role of the pediatrician for giving parents information and support. Once the initial diagnosis has been made, the pediatrician or other primary health care providers should have many important roles vis-à-vis early intervention:

- Monitoring medical problems and making appropriate referrals will be an ongoing need because children with established disabilities can have conditions associated with the disability that require special attention or will have implications for early intervention programming. Some children may have higher risk of hearing or vision problems, oral-motor difficulties, seizures, muscle tone or connective tissue abnormalities, or other medical conditions that could affect learning as well as daily routines related to feeding, sleeping, positioning, or movement.

- Reviewing and interpreting diagnostic and prognostic information in a clear, sensitive, and caring manner also will be an important ongoing role for the pediatrician as the child grows.

- Recommending needed therapies is an important role played by the pediatrician because medical conditions may have consequences for the kinds of interventions that would be optimal.

- Being familiar with the child's progress in early intervention programs and discussing progress with parents allows the pediatrician to become an extra source of support. Regularly sharing early intervention evaluation and progress reports, including the IFSPs, with the pediatrician is recommended.

- Prescribing medications may be helpful for alleviating behavioral symptoms that can interfere with some children's full participation in intervention services and family routines.

- Providing expert information about the child's particular diagnostic condition can be a major resource for helping the family and other intervention providers to evaluate medical and treatment information.

These suggested best practices call for the pediatrician (or other designated medical team member) to participate actively with the family in the child's early intervention experiences by keeping well informed about the early intervention experiences of the child and family, providing medical information, and assisting with medical or therapy referrals that are needed. This kind of active involvement and participation with families of young children, including children with disabilities, are unfortunately not particularly common. For instance, a report about the quality of preventive and developmental services for young children enrolled in Medicaid showed that many parents had developmental concerns that were not addressed by their pediatricians, but having a pediatric clinician or nurse who knew the child well can make an important difference in parents' perceptions of how family-centered the care was (Bethell et al., 2002). There is a clear need for more creative models in pediatric care to address parents' developmental and behavioral questions and concerns. Although uncommon, there are examples of innovative models in which developmental specialists who participate as members of a pediatric clinic can spend more time with families discussing their developmental questions and concerns, but one perplexing problem that has not been solved is funding these positions in the current managed health care environment (Bethell et al., 2002; Eggbeer, Littman, & Jones, 1997).

CONCLUSION

The goal of optimizing the development of young children with disabilities only can be achieved when families are adequately supported in their parenting role. Just as each child is unique, so are the needs of each family. The Developmental Systems Model emphasizes the significant role that parents play in promoting developmental competence (Guralnick, 2001a).

The model also recognizes that families will need various combinations of resources, social supports, and information and services to help them address the stressors associated with parenting in general and parenting a child with a disability in particular. This chapter has described the kinds of supports and services that families would have available to them if a Developmental Systems Model were fully implemented. Existing research substantiates the soundness of an approach that thoroughly supports parents in providing nurturing, responsive, and stimulating environments for their children.

Unfortunately, the distance between current practice and the vision of the Developmental Systems Model is substantial. Many challenges need to be addressed to make the vision a reality. Some of these challenges involve the delivery of the specialized services for children with disabilities. For example,

- Although much is known about effective interventions and instructional practices, this knowledge is often not reflected in actual practice, and the time it takes for new knowledge and recommended practices to be widely implemented is unacceptably long.

- With continuing advances from biomedical, genetic, and neuroscience research about specific disabilities, questions arise about how etiologic-specific information is used to design interventions. Nationally, fewer than 10% of the children entering early intervention had Down syndrome. Similarly, small proportions had vision or hearing impairments (Hebbeler et al., 2001), and yet, entire literatures exist about how to serve children with these conditions. As science continues to advance what is known about early identification and the development of children with rare conditions, additional literatures will emerge increasing the scope of what interventionists must know.

- With the increasing cultural and linguistic diversity of families in the United States, there is a need to consider how interventions should be tailored and how interventionists need to be specially trained to work with families from different cultures (Barrera & Corso, 2002; Lynch & Hanson, 2004). Interventions focused on parental responsivity, for example, will need to develop necessary modifications to reflect cultural sensitivity. Although families are pleased with their early intervention services, programs appear not to serve minority families, low-income families, and families with lower education levels as well as they serve other families (Bailey, Hebbeler, Scarborough, Spiker, & Mallik, 2004).

- Closely related to each of these is the challenge of how best to structure pre- and in-service training for early intervention professionals (Winton, 2000). Given the diversity of young children with disabilities and their families, interventionists need to master a vast range and amount of information and skills. For example, there are an increasing number of reviews of what early interventionists need to know about the health and medical needs of specific groups of children and how these problems can influence a child's response to intervention (McNab & Blackman, 1998; Roizen, 2003). Likewise, parents want the most current information as advances in understanding the genetics of specific conditions continue to grow (e.g., Spiker, 1999). Particularly challenging in the training arena is how to provide the necessary training and support for child care providers and preschool teachers so young children with disabilities can be meaningfully integrated and well served in their programs.

- Despite widespread recognition of the need to coordinate services for families of children with disabilities and a legal mandate to provide service coordination, many families still encounter fragmented service provision. A host of factors continue to operate as barriers to agencies working together effectively that result in poorly coordinated services for individual families (see Chapter 2).

The resources needed by families with disabilities extend beyond the specialized services that make up early intervention and preschool special education. The broader arena of child and family services poses another set of challenges to implementing the Developmental Systems Model. There really is no such thing as an early care *system* in the same sense that we have a K–12 educational system or a health care system. What exists are multiple programs, agencies, and services that operate largely independently, are funded separately, have differing eligibility requirements, usually are located in separate facilities, and keep separate records and data on the children and families they serve (Kagan & Pritchard, 1996; Shonkoff & Phillips, 2000). Coordinating services across programs serving only families with disabilities is challenging enough; coordinating services across the myriad programs that serve families with limited income, mental health needs, job training needs, and other needs when these programs are not integrated at the agency level is truly daunting. Approaches that minimize services provided by professionals and rely more heavily on resources in communities are less troubled by a lack of interagency coordination, but challenges also exist around securing resources. Communities vary in the resources they have available to support families with young children. Many communities need to expand their capacity to meet the needs of children and families by having safer playgrounds or story hours in libraries. These kinds of community resources provide the places in which families with young children can come together and provide their children with learning opportunities.

The road to implementing the Developmental Systems Model may be a long and difficult one, but the promise it holds for young children and their families is worth the journey. Not so many years ago, parents of a newborn with a disability were told that life in an institution was their child's only future. The road was also long between that point and the child with a disability playing with typically developing peers in the neighborhood preschool, but that road has been successfully traveled. The next part of the journey shifts the focus to supporting the family in identifying and securing the full array of resources and services. These should be resources and services to assist them in promoting their child's growth and development and participating as fully as possible in their communities.

REFERENCES

Aber, J.L., Jones, S., & Cohen, J. (2000). The impact of poverty on the mental health and development of very young children. In C.H. Zeanah, Jr. (Ed.), *Handbook of infant mental health* (2nd ed., pp. 113–128). New York: The Guilford Press.

Affleck, G., Tennen, H., & Gershman, K. (1985). Mastery, meaning, and protection from future harm. *American Journal of Mental Deficiency, 89*, 653–656.

Atkinson, L., Scott, B., Chisholm, V.C., Blackwell, J., Dickens, S., Tam, F., & Goldberg, S. (1995). Cognitive coping, affective distress, and maternal sensitivity: Mothers of children with Down syndrome. *Developmental Psychology, 31*, 668–676.

Bailey, D., Hebbeler, K., Scarborough, A., Spiker, D., & Mallik, S. (2004). First experiences with early intervention: A national perspective. *Pediatrics, 113*(4), 887–896.

Bailey, D., Scarborough, A., & Hebbeler, K. (2003). *National Early Intervention Longitudinal Study: Families' first experiences with early intervention.* Menlo Park, CA: SRI International.

Bailey, D.B. (2000). The federal role in early intervention. *Topics in Early Childhood Special Education, 20*, 71–78.

Bailey, D.B. (2001). Evaluating parent involvement and family support in early intervention and preschool programs. *Journal of Early Intervention, 24*, 1–14.

Bailey, D.B., McWilliam, R.A., Darkes, L.A., Hebbeler, K., Simeonsson, R.J., Spiker, D., & Wagner, M. (1998). Family outcomes in early intervention: A framework for program evaluation and efficacy research. *Exceptional Children, 64*, 313–328.

Barakat, L.P., & Linney, J.A. (1992). Children with physical handicaps and their mothers: The interrelation of social support, maternal adjustment, and child adjustment. *Journal of Pediatric Psychology, 17*, 725–739.

Barnett, D., Clements, M., Kaplan-Estrin, M., & Fialka, J. (2003). Building new dreams: Supporting parents' adaptation to their child with special needs. *Infants and Young Children, 16*(3), 184–200.

Barrera, I., & Corso, R.M. (2002). Cultural competency as skilled dialogue. *Topics in Early Childhood Special Education, 22*(2), 103–113.

Bethell, C., Peck, C., Abrams, M., Halfon, N., Sareen, H., & Collins, K.S. (2002). *Partnering with parents to promote the healthy development of young children enrolled in Medicaid.* New York: The Commonwealth Fund.

Blacher, J., Lopez, S., Shapiro, J., & Fusco, J. (1997). Contributions to depression in Latina mothers with and without children with retardation: Implications for caregiving. *Family Relations, 46,* 325–334.

Bornstein, M.H. (Ed.). (1989). *Maternal responsiveness: Characteristics and consequences.* San Francisco: Jossey-Bass.

Botting, N., Powls, A., Cooke, R.W.I., & Marlow, N. (1998). Cognitive and educational outcome of very-low-birthweight children in early adolescence. *Developmental Medicine and Child Neurology, 40,* 652–660.

Boyce, G.C., Smith, T.B., & Casto, G. (1999). Health and educational outcomes of children who experienced severe neonatal medical complications. *Journal of Genetic Psychology, 160*(3), 261–269.

Bradley, R.H., Corwyn, R.F., Burchinal, M., McAdoo, H.P., & Coll, C.G. (2001). The home environments of children in the United States part II: Relations with behavioral development through age thirteen. *Child Development, 72,* 1868–1886.

Bradley, R.H., Corwyn, R.F., McAdoo, H.P., & Coll, C.G. (2001). The home environments of children in the United States, part I: Variations by age, ethnicity, and poverty status. *Child Development, 72,* 1844–1867.

Brady, S.J., Peters, D.L., Gamel-McCormick, M., & Venuto, N. (2004). Types and patterns of professional-family talk in home-based early intervention. *Journal of Early Intervention, 26*(2), 146–159.

Bredekamp, S., & Copple, C. (Eds.). (1997). *Developmentally appropriate practice in early childhood programs* (Rev. ed.). Washington, DC: National Association for the Education of Young Children.

Bricker, D. (2000). Inclusion: How the scene has changed. *Topics in Early Childhood Special Education, 20*(1), 14–19.

Bricker, D. (with Pretti-Frontczak, K., & McComas, N.) (1998). *An activity-based approach to early intervention* (2nd ed.). Baltimore: Paul H. Brookes Publishing Co.

Bristol, M.M., Gallagher, J.J., & Schopler, E. (1988). Mothers and fathers of young developmentally disabled and nondisabled boys: Adaptation and spousal support. *Developmental Psychology, 24,* 441–451.

Bronfenbrenner, U. (1979). *The ecology of human development: Experiments by nature and design.* Cambridge, MA: Harvard University Press.

Brown, W.H., Odom, S.L., & Conroy, M.A. (2001). An intervention hierarchy for promoting young children's peer interactions in natural environments. *Topics in Early Childhood Special Education, 21*(3), 162–175.

Bruce, E.J., Schultz, C.L., Smyrnios, K.X., & Schultz, N.C. (1994). Grieving related to development: A preliminary comparison of three age cohorts of parents of children with intellectual disability. *British Journal of Medical Psychology, 67,* 37–52.

Bruder, M.B. (1997). The effectiveness of specific educational/developmental curricula for children with established disabilities. In M.J. Guralnick (Ed.), *The effectiveness of early intervention* (pp. 523–548). Baltimore: Paul H. Brookes Publishing Co.

Bruder, M.B. (2000). Family-centered early intervention: Clarifying our values for the new millennium. *Topics in Early Childhood Special Education, 20*(2), 105–115.

Bruder, M.B., & Dunst, C.J. (1999). Expanding learning opportunities for infants and toddlers in natural environments: A chance to reconceptualize early intervention. *Zero To Three, 20*(3), 34–36.

Burack, J., Hodapp, R., & Zigler, E. (1998). *Handbook of mental retardation and development.* New York: Cambridge University Press.

Buysse, V., Skinner, D., & Grant, S. (2001). Toward a definition of quality inclusion: Perspectives of parents and practitioners. *Topics in Early Childhood Special Education, 24,* 146–161.

Casby, M.W. (2003). Developmental assessment of play: A model for early intervention. *Communication Disorders Quarterly, 24*(4), 175–183.

Case, R., Griffin, S., & Kelly, W. (2001). Socioeconomic differences in children's early cognitive development and their readiness for schooling. In S. Golbeck (Ed.), *Psychological perspectives on early childhood education: Reframing dilemmas in research and practice* (pp. 37–63). Mahwah, NJ: Lawrence Erlbaum Associates.

Christian, K., Morrison, F.J., & Bryant, F.B. (1998). Predicting kindergarten academic skills: Interactions among child care, maternal education, and family literacy environments. *Early Childhood Research Quarterly, 13*, 501–521.

Cochran, M. (1990). Personal networks in the ecology of human development. In M. Cochran, M. Larner, D. Riley, L. Gunnarson, & C. Henderson (Eds.), *Extending families: The social networks of parents and their children* (pp. 3–33). New York: Cambridge University Press.

Cochran, M.M., & Brassard, J.A. (1979). Child development and personal social networks. *Child Development, 50*, 601–615.

Covey, T.J. (1997). Use of sensorimotor functions for early identification and neurorehabilitation of infants with cerebral palsy and/or cerebral palsy precursors. *Infant-Toddler Intervention, 7*(3), 179–189.

Crnic, K., & Stormshak, E. (1997). The effectiveness of providing social support for families of children at risk. In M.J. Guralnick (Ed.), *The effectiveness of early intervention* (pp. 209–225). Baltimore: Paul H. Brookes Publishing Co.

Crnic, K.A., Greenberg, M.T., Ragozin, A.S., Robinson, N.M., & Basham, R. (1983). Effects of stress and social support on mothers and premature and full-term infants. *Child Development, 54*, 209–217.

Crombie, M., & Gunn, P. (1998). Early intervention, families, and adolescents with Down syndrome. *International Journal of Disability, Development and Education, 45*(3), 253–281.

Demo, D.H., & Cox, M.J. (2000). Families with young children: A review of research in the 1990's. *Journal of Marriage and the Family, 62*, 876–895.

Dinnebeil, L.A., Hale, L., & Rule, S. (1999). Early intervention program practices that support collaboration. *Topics in Early Childhood Special Education, 19*, 225–235.

Duncan, G., & Brooks-Gunn, J. (1997). *Consequences of growing up poor.* New York: Russell Sage Foundation.

Dunst, C.J. (2000). Revisiting "Rethinking Early Intervention." *Topics in Early Childhood Special Education, 20*(2), 95–104.

Dunst, C.J., & Bruder, M.B. (2002). Valued outcomes of service coordination, early intervention, and natural environments. *Exceptional Children, 68*, 361–375.

Dunst, C.J., Bruder, M.B., Trivette, C.M., Hamby, D., Raab, M., & McLean, M. (2001). Characteristics and consequences of everyday natural learning opportunities. *Topics in Early Childhood Special Education, 21*, 68–92.

Dunst, C.J., Hamby, D., Trivette, C.M., Raab, M., & Bruder, M.B. (2000). Everyday family and community life and children's naturally occurring learning opportunities. *Journal of Early Intervention, 23*(3), 151–164.

Dunst, C.J., Leet, H.E., & Trivette, C.M. (1988). Family resources, personal well-being, and early intervention. *Journal of Special Education, 22*, 108–116.

Dunst, C.J., Trivette, C.M., & Jodry, W. (1997). Influences of social support on children with disabilities and their families. In M.J. Guralnick (Ed.), *The effectiveness of early intervention* (pp. 499–522). Baltimore: Paul H. Brookes Publishing Co.

Dwyer, M.C., Chait, R., & McKee, P. (2000). *Building strong foundations for early learning: The U.S. Department of Education's guide to high-quality early childhood education programs.* Washington, DC: U.S. Department of Education.

Eggbeer, L., Littman, C.L., & Jones, M. (1997, June/July). Zero to Three's developmental specialist in pediatric practice project: An important support for parents and young children. *Zero to Three, 3*–24.

Escalona, S. (1982). Babies at double hazard: Early development of infants at biologic and social risk. *Journal of Pediatrics, 70,* 670–676.

Florian, V., & Findler, L. (2001). Mental health and marital adaptation among mothers of children with cerebral palsy. *American Journal of Orthopsychiatry, 71,* 358–367.

Fujiura, G.T., & Yamaki, K. (2000). Trends in demography of childhood poverty and disability. *Exceptional Children, 66,* 187–199.

Garbarino, J., & Ganzel, B. (2000). The human ecology of early risk. In J.P. Shonkoff & S.J. Meisels (Eds.), *Handbook of early childhood intervention* (2nd ed., pp. 76–93). New York: Cambridge University Press.

Garfinkle, A.N., & Schwartz, I.S. (2002). Peer imitation: Increasing social interactions in children with autism and other developmental disabilities in inclusive preschool classrooms. *Topics in Early Childhood Special Education, 22*(1), 26–38.

Gilliam, W.S., & Zigler, E.F. (2000). A critical meta-analysis of all evaluations of state-funded preschool from 1977 to 1998: Implications for policy, service delivery and program evaluation. *Early Childhood Research Quarterly, 15,* 441–473.

Greenberg, M., Lengua, L.J., Coie, J.D., & Pinderhughes, E.E. (1999). Predicting developmental outcomes at school entry using a multiple-risk model: Four American communities. *Developmental Psychology, 35,* 403–417.

Gross, R.T., Spiker, D., & Haynes, C.W. (Eds.). (1997). *Helping low birth weight, premature babies: The Infant Health and Development Program.* Stanford, CA: Stanford University Press.

Guralnick, M.J. (Ed.). (1997). *The effectiveness of early intervention.* Baltimore: Paul H. Brookes Publishing Co.

Guralnick, M.J. (1998). The effectiveness of early intervention for vulnerable children: A developmental perspective. *American Journal on Mental Retardation, 102,* 319–345.

Guralnick, M.J. (2001a). A Developmental Systems Model for early intervention. *Infants and Young Children, 14,* 1–18.

Guralnick, M.J. (Ed.). (2001b). *Early childhood inclusion: Focus on change.* Baltimore: Paul H. Brookes Publishing Co.

Guralnick, M.J. (2001c). A framework for change in early childhood inclusion. In M.J. Guralnick (Ed.), *Early childhood inclusion: Focus on change* (pp. 3–35). Baltimore: Paul H. Brookes Publishing Co.

Guralnick, M.J. (2001d). Social competence with peers and early childhood inclusion: Need for alternative approaches. In M.J. Guralnick (Ed.), *Early childhood inclusion: Focus on change* (pp. 481–502). Baltimore: Paul H. Brookes Publishing Co.

Guralnick, M.J., Hammond, M.A., & Connor, R.T. (2003). Subtypes of nonsocial play: Comparisons between young children with and without developmental delays. *American Journal of Mental Retardation, 108,* 347–362.

Hack, M., Flannery, D., Schluchter, M., Cartar, L., Borawski, E., & Klein, N. (2002). Outcomes in young adulthood for very-low-birth-weight infants. *The New England Journal of Medicine, 346,* 149–157.

Hancock, T.B., & Kaiser, A.P. (2002). The effects of trainer-implemented Enhanced Milieu Teaching on the social communication of children with autism. *Topics in Early Childhood Special Education, 22*(1), 39–54.

Harbin, G.L., McWilliam, R.A., & Gallagher, J.J. (2000). Services for young children with disabilities and their families. In J.P. Shonkoff & S.J. Meisels

(Eds.), *Handbook of early childhood intervention* (2nd ed., pp. 387–415). New York: Cambridge University Press.

Harbin, G.L., & West, T. (1998). *Early intervention service delivery models and their impact on children and families.* Chapel Hill: University of North Carolina, FPG Child Development Center, Early Childhood Research Institute on Service Utilization.

Harris, S.L., & Handleman, J.S. (2000). Age and IQ at intake as predictors of placement for young children with autism: A four- to six-year follow-up. *Journal of Autism and Developmental Disorders, 30*(2), 137–142.

Hauser-Cram, P., Warfield, M., Shonkoff, J.P., & Krauss, M.W. (2001). Children with disabilities: A longitudinal study of child development and parent well-being. *Monographs of the Society for Research in Child Development, 66*(3).

Hebbeler, K. (1994). *Shortages in professions working with young children with disabilities and their families.* Chapel Hill, NC: National Early Childhood Technical Assistance System.

Hebbeler, K. (1997). A system in a system: Sociopolitical factors and early intervention. In S.K. Thurman, J.R. Cornwell, & S.R. Gottwald (Eds.), *Contexts of early intervention: Systems and settings* (pp. 19–38). Baltimore: Paul H. Brookes Publishing Co.

Hebbeler, K., & Gerlach-Downie, S. (2002). Theories of change in the black box of home visiting. *Early Childhood Research Quarterly, 17,* 28–51.

Hebbeler, K., & Spiker, D. (2004, February). *Early intervention in the U.S.: The National Early Intervention Longitudinal Study (NEILS).* Paper presented at the Early Intervention Working Conference: Fragile X Newborn Screening Planning Grant. Palm Springs, CA.

Hebbeler, K., Spiker, D., Mallik, S., Scarborough, A., & Simeonsson, R. (2003). *Demographic characteristics of children and families entering early intervention.* Menlo Park, CA: SRI International.

Hebbeler, K., Wagner, M., Spiker, D., Scarborough, A., Simeonsson, R.J., & Collier, M. (2001). *A first look at the characteristics of children and families entering early intervention services.* Menlo Park, CA: SRI International.

Hemmeter, M.L. (2000). Classroom-based interventions: Evaluating the past and looking toward the future. *Topics in Early Childhood Special Education, 20*(1), 56–61.

Hodapp, R.M., Fidler, D.J., & Smith, C.M. (1998). Stress and coping in families of children with Smith-Magenis syndrome. *Journal of Intellectual Disability Research, 42,* 331–340.

Horn, E., Lieber, J., Li, S.M., Sandall, S., & Schwartz, I. (2000). Supporting young children's IEP goals in inclusive settings through embedded learning opportunities. *Topics in Early Childhood Special Education, 20,* 208–223.

Hwang, B., & Hughes, C. (2000). The effects of social interactive training on early social communicative skills of children with autism. *Journal of Autism and Developmental Disorders, 30*(4), 331–343.

Individuals with Disabilities Education Act (IDEA) Amendments of 1997, PL 105-17, 20 U.S.C. §§ 1400 *et seq.*

Jacobson, J.W. (2000). Early intensive behavioral intervention: Emergence of a consumer-driven service model. *Behavior Analyst, 23*(2), 149–171.

Jimenez, M.V. (1999). Respite care and the family with special needs. *Zero to Three, 19*(5), 20–22.

Kagan, S.L., & Pritchard, E. (1996). Linking services for children and families: Past legacy, future possibilities. In E.F. Zigler, S.L. Kagan, & N.W. Hall (Eds.), *Children, families and government: Preparing for the twenty-first century* (pp. 378–393). New York: Cambridge University Press.

Kaiser, A.P., Hemmeter, M.L., Ostrosky, M.M., Fisher, R., Yoder, P., & Keefer, M. (1996). The effects of teaching parents to use responsive interaction strategies. *Topics in Early Childhood Special Education, 16,* 375–406.

Ketelaar, M., Vermeer, A., Helders, P.J.M., & Hart, H.T. (1998). Parental participation in intervention programs for children with cerebral palsy: A review of research. *Topics in Early Childhood Special Education, 18*(2), 108–117.

Klass, C.S. (1997). The home visitor-parent relationship: The linchpin of home visiting. *Zero to Three, 17*(4), 1–9.

Kochanek, T., & Buka, S.L. (1998). Patterns of early intervention service utilization: Child, maternal, and provider factors. *Journal of Early Intervention, 21,* 217–231.

Kontos, S., Moore, D., & Giorgetti, K. (1998). The ecology of inclusion. *Topics in Early Childhood Special Education, 18,* 38–48.

Krietzmann, J.P., & McKnight, J.L. (1993). *Building communities from the inside-out: A path toward finding and mobilizing a community's assets.* Chicago: ACTA Publications.

Kumin, L., Councill, C., & Goodman, M. (1999). Expressive vocabulary in young children with Down syndrome: From research to treatment. *Infant-Toddler Intervention, 9*(1), 87–100.

Landesman, S. (1986). Quality of life and personal life satisfaction: Definition and measurement issues. *Mental Retardation, 24,* 141–143.

Law, J. (2000). Coping when a child has a disability: Exploring the impact of parent-to-parent support. *Child: Care, Health & Development, 26,* 289–308.

Lee, S., & Kahn, J.V. (2000). A survival analysis of parent-child interaction in early intervention. *Infant-Toddler Intervention, 10*(3), 137–156.

Linn, M.I., Goodman, J.F., & Lender, W.L. (2000). Played out? Passive behavior by children with Down syndrome during unstructured play. *Journal of Early Intervention, 23*(4), 264–278.

Lishner, D.M., Richardson, M., Levine, P., & Patrick, D. (1996). Access to primary health care among persons with disabilities living in rural areas: A summary of the literature. *Journal of Rural Health, 12,* 45–53.

Locke, J.L. (1994). Gradual emergence of developmental language disorders. *Journal of Speech and Hearing Research, 37,* 608–616.

Lovaas, O.I., & Smith, T. (2003). Early and intensive behavioral intervention in autism. In A.E. Kazdin & J.R. Weisz (Eds.), *Evidence-based psychotherapies for children and adolescents* (pp. 325–340). New York: The Guilford Press.

Luiselli, J.K., Cannon, B.O.M., Ellis, J.T., & Sisson, R.W. (2000). Home-based behavioral interventions for young children with autism/pervasive developmental disorder: A preliminary evaluation of outcome in relation to child age and intensity of service delivery. *Autism, 4*(4), 426–438.

Lynch, E.W., & Hanson, M.J. (Eds.). (2004). *Developing cross-cultural competence: A guide for working with children and their families* (3rd ed.). Baltimore: Paul H. Brookes Publishing Co.

Mahoney, G., Kaiser, A., Girolametto, L., MacDonald, J., Robinson, C., Safford, P., & Spiker, D. (1999). Parent education in early intervention: A call for a renewed focus. *Topics in Early Childhood Special Education, 19,* 131–140.

Mahoney, G., & Perales, F. (2003). Using relationship-focused intervention to enhance the social-emotional functioning of young children with autism spectrum disorders. *Topics in Early Childhood Special Education, 23*(2), 77–89.

Mallik, S., & Hebbeler, K. (2002). *Characteristics of early intervention services.* Paper presented at the OSEP National Early Childhood Conference, Washington, DC.

McBride, B.J., & Schwartz, I.S. (2003). Effects of teaching early interventionists to use discrete trials during ongoing classroom activities. *Topics in Early Childhood Special Education, 23*(1), 5–17.

McCathren, R.B., Yoder, P.J., & Warren, S.F. (1995). The role of directives in early language intervention. *Journal of Early Intervention, 19*(2), 91–101.

McConnell, S.R. (2002). Review of available research and recommendations for educational intervention and future research. *Journal of Autism & Developmental Disorders, 32*(5), 351–372.

McCormick, M., McCarton, C., Brooks-Gunn, J., Belt, P., & Gross, R. (1998). The infant health and development program: Interim summary. *Journal of Developmental and Behavioral Pediatrics, 19*, 359–370.

McKinney, B., & Peterson, R.A. (1987). Predictors of stress in parents of developmentally disabled children. *Journal of Pediatric Psychology, 12*, 133–150.

McLoyd, V.C. (1998). Socioeconomic disadvantage and child development. *American Psychologist, 53*, 185–204.

McNab, T.C., & Blackman, J.A. (1998). Medical complications of the critically ill newborn: A review for early intervention professionals. *Topics in Early Childhood Special Education, 18*, 197–205.

McWilliam, R.A. (Ed.). (1996). *Rethinking pull-out services in early intervention: A professional resource.* Baltimore: Paul H. Brookes Publishing Co.

McWilliam, R.A. (2000). Recommended practices in interdisciplinary models. In S. Sandall, M.E. McLean, & B.J. Smith (Eds.), *DEC recommended practices in early intervention/early childhood special education* (pp. 47–54). Denver, CO: Division for Early Childhood.

Mezey, J., Neas, K.B., & Irish, K. (2003). *Coming together for children with disabilities: State collaboration to support quality inclusive child care.* Washington, DC: Center for Law and Social Policy.

Moes, D.R., & Frea, W.D. (2002). Contextualized behavioral support in early intervention for children with autism and their families. *Journal of Autism and Developmental Disorders, 32*(6), 519–533.

Morrison, R.S., Sainato, D.M., Benchaaban, D., & Endo, S. (2002). Increasing play skills of children with autism using activity schedules and correspondence training. *Journal of Early Intervention, 25*(1), 58–72.

Mulick, J.A., & Butter, E.M. (2002). Educational advocacy for children with autism. *Behavioral Interventions, 17*(2), 57–74.

National Research Council. (2001). *Educating children with autism.* Washington, DC: National Academy Press.

Nelson, C.A., & Bloom, F.E. (1997). Child development and neuroscience. *Child Development, 68*, 970–987.

Niccols, A., Atkinson, L., & Pepler, D. (2003). Mastery motivation in young children with Down syndrome: Relations with cognitive and adaptive competence. *Journal of Intellectual Disability Research, 47*(2), 121–133.

Odom, S.L. (2000). Preschool inclusion: What we know and where we go from here. *Topics in Early Childhood Special Education, 20*(2), 20–27.

Oser, C., & Cohen, J. (2003). *Improving early intervention: Using what we know about infants and toddlers with disabilities to reauthorize Part C of IDEA.* Washington, DC: ZERO TO THREE: National Center for Infants, Toddlers, and Families.

Pilkington, K.O., & Malinowski, M. (2002). The natural environment II: Uncovering deeper responsibilities within relationship-based services. *Infants and Young Children, 15*(2), 78–84.

Pinder, G.L., & Olswang, L.B. (1995). Development of communicative intent in young children with cerebral palsy: A treatment efficacy study. *Infant-Toddler Intervention, 5*(1), 51–69.

Powers, L.E. (1993). Disability and grief: From tragedy to challenge. In G.H.S. Singer & L.E. Powers (Eds.), *Families, disability, and empowerment: Active coping skills and strategies for family interventions* (pp. 119–148). Baltimore: Paul H. Brookes Publishing Co.

Pretti-Frontczak, K.L., Barr, D.M., Macy, M., & Carter, A. (2003). Research and resources related to activity-based intervention, embedded learning opportunities, and routines-based instruction: An annotated bibliography. *Topics in Early Childhood Special Education, 18,* 29–39.

Roberts, C., Mazzucchelli, T., Taylor, K., & Reid, R. (2003). Early intervention for behaviour problems in young children with developmental disabilities. *International Journal of Disability, Development and Education, 50*(3), 275–292.

Roberts, R.N., & Akers, A.A. (2002). *Final report: Opening doors into rural communities.* Logan: Utah State University, Early Intervention Research Institute.

Roizen, N.J. (2003). The early interventionist and the medical problems of a child with Down syndrome. *Infants & Young Children, 16*(1), 88–95.

Rosman, E.A., Yoshikawa, H., & Knitzer, J. (2002). Towards an understanding of the impact of welfare reform on children with disabilities and their families: Setting a research and policy agenda. *Social Policy Reports of the Society for Research in Child Development, 16*(4), 1–16.

Saluja, G., Scott-Little, C., & Clifford, R. (2000, Fall). Readiness for school: A survey of state policies and definitions. *Early Childhood Research & Practice, 2*(2). Available at http://ecrp.uiuc.edu/v2n2/saluja.html

Sameroff, A.J., & Fiese, B.H. (2000). Transactional regulation: The developmental ecology of early intervention. In J.P. Shonkoff & S.J. Meisels (Eds.), *Handbook of early childhood intervention* (2nd ed., pp. 135–159). New York: Cambridge University Press.

Sameroff, A.J., Seifer, R., Baldwin, A., & Baldwin, C. (1993). Stability of intelligence from preschool to adolescence: The influence of social and family risk factors. *Child Development, 64,* 80–97.

Sandall, S., McLean, M.E., & Smith, B.J. (Eds.). (2000). *DEC recommended practices in early intervention/early childhood special education.* Denver, CO: Division for Early Childhood.

Sandall, S.R., & Schwartz, I.S. (Eds.). (2002). *Building blocks for teaching preschoolers with special needs.* Baltimore: Paul H. Brookes Publishing Co.

Scarborough, A., Spiker, D., Mallik, S., Hebbeler, K., Bailey, D.B., & Simeonsson, R.J. (in press). A national picture of children and families entering early intervention. *Exceptional Children.*

Shonkoff, J.P., Hauser-Cram, P., Krauss, M.W., & Upshur, C.C. (1992). Development of infants with disabilities and their families. *Monographs of the Society for Research in Child Development, 57*(6), 1–35.

Shonkoff, J., & Marshall, P.C. (2000). The biology of developmental vulnerability. In J.P. Shonkoff & S.J. Meisels (Eds.), *Handbook of childhood intervention* (2nd ed., pp. 35–53). New York: Cambridge University Press.

Shonkoff, J.P., & Meisels, S.J. (Eds.). (2000). *Handbook of early childhood intervention* (2nd ed.). New York: Cambridge University Press.

Shonkoff, J., & Phillips, D. (Eds.). (2000). *From neurons to neighborhoods: The science of early childhood development.* Washington, DC: National Academy Press.

Shonkoff, J., Phillips, D., & Keilty, B. (2000). *Early childhood intervention: Views from the field: Report of a workshop.* Washington, DC: National Academy Press.

Sigafoos, J. (2000). Communication development and aberrant behavior in children with developmental disabilities. *Education and Training in Mental Retardation and Developmental Disabilities, 35*(2), 168–176.

Smith, B., & McKenna, P. (1994). Early intervention public policy: Past, present, and future. In L.J. Johnson, R.J. Gallagher, & M.J. LaMontagne (Eds.), *Meeting early intervention challenges* (pp. 251–264). Baltimore: Paul H. Brookes Publishing Co.

Smith, B.J., Strain, P.S., Snyder, P., Sandall, S.R., McLean, M.E., Ramsey, A.B., & Sumi, W.C. (2002). DEC recommended practices: A review of 9 years of EI/ECSE research literature. *Journal of Early Intervention, 25*(2), 108–119.

Speltz, M.L., Armsden, G.C., & Clarren, S.S. (1990). Effects of craniofacial birth defects on maternal functioning postinfancy. *Journal of Pediatric Psychology, 15*, 177–196.

Spiker, D. (1999). The role of genetics in autism. *Infants and Young Children, 12*(2), 55–63.

Spiker, D., Boyce, G.C., & Boyce, L.K. (2002). Parent-child interactions when young children have disabilities. In L.M. Glidden (Ed.), *International review of research in mental retardation* (pp. 35–70). San Diego: Academic Press.

Spiker, D., & Hebbeler, K. (1999). Early intervention services. In M. Levine, W.B. Carey, & A.C. Crocker (Eds.), *Developmental-behavioral pediatrics* (3rd ed., pp. 793–802). Philadelphia: W.B. Saunders.

Strain, P.S., & Hoyson, M. (2000). The need for longitudinal, intensive social skill intervention: LEAP follow-up outcomes for children with autism. *Topics in Early Childhood Special Education, 20*(2), 116–122.

Taylor, H.G., Klein, N., Schatschneider, C., & Hack, M. (1998). Predictors of early school age outcomes in very low birth weight children. *Developmental and Behavioral Pediatrics, 19*, 235–243.

Trivette, C.M., Dunst, C.J., & Deal, A.G. (1997). Resource-based approach to early intervention. In S.K. Thurman, J.R. Cornwell, & S.R. Gottwald (Eds.), *Contexts of early intervention: Systems and settings* (pp. 73–92). Baltimore: Paul H. Brookes Publishing Co.

U.S. Department of Education. (2002). *Twenty-fourth annual report to Congress on the implementation of the Individuals with Disabilities Education Act.* Washington, DC: Author.

Wade, S.S., Taylor, H.G., Drotar, D., Stancin, T., & Yeates, K.O. (1996). Childhood traumatic brain injury: Initial impact on the family. *Journal of Learning Disabilities, 29*, 652–661.

Warfield, M.E., Krauss, M.W., Hauser-Cram, P., Upshur, C.C., & Shonkoff, J.P. (1999). Adaptation during early childhood among mothers of children with disabilities. *Developmental and Behavioral Pediatrics, 20*, 9–16.

Warren, S.F. (2000). The future of early communication and language intervention. *Topics in Early Childhood Special Education, 20*(1), 33–37.

Wertheimer, R. (2003). *Poor families in 2001: Parents working less and children continue to lag behind.* Washington, DC: Child Trends.

Winton, P.J. (2000). Early childhood intervention personnel preparation: Backward mapping for future planning. *Topics in Early Childhood Special Education, 20*(2), 87–94.

Wolery, M. (2000). Recommended practices in child-focused interventions. In S. Sandall, M.E. McLean, & B.J. Smith (Eds.), *DEC recommended practices in early intervention/early childhood special education* (pp. 29–37). Longmont, CO: Sopris West.

Yoder, D., & Coleman, P. (1990). *Allied health personnel: Meeting the demands of Part H, PL 99-457.* Chapel Hill: University of North Carolina, Carolina Policy Studies Program.

Zeanah, C.H. (Ed.). (2000). *Handbook of infant mental health* (2nd ed.). New York: Guilford Press.

Zigler, E.F., Finn-Stevenson, M., & Hall, N.W. (2002). *The first three years & beyond.* New Haven, CT: Yale University Press.

Zill, N., & West, J. (2001). *Entering kindergarten: A portrait of American children when they begin school.* Washington, DC: National Center for Education Statistics.

CHAPTER 13

MONITORING AND EVALUATION IN EARLY INTERVENTION PROGRAMS

MARJI ERICKSON WARFIELD AND PENNY HAUSER-CRAM

The world of early intervention is continually evolving. The early intervention service system is considerably different today than it was in the 1980s, when early intervention initially received systematic federal support through the Education of the Handicapped Act Amendments of 1986 (PL 99-457). First, the service delivery models have changed. In the past, children were provided with therapeutic services in a center, clinic, or hospital that focused exclusively on children with special needs. Now, children with special needs are included in general community services such as child care, community swim programs, and other "natural environments" in which they play and learn with other children. Services are no longer delivered primarily through direct instruction to the child because parents and other family members and caregivers are considered central to intervention efforts. For example, McWilliam (2000) stressed that because children's actual learning occurs *between* early intervention sessions rather than within a session itself, designing home visits to provide information to caregivers is critical. Indeed, the former medically driven model of service delivery that emphasized direct therapeutic and didactic intervention has been replaced by a Developmental Systems Model (Guralnick, 2001) that recognizes the many important settings in which children develop and the valuable role that the family and other caregivers play in children's optimal functioning.

Second, our knowledge of the demographics of children and families receiving early intervention services is improving; data indicate that early intervention is serving many children and families with multiple and diverse

The preparation of this chapter was supported in part by Grant R40 MC00333 from the Maternal and Child Health Bureau (Title V, Social Security Act), Health Resources and Services Administration, Department of Health and Human Services.

needs. In a representative national sample of children participating in early intervention programs, Hebbeler et al. (2001) reported that the population of children in early intervention differs from the general population of young children in several ways. A higher proportion of males, African American children, families receiving public assistance, and young children in foster care are in the early intervention population. These findings indicate that the population of children in early intervention is disproportionately low income and suggest that a fuller understanding of the implications of poverty on the lives of families of children with disabilities is needed in relation to early intervention service provision (Lukemeyer, Meyers, & Smeeding, 2000; Park, Turnbull, & Turnbull, 2002).

The demographic composition of the United States is changing rapidly, and similar changes in the early intervention population are expected to follow. Given the increasing proportion of Latino/Hispanic families in the United States, as well as increasing numbers of families from various immigrant groups, the responsibility of early intervention providers to be culturally competent as well as knowledgeable about and sensitive to the needs of families from the various cultural groups they serve is imperative (Hauser-Cram & Howell, 2003). Garcia Coll and Magnuson (2000) emphasized how culture can be viewed as a developmental resource. Cultural views of a child's disability and the way in which parents prefer to promote optimal development are as integral to parenting practices as they are to the practices of service providers. Such views may at times collide (e.g., Fadiman, 1997), but they also provide opportunities for creative partnerships between families and early intervention providers.

Furthermore, additional changes in the early intervention population are likely to occur due to technological and medical advances. New diagnostic procedures are resulting in earlier identification of certain disorders, especially those on the autism spectrum (Ehlers, Gillberg, & Wing, 1999). As a result, an increase is expected in the rate at which children with these disorders are referred to early intervention and special education (Safran, 2001). In addition, survival rates for children with serious genetic and neurological conditions (e.g., trisomy 18) are beyond prior expectations (Van Dyke & Allen, 1990). Furthermore, the incidence of children who require medical technology assistance (e.g., mechanical ventilation, tube feeding) is increasing primarily as a result of the improved survival rates of very low birth weight infants (Levy & O'Rourke, 2002). Therefore, early intervention professionals will require basic information about the characteristics of children and families who have not been on their caseloads before, as well as data from evaluation studies on how best to meet their needs.

Finally, the composition and daily lives of families have changed since the 1980s. The most remarkable change is the increased number of mothers of young children in the work force. Between 1976 and 2000, the percentage of women with infants who were employed rose from 31% to 55.2%, which is a 78% increase (Bachu & O'Connell, 2001). Although no census data exist on the employment rates of mothers with young children with disabilities, studies suggest that many are employed and require child care. For example, Booth and Kelly (1998) found that 58% of the children with special needs in their sample were in a child care setting by 15 months of age. In addition, Leiter, Krauss, Anderson, and Wells (2004) conducted a national survey of children with special health care needs and their families and found that about half of the mothers were employed. Of those who were employed, about half worked full time.

In the past, early intervention services were developed based on the assumption that mothers and children would be home during the day and available to either receive early intervention providers in their home or travel to an early intervention program for services. Now that it is not uncommon for mothers of children with disabilities to be working, some children with special needs are being cared for in child care centers, homes, and other alternate arrangements by individuals other than their parents (Kelly & Booth, 1999; Warfield & Hauser-Cram, 1996). From a developmental systems perspective, maternal employment provides both restrictions on service delivery as well as opportunities for promoting integration and inclusion. For example, providing early intervention services in a child care setting may be considered a natural environment for a child with an employed mother and gives early intervention providers the chance to help child care workers become more comfortable caring for children with special needs and including them in typical activities. In contrast, parental work schedules may restrict the times during which the mother (or father) can be involved in early intervention services. Accommodating work schedules may mean that visits have to occur very early or very late in the day (i.e., before or after work), which may not be an optimal time for intervention for the child, the parent, or the provider. Thus, the extent to which early intervention services are well matched to the realities of daily life for families and providers needs to be evaluated to further understand the influence of multiple settings on children's development.

Despite these considerable changes, the goal of early intervention services as defined by legislation, from the Education of the Handicapped Act Amendments of 1986 (PL 99-457) to the Individuals with Disabilities Education Act (IDEA) Amendments of 1997 (PL 105-17), has always been to meet the developmental needs of eligible children and the needs of their families related to enhancing child development. The purpose of this chapter, therefore, is to describe ways in which monitoring and evaluation in the early intervention system can best be matched to this goal given the current service delivery and population realities, what is known about multiple contexts that affect child development, and what has been learned about developing effective evaluations. The chapter begins with a brief review of the three core dimensions of early intervention services that are thought to promote optimal child development (Guralnick, 2001). These core dimensions provide a structure for thinking about how to document and assess the provision of early intervention services and the accessibility of natural learning environments both within the early intervention system and across the multiple contexts that surround children and families.

Next, the chapter discusses the limitations of using traditional approaches to evaluation and presents a multi-tiered model that is designed to reflect the diverse capacities of programs to conduct evaluations. The purposes of each type of evaluation are discussed along with the tasks required to conduct an evaluation at each tier. Examples of questions appropriate for each tier are presented, and studies that represent each evaluation type are discussed. Finally, the chapter provides a practical tool for developing evaluation plans. The building blocks are sets of elements that must be considered in constructing an evaluation that is tailored to specific context and population realities. Thus, the evaluation building blocks are designed to be useful to experienced and inexperienced evaluators alike and to be used by early intervention providers to increase their capacity to incorporate evaluation activities into the operation of their programs.

VIEWING EARLY INTERVENTION IN ECOLOGICAL CONTEXT

From the perspective of developmental systems theory, evaluations of early intervention services, like those of other community-based programs, need to be designed to consider the multiple interacting systems in which children's development is nurtured (Bronfenbrenner, 1986; Lerner, 1991). In considering evaluation of early intervention in particular, Guralnick (2001) emphasized the importance of understanding family interaction patterns in relation to children's development. He delineated three areas of focus that early intervention must support in order to maximize child development: 1) the quality of parent–child transactions, 2) family-orchestrated child experiences, and 3) health and safety provided by the family. Clearly, the family serves as the core setting for the young child with disabilities, but the family is also situated in multiple systems, such as parental social support networks, parental employment systems, community services systems, health services systems, systems of cultural and personal beliefs, and the larger policy and resource environment.

Thus, the extent to which the ecological context across these multiple systems is integrated and inclusive (the two other core components of the Developmental Systems Model [Guralnick, 2001]) will influence how well early intervention can support these critical family interaction patterns. For example, communities can provide therapeutic services through a collaborative process between professionals from different agencies (i.e., integration) and can welcome children with disabilities in typical community activities (i.e., inclusion). This will foster an environment that facilitates collaboration between early intervention providers and families, which can enhance the ability of parents to gain access to learning opportunities that best encourage and engender positive family interaction patterns and nurture children's development (Guralnick, 2001).

A MULTI-TIERED APPROACH TO THE EVALUATION OF EARLY INTERVENTION

Developing evaluations of early intervention that account for the variability in the ecological context of the provision of formal services and informal learning opportunities requires an expansion of the questions asked by evaluators and the methodologies used. Strictly traditional approaches to evaluation are inadequate given their commitment to answering one main question: Does the intervention work? This sole focus on the question of effectiveness has given primacy to the use of experimental designs in which random assignment is utilized to create a treatment group that gets the intervention and a control group that does not (Weiss, 1998). By comparing the outcomes for these two groups, experimental designs utilizing random assignment have been seen as the one design that most clearly attributes the outcomes of the program to the program itself. Concomitant with the use of experimental designs and random assignment has been the use of standardized instruments that often are not normed on the population under study, a reliance on quantitative data collection and analysis, and a view that evaluators are objective, yet powerful outside observers under whom program staff and participants are subordinated. By excluding program staff and participants from playing a role in the process, evaluation came to be viewed as a highly technical endeavor that can only be carried out by those with specialized training.

The primacy of experimental designs has been questioned. In considering evaluation of early intervention services in particular, Shonkoff (2002) maintained that randomized studies would be impractical and difficult to achieve, given the highly individualized focus of such services. Weiss (1998) outlined a variety of conditions in which randomized experiments are problematic. For example, programs that are not well developed or specified and that have little stability are poor candidates for a costly, experimental evaluation. Weiss further detailed criticisms of randomized experiments that are relevant to the consideration of evaluations of early intervention services. Randomized designs require that the program be constant rather than change and improve. Furthermore, they do not account for differences in the quality of the staff that implements the service or treatment and are best used to test services or components one at a time when combinations of services may be more effective. Randomized designs require such strict controls on program operation that the results of the evaluation are generalizable only to the narrow experimental conditions under which it operated, and thus, portability to more typical program operation conditions is unknown. Finally, often little information is generated about how or why the intervention worked or did not work.

These criticisms of randomized designs have propelled evaluators to expand the scope and focus of evaluation research. Jacobs (1988; Jacobs & Kapuscik, 2000) proposed a multi-tiered approach to evaluation that provides a useful framework for evaluation efforts of family support and child welfare programs. This framework is also appropriate for evaluation in early intervention because it sanctions and encourages the use of a wide range of methods to address a comprehensive set of evaluation questions.

The multi-tiered approach has four main characteristics. First, it uses a broad and inclusive definition of evaluation. *Evaluation* is considered "a set of systematically planned and executed activities designed to determine the merit of a program, intervention, or policy, or to describe aspects of its operation" (Jacobs & Kapuscik, 2000, p. 3). Thus, the purpose of evaluation from the perspective of the multi-tiered approach is to address questions about program processes as well as the program's impact on outcomes.

Second, the multi-tiered approach is a developmental model designed so that the demands for technical expertise increase from tier to tier. This allows those new to program evaluation to develop their skills over time and build evaluation capacity into a program's daily operations. Third, the model emphasizes that no one standard evaluation strategy is appropriate for all programs, services, or interventions. Individualized evaluation plans need to be developed for each situation in order to maximize the fit between the program's capacity for evaluation and the goals of the evaluation. Thus, a wide range of methodologies should be utilized including qualitative approaches (e.g., focus groups, case studies, observation studies; Patton, 1987) and mixed method approaches that integrate quantitative and qualitative methods (Caracelli & Greene, 1997; Hauser-Cram, Warfield, Upshur, & Weisner, 2000).

Finally, the multi-tiered approach generates studies that can establish accountability. Evaluations can document accountability by presenting data on the extent to which the program is identifying and serving those who are entitled to services, providing the range of services it is mandated to provide, and establishing some reasonable match between participant need and service receipt. In addition, evaluations that measure participant satisfaction and assess participant and staff perceptions of program effects also can show how a program is being accountable to its constituents and funding agencies.

The various purposes of evaluations common at each tier of the multitiered approach are discussed along with a description of the tasks required to conduct each type of evaluation. In order to apply this approach more specifically to early intervention, examples of evaluation questions pertinent to early intervention are presented. Three types of questions are posed to reflect the Developmental Systems Model (Guralnick, 2001): 1) questions focused on the early intervention system and/or individual early intervention programs, 2) questions focused on the ecological context, and 3) questions focused on both early intervention and the ecological context.

Examples of studies that are representative of each tier also are reviewed briefly. It is important to note that although the tiers are presented separately, most evaluation studies address questions that are representative of multiple tiers.

Tier I: Needs Assessment

Studies at the needs assessment tier focus on defining and measuring a societal problem or trend and the resulting individual needs. Furthermore, they present information about the adequacy of the services currently available to address the identified needs and suggest program or policy options for resolving any unmet need that has been measured. In order to conduct a needs assessment, evaluators must review existing agency, community, county, and/or state level data that will document the existence of the problem under study, indicate why it has come about (if it is a new problem), or determine why it is getting worse (if it is an existing problem for which interventions have been attempted). Needs assessment evaluations also can provide baseline data against which change on the level of unmet needs can be assessed at a later period of time.

Table 13.1 presents some examples of early intervention evaluation questions that could be addressed at this tier. These questions focus on the impact of large-scale demographic shifts on the operation of early intervention and what needs result from those changes.

As mentioned previously, the demographic shifts in the overall U.S. population are being felt in early intervention as programs are now serving greater numbers of children and families from various ethnic groups. Understanding different cultural norms and beliefs is a first step in learning how best to provide services. For example, Skinner, Rodriquez, and Bailey

Table 13.1. Early intervention evaluation questions for Tier I: Needs assessment

Question focus	Examples
Early intervention system/ program questions	• Are all eligible children being identified and assessed? • What needs have become more/less prevalent among early intervention children and families? • Do these needs suggest that changes be made in identification, assessment, and/or monitoring? • Are trained providers available to meet these changing needs?
Ecological context questions	• What changes have occurred in statewide or community populations? • Do these changes suggest modifying early intervention identification, assessment, or monitoring practices? • What changes have occurred in other community programs that influence referral to early intervention?
Combined question	• What new knowledge about needs is generated by examining the identification, assessment, and monitoring efforts conducted by different early childhood programs within a community?

(1999) used qualitative interviews to understand how religious beliefs influence the way in which Latino parents view their child's disability, and Applequist and Bailey (2000) examined Navajo family caregiver perceptions about early intervention services. In addition, Chen and McCollum (2001) conducted qualitative interviews with Taiwanese mothers of infants with Down syndrome. Picture vignettes (i.e., line drawings of an adult and child interacting with and without an object) were used to elicit the mother's thoughts about interacting with her child. These studies provide information about the way in which early intervention services could be more responsive to specific (and in some locations, growing) constituent groups.

Tier II: Monitoring and Accountability

The purpose of an evaluation at the monitoring and accountability tier is to provide a detailed account of the services provided during a selected time period. Details should include information about participants (e.g., personal characteristics, referral information, services and activities outside of early intervention), staff (e.g., education, discipline, staffing patterns, roles on the early intervention team), and the early intervention services themselves (e.g., location, participants, hours, goals, activities, cost). To do this, the record-keeping system of the program being evaluated must be reviewed to determine what gets recorded and how often, as well as whether clear and consistent procedures exist for documenting information. The systems used for storing and retrieving these data must also be assessed to determine whether they are adequate for both conducting the evaluation and respecting participants' privacy. Depending on the capabilities of staff and administrators within the program being evaluated, some form of database training or technical assistance may be required to create a useable system for conducting this type of evaluation or to make improvements to an existing system.

Table 13.2 presents some examples of early intervention evaluation questions relative to monitoring and accountability. The questions are oriented toward documenting all aspects of program operation (e.g., where services are being delivered, who the providers are, who is receiving services, what is being provided) and improving a program's capacity to measure and report this type of information.

Several studies at this tier have been conducted to compare the amount and types of services listed in individualized family service plans (IFSPs) to the services that were actually delivered (Perry, Greer, Goldhammer, & Mackey-Andrews, 2001). Analyses of these data have identified a disconnect between planned and delivered services, raising questions about underutilization of services by certain groups of children and families and the overall success with which early intervention legislation has been implemented

Table 13.2. Early intervention questions for Tier II: Monitoring and accountability

Question focus	Examples
Early intervention system/ program questions	How do children and families enter and exit the early intervention system/program?
	Are there patterns of movement that relate to child, family, and early intervention program characteristics?
	What structural characteristics can be used to describe service provision?
	What structural service characteristics differ by child, family, and early intervention program characteristics?
Ecological context questions	What are the family accommodation activities that describe children and families in early intervention, and how do these differ by child, family, and early intervention program characteristics?
	What are the structural characteristics of the community services/resources that early intervention children and families gain access to, and how do they differ by child, family, and early intervention program characteristics?
Combined questions	What is the early intervention service/family accommodation and activities mix, and how does it differ by child, family, and early intervention program characteristics?
	What is the early intervention/community service mix, and how does it differ by child, family, and early intervention program characteristics?

(Harbin, 2001; Kochanek, 2001). Another study analyzed longitudinal data from the early intervention (Part C) database in North Carolina and found changes in service delivery patterns over time (Buysse, Bernier, & McWilliam, 2002). For example, the proportion of services delivered in the home and in center-based settings has declined over time, whereas the referrals to early intervention from parents have increased (Buysse et al., 2002). Finally, two studies have described the wide variations in early intervention service costs in Massachusetts (Erickson, 1992) and New Jersey (Tarr & Barnett, 2001). Erickson found that differences in the age at which a child enters an early intervention program and variation in the severity of a child's disability significantly influenced the type of services provided and therefore the cost. Tarr and Barnett also found that the service setting and type influenced cost. Other significant predictors of cost were the type of staff providing the service, how providers allocated their time, wage rates, and staff–child ratios. These data are important for initiating studies at the next two tiers.

Other Tier II studies have focused on the ecological context. For example, one study sought to identify and document the extent to which naturally occurring learning opportunities are accessible by children and families receiving early intervention services (Dunst, Hamby, Trivette, Raab, & Bruder, 2000). A second study (Trivette, Dunst, & Deal, 1997) documented the extent to which two types of community resources were available to children and families in early intervention: 1) sources of support such as church, civic and social clubs, community colleges, hospitals, libraries, and respite care programs; and 2) community-sponsored activities such as places to go to enjoy outdoor activities (e.g., playgrounds, hiking trails) and sports (e.g., baseball fields, skating rinks, basketball courts), as well as the existence of other attractions such as children's museums and art centers. Although rare, studies that focus on the neighborhood and community resources provide important information about opportunities that can link with early intervention programs in providing integrated services for families of children with developmental disabilities.

Tier III: Quality Review and Program Clarification

The purposes of evaluations at the quality review and program clarification tier are to develop ways to assess the quality of services and measure the perceived (as opposed to the objective) effects of the intervention in order to provide feedback to reform or improve the program. The tasks involved in developing a Tier III evaluation include expanding the information collected for Tier II evaluations by collecting data from families in the program, program staff, other professionals who interact with the program on a regular basis, and program documents. Table 13.3 presents some

Table 13.3. Early intervention questions for Tier III: Quality review and program clarification

Question focus	Examples
Early intervention system/ program questions	What process/quality characteristics can be used to describe service provision?
	What process/quality service characteristics differ by child, family, and early intervention program characteristics?
	Which process/quality measures are related to parent satisfaction and perceived effects?
Ecological context questions	What family accommodations and activities are related to parent satisfaction and perceived effects?
	Which process/quality measures of community services/ resources differ by child, family, and early intervention program characteristics?
	Which process/quality measures of community services/ resources are related to parent satisfaction and perceived effects?
Combined questions	How well do early intervention services, family accommodations and activities, and community services/resources fit together?
	Does this "goodness of fit" relate to parent satisfaction and perceived effects?

examples of early intervention evaluation questions for studies focused on quality review and program clarification.

Measures of quality can be created that assess whether the program matches the standards that have been set by theory, previous evaluation studies, or legislative guidelines. For example, early intervention services are supposed to be family centered. One study developed a list of family-centered indicators (e.g., use of professional versus lay language, use of a family-centered versus child-centered orientation) and then used content analysis techniques to review a sample of IFSPs to measure the extent to which family-centered indicators were evident in the documents (Boone, McBride, Swann, Moore, & Drew, 1998). The findings suggested that, in contrast to the program and legislative standards, the IFSPs were more child centered than family centered.

Another aspect of quality relates to participant satisfaction with services that have specific characteristics related to performance standards. For example, Romer and Umbreit (1998) examined the services provided to families for 1 year to assess the extent to which they represented services that were coordinated and family centered. They also charted each family's satisfaction with the services they received. They found that when the services were implemented as designed, families were very satisfied. When services did not meet the coordination and family-centered standards, families were quite dissatisfied. Studies at this tier also can focus on the perspectives of the professionals who provide the service. The delivery of services considered to be "best practice" may be difficult to implement if those who are implementing them do not believe in those practices. Campbell and Halbert (2002) asked providers to describe three ways they would change early intervention so that children and families would receive quality services. Their responses conflicted with the current focus on family-centered intervention and services provided in the natural environment.

Evaluations conducted at Tier III are not limited to specific designs. Some program-context questions may be best addressed by using participatory action research (PAR) models (Reason & Bradbury, 2001). This type of critical inquiry has its roots in the work of Paolo Freire (1970) and seeks to understand the subjective experiences of program participants by viewing them as problem-posing collaborators with providers. Thus, for example, a group of parents and providers together might develop a series of questions to explore the way in which community resources relate to family needs and desires as well as their actual and potential links to early intervention services. The collaboration is one that makes the shared interests of all participants explicit and shifts the power away from the "evaluation experts" and toward the participants and providers themselves. Various creative approaches to data gathering and analysis have been developed within the PAR model, including community mapping (Whitmore & McKee, 2001) and Photovoice, in which participants use cameras to document their observations (Wang & Burris, 1997). Few have pursued these approaches in relation to early intervention services.

Tier IV: Achieving Outcomes

The purpose of evaluation at the achieving outcomes tier is to find out whether the program achieved its intended effects. Therefore, this tier is different from the others because the focus is shifted from assessing accountability for services to assessing accountability for outcomes. Table 13.4 presents some examples of early intervention evaluation questions for studies focused on assessing outcomes.

Studies on effectiveness generally require some expertise in evaluation in order to establish and maintain some degree of rigor in the research design. That is not to say that only randomized experimental designs are useful at this tier. In fact, given the mandate to serve all children and families who are eligible, establishing a "no service" control group is unethical. At this tier, therefore, collaboration between early intervention programs and colleges, universities, and other research institutions is important to establish.

Given the limitations of randomized designs, much evaluation of early intervention at Tier IV involves the use of quasi-experiments to compare

Table 13.4. Early intervention questions for Tier IV: Achieving outcomes

Question focus	Examples
Early intervention system/ program questions	• Which measures or combination of measures of early intervention services predict positive changes in child and family well-being? Do some children and families benefit more than others? • Which family outcomes mediate/moderate the effect of early intervention service measures on positive changes in child well-being? Do some children benefit more than others?
Ecological context questions	• Which family accommodations/activities and/or community services/resources singularly or in combination predict positive changes in child and family well-being? Do some children/families benefit more than others? • Which family outcomes mediate/moderate the effect of these factors on positive changes in child well-being? Do some children benefit more than others?
Combined questions	• Are there particular "packages" of early intervention service measures, family accommodations/ activities, and community services/resources that predict positive change in child and family well-being? Do some children and families benefit more than others? • Do any family outcomes mediate/moderate the effect of these packages on positive changes in child well-being? Do some children benefit more than others?

different program options and naturalistic designs to examine the potential effects of services as they are naturally delivered. The Early Intervention Collaborative Study (EICS; Shonkoff, Hauser-Cram, Krauss, & Upshur, 1992) is an example of the latter and involved researchers at several different universities, public health officials, special educators, a parent advisory board, and staff at 29 early intervention programs. The EICS began in the mid-1980s and followed a sample of 190 children and families who had entered an early intervention program in Massachusetts or New Hampshire; children and their families continued to be followed through each child's teen years (Hauser-Cram, Warfield, Shonkoff, & Krauss, 2001). Analyses of the effects of individualized services provided between entry to early intervention and age 3 revealed that greater intensity of services was associated with maternal reports of improved family cohesion and increased helpfulness of social support (Warfield, Hauser-Cram, Krauss, Shonkoff, & Upshur, 2000). In addition, cost effectiveness analyses made two different types of comparisons. First, the gains made by children with different characteristics across various outcome measures were compared with a set level of resources (Warfield, 1994). The findings indicated that children classified as having mild disabilities experienced greater improvement in adaptive behavior, whereas children with more severe disabilities made greater gains in child–mother interaction. These results underscore the ways in which children with different characteristics move toward different goals relative to a common investment of resources.

Second, an analysis of the efficiency of home visiting versus center-based group services for subgroups defined by severity of disability and age at entry was conducted (Warfield, 1995). The service identified as most cost-effective varied by subgroup and outcome measure. For example, home visits were more cost-effective in reducing parenting stress across all subgroups. In terms of improvements in mother–child interaction, however, group services were more cost-effective for children entering early intervention at younger than 1 year of age, whereas home visits were more cost-effective for children entering after 1 year of age.

A different Tier IV study focused on the effectiveness of an intervention designed to improve child behavior and performance by utilizing everyday natural learning opportunities (Dunst et al., 2001). During the pre-intervention phase of the project, parent interviews were conducted to develop a grid matching activity settings, which could serve as sources of learning opportunities, to specific desired behaviors that could be generated in those activity settings. For example, playing in the sandbox at the local park and eating breakfast at the kitchen table were activities identified by parents as both appealing to their children and as useful for working on specific behaviors such as saying hello to other children or using a spoon to eat. During the intervention phase of the study, parents were encouraged to increase the number of times their child participated in the activities they listed and were trained to reinforce and support their child's production of desired behaviors while participating in the activities. Extensive data were gathered on how often the activity settings were used, the extent to which each setting was rated (by parents and independent observers) as interesting and engaging to the child, and how often the child demonstrated the desired behavior. The findings indicated that positive change in child behavior and performance was associated with greater access to activity settings that were characterized as interesting, engaging, and competence producing. This study identified ways in which early intervention providers can work with families to utilize community and family resources to optimize children's functioning.

THE VALUE OF PARTICIPATORY EVALUATION

Participation of the early intervention staff in evaluation efforts often is essential and can be beneficial to an early intervention program, regardless of the tier in which an evaluation is primarily operating. Participatory evaluation is based on the premise that learning can occur within an organization based on staff engagement (Preskill & Torres, 1999). Developed from a constructivist model of individual learning (Bandura, 1986), this approach assumes that knowledge is socially constructed and that individuals operate within organizations according to a series of constructed mental models and maps (Cousins & Earl, 1992). Some of those mental models and maps concern an individual's "theory of change" (Weiss, 1995). Such theories need not be grand, or even explicit, but are used to determine which interventions or supports might be most useful in promoting optimal child development. Therefore, a constructivist model suggests that program planners and service providers develop new knowledge from an interpretive framework rather than on "facts" alone (Kennedy, 1984). By participating in an evaluation, service providers are more likely to ensure that questions relevant to practice are investigated and that new knowledge will be developed and used.

In preparation for writing this chapter, early intervention program directors in Massachusetts were asked about what questions they face on a day-to-day basis that evaluations could address. Their responses fell into three categories. First, some early intervention directors had questions about the relative effectiveness of different service models (e.g., interdisciplinary versus multi- or transdisciplinary models, consultative versus hands-on home visiting models, inclusive playgroups versus playgroups with only children receiving early intervention services). Second, others wanted more information about how best to provide services to children with specific disabilities, such as autism, in terms of the best time to initiate services (e.g., at the time of diagnosis, after a complete assessment has been done) and what service models are the best (e.g., use of Applied Behavior Analysis [ABA] versus floor time versus structured play). Finally, some directors were interested in the effect of the early intervention partnership with parents on improving parent confidence and increasing the quality of the parent–child relationship.

Although these various questions require different types of evaluations, each could benefit from staff involvement in the inquiry process. Staff members can clarify the questions, attempt to make explicit their own belief systems about the phenomena under study, make recommendations about the type of data that would be useful to gather (and why), and consider the implications of the findings for early intervention services and participating families. A critical benefit of the participatory approach is that by designing evaluations (or at least facets of evaluations) together, team members are engaged in the process of learning, and learning contributes to a culture of inquiry within the early intervention system.

EVALUATION BUILDING BLOCKS

The multi-tier and participatory evaluation research models support the need for evaluation to address a wide array of evaluation questions utilizing a broad range of methods. For those charged with planning an evaluation that is right for a particular program at a particular time, however, the range of questions and methods may be so overwhelming as to stop the process before it starts.

Evaluation building blocks are designed to foster the development of evaluation plans that fit particular sets of circumstances (Jacobs & Kapuscik, 2000). The building blocks require that evaluators consider and define eight different program elements and three different evaluation elements in order to help them specify an evaluation approach that suits their needs (see Figure 13.1). Planning an evaluation should be an iterative and collaborative process.

Program Elements

Eight different aspects of the program to be evaluated must be defined before an evaluation can begin.

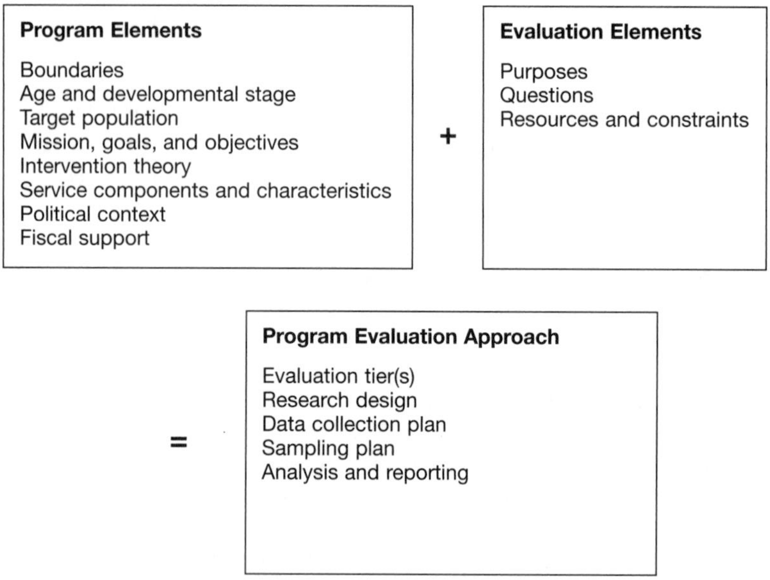

Figure 13.1.   Evaluation building blocks.

1. Boundaries: The boundaries around what will be evaluated must be established. Will the evaluation be focused on multiple early intervention programs, one program, one service type within one program, and so forth? What aspects of the ecological context around the established boundaries will be included in the evaluation?

2. Age and developmental stage: When and how was the program and its different services initiated? How long has it had stable leadership? What is its experience with evaluation? Are there aspects of its operation that are more "ready" to be evaluated at higher tiers than others?

3. Target population: Who are the intended targets of the program? How similar or different are individuals within the target population? What is the size of the population that will be enrolled in the program during the course of the evaluation?

4. Mission, goals, and objectives: What are the program's articulated and/or unspecified expectations for itself and its participants?

5. Intervention theory: What are the underlying theories or assumptions about why the program and its services provided to the target population or subgroups of the target population are expected to produce certain outcomes? Through what mechanisms will the program "work"?

6. Service components and characteristics: What will be the mix of services offered, their structural characteristics (e.g., frequency, intensity, duration, cost), process characteristics (e.g., coordination, learning opportunities in natural environments), and quality (e.g., match between planned and delivered services)? Who/what will determine which services are offered?

7. Political context: To what extent does the program enjoy strong support from its stakeholders? Stakeholders include all individuals and groups who are affected, either directly or indirectly, by the implementation and results of an evaluation (Rossi & Freeman, 1993). These individuals and groups include government officials and private foundations that initiate or fund the program and/or initiate or fund the evaluation, program managers and staff, program participants, evaluators, and the research and policy community.

8. Fiscal support: To what extent can the program's operating budget support the evaluation? Are additional funds required? Where would additional funds come from, and how might they alter the evaluation plan?

Evaluation Elements

Based on the information derived from specifying the program elements, the following three elements of the evaluation need to be defined.

1. Purposes: What are the reasons for undertaking the evaluation, and which stakeholders want to know what?

2. Questions: What questions are most critical and which best address the purposes of the evaluation?

3. Resources and constraints: To what extent do the "evaluation resources" (e.g., data, technical expertise, time, personnel) exist within the program? How easily can the program gain access to the expertise and personnel it needs from other agencies or the surrounding community?

Program Evaluation Approach

Once the purpose of the evaluation and its associated research questions have been specified and the capacities of the program to be evaluated are well understood, the most appropriate evaluation approach can be selected. This may involve identifying a tier or tiers from the multi-tiered approach as the basis from which to start, and/or it may involve investigating how a participatory evaluation project could be initiated. Regardless, a research design, data collection plan, and sampling plan must be proposed as well as a plan for analyzing and disseminating the results. Specific information about research designs, data collection, and sampling are beyond the scope of this chapter but can be found in many research textbooks.

CONCLUSION

The continually evolving world of early intervention presents many challenges to evaluators. The purpose of this chapter is to incorporate the perspective of the Developmental Systems Model (Guralnick, 2001) into the design of early intervention evaluations. A multi-tiered model of evaluation provides a framework on which important questions can be investigated about the effects of early intervention services, their value to parents, and their links to community resources and to other service systems. Given the complexity involved in understanding the interconnected systems in which parents with young children with developmental disabilities operate, those conducting evaluations at any of the multiple tiers may want to utilize the evaluation building blocks as tools for developing and implementing much needed evaluations of early intervention. Evaluations of early intervention can provide a more comprehensive perspective on effective service provision by recognizing that children and families are part of multiple interrelated systems that include not only the immediate contexts in which early intervention services are provided (e.g., home, child care center) but also the other systems affecting the family (e.g., medical services, community resources), as well as the systems of beliefs and values in which families operate. Therefore, although early intervention is only one part of a family's ecological world, it is important to better understand how it helps to promote the optimal development of children with special needs.

REFERENCES

Applequist, K.L., & Bailey, D.B. (2000). Navajo caregivers' perceptions of early intervention services. *Journal of Early Intervention, 23*, 47–61.

Bachu, A., & O'Connell, M. (2001). Fertility of American women: June 2000. U.S. Census Bureau, Current Population Reports, P20-543RV. Historical tables: Table H5. Retrieved May 5, 2004, from http://landview.census.gov/population/socdemo/fertility/tabH5.pdf

Bandura, A. (1986). *Social foundations of thought and action: A social cognitive theory.* Upper Saddle River, NJ: Prentice Hall.

Boone, H.A., McBride, S.L., Swann, D., Moore, S., & Drew, B.S. (1998). IFSP practices in two states: Implications for practice. *Infants and Young Children, 10*, 36–45.

Booth, C.L., & Kelly, J.F. (1998). Child care characteristics of infants with and without special needs: Comparisons and concerns. *Early Childhood Research Quarterly, 13*, 603–621.

Bronfenbrenner, U. (1986). Ecology of the family as a context for human development: Research perspectives. *Developmental Psychology, 22*, 723–742.

Buysse, V., Bernier, K.Y., & McWilliam, R.A. (2002). A statewide profile of early intervention services using the Part C data system. *Journal of Early Intervention, 25*, 15–26.

Campbell, P.H., & Halbert, J. (2002). Between research and practice: Provider perspectives on early intervention. *Topics in Early Childhood Intervention, 22*, 213–226.

Caracelli, V.J., & Greene, J.C. (1997). Crafting mixed-method evaluation designs. In J.C. Greene & V.J. Caracelli (Eds.), *Advances in mixed-method evaluation: The challenges and benefits of integrating diverse paradigms* (pp. 19–32). San Francisco: Jossey-Bass.

Chen, Y., & McCollum, J.A. (2001). Taiwanese mothers' perceptions of parent-infant interaction with children with Down syndrome. *Journal of Early Intervention, 24*, 252–265.

Cousins, J.B., & Earl, L.M. (1992). The case for participatory evaluation. *Educational Evaluation and Policy Analysis, 14*, 397–418.

Dunst, C.J., Bruder, M.B., Trivette, C.M., Hamby, D., Raab, M., & McLean, M. (2001). Characteristics and consequences of everyday natural learning opportunities. *Topics in Early Childhood Special Education, 21*, 68–92.

Dunst, C.J., Hamby, D., Trivette, C.M., Raab, M., & Bruder, M.B. (2000). Everyday family and community life and children's naturally occurring learning opportunities. *Journal of Early Intervention, 23,* 151–164.

Education of the Handicapped Act Amendments of 1986, PL 99-457, 20 U.S.C. §§ 1400 *et seq.*

Ehlers, S., Gillberg, C., & Wing, L. (1999). A screening questionnaire for Asperger syndrome and other high-functioning autism spectrum disorders of school age children. *Journal of Autism and Developmental Disorders, 29,* 129–141.

Erickson, M. (1992). An analysis of early intervention expenditures in Massachusetts. *American Journal on Mental Retardation, 96,* 617–629.

Fadiman, A. (1997). *The spirit catches you and you fall down: A Hmong child, her American doctors, and the collision of two cultures.* New York: Farrar, Straus & Giroux.

Freire, P. (1970). *Pedagogy of the oppressed.* New York: The Seabury Press.

Garcia Coll, C., & Magnuson, K. (2000). Cultural differences as sources of developmental vulnerabilities and resources. In J.P. Shonkoff & S.J. Meisels (Eds.), *Handbook of early childhood intervention* (2nd ed., pp. 94–114). New York: Cambridge University Press.

Guralnick, M.J. (2001). A developmental systems model for early intervention. *Infants and Young Children, 14*(2), 1–18.

Harbin, G.L. (2001). Implementing early intervention policy: Are we making the grade? *Journal of Early Intervention, 24,* 103–105.

Hauser-Cram, P., & Howell, A. (2003). The development of young children with disabilities and their families: Implications for policies and programs. In R.M. Lerner, F. Jacobs, & D. Wertlieb (Eds.), *Handbook of applied developmental science* (Vol. 1, pp. 259–278). Thousand Oaks, CA: Sage.

Hauser-Cram, P., Warfield, M.E., Shonkoff, J.P., & Krauss, M.W., with Sayer, A., & Upshur, C.C. (2001). Children with disabilities: A longitudinal study of child development and parent well-being. *Monographs of the Society of Research in Child Development, 57,* (3, Serial No. 266).

Hauser-Cram, P., Warfield, M.E., Upshur, C.C., & Weisner, T.S. (2000). An expanded view of program evaluation in early childhood intervention. In J.P. Shonkoff & S.J. Meisels (Eds.), *Handbook of early childhood intervention* (2nd ed., pp. 487–509). New York: Cambridge University Press.

Hebbeler, K., Wagner, M., Spiker, D., Scarborough, A., Simeonsson, R., & Collier, M. (2001). *National Early Intervention Study: A first look at the characteristics of children and families entering early intervention services.* Menlo Park, CA: SRI International.

Individuals with Disabilities Education Act (IDEA) Amendments of 1997, PL 105-17, 20 U.S.C. §§ 1400 *et seq.*

Jacobs, F.H. (1988). The five-tiered approach to evaluation: Context and implementation. In H.B. Weiss & F.H. Jacobs (Eds.), *Evaluating family programs* (pp. 37–68). New York: Aldine de Gruyter.

Jacobs, F.H., & Kapuscik, J.L. (2000). *Making it count: Evaluating family preservation services: A guide for state administrators.* Medford, MA: Tufts University.

Kelly, J.F., & Booth, C.L. (1999). Child care for infants with special needs: Issues and applications. *Infants and Young Children, 12,* 26–33.

Kennedy, M.M. (1984). How evidence alters understanding and decisions. *Educational Evaluation and Policy Analysis, 6,* 207–226.

Kochanek, T.T. (2001). Fulfilling the promise of early intervention: Factors related to rates of delivered IFSP services. *Journal of Early Intervention, 24,* 109–111.

Leiter, V., Krauss, M.W., Anderson, B., & Wells, N. (2004). The consequences of caring: Impacts of mothering a child with special needs. *Journal of Family Issues, 25,* 379–403.

Lerner, R. (1991). Changing organism-context relations as the basic process of development: A developmental contextual perspective. *Developmental Psychology, 27,* 27–32.

Levy, S.E., & O'Rourke, M. (2002). Technological assistance: Innovations for independence. In M.L. Batshaw (Ed.), *Children with disabilities* (5th ed., pp. 629–645). Baltimore: Paul H. Brookes Publishing Co.

Lukemeyer, A., Meyers, M.K., & Smeeding, T. (2000). Expensive children in poor families: Out-of-pocket expenditures for the care of disabled children and chronically ill children in welfare families. *Journal of Marriage and the Family, 62,* 399–415.

McWilliam, R.A. (2000). It's only natural . . . to have early intervention in the environments where it's needed. In S. Sandall & M. Ostrosky (Eds.), *Natural environments and inclusion* (pp. 17–26). Denver, CO: Division for Early Childhood of the Council for Exceptional Children.

Park, J., Turnbull, A.P., & Turnbull, H.R. (2002). Impacts of poverty on quality of life in families of children with disabilities. *Exceptional Children, 68,* 151–170.

Patton, M.Q. (1987). *How to use qualitative methods in evaluation.* Thousand Oaks, CA: Sage.

Perry, B.F., Greer, M., Goldhammer, K., & Mackey-Andrews, S. (2001). Fulfilling the promise of early intervention: Rates of delivered IFSP services. *Journal of Early Intervention, 24,* 90–102.

Preskill, H., & Torres, R.T. (1999). *Evaluative inquiry for learning in organizations.* Thousand Oaks, CA: Sage.

Reason, P., & Bradbury, H. (Eds.). (2001). *Handbook of action research: Participatory inquiry and practice.* Thousand Oaks, CA: Sage.

Romer, E.F., & Umbreit, J. (1998). The effects of family-centered service coordination: A social validity study. *Journal of Early Intervention, 21,* 95–110.

Rossi, P.H., & Freeman, H.E. (1993). *Evaluation: A systematic approach* (5th ed.). Thousand Oaks, CA: Sage.

Safran, S.P. (2001). Asperger syndrome: The emerging challenge to special education. *Exceptional Children, 67,* 151–160.

Shonkoff, J.P. (2002). A call to pour new wine in old bottles. *Journal of Early Intervention, 25,* 105–107.

Shonkoff, J.P., Hauser-Cram, P., Krauss, M.W., & Upshur, C.C. (1992). Development of infants with disabilities and their families: Implications for theory and service delivery. *Monographs of the Society of Research in Child Development, 57,* (6, Serial No. 230).

Skinner, D., Rodriquez, P., & Bailey, D.B. (1999). Qualitative analysis of Latino parents' religious interpretations of their child's disability. *Journal of Early Intervention, 22,* 271–285.

Tarr, J.E., & Barnett, W.S. (2001). A cost analysis of Part C early intervention services in New Jersey. *Journal of Early Intervention, 24,* 45–54.

Trivette, C.M., Dunst, C.J., & Deal, A.G. (1997). Resource-based approach to early intervention. In S.K. Thurman, J.R. Cornwell, & S.R. Gottwald (Eds.),

Contexts of early intervention: Systems and settings (pp. 73–92). Baltimore: Paul H. Brookes Publishing Co.

Van Dyke, D.D., & Allen, M. (1990). Clinical management considerations in long-term survivors with Trisomy 18. *Pediatrics, 85,* 753–759.

Wang, C., & Burris, M.A. (1997). Photovoice: Concept, methodology, and use for participatory needs assessment. *Health, Education and Behavior, 24,* 369–387.

Warfield, M.E. (1994). A cost-effectiveness analysis of early intervention services in Massachusetts: Implications for policy. *Educational Evaluation and Policy Analysis, 16,* 87–99.

Warfield, M.E. (1995). The cost-effectiveness of home visiting versus group services in early intervention. *Journal of Early Intervention, 19,* 130–148.

Warfield, M.E., & Hauser-Cram, P. (1996). Child care needs, arrangements, and satisfaction of mothers of children with developmental disabilities. *Mental Retardation, 34,* 294–302.

Warfield, M.E., Hauser-Cram, P., Krauss, M.W., Shonkoff, J.P., & Upshur, C.C. (2000). The effect of early intervention services on maternal well-being. *Journal of Early Education and Development, 11,* 499–517.

Weiss, C.H. (1995). Nothing as practical as a good theory: Exploring theory-based evaluation for comprehensive community initiatives for children and families. In J.P. Connell, A.C. Kubisch, L.B. Schorr, & C.H. Weiss (Eds.), *New approaches to evaluating community initiatives: Concepts, methods, and contexts* (pp. 65–92). Washington, DC: The Aspen Institute.

Weiss, C.H. (1998). *Evaluation* (2nd ed.). Upper Saddle River, NJ: Prentice Hall.

Whitmore, E., & McKee, C. (2001). Six street youth who could. . . . In P. Reason & H. Bradbury (Eds.), *Handbook of action research: Participatory inquiry and practice* (pp. 396–402). Thousand Oaks, CA: Sage.

CHAPTER 14

ENSURING EFFECTIVE TRANSITIONS IN EARLY INTERVENTION

MARCI J. HANSON

All individuals continually experience change throughout their lives. These points of change represent times of transition or in other words, the movement from one form, stage, or point to another. As adults, major life changes (e.g., graduation, landing or losing a job, marriage, separation or divorce, birth of a baby, death of a loved one, moving to a new residence or city) come to mind when transitions are considered. Regardless of whether these transitions constitute positive or traumatic experiences in one's life, they all necessitate major shifts. It is not surprising that most of these events are considered major stressors in life regardless of whether they were planned and initiated or whether they were difficult and unsolicited. Change creates the opportunity for stress because it involves adaptations and adjustments to new circumstances.

For children who are born at risk or with a disability, these transitions occur from the beginning of their lives and often include a number of events or points of change. Consider, as examples, the changes and transitions encountered by the two young children in the following scenarios.

Amy's parents had been longing for a child and were enjoying every minute of their preparation for her birth. However, 8 weeks prior to Amy's due date, her mother was rushed to the hospital, and Amy was delivered prematurely. Due to her low birth weight and prematurity, as well as myriad medical complications, Amy had to spend her early weeks in the neonatal intensive care nursery. Her wizened little body all hooked up to monitors was shocking for her parents to see. When they finally were able to bring Amy home, her parents carefully prepared their home environment to reduce noise and bright lights. That was just the beginning. In fact, special care was needed throughout Amy's first years of life as she returned to the hospital frequently with health concerns. In addition to heath care services, periodic assessments through a high-risk infant follow-up clinic, weekly physical therapy, and visits from an infant vision specialist became part of Amy's routine.

Renaldo was born with Down syndrome, is only 5¹/₂ years old, and is about to enter his fourth "school" experience as he begins kindergarten. When he was 4 months old, he was enrolled in an early intervention program that provided special education support through a home visitor and a consultant to his child care program. At age 3, Renaldo "graduated" from early intervention to a Head Start preschool program in the mornings and another child care program in the afternoons. At age 4, his family moved him to another program that was nearer to their home. Now in his fifth year, he is preparing to enter his neighborhood kindergarten program.

Although not even school age, these youngsters already have been driven and bused to a variety of services operated by different agencies. They and their families are seasoned travelers in the journey of multiple services for children with special needs. Their parents have learned whole new sets of information, terminology, and skills, and these families have been thrust into experiences that they had not anticipated or even knew existed.

These transitions have required a range of adaptations and adjustments for the children and their families. The adjustments include practical and physical factors in that the children and families have to get to new places, learn new rules, and meet new people. The transitions have also necessitated major behavioral and emotional adjustments in that Amy and Renaldo were separated from their parents when they attended the group experiences. Their parents had to learn new skills in caring for their children in a therapeutic way and had to grapple with the new challenges and realities their children's conditions presented to them.

It is evident that these children and their families weathered numerous points of transition in only a few years. Two types of transition are apparent from these examples: vertical and horizontal (Kagan, 1992; Kagan & Neuman, 1998; Rosenkoetter, Whaley, Hains, & Pierce, 2001). *Vertical* transitions occurred as the children moved from service type and agency as they grew and developed over the years (e.g., moved from early intervention services to preschool). Because the children received multiple services by different professionals and agencies during the same time period, *horizontal* transitions across services were necessitated as well. Given the discussion of interagency coordination, collaboration, and professional teaming in other chapters in this volume, this chapter focuses primarily on issues of vertical transition.

These children and their families experience a vast number of transitions on a daily basis—both vertically and horizontally—as families seek services to prevent or remediate their children's risk conditions. Common transition points include moving from the hospital to the family home, entering early intervention infant/toddler services and care, progressing to preschool, and shifting from preschool to kindergarten and elementary school. At each of these points, most children are receiving a variety of services from multiple service providers. These transitions can be frequent and can provoke intense feelings and adjustment demands.

CONTEXTS FOR TRANSITION

When a child has a disability or risk condition, service transitions involve multiple service delivery systems and experiences. Thus, these children and their families potentially interact with more service systems and a wider range of service settings and do so at an earlier point in time than do most children and families. Given the complexity of transition issues, experiences of these children and families, as well as the experiences of the service providers, can best be understood through an ecological model. Bronfenbrenner's (1979) ecological systems framework provides a mechanism for viewing these interactions and experiences. The child, at the minimum, is involved with two *microsystems*—the family and the intervention service system (e.g., early intervention program, child care program, preschool). These systems interact as well as influence one another (*mesosystem* issues). For instance, the early intervention provider and the health care provider have particular services available as governed by their regulatory and funding structures. They may recommend procedures to help the family position and handle their child, feed their child, and interact with their child. The characteristics of the family—their care providers, resources, scheduling issues, cultural and linguistic background, and values and childrearing beliefs—will in turn influence the degree to which the family accepts and implements the service suggestions. Likewise, families and the service delivery systems and settings do not operate in a vacuum. Rather, both are highly influenced by the laws, regulations, policies, and procedures of the systems that govern the services provided, such as school district policies, national laws, public funding for services, and service priorities established by these agencies and administrative structures (*exosystem* issues). On a more global level (*macrosystem*), the cultural and societal mores and supports affect all of these contexts. These may include issues or values pertaining to how individuals with disabilities or risk conditions should be assisted (e.g., federal legislation for special education, inclusive services, early support for children and families) and how young children should be cared for and reared (e.g., family support, external child care).

Although conceptually represented as nesting in one another, these interactions and influences between ecological contexts are dynamic and operate bi-directionally as well.

Bronfenbrenner (1986), as discussed and cited by Diamond, Spiegel-McGill, and Hanrahan (1988), described three steps that characterize transitions as children move from one setting to another. First, prior to the transition or movement, the relationship between the systems (intersecting relationships) must be considered. Variables such as attitudes, expectations, information, and previous interactions all would have a potential effect on the process. Second, once the child has become enrolled in the new setting, reorganization must occur for all parties. For instance, parents and service providers may change their expectations and attitudes about the child's behavior. The third step involves a change in the linkages between the systems. Family members and service providers, for example, ideally develop collaborative relationships or partnerships characterized by effective communication. This framework, thus, illuminates the many factors that play a role in children's transitions, and it also demonstrates the complexity and long-term nature of every transition process. Clearly, transitions constitute an important component of the Developmental Systems Model (Guralnick, 2001).

TRANSITION AS A PROCESS

For purposes of this discussion, the term *transition* relates to "points of change in services and personnel who coordinate and provide services" (Rice & O'Brien, 1990, p. 2). As such, transitions constitute crucial times for decision making regarding the child's services. Though the point of change implies a specific shift in services, *transition is actually a complex and gradual process* rather than a specific event or product. This process begins long before the child moves to another setting or service system, and it extends well after the child has engaged in the new services and activities. This process requires *ongoing monitoring and support* to ensure success.

Ideally, the process of transition should ensure service continuity, reduce family disruptions, prepare children for their program placements, and meet legal requirements (Wolery, 1989). This is a tall order, and as such, it implies a *carefully planned and thoughtful process*. Planning is essential given the complexity of the decisions made at this time, the service shifts, the many players involved in the transition, and the preparations that are needed. Planning should include the exchange of information among participants; the identification of resources, needs, and service options; and an articulation of planning and implementation procedures for ensuring an effective process.

Transition is a two-way process involving close collaboration between professionals and families. Collaboration is an essential ingredient to the process of transition. The roles played by the child's family, the teachers and other personnel, and the services agency personnel all are crucial to the success of this process (Hains, Fowler, & Chandler, 1988).

Because of the magnitude of adjustments made when the child moves from one service setting to another, the *process of transition also can be emotional.* Family concerns may be heightened particularly as the child and family progress from more home-based, family-focused services in the earliest years to increasingly more center-based and child-focused services as the child gets older (Hains, Rosenkoetter, & Fowler, 1991; Hanson, Beckman, et al., 2000).

The process of transition is much more complex than is readily apparent. It involves far more than simply moving the child to a new classroom or a new school. Children and their families are forced to make a series of major adjustments to their schedules, expectations, and social ties, and they must do so in the first few years of the child's life.

COMPONENTS OF THE TRANSITION PROCESS

Each transition in services brings myriad adjustments for children, their families, and service providers. Four major components of the transition process are analyzed in an effort to disentangle the many dimensions of transition and the influences that determine the success or breakdown of the process. These components include personal characteristics and experiences of participants, relationships among participants, procedural variables, and amount and type of support provided (see Figure 14.1).

Personal Characteristics and Experiences

Children, their families, and the professionals who work with them all bring their own personal characteristics and experiences to the transition process. Each person brings his or her own personality, goals, and expectations, as well as style of interaction and way of communicating those goals and expectations.

Child Characteristics and Experiences

Many characteristics of children (personality [e.g., outgoing, withdrawn], ability to interact with peers [e.g., has many friends, communicates well and clearly, has few friends], type and severity of the disability, language and culture) may affect their ability to transition successfully into another

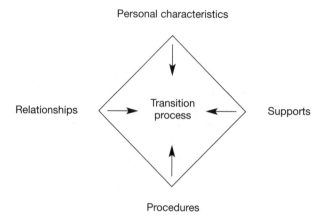

Figure 14.1. Components of the transition process.

learning environment or placement option. When a child has special needs, the characteristics of the disability or risk condition may exert a powerful influence on the transition process and decisions surrounding educational placements. The type and severity of the child's disability will determine the service options that are needed and, in many cases, influence the options that are available. For instance, in a qualitative study of children's transition from infant/toddler to preschool services, Hanson, Beckman, et al. (2000) found that child behavior and developmental level played a key role in the decision-making process. During the transition process, both professionals and families raised issues regarding the child's "readiness" to enter and ability to participate in the new learning environment, specifically with regard to the child's ability to walk, talk, and get along with peers. The child's ability to communicate and function independently (e.g., toilet, feed self, ambulate) and the type of disability often are considered in deciding if a child can enter a more advanced or an inclusive program. One mother of a child diagnosed with pervasive developmental disorder at age 2 lamented, "As soon as you say autistic . . . Well, I've gone where I say speech and language disorder" (cited in Hanson, Beckman, et al., 2000, p. 288). Yet, even children with significant disabilities may be considered "includable" if the child has a winning personality and the ability to get along with peers (Hanson et al., 2001). Thus, characteristics of the child's disability or risk condition may significantly influence the transition both in terms of availability of education placement options and the attitudes and perceptions of the teachers.

The primary language spoken in the family's home also may be a factor in the child's educational placement and the transition process. In many parts of the United States, for instance, a large proportion of students enrolled in the public schools are non-native English learners. In California, for example, approximately 40% of the school-age population are English learners (U.S. Census Bureau, 2003). Finding appropriate interpreters and professionals trained both in a specialty (e.g., physical therapy, occupational therapy, speech therapy) and who also are fluent speakers of the family's primary language often is difficult to achieve. The child and family's cultural practices may vary too much or be at odds with the expectations held by the classroom personnel (Hanson, Gutierrez, Morgan, Brennan, & Zercher, 1997).

Family Characteristics and Experiences

Although the child's disability and English proficiency may be factors in the transition process and placement decisions, other factors may play more subtle roles (e.g., the child and family's racial, ethnic, and cultural identity).

When families enter the transition process having experienced discrimination on the basis of race, gender, or ability level, they bring that history with them. Understandably, they may be more sensitive about assessment or placement issues, and their styles of interaction may be affected by their previous experiences. Statistics on the over-representation of children of color in disability categories and in special education placements underscore the very real issues of prevention and discrimination in educational decision making (Bowe, 1995; U.S. Department of Education, 2001).

The family's socioeconomic status also may limit the family's ability to collaborate fully and meaningfully in the transition process. Opportunities to participate and contribute to the transition process will be seriously compromised for families who are homeless, who are unable to find transportation or child care for other children, who are unable to leave work to participate, or who feel threatened and devalued in the professional services setting.

Similarly, families who do not speak English or whose literacy skills are limited also may encounter difficulties in participation. It is incumbent upon professionals to "go the extra mile" to provide interpretation and translation services, as well as provide information in modes that are meaningful and understandable to the family, in order to support each family's full participation in the transition process.

Service Provider Characteristics and Experiences

Practitioners also bring their attitudes, expectations, experience, and cultural and linguistic background to the transition process. When these are in sync with those of the family with whom they are working, a more favorable outcome is likely to be achieved. For instance, if the parents desire a program that emphasizes play and social interactions and this philosophy of education also matches that of the receiving program and teachers, then a more harmonious transition may be achieved. Often, however, families and teachers may differ on their expectations for the child, their philosophy of how children learn, and with respect to the skills the child needs to participate effectively in the new environment.

Teachers often function as powerful gatekeepers in the transition process (Hanson, Lieber, Horn, & Beckman, 2000). Their attitudes and experience with children with various types of disabilities or their lack of experience with a child with special needs can have a significant effect on whether the child is placed in a given setting and on the child's adaptation to the new environment. Hanson, Beckman, et al. (2000) noted that often the teacher in an infant/toddler early intervention program functioned as a key guide for the family as they made the transition process. These teachers were instrumental in providing families with the information that they needed and in facilitating meetings and communication between the sending and receiving sites. In other cases, the service coordinator helped families and children prepare for the service shift.

Given the tremendous influence that professionals—teachers in particular—exert during the transition process, professional personnel preparation must emphasize the development of communication skills and strategies for partnering with families in the education process. Likewise, professionals must receive training on the provision of culturally competent and respectful services given the diversity of the children and families with whom they are working.

Relationships Among Participants

Effective transitions are characterized by collaborative relationships between families and service providers. The family knows the child best and is ultimately responsible for making decisions related to the child's services and care. Professionals, however, hold the specialized knowledge that families need to optimize the child's development. Thus, the success of the transition process will be greatly influenced by the effectiveness of the communication process between families and service providers. When practitioners are trained to deliver services in a manner that is culturally competent and respectful of family variability, the communication process will be enhanced. The delivery of family-centered or family-based services constitutes a major provision of the Division for Early Childhood (DEC) recommended practices (Sandall, McLean, & Smith, 2000).

Procedural Variables

Transition policy is an integral component of the Individuals with Disabilities Education Act (IDEA) Amendments of 1997 (PL 105-17). A written transition plan is stipulated at age 3 for eligible children with disabilities as these children transition from infant/toddler early intervention services to preschool services. In subsequent years, attention to transition services is likewise emphasized, and service systems are charged with developing coordinated activities to support the transition of children as they move from one set of services and programs to another.

These transition policies have necessitated the analysis and development of new practices and procedures for service providers and service systems. Attention in the field, thus, largely has been focused on this component of the transition process. Service systems have endeavored to develop activities and procedures to guide this process, and, as a result, a wide range of strategies have been developed to enhance interagency collaboration and cross-agency linkages (Rosenkoetter, Hains, & Fowler, 1994).

Amount and Type of Support

Support is a personal matter as the needs of each individual vary from one another and from one situation to the next. Like relationships and communication styles, one size does not fit all. Support is cloaked in many forms, and different individuals will need different types of assistance at different points in their transition journey.

Support may be offered through more formalized or systematic attempts by "sending" service providers to prepare children and families. Such supports may focus on teaching children the skills that they will need to succeed in the next environment. Supports also may be delivered by providing families with the information on instruction, laws, and placements that will aid them in negotiating the new system. Support also can be informal, with family members, friends, or professionals listening to families, encouraging families, and bolstering and coaching families as they interact with new professionals and service delivery systems in the service setting to which the child is transitioning.

IMPLEMENTATION ISSUES: CHALLENGES TO THE TRANSITION PROCESS

Every transition necessitates a shift or adjustment that poses challenges to the participating individuals and systems. These challenges may be magnified for children who have a disability or whose development is at risk because they are required to make many transitions from one service system type or level to another. Some challenges noted in the professional literature include 1) the shift from one service system or agency to another, 2) differences in eligibility requirements for services, 3) new demands for child participation, 4) differing expectations for child behavior and "readiness," 5) differences in type and level of staff involvement and training, and 6) philosophical shifts in intervention models across services and agencies (Fowler, Hains, & Rosenkoetter, 1990; Hains et al., 1988; Noonan & Ratokalau, 1991; Shotts, Rosenkoetter, Streufert, & Rosenkoetter, 1994).

Systems Issues—Continuity of Services

Wolery (1999) suggested that continuity of services is important in minimizing disruptions to children and families as they transition across and between services. Individual children may require a variety of services from different agencies. Those agencies and services also will change as the child grows older and moves on to different educational settings. IDEA requires collaboration among state and local agencies and service providers; the amendments of 1997 further emphasize the promotion of a more seamless *system* of early intervention services. A number of factors, however, produce challenges to achieving a seamless system (Sainato & Morrison, 2001). Different agencies require different eligibility requirements for participation. Some agencies serve only children with disabilities or certain types of disabilities, whereas others also serve children at risk or children who are typically developing. Services also differ in structure and in the requirements and demands for child participation. For instance, as the child moves from preschool to the more structured and group-centered approaches offered in kindergarten and elementary school, less emphasis may be placed on support for individual child needs and family issues. The availability of and support for inclusive services, likewise, will vary across systems and programs. In some systems, inclusion is an established practice and a priority. For others, such as a private child care program, the staff members may have less background training and experience in working with children with special needs and, thus, may be less willing or able to admit children and assist them in making the transition to such services.

Philosophical Issues

A related issue is the philosophical approach of the service agency and the service practitioners within it, which greatly affects service delivery options. For instance, in a study of preschool inclusion, researchers found that community and classroom cultural values that supported diversity at all levels also facilitated the inclusion of children with disabilities (differing abilities; Hanson et al., 1998).

Another contemporary focus is on readiness—related to children and with respect to service systems. The 1997 National Education Goals Panel has defined priorities in getting children ready for school and schools ready for children. Characteristics of "ready schools" included those that facilitated smooth transitions between the child's home and school, continuity across services (from early childhood to elementary), and a comprehensive focus on the community as well as children and their families (Pianta, Cox, Taylor, & Early, 1999; Sainato & Morrison, 2001). The emphasis is on preparing educational environments to appropriately serve a wide variety of children rather than to require children to achieve some behavior in order to participate.

Training and Personnel Preparation Issues

A major transition for children may be between services aimed at serving all children and staffed primarily by individuals with a general education or child development background and those services aimed at a particular specialization and staffed by professionals with training in special education or related fields. A number of survey studies have documented the attitudes and practices of general educators with respect to serving children with special needs (Buysse, Wesley, Keyes, & Bailey, 1996; Dinnebeil, McInerney, Fox, & Juchartz-Pendry, 1998). Understandably, those educators who have not received training or experience working with children with special needs may feel less comfortable. Thus, personnel preparation is an essential need to address this issue.

CREATING SUCCESSFUL TRANSITIONS

Successful transitions are characterized as those that promote

> (a) placement decisions that meet individual needs; (b) uninterrupted services; (c) nonconfrontational and effective models of advocacy that families can emulate throughout their children's lives; (d) avoidance of duplication in assessment and goal planning; and (e) reduced stress for children, families, and service providers. (Shotts et al., 1994, pp. 395–396)

These goals represent a tall order for agencies and professionals in the field of human services. Transitions, as previously discussed, involve many components and are processes rather than events that involve preplanning or preparation prior to the transition, as well as follow-up after the transition has occurred (see Figure 14.2).

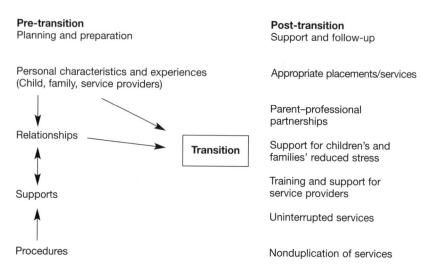

Pre-transition
Planning and preparation

Post-transition
Support and follow-up

Personal characteristics and experiences
(Child, family, service providers)

Appropriate placements/services

Relationships

Parent–professional
partnerships

Transition

Support for children's and
families' reduced stress

Supports

Training and support for
service providers

Uninterrupted services

Procedures

Nonduplication of services

Figure 14.2. The transition process.

The charge of this volume is to provide a blueprint for optimal services; however, with respect to transition (or other components; see Chapter 1), the details of the blueprint must be completed by agencies or individuals in their own way to achieve the goal of successful transitions. Consequently, a set of tenets is proposed that optimize the likelihood of successful transition experiences for children and their families and for the professionals with whom they work. Specific recommendations in each area are offered and tied to research literature that may be useful as communities develop the details and strategies of the transition component of the Developmental Systems Model (Guralnick, 2001).

#1: Transition Is Viewed as a Process in Successful Transition Experiences

Transition is not just an event or a product of a meeting. Transition is a process that begins long before the child shifts to a new set of services, and it continues after the child physically has moved to the new services setting(s). Though this perspective on transition has been presented in the literature for many years (Diamond et al., 1988; Hains et al., 1991; Noonan & Kilgo, 1987), the reality of the experience for many families still differs from this orientation. For families whose children were making the transition from infant/toddler to preschool services, for instance, transition was viewed as a formalized, "marker event," often fraught with anxiety given the magnitude of the decisions made at the transition meeting (Hanson, Beckman, et al., 2000).

The transition process is procedural and emotional (Hanson, Beckman, et al., 2000). It requires the implementation of procedures defined by agency and legal regulations regarding the exchange of information, eligibility for services, placement decisions, consent, and so forth. The process also involves emotional adjustments, particularly for families. Typically, children and families must adapt to services that are more child centered as the child grows older, which often entails leaving behind services that were more family centered and family involved. The following quotations reflect this emotional adjustment for families. One mother stated, "I'm going to miss the program. Because it's like meeting someone and—and spending all that time with them and then knowing that you're not going to see them anymore." Another mother related, "I wish I could just keep her in the program because I've gotten to know all the people there. And they've been a real good supportive team for—it's not just me, but the whole family as well" (Hanson, Beckman, et al., 2000, p. 285).

Recommendation: Focus on Relationships

Agency personnel and direct service providers typically are aware of the paperwork and accounting demands related to the transition process. The human or emotional aspects may be less salient. The preceding discussion of the components of the transition process highlights the dimensions that must be considered in this process. The characteristics of children, families, and service providers all interact and will affect the process and the outcomes. The *relationships* among the major players and the resources and supports that are available can contribute to the smoothness and overall success of the experience for all of the participants. Kalmanson and Seligman acknowledge the fundamental importance of relationships to successful intervention efforts: "The success of all interventions will rest on the quality of the provider–family relationship, even when the relationship itself is not the focus of the intervention" (1992, p. 48).

Many children and families will experience a close *match* or *fit* between their needs, goals, and expectations and those of the receiving agency or service. In these circumstances, children's cultural and language backgrounds will be compatible with those of the new setting; the child will have the prerequisite skills needed to fully benefit and participate; and the families and professionals will share similar philosophies on how children learn and their learning priorities. Of course, this match/fit does not always occur. When transition is recognized as a process requiring behavioral and emotional adjustments and adaptations, however, the likelihood of a more successful experience will be enhanced.

#2: Successful Transitions Are Built on a Foundation of Effective Communication and Collaborative Partnerships

Each effective transition is built on a foundation of respectful, culturally competent, and family-centered services characterized by effective communication and collaboration. Even when a mismatch occurs between family goals and expectations and those of service providers, conflict can be prevented or overcome if a respectful working relationship has been established between the families and service professionals (Hains et al., 1991; Rosenkoetter et al., 1994). Collaboration between professionals and families and the roles of the child's family, the sending and receiving teachers and other personnel, and service agencies are crucial to a successful transition process (Hains et al., 1988).

Communication and effective collaboration are more likely to be achieved through parent–professional partnerships. This partnership is "an association between a family and one or more professionals who function collaboratively using agreed upon roles in pursuit of a joint interest or common goal" (Dunst & Paget, 1991, p. 29). Optimal partnerships are those that foster *empowerment* or *enablement* of family members to accomplish their own goals and demonstrate competence (Dunst, Trivette, & Johanson, 1994). Clear, respectful communication is essential to fostering and maintaining such partnerships (Edelman, Greenland, & Mills, 1992a, 1992b). Professional dispositions or attitudes and family-centered philosophical beliefs and values are more likely to enhance these collaborative relationships in early intervention settings (Dinnebeil, Hale, & Rule, 1996; McWilliam, Tocci, & Harbin, 1998).

Recommendation: Enhance the Role of Families in Partnerships

Families must be viewed as equal partners in the transition process in order for their voices to be fully heard and their participation to be facilitated. Although this philosophy is the ideal, practice often falls quite short of this goal and transition becomes a professionally driven event during which parents' information and choices are circumscribed (Hanson, Beckman, et al., 2000). However, a number of strategies can enhance family participation in the process and in decision making (Hanson, Beckman, et al., 2000). Families' participation can be facilitated when planning is undertaken prior to the transition. Professionals establish procedures for getting to know the children and families and for exchanging valuable information. Families need this information in the language and formats that they prefer and find meaningful. The assistance of a key person or guide also can enhance families' participation. This guide may be another parent, a parent group, or a professional such as the sending teacher. Another strategy is to devise a mechanism for "bringing the child to the process." Professionals may easily lose sight of the needs and circumstances of individual children and their families, particularly at the end of a school year during which many children are making transitions. Some families have found it useful to bring a photograph, school records, videotape, child art or school work, or other records of their child's behavior and accomplishments to meetings that they hold with professionals. When professionals recognize the strengths and resources of families and focus on families as pivotal decision makers for their children, family participation is enhanced. These strategies allow families to play a more active and empowered role in planning meetings.

Recommendation: Enhance the Role of Professionals in Partnerships

Although service agency professionals often hold a disproportionate amount of the decision-making power during transitions because they control access to the service resources and assets, professionals can serve as major facilitators of a collaborative and inclusive transition process. All professionals have the opportunity to produce an environment in which families are embraced as full partners in a process of planning, deciding, and implementing service goals for children. Furthermore, teachers often take or are assigned primary responsibility for preparation of children for transitions (Hanline, 1993).

Sending professionals, such as the service coordinator, the teacher, or professionals from the services in which the child is enrolled, may be particularly instrumental in this process. These individuals typically know the child and family best and can help families to gain access to or procure information, understand laws and procedures, and emotionally and behaviorally prepare children for the next environment. Sending professionals may provide information on the child's behavior and development, initiate contact with the receiving service, visit the new environment, and make specific recommendations to families on issues to consider in the decision-making process. They essentially serve as a liaison between the family and the receiving program. This role is reflected in one parent's comment during transition, "She's given me contact people . . . she's done her job above and beyond the call of duty in my eyes because she was very helpful" (Hanson, Beckman, et al., 2000, p. 289). A service coordinator, speaking from the other side of the parent–professional dyad, echoes the supportive and informative role of the sending professional in her statement, "I'm there for support . . . for the parents to have a familiar face . . . [to] kind of hold their hand . . . " (Hanson, Beckman, et al., p. 289). This sending role, thus, not only involves compiling and providing information around procedural issues but also centers on supplying emotional support and guidance through the transition process. The sending professional may function as a navigator or guide with the amount of assistance dictated by the needs and preferences of the family.

Receiving professionals also can ease or enhance the transition process for children and families. These individuals also can participate actively in the process and openly embrace family participation through providing information and opportunities for pre- and post-transition visits, reviewing child records, and preparing their service/educational environment (e.g., procuring equipment and materials, making adaptations or modifications) to address the child's needs. Their skills at communicating and collaborating with families will play a major role in the process. These individuals may need to acquire new information and training on the child's special needs, or they may need to procure appropriate interpretation and translation services, for example, in order to communicate effectively and respectfully with the family.

#3: Successful Transitions Require Preparation for Children, Families, and Professionals

Few individuals make major transitions of any kind without gathering more information, contemplating or weighing options, and making active decisions. In fact, when transitions are thrust on individuals without preparation, the consequences are likely to include emotional upheaval and distress. Transitions for young children through the service maze require careful planning and preparation as well enhancing smoother and more successful shifts.

Recommendation: Prepare Children

A number of efforts have focused on assessing and teaching the skills needed by the child in the next environment (Byrd & Rous, 1991; Rous, Hemmeter, & Schuster, 1994). Through observations and analyses of the skills that children need in kindergarten and elementary school in order to fully participate, professionals have argued that young children with special needs should be given training on survival skills that are useful in the "next" environment (Chandler, 1992; Conn-Powers, Ross-Allen, & Holburn, 1990; Vincent et al., 1980). Others have questioned the developmental appropriateness of this instruction (Atwater, Orth-Lopes, Elliott,

Carta, & Schwartz, 1994; Hanline, 1993) and whether the sending program has the time and resources to put into this effort.

Atwater, Orth-Lopes, et al. (1994) reviewed the research literature in this area and recommended against teaching pre-academic or readiness skills that may not be developmentally appropriate. Rather, they concluded that it may benefit children to receive teaching in generic functional skills aimed at supporting children's increased independence and abilities to engage with peers in play, social, and instructional activities. Examples of these skills may include behaviors such as completing a task independently, playing cooperatively, and listening to and following group activity instruction.

Systematic teaching strategies have been developed and employed successfully by a number of researchers in efforts to teach functional skills to facilitate children's transitions. These studies, aimed at preschool to kindergarten transition, focused on children's positive and independent participation in classroom activities (Rule, Fiechtl, & Innocenti, 1990), appropriate engagement during group activities (Sainato, Strain, & Lyon, 1987), engagement during independent activities (Hains, 1992; Sainato, Strain, Lefebvre, & Rapp, 1990), and appropriate behavior during in-class transitions (Connell, Carta, Lutz, Randall, & Wilson, 1993; Sainato, Strain, Lefebvre, & Rapp, 1987). Carta, Atwater, and Schwartz (1991, 1992) also developed teaching strategies that can be folded into existing early childhood curricula at the preschool and kindergarten levels for the purpose of encouraging children's appropriate engagement in group and independent activities, as well as appropriate behavior during in-class transitions. Strategies such as teacher prompting, pacing, and organizing elements of the physical setting were employed successfully to enhance children's skills in the target areas. This model was expanded in Project SLIDE (Skills for Learning Independence in Diverse Environments; Carta, Elliott, et al., 1992) for enhancing the transition of children into kindergarten through promoting group participation and independence skills.

In addition to skills aimed at group interaction and independence, Atwater, Orth-Lopes, et al. (1994) noted that self-help and social interaction skills also foster children's successful transitions. Their review of recommended teaching regimens included the Hawaii Preparing for Integrated Preschool (PIP) Curriculum (Noonan, Yamashita, Graham, & Nakamoto, 1991), which identifies strategies for teaching self-help skills and social interaction skills, and the strategies developed by McEvoy and colleagues for fostering positive social interactions and friendships between children (McEvoy et al., 1988; McEvoy, Odom, & McConnell, 1992; McEvoy, Twardosz, & Bishop, 1990).

Although the development of skills in social interaction, self-help, participation in group activities, and independent performance may facilitate the transition of children into classroom experiences, these skills should not be seen as prerequisites for children to participate in the new classroom or inclusive experiences (Salisbury & Vincent, 1990). Instruction aimed at assisting children to achieve skills that will be useful in their next educational environment should be focused on functional skills rather than pre-academic or "readiness" skills (Atwater, Orth-Lopes, et al., 1994). Furthermore, children with disabilities may be less likely to generalize skills to new environments without systemic instruction and support. Sainato and Morrison (2001) discussed the concept of naturalistic instruction that emphasizes the delivery of intervention and instruction during routine classroom events and activities. In addition, strategies are reviewed for supporting children both before and after transition.

Recommendation: Prepare Families

Families also make the transition to new services with their children. They typically are faced with new terminology to learn, new situations and systems to navigate, new rules and schedules to meet, new demands for participation, and new professionals with whom they must establish working relationships. Families will need to secure new information and knowledge in order to meet the needs of their children as they make the transition to new environments. Families who have less "know-how" at navigating the services systems due to the language they speak, their immigration status, their socioeconomic status, their literacy level, or their education level may be at a disadvantage in securing the services and information that they need. Studies have suggested that families' access to information related to education laws and regulations, placement options, and procedures for decision making were pivotal in influencing their ability to participate in and have an effect on the decision-making process for their children (Hanson, Beckman, et al., 2000; Hanson et al., 2001).

Families need to have access to service delivery systems that provide information in different modes (e.g., written, verbal) and in the families' primary languages through trained, professional interpreters and translators. Attention to the literacy level of families is warranted to ensure that they are given materials that are understandable.

Family advocates or guides are useful to some families as well. These individuals may be other parents who are involved in parent-to-parent support networks or they may be sending teachers or service coordinators who are familiar with the child and family's background, strengths, and needs. Individuals who function as cultural guides also may be needed for those families who are new to this country, whose values and beliefs may be different from those of the dominant culture, or who are unfamiliar with the educational protocol in this country (Hanson, Beckman, et al., 2000; Lynch & Hanson, 2004).

Recommendation: Provide Staff with Training and Encourage Collaboration

Practitioners who provide services to young children with disabilities or risk conditions and their families come from a variety of training and educational environments. Some individuals will have completed highly technical training programs in specialized areas (e.g., special education, speech and language therapy, physical or occupational therapy). Other practitioners may have a background primarily in child care, which may or may not have included extensive academic training. The training of personnel for one age group or type of services (e.g., providing infant/ toddler services versus preschool services versus kindergarten) also may differ widely and emphasize different goals (Fowler et al., 1990). The potential for differences in training and orientation of personnel providing services to young children necessitates coordination across fields (e.g., early childhood education and special education) and preparation specifi- cally related to children with special needs and transition issues. Models that provide transition team training for parents and professionals have ensured more successful transitions (Rous et al., 1994). Likewise, teachers who have had less experience with children with special needs often are responsive to having these children in their class but may receive little or no support for doing so. Wolery (1999) suggested that in order for teachers to be successful in helping children to make transitions, they and other staff members also must be given resources, such as training, ongoing technical assistance, and time for planning, in order to meet their own needs related to supporting the transition process.

#4: Procedural Supports Enhance Successful Transitions

Perhaps more attention has been devoted to addressing procedural issues than any other component. Given the focus on coordination and collabora- tion across systems and services in IDEA, a number of research and policy efforts specifically have addressed this dimension. They underscore the importance of collaboration as influential and essential in the transition process. Collaboration between professionals, and between families and professionals, may take many forms and occur at different levels (Rosen- koetter et al., 1994). Strategies must be adapted to address different types of services and systems and meet the needs of the range of children and families served in terms of cultural, linguistic, ethnic, racial, and socioeconomic backgrounds.

Recommendation: Encourage Interagency Coordination and Continuity of Services

Because the child's services often cross agencies during transition, issues regarding interagency coordination are heightened. Cross-agency linkages are crucial in order to establish lines of responsibility and coordinate all facets of the process including child find, referral and assessment, eligibility requirements, individualized family service plan (IFSP)/individualized education program (IEP) processes, and follow-up and evaluation services (Fowler et al., 1990; Rosenkoetter et al., 1994; Rous et al., 1994; Shotts et al., 1994).

This continuity of services across agencies is crucial to successful transitions (Wolery, 1999). Rosenkoetter and colleagues (1994) provided suggestions for implementing interagency and intra-agency collaborative processes.

Recommendation: Focus on Transition Planning and Policies

An interagency committee whose function it is to review and develop policies and procedures can be beneficial for planning (Rous et al., 1994). Some agencies or communities employ a transition coordinator whose job it is to monitor this process and foster effective working relationships among service participants (Rosenkoetter et al., 1994).

Recommendation: Prepare for the Exchange of Information

Prior to decision making and meetings about future placement, all participants (family members and professionals) must have information about the child, family concerns, and priorities (Hains et al., 1991; Shotts et al., 1994). Many communities or school systems have employed a planned approach for exchanging information with the use of materials and planning guides aimed at facilitating this process (Hanline, 1993; Hanline & Knowlton, 1988). The development of a transition plan and an established means of communication between families, the sending professionals, and the receiving professionals facilitates the transition process (Hains et al., 1988; Hains et al., 1991; Hanline & Knowlton, 1988; Rosenkoetter et al., 1994).

Recommendation: Provide Opportunities for Parent Involvement

Information should be provided to families in formats that match the needs of the family (e.g., written versus oral, group versus individual), include opportunities for program visitation, and include options for supplemental services (Rous et al., 1994). Families often have greater opportunities for participation in early intervention programs than in subsequent programs given the IFSP process (Fowler et al., 1990). However, opportunities for their involvement at all levels are crucial to the success of their children's transitioning. Indeed, parental attitudes can be crucial to successful transitions (Pianta et al., 1999).

Although programs and services agencies typically embrace parental involvement, the reality for many families is that their socioeconomic status, culture, and language may play powerful roles in their experiences with service delivery systems (Harry, 1992a, 1992b). Families' opportunities to obtain or exchange information, gain access to services, effectively communicate, and form working relationships with professionals may be severely circumscribed. The importance of training and assisting service agency administrators and personnel to provide services in a culturally competent and respectful manner cannot be underscored enough (Lynch & Hanson, 2004).

CONCLUSION

The recommendations made in this chapter are not new. Many have been discussed in various forms since the 1990s. In fact, the issue of transition has received a great deal of research and policy attention. Barriers or challenges to implementation have been identified, and a number of strategies have been developed to address various service components. Although refinements and new ideas are always welcome in the service delivery process, a substantial body of literature and practical strategies exist. Still, services often fall short and transitions for children and their families do not run smoothly.

The missing ingredient often is the commitment to making these procedures work. This commitment is required of all participants in the transition process: teachers and other personnel, families, and administrators and policy makers. It is a commitment of time and energy to work with families through relationships; time to plan; openness to different points of view and different values; and the fostering of creative and multiple service options for individual children, rather than the provision of a predetermined menu. Teachers and other professionals who provide services to young children must be committed to serving *all* children. They must provide respectful, family-centered, culturally responsive services, and they must commit time to get to know children and their families and listen to their perspectives and needs. Families must be committed to becoming involved in their child's education and communicating their needs. That involvement may necessitate gathering new information, and it may require becoming familiar with new educational values and practices as well as new laws and regulations. Administrators, service agency personnel, and policy makers must be committed to providing the leadership and resources that are necessary to ensure and sustain adequate planning and preparation as children and their families make the transition across services (Hanson & Bruder, 2001).

Transition is a complex, multifaceted process. No magic is needed for its success. Rather, service systems and service providers must be responsive to the wide range of child and family needs represented by the diverse population of families served. Melton, Limber, and Teague articulated this obligation well in their credo: "Families should be able to get help where they are, when they need it, and in a form that they can use with ease and without stigma" (1999, p. 196).

REFERENCES

Atwater, J.B., Carta, J.J., Schwartz, I.S., & McConnell, S.R. (1994). Blending developmentally appropriate practice and early childhood special education: Redefining best practice to meet the needs of all children. In B.L. Mallory & R.S. New (Eds.), *Diversity and developmentally appropriate practices: Challenges for early childhood education* (pp. 185–201). New York: Teachers College Press.

Atwater, J.B., Orth-Lopes, L., Elliott, M., Carta, J.J., & Schwartz, I.S. (1994). Completing the circle: Planning and implementing transitions to other programs. In M. Wolery & J.S. Wilbers (Eds.), *Including children with special needs in early childhood programs* (Vol. 6, pp. 167–188). Washington, DC: National Association for the Education of Young Children.

Bowe, F.G. (1995). Population estimates: Birth to 5 children with disabilities. *Journal of Special Education, 28*(4), 461–471.

Bronfenbrenner, U. (1979). *The ecology of human development.* Cambridge, MA: Harvard University Press.

Bronfenbrenner, U. (1986). Ecology of the family as a context for human development: Research perspectives. *Developmental Psychology, 22,* 723–742.

Buysse, V., Wesley, P., Keyes, L., & Bailey, D.B. (1996). Assessing the comfort zone of child care teachers in serving young children with disabilities. *Journal of Early Intervention, 20*(3), 189–203.

Byrd, M.R., & Rous, B.S. (1991). *Helpful entry level skills checklist—Revised.* Lexington, KY: Child Development Centers of the Bluegrass.

Carta, J.J., Atwater, J.B., & Schwartz, I.S. (1991). *Early classroom survival skills: A training approach.* Paper presented at the New Directions in Child and Family Research: Shaping Head Start in the 90s conference, Arlington, VA.

Carta, J.J., Atwater, J.B., & Schwartz, I.S. (1992). *Classroom survival skills interventions: Demonstration of short- and long-term effects.* Poster presented at the meeting of the Association for Behavior Analysis, San Francisco.

Carta, J.J., Elliott, M., Orth-Lopes, L., Scherer, H., Schwartz, I., & Atwater, J. (1992). *Effective instructional strategies to facilitate in-class transitions, group instruction, and independent performance activities* (2nd ed.). Kansas City: Juniper Gardens Children Project, University of Kansas.

Chandler, L.K. (1992). Promoting children's social/survival skills as a strategy for transition to mainstreamed kindergarten programs. In S.L. Odom, S.R. McConnell, & M.A. McEvoy (Eds.), *Social competence of young children with disabilities: Issues and strategies for intervention*. Baltimore: Paul H. Brookes Publishing Co.

Connell, M.C., Carta, J.J., Lutz, S., Randall, C.C., & Wilson, J. (1993). Building independence during in-class transitions: Teaching in-class transition skills to preschoolers with developmental delays through choral-response-based self-assessment and contingent praise. *Education and Treatment of Children, 16*(2), 160–174.

Conn-Powers, M.C., Ross-Allen, J., & Holburn, S. (1990). Transition of young children into the elementary education mainstream. *Topics in Early Childhood Special Education, 9*(4), 91–105.

Diamond, K.E., Spiegel-McGill, P., & Hanrahan, P. (1988). Planning for school transition: An ecological-developmental approach. *Journal of the Division for Early Childhood, 12*, 245–252.

Dinnebeil, L.A., Hale, L.M., & Rule, S. (1996). A qualitative analysis of parents' and service coordinators' descriptions of variables that influence collaborative relationships. *Topics in Early Childhood Special Education, 16*, 322–347.

Dinnebeil, L.A., McInerney, W., Fox, C., & Juchartz-Pendry, K. (1998). An analysis of the perceptions and characteristics of childcare personnel regarding inclusion of young children with special needs in community-based programs. *Topics in Early Childhood Special Education, 18*(2), 118–128.

Dunst, C.J., & Paget, K.D. (1991). Parent–professional partnerships and family empowerment. In M. Fine (Ed.), *Collaborative involvement with parents of exceptional children* (pp. 25–44). Brandon, VT: Clinical Psychology Publishing Co.

Dunst, C.J., Trivette, C.M., & Johanson, C. (1994). Parent–professional collaboration and partnerships. In C.J. Dunst, C.M. Trivette, & A.G. Deal (Eds.), *Supporting and strengthening families: Methods, strategies and practices* (Vol. 1, pp. 197–211). Cambridge, MA: Brookline Books.

Edelman, L., Greenland, B., & Mills, B.L. (1992a). *Building parent/professional collaboration: Facilitator's guide*. St. Paul, MN: Pathfinders.

Edelman, L., Greenland, B., & Mills, B.L. (1992b). *Family centered communication skills: Facilitator's guide*. St. Paul, MN: Pathfinders.

Fowler, S.A., Hains, A.H., & Rosenkoetter, S.E. (1990). The transition between early intervention services and preschool services: Administrative and policy issues. *Topics in Early Childhood Special Education, 9*(4), 55–65.

Guralnick, M.J. (2001). A developmental systems model for early intervention. *Infants and Young Children, 14*(2), 1–18.

Hains, A.H. (1992). Strategies for preparing preschool children with special needs for the kindergarten mainstream. *Journal of Early Intervention, 16*, 320–333.

Hains, A.H., Fowler, S.A., & Chandler, L.K. (1988). Planning school transitions: Family and professional collaboration. *Journal of the Division for Early Childhood, 12*(2), 108–115.

Hains, A.H., Rosenkoetter, S.E., & Fowler, S.A. (1991). Transition planning with families in early intervention programs. *Infants and Young Children, 3*(4), 38–47.

Hanline, M.F. (1993). Facilitating integrated preschool service delivery transitions for children, families, and professionals. In C.A. Peck, S.L. Odom, & D. Bricker (Eds.), *Integrating young children with disabilities into community programs: Ecological perspectives on research and implementation* (pp. 133–146). Baltimore: Paul H. Brookes Publishing Co.

Hanline, M.F., & Knowlton, A. (1988). A collaborative model for providing support to parents during their child's transition from infant intervention to preschool special education public school programs. *Journal of the Division for Early Childhood*, *12*(2), 116–125.

Hanson, M.J., Beckman, P.J., Horn, E., Marquart, J., Sandall, S., Greig, D., & Brennan, E. (2000). Entering preschool: Family and professional experiences in this transition process. *Journal of Early Intervention*, *23*, 279–293.

Hanson, M.J., & Bruder, M.E. (2001). Early intervention: Promises to keep. *Infants and Young Children*, *13*(3), 47–58.

Hanson, M.J., Gutierrez, S., Morgan, M., Brennan, E.L., & Zercher, C. (1997). Language, culture and disability: Interacting influences on preschool inclusion. *Topics in Early Childhood Special Education*, *17*(3), 307–336.

Hanson, M.J., Horn, E., Sandall, S., Beckman, P., Morgan, M., Marquart, J., Barnwell, D., & Chou, H.Y. (2001). After preschool inclusion: Children's educational pathways over the early school years. *Exceptional Children*, *68*, 65–83.

Hanson, M.J., Lieber, J., Horn, E., & Beckman, P. (2000). *Gatekeeping*. Presentation to the Council for Exceptional Children's Division of Early Childhood Annual International Early Childhood Conference on Children with Special Needs, Albuquerque, NM.

Hanson, M.J., Wolfberg, P., Zercher, C., Morgan, M., Gutierrez, S., Barnwell, D., & Beckman, P.J. (1998). The culture of inclusion: Recognizing diversity at multiple levels. *Early Childhood Research Quarterly*, *13*(1), 185–209.

Harry, B. (1992a). *Cultural diversity, families, and the special education system: Communication and empowerment*. New York: Teachers College Press.

Harry, B. (1992b). Restructuring the participation of African-American parents in special education. *Exceptional Children*, *59*, 123–131.

Individuals with Disabilities Education Act (IDEA) Amendments of 1997, PL 105-17, 20 U.S.C. §§ 1400 *et seq.*

Kagan, S.L. (1992). The strategic importance of linkages and the transition between early childhood programs and early elementary school. In U.S. Department of Education (Ed.), *Sticking together: Strengthening linkages and the transition between early childhood education and early elementary school* (Summary of a National Policy Forum). Washington, DC: U.S. Department of Education.

Kagan, S.L, & Neuman, M.J. (1998). Lessons from three decades of transition research. *The Elementary School Journal*, *98*(4), 366–379.

Kalmanson, B., & Seligman, S. (1992). Family–provider relationships: The basis of all intervention. *Infants and Young Children*, *4*(4), 46–52.

Lynch, E.W., & Hanson, M.J. (Eds.). (2004). *Developing cross-cultural competence: A guide for working with young children and their families* (3rd ed.). Baltimore: Paul H. Brookes Publishing Co.

McEvoy, M., Nordquist, V.M., Twardosz, S., Heckman, K.A., Wehby, J.H., & Denny, R.K. (1988). Promoting autistic children's peer interaction in an integrated early childhood setting using affection activities. *Journal of Applied Behavior Analysis*, *21*, 193–200.

McEvoy, M., Odom, S.L., & McConnell, S.R. (1992). Peer social competence interventions for young children with disabilities. In S.L. Odom, S.R. McConnell, & M.A. McEvoy (Eds.), *Social competence of young children with disabilities: Issues and strategies for intervention* (pp. 113–133). Baltimore: Paul H. Brookes Publishing Co.

McEvoy, M., Twardosz, S., & Bishop, N. (1990). Affection activities: Procedures for encouraging young children with handicaps to interact with their peers. *Education and Treatment of Children*, *13*, 159–167.

McWilliam, R.A., Tocci, L., & Harbin, G. (1998). Family-centered services: Service providers' discourse and behavior. *Topics in Early Childhood Special Education*, *18*, 206–221.

Melton, G.B., Limber, S.P., & Teague, T.L. (1999). Changing schools for changing families. In R.C. Pianta & M.J. Cox (Eds.), *The transition to kindergarten* (pp. 179–213). Baltimore: Paul H. Brookes Publishing Co.

National Education Goals Panel. (1997). *Getting a good start in school.* Washington, DC: Government Printing Office.

Noonan, M.J., & Kilgo, J.L. (1987). Transition services for early age individuals with severe mental retardation. In R.N. Ianacone & R.A. Stodden (Eds.), *Transition issues and directions* (pp. 25–37). Reston, VA: Council for Exceptional Children.

Noonan, M.J., & Ratokalau, N.B. (1991). Project Profile–PPT: The Preschool Preparation and Transition Project. *Journal of Early Intervention, 15*(4), 390–398.

Noonan, M.J., Yamashita, L., Graham, M.A., & Nakamoto, D. (1991). *Hawaii Preparing for Integrated Preschool (PIP) Curriculum.* Honolulu: Department of Special Education and University Affiliated Program, University of Hawaii, Manoa.

Pianta, R.C., Cox, M.J., Taylor, L., & Early, D. (1999). Kindergarten teachers' practices related to the transition to school: Results of a national survey. *The Elementary School Journal, 100,* 71–86.

Rice, M.L., & O'Brien, M. (1990). Transitions: Times of change and accommodation. *Topics in Early Childhood Special Education, 9*(4), 1–14.

Rosenkoetter, S.E., Hains, A.H., & Fowler, S.A. (1994). *Bridging early services for children with special needs and their families.* Baltimore: Paul H. Brookes Publishing Co.

Rosenkoetter, S.E., Whaley, K.T., Hains, A.H., & Pierce, L. (2001). The evolution of transition policy for young children with special needs and their families: Past, present, and future. *Topics in Early Childhood Special Education, 21*(1), 3–15.

Rous, B., Hemmeter, M.L., & Schuster, J. (1994). Sequenced transition to education in the public schools: A systems approach to transition planning. *Topics in Early Childhood Special Education, 14*(3), 374–393.

Rule, S., Fiechtl, B.J., & Innocenti, M.S. (1990). Preparation for transition to mainstreamed post-preschool environments: Development of a survival skills curriculum. *Topics in Early Childhood Special Education, 9*(4), 78–90.

Sainato, D.M., & Morrison, R.S. (2001). Transition to inclusive environments of young children with disabilities: Toward a seamless system of service delivery. In M.J. Guralnick (Ed.), *Early childhood inclusion: Focus on change* (pp. 293–306). Baltimore: Paul H. Brookes Publishing Co.

Sainato, D.M., Strain, P.S., Lefebvre, D., & Rapp, N. (1987). Facilitating transition times with handicapped preschool children: A comparison between peer-mediated and antecedent prompt procedures. *Journal of Applied Behavior Analysis, 20,* 285–291.

Sainato, D.M., Strain, P.S., Lefebvre, D., & Rapp, N. (1990). Effects of self-evaluation on the independent work skills of preschool children with disabilities. *Exceptional Children, 56,* 540–549.

Sainato, D.M., Strain, P.S., & Lyon, S.R. (1987), Increasing academic responding of handicapped preschool children during group instruction. *Journal of the Division for Early Childhood, 23,* 23–30.

Salisbury, C.L, & Vincent, L. (1990). Criterion of the next environment and best practices: Mainstreaming and integration 10 years later. *Topics in Early Childhood Special Education, 10*(2), 78–89.

Sandall, S., McLean, M.E., & Smith, B.J. (2000). *DEC recommended practices in early intervention/early childhood special education.* Longmont, CO: Sopris West.

Shotts, C.K., Rosenkoetter, S.E., Streufert, C.A., & Rosenkoetter, L.I. (1994). Transition policy and issues: A view from the states. *Topics in Early Childhood Special Education, 14*(3), 395–411.

U.S. Census Bureau. (2003). *California quick facts.* Retrieved March 26, 2003, from http://quickfacts/census.gov/qfd/states/0600o.html

U.S. Department of Education, Office of Special Education Programs. (2001). *Twenty-third annual report to Congress on the implementation of the Individuals with Disabilities Education Act.* Retrieved March 15, 2003, from http://www.ed.gov/offices/OSERS/OSEP/Research

Vincent, L.J., Salisbury, C., Walter, G., Brown, P., Gruenwald, L.J., & Powers, M. (1980). Program evaluation and curriculum development in early childhood/special education: Criteria for the next environment. In W. Sailor, B. Wilcox, & L. Brown (Eds.), *Methods of instruction for severely handicapped students* (pp. 303–328). Baltimore: Paul H. Brookes Publishing Co.

Wolery, M. (1989). Transitions in early childhood special education: Issues and procedures. *Focus on Exceptional Children, 22*(2), 1–16.

Wolery, M. (1999). Children with disabilities in early elementary school. In R.C. Pianta & M.J. Cox (Eds.), *The transition to kindergarten* (pp. 253–280). Baltimore: Paul H. Brookes Publishing Co.

PRACTICES: INTERNATIONAL PERSPECTIVES

CHAPTER 15

EARLY INTERVENTION IN AUSTRALIA

The Challenge of Systems Implementation

CORAL KEMP AND ALAN HAYES

Early intervention services provision in Australia has been strongly influenced by research, policy, and practice in the United States. The influence is reflected in views of what constitutes good practice; the progressive move from highly directive, professionally focused services to more naturalistic interventions and support services sensitive to the needs of families; and the concern, wherever possible, to provide interventions within generic early childhood services. Keynote speakers invited to conferences on early intervention or special education frequently are prominent authors and researchers from the United States. In turn, Australian policy makers have generally supported the same principles of *best practice* or *recommended practice* that have been developed and adopted over the years in the United States. Each new and exciting development within the field seems to be embraced with enthusiasm in Australia. What is not occurring with the same certainty is the translation of best practice into qualitatively better services for Australian children and families.

The Developmental Systems Model (Guralnick, 2001) acknowledges the need for a well-articulated early intervention system, including screening and referral, intake, assessment, monitoring, intervention, transition planning, and program evaluation. Such a system is designed to ensure that children who are vulnerable and their families are directed to the level of service that will meet their individual needs and to ensure that the stressors that may be associated with child and family factors are adequately addressed. For those interested in early intervention provision in Australia, such a system is likely to be appealing for two reasons. First, it moves beyond the *ad hoc* way in which all services related to early intervention have been delivered in Australia. Second, the proposed model emphasizes principles that have general acceptance within the field. These principles include the following: 1) the pivotal role of the family in promoting the development of children, 2) the integration of services within and across agencies, and 3) the delivery of services within inclusive environments, wherever possible.

The purpose of this chapter is to examine current service provision in Australia in relation to the following: 1) target populations, 2) range of available services, 3) professions and agencies providing services and their interrelationships, 4) availability of services across the target populations, and 5) quality control and accountability. The chapter discusses the effect of each of these on the potential effectiveness of early intervention provision, and the conclusion is that barriers to a systems approach are inherent in current early intervention provision in Australia. These barriers are similar to those identified by Guralnick (2001) in his overview of the Developmental Systems Model and include the following: 1) problems with coordination within and across agencies providing services, including screening, assessment, monitoring, and intervention; 2) lack of appropriate professional training courses to prepare personnel for working in early intervention related services; 3) multiple and uncoordinated funding sources; and 4) lack of independent Australian research, including evaluation research, guiding early intervention policy and provision. Suggestions for minimizing these barriers are addressed, and the potential for an approach to early intervention provision in Australia that is congruent with the Developmental Systems Model is discussed.

The data used in this chapter were gathered from a number of sources. Information relating to government policy and provision was obtained through government-commissioned reports and papers, available in both hard copy and on government web sites; papers published in Australian journals; papers presented at conferences; and locally published books and book chapters. Information on services was sought through direct contact with individual service providers and through questionnaires sent to targeted state government departments. These questionnaires sought information relating to the following: 1) populations in receipt of early intervention services, 2) service providers, 3) sources of funding, 4) referral procedures, 5) professionals working in the field, 6) models of service delivery, and 7) possible gaps in services. Additional information was obtained through state government-initiated reports and, in the case of professional qualifications, through a database of federally funded programs managed by the New South Wales Department of Education and Training. Information on pre- and postservice university training programs in the area of early childhood special education was obtained through the Internet (*Good Universities Guide*, n.d.). This was followed up by perusal of the web sites of all universities offering courses in the areas of education and disability.

POPULATION AND GOVERNMENT

In order to discuss the provision of early intervention services in Australia, it is useful to include a brief overview of the way in which the nation's population is distributed and governed. Most of Australia's population is concentrated in the east, particularly in the southeast, and to a lesser extent in the southwest of the country. The most populous state is New South Wales with 6.5 million people. More than half the country's population lives in either New South Wales or Victoria. People generally live in urban areas, principally in the state and territory capital cities, with a declining number (14% of the population) residing in rural areas (Australian Bureau of Statistics, 2002). There are, however, still many remote towns and settlements, most of which have limited support services (Bailey & du Plessis, 1996).

Australia has a federal system of government whereby the commonwealth government collects most of the taxes and allocates money to each state and territory for the operation of government, including the provision of education, health, and community services. Even though federal law and policy dictate, to some extent, how these monies should be spent, state and territory governments have considerable discretion in relation to program implementation.

Australia has no laws that mandate early intervention services or dictate the way in which intervention services must be delivered to infants and young children with disabilities (Hayes, 1991). Instead, Commonwealth and State Disability Discrimination Acts prohibit discrimination against people with disabilities, including educational discrimination. Such laws support the rights of people with disabilities to have access to services and facilities to which they are entitled.

TARGET POPULATION FOR EARLY INTERVENTION

Definitions of early intervention in Australia, even though influenced by overseas definitions, also have reflected the nature of the populations served in Australian early intervention programs. Historically, these populations have been children with established disabilities or delays. Reflecting this traditional focus, Ashman and Elkins defined *early intervention* as, "a program provided for young children with a disability or an impairment to optimise their chances for enrollment in regular education programs" (1998, p. 524).

Traditionally Targeted Populations

Although limited funding was provided for young children from disadvantaged backgrounds, including indigenous preschool populations, even before the establishment of the first comprehensive early intervention programs for children with disabilities (see Braithwaite, 1983; Teasdale & Whitelaw, 1981), these were not generally referred to, or funded as, early intervention programs. Similarly, neither children born with very low birth weight nor those whose mothers had been involved in substance abuse have been traditional recipients of comprehensive early intervention services in Australia, even though these children are known to have an increased risk of developing disabilities or learning or behavior difficulties (Blair & Ramey, 1997; Olson & Palmer, 1997).

In reviewing early intervention in Australia, Pieterse, Bochner, and Bettison (1988) included an overview of the services provided by each of the states and one Australian territory. In outlining the early intervention services provided, reference was predominantly made only to early intervention services for children with developmental delay and established disability. Jacob (1988), however, stated that unlike children in the other Australian states, Tasmanian children whose development was at risk because of environmental disadvantage were able to gain access to early intervention services. Moore (1988) indicated that even though children born with very low birth weight were monitored by hospitals, there was no routine provision of early intervention for this population in Victoria. This situation is likely to remain not only in Victoria but also more generally in Australia. Again, Tasmania, with its small population and geographical area, is likely to be an exception. A paper describing services for premature infants in Tasmania indicated that infants are not only monitored but also referred to both preventive and, if necessary, comprehensive intervention services (O'Keeffe & Maeder, 2002).

Influence of Funding Systems on the Nature of Populations Served by Comprehensive Early Intervention Programs

Over the years, funding for early intervention programs in Australia has been submission based (Bettison, 1988; Linfoot, 1992) and generally renewable on an annual basis (Linfoot, 1992) with applications for funding that targets children with established disabilities. Most funding for early intervention programs is allocated by state and territory governments and delivered by their departments of education, health, and/or community services, or it is allocated to community-based programs through government departments. The exact nature of the distribution differs from state to state. Direct commonwealth funding for disability services, including early intervention, is intended to support nongovernmental programs and is distributed by departments of education in all states and territories, except for Victoria, where it is distributed by the Department of Human Services (*Commonwealth Programs for Schools*, n.d.). These federal grants are not intended to provide core funding but to *top up* (i.e., supplement) existing funding. Federal top up funding targets individuals with established disabilities, including those with physical, sensory, intellectual, social, and emotional impairment (*Commonwealth Programs for Schools*, n.d.). The guidelines suggest that the recipients of this funding should either have a disability or be able to satisfy the criterion for enrollment in special education programs within the Department of Education in their state of residence once they reach school age. Documentation from relevant qualified professionals (generally medical practitioners or psychologists) supporting the diagnoses for individual children must be available for all children included in applications for federal funding (e.g., New South Wales Department of Education and Training, 2002). Even though the interpretation of federal guidelines differs across states, this particular source of funding generally supports children with established disabilities rather than children who are at environmental or biological risk.

Although the funding from state and territory governments supports programs rather than individual children, the criteria for funding still relate to the disability label. Because funding is not tied to specific children or families, however, it is easier for these programs to accept children without a disability diagnosis. This allows programs to accept children prior to diagnosis and to accept children who are developmentally at risk.

A CHANGING VIEW OF EARLY INTERVENTION

Interest in early intervention or prevention has been increasing since the late 1990s in Australia. This has resulted in a broader definition of early intervention and its target population, with an increased focus on children at risk. This new definition relates to intervening early, both in life and in the pathway to vulnerability, and is no longer used exclusively to describe programs for infants and young children with disabilities or delays (Consortium on Developmental Crime Prevention, 1999). It may also be applied to programs for other populations of infants and young children. Recently,

the New South Wales parliament conducted an inquiry into early intervention for children with learning difficulties. This attracted submissions from
individuals and organizations representing the interests of children with
disabilities and those with specific learning problems (Standing Committee
on Social Issues, 2002a). The Australian Network for Promotion, Prevention, and Early Intervention for Mental Health (AUSEINET), funded by
the Commonwealth Department of Health and Aging, was launched in
1997. Included in its directory of services (Australian Early Intervention
Network for Mental Health in Young People, 1998) are some of the
services available for infants and young children with disabilities, but the
focus is on mental health issues, including services for older people with
mental health problems and adolescents at risk for suicide.

In addition to the change in the use of the term *early intervention*,
which now relates more to prevention in such areas as learning difficulties,
mental health problems, and child abuse, there has been a renewed
acknowledgment of the importance of the early years to human development (Foley et al., 2000; Press & Hayes, 2000). The wider public awareness
of the research on early brain development, and particularly the lifelong
effect of abuse and neglect, has drawn considerable attention to the importance of early intervention (Consortium on Developmental Crime Prevention, 1999; Cynader & Frost, 1999; Nelson, 2000; Shonkoff & Marshall,
2000; Shonkoff & Phillips, 2000). In turn, this has led to a much greater
prominence of interest in early intervention on the part of politicians and
policy makers (Press & Hayes, 2000). Consequently, there has been an
increased interest in the influences on children in the early years of life,
including the importance of family and early care. The interest in early
human development and an economically motivated determination to
invest in prevention have influenced the commonwealth, state, and territory governments to develop initiatives that focus on the needs of young
families, in particular those who are disadvantaged and vulnerable. The
federal initiative, "Stronger Families and Communities Strategy," has
funded numerous projects providing support for families with young children, especially when there is economic or another form of disadvantage,
including the presence of children at risk. The home visiting programs
established through Good Beginnings, a nongovernmental community
organization (Pritchard, 2002), have been funded, in part, by this initiative.
These programs use trained volunteers to support families with children
under school age, particularly when these families are under stress. Initially,
funding was available to support programs at four sites, but currently 38
programs operate across Australia (Polglaise & Paino, 2002).

State and territory governments also have supported family-focused
initiatives. For instance, many have either established or are planning
offices that will specifically target the needs of children. These initiatives

have included the use of schools as community centers in disadvantaged areas in New South Wales and Tasmania (Ambikapathy, 2002). The New South Wales government has established the Families First project, initially in disadvantaged areas, as an initiative aimed at achieving a better-coordinated approach to early intervention and family support. It is anticipated that Families First will eventually be available in all areas of New South Wales. The aim of this project has been to support parents and caregivers in raising children, which will reduce the risk of child neglect and thus have long-term benefits for the community (Office of Children and Young People, 1999). The focus of the Families First project is children up to 3 years old and the education and support of their families. Several government and nongovernmental agencies participate in the project, which aims to enhance parenting skills and assist families to *take control* and to develop coordinated service networks (Office of Children and Young People, 1999).

Implications for the Establishment and Maintenance of a Developmental Systems Model of Early Intervention

The Developmental Systems Model (Guralnick, 2001) targets children who are vulnerable and their families. Accepted practice in North America defines *children who are vulnerable* as those at biological risk of disability, those with established disabilities, and those who are socially disadvantaged (Guralnick, 1997). Even though the importance of parent–child interactions is acknowledged for all three populations, the risk factors and the degree and type of intervention needed across these populations will differ. It would be unlikely, however, that any service provider or funding agency in Australia would deny the importance of some level of intervention with the families of children in each of the categories.

Acknowledging the need is an important first step. The changing use of the term *early intervention* and the focus on a broader range of infants and young children who are vulnerable in papers presented at national conferences reflect a more inclusive approach to early intervention in Australia. The resulting practice might also represent a failure to discriminate between the comprehensive and/or more intensive programs needed for children with established disabilities, particularly those with higher support needs, and services for children whose development needs to be monitored because of biological and/or environmental risk. The latter may have only mild delays and/or risks to intellectual, physical, or social and emotional development and would not require the same degree of professional support. Access to early intervention services in Australia appears to depend more on the availability of programs, the agency involved, and the funding source for these services than on the specific needs of the clients.

The availability of services such as those provided through Good Beginnings and Families First shows that support is available to Australian families with young children who are vulnerable. This is a positive development and one that has been long overdue. It is also important, however, that a consistent approach is taken to identify programs that best meet the needs of the range of children and their families who are in need of early intervention services. It is definitely not a case of *one size fits all*. A more systematic approach to identification, assessment, and referral, such as the Developmental Systems Model (Guralnick, 2001), has the potential to ensure a more equitable and successful early intervention service system in Australia. What is still lacking, however, is a comprehensive national framework for early intervention that enables better planning and coordination of services across the nation.

SERVICE PROVISION

Referral to Services

Children are referred to early intervention services via a number of routes. Respondents from various states and territories reported that children were referred to early intervention by pediatricians, general practitioners, early childhood health nurses, preschools, child care services, and self-referral. Children are more likely to receive an assessment by a cross-disciplinary team if they have a moderate to severe level of disability, and some services require such assessments prior to, or at the time of, enrollment in a program. Parents frequently report these to be difficult experiences but generally acknowledge that they are necessary for access to the appropriate funding for an early intervention, preschool, or school program. Even though efforts are being made to improve intake and assessment systems, these appear to be isolated endeavors. Parents are still reporting that their children's pediatricians or neurologists are not referring them for cross-disciplinary assessments or for interventions, even when the threat to the child's development is great.

Models of Service Delivery

In Australia, a wide range of intervention services is available for children with established disabilities or those at risk of developing disabilities or developmental delays. The models available are influenced by the age of the children; the context in which the service is delivered; the location of the service; the organization or government department responsible for the service; the personnel employed; and, in some cases, the specific disability or the level of the child's disability.

Officers from government departments indicated that a range of services was provided in their states and territories, including home- and center-based services or a combination of the two, itinerant support programs within generic early childhood services, parent support programs such as home visiting programs, clinical and home-based therapy programs, and special playgroups. These services were provided by a range of professionals including teachers, therapists, psychologists, and social workers, in some cases with the assistance of teacher and/or therapy aides.

Metropolitan areas, in particular the capital cities in each state and territory, arguably have the best range of services, whereas gaps are frequently identified in the services available in rural and remote areas (Bailey & du Plessis, 1996; Cocks, 1988; Fyffe, Gavidia-Payne, & McCubbery, 1995; Goodfellow, 1988; Hayes, 1991; Rouse, 1988). Rural and remote areas have difficulty attracting the appropriate professionals, in particular physio-, speech, and occupational therapy staff. Also, services from specific disability organizations, even though readily available in the major cities, are more difficult to gain access to in regional areas. In more remote areas, access may be limited to *any* specialist services for children with disabilities or developmental delays (Bailey & du Plessis, 1996; Kemp, 2001).

Service Providers

In the mid-1970s, when *early intervention* became a commonly used term in reference to the early development and education of infants and young children with intellectual disabilities and multiple disabilities, the first programs were established as model programs in universities and training colleges. The first of these were set up in New South Wales and Victoria and relied on submission-based government funding. The models developed were subsequently adopted and adapted in community settings. This has meant that early intervention services in these states, although primarily funded through government agencies, are generally managed by nongovernmental organizations. Some of these are small, local organizations that were developed on the basis of perceived community need, and others are part of larger disability organizations that are more broadly based. Such programs, even though receiving funding from government sources, also have access to private funding. This is particularly true of programs that provide services to specific categories of disability (e.g., cerebral palsy, physical impairment, sensory impairment, autism).

Early intervention in Australia is aimed at children before they reach compulsory school age, which is age 6 in all states of Australia (Ministerial Council on Education, Employment, Training, and Youth Affairs, 1997).

Children may begin a school program before the age of 6 and as young as 3 years of age for some children with disabilities (see New South Wales Department of Education and Training, 1999). Full-time school-based programs for children younger than age 6 would not receive early intervention funding. In states and territories across Australia, most government departments involved in service provision in the areas of health and education would claim to offer early intervention services. Even though education departments are lead providers of early intervention services in some states, they take only a small role in others. In Queensland and Tasmania, the education departments take responsibility for early intervention provision from the point of diagnosis, which may be at birth for some children. In Queensland, eligibility for services depends on a diagnosis of disability, with the level of service dictated by the severity of disability. Early intervention centers have been established in both states, with therapy and other associated services being provided by other government departments or community organizations. In other states or territories, departments of education may provide early intervention programs to children from 3 years of age (e.g., New South Wales, Australian Capital Territory), but places in these programs are subject to availability.

Departments of education in all states offer generic preschool services from the age of 4 and as early as the age of 3 in some states (Fleer & Udy, 2002). These services are not universally available and are sometimes limited to more disadvantaged areas. Preschool services also are offered by local government and community organizations. All preschool services provide an excellent opportunity for the inclusion of children with disabilities along with typically developing children. Even though the provision of additional staff or consultancy services to cater to children with delays or disabilities is the responsibility of the relevant department, wherever the government provides preschool services, additional funds for community-based preschools are provided through a mixture of state and federal funding. The state government in New South Wales has adopted a brokerage system whereby a peak organization is responsible for the allocation of state money for supporting preschools in which children with disabilities and developmental delays are integrated.

In addition to preschool services, the commonwealth government subsidizes other early childhood services, such as child care, occasional care, and family child care, in order to ensure that they are affordable, particularly for families with low incomes. Targeted federal funds are provided to these centers to enable a child with a disability to gain access to the center and also to provide consultancy services relevant to programming for children with special needs. The difficulties associated with this funding were highlighted by a report on child care in Australia (Commonwealth Child Care Advisory Council, 2001). The report recommended that sources of funding should be more flexible and responsive to differing community needs. Generally, funding to allow a child with a disability to be accommodated in a center is used to provide for an extra member of staff to be present at the center for the time the child is attending. The staff member, who is unlikely to have any training in special education, has to be recruited by the individual center. Funds are limited and often unavailable when needed.

Views Relating to Quality of Service Provision

There is now a set of common beliefs about best practice that is promoted by the agencies involved in both the delivery and the funding of early intervention services (see Beamish & Bryer, 1999; New South Wales Government, 1994). These practices, which have emanated from the United States, focus on the pivotal role that parents play in the facilitation of their children's development.

The importance of a family-focused approach to early intervention has been acknowledged for some time in the Australian literature (Dempsey & Carruthers, 1997; Fyffe et al., 1995; Gavidia-Payne, 1995; Kemp, 1992; Sims, 1995). Although the importance of family participation in early intervention has been acknowledged since the first comprehensive programs were established in Australia (Pieterse, 1988), the move over the years from a more rigid behaviorist approach to less intrusive interventions (Carter & Kemp, 1992) and the acknowledgment of the importance of the caregiving environment to children's development (Foley et al., 2000; Gauntlett, Hugman, Kenyon, & Logan, 2000) have changed the ways in which families have participated in early intervention provision in this country. There has also been acknowledgment that programming within the daily routines and activities in which children engage is a more acceptable and fruitful approach (Hayes, 1991), and this, of course, often means a focus on teaching through play (Copeland, 1995).

A participatory action study conducted by Beamish and Bryer (1999) in Queensland involved the following: 1) the generation of a set of quality practices in programs for infants and preschoolers with disabilities and their families and 2) a validation and rating of the degree of implementation of the listed practices by practitioners working in the field, as well as relevant parents and caregivers. The 31 quality indicators identified by the "experts" included the range of therapy and educational services targeted, assessment procedures, evidence of family-based practices, individualized education plans, team relationships, case management processes, service access, transition plans, and the training and professional competencies of the staff. Even though the families and practitioners responding to the questionnaire validated all 31 indicators, 13 of the indicators were given a frequency rating of less than 50%. Staff training, their professional competencies, and the extent of their feedback to families were rated lowest in terms of their frequency of implementation. It is difficult to say whether these findings are representative of Australia as a whole, but they do highlight the need for improved training of personnel to work in early intervention. It seems, therefore, that even though early intervention stake-holders in Australia might recognize good early intervention practice, they are not confident that such practice is universally available.

Coordination of Early Intervention Services

In Australia, cross-disciplinary services (i.e., those employing a range of different professions) are generally provided by community-based agencies. Even though state government departments all claim to provide early intervention services, there is frequently a problem with any one department providing the full range of professions needed for a comprehensive service. For instance, departments of education typically do not employ therapists, and departments of health typically do not employ teachers. Frequently, however, the services of one government department occur in isolation from the services offered by others. In situations in which the populations and departments are small, closer collaboration among agencies and professionals is likely. In Queensland, Tasmania, and the Australian Capital Territory, the departments of education play an important role in the provision of early intervention services, and these departments are supported with therapy services by the departments of health and community services. Wherever there is a paucity of services, such as in the situation of remote or rural locations, much more cooperation among service providers is likely (McRae, 1997). Even with a demarcation in relation to the services provided by the various departments or agencies, this is unlikely to be an issue in areas in which few services exist.

Echoing earlier national reviews (Hayes et al., 1981; Watts et al., 1981), Bettison (1988) described the development of Australian early intervention services as being ad hoc with inevitable inequalities and gaps in service in every state. All of these early reviews acknowledged that the system for funding early intervention was complex and difficult to navigate and that numerous government and community organizations provided services. As such, coordination of services has always been, and remains, problematic in the provision of early intervention in Australia (Ashby & Taylor, 1988; Bettison, 1988; Bottroff, 1988; Cocks, 1988; Hayes, 1991; Moore, 1988; Rouse, 1988). Recognition of the importance of the provision of coordinated services so that the duplication of services and service gaps might be avoided has resulted in many attempts, both formal and informal, to coordinate services. Because of the number of organizations delivering early intervention in New South Wales, and the fact that no one department has responsibility for the provision or coordination of services, coordination is a particular problem in this state. An interdepartmental working party was established in 1983 in the Northern Metropolitan area of Sydney, New South Wales, for the purpose of preparing guidelines for the management of early intervention. Included in the working party were representatives from all relevant government departments and the principal community-based organizations involved in early intervention service provision in the region. Part of the brief was that one department should be nominated to take responsibility for early intervention services. In its report (Northern Metropolitan Early Intervention Interdepartmental Working Party, 1985), the working party recommended that rather than nominate one government department, more effort should be made to coordinate across departments and community-based organizations. This outcome was not surprising given the interests and biases of the members of the working party. The reason for this decision, as provided by the working party, was that the nomination of one department might lead to the "limited availability of some services that are more frequently available through another department" (p. 31).

The Early Childhood Coordination Project was launched in New South Wales in 1991 with the specific goal of improving the provision of early intervention to families by coordinating both the planning and delivery of services across regions (McRae, 1997; New South Wales Government, 1994). Following the trial of the project in pilot areas, a comprehensive system of area and local committees was established across the state with the aim of coordinating services across government and community agencies. Although a government commissioned evaluation of the project supported its continuation (McRae, 1997), several specific problems were reported, including variability among departments in the level of support for and commitment to the project and problems relating to accountability. A survey of service providers and consumers of early intervention in the state revealed problems with both duplication of and gaps in services. Of the families surveyed for this report, 80% indicated that they used more than one service, with 40% using three or more. The situation in New South Wales mirrored that observed earlier in Queensland (Hayes, 1991).

The report of a New South Wales parliamentary inquiry into early intervention for children with learning disabilities included strong criticisms of children's services in this state (Standing Committee on Social Issues, 2002b). Following submissions from major stakeholders relating to the poor coordination of services for children with all types of difficulties, the committee reported that services were fragmented. They correctly identified participation by three levels of government (federal, state, and local), four agencies within state government, and numerous nongovernmental organizations as the prime contributor to the problems with service coordination. The committee noted that professions tended to work almost exclusively within their own area and that this contributed to the fragmentation of service provision. The report stated, "There is clear evidence that early intervention services have the greatest impact when they address a broad range of issues and are provided as part of a coordinated network" (p. 8).

IMPLICATIONS FOR THE ESTABLISHMENT AND MAINTENANCE OF A DEVELOPMENTAL SYSTEMS MODEL OF EARLY INTERVENTION

Australian early intervention stakeholders clearly value the core principles of the Developmental Systems Model (Guralnick, 2001)—developmental framework, integration, and inclusion. Over the past few years, the focus of Australian literature, government, and community agency policy has been on the importance of the role of parents in the development of their children. This has included an acknowledgment of the difficulties involved in raising young children, the importance of parent–child interactions, and the additional stresses incurred when economic disadvantage, disability, problems with mental health, and lack of extended family and community support also are present. The Commonwealth Government Stronger Families and Communities Strategy is an example of government commitment to supporting families with young children. Furthermore, few comprehensive services for children with established disabilities would admit to not having an individualized family service plan or a family-focused approach to service provision. A report on the New South Wales Early Intervention Coordination Project (McRae, 1997), which surveyed consumer satisfaction with early intervention services in New South Wales, revealed a high level of satisfaction with the early intervention services received and with the level of family centeredness. Similarly, a survey by Beamish and Bryer (1999) of families and service providers in Queensland and another by Dempsey and Carruthers (1997) of families and service providers in New South Wales also indicated high levels of implementation of practices associated with family centeredness. Other surveys, however, have been less positive and have revealed some dissatisfaction with professional responsiveness to individual family needs (Bailey & du Plessis, 1996; Fyffe et al., 1995).

The concern in all states and territories to improve the coordination of services across agencies is evidence of the recognition that such coordination is important if duplication and gaps in services are to be minimized. Unfortunately, despite numerous committees and projects established to tackle problems of agency coordination, there is still clearly a problem with coordination of services, especially in the major cities that have many services and competing interests. There is also evidence of problems with the integration of services within agencies (Standing Committee on Social Issues, 2002b). This is likely to be particularly problematic within disability organizations that focus on one disability area (e.g., physical disability) and in which one profession dominates. In such cases, the employment of professions outside of the disability area may create problems for the integration of services. Funding policy may also impinge on service integration. For instance, in New South Wales Commonwealth, funding for early intervention targets educational rather than therapy programs and is used by some organizations to pay for teachers. The fact that this money is not necessarily recurrent and is limited to a small amount per child means that the educational program may be seen as an *add on*, and teachers may be considered to be relatively unimportant in the organization. This is likely to affect the way in which the services are prioritized and delivered, including the degree of integration of services.

Low-cost, generic early childhood services are available to most children and their families in Australia (Foley et al., 2000). The focus of federal funding on programs promoting the inclusion of children with disabilities in generic early childhood services also is evidence of government commitment to inclusive services for children with established disabilities and those at risk of disability or delay. The dominance of specific disability service providers and the fact that most comprehensive early intervention programs have a major center-based component, however, means that a majority of government funding is supporting segregated rather than inclusive programs. Llewellyn, Thompson, and Fante (2002) identified a number of challenges to the inclusion of children with disabilities in early childhood services following surveys of 1,195 children's services in metropolitan and regional areas of New South Wales. Among the impediments to inclusion identified by the authors were 1) the multiple sources of government funding and the need for a diagnosis in order to be deemed eligible for funding, 2) the inability of services to employ staff capable of meeting the needs of children with disabilities, and 3) the philosophical and geographic distance between specialist and generic services. The fact that fewer than 15% of the children were integrated in early childhood services other than preschools provides further evidence of the difficulties of funding and supporting inclusion in services such as long-term child care, occasional care, family child care, and mobile services.

Although Australia has a great deal of philosophical support for the three core principals of the Developmental Systems Model (Guralnick, 2001), clearly this does not always translate into practice. Major impediments to the implementation of these principles are 1) problems with agency commitment to coordination; 2) a complex, fragmented funding system; and 3) the lack of appropriate training of personnel working in the field, including those who are guiding policy development in the area. In addition, Australian research to guide the development of services within the Australian context is limited.

RESEARCH, PROGRAM EVALUATION, AND TRAINING

It is evident that what is considered to be best practice is not extensively based on empirical evidence but rather reflects current trends or expert opinion. As stated at the outset, Australia has largely adopted and adapted early intervention programs developed in the United States. There is a dearth of research on early intervention provision in Australia, and the contribution of the Australian literature to accepted best practice is limited. Much of the available Australian research is process rather than outcome evaluation research, the majority of which is by way of government-commissioned report. Some of these reports are never released, and others appear to have limited impact because of the funding implications. Clearly, more strategic and independent research is necessary to provide a solid informational database that can be used to inform the nature of early intervention service provision in Australia.

Program accountability also is of concern. In New South Wales, where most comprehensive early intervention programs are provided by nongovernmental organizations, the application and accountability process for basic funding is time consuming, and the decision process is not always transparent. Until recently, the applications for state government funding were to be submitted annually, and such submissions have varied from year to year in relation to their timing and the information solicited. In 2000, the annual submissions for funding were replaced by accountability returns, which essentially focused on financial rather than program accountability. From time to time, expressions of interest have been solicited with the view to extending funding where it is needed, but sometimes the submission process is bypassed altogether with monies being directly allocated to targeted early intervention programs. This can leave unsuccessful applicants frustrated by the time-consuming exercise, and the danger is that organizations from more affluent areas can be allocated funds to provide services in less affluent communities in which they have had no history of service provision. Given that accountability has never included rigorous program evaluation, unsuccessful applicants can only wonder about the decision-making process and the political influences.

One of the major impediments to implementing the Developmental Systems Model (Guralnick, 2001) in Australia is the lack of adequately trained personnel working in the area of early intervention. Apart from basic training related to facilitating growth within and across developmental areas, additional skills also are required. If part of the role of the early intervention service provider is to assess the family- and child-related stressors, then the skills for such an assessment must be an important part of the early interventionist's repertoire. Similarly, if the ability to work as part of a cross-disciplinary team in both the assessment and intervention process is important, then team-related skills ought to be included in an initial training program. Personnel training has been identified as an area of concern in the United States (Bailey, 1996; Klein & Gilkerson, 2000; Malone, Straka, & Logan, 2000; Winton, 2000). The situation may be even more critical in Australia.

The 2002 database containing the qualifications of the staff working in programs receiving federal funding for early intervention and preschool services for children with disabilities in New South Wales (393 projects) provides a disturbing picture of the level of training for staff working with children in both inclusive and segregated services. Of those employed specifically by early intervention services ($N = 521$), separate from those employed by preschools integrating children with disabilities, a minority have been trained in special education (23.4%) and even fewer have been trained in both early childhood and special education (7.7%). Although individual staff members claim to have a qualification in special education, this is frequently not a named qualification in either special education or early childhood special education. The information provided by respondents would suggest that sometimes their special education training consists of a small number of electives in special education taken as part of their generalist training. Although 145 of the staff employed by early intervention services are qualified therapists, only 3 have had additional training in special education. Personnel with general education qualifications (8%) also are employed in early intervention services. Very few staff members (26) have qualifications in social work or psychology, and no medical practitioners are listed as working in early intervention services. The qualifications of personnel working in preschools that are supported by federal money to integrate children with disabilities in New South Wales are even poorer. Of these personnel, 25% are untrained, only 7% have any special education training, and only 6 of the 1,018 staff members are qualified in one of the related therapies.

Very few university courses across Australia specifically target training in early intervention. Although institutions advertise early intervention courses, some are equivalent to 6 months of full-time study. When the courses involve a year or more of study, a closer inspection of the content reveals that very few units are specifically relevant to early intervention. Early intervention has a cross-disciplinary focus and therefore requires cross-disciplinary training. Such preservice training is not generally available in Australia.

CONCLUSION

Australia has many examples of exemplary practice in early intervention. Unfortunately, access to best practice is not universal. As in other areas of early childhood in Australia, the lack of a national framework contributes both to the lack of uniformity in the availability of services across the nation as well as to the lack of coordination of the services offered within the states and territories (Press & Hayes, 2000). In addition, the lack of a national framework also leads to problems with the articulation of early intervention and the services that are provided by schools and other community services later in life.

Several Australian researchers have examined the problems of transition and articulation (see Chadwick & Kemp, 2002; Green & Kemp, 1998; Hawke & Hayes, 1993; Kemp & Carter, 2000). Their findings resonate with the pleas of Brooks-Gunn (2003) and Farran (2000) for a clearer recognition of the factors that sustain the impact of early intervention. They collectively highlight the need for any framework for early intervention to consider the developmental supports that are needed to sustain the effects of early intervention across the years that follow. A developmental systems approach to early intervention would assist with the provision of quality intervention services to all children who are vulnerable and their families as well as stimulate a national focus on an articulated system of supports following early intervention that sustains the benefits of best practice. The Developmental Systems Model (Guralnick, 2001) provides an excellent basis for such a national framework, given its congruence with the priorities identified by Australian policy makers and practitioners.

Guralnick (2001) identified the action needed to develop the critical components of the Developmental Systems Model. Because many of the barriers to the implementation of such a system are common to both countries, Guralnick's suggestions for change provide a useful guide for the Australian context. In order to overcome the barriers to implementing his model, political will is required to ensure that it is effectively implemented to achieve both coordination and articulation of services.

The development of highly specific training for early intervention service provision is another aspect of a national framework that is critical to the operation of more professional, yet family-focused, services. This training also will contribute to better-integrated services, with levels of support provided according to need. A nationally coordinated approach to education and training has implications beyond those typically associated with early intervention, if the development of more inclusive services is to be a priority. Increased funding for independent research, a requirement for objective program evaluation, and a transparent and comprehensive funding system for early intervention would contribute to enhancing the quality of Australian services.

Finally, those who are developing government policy in the area of early intervention should also have access to cross-disciplinary training and possess a healthy respect for the findings of independent, objective research. To be effective, a national framework must be strongly informed by the research literature and provide an explicit base for the development of early intervention services that are first and foremost evidence based. National developments, such as the establishment of the Australian Research Alliance for Children and Youth (ARACY), recognize the importance of early intervention as well as the need for better coordination of cross-disciplinary research, particularly for children who are vulnerable, their families, and their communities. Equal weight is given by ARACY, however, to the need to develop and appropriately evaluate early intervention services that are evidence based and that inform national policies and practices. Again, a national framework for early intervention incorporating the key elements of Guralnick's (2001) Developmental Systems Model, with strong connections between research, policy, and practice, is a vital next step for the further development of early intervention in Australia. This step would seem entirely consistent with international best practice.

REFERENCES

Ambikapathy, P. (2002, September). *The role of the commissioner for children in Tasmania with respect to advocacy for early childhood services in health, welfare, care, protection and development.* Paper presented at the Early Childhood Intervention Australia Biennial Conference, Hobart, Australia.

Ashby, G., & Taylor, J. (1988). Early intervention in Queensland. In M. Pieterse, S. Bochner, & S. Bettison (Eds.), *Early intervention for children with disabilities: The Australian experience* (pp. 33–42). Sydney: Special Education Centre, Macquarie University.

Ashman, A., & Elkins, J. (Eds.). (1998). *Educating children with special needs.* Sydney: Prentice Hall.

Australian Bureau of Statistics. (2002, June). *Population distribution: Year book Australia 2002.* Retrieved February 3, 2003, from http://www.abs.gov.au/ausstats.

Australian Early Intervention Network for Mental Health in Young People. (1998). *National stocktake of early intervention programs.* Bedford Park, South Australia: Author.

Bailey, D.B., Jr. (1996). An overview of interdisciplinary training. In D. Bricker & A.H. Widerstrom (Eds.), *Preparing personnel to work with infants and young children and their families: A team approach* (pp. 3–21). Baltimore: Paul H. Brookes Publishing Co.

Bailey, J., & du Plessis, D. (1996). Isolated parents' and service providers' perceptions of the education of their children with disabilities. Sydney: The Australian Association of Special Education.

Beamish, W., & Bryer, F. (1999). Practitioners and parents have their say about best practice: Early intervention in Queensland. *International Journal of Disability, Development, and Education, 46,* 261–278.

Bettison, S. (1988). Overview of early intervention services in Australia. In M. Pieterse, S. Bochner, & S. Bettison (Eds.), *Early intervention for children with disabilities: The Australian experience* (pp. 3–5). Sydney: Special Education Centre, Macquarie University.

Blair, C., & Ramey, C.T. (1997). Early intervention for low-birth-weight infants and the path to second-generation research. In M.J. Guralnick (Ed.), *The effectiveness of early intervention* (pp. 77–97). Baltimore: Paul H. Brookes Publishing Co.

Bottroff, V. (1988). Early intervention in South Australia. In M. Pieterse, S. Bochner, & S. Bettison (Eds.), *Early intervention for children with disabilities: The Australian experience* (pp. 43–53). Sydney: Special Education Centre, Macquarie University.

Braithwaite, J. (1983). *Explorations in early childhood education.* Hawthorne, Victoria: Australian Council for Educational Research.

Brooks-Gunn, J. (2003). Do you believe in magic?: What we can expect from early childhood intervention programs. *Society for Research in Child Development Social Policy Report, 17*(1), 3–15.

Carter, M., & Kemp, C. (1992). On maintaining your centre of gravity over your base of support: A response to Hinton and Ballard. *Australasian Journal of Special Education, 15,* 41–43.

Chadwick, D., & Kemp, C. (2002). Critical factors of successful transition to mainstream kindergarten for children with disabilities. *Australasian Journal of Special Education, 26,* 50–68.

Cocks, E. (1988). Early intervention in Western Australia. In M. Pieterse, S. Bochner, & S. Bettison (Eds.), *Early intervention for children with disabilities: The Australian experience* (pp. 55–62). Sydney: Special Education Centre, Macquarie University.

Commonwealth Child Care Advisory Council. (2001, September). *Child care beyond 2001: A report to the Minister for Family and Community Services.* Canberra, Australian Capital Territory: Commonwealth Australia.

Commonwealth programs for schools. Administrative guidelines for schools, 2001–2004. (n.d.) Retrieved September 7, 2002, from http://www.dest.gov.au/schools/guidelines/quadrennial/2001-04/Guidelines2002.pdf

Consortium on Developmental Crime Prevention. (1999). *Developmental and early intervention approaches to crime in Australia.* Canberra, Australian Capital Territory: National Crime Prevention, Commonwealth Attorney General's Department.

Copeland, I. (1995). Developmentally appropriate practice and early childhood special education. *Australian Journal of Early Childhood, 20*(4), 1–4.

Cynader, M.S., & Frost, B.J. (1999). Mechanisms of brain development: Neuronal sculpting by the physical and social environment. In D.P. Keating & C. Hertzman (Eds.), *Developmental health and the wealth of nations: Social, biological and educational dynamics* (pp. 153–184). New York: The Guilford Press.

Dempsey, I., & Carruthers, A. (1997). How family-centered are early intervention services?: Staff and parent perceptions. *Journal of Australian Research in Early Childhood Education, 1*, 105–114.

Farran, D.C. (2000). Another decade of intervention for children who are low income or disabled: What do we know now? In J.P. Shonkoff & S.J. Meisels (Eds.), *Handbook of early childhood intervention* (2nd ed., pp. 510–548). New York: Cambridge University Press.

Fleer, M., & Udy, G. (2002). Australian Bureau of Statistics. Early years education in Australia. *Year Book Australia 2002*. Retrieved December 6, 2002, from http://www.abs.gov.au/ausstats/ABS9640.nsf

Foley, D., Goldfeld, S., McGloughlin, J., Nagorcka, J., Oberlaid, F., & Wake, M. (2000, February). *A review of the early childhood literature.* (Available from the Department of Family and Community Services, Commonwealth of Australia.)

Fyffe, C., Gavidia-Payne, S.T., & McCubbery, J. (1995). Early intervention and families in rural Victoria. *Australian Journal of Early Childhood, 20*(4), 34–39.

Gauntlett, E., Hugman, R., Kenyon, P., & Logan, P. (2000, March). *A meta-analysis of the impact of community-based prevention and early intervention action.* Retrieved September 7, 2002, from http://www.facs.gov.au/internet/facs internet.nsf/aboutfacs/respub s/research-PolicyResPaperSeries.htm

Gavidia-Payne, S.T. (1995). Contemporary perspectives in the study of families of young children with disabilities: Implications for policy and practice. *Australian Journal of Early Childhood, 20*(4), 11–18.

Good Universities Guide. (n.d.). Retrieved July 17, 2002, from http://www.thegood guides.com.au

Goodfellow, J. (1988). Early intervention in New South Wales. In M. Pieterse, S. Bochner, & S. Bettison (Eds.), *Early intervention for children with disabilities: The Australian experience* (pp. 7–20). Sydney: Special Education Centre, Macquarie University.

Green, I., & Kemp, C. (1998). Transition: Support issues for teachers integrating young children with disabilities into mainstream classes. *Special Education Perspectives, 7*(1), 4–16.

Guralnick, M.J. (1997). Second generation research in the field of early intervention. In M.J. Guralnick (Ed.), *The effectiveness of early intervention* (pp. 3–20). Baltimore: Paul H. Brookes Publishing Co.

Guralnick, M.J. (2001). A developmental systems model for early intervention. *Infants and Young Children, 14*(2), 1–18.

Hawke, A., & Hayes, A. (1993). Beyond early intervention: An initial follow-up of children who participated in an early intervention program in a Queensland provincial city. *Australasian Journal of Special Education, 17*, 33–41.

Hayes, A. (1991). The changing face of early intervention: Following fads and fashions? In K. Marfo (Ed.), *Early intervention in transition: Current perspectives on programs for handicapped children* (pp. 271–298). New York: Praeger.

Hayes, A., Steinberg, M., Cooksley, E., Jobling, A., Best, D., & Coulston, A. (1981). *Special preschools: Monitoring a pilot project. Project Report.* St. Lucia, Queensland: Fred and Eleanor Schonell Educational Research Centre.

Jacob, A. (1988). Early intervention in Tasmania. In M. Pieterse, S. Bochner, & S. Bettison (Eds.), *Early intervention for children with disabilities: The Australian experience* (pp. 63–66). Sydney: Special Education Centre, Macquarie University.

Kemp, C. (1992). Distinctive features of early intervention services within early childhood education. *Special Education Perspectives, 1*(1), 3–14.

Kemp, C. (2001). Interview with student and practitioner, Natalie Fazldeen. *Early Links, 6*(2), 12–16.

Kemp, C., & Carter, M. (2000). Demonstration of classroom survival skills in kindergarten: A five-year transition study of children with intellectual disabilities. *Educational Psychology, 20*, 393–411.

Klein, N.K., & Gilkerson, L. (2000). Personnel preparation for early childhood intervention programs. In J.P. Shonkoff & S.J. Meisels (Eds.), *The handbook of early childhood intervention* (2nd ed., pp. 444–483). New York: Cambridge University Press.

Linfoot, K. (1992). The delivery of early intervention services for infants and preschool children: A ten year retrospective. *Australasian Journal of Special Education, 16*(1), 42–47.

Llewellyn, G., Thompson, K., & Fante, M. (2002). Inclusion in early childhood services: Ongoing challenges. *Australian Journal of Early Childhood, 27*(3), 12–23.

Malone, D.M., Straka, E., & Logan, K.R. (2000). Professional development in early intervention: Creating effective inservice training opportunities. *Infants and Young Children, 12*(4), 53–62.

McRae, D. (1997, September). *The early intervention co-ordination project in New South Wales: An evaluation.* Unpublished report.

Ministerial Council on Education, Employment, Training, and Youth Affairs. (1997). *National report on schooling in Australia.* Melbourne: Curriculum Corporation.

Moore, T. (1988). Early intervention in Victoria. In M. Pieterse, S. Bochner, & S. Bettison (Eds.), *Early intervention for children with disabilities: The Australian experience* (pp. 21–31). Sydney: Special Education Centre, Macquarie University.

Nelson, C.A. (2000). The neurobiological bases of early intervention. In J.P. Shonkoff & S.J. Meisels (Eds.), *Handbook of early childhood intervention* (2nd ed. pp. 204–227). New York: Cambridge University Press.

New South Wales Department of Education and Training. (1999). *Who's going to teach my child: A guide for parents of children with special learning needs.* Sydney: Author.

New South Wales Department of Education and Training. (2002). *Intervention support program: Guidelines 2003.* Sydney: Author.

New South Wales Government. (1994). *Disability direction: Tomorrow's blueprint. Coordinating early intervention services.* Sydney: Author.

Northern Metropolitan Early Intervention Interdepartmental Working Party. (1985, August). *Early intervention guidelines: Report of the working party on establishment, implementation and operation of all programs of an early intervention nature for the northern metropolitan region.* Unpublished report.

Office of Children and Young People. (1999). *Families first state framework.* Sydney: New South Wales Government.

O'Keeffe, F., & Maeder, D. (2002, September). *Monitoring and supporting premature babies.* Paper presented at the Early Childhood Intervention Australia Biennial Conference, Hobart, Australia.

Olson, H.C., & Palmer, F.B. (1997). Early intervention for children prenatally exposed to alcohol and other drugs. In M.J. Guralnick (Ed.), *The effectiveness of early intervention* (pp. 109–145). Baltimore: Paul H. Brookes Publishing Co.

Pieterse, M. (1988). Services for children with disabilities and model programs. Introduction. In M. Pieterse, S. Bochner, & S. Bettison (Eds.), *Early intervention for children with disabilities: The Australian experience* (pp. 77–80). Sydney: Special Education Centre, Macquarie University.

Pieterse, M., Bochner, S., & Bettison, S. (Eds.). (1988). *Early intervention for children with disabilities: The Australian experience.* Sydney: Special Education Centre, Macquarie University.

Polglaise, L., & Paino, K. (2002, September). *Volunteer home visiting and professional family support program.* Paper presented at the Early Childhood Intervention Australia Biennial Conference, Hobart, Australia.

Press, F., & Hayes, A. (2000). *OECD thematic review of early childhood education and care policy: Australian background report.* Retrieved July 10, 2002, from http://www.facs.gov.au/internet/facsinternet.nsf/childcare/servicesoecd_review_early _childhood_ed.htm

Pritchard, P. (2002, September). *How wide is my family?* Paper presented at the Early Childhood Intervention Australia Biennial Conference, Hobart, Australia.

Rouse, J. (1988). Early intervention in Northern Territory. In M. Pieterse, S. Bochner, & S. Bettison (Eds.), *Early intervention for children with disabilities: The Australian experience* (pp. 67–73). Sydney: Special Education Centre, Macquarie University.

Shonkoff, J.P., & Marshall, P.C. (2000). The biology of developmental vulnerability. In J.P. Shonkoff & S.J. Meisels (Eds.), *Handbook of early childhood intervention* (2nd ed., pp. 35–53). New York: Cambridge University Press.

Shonkoff, J.P., & Phillips, D.A. (Eds.). (2000). *From neurons to neighborhoods.* Washington, DC: National Academy Press.

Sims, M. (1995). Early intervention: Where have we been and where are we going? *Australian Journal of Early Childhood, 20*(4), 40–46.

Standing Committee on Social Issues Legislative Council New South Wales Parliament. (2002a). *Foundations for learning: A new vision for New South Wales* (Issues Paper 4).

Standing Committee on Social Issues Legislative Council New South Wales Parliament. (2002b). *Early child development: A co-coordinated approach. First Report on early intervention for children with learning difficulties* (Report 27).

Teasdale, G.R., & Whitelaw, A.J. (1981). *The early childhood education of Aboriginal Australians: A review of six action-research projects.* Hawthorne, Victoria: Australian Council for Educational Research.

Watts, B.H., Elkins, J., Conrad, L.M., Andrews, R.J., Apelt, W.C., Hayes, A., Calder, J., Coulston, A.J., & Willis, M. (1981). *Early intervention programs for young handicapped children in Australia 1979–1980.* St. Lucia, Queensland: Fred and Eleanor Schonell Educational Research Centre.

Winton, P.J. (2000). Early childhood intervention personnel preparation: Backward mapping for future planning. *Topics in Early Childhood Special Education, 20,* 87–94.

CHAPTER 16

A DEVELOPMENTAL COMMUNICATIONS MODEL WITHIN THE EARLY INTERVENTION SYSTEM IN AUSTRIA

MANFRED PRETIS

Whenever parents enter an early intervention system after having gone through several steps of screening and/or comprehensive interdisciplinary assessment (Guralnick, 2001), their emotional situation can be described as highly anxious, fluctuating between the hope of obtaining adequate support and the fear that the diagnosis may be more serious (Pretis, 2001a). This emotional ambiguity requires highly transparent communication between professionals and parents because the involvement of parents in the psychosocial environment is of crucial importance for both the long-term effects of the intervention and on the development of the child (Kuehl, 2002).

This chapter provides a description of communication strategies for professionals within the different phases of the early intervention process in Austria, and it is based on the assumption that parents enter the early intervention system voluntarily and have a basic interest in the development of their child. It is hoped that this systemic model could serve as a guideline for many components of the early intervention system, including the Developmental Systems Model (Guralnick, 2001). Austria's developmental communications model is based on a partnership model of early intervention that emphasizes the importance of shared and defined responsibility between parents and professionals (Speck, 1983). The partners, especially the professionals, require a model that includes 1) transparency of communication; 2) parental competence in child rearing; 3) definition of responsibilities, functions, and goals; and 4) contract-based interventions. The model (as an abstract reduction of reality) relies on continuous exit and feedback strategies and defines early intervention as a process of interaction.

A structured communication model is necessary, especially within the current European discussion concerning quality criteria in early intervention (Pretis, 2002b), because organizations providing services are increasingly obliged to define their standards and procedures. Within this context, particularly in urban areas with easy access to services and information media (the Internet), a new model of interaction between parents and services—the consumer model—has been developed. Children with disabilities or their parents tend to *consume* and/or compare services. In some European countries, people with disabilities with the financial means also employ professionals rather than use existing intervention services.

DEVELOPMENTAL COMMUNICATIONS MODEL

Parents of children with developmental delays or social risks enter early intervention intake structures with a high level of stress. Therefore, professional communication strategies should, at a minimum, provide a secure base for the parents by providing stress reduction, transparency, and intersubjectivity in terms of quality control. A set of defined communication rules has two functions: 1) to give structure to the parents in terms of defined interventions and 2) to provide a theoretical framework for the inexperienced professional.

Early intervention, despite the variety of approaches and applied methods, can be described by means of defined communication steps. Generally, in Austria, early intervention (within one monitoring period) will be *prescribed* for 1 year, and children at biological and/or social risk or with an established disability will remain in the program, on average, for 2 years (Pretis, 2002a). These programs are mostly free of charge and provided by decentralized services (mostly nongovernmental organizations). Intake into the program requires a defined medical or psychological diagnosis and at least minimal cooperation by the parents. Furthermore, 20% of the children at biological and/or social risk or with an established disability do not need any further special educational support (e.g., specialized child care centers, special education in school; Pretis, 2000a).

Despite heterogeneous forms of service provision (88 centers provide early intervention), every professional contact consists of a set of hierarchical steps including 1) first contact, 2) attachment, 3) assessment or diagnostic procedures, 4) goal-oriented work, 5) reflection, and 6) final evaluation. Table 16.1 shows the basic requirements for both parents and professionals within the different phases.

Table 16.1. Hierarchical steps within the process of early intervention

Step	Goal	Basic service requirements	Basic professional requirements	Basic parental requirements
1) **First contact**	Information, first contact with the child, collection and assessment of available data, defining basis of cooperation with the parents	Accessibility of the service, information management system	Knowledge about the structure of the service and the intervention process, capacity to reflect on personal function and role, empathy	Minimal interest, ability to communicate their needs, voluntary acceptance of the necessity of the offered service, intellectual capacity to understand the formal requirements
2) **Attachment** (first and second months)	Definition of a minimal consensus, gradual increase in attachment to the child by means of child-centered activities	Defined framework agreement on when, where, with whom, and what; continuity of contact	Capacity to form relationships and to perceive and handle emotions, empathy, patience; at ease with the model used	Respect of terms, minimal interest in questions of child-rearing, reliable in keeping appointments
3) Goal-oriented **diagnostic** phase (third month)	Contracting goals with the parents in terms of 1) child-centered work, 2) family work, and 3) inter-disciplinary work	Adequate pedagogical assessment instruments (e.g., question-naires, screening tests), defined time frame	Knowledge on how to assess the needs of the child, the parents, and the interdisciplinary team; ability to communicate goals	Minimal motivation, perceptive of the judgment of others, respect of the professional partner's assessment
4) **Phase of goal-oriented work** (fourth through sixth months)	Supporting the resources of the child, the parents, and the relevant environment with suitable methods	Adequate means and techniques, support from the interdisciplinary team	Knowledge about techniques and methods of developmental support, the ability to work in a team, and the ability to counsel; stable personality	Minimal consensus concerning the methods

(continued)

Table 16.1.   *(continued)*

Step	Goal	Basic service requirements	Basic professional requirements	Basic parental requirements
5) **Reflection** on goals (sixth month)	Reflection on the ongoing process: Are we doing the right thing? Are we applying the right methods? Can we explain our interventions?	Defined time frame and adequate techniques (e.g., video, rating scales)	Capacity for personal reflection and reflection on others, capacity to evaluate intervention processes, ability to formulate and accept requests, ability to differentiate between personal and professional goals	Capacity to reflect on the work with the child and on changes within the family system, capacity to define wishes
6) **Continued goal-oriented work** (sixth through eleventh months)	See 4	See 4	See 4	See 4
7) **Final evaluation** (twelfth month) = possible new diagnostic phase (see 3)	End of goal-oriented work, assessment of the outcomes, definition of further steps, ease of transition into other systems	Information concerning further steps and services, structures to avoid lack of information during phases of transition	Capacity to finish processes and to establish new structures, ability to terminate professional relationships	Interest in the future development of the child, sufficient self-esteem to deal with challenging situations, acceptance of other support services

From Pretis, M. (2001a). *Fruehfoerderung planen, durchführen, evaluieren* (Planning, performing, and evaluating early intervention) (p. 36). Muenchen: Reinhardt; reprinted by permission.

First Contact

Many times, parents are confronted with repetitive questions about their children, and parents are often too tired to describe their worries or stress. Professionals tend to interpret parents instead of listening, especially in this first phase of early intervention (see Table 16.2). In the first 2 months of early intervention, the professional should be concerned not only with collecting information but also with creating a basis for cooperation that means respecting the existing interaction pattern in the family.

Table 16.2. Starting the process of early intervention

Associated questions		Feedback/exit strategies
1. Identification and function of professional, brief information concerning the intake process: Does the client need this specific service? Yes	No	Information about alternatives Referral to the responsible service; when possible, name of contact people with telephone numbers
2. Do the parents have enough information about the service? Yes	No	Brief information about the service: who are we, what services do we offer? Or, information folder by mail
3. Is it convenient for us to talk now? Yes	No	Organize the possibility to call again when it is convenient.
4. A short description of the problems and reasons why our service was contacted: Is our service responsible? Yes	No	Do we need more information (e.g., screening, interdisciplinary assessment)?
5. Information about the next steps (i.e., definition of the setting, continuity, attachment phase with the child): Do the parents want this service? Yes	No	Offer information on alternatives or the possibility to start at a later date. Give more information about the service.
6. Are we able to define the next steps (i.e., when, who, what; e.g., administrative procedures in most European systems)? Yes	No	How can we stay in contact?
7. Are both parties clear about the next steps? (Careful! Parents may be very stressed in such situations.)	No	Do parents need clear instructions? Feedback possibilities: telephone numbers, directions, fax numbers

From Pretis, M. (2001a). *Fruehfoerderung planen, durchführen, evaluieren* (Planning, performing, and evaluating early intervention) (pp. 42–43). Muenchen: Reinhardt; reprinted by permission.

Attachment

In early intervention, creating rapport with the child and the family is seen as a professional process (see Table 16.3). The professional has to establish a secure base for the child and family to enable goal-oriented work. Basic features of attachment are 1) reduction of distress by means of anticipation (e.g., by using rituals for the child), 2) respect and care for family values (especially if professionals work in home-based programs), 3) nonintrusion into the world of the child and family (e.g., observing how

Table 16.3. Attachment-related communication strategies

Associated questions		Feedback/exit strategies
1. Do we have minimal consensus about the setting? Yes	No	What do we need to reach a minimal consensus concerning the setting? Is there a personal problem between professional and parents? Are there any alternatives?
2. Is it possible to discuss the expectations of the early intervention? Yes	No	If the parents do not show any interest, then early intervention may not be suitable. Possible alternatives should be discussed (e.g., child care center).
3. Is it possible to identify associations of the child and family (e.g., strengths, likes)? Is there a consensus within the interdisciplinary team (e.g., about family functioning)? Yes	No	Analysis: Why it is so difficult to recognize positive resources? Possible alternative: psychotherapy for the family.
4. Are there any signs of relaxation after the first units of early intervention? Yes	No	What can we do to create a low-stress/relaxing environment for the family and the child?
5. Can an individual identify rituals within the early intervention units (e.g., a coffee break after the work has been done, recognition of toys, recognition of the structure of the unit)? Yes	No	Active implementation of structure and rituals during the units
6. Start of the diagnostic procedure within early intervention (definition of pedagogical goals)		

From Pretis, M. (2001a). *Fruehfoerderung planen, durchführen, evaluieren* (Planning, performing, and evaluating early intervention) (p. 61). Muenchen: Reinhardt; reprinted by permission.

the child is *constructing* his or her world), 4) show of confidence and professional competence (e.g., by clear definition of the steps), and 5) self-disclosure (e.g., giving information about personal and professional background).

Both parents and professionals often are too impatient to establish attachment. Parents show dissatisfaction, especially in instances involving children with established disabilities (e.g., Down syndrome), if the professional does not immediately start with the program (Pretis, 1998b). Pretis (2000b) pointed out that the activity of the child is one of the basic principles in most European early intervention systems. This implies that, in the first contact, professionals should observe the child's strategies and how the child interacts with his or her surroundings.

Diagnostic

The huge challenge in the field of pedagogical diagnostics presents itself in three ways in this process. The first challenge is focusing on the resources of the child and the family. Traditional medical and psychological diagnostics tend to describe *impairments* of the child in order to compensate for them. Pedagogical diagnostics tend to assess potential skills in order to reach developmental goals with these additional skills. Even though there is not yet a systematic methodology for a resource-oriented diagnostic process, experts should still use a positive method for describing the child and family.

The second challenge is describing prognostic goals based on diagnostic status (see Table 16.4). These goals depend to a great extent on the theoretical background of the professional (e.g., Piaget, behavioral approaches). As of 2004, there is no recognized pedagogical algorithm for how to define goals based on pedagogical assessments. At least three groups of approaches can be recognized: 1) descriptive—abilities and impairments of the child by means of standardized methods; 2) reconstructive—functional assessment and reconstruction and how the child interacts in a meaningful way with the environment; and 3) relation-based—how the child is interacting with the professional and what the professional can offer based on his or her interaction skills (Pretis, 2001a). There cannot be an assessment of the child and/or the family without interaction. This means that every attribution, assessment, and test in the diagnostic process is regarded as a possible way to interact and exchange. Only a minimum consensus within the interaction process enables a goal-oriented contract between parents and the professional (see Table 16.3).

The third challenge is recognizing that defined pedagogical goals only correlate to a limited extent with intervention methods. A defined goal can be reached by different methods, and in turn, a variety of methods can be used to reach one goal (Petermann, Kusch, & Niebank, 1998).

Numerous standardized tests, rating scales, and questionnaires are used in this field (see Guralnick, 2001); however, it is worth mentioning that this diagnostic process—because of the complexity of the early intervention process—has to include at least the following features: 1) child orientation and developmental goals of the child; 2) family orientation, family functioning, and support of siblings; and 3) interdisciplinary cooperation. These

Table 16.4.   Pedagogical diagnostics as a process of interaction

Associated questions		Feedback/exit strategies
1. Is there a secure attachment toward the parents and the child that enables open discussion concerning goals and methods of early intervention? **Yes**	**No**	What emotional needs do the parents have (e.g., grieving, emotional support)?
2. Is there a consensus about the applied methods of goal definition (e.g., child-centered, family oriented, interdisciplinary)? **Yes**	**No**	Are there alternative methods?
3. Is there a consensus about the goal of the diagnostic process and how the results will be managed (e.g., availability of data)? **Yes**	**No**	What worries do parents have? How can these worries be alleviated?
4. Are we able to implement what we have planned (time wise/ methods)? **Yes**	**No**	Are there any alternatives (e.g., existing data, external expert)?
5. Are we able to define a working "contract" (i.e., who will be responsible for what during the early intervention process)? **Yes**	**No**	What prevents this process, and how can we overcome it?
6. Concrete pedagogical diagnostic and goal-definition process		

From Pretis, M. (2001a). *Fruehfoerderung planen, durchführen, evaluieren* (Planning, performing, and evaluating early intervention) (p. 75). Muenchen: Reinhardt; reprinted by permission.

three aspects also should be part of the professional documentation and the contract between the parents and the professional.

Goal-Oriented Work

The result of the pedagogical diagnosis is a contract between parents and the professional (and the interdisciplinary team) that states what will be done and how it will be done (see Table 16.5). Even though most parents tend to be impatient about when the actual work will begin, it is crucial to define the previous steps first (i.e., first contact, attachment, diagnostic phase). Only defined goals on a transparent behavioral level (Pretis, 1998a),

Table 16.5. Communication strategies during the goal-oriented work

Associated questions		Feedback/exit strategies
1. Welcome being "here and now." Am I able to follow my prepared intervention plan? **Yes**	**No**	Urgent issues have to be discussed. Framework conditions require modification (e.g., child is sick, child is sleeping).
2. Is it possible to briefly reflect on what happened over the past week/after the last unit? **Yes**	**No**	Why not? What open questions have to be solved immediately?
3. Am I able to get in contact with and motivate the child? **Yes**	**No**	What kind of setting do we need to promote a good working relationship?
4. Does the child display recognition when going through known situations or doing known activities? Does the child anticipate activities (e.g., ritual at the beginning of the unit, pedagogical toys)? **Yes**	**No**	Possible modulation of the activity level of the child: repeating situations that can be easily recognized by the child
5. Are we able to start with something new? **Yes**	**No**	Repetition of the known activities with possible slight modification
6. Is it possible to change the child's activity by introducing a slight variation (e.g., toy)? **Yes**	**No**	Strengthen the child's independent activities.
7. Is it possible to initiate activities that are based on your professional goals? **Yes**	**No**	Finish this circle of activities. Look for explanations about why it is not possible.
8. Is it possible to finish activities that are based on your professional goals? **Yes**	**No**	How can I define clear changes in the setting? Give clear instructions.
9. Finish and start with a new activity circle (e.g., parent work) **Yes**	**No**	Which factors contribute to the fact that parent or family work is not assessed as effective?
10. It is possible to start and continue parent work? **Yes**	**No**	What kind of setting do we need?

(continued)

Table 16.5.—*continued*

11.	Similar structure to child-oriented work Can the parent or the professional address pertinent questions? Yes	No	Possible termination of the unit Definition of the setting for the next unit Is our working contract still relevant?
12.	Are we able to finish the unit? Yes	No	What is unclear? What still needs to be discussed?
13.	Finish on time; say good-bye.		

From Pretis, M. (2001a). *Fruehfoerderung planen, durchführen, evaluieren* (Planning, performing, and evaluating early intervention) (pp. 108–109). Muenchen: Reinhardt; reprinted by permission.

which are operationalized, are able to show the efficiency of early intervention. There is still some resistance to the definition of operationalized goals, especially in German-speaking countries. This resistance may be explained by the fact that evaluation is often interpreted as control. As a result, professionals tend to use "philosophical models and goals" (e.g., promotion of the autonomy of the child; Weiss, 1995), which are difficult for professionals and parents to evaluate.

Despite the heterogeneity of the applied methods—either oriented toward therapeutic concepts (e.g., physiotherapy, occupational therapy, speech therapy) or toward pedagogical concepts (e.g., Montessori)—they should be based on a theoretical model, include a hypothesis, and include a pattern of clearly defined interventional behavior that can be observed and described (Pretis, 2002b). This is important because early intervention, especially in Austria and more generally in Europe, tends to rely on abstract terms that include an *all-or-nothing* holistic approach.

Even though there is a need to define a *philosophy* of early intervention, this does not mean that the applied methods cannot be put into practice. There is a consensus that well-structured and comprehensive programs show the most benefit. On average, one unit of early intervention in Austria takes 90 minutes, is mostly home-based, and includes goal-oriented work with the child and family work with the parents (mother) and siblings. Furthermore, interdisciplinary work (e.g., with the pediatrician) is included in the concept of early intervention (see Pretis, 2000a).

Reflection

The contract between parents and the professional should include a process of reflection at least every 6 months during the intervention. The failure of early intervention highly correlates with a lack of communication between parents and professionals concerning expectations, goals, and outcomes of the process (Pretis, 1998a). This is especially the case when inexperienced

Table 16.6. Structure of a reflection unit during the goal-oriented work

Associated questions		Feedback/exit strategies
1. Based on our relationship, are we able to reflect on the ongoing process? Yes	No	How can we create an acceptable working relationship?
2. Discussion concerning the goals and expectations of early intervention. Is there a consensus on these expectations and goals? Yes	No	Analyze the documents (e.g., contract, diagnostics). How can we explain our different perception of reality?
3. Do we remember concrete steps and procedures of the process? Yes	No	Analyze the preparation documents.
4. Are we able to specify to what extent the goals have been reached? What has supported/inhibited the ongoing process? Yes	No	How can we explain these differences in perception? What do we need to achieve a relative agreement? (Possible assessment by external expert.)
5. Are we able to follow our contracted goals? Yes	No	Modify the goals (e.g., new diagnostic strategies; see above). Early intervention is no longer necessary.
6. Continuous early intervention process.		

From Pretis, M. (2001a). *Fruehfoerderung planen, durchführen, evaluieren* (Planning, performing, and evaluating early intervention) (p. 127). Muenchen: Reinhardt; reprinted by permission.

professionals have to work with multiproblem families (e.g., family with young children, single-parent families, families with children with multiple disabilities; Strothmann & Zeschitz, 1983).

This process of reflection includes self-evaluation by the professional (What did I reach?) to the parents (see Table 16.6) and structured interaction with the parents, including fathers, if possible. One of the adverse side effects of early intervention is that fathers often feel excluded, which may decrease their perceived competence to rear their child and may lead to conflicts within the family. Krais (1983) was one of the first fathers from a German-speaking country who described the process of conditioned helplessness followed by tendency toward withdrawal.

Final Evaluation

In a traditional sense, *evaluation* can be defined as a process of assessment (i.e., to what extent a social program has been able to reach its defined goals). In most cases, this assessment correlates with financial aspects and whether a program is effective and efficient. Because of methodological limitations (how to measure the preventive effect; e.g., in children with progressive diseases), more extended models of evaluation have been developed and applied to the disability field, taking into account increasing self-evaluation (e.g., Spiegel, 1993), conceptual evaluation (whether the ongoing process correlates with the conceptual hypothesis), structural evaluation (whether there are adequate means to reach the goals [e.g., infrastructure, qualification of staff, financial and legal frameworks]), process evaluation (what is being done, how interventions are described, and how interventions are explained and justified), and outcome evaluation (how differences and outcome parameters are described and what criteria are used to assess success; Pretis, 2001b). Evaluation in this context functions to assess what happened during the intervention and what effects can be attributed to the early intervention process. It also functions to assess what kind of intervention will be adequate for the future. As pointed out in our Austrian sample (Pretis, 2000a), 20% of children (most were birth to 3 years old; some were birth to 6 years old) did not need further special educational support.

CONCLUSION

Effective early intervention processes—organization or intake strategies or communications strategies—are associated with increased transparency, comparability, and, hopefully, quality control. Current discussion of quality control, especially in Europe, primarily emphasizes *product parameters* because the methods are based on industrial production approaches (e.g., total quality management). Early intervention is regarded as a relation-based process, which therefore requires a set of social interaction and communication rules. These rules have to be open and dynamic and adjusted for individual circumstances, but also they have to provide a structured framework that allows transparency, intersubjectivity, and participation of the subjects (in terms of feedback loops). In Austria, a growing number of early intervention services rely on this model. It is useful to know about this developmental communications model so that those interested can consider its use.

REFERENCES

Guralnick, M.J. (2001). A developmental systems model for early intervention. *Infants and Young Children, 14*(2), 1–18.
Krais, R. (1983). Brief eines Vaters. In O. Speck & A. Warnke (Eds.), *Fruehfoerderung mit Eltern* (Letter of a father) (pp. 21–24). Muenchen: Reinhardt.

Kuehl, J. (2002). Was bewirkt Fruehfoerderung? Über die Schwierigkeit, Wirkungszusammenhaenge zu objektivieren. (Which effect does early intervention show? About the difficulty to find objective impact.) *Fruehfoerderung interdisziplinaer, 21*, 1–10.

Petermann, F., Kusch, M., Niebank, K. (1998). *Entwicklungspsychopathologie. Ein Lehrbuch.* (Developmental psychopathology. A textbook.) Weinheim: Beltz.

Pretis, M. (1998a). Das Konzept der Partnerschaftlichkeit in der Fruehfoerderung. Vom Haltungsmodell zum Handlungsmodell. (The concept of partnership within Early Intervention.) *Fruehfoerderung interdisziplinaer, 17*, 11–17.

Pretis, M. (1998b). Evaluation interdisziplinaerer Fruehfoerderung und Familienbegleitung bei Kindern mit Down-syndrom. Bedingungs-und Wirkfaktoren, kovariierende Variablen. (Evaluation of interdisciplinary early intervention in children with Down's syndrome. Context and impact factors.) *Fruehfoerderung interdisziplinaer, 17*, 29–40.

Pretis, M. (2000a). *Fruehfoerderung in Oesterreich.* (Early intervention in Austria.) Graz: SHFI.

Pretis, M. (2000b). Early intervention in children with Down's syndrome. From evaluation to methodology. *Infants and Young Children, 12*, 23–31.

Pretis, M. (2001a). Fruehfoerderung planen, durchführen, evaluieren (Planning, performing, and evaluating early intervention.) Muenchen: Reinhardt.

Pretis, M. (2001b). Towards future paradigms and challenges of early intervention? *Speicalusis ugdymas/Special Education, 2*, 55–63.

Pretis, M. (2002a, March 14). *Fruehfoerderung in Oesterreich—Zwischen paedagogischer Notwendigkeit und Finanzierbarkeit.* (Early intervention in Austria—between pedagogical necessities and financial possibilities.) Paper presented at the Tagung der Ambulanten Erziehungshilfe, Klagenfurt.

Pretis, M. (2002b). Was ist "gute" Arbeit in der Fruehfoerderung? 10 Thesen zur Qualitaet und zur Qualitaetsentwicklung. (What do we mean by "good" work in early intervention?) *Fruehfoerderung interdisziplinaer, 21*, 29–40.

Speck, O. (1983). Das gewandelte Verhaeltnis zwischen Eltern und Fachleuten in der Fruehförderung. (The changed relationship between parents and professionals in the field of early intervention.) In O. Speck & A. Warnke (Eds.), *Fruehfoerderung mit den Eltern* (Early support with the parents) (pp. 13–20). Muenchen: Reinhardt.

Spiegel, H. (1993). *v. Aus Erfahrung lernen.* (Learning from experience.) *Qualifizierung durch Selbstevaluation.* Muenster: Votum.

Strothmann, M., & Zeschitz, M. (1983). Grenzen elterlicher Kooperation in der Fruehfoerderung. Eine Analyse der Randbedingungen von Abbruechen innerhalb eines Modelversuches zur Fruehfoerderung. (Limits of parental cooperation within earl intervention.) In O. Speck & A. Warnke (Eds.), *Fruehfoerderung mit den Eltern* (Early support with the parents) (pp. 85–115). Muenchen, Reinhardt.

Weiss, H. (1995). Bedingungs-und Wirkungszusammenhaenge in der Fruefoerderung. (Causality and impact in the field of early intervention.) *Fruehfoerderung interdisziplinaer, 14*, 59–71.

CHAPTER 17

THE INFANT DEVELOPMENT PROGRAM'S EARLY ASSESSMENT AND EARLY INTERVENTION MODEL IN BRITISH COLUMBIA

HILLEL GOELMAN, DANA BRYNELSEN,
MARI PIGHINI, AND GERARD M. KYSELA

The Developmental Systems Model (Guralnick, 2001) is an important contribution to the continued understanding of both the principles and practices of early assessment and intervention. The clarity and detail of the model provides researchers and clinicians with an opportunity to examine their own current assessment and intervention methods and to fine tune and customize their existing practices and procedures. This chapter compares the Developmental Systems Model with the approach currently being used by the Infant Development Program (IDP) in British Columbia. The chapter begins with a brief overview of the history and current status of early intervention in Canada with specific reference to the IDP in British Columbia. The next section describes the current assessment and intervention model that is used by the IDP in British Columbia. The third section begins by placing both models into the context of recent developments in early intervention followed by a discussion of the similarities and differences between the IDP model and the Developmental Systems Model. The last section offers some thoughts and reflections on future developments in this area.

The authors acknowledge the British Columbia Ministry of Children and Families, the *Human Early Learning Partnership*, and the Social Sciences and Humanities Research Council of Canada for their generous grant support. The authors would also like to acknowledge the valuable help provided by Jacqueline Smit Alex for her editorial comments and D'Anne Rathie for her ongoing administrative support.

AN OVERVIEW OF EARLY INTERVENTION
SERVICES IN CANADA AND BRITISH COLUMBIA

Early childhood intervention in Canada traditionally consists of multidisciplinary services provided to children from birth to 5 years of age (Marfo, 1991, 1995). Typically, early childhood intervention attempts to promote child health and well-being, enhance emerging child competencies; minimize developmental delays; remediate existing or emerging disabilities; prevent functional deterioration; promote adaptive parenting; and promote overall family functioning, resilience, and adaptation (Kysela, Drummond, McDonald, & Fleming, 2004; Meisels & Shonkoff, 2000).

Although almost all program delivery is the responsibility of the provincial or territorial governments, since the late 1990s the federal Government of Canada has stimulated and initiated a number of important developments that affect early intervention services. After years of discussions and planning, in 1999, the Government of Canada announced a National Children's Agenda in partnership with territorial and provincial governments (Government of Canada, 2001, 2002). This agenda was intended to assign a high priority to the needs of young children and their families and to provide programs and funds to advance the agenda. Based on the commitments identified in the agenda, in 2000, a federal/provincial/territorial Early Childhood Development Agreement was announced with four key foci: promoting healthy pregnancy, birth, and infancy; improving parenting and family supports; strengthening early childhood development, learning, and care; and strengthening community supports. Through this agreement, the federal government has attempted to develop and expand early intervention programs in part by implementing programs at the local level and in part by providing funding to the provinces/territories to set their own priorities. The agreement made it clear that funds were to be used to support effective programs that would 1) focus on early intervention and prevention; 2) value diversity in terms of the children's abilities, ethnicity, and language; 3) provide community support to the families and children; and 4) provide a cross-sectoral form of service delivery from different professions and disciplines.

In addition to the transfer of funds to provinces and territories, the federal government did provide some direct services to local communities. These federally funded and administered programs include 1) *Canada Prenatal Nutrition Program* (CPNP), which provides health and nutritional information to pregnant women; 2) *Family-Centered Maternity and Newborn Care: National Guidelines*, which are materials designed to educate parents about appropriate care of newborns; 3) *The Fetal Alcohol Syndrome/Fetal Alcohol Effects (FAS/FAE) Initiative*, which is designed to reduce the incidence of and to help mitigate the impacts of FAS/FAE on children and their families; 4) *The Folic Awareness Campaign*, which is intended to inform parents of the importance of folic acid in the prevention of certain developmental defects; 5) *The Healthy Pregnancy Marketing Strategy*, which is a community-based program to help disseminate information to prospective parents on how to maintain healthy lifestyles; 6) *The Postpartum Parent Support Program* (PPSP), which is delivered by community health nurses and other health care professionals to provide parent education to parents of young infants; 7) *The Back to Sleep Awareness Campaign*, which is designed to raise public and professional awareness of Sudden Infant Death Syndrome (SIDS); 8) *Aboriginal Head Start*, which consists of half-day preschool programs for aboriginal children on-reserve both in urban and rural settings; 9) *The Community Action Program for Children* (CAP-C), which addresses the health and development of children from birth to 6 years who are at risk, including children in families with low incomes; children living in families with a teenage parent; children experiencing developmental delays or social, emotional, or behavioral problems; and children who are abused and neglected; 10) *The First Nations and Inuit Child Care Initiative*, which is managed by local Aboriginal communities in order to provide accessible, affordable, and quality child care programs to these communities; and 11) *Brighter Futures*, which is a program targeted at improving the health of First Nations children with particular reference to injury prevention, healthy infants, and parenting skills.

Although these initiatives address early child development and parenting issues for communities that are at risk, it is important to note that these federal initiatives are mostly *primary prevention* programs and not specific *secondary* or *tertiary early intervention* programs for infants and young children who are at risk for developmental delays or who have identified disabilities. At a provincial level, British Columbia, Alberta, Saskatchewan, Newfoundland, and Prince Edward Island have developed IDPs to specifically target the needs of this latter group of infants and young children and their families. These programs were originally local or community initiatives and have provided services to families since the early 1970s (Brynelsen, Cummings, & Gonzalez, 1993). Programs and services have continued to expand in the different provinces since the 1970s and 1980s (Marfo, 1995). Nevertheless, and "because there is no legal mandate federally or provincially, for the specific provisions of these services, no standard or provincial database exists" (Brynelsen, 2003; Brynelsen et al., 1993, p. 166)

Infant Development Program

The IDP of British Columbia has provided early intervention services in British Columbia since 1972. The program has grown from one staff person and 15 families to 52 programs in all regions of the province with 108 staff who conducted more than 28,000 home visits in 2001–2002. In the years that IDP has been in operation, it has provided service to more than 43,000 children (Brynelsen, 1990; Office of the Provincial Advisor for Aboriginal Infant Development Programs, 1984, 2002). The IDP of British Columbia follows provincial guidelines for the operation of IDPs through the province. To date, British Columbia is one of the few provinces in Canada that continues to have a full-time coordinator or Provincial Advisor. Together, with the recently appointed Aboriginal IDP Provincial Advisor, they "advise, train, monitor local staff and encourage standard practices" (Brynelsen et al., 1993, p. 166). The Provincial Advisors are accountable to the Provincial Steering Committee and to the British Columbia Ministry of Children and Family Development.

The IDP of British Columbia delivers family-centered services for children from birth to 3 years who are at risk for or have established developmental disabilities based on the following principles: the early years are important, early intervention can alleviate the impact of delay or disability, and the family unit is essential to the healthy development of the child (Brynelsen et al., 1993). The provincial Ministry of Children and Family Development funds individual IDPs (Ministry of Children and Family Development, Early Childhood Development Branch, 2002). Programs are sponsored by nonprofit community service societies, associations for community living, child development centers, and community societies with special focus on early intervention (Brynelsen, Krausert, Oldfield, Stewart, & Wolverton, 2003). IDP is just one of the home visiting programs that is delivered in many communities in British Columbia. Unlike other programs serving young children and families, IDP *specifically* targets prevention and intervention for young children and is based on the premise that home visiting is an effective and cost-efficient way to support families with children with special needs. In order to be eligible for IDP services, the child must be between birth and 3 years of age and have a diagnosis of or be at risk for developmental delay and/or developmental disabilities, and the family must be participating voluntarily (as opposed to a court- or government-mandated referral). Health practitioners and social- and community-based agencies make referrals to the program, and parents also can self-refer. In some communities, the family is placed on a waiting list that could range from 2 weeks to 6 months. The IDP's top priorities are to assist families to make optimum use of available supports and services, to enhance their knowledge of their child's overall growth and development, and to learn skills that will facilitate their child's development (Brynelsen et al., 2003).

As a program that has always embraced family-centered practice, IDP has opened its doors to all families whose children meet the previously mentioned criteria. Families form long-term meaningful relationships with staff. Services to children and families are individually determined based on pre-identified family needs and through a variety of tools, including the Parent Checklist for Home Visit (Brynelsen et al., 2003) and the Family Needs Survey (Dunst & Trivette, 1994). In addition to looking into the family's needs, IDP consultants also attempt to build on the strengths of both the child and the family. One such strength is the family's level of commitment to the program as demonstrated by the amount and intensity of contact with the IDP consultant as well as the family's willingness to be flexible in allotting time for program participation. All of these features are within the control and willingness of the individual family (Brynelsen, 2003).

Collaborations

The program owes much of its success to its strong collaborations with others in the health and early childhood communities. IDP has strong linkages with community health nurses and family physicians for referrals, diagnosis, and follow-up. Most programs have consulting therapists available and work closely with physiotherapists, occupational therapists, and speech-language pathologists. There is also close collaboration with inclusive community programs—as opposed to segregated programs—that are also accessible to parents of children with special needs. These programs, which in many communities are sponsored or initiated by the IDP (Brynelsen et al., 2003), might provide specific parenting or skill-based support for families of young children at risk or with developmental disabilities and include programs such as "Parent–Child Mother Goose" or "Watch, Wait and Wonder."

The IDP has also maintained strong links with postsecondary professional programs that provide ongoing training and support for staff, such as the ID/SC Certificate and Diploma Programs and the Summer Institutes, all of which are offered at the University of British Columbia. The five courses in the Certificate Program and the ten courses in the Diploma Program are offered in a variety of different distance and face-to-face formats. The majority of consultants hold at least a bachelor's degree. In some of the more isolated rural and/or aboriginal communities, IDP staff continue to develop professionally, working toward the completion of a certificate or diploma equivalent in level to infant development/early childhood programs. Overall, the IDP consultants are well trained, connected, and supported, with ongoing professional development throughout the year (Brynelsen, 2003).

Characteristics of Children in the Program

Since the 1980s, the number of IDPs has increased from 26 to 52—an increase of more than 100%—and caseloads have increased from 1,400 to

2,493 infants. In addition, some notable changes in the numbers of young children who have been identified with disabilities or delays in the first few years of life are due to an increase in the awareness, knowledge, and skills of many health, education, and social services professionals (Office of the Provincial Advisor for Aboriginal Infant Development Programs, 1984, 2002). These professionals have a greater understanding of developmental disabilities and the impact of early intervention. As a result, more newborns who are at risk are identified at birth, and more infants are identified with a disability in their early months (Brynelsen, 2003). For example, in 2001–2002, 43% of all referrals were identified in the first 6 months of life. In the 1980s, the large majority of infants likely to experience developmental problems were identified between 12 and 18 months (Office of the Provincial Advisor for Aboriginal Infant Development Programs, 1984, 2002).

"A traditional" referral of infants and toddlers with developmental delays or a diagnosed disability continue to make up 56% of all caseloads. The developmental delay category, which makes up to 25% of the caseload, includes toddlers who show significant overall delays or 2- to 3-year-old children with specific areas of delay, such as language or behavior. What is notable, however, is that once assessed, many of these children are identified as having delays in more than one developmental area. Also, some conditions emerge only as children grow older, and ongoing monitoring of their developmental status and ready access to diagnosticians is of great importance for every child and family referred to the IDP (Brynelsen, 2003; Office of the Provincial Advisor for Aboriginal Infant Development Programs, 2002). It has been reported that approximately 3%–7% of caseloads include children with cognitive delays, children living with at-risk conditions (e.g., a physical illness or mental illness), or children living in extreme poverty. Since the 1990s, IDP has also seen a significant increase in the number of immigrant families, refugee families, and/or families who speak English as a second language. In some communities, these families account for up to 60% of the IDP caseload. In addition to language and financial barriers, IDP consultants are confronting new issues such as the fact that new immigrant families in some cultures may consider it foreign to bring in an outside professional to deal with what they see as essentially a "family matter." In some cases, the specific needs of an individual within the family may play a secondary role to the family unit as a whole (Brynelsen, 2003; Office of the Provincial Advisor for Aboriginal Infant Development Programs, 2002).

Cultural and Related Issues

IDP staff have become increasingly aware of and sensitive to cultural, linguistic, ethnic, and national diversity. There is a growing need for specific training that allows them to deal with diverse patterns of parent–child attachment patterns and differences in parenting styles. One of the primary challenges that has been identified by IDP consultants is a perceived lack of knowledge about child development and disability among key groups. For example, IDP consultants have found that many individuals with whom they deal in some professional communities adopt a benign "wait and see" attitude, characterized by statements such as, "Don't worry, your child will outgrow this." Similarly, IDP consultants have found that many parents and the public in general are largely unaware of what constitutes typical and atypical development, the definition and identification of risk factors, and general knowledge about disabilities. Perhaps the greatest obstacle is the lack of an early developmental screening system used throughout all of British Columbia. Regular, standard, and widely used developmental screening would enable early identification and could provide early intervention at a time when children would benefit the most (Brynelsen, 2003).

Professional Training

Just as the federal government has demonstrated increased interest in early childhood development, the provincial government in British Columbia has also shown a greater awareness of the importance of the early years. Beginning in the 1990s, the provincial government has devoted increasing resources to professional training of early childhood educators and has developed an "Integrated Service Delivery and Integrated Case Management" approach to all children's services (Ministry of Children and Families, 1998). Wage enhancement grants and operating grants to child care programs were implemented, resulting in the highest quality of group child care programs in Canada in 1998 (Goelman, Doherty, Lero, LaGrange, & Tougas, 2000).

The IDP Approach to Early Assessment and Intervention

The IDP uses an approach that comes out of family-centered and evidence-based practice rather than from the implementation of a specific early intervention system (see Figure 17.1). The process begins when there is a referral to the IDP from a family member or from a community professional. Following telephone contact, an IDP consultant may also arrange a family visit to explain the program. If the family declines, then the consultant can assist the family in seeking other services. If the family decides that it wishes to work with the IDP consultant, then the assessment process begins with a family needs assessment. The family and the IDP consultant will then decide whether it is appropriate to proceed to a

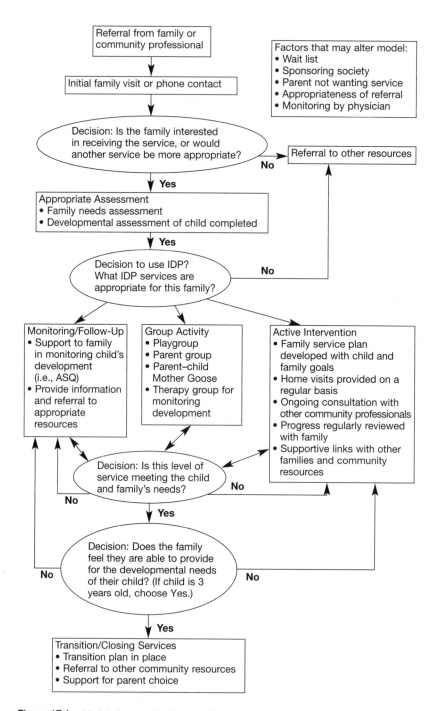

Figure 17.1. Model of service for the Infant Development Program (IDP) of British Columbia.

developmental assessment of the child and/or whether they wish to consult with other health care and/or intervention professionals. The IDP consultant and the family also look at the different services that may be appropriate for them. At this point, the family has a choice to proceed with receiving IDP services, or, if IDP does not provide the services that the family needs for their child, then the IDP consultant can assist the family in obtaining a referral to other resources.

If the family decides to work with IDP, then they may choose from among three levels of service: 1) monitoring the child's development and/or periodic follow-up assessments, 2) enrolling the child in an appropriate program or group activity, and 3) conducting active intervention with the child. These services differ in terms of intensity and frequency of the work and also in the extent to which the services are provided to individual children at home or in group or program settings outside of the home. In the monitoring and follow-up stage, tools such as the *Ages & Stages Questionnaires®* (ASQ), *Second Edition* (Bricker & Squires, 1999), are administered, which can provide families with information on the developmental status of their child and can guide referrals to appropriate resources. With active intervention, the family follows a service plan developed with child and family goals and they receive regular home visits from the IDP consultant, as well as ongoing consultation with other professionals. Group activity involves the family's participation in playgroups, parent groups, and more specific groups such as the "Parent–Child Mother Goose" program or a therapy group for monitoring the child's development.

The IDP consultant and the family periodically evaluate whether the level of service chosen is meeting the child and family's needs. As the child grows and develops, a decision may be made, for example, to shift from the active intervention level to the monitoring and follow-up level. The next step is transition and closing services, which involve two possible scenarios. In the first scenario, after receiving services for a period of time, the family evaluates whether they feel that they have the capacity to provide for the developmental needs of their child without the IDP support. In the second scenario, the child is referred to a group program because he or she is older than 3 years. The transition includes a plan for the child developed in conjunction with the family, which may include preschool (with or without special needs support) or referrals to other community resources. In these situations, the IDP consultant supports the parent's choice(s) and, as much as possible, becomes a liaison between IDP and the next services.

Some factors may alter this model in terms of the sequence of events or the nature and/or level of services provided: 1) there may be long waiting lists for specific services (e.g., speech and hearing assessment), which often result in delays in decisions and referrals; 2) financial, staffing, or administrative difficulties within specific agencies can disrupt service delivery; 3) some parents may be reluctant to participate in an intervention program or to receive suggestions for specific assessments and/or interventions; 4) a professional in a specific community may have erred and made an inappropriate referral; 5) a professional may spend more time on passive monitoring of the child's progress rather than actively tracking the child's development and/or changes in the family's attitudes; 6) some agencies sponsoring IDPs may not be fully practicing family-centered care and have intake, assessment, or multidisciplinary procedures that affect the capacity of the IDP to implement this model; and 7) accreditation procedures may also affect the model with an emphasis on institutional requirements and can reduce the potential impact on families receiving service (Brynelsen, 2003).

The IDP Approach and the Developmental Systems Model

Both the IDP approach and the Developmental Systems Model (Guralnick, 2001) can be traced to the same ideological and theoretical underpinnings. Meisels and Shonkoff have summarized these as

> A belief in society's responsibility to provide care and protection to young children; a commitment to the special needs of children who are particularly vulnerable as a result of a chronic disabling condition or as a consequence of growing up in poverty; and a sense that prevention is better than treatment and that earlier prevention is better than later remediation. (2000, p. 13)

In addition to seeing both models as expressions of similar theoretical assumptions about early intervention, both models also subscribe to the same body of principles that guide early identification and early intervention programs (Meisels & Atkins-Burnett, 2000). For example, both models hold that early assessment should 1) follow a specific sequence, 2) involve multiple sources of information, 3) include observations of the child with his or her primary caregiver, 4) be seen as a first step in designing an appropriate intervention process, 5) be based on an understanding of both typical and atypical development, and 6) identify both strengths as well as limitations of the child.

It was very instructive to go through the process of examining the Developmental Systems Model through the lens of the IDP approach and vice versa. The authors of this chapter agree that the Developmental Systems Model can "provide a framework for community-based early intervention services and supports for vulnerable children and families" (Guralnick, 2001, p. 2). In this way, the IDP is not seen as an alternative approach to the Developmental Systems Model but as an example of one of the ways in which the Developmental Systems Model framework can be implemented in a way that meets the needs of specific communities. The IDP approach shares the same fundamental principles as the Developmental Systems Model. Central to both is the importance of family dynamics, including patterns of interaction, parental responsiveness to their children, the types of experiences in which the family engages, and providing for the basic health and well-being of the children. The Developmental Systems Model also identifies a number of the specific family stressors that IDP consultants are trained to observe, including the need for accurate information, family distress, financial pressures, or the lack of self-confidence parents might have in their parenting abilities.

Another shared core principle is the commitment to the provision of integrated services to children and families. Many jurisdictions are plagued by gaps and overlaps in services, resulting in parents experiencing fragmentation and confusion among the different service providers. In order to support children with multiple biologic and/or environmental risk factors who live in complex family systems, it is imperative that early intervention be able to provide a coordinated and coherent response to the needs of individual families.

The Developmental Systems Model framework and the IDP approach include most of the same decision points and specific activities with some slight differences in their sequencing. Decision making, monitoring the progress of the child, and evaluating the efficacy of specific programs and interventions are prominent features of both models. Both begin with a referral (or self-referral) to the early intervention program, and a series of individual and family assessments are conducted at different stages in order to determine the appropriate next steps to take. Both systems also include procedures for ending the delivery of early intervention services at the appropriate time.

There are some relatively minor differences in the two approaches. For example, the Developmental Systems Model includes many more steps and decision points between the initial referral and the child's actual entry into an early intervention program. This may be due to the different origins and intentions of the two approaches. The IDP approach is the result of 30 years of practice and refinement within specific—and extremely diverse—community settings. The IDP approach has a much more iterative quality to it in contrast to the seemingly linear approach reflected in the Developmental Systems Model's flow chart. As a result, the IDP approach seems to allow for a more easily implemented movement for families between the various levels of service, monitoring, group activities, and active intervention. The Developmental Systems Model refers to an apparently homogeneous and self-contained "early intervention program," whereas the IDP approach is based more on the notion of customizing a set of specific responses and supports from different but complementary services agencies. One of the primary roles played by IDP consultants is to coordinate the type and frequency of different support services rather than providing a one-stop early intervention program that can respond to all needs of all children with disabling conditions.

These are relatively minor differences, however, and they stem from the fact that the Developmental Systems Model was developed in order to describe a framework for a comprehensive system of assessments and intervention that could be adapted in different settings. In contrast, the IDP approach is an actual, currently operating program that has had to grow, evolve, and adapt itself within specific policy and programmatic contexts. The Developmental Systems Model holds great value for the IDP approach in a number of ways. It provides a highly detailed and comprehensive blueprint of the critical activities and decisions that must be made by early intervention professionals. This blueprint will be very useful as a template for monitoring the presence or absence of the critical features that are needed in an early intervention program. It will also help to challenge early intervention professionals to articulate and to justify their practice and decision making, not only on the basis of past experience but also on the basis of a comprehensive system that draws on an expert interpretation of many years of early intervention research. In summary, the blueprint will greatly enrich the field and will provide opportunities to continue to share the many different ways in which different communities adapt, revise, and implement features of the Developmental Systems Model.

FUTURE DIRECTIONS, FUTURE CHALLENGES

This chapter began with an overview of early childhood and early intervention services in Canada, and it returns to this broader context in order to consider future directions in these areas. The expansion and further development of early intervention services in Canada will continue to be hampered by the conflicting mandates of the federal, territorial, and provincial governments and the absence of a national strategy or national standards regarding best practices.

Most existing federally funded programs emphasize prevention programs for all parents and families but provide no support specifically for children with disabilities. The provincial/territorial programs focus on intervention, but there is little, if any, systematic coordination with the federal prevention programs, and there is tremendous variability in programs across provinces and territories in almost all aspects of early intervention services. These differences extend to eligibility factors (e.g., child's age); the absence/presence of screening procedures; and the type, intensity, focus, and duration of these programs.

Although the IDP in British Columbia is a universal program provided to all children with special needs from birth to 3 years, there is no such universal program for children older than 3. As a result, very few spaces exist in licensed child care facilities for children who are 3–5 years old with special needs. There is a sharp drop in the number of services available for children who are preschool age, and this represents a major disruption in what should be a strong continuum of services for all children with disabilities from birth up to and including school entry.

Although advances have been made in developing both preservice professional training programs for IDP consultants, the continuing professional development of IDP consultants remains a critical need for the future. Continuing in-service training is required in large part due to changes in the nature and size of IDP consultants' workload. For example, the number of children diagnosed with "low incidence" disorders such as autism has increased, as well as the number of children facing a wider range of environmental hardships including social, familial, and economic pressures. Children being diagnosed with rare disorders and parents facing health, social, and economic hardships has also increased. Continuing professional development is needed due to the increasing complexity of the kinds of disabling conditions in children that are becoming more prevalent. Although neonatal nurseries have developed the technology to dramatically increase the survival rates of very low birth weight and preterm infants, these children face multiple and complex developmental disabilities that must be addressed by IDP and other professionals (Brynelsen, 2003). These complexities require greater understanding and knowledge that can only be provided through continuing professional education.

There is no universal screening system anywhere in Canada in spite of the fact that research shows that early detection makes a difference in early intervention (e.g., Meisels & Shonkoff, 2000). Both the Developmental Systems Model and IDP model could provide the practical and empirical "evidence-based research" that can inform and direct provincial and federal policies. The implementation of universal screening as a means of identifying young children when early intervention can have its greatest impact, and the provision of affordable, accessible, and high quality child care for children of all abilities, must be a higher priority for all levels of government in Canada. As pointed out in a position paper by the Society for Children and Youth of BC:

> Inclusion in society is a fundamental human right, yet many children with disabilities and other special needs are excluded from full inclusion in community life, education (and as they grow older, employment), recreation and play, and even family life. Parents and siblings may also experience barriers to inclusion. (2002)

One of the major barriers to early intervention programs in general is the inadequate level of financial support given to early screening and intervention. Without the means, personnel, and related resources needed to deliver high quality early intervention programs, large numbers of children and their families will continue to face obstacles to these programs. Another barrier is the inadequate level of supports to families in many programs. Both the IDP and Developmental Systems Model strongly advocate the role of families and family support in order to help provide the optimal environmental opportunities for their children. Beyond the limited provision of specialized early intervention programs for children and families, society must also ensure more opportunities for recreation and play for children with special needs. The absence of such facilities and programs will mean the continued exclusion of the large majority of young children with special needs for whom play and peer socialization are critical factors in their development. Finally, in Canada, there is still a dearth of evidence-based, policy-relevant research on best practices in early intervention and on the longitudinal impact of early intervention. It is critical that professionals and parents all have access to the most recent information and in the most accessible format in order to help communities, parents, and professionals make the most effective choices regarding young children with special needs.

Guralnick's (2001) Developmental Systems Model provides the field with an important point of reference regarding the current status of early screening and intervention. Certainly, it will continue to stimulate much discussion and reflection in the field and will, no doubt, further refinements to program delivery in these areas. Hopefully, in 10 years, when a retrospective volume on early screening and intervention models is published, researchers, policy makers, professionals, and parents will be able to look back and cite significant positive changes in the field and the reduction of barriers to service that currently exist.

REFERENCES

Bricker, D., & Squires, J. (with Mounts, L., Potter, L., Nickel, R., Twombly, E., & Farrell, J.). (1999). *Ages & Stages Questionnaires® (ASQ): A parent-completed, child-monitoring system* (2nd ed.). Baltimore: Paul H. Brookes Publishing Co.

Brynelsen, D. (1990). *Historical perspective of IDP programs.* Paper presented at the Atlantic Conference; Early Intervention: Current Issues and Future Directions, Halifax, Nova Scotia.

Brynelsen, D. (2003). Interview with Dana Brynelsen, Provincial Advisor of the Infant Development Programs of British Columbia, July 9, 2003, and July 18, 2003. Vancouver, British Columbia.

Brynelsen, D., Cummings, H., & Gonzalez, V. (1993). Infant development programs. In R. Ferguson, A. Pence, & C. Denholm (Eds.), *Professional child and youth care* (2nd ed., pp. 162–187). British Columbia: UBC Press.

Brynelsen, D., Krausert, P.L., Oldfield, J., Stewart, M., & Wolverton, A. (2003). *British Columbia IDP PowerPoint* Presentation. Vancouver, British Columbia: Infant Development Programs.

Dunst, C., & Trivette, C.M. (1994). Aims and principles of family support programs. In C. Dunst, C.M. Trivette, & A.G. Deal (Eds.), *Supporting and strengthening families: Methods, strategies, and practices* (Vol. 1, pp. 30–48). Cambridge, MA: Brookline Books.

Goelman, H., Doherty, G., Lero, D., LaGrange, A., & Tougas, J. (2000). *Caring and learning in child care centres across Canada.* Guelph, Ontario: University of Guelph Centre for Families, Work, and Well-Being.

Government of Canada: Federal/Provincial/Territorial Early Childhood Development Agreement. (2001). *Early childhood development activities and expenditures: Government of Canada report 2001.* Retrieved September 8, 2003, from http://socialunion.gc.ca/ecd_e.html

Government of Canada: Federal/Provincial/Territorial Early Childhood Development Agreement. (2002). *Early childhood development activities and expenditures: Government of Canada report 2002.* Retrieved September 8, 2003, from http://socialunion.gc.ca/ecd_e.html

Guralnick, M. (2001). A developmental systems model for early intervention. *Infants and Young Children, 14*(2), 1–18.

Kysela, G.M., Drummond, J., McDonald, L., & Fleming, D. (2004). In R. DeV. Peters, B. Leadbeater, & R.J. McMahon (Eds.), *Resilience in children, families and communities: Linking context to practice and policy.* New York: Kluwer Academic/Plenum.

Marfo, K. (Ed). (1991). The evolution and current status of early intervention in Canada. In K. Marfo (Ed.), *Early intervention in transition: Current perspectives on programs for handicapped children* (pp. 235–270). New York: Praeger Publications.

Marfo, K. (1995). Linking the research, policy and practice in early intervention. In I.S. Hope (Ed.), *SpecialLink national early intervention symposium: Charting new waters* (pp. 9–18). Wreck Cove, Nova Scotia: Breton Books.

Meisels, S.J., & Atkins-Burnett, S. (2000). The elements of early childhood assessment. In J.P. Shonkoff & S.J. Meisels (Eds.), *Handbook of early childhood intervention* (2nd ed., pp. 231–257). New York: Cambridge University Press.

Meisels, S.J., & Shonkoff, J.P. (2000). Early childhood intervention: A continuing evolution. In J.P. Shonkoff & S.J. Meisels (Eds.), *Handbook of early childhood intervention* (2nd ed., pp. 3–31). New York: Cambridge University Press.

Ministry of Children and Families. (1998). *Integrated service delivery and integrated case management policy manual.* British Columbia: Author.

Ministry of Children and Family Development, Early Childhood Development Branch. (2002). *Early childhood development branch update.* British Columbia: Author.

Office of the Provincial Advisor for Aboriginal Infant Development Programs. (1984). *Biennial statistics April 1, 1983–March 31, 1984.* Presented by the Provincial Steering Committee, Infant Development Program of British Columbia (Unpublished manuscript).

Office of the Provincial Advisor for Aboriginal Infant Development Programs. (2002). *Biennial statistics April 1, 2001–March 31, 2002.* Presented by the Provincial Steering Committee, Infant Development Program of British Columbia (Unpublished manuscript).

Society for Children and Youth of BC. (2002). *Position statement 9 on children with disabilities or other special needs.* Burnaby, British Columbia: The Volunteer Advocacy Group for Children and Youth.

Werner, E.E. (2000). Protective factors and individual resilience In J.P. Shonkoff & S.J. Meisels (Eds.), *Handbook of early childhood intervention* (2nd ed., pp. 115–132). New York: Cambridge University Press.

CHAPTER 18

EARLY INTERVENTION IN THE UNITED KINGDOM

Current Policy and Practice

BARRY CARPENTER AND PHILIPPA RUSSELL

INTRODUCTION

Since the 1980s, there has been an unprecedented interest in, and development of, a range of initiatives around early intervention in the United Kingdom. The concept of "early intervention" has been expressed in a multiplicity of definitions and sometimes with varying intended outcomes. For example, in education, early intervention is seen as providing appropriate early support both to promote optimum development in early childhood and in order to prevent subsequent educational failure. For children with difficult disruptive behavior (in particular, those coming from families perceived as dysfunctional or troubled), early intervention is linked to a variety of initiatives to reduce subsequent antisocial behavior.

Historically, early intervention was regarded as a service that targeted individual *children*. Since the 1970s, however, there has been a growing emphasis on *parents* as partners in any early intervention program and a parallel recognition that high-quality family support is an essential element within any early intervention program.

The growth of interest in parents and families as "change agents" for young children with special educational and other special needs has led to an increase in the range of early intervention programs (Cameron, 1986; Lovaas, 1987) that specifically engage parents as co-educators and key players in both the design and subsequent "roll out" of any early intervention program. There has also been a growing interest in the use of early intervention through parent group support or education programs (e.g., Sure Start) to target disadvantaged families whose children may be at risk.

The interventions aim to improve parents' confidence, competence, and economic circumstances. They focus on parent education and on the whole family as well as on the individual child.

There is considerable and ongoing debate about which approach to early intervention is most effective. There is general recognition within the United Kingdom, as well as in the United States, that a large population of children and families are vulnerable and confront service providers with a diverse range of risk factors and developmental delays. The UK government has now firmly committed itself to the creation of a National Centre for Early Intervention within its 10-year strategy for special educational needs. The creation of such a center acknowledges that, notwithstanding a rapid increase in scientific knowledge about the foundations for early childhood development and a parallel increase in evidence-based interventions to address a range of difficulties and disabilities, there is an ongoing debate about which tools and approaches are most effective for particular groups of children.

Historically, early intervention in the United Kingdom has developed along two distinct tracks, each characterized by a different focus. The first is represented by a range of early interventions primarily designed to address social deprivation and disadvantage and to improve parenting skills (e.g., Sure Start). The interventions associated with the second have primarily focused on children with learning or other disabilities (e.g., Early Bird; Shields, 2001). These interventions also have a focus on parents, but they are more likely to assume an educational role and to involve parents as partners within a structured teaching or therapy program. There is likely to be greater synergy in the future between the two broad approaches.

Establishing a comprehensive model of early intervention, which integrates health, social care, and educational interventions within a common protocol, has been challenging. There is recognition that, although some children have very complex needs, they and their families will nonetheless need interventions that take account of wider child development and family functioning. A variety of approaches have been developed and are explored next. The majority of these approaches are conceptualized as developmental models and locate any specific programs or interventions within wider policies for community and family support.

NATIONAL POLICY CONTEXT IN THE UNITED KINGDOM

The UK government, through early intervention programs, aims to enable children and families to escape social exclusion. An important element in tackling social exclusion is ensuring that children with disabilities have their needs recognized and that these needs are addressed promptly and effectively. Many families will need additional support when seeking help for their children from professionals across a range of services. For some families, social disadvantages such as low income, poor housing, or parents' mental health needs may make any active partnership with professionals problematic without tackling the problems in the wider family context.

Early intervention that addresses social exclusion and maximizes children's development (and thereby their life chances) is a key theme within the government's Green Paper, *Every Child Matters* (Department for Education and Skills, 2003c). The proposals in the Green Paper set out to "reform children's services for the 21st century" (p. 4) and give early intervention a new urgency and a high priority across all children's services. To address social inclusion in early years services, the government has introduced a wide range of initiatives and programs to support families and young children, and these have helped to raise the profile of effective intervention in the early years. Of particular importance are the local Sure Start programs, the Neighbourhood Nurseries, the Early Excellence Centres Programme, and the Early Years Development and Childcare Partnerships.

Local authorities were required to establish a network of early years Area Special Educational Needs Coordinators (Area SENCOs) by 2004. Area SENCOs provide day-to-day support concerning early intervention and appropriate intervention measures for other SENCOs who are based in a range of early years settings. A key part of the Area SENCO's role is to build links between different settings and services, whether provided by the Local Education Authority (LEA), social services, health departments, or the voluntary sector. Although this provision is directed primarily at children age 3 years and older, the network links with earlier identification and intervention services and assists in the creation of a seamless transition from birth through school age for children with and without disabilities and their families. The importance of early identification is further reinforced within the revised *Special Educational Needs (SEN) Code of Practice* (Department for Education and Skills, 2001b), which recognizes the importance of developing a continuum of special educational interventions from birth through a child's educational life.

The entitlement of young children with disabilities to support and to appropriate education right from the start is reinforced by the Special Educational Needs and Disability Act 2001, which introduces a new Part 4 into the Disability Discrimination Act 1995, thereby creating disability rights in education. Early years, as well as the school and post-16 stages of education, are covered, and all providers and local authorities must develop accessibility plans to improve access progressively to the curriculum, the physical environment, and information. The Foundation Stage of the National Curriculum, the Early Learning Goals, and the introduction of the Foundation Profile to record young children's progress all offer new opportunities for identifying difficulties at an early age, providing appropriate early intervention, and ensuring the active involvement of parents.

Major modernization and reorganization of the National Health Service (NHS) also have implications for early intervention services. The government's National Service Framework will develop new national standards for children across the NHS and social services and interface with education. These standards will provide a coherent and integrated approach to providing services for children with disabilities and will interrelate with *Together from the Start*, the new guidance on early intervention. However, a commitment by government to develop better "joined-up" services in the best interest of effective early intervention raises important issues about how early intervention can be conceptualized in a way that permits a diversity of agencies to deliver appropriate support.

DEFINING EARLY INTERVENTION

Several definitions have influenced the way in which early intervention has developed in the United Kingdom over several decades. Eurlyaid, the European Association on Early Intervention, stated that

> Early intervention can be defined as all forms of child-orientated training activities and parent-orientated guidance activities that are implemented in direct and immediate consequence of the identification of the developmental condition. Early intervention pertains to the child as well as to the parents, the family and the broader network. (Heinen, 1997, p. 17)

Sheila Wolfendale (2000), in an analysis of early intervention, stated that early intervention typically has four primary goals: 1) to support families in supporting their children's development; 2) to promote children's development in key domains (e.g., cognitive, social, physical, emotional, linguistic) through the early years curriculum and other learning opportunities; 3) to promote children's coping confidence; and 4) to prevent the emergence of future problems.

In effect, UK debates about the nature of early intervention are distilled within Michael J. Guralnick's overarching and perceptive definition, "Early intervention is best conceptualized as a system designed to support family patterns of interaction that best promote children's development" (2001, p. 1). As Carpenter (in press) noted,

> This definition offers a basis for re-defining early intervention at the beginning of the 21st century. Its simplicity and its focus on the family as an empowered unit in its own right suggest a natural support process. It asserts the family as the context for the nurture and development of the child. Yet these family-focused approaches must be set within the ever-changing scenario that surrounds early intervention.

EARLY INTERVENTION: THE EFFICACY DEBATE

Since the 1980s, early intervention has resulted in achievements for children, their families, and professionals. For the children, there have been improvements in many aspects of their development, including increased opportunities for wider participation and a greater awareness of the range and nature of special educational needs that exist in very young children. For their families, early intervention has offered support at an emotional and practical level, information on disability or any special health needs, and access to services. It also has offered skills for home-based interventions, advocacy, and an increased awareness of family perspectives and needs.

The United Kingdom has not carried out any long-term cost-benefit analyses of early intervention programs similar to the High Scope evaluation in the United States. However, there is growing concern about what constitutes "value for money" and the relative efficacy of different programs. As the government observed in *Every Child Matters* (Department for Education and Skills, 2003c),

> Society as a whole benefits through reduced spending on problems that can be avoided and through maximising the contribution to society of all its citizens. For instance, a child with a conduct disorder at age 10 will cost the public purse around £70,000 by age 28—up to ten times more than a child with no behavioural problems. (Section 1.6)

The principle (and the long-term benefits) of early intervention are well recognized, and the proposals to create the National Centre for Early Intervention have been warmly welcomed. But there remains an ongoing debate about the optimum timing and nature of early intervention for particular groups of children.

The Impact of Changing Patterns of Childhood Disability

The need for a developmental approach to early intervention in the United Kingdom has been given fresh credence by the changing nature of childhood disability. With technological progress and developments in neonatal care, the survival rates of young children with complex disabilities or health care needs are increasing rapidly. The Department of Health (2003), in *Emerging Findings* from the Children's National Service Framework, emphasized the importance of developing holistic support for families in early intervention programs to maximize development and progress and involve parents at every stage. The *Emerging Findings* (Department of Health, 2003) noted that one third of parents with children younger than 2 years old with disabilities now use more than three pieces of equipment daily to provide basic care (e.g., suction tubes, oxygen masks, mobility aids, feeding tubes). There also has been a marked increase in the numbers of children with autism spectrum disorders, attention-deficit/hyperactivity disorder (ADHD), and/or other behavioral difficulties.

Children become "doubly" vulnerable when their social circumstance is combined with a disability (i.e., environmental and biological risk). The numbers of these children are increasing, and they are especially susceptible to significant developmental problems. There has been growing concern about the developmental and other consequences to children who have been affected by their mother's use of illegal drugs during pregnancy and about the implications of smoking on unborn infants and neonates. The gap between rich and impoverished has grown at a faster rate in the United Kingdom than in any other country in Europe and is second only to New Zealand in the world. Mittler (2000) presented some staggering facts. On a daily basis in the United Kingdom, more than 400 children will see their parents divorce; 300 children will be homeless and need accommodation; 81 children will be taken into care by Social Services; 87 children will be added to child protection registers; and 150 children will be born to teenage mothers.

Ironically, some children with disabilities may themselves be victims of improvements in neonatal and medical care. A review of 25 studies of infants born after assisted conception (Helmerhorst, Peerquin, Donker, & Keirse, 2004) noted the greater risk of perinatal morbidity (and thereby possible later ill health, disability, or special educational needs). This study found the risk to be greatest in single pregnancies rather than multiple gestations, which are most commonly associated with postnatal difficulties. Helmerhorst et al. noted that

> 25 years after the birth of the first baby conceived by in vitro fertilisa-
> tion, our data draws attention to a number of challenges. Firstly,
> emphasis needs to shift, more than it has already, from achieving a
> successful pregnancy to achieving a successful outcome [for the child].
> (2004, p. 263)

In effect, the increase in assisted conception raises new challenges for neonatal and other child health services. As Helmerhorst et al. (2004) observed, there is a need to narrow the gap in positive outcomes between children of assisted pregnancies and those of other pregnancies. There are implications for neonatal and early intervention services if infants who are very small and vulnerable continue to survive.

There also are implications (practical and ethical) for screening and earlier intervention for young children who are born after assisted conception and for ensuring that they have appropriate support during their early years. Because of the potential risk to the well-being of infants born through in vitro fertilization, the government has now issued new guidelines to restrict the numbers of embryos implanted during any one course of treatment.

Children at Risk of Social Exclusion

In *Every Child Matters*, the government noted that, "Overall, this country is still one where life chances are unequal. This damages not only those children born into disadvantage but our society as a whole" (Department for Education and Skills, 2003c, p. 6). The same report noted that family patterns are changing. There are more uncertainties and risks; more single parents without supportive family networks; and clear evidence that negative outcomes for children are frequently associated with a number of key factors, including low income and parental unemployment, homelessness, poor parenting, poor education opportunities, low birth weight, substance abuse, and community factors such as living in a disadvantaged neighborhood.

In the case of a child with disabilities, all of these factors will exacerbate any problems experienced by parents with regard to their child's individual needs. In the United Kingdom, there have been growing concerns about the association between families with a child with disabilities and poverty. The government has committed itself to ending child poverty within 5 years, but Gordon, Parker, Loughran, and Heslop (2000) noted that 55% of families with a child with disabilities live, or have lived, in poverty. Dobson and Middleton (1998) estimated that the cost of raising a child with disabilities is three times that of raising a child without disabilities.

Russell also outlined the considerable financial and social disadvantage that families experience because of the additional costs associated with disability. She commented that

> We need to review the circumstances [of families with disabled children] to ensure that they have the quality of life they deserve. Investment in families with a disabled child and avoiding family breakdown will have direct benefits for the community and the economy as well as for parents and children. They can "pay back" the cost of enhanced family support through tax and pension contributions. Importantly and additionally, we cannot improve the efficacy of any interventions

unless we address the context within which they are to be delivered. (2003, p. 4)

Mental Health of Young Children

Increasing numbers of children are experiencing mental health problems. A survey showed that 10% of children ages 5–15 years experience clinically defined mental health problems (Department for Education and Skills, 2001a). This same study conjectured that the roots of these problems could have begun earlier for many of the children. This study identified the problems that young children and their families could face—emotional disorders (e.g., anxiety states, phobias, depression), conduct disorders (e.g., aggression, defiance, antisocial behavior), hyperkinetic disorders (e.g., disturbance of activity and attention), developmental disorders (e.g., delay in acquiring certain skills such as speech, social ability, or bladder control), attachment disorders (e.g., children who are markedly distressed or socially impaired as a result of an extremely abnormal pattern of attachment to parents or major caregivers), eating disorders (e.g., food refusal), and habit disorders (e.g., sleeping problems, soiling, spontaneous urination). The Office of National Statistics (Melzer, 2000) concluded that whereas one in five children may have special educational needs at some point in their life, children with a special educational need are three times more likely to have mental health problems. Melzer, Gatward, Goodman, and Ford (2000) noted that poverty and social disadvantage are frequent indicators of a stressful life.

EARLY INTERVENTION: THE IMPACT OF DISABILITY ON FAMILIES

Despite extensive literature on working with families of children with disabilities, ample evidence still shows that their needs are not appropriately met. McConachie (1997) remained critical of professionals and of the poor support given to parents following the diagnosis of their child's disability or other special need. Such claims challenge professionals to reflect on their practice, their current approaches to families, and their commitment level to family-centered services.

Is there confidence that professionals have the necessary insights into the impact that the birth of, and life with, a child with disabilities has on family life? They may know what families need but not understand the range of emotions experienced and their impact on the parents' views of a particular intervention or support program. Manuel stated that, "What is so often not recognised is that Mums and Dads and brothers and sisters have love for the child. They don't necessarily want to abandon the child.

Because this is their child" (1996, p. 3). *Abandon* may be an inappropriate word to use in the 21st century in the context of government commitment to improving the quality and availability of early intervention services. Yet, examples still can be found of parents who have been put under pressure to relinquish responsibility for their child (Carpenter, 2001).

Refocusing Professional Perspectives

"Professional distancing" can be as damaging as overinvolvement when it ignores the feelings of families. To be effective, professionals need to respect each and every family at every particular moment by acknowledging their unique expertise and their right to determine priorities (Treloar, 1997). A family-centered and developmental approach to early intervention prioritizes empathy and respect. In order to provide effective early intervention services for families, professionals must understand and respect the various roles in families undertaken by different family members, which may differ according to situations and cultures. Families may not fit stereotypical assumptions, but they will provide the key to support themselves—if professionals understand the context within which families will care for their child and their wishes and aspirations.

Family Contributions to Early Intervention

Family dynamics may mean that services need to be very flexible. It is inappropriate for one parent to be consistently unsupported at meetings because a partner or other family member can never be available at the professionals' preferred time for a meeting. Mothers play a pivotal role in families, and research studies have shown that they carry the bulk of responsibility for household chores and child care (Hornby, 1995). Hauta-mäki (1997) produced findings from a cross-Nordic study in which she contrasted the situation of more than 1,000 mothers of children with Down syndrome with mothers of children without disabilities. She found that the mothers of the children with Down syndrome had increased caregiving responsibilities, had often amended their "life project" goals, and had more restricted leisure activities and different work patterns. When they did work, they had high levels of sick leave. In her international study, Mittler (1995) found that mothers typically remained the major caregivers throughout all regions of the world.

Fathers matter, too. Carpenter and Herbert (1995) suggested that if professionals are to include those whom McConkey (1994) described as "hard to reach parents," then services need to take into account the life pattern of fathers. Fathers need to be offered increased access to information and support, be provided with the opportunity to network with other fathers, and have their own needs for information and emotional support within the family met.

In order to achieve these aims, greater training and awareness among professionals is essential. In his collection of essays by fathers, Meyer (1995) told how the birth of a child with disabilities brings about a life-transforming experience. For some, it is a challenge that enables them to display previously unacknowledged aspects of their personality. For others, it causes relentless stress, disorientates their life goals, and affects their work patterns. Bray, Skelton, Ballard, and Clarkson (1995) identified two main types of love within their cohort of fathers—unconditional and trans-forming. Some fathers showed devotion by accepting their children as they are and patiently standing by them through all of their endeavors. Others focused on transforming acts such as converting a room or building a playhouse.

Sheila West (2000) concluded that the fathers whom she interviewed felt that they were *just shadows*. Although there is some evidence that professionals are beginning to consider fathers' needs, four themes con-stantly recur throughout research and are of major significance within any effective early intervention program: 1) the absence of someone to talk to; 2) very little direct advice (e.g., on behavior management); 3) poor information; and 4) professionals' reluctance to discuss their child's future.

Siblings also have an important (but often neglected) role within any early intervention program; Newson and Davies (1994) and Glynne-Rule (1995) found that siblings seldom had full information on their brother or sister's disability. Some siblings experienced bullying and teasing, and many provided significant caregiving (after their parents). However, other studies (Byrne, Cunningham, & Sloper, 1988; Tritt & Esses, 1988) found that siblings of children with disabilities showed no difference in terms of emotional or behavioral disturbance when compared with other children. Siblings of someone with disabilities also have been found to be well adjusted and mature and to show a responsible attitude beyond their chronological age (Dale, 1996; Seligman & Darling, 1989). The emergence of literature specifically directed at siblings to help them understand their brother or sister's disability has been particularly helpful.

Grandparents also are an important source of support and advice for families, particularly in minority ethnic communities (Mirfin-Veitch & Bray, 1997). They can offer a range of practical help and also provide the emotional support so important to families, but their role within early intervention programs has been variable.

"Significant Others" in Early Support and Intervention

The literature on "significant others" in the lives of children with disabili-ties is sparse. Mittler noted that the support available to families (particu-larly in their local community) is "crucial in determining their quality of life" (1995, p. 87). However, in this international study, reactions of friends and neighbors varied, with some families reporting that they felt isolated by their neighbors. Carpenter (1997) examined family support strategies, and all of the families reported that their life would have been seriously altered without the input of "significant others." This is further indicated both by the increasing fragmentation of families and family support within the United Kingdom and by the success of community support schemes such as Home Start (which uses a wide range of trained volunteers to support families who are vulnerable). The development of Independent Parental Supporters for children with special educational needs (Russell, 2003) is another initiative that relies on proactive and informed "significant others."

Developing Family Support: The Challenge for Professionals

For many years, a variety of professionals have encouraged families to accept their children with disabilities and have attributed their reluctance to do so to a bereavement response. But although many of the similarities between grief and parenting a child with a disability may be endorsed, the reality at the sadness of having a child with a disability is constantly renewed, regardless of the pleasures gained from each positive development. Bowdery, the mother of a young man with disabilities, reminded professionals that the ever-unfolding pattern of life brings new and painful insights, "Just occasionally, there is a tantalising glimpse of the son that might have been. This is not the baby, the adolescent or adult I thought I would have" (1997, p. 7).

Parent empowerment was rigorously discussed by Dempsey (1993) and offers the best antidote to what Carpenter termed "the chronic vulnerability of families with children with disabilities" (1997, p. 92). The lack of professional understanding of the real lives of families of children with disabilities has led parent support organizations in the United Kingdom to produce models of service delivery that are "family friendly" and ensure real partnership between parents and professionals. Given the multiplicity of professionals, the "key worker" role is seen as pivotal in offering direct meaningful support to families and synthesizing the complex web of professional agencies that can overwhelm families. Limbrick (1997) saw the role of the key worker as part of a family-focused approach based in a supportive relationship built on honesty, respect, trust, and confidentiality—and defined by the parents' agenda.

Lifelong Support

McConachie (1997) pointed out that many professionals have had little training in working together, let alone with families. Thus, effective, interdisciplinary collaboration is not always the reality for many multiprofessional teams working with the families of children with disabilities. The shift toward family-centered service delivery reflects a move away from earlier efforts by professionals to involve parents in their children's specialized care, which assumed parental approval of professional recommendations. McGonigel and Garland (1988) noted that early approaches often were overly directive, and Basil (1994), writing from the Spanish context, described how many teachers endeavored to transplant their skills onto parents. Pivotal to the family-centered model is its focus on the needs of the entire family rather than on the needs of the child, the respect for family diversity, and the emphases on flexible and responsive services and on parental choice and decision making (Carpenter, Conway, & Woodgate, 2003). The family-centered approach is not a panacea; it will not instantly bring about quality services, but it will reposition the family at the heart of service delivery as the most informed source of knowledge about the child and family. As Beckman and Beckman Boyes stated,

> Like other families, we have experienced our share of competent professionals and our share of incompetent professionals; felt good about the services that Jacob was receiving, and felt that he was entitled to more; and met sensitive, caring professionals, and insensitive ones. We have waited for days to have a phone call returned, travelled miles to appointments, and feared the reactions of other children. (1993, p. 3)

The need for culturally sensitive early intervention as a universal concept is highlighted by the work of Srinivasan and Karlan who reminded professionals that the "diverse child-rearing goals and practices of Indian culture are not compatible with western conceptualisation of effective early intervention" (1997, p. 367). Nevertheless, if professionals do not start to adopt early intervention as a fundamental and valuable component in their repertoire of support services to families of children with disabilities, they will see its demise, and families will pay the price.

It is important not to lose sight of the fact that the impact on families of children with disabilities and their need for support is life long. The reality for them is that they face recurrent and unpredictable challenges. Not only do they require appropriate early intervention to provide support in the years after their child's birth, but also they will require access to ongoing support. Sainsbury raised issues about the lifelong implications of disability not only for families but also for society as a whole:

> The severity of handicaps that affect surviving children is becoming greater. Families cannot support the attention their children need without help from the state, but statutory funds are not rising with numbers. None of the £43 billion health budget is allocated towards care over a lifetime of disability. Health and social services do not connect to work at the problem together and there is little political

will to improve services. My son and my family, like parents and children all over the country, are living out society's forgotten ideals. (1998, p. 23)

These families do not seek sympathy and do not wish to be patronized but want to be valued and treated as equals. They are not interested in being converted to particular educational ideologies or medical or therapeutic doctrines but desire recognition of the individuality of their children and the uniqueness of their families. If these families' needs are to be met, then a coordinated and coherent approach is necessary.

Toward a Transdisciplinary Approach

Effective early intervention demands new patterns of working that are neither multiprofessional nor interdisciplinary but are transdisciplinary. The Australian researcher Paul Pagliano defined this approach:

> In a transdisciplinary team the roles are not fixed. Decisions are made by professionals collaborating at a primary level (rather than at a secondary level as in a multi-disciplinary team). The boundaries between disciplines are deliberately blurred to employ a "targeted eclectic flexibility." (1999, p. 2)

What are the challenges and opportunities that emerge? It has to be recognized, as Randall and Parker stated, that

> The severity of the child's disorder, at any level, can leave parents exhausted to a degree that is dependent on their stress tolerance. Many of them experience chronic pessimism and risk breakdowns in their functioning. Early intervention should seek to divert this bleak outcome. It should seek it vigorously and with great endeavour. (1999, p. 121)

Gary Mesibov (2001), in his analysis of the effect of early intervention, stated that its greatest contribution was engagement. He based this assumption on neuropsychological research. Very young children with autism may "block off" certain experiences and thus limit their brain growth and development. Mesibov stated that "it is important to do something and do it with a degree of intensity" (p. 189). Hendriks (2001), in a major Dutch study, criticized the focus that early intervention had on outcomes for the child. These outcomes, he stated, can no longer be regarded as a sole criterion for the efficacy of early intervention. If professionals move toward family-focused service delivery, then outcome measures should similarly be family focused. Thus, evaluation is only effective if it is conducted jointly by the family and the professional. This would endorse collaborative working—professionals and parents would be mutually valued, and there would be a shared agenda with shared goals. All of these are principles for good practice in early intervention (Carpenter, 1997).

The suggested redefinitions complement the Developmental Systems Model for early intervention that Guralnick (2001) published. The four key aims of this approach are 1) to guide early intervention programs for children who are vulnerable and their families, 2) to maximize family patterns of interaction, 3) to address potential stressors related to risk and disability conditions, and 4) to advocate community-based services.

These goals are only possible if professionals can cut through role-specific rhetoric and jargon and truly embrace partnership. This does not come automatically; it involves work. Fialka and Mikus spoke of the "dance toward partnership" and reminded us that "the only magic to forming partnerships is to slowly, tenderly and persistently share our dreams with each other, for it is our children who give us the reason and opportunity to strengthen our partnerships with others" (1999, p. 63).

Skilled professionals will no longer be solely concerned with their own disciplinary boundaries but with their capabilities as empathetic human beings and how their disciplinary skill base can enhance the lives of the families that they support. They will need to use an empowerment approach (Appleton & Minchcom, 1991) that recognizes the family as a system, with its own social network and the right to a choice of services and varying levels of engagement. Negotiation (Dale, 1996) will be a key feature of their practice, and, when there are differences between professionals and families, there will be joint decision making based on shared perspectives. Thus, partnerships with families becomes a dynamic, not a static, concept, which is multilevel rather than linear in its approach.

Open and honest sharing of ideas, knowledge, and skills can lead to a more collaborative team process and result in better services for the child. It is necessary, however, to begin to address more fully ways of fostering reflective practitioners who feel comfortable and valued in working within families. A first step to achieving this has been reported in a training program, "Celebrating Families," in which professionals are trained by and with families to improve and deepen their insights into family needs (Carpenter, Addenbrooke, Attfield, & Conway, in press).

DEVELOPING A FRAMEWORK FOR POSITIVE EARLY INTERVENTION: PUTTING VALUES INTO ACTION

As noted previously, since the 1990s, there has been an unprecedented interest in early intervention in the United Kingdom. This interest in (and commitment to) early intervention has been accompanied by a recognition that programs are unlikely to be effective unless families are fully involved, are both valued and supported in their parenting roles and within any intervention program, and have relevant and accessible information on which to make decisions about their and their children's lives.

It also has been widely recognized that although all children should have the best possible start to life, young children with disabilities often receive interventions from a fragmented and uncoordinated range of services. Furthermore, such services frequently place unreasonable and additional burdens on families because of the complexity of assessment and eligibility access criteria. Early identification and intervention are key themes in the government's Special Educational Needs Action Plan (Department for Education and Skills, 2004). They are central to other government initiatives such as Quality Protects (a program of targeted funding to improve the life chances of children who are disadvantaged or vulnerable) and Sure Start.

The government, therefore, established a multi-agency working party to produce *Together from the Start* (Department for Education and Skills, 2003b), the first practical guidance for professionals working with children with disabilities from birth to 3 years and their families. The guidance was launched in 2003, simultaneously with guidance on the development of early intervention/support services for deaf children and their families. This parallel document addresses the particular issues for the early identification of deafness in children and for their families in the context of the introduction of universal newborn hearing screening.

Together from the Start started from the belief that

> Effective early intervention and support can produce improvements in children's health, social and cognitive development and help tackle some of the many social and physical barriers that families of disabled children face to full participation in society. (Department for Education and Skills, 2003b, p. 3)

It also has a strong family focus, recognizing that

> It is not only disabled children's impairments which determine the quality of life but also disabling attitudes and a disabling environment, which can result in unequal access to community services and facilities. Effective intervention strengthens the ability of families to provide effective support to their children and improves outcomes for the whole family. (Department for Education and Skills, 2003b, p. 7)

Together from the Start also acknowledges the challenge of a rapidly changing population of young children with disabilities, including those with very complex multiple disabilities (in part because of the increased survival of very preterm infants due to improvements in neonatal care) and a significant reported increase in the prevalence of autism spectrum disorders and ADHD.

The specific aims of the guidance are to promote effective early intervention services for meeting the needs of very young children with disabilities and their families, to identify and promote existing examples of effective partnership, and to support the strategic development of services for this population. The key barriers to early intervention are identified as a lack of sensitivity around the initial diagnosis, inconsistent patterns of provision, lack of coordination between a range of multiple service providers, and the current exclusion of children and families from some mainstream and community services and facilities.

Extensive consultation with parents, relevant professionals, and services offered some key messages about improving the quality and coherence of services, namely, earlier diagnosis and a "joined-up" or transdisciplinary approach to assessment, effective coordination of service provision with transparency in information sharing, parent/family-held records, the introduction of key workers who can provide a single gateway to multidisciplinary services, effective communication between professionals, and emotional support that recognizes the pressures and challenges facing parents who want to be active partners in the care and development of their child.

An interesting and initial challenge for the working party was deciding which children have disabilities. Many parents said they found current definitions of *disability* to be very negative and irrelevant to very young children. It was also acknowledged that, in the case of very young children, it would not always be possible to determine whether an impairment would be long term. A working definition was therefore developed:

> A child under 3 years of age shall be considered disabled if he or she
> 1) Is experiencing significant developmental impairment or delays, in one or more of the areas of cognitive development, sensory or physical development, communication development, social, behavioural or emotional development, or 2) Has a condition which has a high probability of resulting in developmental delay. (Department for Education and Skills, 2003b, p. 6)

The introduction of guidance on early intervention must be put in the broader context of the government's wider policy agenda. The creation of the Disability Rights Commission in 2000 and related disability discrimination legislation (together with the National Service Framework for children's health care and a strong focus on inclusion within education services) focused attention on the high risk of social exclusion for young children with disabilities and their families. In *Together from the Start*, the government affirmed that

> An important element in tackling social exclusion is ensuring that disabled children have their needs recognised and that these needs are addressed promptly and effectively. Families also need support when seeking help from professionals across a range of services. Their reasonable expectation is that agencies will work closely together and flexibly to improve the provision made for their children. (Department for Education and Skills, 2003b, p. 8)

The national policy agenda for young children and their families has provided a number of new opportunities such as Sure Start programs and the development of Neighbourhood Nurseries. *Together from the Start* presented the common themes with regard to parents' roles and rights within the new initiatives:

- Rights and responsibilities: Parents have rights and responsibilities in relation to the development and care of their child. They have the right to be respected as the primary caregivers of their child.

- Respect: Parents have unique knowledge about their child.

- Informed choice: Parents have the right to be provided with unbiased, accurate, and up-to-date information in order to be able to make informed and appropriate choices for their child.

- Individuality: There are many common issues for parents of children with disabilities, but no two families are the same. Families can be diverse in terms of their experience, resources, and expectations, as well as their cultural, religious, and linguistic influences.

- Equality: Optimum support for a child with disabilities can occur only when parents are considered to be valued and equal partners alongside the range of professionals working with them and their child.

Outcomes from *Together from the Start:* The Development of the Role of the Key Worker

Creating family-friendly services will necessitate fresh thought about what makes services "work" for families. Both *Together from the Start* and the National Service Framework endorse the potential of the role of key worker (discussed previously in this chapter) with different models currently being developed within the government-funded and evaluated Early Support Pilot Projects.

Together from the Start defined the role of the key worker as

> A source of support for the families of disabled children and a link by which other services are accessed and used effectively. The key worker has responsibility for working together with the family and with professionals from their own and other services and for ensuring delivery of the [Family Service] Plan for the child and family. Workers performing this role may come from a number of different agencies, depending upon the particular needs of the child. (Department for Education and Skills, 2003b, p. 17)

Together from the Start and the National Service Framework envision key workers being allocated to all families of children with complex needs, with a possible expansion to other families in the future. The key workers' central roles will be to provide a single reference point for information; to assist in coordination and facilitating access to relevant services; to anticipate children's and families' emotional, practical, and social needs; and to play a role in the implementation of the Family Service Plan.

Sloper, Jones, Triggs, Howarth, and Barton (2003), in a paper on the role of key workers for the National Service Framework External Working Group on Disabled Children, noted the need both to explore different options around implementation of the role and to consider core competencies (e.g., specific training in working with young children and their families; relevant knowledge of local and national services for the children they work with and how to gain access to them; counseling, communication, and negotiation skills). In many instances, key workers will, logically, be chosen from the main service working with the child (e.g., health, education); however, *Together from the Start* acknowledged that, on occasions, the role of the key worker may blur with that of advocate, and in those circumstances, an independent person may be needed to perform the role.

Making Sense of Multi-Agency Assessment and Support: The Family Service Plan

An immediate task for the key worker, on being allocated to a family, will be the implementation of the Family Service Plan. The Family Service Plan is a written summary of assessment outcomes provided in an accessible format and which gives key information on actions by different professionals. It specifies services and support (with review arrangements) and states who the family's key worker will be. *Together from the Start* represents a major step forward in exploring optimum models for effective early education and support. Once evaluated, the 27 Pilot Projects will lead to a national dissemination program to improve the delivery of services to children younger than 3 years old and their families.

A number of specific products are being developed to help implement the key lessons from the Pilot Projects:

- Early Support Professional Toolkit: This will assist service providers and offer practical guidance, case studies, and examples of regional and national development.

- Early Support Family Toolkit: This will both provide parents with information on their child's disability and act as a lever to improve services by helping families understand what good services look like and, hence, what to request. The Toolkit will give parents templates for Family Service Plans, Family Held Records, and a Log of Professional

Contacts, along with a standard bank of information tailored for a range of different populations.

- Early Support Service Audit Tool: This will enable service providers to measure the quality of the service they are providing and to plan for improvement. The Service Audit Tool will provide a multi-agency, pan-disciplinary instrument to audit current service provision at the local level, plan for development, and inspect service provision.

- Early Support Monitoring Protocol for Deaf Children: This will provide a standard developmental profile for parents and professionals to use in tracking the development of deaf children in the first 3 years of life.

Sure Start

Sure Start is a "flagship" government program, creating multi-agency universal support systems for families with young children in disadvantaged communities. The program provides a range of support services for families and children, with a strong focus on developing the capacity of local professionals and parents and improving the life chances of children who are potentially vulnerable. Sure Start has its own Public Service Agreement with the UK Treasury, with specific targets that include increasing the proportion of young children meeting early learning goals for personal, social, and emotional development; increasing the proportion of young children with satisfactory speech and language development at 2 years old and those reaching early learning goals for communication, language, and literacy; and reducing by 12% the proportion of young children living in households in which no one is working.

Sure Start–funded Children's Centres must be located in and serve families in disadvantaged areas. They bring together locally available services and integrate management and staffing structures (not necessarily on one site). All Children's Centres must offer early education integrated with child care, family support (including outreach services for parents), and child and family health services.

The Sure Start Children's Centres are intended to act as a hub for local community services for parents and as providers of child care services for children of all ages. Their services can include early education integrated with child care for infants and children until they reach school age, child care suitable for working parents (i.e., 5 days per week, 48 weeks per year if required), early identification of children with special needs and disabilities, and inclusive services and support for the families of these children.

Active parental involvement is a key theme with Sure Start. Schemes are expected to develop specific strategies to include fathers and families from minority ethnic groups in planning local services. Family support and health advice must be available at times suitable for working parents, and all services are expected to be accessible to children with disabilities and their families.

Sure Start expects all young children's services to work from a shared set of key principles:

- Working with parents and children: Every family should have access to a range of services that will deliver better outcomes for both children and parents, meeting their needs and stretching their aspirations.

- Services for everyone: Families have distinctly different needs— between different families, in different locations, and across time in the same family. Services should recognize and respond to these varying needs.

- Flexibility at the point of delivery: All services should be designed to encourage access. Families should receive support through a single point of contact.

- Starting very early: Services for young children and parents should start at the first antenatal visit. This means not only advice on health in pregnancy but also preparation for parenthood, decisions about returning to work (or starting work) after birth, advice on child care options, and information on available support services.

- Respect and transparency: Services should be customer driven.

- Being community driven and professionally coordinated: All professionals with an interest in children and families should routinely share expertise with, consult with, and listen to parents and local people to determine their service priorities

- Being outcome driven: The core purpose for all services for children and parents should be better outcomes for children. The government should acknowledge this by reducing bureaucracy and simplifying funding to ensure a "joined-up" approach with partners (Department for Education and Skills, 2003a).

The Sure Start program is being considerably extended. Early messages from its evaluation suggest that the provision of flexible early education and intervention services linked to active community development and parent education and support can have impressive outcomes for otherwise disadvantaged and socially excluded communities. All Sure Start programs offer Portage Home Teaching Programmes for young children with special educational needs or disabilities. Portage is expected to be more widely available in the near future because the government is considering requiring Portage or similar home teaching schemes to be available in all areas.

EARLY INTERVENTION AND WIDER STRATEGIC PLANNING

All of the previous initiatives were introduced within the wider context of a range of policy initiatives, including new frameworks for the inspection, regulation, and accreditation of services and the development of Local Strategic Partnerships introduced to create improvements in local coordination of children's services. New disability rights legislation and the creation of the Disability Rights Commission in 2000 provided an important incentive to review the extent to which young children with disabilities might be discriminated against in gaining access to early years services. Similarly, the creation of Children's Trusts (bringing together education, health, and social services within one organizational structure locally) provide the opportunity to pilot the design, commissioning, and delivery of well-integrated services for young children with disabilities and their families.

The government's Special Educational Needs Strategy (Department for Education and Skills, 2004) probably provides the most favorable environment in many years with regard to the developmental early intervention services within the United Kingdom. The program sets out a strategy that has a clear focus on improving service outcomes for the very youngest children with disabilities and their families. Key goals are better integration of services, improved information and support for parents, and new ways for professionals to work. Recognizing the need for families to lead "ordinary lives," the strategy also promotes better coordination of child care and early education and the creation of local networks to provide specialist advice and support to professionals. The current evaluations of Sure Start, Early Excellence Centres, and the Early Support Pilot Projects demonstrate a commitment to creating an evidence base for early intervention—with the prospect of a National Centre underlining the need for an ongoing agenda of development, training, and research in this area.

If *Together from the Start* works well and leads to better coordinated and preventive children's services, then children with disabilities may well benefit the most. A key factor in positive outcomes for children with disabilities will be the active partnership and confidence of parents and a recognition of their key role as educators, advocates, and co-workers alongside relevant professionals.

CHALLENGES AND OPPORTUNITIES FOR THE FUTURE

Professionals are being faced with children with increasingly complex learning disabilities. They challenge special educators to devise new and innovative methods of teaching. Their families require services to devise new strategies for sustaining and upholding them. These self-defining families (Carpenter, 1997) will require early intervention that can enable them to work with professionals toward meeting the needs of their children.

The challenge is to enable and empower families, but are professionals ready to align their practices with family need? With all of the competing pressures on resources in services, can there be a philosophical shift? Perhaps inspiration can be gained from Mencap:

> We believe that it should not be regarded as an exotic idea for disabled children and those close to them to aspire to a quality of life comparable to that enjoyed by others who do not live with a disability. In our view it is unacceptable at the beginning of the 21st century for the lives and experiences of disabled children and their families to be bereft of those features that many of us take for granted; features which make an ordinary and reasonable quality of life. Families are our greatest resource and if they are not seen as a resource they become problems. (2001, p. 21)

For the sake of children with disabilities and their families, professionals need to rescue early intervention from the clutches of political debate and economic scrutiny. Early intervention is society's response to its social responsibility. It is the means by which, in the early years, we will sustain our families who are undertaking that most complex of tasks—rearing a child with a disability. Their endeavors are to be applauded; they deserve our unquestionable support.

The United Kingdom has major opportunities to promote a developmental model of early intervention that values families and promotes a transdisciplinary approach to working with young children with disabilities or special educational needs. These opportunities include The National Service Framework; prioritization of early intervention and family support within *Every Child Matters*; an expansion of the Sure Start program and related early years initiatives; a new 10-year Special Educational Needs Strategy; the establishment of a National Centre for Excellence in Early Intervention; and a Foundation Stage to the National Curriculum within which there is particular interest in providing early intervention for children with disabilities or special educational needs. These should lead to greatly improved arrangements for the earlier identification and subsequent appropriate early intervention for children with disabilities and the wider range of children and families experiencing problems in the early years. The implementation of *Together from the Start* and the key messages emerging from the Early Support Pilot Projects should put high-quality early intervention firmly on the government's agenda. As the government's Special Educational Needs Strategy emphasized,

> Early intervention at all educational stages and phases is the cornerstone of our strategy. So while we have a particular focus on early years and the importance of a good start for children with special educational needs, early intervention is equally important once a child is in school. (Department for Education and Skills, 2004, p. 9)

However, the success of the growing number of targeted early intervention programs will be wholly effective only if they are developed within the wider context of strategic planning for *all* children and families. As Baroness Ashton, the government minister with responsibility for special educational needs and Sure Start, noted,

> Our mixture of universal support for parents and more targeted support and earlier intervention for disadvantaged families and their young children will help all parents balance their work and family life more effectively to ensure all children get a sure start in life . . . , we believe that early multi-agency support right from the start will improve the life chances of children and maximise the skills and commitment of families. (Department for Education and Skills, 2003a, p. 39)

REFERENCES

Appleton, P.L., & Minchcom, P.E. (1991). Models of parent partnership and child development centres. *Child: Care, Health and Development, 17,* 27–38.

Basil, C. (1994). Family involvement in the intervention process. In J. Brodin & E. Bjorck-Akesson (Eds.), *Methodological issues in research in augmentative and alternative communication* (pp. 56–84). Jonkoping, Sweden: Jonkoping University Press.

Beckman, P.J., & Beckman Boyes, G. (Eds.). (1993). *Deciphering the system: A guide for families of young children with disabilities.* Cambridge, MA: Brookline Books.

Bowdery, S. (1997, June). *Happy birthday, Matthew: A parent's perspective: On-going grief when your child has a disability.* Paper presented at the Child Bereavement Trust Conference, Portrait of Family Grief, London.

Bray, A., Skelton, E.J., Ballard, L., & Clarkson, J. (1995). Fathers of children with disabilities: Some experiences and reflections. *New Zealand Journal of Disability Studies, 1*(1), 164–176.

Byrne, E.A., Cunningham, C.C., & Sloper, P. (1988). *Families and their children with Down syndrome: One feature in common.* London: Routledge.

Cameron, R.J. (Ed.). (1986). *Portage: Preschoolers, parents and professionals: Ten years of achievement in the UK.* Windsor: NFER-Nelson.

Carpenter, B. (1997). *Families in context: Emerging trends in family support and early intervention.* London: David Fulton.

Carpenter, B. (2001, September). *What do we mean by early intervention? Doubts and definitions.* Paper presented at the British Institute of Learning Disabilities Conference, Cork, Ireland.

Carpenter, B. (in press). Early intervention—need or necessity?: An overview of emerging trends. *Tizard Learning Disability Review.*

Carpenter, B., Addenbrooke, M., Attfield, E., & Conway, S. (in press). Celebrating families: An inclusive model of family-centred training. *British Journal of Special Education.*

Carpenter, B., Conway, S., & Woodgate, A. (2003). Happy families. *Special Children, 157,* 34–37.

Carpenter, B., & Herbert, E. (1995). Including fathers: Parent–professional considerations of the role of fathers in early intervention. *Network, 4*(4), 4–11.

Dale, N. (1996). *Working with families of children with special needs.* London: Routledge.

Dempsey, I. (1993). The measurement of parent empowerment. In M. Arthur, R. Conway, & P. Foreman (Eds.), *Quality and equality in intellectual disability* (pp. 63–91). Newcastle, New South Wales: ASSID.

Department of Health. (2003). *National service framework (children): Emerging findings (Report of the external working group on disabled children).* London: Author.

Department for Education and Skills. (2001a). *Promoting children's mental health within early years and school settings.* Nottingham, England: Author.

Department for Education and Skills. (2001b). *The SEN [special educational needs] code of practice, revised edition.* Nottingham, England: Author.

Department for Education and Skills. (2002). *Developing early intervention/support services for deaf children and their families.* Nottingham, England: Author.

Department for Education and Skills. (2003a). *Sure Start: Start-up guidance for children's centres.* Nottingham, England: Author.

Department for Education and Skills. (2003b). *Together from the start: Practical guidance for professionals working with young disabled children (birth to third birthday) and their families.* Nottingham, England: Author.

Department for Education and Skills. (2003c). *Every child matters.* London: The Stationery Office.

Department for Education and Skills. (2004). *Removing barriers to achievement: The government's strategy for special educational needs.* Nottingham, England: Author.

Disability Discrimination Act 1995. Retrieved from http://www.legislation.hmso .gov.uk/acts/acts1995.htm

Dobson, B., & Middleton, S. (1998). *Paying to care: The cost of childhood disability.* York: Joseph Rowntree Foundation.

Fialka, J., & Mikus, K.C. (1999). *Do you hear what I hear? Parents and professionals working together for children with special needs.* Ypsilanti, Michigan: Proctor Publications.

Glynne-Rule, L. (1995, April 14). Support for the disabled. *Times Educational Supplement.* Retrieved from http://www.tes.co.uk/search/search_display .asp?section=Archive&sub_section=Friday&id=11668&Type=0

Gordon, D., Parker, R., Loughran, F., & Heslop, P. (2000). *Disabled children in Britain: A reanalysis of the KOPCS disability surveys.* London: The Stationery Office.

Guralnick, M.J. (2001). A developmental systems model for early intervention. *Infants and Young Children, 14*(2), 1–18.

Hautmäki, A. (1997). Mothers—stress, stressors and strains: Outcomes of a cross-Nordic study. In B. Carpenter (Ed.), *Families in context: Emerging trends in family support and early intervention* (pp. 63–81). London: David Fulton.

Heinen, H. (Ed.). (1997, October). *Early intervention for children with developmental disorders*. Leuven, Belgium: Alefpo/Europe.

Helmerhorst, F., Peerquin, D., Donker, D., & Keirse, M. (2004). Perinatal outcome of singletons and twins after conception: A systematic review of controlled studies. *British Medical Journal, 328*, 261–264.

Hendricks, L. (2001). *Therapeutic toddler classes in Dutch rehabilitation centres*. Nijmegen: University Press.

Hornby, G. (1995). *Working with parents of children with special needs*. London: Cassell.

Limbrick, P. (1997). Keyworking: Parent support. In P. Limbrick (Ed.), *Who supports the parents?: Five year review for parents, professionals and funders* (pp. 18–29). Todmorden, W. Yorkshire: One Hundred Hours.

Lovaas, O.I. (1987). Behavioural treatment and normal intellectual functioning in autistic children. *Journal of Consulting and Clinical Psychology, 55*, 3–9.

Manuel, P. (1996, December). *A parent's perspective*. Paper presented at the National Children's Bureau Conference, London.

McConachie, H. (1997). Do UK services really support parents? *Opportunity, 15*, 1–2.

McConkey, R. (1994). Early intervention: Planning futures, shaping years. *Mental Handicap Research, 7*(1), 4–15.

McGonigel, M.J., & Garland, C.W. (1988). The individualised family service plan and the early intervention team: Team and family issues and recommended practices. *Infants and Young Children, 1*(1), 10–21.

Melzer, D. (2000). *The development and well-being of children and adolescents in Great Britain*. London: Office of National Statistics.

Melzer, H., Gatward, R., Goodman, R., & Ford, T. (2000). *Mental health of children and adolescents in Great Britain*. London: The Stationery Office.

Mencap. (2001). *No ordinary life: The support needs of families caring for children with profound and multiple learning disabilities*. London: Royal Society for Mentally Handicapped Children and Adults.

Mesibov, G. (2001, May). *The spirit of TEACCH*. Keynote address to the International Autism Conference, Charlotte, North Carolina.

Meyer, D.J. (Ed.). (1995). *Uncommon fathers: Reflections on raising a child with a disability*. Bethesda, MD: Woodbine House.

Mirfin-Veitch, B., & Bray, A. (1997). Grandparents: The supporting role. In B. Carpenter (Ed.), *Families in context: Emerging trends in family support early intervention* (pp. 76–88). London: David Fulton.

Mittler, H. (1995). *Families speak out: International perspectives in families' experiences of disability*. Cambridge, MA: Brookline Books.

Mittler, P. (2000). *Working towards inclusive education: Social contexts*. London: David Fulton.

Newson, E., & Davies, J. (1994). Supporting the siblings of children with autism and related developmental disorders. In P. Mittler & H. Mittler (Eds.), *Innovations in family support for people with learning disabilities* (pp. 66–90). Chorley, Lancashire: Lisieux Hall.

Pagliano, P. (1999). Designing the multisensory environment. *PMLD Link, 12*(2), 2–6.

Randall, P., & Parker, J. (1999). *Supporting the families of children with autism*. Chichester: John Wiley.

Russell, P. (2003). *Disabled children, their families and child poverty, Briefing Paper*. London: End Child Poverty and Council for Disabled Children.

Sainsbury, K. (1998, March 20). Whose life is it? *Guardian*, 24.

Seligman, M., & Darling, R.B. (1989). *Ordinary families, special children: A system approach to childhood disability*. New York: The Guilford Press.

Shields, J. (2001). *The NAS early bird programme*. London: National Autistic Society.

Sloper, P., Jones, L., Triggs, S., Howarth, J., & Barton, K. (2003). Multi-agency care co-ordination and key worker services for disabled children. *Journal of Integrated Care, 11*(1), 9–15.

Special Educational Needs and Disability Act 2001. http://www.legislation.hmso.gov.uk/acts/acts2001.htm

Srinivasan, B., & Karlan, G.R. (1997). Culturally responsive early intervention programs: Issues in India. *International Journal of Disability, Development and Education, 44*(4), 367–385.

Treloar, R. (Ed.). (1997). *Recommended practices in family-centred early intervention*. Australia: New South Wales Ageing and Disability Department.

Tritt, S.G., & Esses, L.M. (1988). Psychosocial adaptation of siblings of children with chronic medical illness. *American Journal of Orthopsychiatry, 58*(3), 211–220.

West, S. (2000). *Just a shadow? A review of support for the fathers of children with disabilities*. Birmingham: The Handsel Trust.

Wolfendale, S. (2000). Special needs in the early years: Prospects for policy and practice. *Support for Learning, 15*(4), 147–151.

CHAPTER 19

EARLY INTERVENTION SERVICES IN GREECE

Present Situation and Future Prospects

EFTHALIA N. KADEROGLOU AND MARIA DROSSINOU

Greece is a European country that lies at the Southeastern part of the Mediterranean Sea. Twelve million people inhabit the country; more than 50% of them are located in the capital of Athens. Greece has an extensive coastline and hundreds of islands in the surrounding Aegean and Ionian Seas. Hellenic history and culture cover thousands of years, and from ancient times, Greeks have been deeply concerned with the discipline of education. Eternal teachers such as Socrates, Plato, and Aristotle were the first philosophers to explore the aims and structure of education as a science, and their work still enlightens philosophers and educators throughout the world. The term *pedagogy* is an offspring of the Hellenic spirit, and it was widely used by eminent academics of the 18th century such as Kant and Herbart who re-established it as an international term (*pädagogik, pédagogie, pedagogia*).

Equally, modern Greece declares through its Hellenic Constitution amendments of 2001 that

> Education is the country's basic mission aiming at moral, spiritual, professional and physical training of the Greeks that will result in the development of a national and religious conscience that will aid them to fulfill a free and responsible identity of citizenship. All Greeks are entitled to a free education, which is offered to them in public schools at all levels. The country shall support distinguished students and those deserving assistance or special care according to their abilities. (Article 16)

The very first attempts to implement Article 16 in regard to the education of people with special needs were initiated at the beginning of the 20th

481

century, more than 70 years after the Constitution of Rights was established. In 1906, the Home for the Blind was the first special school established in modern Greece. In 1937, the National Foundation for the Deaf made the first attempt to educate and care for people with hearing impairments; soon after, a small number of public elementary schools for children with disabilities were established (Imvrioti, 1939; Kalantzi, 1984).

In the years that followed, the Hellenic economy was deeply strained by World War II and the Hellenic Civil War until 1950. This afforded no luxury of special provisions that could have been designed to meet the different educational needs of children and adults. Until the early 1970s, special education has been left in the hands of charity organizations and isolated initiatives stemming from the private sector (Drossinou, 2001b; Kalantzi, 1984).

At the beginning of the 1970s, the Hellenic Ministry of Education and Religious Affairs (HMERA) started to undertake a more active role regarding the education of children with special educational needs. At that time, a 2-year in-service training program in special education was initiated for teachers, and in 1976, HMERA founded the Directorate of Special Education and appointed the first special education counselors to provide further guidance and support to special education teachers.

LEGISLATION

In March 1981, the first law concerning special education (1143/81) was accepted by consensus of all political parties at the Hellenic Parliament. This law was enriched and refined and resulted in Law 1566 (L.1566) of 1985, which concerned the general education policy of the country. During the 1980s, Greece witnessed a more systematic development of educational provision for children with special needs (Kalantzi, 1984). Since the late 1980s, HMERA's priorities have been defining special educational needs as well as the structure and implementation of a special educational provision within the public school system through public special schools and special classes functioning within the ordinary schools (Drossinou, 2001c; HMERA Pedagogical Institute, 1995, 1996, 2000a, 2000b, 2000c, 2000d, 2000e; Kalantzi, 1975).

According to the 1994 informational report of the Special Education Directorate of HMERA, Greece has no specific statistical information concerning the number of children with special educational needs; therefore, HMERA is still obliged to estimate that 10% of the school-age population is experiencing some form of disability. According to this estimate, 176,000 children belong in this group (HMERA, 1994). Figures resulting from the Eurydice Program funded by the European Community

(EC) indicate that a total of only 13,595 children with diverse special needs attended all levels of compulsory schooling for the 1999–2000 school year (Efstathiou, 2001a; Markakis & Fragulitaki, 2000; Pepin, 1994).

It has to be stressed that kindergartens that provide early childhood education beginning at age 4 years are not compulsory. Thus, it is fairly easy for one to understand that the previous figures do not necessarily include the fragile age group of children from birth to 6 years of age. Until recently, special educational needs in Greece were addressed after the age at which children entered school (6 years and older).

Between 1995 and 2000, HMERA brought forth 40 different bills for the reformation of special education services. This was done without an efficient dialogue between HMERA and collective bodies of special education, parent organizations, and scientific associations, and it thereby resulted in some harsh criticism (Xanthopoulos, 2001; Zoukis, 2001).

In March 2000, a new law concerning special education provision was passed. The need to follow the ideological trends of educational inclusion for all children in one school resulted in this latest revision of the law. The new Law 2817 (L.2817) describes the available educational services for children with special educational needs. L.2817 defines itself as inclusion oriented and, depending on its implementation, could become the cornerstone of a new era in the field of support and educational provision for children with special needs in Greece. Haroupias (2001) questioned the correct implementation of L.2817, highlighting that on various occasions the implementation of the law has been inadequate. He noted that L.1566 of 1985 asked for the establishment of a special education council (SEC) that would be responsible for the implementation of all decrees concerning special education provision. Unfortunately, SEC was never formed.

EMERGENCE OF EARLY INTERVENTION

L.2817 brings up certain issues that imply a meager attempt to begin a form of early intervention services. More specifically, Article 2 of L.2817 provides a definition of people with special educational needs as those experiencing any of the following: mental deficiency or immaturity; severe visual or hearing problems (e.g., blind, deaf, hard of hearing); severe neurological or orthopedic problems or general health problems; speech and language problems; specific learning difficulties (e.g., dyslexia, dysarithmesia); and complex cognitive, emotional, and social difficulties including those associated with autism and other pervasive developmental disorders. Article 3 expands the target population, clarifying that it includes people of preschool, school, and adolescent age that might not be included in one of the previous categories but could be in need of special approaches and care. Article 6 declares that children in all of the previous categories are entitled to special education services in the context of the aims of primary, secondary, and vocational education. Article 7 of L.2817 states that special educational provision, which includes diagnosis and assessment of special needs, pedagogical and psychological intervention and support, physiotherapy, occupational therapy, speech therapy, social work, and counseling, will be offered to all people in need until they are 22 years old (Law 2817, 2000).

Although the definition of Article 3 includes children from birth to 6 years for the first time, the use of the term *preschool age* does not clearly define the lower age limit of these children. Bearing in mind that preschool education begins at age 4, together with the noncompulsory status of public kindergartens, it is evident that L.2817 is not intended to entitle early care and support services to children from birth to 4 years.

A second point that is worth mentioning is the funding of the Centers for Diagnosis, Assessment, Evaluation, and Support (CDAES). These centers, as described in L.2817, should be responsible for the official statement of special educational needs of the school-age population as well as for the design of the necessary educational provision and support for each individual child. These centers must assess each child in the center's geographical area of responsibility and decide the placement of children with established disabilities and children at risk. Placement can occur in one of the three different types of school settings: regular classroom, inclusion class, or special school class. Interesting enough, the complex job description of the multidisciplinary team of CDAES, among other aspects, includes the recommendation of a structured program of early intervention for all people belonging to the target population. This statement uncovers a vague attempt at placing the first foundations for early intervention provision on the Greek public educational system.

In the pilot phase of the implementation of L.2817, HMERA announced the establishment of 21 CDAES: four in the Attica prefecture; two in Peloponnese; four in Macedonia; three in Thrace; and the rest in the Cyclades, Dodekanissos, Lesvos, Crete, Larissa, Fthiotida, Ioannina, Corfu, and Aetoloakarnania. Nonetheless, certain issues concerning the functioning of CDAES have raised considerable criticism. An important issue that has been expressed by several collective bodies involved in special education provision is the doubt that there will be equal development of CDAES in each one of the 53 prefectures of the country. A major reason is the country's long-existing uneven distribution of relevant infrastructures that has created enormous problems in educational services. The repetition of the same scenario is a major concern with respect to the educational reformation of L.2817. Unfortunately, these facts stem from the suffocating administrative centralization and have created cumulative problems that are well documented by numerous denunciations from parents across the country (Drossinou, 2001a). In addition, special educators also criticized the interdisciplinary model that CDAES adopted as a discipline-referenced model that relies on isolated services in which students receive assessment in an unnatural environment away from the flow of the school's educational process (Efstathiou, 2001b; Xanthopoulos, 2001).

A third point of discussion is about the development of the Multipower Resource Centers of Special Education (MRCSE) that L.2817 presents. The possibility for the establishment of counseling services for infants and their families lies in this new infrastructure (Law 2817, 2000). This point is of major importance because it is the first time that a Greek law has mentioned special needs in infancy and the importance of early help and guidance for the whole family. Under the broad term of *counseling*, an individual could infer that different types of family-centered early intervention practices could be embraced by these services once they are established (Cameron, 1986; Daly, Addington, Kerfoot, & Sigston, 1985). Because the establishment of the counseling services at MRCSEs depends on a future ministerial decree, none of these services are yet granted.

Because L.2817 claims to be inclusion oriented, certain actions were thought to provide evidence of this. In furtherance of this goal, L.2817 states that certified special educators will be appointed to every school that includes a minimum of eight children with established disabilities that need special support. In 2001, HMERA *inaugurated* 35 new inclusion classes within the general public kindergartens. These classes were expected to cover the needs of an additional 350 children in the 4- to 6-year-old age group (Drossinou, 2001a).

DEVELOPMENTAL SYSTEMS MODEL FOR EARLY INTERVENTION

Since the 1980s, international literature has produced a tremendous amount of information on issues concerning early intervention models and practices. Considerable light has been shed on the scientific foundations of early childhood development; models of early intervention have been refined; and understanding their limitations has compounded (Guralnick, 1997; Harbin, McWilliam, & Gallagher, 2000). EC countries reached a general consensus for a definition of *early intervention* regardless of variations in social and economic conditions:

> The aim of giving help at an early stage to a child with disabilities or whose development is delayed, is to encourage and stimulate their sensory-motor, emotional, social and intellectual development, so that their individual aptitudes and capacities can develop and they can

participate in life and environment actively and independently. (Peterander, 1996, p. 8)

Current international trends that reflect contemporary thinking that is consistent with empirical information have shown a shift in the focus of early intervention. The target is no longer solely the child but rather the complex system of the whole family. It has been stressed that family-focused early intervention has to be incorporated into the unique life of each community. Guralnick (2001) developed such a model, applying a developmental framework on which early intervention organizes critical components that are flexible enough to be applied to any community-based early intervention service system. According to the Developmental Systems Model, three core principles guide the system's design in order to provide the best quality of services and tackle most of the practical issues of service provision (see Chapter 1). The first principle of the model is the developmental framework that needs to address stressors on typical family patterns of interaction that might result from either child or family characteristics. The model is clearly focused on the family as a whole in an attempt to strengthen the family's abilities to interact with the child effectively and, therefore, maximize the child's development and well-being. The second principle of the model refers to the integration of an array of relevant and necessary disciplines and coordination of services as a meaningful foundation for collaboration efforts. This principle is especially important for interdisciplinary assessments, the assessment of potential stressors, and the successful implementation of intervention plans. The third core principle is inclusion, which is an increasingly accepted value that encourages the provision of support and services to children and families in natural environments and in typical community activities.

These principles are applied to the major components of early intervention systems including screening, monitoring, points of access, comprehensive interdisciplinary assessment, eligibility, preventive and regular early intervention programs, assessments of stressors, developing and implementing programs, monitoring, outcome evaluations, and transition. This chapter depicts the circumstances under which early intervention functions in Greece for each of these components.

HELLENIC EARLY INTERVENTION PROVISION: A GUIDED TOUR

Screening

In Greece, developmental screening is occasionally offered at the pediatric clinics of state hospitals or at the medico-pedagogical centers that function under the auspices of the Hellenic Ministry of Health and Social Welfare

(HMHSW). Apart from these institutions, mental health centers also might be engaged in developmental screening. All of these institutions are centrally administered by the HMHSW, which poses many problems in the institutions' functioning. Pediatric clinics, medico-pedagogical centers, and mental health centers are found only in major cities, leaving most of the 53 prefectures without efficient primary health care. Moreover, the existing institutions are usually understaffed because of the monstrous urbanization in Athens. Although many attempts have been made to provide incentives for citizens to move to and work in other parts of the country, the problem still remains, creating enormous heterogeneity in terms of offered services simply because human resources are scarce in most provinces of the country. The centralized administration of all health and support services, coupled with a rigid bureaucratic procedure for staff appointments, worsens the situation. Job positions in health and support settings throughout the country are often left vacant for months (HMHSW, 2003). Families in rural parts of the country, especially the islands, are either left unattended or are obliged to wait for an appointment for several months (Efstathiou, 2001b). For all of the aforementioned reasons, it is fairly easy to understand why the screening procedure is skipped in most cases.

Similarly, localized services of the newly established CDAES are run by the central administration of HMERA and are equally scarce. Of course, CDAES is designed to meet the needs of children with established disabilities starting at the age of 4 in an attempt to create the best possible schooling environment according to their needs. Therefore, CDAES is by nature not responsible for general screening. Apart from the problems that a centralized administration of services creates for various parts of the country, screening also may be hindered by a possible lack of interest in or awareness of the value of developmental observation by health care providers.

Monitoring

Similar to the screening process, monitoring is also rather poor in Greece. No specific protocols are put forward by HMHSW or other professional organizations for the monitoring of children at risk. Some of the reasons for the country's poor monitoring system might be the families' limited access to information; scarcity and uneven distribution of primary health care services; and lack of appropriate knowledge and skills of primary care physicians, who should play a leading role in developmental surveillance.

Point of Access

In the absence of a clear and cohesive model of developmental screening and monitoring, parental concerns often are underestimated and left unattended for a critical amount of time. Most of the time, after a period of frustration and impatience, families self-refer either to the existing organizations mentioned previously or to health professionals and/or early intervention providers of the private sector.

The medico-pedagogical centers and the centers for mental health that cannot fulfill their mission because of lack of specialized personnel refer the families to pediatric or child psychiatric clinics for interdisciplinary assessment for the child and family. If these services are remote for the family, then they might prefer to visit health professionals from the private sector and skip the long hospital waiting lists. These professionals might recommend an interdisciplinary assessment, sending the family back to the national health system, or they may directly refer them to early intervention providers. Accordingly, some of these early intervention providers might stress the need for interdisciplinary assessment of the child and family; others will not, depending on their ethics and level of good practice.

Comprehensive Interdisciplinary Assessment

When a child is born with a disability or displays a developmental delay, the family is forcefully thrown off balance. The first diagnosis is one of the most important, if not the most important, phase regarding early intervention because it has a decisive influence on the necessary immediate measures and future course of help, education, and support given to the child and his or her family. Through this process, a child's health and developmental profile will be generated along with diagnostic or etiologic information and a description of family functioning.

This chapter has already discussed that a family's general route toward acquiring an interdisciplinary assessment of their needs, strengths, and stressors can be difficult. Even when a late diagnosis is made (at 36–60 months of age), a family usually receives information solely from the medical point of view (e.g., genetic causes, cerebral dysfunction). A medical treatment (e.g., operation, seeing or hearing aids, medication) might be offered. As in many other countries, early cooperation between medicine, pedagogy, and psychology is weak.

Members of the assessment team are usually psychiatrists, neurologists, and occupational therapists (Kottaridi, Kappi, & Adam, 1998). The pedagogical and psychological aspect of the diagnosis that would enrich assessment with descriptions of the child and family's strengths and weaknesses along with clear objectives that concern early intervention are rarely found in Hellenic pediatric clinics.

Similarly, the medico-pedagogical centers and mental health centers, although designed to be staffed as interdisciplinary teams, are understaffed and have been unable to play an active role in designing and conducting individualized family service plans. Their participation is unfortunately inadequate at the diagnostic phase, merely because of inadequate human resources.

In addition, interdisciplinary teams in all health and support services settings are followed by their model design ghosts: Child skills are not assessed in natural environments, and assessments often are test specific. Moreover, the structure of the interdisciplinary team sometimes promotes competitive professional interactions that can result in disjointed programmatic outcomes (Albano, Cox, York, & York, 1981; Giangreco, 1986; Giangreco, York, & Rainforth, 1989; York, Rainforth, & Giangreco, 1990).

Eligibility

Early intervention programs in Greece are provided both by the public and private sectors. The public sector, through the institutions that have been described, is unable to provide intervention covering the large numbers of children and families that are in need of such services. Each interdisciplinary assessment team in Greece usually ends its role in relation to the families by giving some suggestions on treatment, leaving the actual implementation to special educators and therapists. A small number of children might be directed to a few institutions that were funded by parent associations and provide early intervention through separate and parallel therapies, including Hellenic Society for the Protection and Rehabilitation of Disabled Children (ELEPAP) and Center for Rehabilitation of Spastic Children (KASP), which aim primarily to provide services to children with physical disabilities; Center for the Education and Rehabilitation of the Blind (KEAT), which provides services to children with vision problems; and the Institution for the Deaf, which provides services for children with hearing problems. Unfortunately, most of these institutions enroll children with established disabilities starting from the age of 4. KEAT and the Institution for the Deaf are the only institutions that provide counseling services to families and home-based programs aiming to educate and train parents on how to enhance their communication patterns with their children (ELEPAP, 2002; KASP, 2002; KEAT, 2002). Similarly, the Research Institution for the Child–Spiros Doxiadis and the Hellenic Portage Association are non-governmental organizations (NGOs) that have been trying to promote home-based early intervention, which strengthens families by gradually educating them to organize better parent–child transactions (Kaderoglou, 2001; Kaderglou & Vayona, 2003; Portage-Hellas, 2002; Thomaidis & Kaderoglou, 1997; Thomaidis, Kaderoglou, Stefou, Damianou, & Bacoula, 2000). Unfortunately, the parents must pay high fees for these services because of very little state compensation. All of these NGOs are headquartered in Athens, making these meaningful and efficient services available mainly to residents of Athens.

An alternative to early intervention in all areas of the country started with the implementation of L.2817. According to the law, children with less severe disabilities can enroll in an inclusion class after a CDAES formal assessment. Nonetheless, the first year of the implementation of L.2817 has brought very poor feedback. The scarcity of CDAES, their long waiting lists, and their inability to provide immediate solutions to establish new inclusion classes in districts where families in need live or to appoint accredited special educators to the existing ones have created more problems than they have solved. These cumulative problems are well documented by numerous criticisms from parents across the country that reached the office of the Administration of Special Education of HMERA (Drossinou, 2001a).

For the aforementioned reasons, the majority of children that actually go through the diagnostic phase are referred to freelance therapists that are capable of addressing the immediate needs of this population. The referrals are carried out with a general anticipation of improvement of the child's development. However, short- and long-term goals are not usually clearly defined. In addition, these referrals have no specific eligibility criteria. A crude rule-of-thumb is followed: Children with motor disabilities need physiotherapy and occupational therapy; children with mental retardation need special education programs, speech therapy, and occupational therapy; and children with language disorders or specific learning difficulties need speech therapy, among other things.

Entrance into an Early Intervention Program

In the absence of a clear legal framework and adequate government services, early intervention provision in Greece depends mainly on independent private establishments. Naturally, such establishments have their own organization and are responsible for their own finances, administration, and promotion of services. Furthermore, they are based on their own concepts and principles of early intervention, mirroring the theoretical and ideological orientation of their owners. Indeed, the 1990s brought an outburst of services in Greece claiming to provide early intervention. These services were and continue to be clustered in the capital of Athens, Thessaloniki, and in a few other major cities. For the most part, these are private offices of freelance therapists that offer special education programs, speech therapy, occupational therapy, physiotherapy, or a combination of these approaches. Some private centers employ specialists from a wide array of disciplines, whereas others concentrate on one or two types of therapeutic services. Integration of various therapies is not a task that can be easily achieved in these centers because rarely is there a service coordinator who will work closely with the family to develop the program.

Preventive Intervention Program

In Greece, early intervention is perceived merely as a separate provision of discipline-specific therapeutic services. This constitutes perhaps the biggest barrier to a well-integrated and well-coordinated developmental model of early intervention in which the involvement of families would be of central importance, and the coordination and collaboration of different disciplines would give their input in the context of naturalistic environments. The absence of clear eligibility criteria for early intervention stems from this theoretical perception that, unfortunately, applies to most of the existing interdisciplinary assessment teams. The inefficiency of the existing assessment procedure caused by the centralization of services, along with the absence of clear eligibility criteria, is clearly leaving no space for the luxury of preventive early intervention programs. Children at risk who do not display established disabilities often simply exit the system or never participate in any program whatsoever.

Assessment of Stressors

The Developmental Systems Model (Guralnick, 2001) stresses that effective early intervention programs are those that, while working in partnership with families, are able to address potential stressors that are influencing the levels of the family's patterns of interaction and therefore child development. These programs coordinate services, provide counseling, arrange parent groups, or make financial assistance amenable to each family's special pattern of stressors.

The stressors that may be affecting family interaction patterns are rarely assessed; the intervention in Greece is mainly child focused and concentrates on the impairments children exhibit. Therefore, stressors that are related to information needs, interpersonal and family stress, resource needs, and confidence threats are generally not assessed. In cases in which the interdisciplinary team of a hospital, a medico-pedagogical center, or a mental health center does include specialists from social work or psychology, information might be gathered through interviews and discussions about the family's perceptions of their child's development, the family's social support network, the family's adaptability and stability, or parent–child related interactions.

Similarly, when qualified personnel are available, family characteristics such as stressors related to the marital relationship, the family's financial resources, and parental mental health, as well as the child's influence on these characteristics, might be assessed. Although this information would be meaningful for better design and implementation of a comprehensive intervention program, it is usually kept idle in records simply because there is no alternative early intervention scheme except the one that will be organized by the individual therapists themselves. Moreover, all of the previous information regarding potential stressors that may negatively influence the three family patterns of interaction is elicited in a one-way information flow. Sadly, the aim of all services is to gather information; it is seldom to provide and share information with the parents who are regarded as passive recipients of child-focused therapies. The overall philosophy of building a relationship with the families is bypassed in existing services. This could be a reflection of various disciplines' professional training or simply that the rigidity of the existing system leaves no room for alternatives in early intervention, thus no frame of mind for partnership with parents. In this framework, it is easily understood that even the basic information needs of the family (e.g., implications regarding diagnosis, comprehension of the child's asymmetrical development) often are left unattended.

Developing and Implementing Programs

Because suggestions to strengthen families are generally not discussed, early intervention providers offer the program's content of child-focused therapies, decide on the intensity of the educational-therapeutic scheme, and define the parental role primarily as the child's transporter. Often, families are subject to a great deal of discomfort because they are obliged to bring their child to these centers two or three times per week. Families residing in rural areas often have to travel for 1 or 2 hours to reach centers in the nearest city. The difficulty of weekly transportation, coupled with economic burdens, makes commitment to an intervention program very fragile (Konstantopoulou, 2001). Most parents are treated as recipients of services and simply quit a program if it does not match their needs or when stressors in family life have become unbearable.

Monitoring and Outcome Evaluations

Unfortunately, there is neither legal framework to control and ensure the quality of the private establishments' services nor any evidence through independent research regarding their evaluations of effectiveness. As noted previously, whether concrete approved interventions for each specific child are developed with interdisciplinary cooperation is rather dubious. In most cases, the program is designed by the owner of the center, who usually offers a synthesis of different therapeutic sessions. Core principles of developmental framework, integration, and inclusion do not seem to fit into this framework. The monitoring process that might take place is an occasional follow-up assessment through the interdisciplinary teams of pediatric and child psychiatric clinics, at the medico-pedagogical centers, and at mental health centers. More often, families are frustrated and overwhelmed by the problematic procedures of the health care system and choose a simpler way in order to receive some feedback about their child's development. They may visit the health clinicians in the private sector that had originally referred them for early intervention to the therapists. Unfortunately, although this route is quicker, it is not the best for this purpose. Parents rarely receive a written report of their child's assessment with specified child outcomes.

Transition

Neither therapists in the private sector nor state establishments have a planning process for the transitions that children or their families might experience. The model of early intervention in Greece is not conceptualized as a system designed to strengthen families in ways that would best promote a child's development. Therefore, such a model is by nature indifferent with respect to encouraging the family's full participation in the natural environments at home and school and in community life.

RECENT LEGISLATION

In January 2003, the HMHSW (2003) presented a bill that concerned the reconstruction of all offered social services infrastructures. The overall spirit of L.3106 that was finally passed on January 21, 2003, concerns the decentralization of all offered social services. Health, social care, and support services are now becoming a responsibility of the local authorities in each and every prefecture of the country. The shift from central-based administration of services to locally- and community-based support is intended to help alleviate many of the cumulative problems of the past. Flexibility of services is desirable, and it acknowledges the effectiveness of a small range of services being tailored to local needs. This is a fundamental characteristic of the new Law 3106 (L.3106, 2003). Nonetheless, questions already have arisen about the viability of the existing services. Local authorities stress that decentralization must occur not only in philosophy but also in terms of the financial flow toward all provinces of the country.

In general, L.3106 adds nothing new to the foggy landscape of early intervention provision in Greece. Would the general spirit of the law actually inspire local communities to create their own early intervention programs? Because future establishment of new localized social services depends on secure financial resources and economic research, the cost of early intervention could be examined and justified on economic grounds.

Barnett and Escobar (1990) have shown empirical evidence that indicates that early intervention for children at risk can be a sound economic investment. Guralnick (1997), in reviewing available evidence (Goodman, Cecil, & Barker, 1984; Guralnick & Bennett, 1987; Shonkoff & Hauser-Cram, 1987; Thomaidis & Kaderoglou, 1997; Thomaidis et al., 2000) found a substantial basis for concluding that early intervention can produce immediate benefits for children with established disabilities.

FUTURE PROSPECTS: WHAT NEEDS TO BE DONE

Clearly, some steps have been made toward the implementation of L.2817. HMERA showed some good intentions and actions that might provide early educational support to children with special needs for the 4- to 7-year-old age group. Obviously, this is only the beginning of a long process of establishing the necessary infrastructures that the field of early intervention needs (Bricker & Woods Cripe, 1993; Cameron, 1986; Dunst, Trivette, & Deal, 1994; Meisels & Wasik, 1990; Odom & McEvoy, 1988). Certainly, HMERA should reconsider its administrative centralization by offering a voice to all local infrastructures of L.2817, starting from CDAES, the schools of each and every district, the educational community, and parent organizations. All parties must be invited to play an active part in the decision-making process regarding the services that will be offered. Of course, decentralization of educational services should be reinforced with greater resource allocation to local communities in every prefecture of the country. Above all, HMERA and HMHSW should put their collaborative efforts into designing a framework for early intervention provision with clear statutes that should be followed by both public and private practices. Presented next are some suggested courses of action.

Screening

1. Develop a conscious campaign for medical staff of pediatric clinics throughout the country about the necessity and value of early intervention.

2. Establish information campaigns for health professionals on the importance of developmental screening.

3. Obtain mutual agreement from HMHSW and HMERA with respect to protocols that will capture core information on child development useful for screening purposes and that will be used in all interdisciplinary assessment teams governed by both ministries.

Monitoring

1. Organize electronic transfer of medical, educational, and psychological reports of children between pediatric clinics, CDAES, medico-pedagogical centers, and all other relevant services through access networks.

2. Develop protocols with clearly established entrance and exit criteria for the monitoring process.

3. Model available tools specific to different risk categories and in-service training of personnel on their use.

Point of Access

1. Establish counseling services for infants and their families in every MRCSE by immediate ministerial decree. (Short-term counseling services, child care intervention, and home-based early intervention could be some of the options that CSIF might offer.)

2. Establish the liaison mechanisms and good communication among the existing medico-pedagogical centers, CDAES, and pediatric clinics.

3. Encourage local authorities to design and conduct small-scale early intervention programs.

4. Create community-based directories that will include different early intervention options. List these community options on web sites, develop a help line as a source of immediate information, distribute leaflets and posters, and establish information desks in every community.

Comprehensive Interdisciplinary Assessment

1. All infrastructures involved in assessment of children at risk or children with established disabilities governed by HMERA and HMHSW must ensure the representation of early childhood special education and psychology on their interdisciplinary teams.

2. Establish small local community assessment teams in close cooperation with other independent specialists (e.g., psychiatrists, geneticists, neurologists).

3. Enhance the liaisons with the existing medico-pedagogical centers, CDAES, and pediatric clinics to meet the diagnostic needs of children younger than 4 years of age.

4. Organize electronic transfer of medical, educational, and psychological reports of children between CDAES, medico-pedagogical centers, and counseling centers for infants through access networks.

Eligibility

1. Establish clear criteria for entering an early intervention program.

2. Discuss each of the available options with the family in order to find the one that best matches the family's unique needs.

Entrance into Early Intervention Programs

1. Encourage communities to establish small-scale, manageable, and flexible programs of early intervention.

2. Create mobile early intervention services with CDAES or counseling services in order to provide home training at a local level.

3. Provide guidelines with the Pedagogical Institute for an effective fusion of preschool educational programs of inclusion classes with early intervention programs that are activity oriented.

4. Continue further expansion with HMERA of inclusion classes for children with special needs in general kindergarten classrooms, ensuring the availability of specialized and support personnel.

5. Consider the paramount importance of the role of a service coordinator in a community-based program. This person will act as the medium between the interdisciplinary assessment team and the family in the process of the actual implementation of comprehensive intervention.

Preventive Intervention Program

1. Identify available preventive services (e.g., short-term counseling, parent support groups) with communities.

2. Include these service options in communities' directories and review them periodically.

Assessment of Stressors

1. Ensure cooperation between Greek Universities' Schools of Special Education (undergraduate and postgraduate courses) and existing service agencies on a local level in order to conduct local surveys on families' potential stressors.

2. Work with community programs of early intervention to produce protocols in order to identify the four categories of stressors on families with children at risk or those with established disabilities.

3. Train all related disciplines' professionals skills that will help them form a partnership with families. Listening skills should be a priority, and training in conducting interviews should include adopting a sensitive nonjudgmental manner.

4. Train professionals skills that involve families in the decision-making process. Professionals must also be efficient in establishing reciprocal communication by contributing information about critical elements of parent–child transactions in a simple comprehensible manner that avoids scientific terminology.

Developing and Implementing Programs

1. Organize alternative options with local service coordinators based on the assessment of each family's stressors.

2. Discuss and justify suggestions for different options with parents. Issues on timing, intensity, efficiency, and parental roles for each comprehensive intervention program should be explained in simple terms.

3. Make listings of community programs and information packages on specific disorders available at a local level.

4. Following the example of an innovative initiative of HMHSW, provide information on available services using Web technologies. The Map of Social Support Services has a web site that provides a useful inventory of available services across the nation (http://www.cecl.gr/English/hellenicconstitution.htm), and individuals can gain access to it by using key words that apply to each target population or each prefecture of the country (HMHSW, 2002).

Monitoring and Outcome Evaluations

1. With collaboration between HMHSW and HMERA, invite collective bodies providing early childhood special education service, relevant disciplines' professional organizations, and parent associations for an open discussion on the design of an early intervention monitoring and outcome evaluation system. This cooperation could result in guidelines for the implementation of a rational system capable of capturing core information on a family's stressors, monitoring stressors over time,

and monitoring changes in children's developmental patterns and transitions that might affect family functioning. A meaningful outcome evaluation system for early intervention services also can be agreed on.

2. Incorporate into every early intervention program the previous guidelines in separate protocols regarding parent satisfaction and child outcomes.

Transition

It goes without saying that if local communities throughout the country are proven to be capable of initializing early intervention services that focus on the empowerment of the family, then transition planning can be a built-in component.

CONCLUSION

The family as an entity needs and has the right to receive quality early intervention services based on specific needs. Setting higher standards, adopting a holistic approach, involving and empowering families, following a code of practice, and establishing a built-in evaluation procedure can ensure better quality (Bruder & Bologna, 1993; Dunst et al., 1994; European Disability Forum, 2002; Heinen, 2000; Lanners & Mombaerts, 2000; Peterander, 2000). The year 2003 was proclaimed to be the European Year of People with Disabilities. During this year the opportunities for massive public campaigns were substantial and could be used as a stepping stone toward an expanded political and social agenda that promotes the goals of equality and inclusion. In this spirit, Greece's national goal could be the encouragement of local authorities to draft plans of action toward the establishment of a variety of community-based early intervention services. HMHSW has given the green light for a new design of local administration and management of support services adapted to the needs of each community. Therefore, local authorities exercising their managerial and political capacities must secure the necessary funding for these purposes.

Greece held the precedence of the EC for the first 6 months of 2003. It was believed that during that period Greek authorities had a golden opportunity to awaken the spirit of their ethnic tradition and heritage and rediscover the high ideals that taught the world about solidarity and the society's collective responsibility toward one another by investing in people and fragile social groups such as children in need and their families. Unfortunately, the Greek government showed this spirit mainly through athletics as Greece focused and gave major priority in welcoming the Olympic games back in their birthplace during the summer of 2004. Nonetheless, the new government that was elected in March 2004 has changed HMHSW's name to "Hellenic Ministry of Health and Social Solidarity" (HMHSS) and accordingly has declared that early intervention services will be one of the ministry's highest priorities. Definitely, all parties involved are required to collaborate effectively in an effort to present and implement a new social network of services and supports for all. Legislation is not enough; this national goal is a challenge that needs commitment, synesthesia, and hard work on behalf of all people who strive to alleviate the discrepancy between ideals of ancient Greece and the practices of modern Greece in favor of present and future generations.

REFERENCES

Albano, M.L., Cox, B., York, J., & York, R. (1981). Educational teams for students with severe and multiple handicaps. In R. York, W. Schfield, D. Donder, D. Ryndak, & B. Reguly (Eds.), *Organizing and implementing services for students with severe and multiple handicaps* (pp. 23–24). Springfield, IL: State Board of Education.

Barnett, W.S., & Escobar, C.M. (1990). Economic costs and benefits of early intervention. In S.J. Meisels & J.P. Shonkoff (Eds.), *Handbook of early childhood intervention* (pp. 605–632). New York: Cambridge University Press.

Bricker, D., & Woods Cripe, J.J. (1993). *An activity-based approach to early intervention.* Baltimore: Paul H. Brookes Publishing Co.

Bruder, M.B., & Bologna, T. (1993). Collaboration and service coordination for effective early intervention. In W. Brown, S.K. Thurman, & S.F. Pearls (Eds.), *Family-centered early intervention with infants and toddlers: Innovative cross-disciplinary approaches* (pp. 103–127). Baltimore: Paul H. Brookes Publishing Co.

Cameron, R.J. (1986). *Portage: Pre-schoolers, parents and professionals. Ten years of achievement in the UK.* London: NFER-NELSON.

Daly, B., Addington, J., Kerfoot, S., & Sigston, A. (Eds.). (1985). *Portage: The importance of parents.* London: NFER-NELSON.

Drossinou, M. (2001a). New educational priorities and proposals for implementations of special education in public schools. *Special Education Issues, 13,* 40–47.

Drossinou, M. (2001b). Social attitudes of inclusion and integration of people with disabilities vs. philanthropy in modern society. *School and Home, 6(7),* 435–436.

Drossinou, M. (2001c). Special classes or inclusion classes? *Social Work, 64,* 225–239.

Dunst, C., Trivette, C., & Deal, A. (1994). *Supporting and strengthening families.* Cambridge, MA: Brookline Books.

Efstathiou, M. (2001a). The democratic shortfalls and the statutory dysfunctions as political staking of the new law about special education (L.2817). *Special Education Issues, 13,* 19–24.

Efstathiou, M. (2001b). Unaccessible education reproduces social exclusion. *Special Education Issues, 12,* 15–20.

ELEPAP. (2002). *Informational newsletter from parent association of ELEPAP.* Thessaloniki, Greece: Author.

European Disability Forum. (2002, March). *The Madrid declaration*. Paper presented at the European Congress on Disability, Madrid, Spain.

Giangreco, M.F. (1986). Delivery of therapeutic services in special education programs for learners with severe handicaps. *Physical and Occupational Therapy in Pediatrics, 6*(2), 5–15.

Giangreco, M.F., York, J., & Rainforth, B. (1989). Providing related services to learners with severe handicaps in educational settings: Pursuing the least restrictive option. *Pediatric Physical Therapy, 1*(2), 55–63.

Goodman, J., Cecil, H., & Barker, W. (1984). Early intervention with retarded children: Some encouraging results. *Developmental Medicine and Child Neurology, 26*, 47–55.

Guralnick, M.J. (Ed.). (1997). *The effectiveness of early intervention*. Baltimore: Paul H. Brookes Publishing Co.

Guralnick, M. (2001). A developmental systems model for early intervention. *Infants and Young Children, 14*(2), 1–18.

Guralnick, M.J., & Bennett, F.C. (1987). *The effectiveness of early intervention for at-risk and handicapped children*. Orlando, FL: Academic Press.

Harbin, G.L., McWilliam, R.A., & Gallagher, J. (2000). Services to young children with disabilities: A descriptive analysis. In S.J. Meisels & J.P. Shonkoff (Eds.), *Handbook of early childhood intervention, 2nd edition* (pp. 387–415). Cambridge: Cambridge University Press.

Haroupias, A. (2001). A special education counsellor's opinion about Law 2817/2000. *Special Education Issues, 13*, 62–65.

Heinen, H. (2000). EURLYAID: A European working party on early intervention. *Infants and Young Children, 12*(30), 1–3.

Hellenic Constitution amendents of 2001. (Available on-line at http://www.cecl.gr/English/hellenicconstitution.htm)

Hellenic Ministry of Health and Social Welfare (HMHSW). (2002). *Information package*. Athens: Author.

Hellenic Ministry of Health and Social Welfare (HMHSW). (2003). *Introductory report regarding the bill about the re-construction of the national social care system*. Athens: Hellenic Parliament.

HMERA. (1994). *Informational report on special education*. Athens: Author.

HMERA Pedagogical Institute. (1995). *Special education in Greece: Research and recording of the views and attitudes of the staff in special education units. Preliminary report*. Athens: OEBD.

HMERA Pedagogical Institute. (1996). *Teacher's book: Activities for Educational Readiness*. Athens: OEBD.

HMERA Pedagogical Institute. (2000a). *Emotional organization*. Athens: OEBD.

HMERA Pedagogical Institute. (2000b). *Cognitive abilities*. Athens: OEBD.

HMERA Pedagogical Institute. (2000c). *Oral communication*. Athens: OEBD.

HMERA Pedagogical Institute. (2000d). *Psycho kinetics*. Athens: OEBD.

HMERA Pedagogical Institute. (2000e). *Teacher's book. Activities for educational readiness*. Athens: OEBD.

Imvrioti, R. (1939). *Abnormal and retarded children*. Athens.

Kaderoglou, E. (2001). Family-centered early intervention on seven children within the autistic spectrum. In M. Ainscow & P. Mittler (Eds.), *Including the excluded. Proceedings of the 5th international special education congress*. Manchester, England: Inclusive Technology (CD-ROM).

Kaderoglou, E., & Vayona, S. (2003). Observing families of prechool children with pervasive developmental disorders. In *Mental health and mental retardation: A lifespan multidisciplinary approach* (book of abstracts of the 4th MH-MR European

Congress, the 3rd SIRM National Congress and International Society on Early Intervention Congress). Rome: MH-MR.

Kalantzi, K. (1984). Special education past and present. *New Paedia, 32,* 6.60.

KASP. (2002). *Informational brochure.* Athens: Author.

KEAT. (2002). *Informational brochure.* Kalithea, Greece: Author.

Konstantopoulou, P. (2001). Formation of inclusion classes in secondary education for meeting the needs of learning difficulties. *Special Education Issues, 13,* 25–35.

Kottaridi, Y., Kappi, C., & Adam, E. (1998). *Disabled children and their families in Mediterranean countries. A preliminary study in Greece.* Athens: EKKE.

Lanners, R., & Mombaerts, D. (2000). Evaluation of parents' satisfaction with early intervention services within and among European countries: Construction and application of a new parent satisfaction scale. *Infants and Young Children, 12*(3), 61–70.

Law 1143. (1981). Special education provision. *Governmental Newspaper of Hellenic Democracy.*

Law 1566. (1985). Education of people with special needs. *Governmental Newspaper of Hellenic Democracy.*

Law 2817. (2000, March). Education of people with special educational needs. *Governmental Newspaper of Hellenic Democracy.*

Law 3106. (2003). Re-construction of the national social care system. *Governmental Newspaper of Hellenic Democracy.*

Markakis, E., & Fragulitaki, A. (2000). *Eurydice program.* Athens: HMERA.

Meisels, S., & Wasik, B. (1990). Who should be served? Identifying children in need of early childhood intervention. In S.J. Meisels & J.P. Shonkoff (Eds.), *Handbook of early childhood intervention* (pp. 605–632). New York: Cambridge University Press.

Odom, S.L., & McEvoy, M.A. (1988). Integration of young children with handicaps and normally developing children. In S.L. Odom & M.B. Karnes (Eds.), *Early intervention for infants and children with handicaps: An empirical base.* Baltimore: Paul H. Brookes Publishing Co.

Pepin, L. (1994). *Pre-school and primary education in the European union.* European Community, Luxemburg: Eurydice.

Peterander, F. (1996). *HELIOS II. Early intervention. Final report. Information, orientation and guidance of families.* Munich, Germany: Druck-Service Schwarz GmbH.

Peterander, F. (2000). The best quality cooperation between parents and experts in early intervention. *Infants and Young Children, 12*(3), 32–45.

Portage-Hellas. (2002). *Informational newsletter.* Athens: Hellenic Portage Association.

Shonkoff, J., & Hauser-Cram, P. (1987). Early intervention for disabled infants and their families: A quantitative analysis. *Pediatrics, 80,* 650–658.

Thomaidis, L., & Kaderoglou, E. (1997). Early intervention for children with special needs: Implementation of the Portage program in Greece. *Paediatrics, 60,* 574–581.

Thomaidis, L., Kaderoglou, E., Stefou, M., Damianou, S., & Bacoula, C. (2000). Does early intervention work? A controlled trial. *Infants and Young Children, 12*(3), 17–22.

Xanthopoulos, X. (2001). Law 2817/2000 and activities of P.E.S.E.A. *Special Education Issues, 9,* 72–75.

York, J., Rainforth, B., & Giangreco, M.F. (1990). Transdisciplinary teamwork and integrated therapy: Clarifying the misconceptions. *Pediatric Physical Therapy, 2*(2), 73–79.

Zoukis, N. (2001). Opinion of the director of secretariat of "Maraslion School for Primary Education" (school of in-service training in special education for pre-school and primary school educators) about L.2817. *Special Education Issues*, *13*, 59–61.

CHAPTER 20

EARLY CHILDHOOD
INTERVENTION IN ISRAEL

MICHAL AL-YAGON AND MALKA MARGALIT

Since the 1980s, Israel has witnessed remarkable progress in the development of services for young children at risk and their families. Two main factors contributed to this trend: marked development in the theoretical understanding of children at risk and their families (Guralnick, 2001; Sameroff & Fiese, 2000; Shore, 1997) and parental demands for effective and earlier intervention with their young children. It has been commonly accepted that mothers and fathers want the best for their children and wish to ensure that everything be done to help their children develop to their maximum potential. There is a growing need for parents in Israel to feel confident that every innovative educational method, new therapeutic approach, or bit of recent knowledge will be available and accessible to support children's options to lead fuller and better lives, regardless of the severity of the child's disability and the family's location or economic constraints. The goals of this chapter are to discuss early childhood intervention programs in Israel within the Developmental Systems Model (Guralnick 2001), accentuating contemporary family-resilience approaches (Patterson, 2002).

Early childhood intervention programs in Israel serve a diverse population of children and families, representing different subcultures as well as new immigrants from different countries, languages, and cultures. To address the multiple childhood risk factors associated with family vulnerability (e.g., poverty, unemployment, immigration) and children's developmental disabilities, public and private agencies in Israel have developed a broad range of diverse interventional solutions. These programs share a developmental framework and an awareness of the centrality of families

The authors thank Dee B. Ankonina for her editorial contribution.

in the intervention process. In accord with Brooks-Gunn's (2003) emphasis, these programs are based on what is known about the normative development of young children. The special focus in Israel on promoting early intervention programs reflects the combined outcomes of the following: 1) cultural awareness about the importance of general early education programs, which have resulted in a comprehensive system of preschool education throughout the country, and 2) Israel's national health system's comprehensive early screening system that assesses the developmental milestones of all infants. This chapter provides a few examples of early childhood intervention centers and programs in Israel that demonstrate cooperation between governmental ministries such as education, health, welfare, and immigration, as well as collaboration with parents' organizations and individuals' initiatives. The chapter then examines the programs' characteristics within the framework of Guralnick's (2001) Developmental Systems Model.

ISRAELI INTERVENTIONS TARGETING SPECIFIC DEVELOPMENTAL DISABILITIES

Many early intervention programs in Israel serve children with different developmental disabilities such as mental retardation, hearing impairment, autism, and cerebral palsy. Several of these programs were originally established by parents as nonprofit organizations and later received government recognition and funding. Others were instigated by government policy or private initiation. The richness and uniqueness of the different programs make them extremely difficult to summarize. However, short, general descriptions of several different early childhood intervention programs are provided. Each program is unique in its goals and characteristics; yet, each also represents the general approaches in the country, regardless of the diverse difficulties related to the different disabilities and children at risk.

Micha: The National Council for the Education of Children Who Are Hearing Impaired, Tel Aviv

This nonprofit organization provides early intervention for young deaf children (from birth to school age) and their families and operates several branches nationally. The Tel Aviv center delivers intensive and comprehensive education and rehabilitation services such as nursery, preschool, and individual and group inclusion programs, as well as a variety of interdisciplinary evaluations and treatments. Moreover, this center's strong emphasis on the parents' contribution and cooperation has led to the development of a broad network of parental services including information provision, parental training in communicative skills, monitoring, and counseling.

Shalva: Center for Children Who Are Mentally and Physically Challenged, Jerusalem

Shalva is a nonprofit organization and was established by parents and for parents to improve the quality of life for their children and youth with developmental disabilities. The center focuses on after-school and leisure activities, promoting the children's autonomy and personal independence. The center's multidisciplinary staff delivers several therapies and programs for children with developmental disabilities—those with motor impairments. In accord with the center's interventional approach, the "Me and My Mommy" early childhood intervention program provides a comprehensive multidisciplinary intervention for children with developmental delays (from birth to 3 years of age) and their mothers. This individualized comprehensive program for mother–baby dyads is adapted to the identified developmental needs and tailored to the babies' level of functioning. It includes speech therapy, occupational therapy, aqua treatment, a sensory (Snoezelen) room, and computers. The "Me and My Mommy" program's interdisciplinary team places special emphasis on mothers' peer support and on facilitation of the parent–child transactions in terms of reciprocity and affective warmth. The team models developmental tasks and instructs mothers to continue the directed activities at home.

Aaron De Lowe Early Intervention Center in Beit Issie Shapiro—Avi Nonprofit Organization, Ra'anana

This center provides early intervention, interdisciplinary evaluation, and treatment for children with developmental disabilities (from 6 months to 4 years). The center is part of Beit Issie Shapiro, which was founded as a nonprofit organization and later received partial support from various governmental ministries. The early intervention program consists of a group of four preschools and nursery schools divided according to ages and functioning ability. In line with the center's emphasis on the family's contribution and collaboration, its broad range of services incorporates parental groups, supervision, and counseling; family therapy; and groups for other family members such as siblings and grandparents. Additional treatments include aqua treatments, sensory (Snoezelen) rooms, alternative medical services, and dental services.

Maagan: Support Scheme and Preschool/Child Care Center

This government-initiated national project targets children at high risk from birth to 5 years with developmental delays or transient disabilities due to immigration; these children attend general preschools in their communities. Multidisciplinary professionals provide teacher and parent counseling for early childhood intervention, focusing on each child's unique difficulties. These inclusive interventions comprise appropriate instruction and treatment at the preschool as well as referral to treatments and interventions outside of the preschool.

Makom Meyuchad: Internet Support Center for Parents of Children with Special Needs

The constant search for innovative, technology-supported approaches to empower families led the Center for Educational Technology together with Kesher (a voluntary organization that provides information by telephone to support decision making by individuals and families) to develop an Israeli Internet site "Makom Meyuchad" ("Special Place"). This site provides parents with useful and updated information on educational opportunities, rights and provisions, laws, health, accessibility, leisure, and so forth and also supplies links to relevant organizations and virtual support groups. A special section is devoted to early education for students from birth to 3 years. This site is still at the formative stage, but it is already raising critical questions about the role of the Internet and virtual connections in early interventions and in models of parents' learning and usage.

ISRAELI INTERVENTIONS TARGETING FAMILY VULNERABILITIES

Myriad projects targeting families at risk receive support from ministries such as education, health, welfare, and immigration. These projects focus on children and families with adversities related to new immigration, neglect, and disadvantage.

First Steps Program

This government-funded national project aims to train parents at risk (due to family adversity or a history of maltreatment and neglect) to care appropriately for their infants during the first year of life. The project focuses on infant developmental phases and parental empowerment.

The "Or" Preschool Intervention Project

This government-funded national project in the preschool centers on communities at high risk because of family adversities such as poverty and parental psychopathology and a history of maltreatment emphasizes the importance of professional intervention by social workers and teachers. Each target child receives individual intervention, three times per week, during preschool hours. This intervention focuses on emotional and social aspects such as social initiation, cooperation, and social motivation.

Multicultural Approach to Immigrant Absorption

This education ministry–funded national project focuses on providing support to new immigrant children who attend general preschools and their parents. Teachers receive special training and counseling to empower them to cope with new immigrant preschoolers and their families. The training project aims to provide teachers with a new, positive approach to immigrant cultures and languages with skills for promoting cultural and linguistic preservation within the preschools. In addition, preschools with a high proportion of new immigrants obtain extra counseling from a special counselor.

Although the aforementioned centers and programs focus on different disabilities and risk factors, they place similar emphasis on finding a balance between the two major aspects of the early childhood intervention: providing an answer to the children's difficulties and promoting family strengths (Turnbull & Turnbull, 2001).

FROM A PROBLEM-ORIENTED APPROACH TO A NURTURING-STRENGTHS APPROACH

The resilience models have moved from identifying resilient individuals and families to examining processes contributing to resilient adaptation among individuals from diverse backgrounds of adversity and with diverse disorders (Margalit, 2003; Wenz-Gross & Siperstein, 1998). *Resilience* refers to a dynamic process wherein the individual displays positive adaptation despite experiences of significant adversity (Luthar & Cicchetti, 2000). The shift in early intervention approaches (Blackman, 2002) from a focus on the acquisition and practice of developmental skills to focus on promoting a broad-based functional and social competence calls for analyzing the dynamic processes within the programs that might modify the negative effects of vulnerability factors through strengthening protective factors at the individual, family, and community levels.

Vulnerability and protective factors can be identified among Israeli children and their families who participate in early childhood intervention programs (Al-Yagon, 2003; Margalit, Al-Yagon, & Neuberger, 1996). At the individual level, these children manifest considerable diversity in their developmental disabilities (i.e., vulnerability factors). Their protective factors can include an easygoing temperament, secure attachment style, and high sense of coherence. At the family level, the Israeli families involved in early childhood interventions exhibit a variety of risk factors such as poverty, immigration, and a low level of social support. At the same time, various families demonstrated protective factors such as high family cohesion and effective communication style in the family system. At the community level, vulnerability factors may include exposure to neighborhood violence, whereas the protective factors may entail supportive relationships with adults in the early childhood intervention programs and availability of satisfactory services. Although all Israeli early childhood programs' policy states the importance of providing support for parents of targeted children at high risk (i.e., the family level of the resilience framework), they differ in their interpretations of how such support should be implemented and in their understanding of the concept of family-centered programs. In the different centers, parents may be involved through organized parent counseling groups, individual parent counseling, informal mothers' peer meetings, and other solutions per need.

The resilience framework, taken together with research of early childhood development (i.e., the biological aspects of developmental vulnerability; Shonkoff & Marshall, 2000; Shore, 1997), highlights the importance of a comprehensive early intervention system of community-based services (Guralnick, 1998; Luthar & Cicchetti, 2000; Sameroff & Fiese, 2000). The remainder of this chapter examines the Israeli early childhood intervention programs in terms of the construct and core principles presented by the Developmental Systems Model (Guralnick, 2001). These issues are illustrated using the aforementioned examples of Israeli early childhood interventions. Finally, the chapter discusses future trends.

The First Phase: Screening and Referral

According to the Developmental Systems Model (Guralnick, 2001), children and families enter the intervention system through a process of screening or referral. In the early childhood intervention programs in Israel, parents most frequently initiate referrals as a result of their concerns and awareness of their child's atypical development and difficulties. In addition, because the Israeli health system for young children is quite regulated, professionals such as pediatricians and child care workers may recommend seeking additional screening and information. The directors of Israeli early childhood intervention centers recognize the important role of parental concerns in the referral process.

The public well-baby care centers ("Tipat Chalav") that operate throughout the country afford an additional, unique source of referral in Israel. In accord with Israeli national health policy, all infants and children up to age 5 receive free, routine formal and informal developmental screenings at regular intervals to evaluate developmental delays in cognitive, motor, sensory, and language domains. Trained nurses and pediatricians refer parents to the appropriate agencies (child development centers operated by health maintenance organizations or specialized centers) to seek further information, assessment, and treatment. It should be noted that children who are highly vulnerable, such as premature and low birth weight infants, are routinely referred to child development centers for ongoing monitoring immediately after postnatal discharge from the hospital. The screening and assessment phase in Israel is well organized with equal accessibility options regardless of the family economic or education levels or the distance from the center of the country. However, the parental role in the screening process should be reconsidered. Most screening systems in Israel regard the parents as an important source of information; yet, families complained that the various agencies sometimes did not treat them as partners in the process of helping the child and did not provide them with the empowerment they needed, especially at the screening stages.

The Second Phase: Monitoring

The monitoring phase focuses special attention on children who do not meet screening criteria for referral. The monitoring phase enables maintenance of contact with children (referred by parents or professionals) who pass initial screenings but who may demonstrate subsequent developmental difficulties (e.g., premature or low birth weight infants). Most Israeli early intervention programs and centers do not continue to monitor referred children who did not meet initial screening criteria for referral. Several centers regularly continue to monitor a variety of at-risk groups such as premature or low birth weight infants, as well as children who were referred because of parental concerns. However, informal discussions with parents reveal their frustration and anger due to a feeling that many times professionals do not listen to their concerns and sometimes judge them as over-anxious or unrealistic in their expectations, especially when these expectations are not fulfilled. Unsurprisingly, when parents' concerns about atypical development were later verified in terms of an identified disability, they felt annoyed and hurt by professionals' initial denial of services and negative attitudes. It seems that many centers throughout the country are not able to monitor children whose diagnosis is not validated, and they do not continue to monitor children's development because of financial resource limitations.

The Third Phase: Point of Access

Once a concern or risk has been validated, children and families enter a new phase of services. At this stage, Israeli families often turn to or are referred to a specific center in order to begin the assessment and intervention process. However, Guralnick's (2001) recommendation to offer families multiple points of entry has not been fully implemented in the Israeli systems. In many cases, children and parents were not able to obtain appropriate services within their own neighborhood or local community. For example, Micha Tel-Aviv, which treats children with hearing impairments, and Aaron De Lowe, which treats children with developmental delays, each serve children and families from a wide range of geographical areas and population sectors (e.g., Jews, Arabs). Many young children who cannot obtain services in their neighborhoods must travel, causing inconvenience, fatigue, and social alienation from their local peers.

With regard to the three primary tasks of the first point of access described in the Developmental Systems Model (Guralnick, 2001), the current situation in the Israeli early childhood intervention programs reveals partial similarity. Most of the programs do emphasize the first task, with a focus on collecting comprehensive information from different sources such as the pediatrician and community social worker. The second task—the focus on categorizing children—is generally addressed during the initial decision-making process and is related to selecting the appropriate center or program with special expertise in that particular area of risk and disability. For example, children at high risk from vulnerable families may be referred to a community intervention or preventive project such as the First Steps Program or the "Or" Preschool Intervention Project. Children with developmental delays or identified disabilities, however, may be referred to a center or program specializing in that domain (e.g., Micha, for children with hearing impairments; Shalva or Aaron De Lowe for children with developmental disabilities, Down syndrome, and specific genetic syndromes). Center staff will perform the comprehensive interdisciplinary assessment, as described in the fourth phase.

The Fourth Phase: Comprehensive Interdisciplinary Assessment

The comprehensive interdisciplinary assessment has been considered to provide the most costly and time-consuming, yet vital, components of most early intervention programs. Moreover, researchers asserted that these assessments must include active participation of the child's family, information about the context in which the child and family live, and an intervention-oriented application of assessment data that will empower children and families to reach their potential (Meisels & Atkins-Burnett, 2000). Likewise, the early childhood intervention programs and centers in Israel emphasize this phase and focus on its essential contribution for later prevention and intervention planning. Professionals from several early childhood intervention programs value the facilitating role of comprehensive interdisciplinary assessment on subsequent plans and recommendations. The programs that target developmental disabilities place major emphasis on a comprehensive interdisciplinary assessment team process that includes the child's health and development profile as well as an evaluation of the family's functioning within their home and neighborhood. An essential part of this comprehensive interdisciplinary assessment process comprises the attempt to generate a diagnosis, including a developmental profile and a family profile. In some cases, however, the need for referral to a different agency will be indicated after the comprehensive interdisciplinary assessment.

The Israeli early childhood programs attribute great importance to the assessment stage; yet, the valuable time spent during these processes cannot be ignored. Thus, several programs have invested creative efforts toward increasing the efficiency of the process. For example, at the Aaron De Lowe Early Intervention Center, the interdisciplinary team members conduct the assessment with the child and parents in a special room. The process includes planned observations of the child–parent interaction and interaction with the staff along a variety of tasks, as well as parent–staff collaboration in completing a battery of questionnaires. Moreover, the team invites the parents to bring in a videotape that depicts their child in a daily activity.

In contrast to the strong interdisciplinary focus in the assessment process characterizing the majority of Israeli early intervention centers for children with developmental disabilities, projects targeting families at high risk reveal a lower capability to provide such a comprehensive interdisciplinary assessment because of budgetary limitations. The restricted interdisciplinary focus in these projects may impede the assessment process as well as the design and planning of appropriate early intervention programs. Several professionals in these programs, however, claimed that the outcomes, in terms of more investment in the immediate intervention activities without the delay needed for the extended assessment, have clear advantages. In addition, an ongoing evaluation through the intervention processes has occasionally established additional advantages. These procedural outcomes, emerging from different policies and budgets, call for evaluative studies to compare the advantages and disadvantages of the different approaches.

The Fifth Phase: Early Intervention Program Eligibility

In this phase, most of the children will meet eligibility criteria and formally enter the early intervention program. Conversely, in several cases, the comprehensive interdisciplinary assessment team may fail to find evidence of delays or disabilities. Nevertheless, in accord with the Developmental Systems Model (Guralnick, 2001), the concerns that brought the child to the team should not be ignored; children and families should stay within the system. As recommended by the Developmental Systems Model, two options exist: referral to a monitoring program or referral to a preventive intervention program.

An examination of the current early childhood intervention programs in Israel reveals that only a few of the ineligible children continue to be monitored or referred to preventive programs because of budget limitations. For example, Micha Tel-Aviv monitors children with mild hearing impairments who fail to meet eligibility criteria for entry into the intervention center, considering them at risk for hearing decline and ensuing difficulties. Also, as mentioned previously, the Israeli child development centers do often provide monitoring services for children and families who do not meet eligibility criteria for intervention. Yet, the majority of early childhood intervention centers and programs, whether they target children with disabilities or children from high-risk communities, do not provide formal monitoring or prevention programs for children who do not meet eligibility requirements for entrance into early intervention programs. Taken together with research that emphasized the importance of early childhood prevention (Luthar & Cicchetti, 2000; Rutter, 2000; Werner, 2000), the undersupply of Israeli monitoring and preventive options for children who are at risk calls for the establishment of additional programs.

The Sixth Phase: Entering the Early Intervention Program

During this phase, children and families enter into the formal process that ultimately will result in the provision of resource supports, social supports, information, and services. This phase includes assessment of the stressors or risk factors that may influence the ability of the child and family to participate in the intervention plan. Indeed, most of the aforementioned Israeli early childhood interventions enroll children almost immediately into a preliminary intervention program that allows for assessment of the information they define as critical. For example, Micha Tel-Aviv views the assessment of hearing impairment as a prerequisite for intervention, and this is comprehensively addressed in initial interactions with the child who is accepted into the program. In other cases, intervention centers utilize the developmental information gathered previously by the child development centers as a basis for the preliminary intervention. These preliminary interventions enable the interdisciplinary staff to assess stressors without delay at the beginning of the intervention.

According to the Developmental Systems Model (Guralnick, 2001), a service coordinator would be selected or reconsidered at this phase to work closely with the family and jointly develop the program. The model also emphasizes the special attention that should be devoted to building a long-term partnership with the families during this phase of the process. It is quite disappointing that the examination of the process of intervention management among the Israeli programs demonstrates that only a few programs use a service coordinator (or case manager) to work closely and continuously with the family and coordinate the interventions as well as the assessment of family stressors. With regard to the formation of a partnership with families, most Israeli programs emphasize this component and integrate family members' perspectives and preferences when establishing the aims of intervention. However, additional research is needed to determine the best ways to listen to families and their perspectives with respect to how they view the partnerships.

The Seventh Phase: Assessment of Stressors

The assessment of stressors in order to acquire information to promote optimal family patterns of interaction is considered one of the most critical and complex components of community service and support, and it consists of the following assessment categories: information needs, interpersonal and family distress, resource needs, and confidence threats (Guralnick, 2001). Wide consensus exists among the Israeli early intervention programs and centers regarding the importance of this component to the intervention process. Israeli early intervention programs employ a combination of interviews, discussions, and questionnaires to collect important information on family patterns of interaction, interpersonal and family distress, resources, and social supports. This information is essential for developing priorities for intervention focusing on the child and family's needs. In addition, they provide information to the parents including written explanations for children's difficulties and needs. Along the lines of researchers' suggestions (Kelly & Barnard, 2000), Israeli programs emphasize the contribution of the interview process to the establishment of a partnership with families. In addition, some Israeli programs have developed unique processes to enhance collaboration, such as asking parents to bring a short videotape of their child's daily activity or conducting part of the meetings with family members in the family's own home. Israeli programs, on the whole, consider the family's perceptions about their child's development to be a valuable step within the process of assessing stressors (Dromi & Ingber, 2002).

The Eighth Phase: Developing and Implementing a Comprehensive Program

The eighth phase refers to the process of developing and implementing a comprehensive program according to the assessment of stressors and definition of both the child's and the parents' needs. This phase consists of determining child-focused services (related to program content and intensity) as well as family-focused recommendations (e.g., participation in a parent group). Likewise, most Israeli early childhood interventions that target children with disabilities demonstrate a focus on both child and family services. However, these programs differ in the variety, timing, and intensity of services that they provide and in the emphasis they place on each of the two populations (i.e., children and families).

Unfortunately, because of budget problems, the community programs targeting Israeli populations who are at risk are less able to provide a comprehensive focus on both child and family services. Most of these projects, working with children from impoverished or abusive families, focus on the child directly or indirectly via teacher guidance.

The Ninth Phase: Monitoring and Outcome Evaluations

It has long been assumed that programs' structure and expectations for outcomes play an essential role in evaluating success (Hauser-Cram, Warfield, Upshur, & Weisner, 2000). At this stage, all those involved are expected to evaluate how both children and families are progressing in order to adjust plans accordingly. This phase also refers to the continuing evaluation of child and family stressors, which may change periodically (e.g., because of life events, transitions), as well as evaluation of changes in children's developmental patterns.

Examination of the implementation of this phase among the Israeli early childhood programs and centers demonstrates similar trends. For example, several Israeli programs (e.g., Shalva Jerusalem, Micha Tel-Aviv, Aaron De Lowe Center) emphasize the importance of regular meetings between the parents and interdisciplinary staff focused on evaluating both the child's and family's progress and stressors. Moreover, several other programs have developed a well-designed evaluative process focusing on the contribution of parents' expectations to the process of early intervention (i.e., Dromi & Ingber, 1999). The Israeli community programs targeting populations who are at high risk have implemented these components less effectively because of lower familial cooperation and because of economic constraints (e.g., fewer staff). Taken together, these data call for expanding the monitoring and outcome evaluation procedures depicting the community programs that target populations who are at high risk so that they resemble the procedures demonstrated among the Israeli early childhood intervention centers.

The Tenth Phase: Transition Planning

The importance of transition planning is widely recognized in order to enhance successful adjustment to a new setting (e.g., Pianta & Cox, 1999). The transition programs in Israeli early childhood intervention programs implement several activities to support the successful moves, such as visits to the new early intervention center, communication with the staff in the new setting, and a transition that is conducted in gradual steps.

DISCUSSION AND FUTURE DIRECTIONS

This chapter has provided an examination of the relevance and implementation of the Developmental Systems Model (Guralnick, 2001) with regard to early childhood intervention programs and centers in Israel. It has presented several examples of Israeli programs for early childhood intervention that demonstrate diverse solutions developed in Israel to serve children and families with different vulnerability factors and disabilities. The early childhood intervention landscape in Israel reveals similarities to Guralnick's (2001) model in the majority of phases. However, detailed examination of the procedures at the different centers revealed that professionals attributed different meanings to similar concepts and phases, reflecting professionals' unique philosophies and different training traditions. Parents' partnerships, family support, and follow-up monitoring hold different emphases in the different centers. Longitudinal, comprehensive studies are needed to investigate the contributions made by the different approaches to the development of the children and to the empowerment of the families.

The current unsatisfactory solutions for those Israeli children who did not meet eligibility criteria for entrance into early intervention programs call for appropriate innovative answers, focusing on monitoring and preventive intervention options. Similarly, the current exploration pinpoints the need to expand the family focus of interventions targeting populations who are high risk such as families facing disadvantage or adversity. In addition, and regardless of the national educational policy involving inclusion, several centers focus on serving children with disabilities without planning for inclusion opportunities. The conclusions of the current examination call for additional exploration of the following four critical aspects: the resilience framework, programs' family focus, technology integration, and teachers or professionals' training.

The Resilience Framework

Studies in early intervention demonstrated the growing research interest in family resilience either as an expression of interest in the family strengths versus deficits approaches (the characteristics of resilient parents) or as attempts to explain and predict positive outcomes and unexpected competent functioning among families at risk (Patterson, 2002). This shift from a focus on a problem-solving approach to one accentuating the need to nurture strengths (Luthar & Cicchetti, 2000) should be considered an exemplification of the third wave of resilience research (Richardson, 2002).

The first and the second waves of resilience examined the resilient individuals as presenting unique personal and interpersonal traits and characteristics (Werner & Smith, 1982). These studies pinpointed attention toward critical factors such as patterns of attachment and temperament (e.g., Al-Yagon, 2003). The third wave presented a nonlinear construct of resilience in terms of a multidisciplinary identification of motivational energy and processes within individuals and groups (Richardson, 2002). This wave emphasized the dynamic role of families' goals and their feelings of control during the process of promoting resiliency. Antonovsky's (1987) conceptualization of factors predicting the development of a strong sense of coherence further supports this conceptualization, pointing to the importance of information dissemination to enhance the understanding of individuals in times of stress and the importance of partnership with supporting agencies that enable participation in critical decision making.

Following initial phenomenological research (i.e., the first wave in the resilience conceptualization), most intervention programs in Israel acknowledged the importance of identifying vulnerability and protective factors that contribute to positive adjustment (i.e., the second wave). However, relatively few investigations have examined the sources of energy needed for resilient processes among children and families who are at risk (i.e., the third wave). In applying the resilience framework to early childhood intervention, programs would do well to examine the individualized energy sources or motivation that would help reintegrate positive outcomes among children and families who are at risk. Future studies need to identify the predictive factors that will enhance the probabilities for successfully energizing parents and children.

Family-Focused Programs

General consensus has emerged from large numbers of programs as well as research studies asserting the significant contribution of family functioning to childhood adjustment (e.g., Campbell, 1998; Patterson, 2002). Although this chapter indicates that the vast majority of Israeli early childhood interventions targeting children with disabilities provide varied services to support the families, only limited parental support programs are available to Israeli families who are at high risk and are confronted with vulnerability factors such as unemployment and immigration. In addition, among the centers that provide parental support, different centers gave different interpretations to the meaning of a partnership with parents. Research findings emphasizing the contribution of family difficulties to children's later maladjustment (Campbell, 1994, 1998; Denham et al., 2000; Greenberg, Speltz, & DeKlyen, 1993) clearly suggested the need to establish more systematic services for the families. For example, with regard to studies' recommendations that focused on secure early attachment as a protective factor for children who are at risk (Al-Yagon, 2003; Svanberg, 1998; Werner, 1993), interventions may offer parent training to improve the quality of parent–child relationships and the formation of a secure attachment style with their children.

Technology Integration and Internet Challenges

The *technology revolution* is widely perceived as having important implications for virtually all facets of our society. Computers and the Internet are becoming a part of our everyday lives, entering our work and home environments, enabling social interactions and vast information sharing that is not limited by the boundaries of time and place. The establishment of the Israeli site for families of children with special needs (Makom Meyuchad) is opening up the classic conceptualization of empowerment and support to new possibilities.

However, researchers must investigate the meaning of support by virtual friends—other parents who share similar difficulties—and of empowerment via on-line resources, as well as the ability for information processing among parents with lower educational levels and among distressed parents. Seating a parent in front of a computer may not suffice. Planned instruction and supported experimentation can enhance parents' utilization of such a site and realization of the potential of such technologies within intervention programs. This area remains in its initial stages, but the Center for Educational Technology is working with various centers and the academic support of Tel-Aviv University to search for new implementations of the Internet to supplement the early intervention programs. Future studies will do well to explore how to integrate these extended options into the current intervention procedures and parental support and monitoring.

Teacher and Professional Training Programs

The inclusion policy in Israel is well accepted and supported by the Israeli Law of Inclusion. However, teachers from early education systems require additional support and specialized training to translate good intention into empowering practices. General preschool teachers, who teach children with diverse abilities and needs, would benefit from guidance and instruction in effective education methods for those children. Moreover, these teachers must expand their professional knowledge about disabilities, high risk, and treatment modes as well as their attitudes toward the child in order to promote successful inclusion (Al-Yagon, 2002; Hegarty, 1993). Even the inclusion of very young infants is now a possibility because of the expansion of early education in small systems around the country. Future studies are needed to evaluate the teacher training programs' effectiveness in promoting the successful inclusion of young children and infants with vulnerability factors or disabilities. In addition, professionals in early intervention centers often hesitate to develop working relationships with general preschool teachers. Disagreements and misunderstanding between the two groups of professionals of the clinical systems and the educational systems may be avoided if the clinical professionals are trained to recognize the uniqueness of the educational systems, their language, and culture.

Finally, an examination of the current situation among the Israeli programs for early childhood intervention reveals the paucity of preventive programs focusing on children raised in families and communities with a variety of adversities. The reasons for this derive mainly from budgetary issues. However, Israeli policy makers would do well to reconsider budgetary allotments in light of research recommendations concerning the substantial contribution of early preventive programs to reducing maladjustment in later development (Guralnick & Neville, 1997; Svanberg, 1998; Winett, 1998). Evaluative research is needed for examining these new trends.

REFERENCES

Al-Yagon, M. (2002, June). *Early intervention among preschool children in Jaffa*. Paper presented at the Price-Brodie Initiative conference, Tel-Aviv, Israel.

Al-Yagon, M. (2003). Children at-risk for developing learning disorders: Multiple perspectives. *Journal of Learning Disabilities, 36*(4), 318–335.

Antonovsky, A. (1987). *Unraveling the mystery of health.* San Francisco: Jossey-Bass.

Blackman, J.A. (2002). Early intervention: A global perspective. *Infants and Young Children, 15*(2), 11–19.

Brooks-Gunn, J. (2003). Do you believe in magic? What we can expect from early childhood intervention programs. *Social Policy Report, 17*(1), 3–14.

Campbell, S.B. (1994). Hard-to-manage preschool boys: Externalizing behavior, social competence, and family context at two-year follow-up. *Journal of Abnormal Child Psychology, 22,* 147–166.

Campbell, S.B. (1998). Developmental perspectives. In T.H. Ollendick & M. Hersen (Eds.), *Handbook of child psychopathology* (pp. 3–35). New York: Plenum Press.

Denham, S.A., Workman, E., Cole, P.M, Weissbrod, C., Kendziora, T., & Zahn-Waxler, C. (2000). Prediction of externalizing behavior problems from early to middle childhood: The role of parental socialization and emotional expression. *Development and Psychopathology, 12,* 23–45.

Dromi, E., & Ingber, S. (1999). Israeli mothers' expectations from early intervention with their preschool deaf children. *Journal of Deaf Studies and Deaf Education, 4,* 50–68.

Dromi, E., & Ingber, S. (2002). *The relationships between child, mother and family characteristics and mothers' expectations from early intervention with their hearing impaired children.* Manuscript submitted for publication.

Greenberg, M.T., Speltz, L., & DeKlyen, M. (1993). The role of attachment in the early development of disruptive behavior problems. *Development and Psychopathology, 5,* 191–213.

Guralnick, M.J. (1998). The effectiveness of early intervention for vulnerable children: A developmental perspective. *American Journal on Mental Retardation, 102,* 319–345.

Guralnick, M.J. (2001). A developmental systems model for early intervention. *Infants and Young Children, 14*(2), 1–18.

Guralnick, M.J., & Neville, B. (1997). Designing early intervention programs to promote children's social competence. In M.J. Guralnick (Ed.), *The effectiveness of early intervention.* Baltimore: Paul H. Brookes Publishing Co.

Hauser-Cram, P., Warfield, M.E., Upshur, C.C., & Weisner, T.S. (2000). An expanded view of program evaluation in early childhood intervention. In J.P. Shonkoff & S.J. Meisels, (Eds.), *Handbook of early childhood intervention* (2nd ed., pp. 487–509). New York: Cambridge University Press.

Hegarty, S. (1993). Reviewing the literature on integration. *European Journal of Special Needs Education, 8*(3), 194–200.

Kelly, J.F., & Barnard, K.E. (2000). Assessment of parent–child interaction: Implications for early intervention. In J.P. Shonkoff & S.J. Meisels (Eds.), *Handbook of early childhood intervention* (2nd ed., pp. 258–289). New York: Cambridge University Press.

Luthar, S.S., & Cicchetti, D. (2000). The construct of resilience: Implications for interventions and social policies. *Development and Psychopathology, 12,* 857–885.

Margalit, M. (2003). Resilience model among individuals with learning disabilities (LD): Proximal and distal influences. *Learning Disabilities Research and Practice, 18*(2), 82–86.

Margalit, M., Al-Yagon, M., & Neuberger, S. (1996). *Mothers' coherence, family climate, and preschool children with learning disabilities: Risk and resilience.* Paper presented at the annual IARLD conference, Detroit, MI.

Meisels, S.J., & Atkins-Burnett, S. (2000). The elements of early childhood assessment. In J.P. Shonkoff & S.J. Meisels (Eds.), *Handbook of early childhood intervention* (2nd ed., pp. 231–257). New York: Cambridge University Press.

Patterson, J.M. (2002). Understanding family resilience. *Journal of Clinical Psychology, 58*(3), 233–246.

Pianta, R.C., & Cox, M.J. (Eds.). (1999). *The transition to kindergarten.* Baltimore: Paul H. Brookes Publishing Co.

Richardson, G.E. (2002). The metatheory of resilience and resiliency. *Journal of Clinical Psychology, 58*(3), 307–321.

Rutter, M. (2000). Resilience reconsidered: Conceptual consideration, empirical findings, and policy implications. In J.P. Shonkoff & S.J. Meisels (Eds.), *Handbook of early childhood intervention* (2nd ed., pp. 651–682). New York: Cambridge University Press.

Sameroff, A.J., & Fiese, B.H. (2000). Models of development and developmental risk. In C.J. Zeanah, Jr. (Ed.), *Handbook of infant mental health* (2nd ed., pp. 3–29). New York: The Guilford Press.

Shonkoff, J.P., & Marshall, P.C. (2000). The biology of developmental vulnerability. In J.P. Shonkoff & S.J. Meisels (Eds.), *Handbook of early childhood intervention* (2nd ed., pp. 35–53). New York: Cambridge University Press.

Shore, R. (1997). *Rethinking the brain: New insights into early development.* New York: Families and Work Institute.

Svanberg, P.O.G. (1998). Attachment, resilience, and prevention. *Journal of Mental Health, 7,* 543–578.

Turnbull, A., & Turnbull, R. (Eds.). (2001). *Families, professionals, and exceptionality: Collaboration for empowerment.* Upper Saddle River, NJ: Merrill/Prentice Hall.

Wenz-Gross, M., & Siperstein, G.N. (1998). Students with learning problems at risk in middle school: Stress, social support, and adjustment. *Exceptional Children, 65,* 91–100.

Werner, E.E. (1993). Risk, resilience, and recovery: Perspectives from the Kauai longitudinal study. *Development and Psychopathology, 5,* 503–515.

Werner, E.E. (2000). Protective factors and individual resilience. In J.P. Shonkoff & S.J. Meisels (Eds.), *Handbook of early childhood intervention* (2nd ed., pp. 115–132). New York: Cambridge University Press.

Werner, E.E., & Smith, R. (1982). *Vulnerable but invincible: A study of resilient children.* New York: McGraw-Hill.

Winett, R.A. (1998). Prevention: A proactive-developmental-ecology perspective. In T.H. Ollendick & M. Hersen (Eds.), *Handbook of child psychopathology* (pp. 637–672). New York: Plenum Press.

CHAPTER 21

EARLY INTERVENTION FOR CHILDREN WITH SPECIAL NEEDS

The Italian Paradigm

ENNIO DEL GIUDICE, MICHELE BOTTOS,
BEATRICE DALLA BARBA, LORENZO PAVONE,
MARTINO RUGGIERI, AND SALVATORE OTTAVIANO

A short historical preface is mandatory to understand sociological, educational, and health care issues regarding specific aspects related to early intervention in Italy. Even though Italy is one of the seven most industrialized countries of the world, wealth and welfare are not evenly distributed throughout the nation, and the administrative division of the country into 20 regions further emphasizes the uneven distribution. Italy has always been an ensemble of states of small or medium size. The biggest one was the Kingdom of Naples—also called the Kingdom of the Two Sicilies—that included all of the present southern regions together with the island of Sicily. After the unification of Italy in 1860, the Italian south or Mezzogiorno retained its rural characteristics so that the subsequent process of industrialization mainly involved the northern regions. In fact, most of the manpower for northern industries always came from the south of Italy. The situation has evolved in such a way as to promote the buildup of widespread wealth in northern Italy but with a high unemployment rate in the south. The legislative trend toward devolution contributed to heightening this unevenness (e.g., Law 59/97 concerning the reform of the Italian civil service). As a result of this complex sociopolitical situation, the situation in the Mezzogiorno is still a strong and deeply felt problem present during current electoral campaigns.

This chapter is dedicated to the memory of Michele Bottos, M.D., who brought important contributions to the fields of child neurology and developmental pediatrics.

The concept of early intervention (birth to 3 years) as a specifically dedicated program or an integrated system of services for children with special needs and their families is not present as such in the Italian legislation. Because the educational system only accepts children beginning at age 3 years, the health system should take into account any needs coming from an established or potential disability in the birth-to-3-years age range. Health care is provided to the entire population by the Italian National Health Service (INHS), whose financial and organizational architecture is similar to that of the British National Health Service. The population has unlimited health care coverage, which is provided by a local health agency (LHA) responsible for a geographically defined catchment area. LHAs are set out in several single functional units called health districts, which cover an average population of 60,000 inhabitants.

To better understand how children with special needs and their families can receive help from INHS, one should take into account legislative issues concerning the structure and function of INHS as well as the health and social services needs of people with disabilities. Main characteristics of the present setup are as follows: devolution of political powers to regions, managerial issues, and competition in health services provision (Fattore, 1999). INHS has become almost completely decentralized, reflecting closely the political and administrative division of Italy into 20 regions. Regional authorities assign the available resources according to local needs but sometimes interpret the central government's directives for controlling their health care budgets at their own discretion. In fact, each LHA has a defined budget for health care, which should be assigned by the regional political health authority based on the number of inhabitants, as well as the number of health facilities located in the catchment area. Other health-related indicators also should be considered. As a result of the fragmentation of INHS into 20 multifaceted regional systems, profound interregional differences in health care expenditures occur, which may aggravate the pre-existing inequalities between the northern and southern Italian regions. As far as the legislation for children with disabilities is concerned, the Italian government has focused attention on them in a systematic way only since 1992 when Law 104/92 came forth. That was a so-called Legge-Quadro (i.e., a comprehensive body of principles for the health care, social integration, and civil rights of people with disabilities). Likewise, in 2000, the Italian parliament promulgated Law 328/00, another Legge-Quadro, for the implementation of an integrated system of social services and interventions. This latter law will undoubtedly bring substantial advantages to children with special needs in the way of proper management of potential stressors on their families due to family characteristics and family patterns of interaction.

PROVISION OF SERVICES FOR CHILDREN WITH SPECIAL NEEDS IN LIGHT OF A DEVELOPMENTAL SYSTEMS MODEL

The health district delivers two main services that are of utmost importance to early intervention: child health care and habilitative or rehabilitative treatments. The first and most important is the free-of-charge provision of pediatric health care to the entire population. Every newborn is immediately assigned a pediatrician whom the family may choose from among those on a district list; that is why health agencies always make use of the term *free choice pediatrician* (FCP). Apart from providing diagnosis and treatment for any illness, FCPs regularly schedule follow-up visits for the child, which are called *bilanci di salute* or health accounts. Health districts also provide habilitative or rehabilitative treatments either through a public rehabilitation unit or a private rehabilitation center. In this latter case, a private center has to get an accreditation from the LHA. In general, private accredited centers are, on the whole, more common in southern Italy.

Because there exist no homogeneous programs for early intervention in Italy, existing services will be inserted into the various elements of the conceptual model designed by Guralnick (2001). Figure 21.1 shows a schematic outline of the provision of services for children with special needs, which applies roughly to all of Italy. The pivotal role of FCPs allows for a starting point for referral. If the family pediatrician detects a

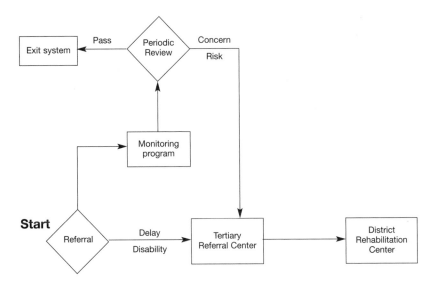

Figure 21.1. A simplified diagram outlining the provision of services for early intervention in Italy.

developmental delay or disability, then he or she usually sends the patient to a tertiary referral center—which usually is a university-based center or a tertiary hospital—for a diagnostic workup.

Children with developmental problems of an uncertain nature are monitored either by the pediatrician alone or with the help of a child neuropsychiatrist[1] until a definite concern emerges or, alternatively, disappears. Regarding monitoring, all neonates considered to be at risk for subsequent neurodevelopmental disabilities, such as premature birth or low birth weight, are offered a follow-up program. A high-risk infant follow-up is usually provided for children up to 3 or 5 years of age by the neonatal unit or by the nearest main hospital. Obviously, if a definite concern comes out at some future point, then children would be sent to a tertiary referral center for further diagnostic workup. A special case would be a newborn leaving the intensive care unit with an established disability. Once discharged from the hospital, the infant would be immediately sent to either the district rehabilitative unit or to an accredited center to begin treatment (e.g., physical therapy). The infant will get his or her own FCP. In this case, a special follow-up schedule called *bilanci di salute per bambini con bisogni speciali* or health accounts for children with special needs is set.

Two crucial elements of the Developmental Systems Model (Guralnick, 2001), namely a definite point of access and the comprehensive interdisciplinary assessment, do not exist as such in the Italian system. Children with developmental delays or disabilities are directly referred to a tertiary referral center where an in-depth diagnostic workup takes place. Moreover, a proper interdisciplinary assessment team devoted to children with special needs and their families is not always available before entering a treatment program. In fact, once a diagnosis has been made of a condition that entails a developmental delay or disability, the child is rapidly sent to the district rehabilitation unit or center nearest his or her home. The center is the pivotal point that contains in itself more than one element of the Developmental Systems Model, namely confirmation of early intervention program eligibility, development and implementation of a program, and monitoring and outcome evaluations.

As far as assessment of stressors is concerned, it should be said that even this crucial and complex component of a Developmental Systems Model thoroughly relies on each individual professional team working for

---

[1]In Italy there is a unique medical specialty called *child neuropsychiatry*, which is separate and autonomous from pediatrics. A child neuropsychiatrist is supposed to cover both child psychiatry and child neurology.

the rehabilitation center. This also means that the quality of assessment might exhibit considerable interregional differences reflecting geographical inequalities. Regardless, the promulgation of Law 328/00 for an integrated system of social services and interventions offers a powerful tool to relieve interpersonal and family distress. As a consequence, psychosocial assessment and intervention are becoming more effective throughout the whole country.

Coming back to the functions and duties of district rehabilitation units or centers, an individualized plan of treatment is usually developed either by a child neuropsychiatrist or a physiatrist that is almost exclusively child focused and center based. Implementation occurs through individual sessions lasting an average of 50 minutes. The schedule is organized on a weekly basis and goes from a minimum of one to a maximum of six sessions, depending on the severity of impairment. Treatment is provided by physiotherapists and speech-language pathologists (SLPs), as well as by psychomotricity therapists, for children birth to 3 years. (Psychomotor therapy or rehabilitation—also called *psychomotricity*, from the French word *psychomotricité*—a method of intervention that began in France, is focused in the body to work on cognitive dysfunction or neurological disorders. The available literature on psychomotricity is almost exclusively in French. See http://www.psychomot.org and http://www.psychomotricite.com for information on this rehabilitative technique.)

Parents are provided with psychological help or support during the overall treatment period if it becomes evident that their coping abilities are inadequate. Unfortunately, especially in southern Italian regions, parents are not often allowed to attend individual treatment sessions; moreover, discussions with therapists about a child's progress and failures are scant. Also because of this, critical issues such as monitoring and outcome evaluation could be somewhat neglected. This would not apply to centers located in better-organized regions such as Emilia-Romagna or Lombardy. Finally, transition-planning issues have not been uniformly dealt with throughout the country: They might be left entirely to individual family coping abilities or taken care of by a sensitive team who do so because of personal motivation.

After almost exclusively focusing on center-based early intervention programs, it is worthwhile to briefly mention the few existing examples of home-based early intervention. The first person to introduce a home-based curriculum in Italy was Salvatore Ottaviano at the Department of Child Neurology and Psychiatry of La Sapienza University in Rome. He has worked with the Italian translation of the *Carolina Curriculum for Infants and Toddlers with Special Needs* (CCITSN; Johnson-Martin, Jens,

Attermeier, & Hacker, 1991, 1997). His preliminary data came from a sample of 30 children, ranging in age from 1 month to 18 months, who exhibited a developmental delay (Down syndrome, 4; 4p- syndrome, 1; hypoxic-ischemic encephalopathy, 25). All of the children were regularly assessed by the Italian version of the Brunet-Lézine psychomotor development scales (Brunet & Lézine, 1955, 1967). Baseline mean developmental scores showed a 7.5 point increase by the end of the intervention (S. Ottaviano, personal communication, 2002). According to Ottaviano, these results are comparable with those of McCormick, McCarton, Tonascia, and Brooks-Gunn (1993), in which an increase of 7.2 points on the Stanford-Binet scales had been reported. A further experience with the same curriculum was carried out in Naples at the Department of Pediatrics, Federico II University, by Ennio Del Giudice and his team (Del Giudice et al., in press). The aim of the study carried out in Naples was to assess whether the CCITSN could be of greater benefit—in terms of developmental gain—to infants with Down syndrome than the standard INHS neurodevelopmental approach. INHS treatment included traditional physiotherapy aimed at improving motor control and skills as well as psychomotor therapy.

A total of 47 infants with Down syndrome were enrolled in the aforementioned study. All children and their families were randomly assigned either to the new curriculum (i.e., CCITSN) or to the standard INHS program. Parents in the CCITSN group were trained to utilize daily routines to implement curricular items. Both groups were followed prospectively for 12 months. The primary outcome of effectiveness was the developmental quotient (DQ) of Brunet and Lézine's (1955, 1967) developmental scales, and secondary outcomes were its single components (language, socialization, posture, coordination). Twenty-four children were assigned to CCITSN, and 23 were assigned to INHS. At baseline, there were no significant differences between the two study groups in terms of social and environmental data, pregnancy and delivery, and breast-feeding and age at the beginning of the intervention. Moreover, CCITSN and INHS groups had comparable mean developmental levels at the beginning. An overall trend toward better psychomotor performances for infants assigned to the CCITSN group was clearly shown. After completion of the 12-month intervention, mean DQ of the CCITSN group was 12.31 points higher than that of the INHS group (95% CI: 1.53 to 23.57; p < 0.05). Throughout the study, mean DQ was higher in the CCTISN group than it was in the INHS group with a mean difference of 8.48 points (95% CI: 3.45 to 13.5; $p < 0.001$). Likewise, all mean scores of secondary outcome measures were consistently higher in the CCITSN group. A good home-based and parent-implemented intervention program such as CCITSN might be valuable in the Italian sociocultural context, which strengthens the point that direct parent involvement contributes to better developmental outcomes for children with disabilities. It should be noted that a commitment to involving parents in intervention is not a common practice in Italy and many other countries. Nonetheless, it could be an effective and cost-efficient way of providing services to young children with Down syndrome and other developmental disabilities.

EARLY INTERVENTION FOR NEUROMOTOR DISABILITIES IN NORTHERN ITALY

Historical Review of Early Intervention

In Italy, the history of the provision of intervention for children with neuromotor disabilities could have started in 1954 when the first services for children with disabilities were established by law (Bottos & Orlandi, 1997). In those years, however, Italy, as well as other European countries, followed the conceptual trend that dictated that the best intervention would be provided by residential institutions. Chronic disabling conditions were viewed as conditions that could be treated and healed with adequate intervention. Institutions were places in which all of the various types of professionals—physiotherapists, SLPs, as well as others—could be concentrated in order to set up an intensive treatment, thus providing the best chances for achieving optimal therapeutic results. The institutional lifestyle was planned on the availability of therapy, according to an acute medicine model that can be defined as adapting life to therapy. This would be appropriate for acute diseases such as bronchopneumonia: For a 2- or 3-week period, the primary goal is the treatment of the acute disease, so life is first adapted to therapy (e.g., rest in bed, antibiotic therapy) and then the patient resumes his or her previous life. Developmental disabilities in children, however, are not, of course, acute diseases; they persist for the duration of the child's life, so therapy will not be limited to just a 2- or 3-week period.

An approach that only promotes therapy inevitably leads to the lack of fundamental life experiences and consequently to a deterioration of the quality of life for the child and family. This being so, children who lived in residential institutions, even though theoretically receiving the best treatment, nearly always had a poorer functional outcome than their peers who remained at home. Fortunately, the approach of people such as Milani Comparetti (1981, 1982a, 1982b; Milani Comparetti & Gidoni, 1971, 1976) and Boccardi (1987, 2003) prevailed. The point was progressively grasped that the best technical intervention could not compensate for the lack of social and family experiences. To clarify this concept, an example follows: Since 1975, Italian legislation has stated that all children (with and without disabilities) must attend the same mainstream inclusive schools. Until then, special schools (i.e., those devoted only to children with disabilities) had been based on the concept that special intervention could provide a better outcome for children with special needs (e.g., motor, intellectual), once more embracing the institutional two-step theory. The idea was that intensive intervention (e.g., special education, physiotherapy, occupational therapy inside the schools) could enable children to cope with their life needs on their own. Thereafter, it became evident that granting each individual child the opportunity of normal life experiences, as far as possible, was far more important than the best special education. In this way, Italy has shifted from an adapting life to therapy model to an alternative: adapting therapy to life. This does not mean giving up therapy but rather adapting therapeutic interventions such as physiotherapy and speech-language pathology, which are still necessary for the treatment of an impairment, to reflect a lifestyle of a child without disabilities. In the beginning, the integration of all children into mainstream schools resulted in rather controversial results, but it is worth noting that many Western countries are now using the Italian model by reducing, as much as possible, the number of special schools (Armstrong, 2001). Furthermore, even though only a few studies confirmed that the outcomes of children with disabilities integrated into mainstream schools were better than those of controls attending special schools (Bottos, Feliciangeli, Sciuto, Gericke, & Vianello, 2001), and although integration often entailed some troubles, not a single child with a disability or his or her family wished to go back to a special school.

A further argument forced professionals to abandon the institutional approach when early intervention was started. Beginning in the mid-1960s to early 1970s, early assessment of infants in order to detect developmental disabilities was started by pediatricians, nurses, physiotherapists, child neurologists, and physiatrists in northern and central Italy. When it came to intervening, all professionals realized that young children could no longer be institutionalized for treatment. A network was then developed to set up local outpatient district units in order to provide treatment for children and their families close to the areas where they lived. This district-unit–centered organization was again inspired by Milani Comparetti, who conceived a system for early diagnosis and intervention based on a strict cooperation between basic pediatric units (family pediatricians and nurses) and units specializing in the treatment of children with disabilities (e.g., child neuropsychiatrists, physiatrists, physiotherapists). He proposed that all infants should undergo developmental screening at 3 months of age, which is the same time they receive their polio vaccination, which is compulsory by law. Keeping in mind the difficulties related to the predictive value of early neurodevelopmental examination with a high false positive rate (Allen & Capute, 1988; Amiel Tison, 1988; Bierman-Van Eendenburg, Jurgens-Van Der Zee, Olinga, Hiusjes, & Towen, 1982), Milani Comparetti introduced a new conceptual method for early developmental assessment. According to his method, different reflexes and reactions were specific to stages of motor development, and the competition of patterns influenced the emergence of a specific developmental stage (Milani Comparetti, 1965; Milani Comparetti & Gidoni, 1971). Following this approach, he prepared a very simple chart that could be easily filled in by pediatricians or nurses at the time of the polio vaccination (Milani Comparetti & Gidoni, 1971). When deviations from harmonic or optimal development were found, the infant was referred to a child neuropsychiatrist or physiatrist. If the suspected delay or disability turned out to be confirmed, then early intervention would eventually be started.

Overall Functional Organization

As a consequence of the aforementioned historical changes, a three-level system has been progressively developed: hospital services, district units, and university-based centers. Infants admitted to neonatal intensive care units (NICUs) because of low or very low birth weight are hospitalized until all of their problems are solved. NICUs can provide complete diagnostic services such as biochemical studies, electroencephalograms, and imaging studies. The pediatric staff of the NICU follows up with infants after they are discharged from the hospital if they have abnormal neuroimages or significant risk factors such as severe respiratory distress syndrome with long-lasting assisted ventilation or neonatal convulsions. Once the diagnostic workup is completed, an infant is referred to the family pediatrician. If a neurological problem is suspected, then an assessment by a neuropediatrician or a physiatrist with specific competence in the diagnosis and treatment of children with disabilities is recommended. After confirmation of a disability, children are referred to the district unit of the area in which they live: A full clinical report is sent including a suggested schedule of follow-up visits in the outpatient facilities. Some hospital rehabilitation units also provide treatment to infants and children when they are discharged, although not very often. If necessary, habilitative treatment starts as early as at the time of discharge or even during hospitalization. The work is then carried out by professionals (e.g., psychologists, physiotherapists, SLPs) from the district rehabilitation unit. District units are nonhospital units and provide all of the necessary services for infants and children with disabilities through the INHS. They are present throughout the country, covering local catchment areas from 30,000 to 100,000 inhabitants so that families do not have to travel too far to get services. Units for motor, psychiatric, intellectual, and sensory disabilities are usually separate. If the same child has motor as well as intellectual and sensory impairments, then the child is usually seen in the motor disabilities unit, and interdisciplinary work is started. Sometimes habilitative or rehabilitative services are not directly provided by INHS district units but by private (charity) units, which are indirectly supported by the INHS as well. This kind of institution is especially widespread in some regions, depending on the history of the different areas (e.g., a larger number is likely in the northeast of Italy, where the Catholic church had a very strong influence). The standards of the services provided by both charities and INHS units vary greatly. Generally speaking, both provide better standards in the northern and central parts of Italy. Finally, some units traditionally play a supportive role because of their specific knowledge in computer science, aiding devices, and orthoses. Children are also referred to tertiary, university-based facilities whenever high-standard technology for diagnosis is needed. Sometimes parents themselves wish to pursue an in-depth evaluation at a university center even though it rarely bears a significant contribution to the intervention.

Several types of physicians are involved in the provision of services for children with disabilities, namely neurologists, neuropediatricians, child neuropsychiatrists, and physiatrists. Neurologists and neuropediatricians provide their services through a hospital (e.g., prescribe drug treatment for epileptic seizures). Most doctors involved in district units are child neuropsychiatrists and physiatrists. The former mainly handle psychological problems associated with a chronic disabling condition, whereas the latter are specifically involved in planning habilitative or rehabilitative programs together with physiotherapists. Other professionals, such as physical therapists, SLPs, occupational therapists (OTs), psychologists, and social workers, are also involved. Teachers are not part of the district units, but they are provided directly by the educational system. A close collaboration is established for each child between the different professionals involved in carrying out the habilitative plan, including teachers. Several kinds of treatment are provided, including physical therapy, speech-language therapy, and psychotherapy (for children and parents).

A New Conceptual Framework for Diagnosis and Intervention

The aforementioned approach for early developmental assessment by Milani Comparetti views newborns and infants as goal-directed motivated organisms (Milani Comparetti & Gidoni, 1976). The shift of emphasis from pure elicitation of reflexes and reactions to achievement of functional performances, thanks to the interaction with the environment, brought new and interesting methodological issues. In light of these concepts, different groups began to study the infant's spontaneous motility—general movements according to Prechtl and colleagues (Prechtl, Ferrari, & Cioni, 1993)—and quality of motor patterns—following Milani Comparetti's intuitions, with encouraging results (Ferrari, Cioni, & Prechtl, 1990). Milani Comparetti stressed the importance of positive developmental reactions as opposed to classical abnormal or deviant neurological signs. This view is similar to Brazelton's (1984) concept of optimal performance in which the examiner must stay at the infant's side and make adjustments to see if the infant is capable of modifying his or her performance in response to the modification of environmental or social conditions. In contrast to this concept, the classical neurological perspective views the infant as a living organism generating preprogrammed reflexes or reactions without taking into account the influences of the environment or even the infant's motivations. On the whole, the classical neurodevelopmental approach has to be considered a good evaluation of the infant's current neurological status but cannot provide reliable information on long-term prognosis. In 1996, two of the authors and their collaborators proposed a new diagnostic or intervention procedure taking into consideration both Milani Comparetti's approach to early diagnosis and intervention and Brazelton's concept of optimal performance (Bottos, Dalla Barba, D'Este, & Tronick, 1996). According to this method, neuromotor performances should link up with behavioral performances in order to assess the modifiability of motor performances in response to environmental inputs. To be able to achieve his or her functional goals, any given infant must modulate his or her physiological or neurological status, process environmental information, and generate behavioral strategies suitable to environmental conditions. In light of this view, neurobehavioral performances should be seen as functionally motivated consequences of infant–environment interaction. This being so, the critical feature of any given performance to be evaluated is not simply the normality or abnormality of movement but the ability of the infant to adapt and modify his or her performance in response to environmental demands. Neonatal and primary reflexes bear a poor prognostic significance if considered in terms of their presence or absence. Individual motor performances should not be considered normal or abnormal in themselves; rather, their modifiability and adaptability reflect central nervous system residual potential for a favorable outcome. The assessment scale developed by Bottos and his group called the Neurobehavioral Assessment Scale (NAS) differs from the traditional neurological examination in the way items are administered, evaluated, and scored (Bottos et al., 1996). Each item may be administered several times; the examiner should elicit the infant's best performances through a number of maneuvers. Each item is scored on a 5-point scale that rates the quality of the response as well as the adaptability or modifiability of the infant's performance throughout the examination. For instance, the control of the behavioral state is scored according to the following numerical scale:

1—The infant shows a prompt reaction to the more disturbing maneuvers such as being undressed, and even though the infant will eventually reach a crying state, the infant is able to calm down alone or to be comforted by minimal examiner intervention (e.g., vocal consolation) and achieve an alert state.

2—Crying or agitation is marked only during distressing phases, and consolation is very quickly achieved through mild examiner intervention (e.g., restraining one or both arms).

3—Even in the moderately distressing examination phases, such as putting the infant in the prone position, the infant shows an overall poor behavioral state organization (e.g., difficulty in emerging from a state of sleep, apathy, or accentuated irritability). Consolation or arousal from these states requires prolonged examiner intervention (e.g., holding and cuddling the baby).

4—The infant cries or does not respond during the entire examination, with no behavioral state modifications, and consolation is achieved only after the infant has been held by the examiner and cuddled, wrapped in a blanket, and rocked.

5—The infant shows an uncontrollable alteration in behavioral states, and consolation is not achieved, even after prolonged examiner attempts.

Each score indexes the quality of the infant's performance and the responsiveness of the infant to the maneuvers performed by the examiner. These administration and scoring features are unique to the NAS. Not only does the examiner carry out standard maneuvers in order to get responses (e.g., reflexes, reactions)—that are judged normal or abnormal according to a standard criterion—but also the examiner plays an active role, modifying his or her behavior in order to elicit the infant's best performance (Brazelton, 1984). In this way, the NAS tests the modifiability of the infant's performances in response to changes of environmental inputs (i.e., affordabilities including examiner's scaffolding behavior). The entire procedure allows the examiner to test the effectiveness of maneuvers in modifying the infant's responses so as to perform a neurodevelopmental diagnosis and also lay the basis for an adequate intervention. Consequently, the scale is an instrument for early diagnosis and early intervention. An additional goal of assessment is to give parents the opportunity to achieve a better understanding of their infant who is at risk. Assessing and reassessing the infant in search of competencies rather than incompetencies allows parents to learn about and appreciate their infants, as well as to observe obtainable performances during daily handling. This promotes parents' sense of competence as caregivers and facilitates their active involvement in the development of their infant's functioning (Nugent, 1985). This holds true not only in cases in which progressive normalization occurs with the consequent formulation of a positive prognosis but also in more difficult situations. Physiotherapy will then be much more effective if parents have already been trained to look at their infant as an individual with competencies and incompetencies rather than as a mixture of more or less understandable neurological responses that appear to have little functional implication for how parents can interact with their infant.

Which Intervention: Physiotherapy or Assistive Technology?

The adapting therapy to life model determines many consequences not only in terms of educational policies but also in terms of possible therapeutic approaches. A traditional approach invariably aims at recovering motor function in children with neuromotor impairment, no matter how long it will take. Even though a significant percentage of children with cerebral palsy will never achieve independent walking (Sala & Grant, 1995; Trahan & Marcoux, 1994)—and many who do frequently lose it (Bottos, Feliciangeli, et al., 2001; Murphy, Molnar, & Lankasky, 1995; Pimm, 1992)—traditional management is almost exclusively focused on motor habilitation to achieve walking through physical therapy. In fact, an ambulatory prognosis can be outlined quite early (Badell Ribera, 1985; Bleck, 1975; Bottos et al., 1995; Campos da Paz, Burnett, & Braga, 1994; Crothers & Paine, 1988; Fedrizzi et al., 2000; Souza & Ferraretto, 1992; Trahan & Marcoux, 1994; Watt, Robertson, & Grace, 1989). Children with cerebral palsy who do not achieve basic functional performance such as independent sitting and/or crawling by the age of 3 have little, if any, chance to achieve independent walking with motor training. Furthermore, there is no general agreement on the effectiveness of physiotherapy (Butler & Darrah, 2001). Traditional approaches should then be critically revised. Many habilitative methods are based on the premise that the more you treat the more you get (in terms of favorable outcome). Doman-Delacato and akin techniques do not set limits to the length and the intensity of treatment (even 8 hours per day for 365 days a year is acceptable) (American Academy of Pediatrics, 1999). A given skill will be practiced for as much time as it will take to achieve it. Consequently, aims and means are inverted: Instead of therapy for life, there is life for therapy (Bottos, 1987, 2003; Bottos & Orlandi, 1997).

When the prognosis for independent walking is poor, considerable attention is focused not only on physical therapy but also on surgical procedures and ambulatory aids in an attempt to promote eventual ambulation. Even though there is no need to give up motor training, it is mandatory at the same time to develop strategies that can help to achieve the greatest degree of autonomy and quality of life in a reasonable amount of time. There could be an illusion of full recovery for a child who is able to perform well during treatment sessions but who otherwise is passively carried by an adult while waiting for independent walking. This false impression delays real motor autonomy, which could be more quickly achieved by means of technological aids. This delay will markedly influence the onset of an independent personality: A child who is not able to move independently cannot disobey his or her parents and therefore experience the consequences of autonomous decisions. Lack of autonomy will set up a vicious circle of dependence: The child learns to give up rather than to keep trying and learning. However, if the child has the opportunity to use a mobility aid, which allows independent movement early in life, a virtuous circle is more likely to be activated. The child will make decisions, which will likely lead to the development of a more independent personality. The increasing knowledge of the possibilities offered by technological aids together with a clearer knowledge of the natural history of the different forms of cerebral palsy allow a more reliable early functional prognosis (Badell Ribera, 1985; Bleck, 1975; Bottos et al., 1995; Campos da Paz et al., 1994; Crothers & Paine, 1988; Fedrizzi et al., 2000; Souza & Ferraretto, 1992; Trahan & Marcoux, 1994; Watt et al., 1989), thus enabling professionals to make more appropriate and timely therapeutic decisions. The endless pursuit of a treatment that awaits a radical improvement—regardless of how long this improvement may take and how much it will cost in terms of time spent in therapy—can no longer be accepted. In contrast, the approach outlined here, even though it does not preclude motor recovery, aims at achieving the greatest possible autonomy and the highest quality of life for a given child, taking into consideration all aspects of the child's development. Reducing the importance of physical therapy in the treatment of children with disabilities by bypassing motor and language impairments with the help of technological aids constitutes a fundamental issue with enormous consequences from a psychological point of view. For instance, early utilization (third year of life) of a powered wheelchair probably grants the child better autonomy, but at the same time, parents realize they are giving up dreams of normalization (Bottos,

Biolcati, Sciuto, Ruggeri, & Feliciangeli, 2001). Dream of normalization, however, can be maintained with full-time physiotherapy.

Planning Treatment

Research findings are now forcing professionals involved in early diagnosis and treatment of children with cerebral palsy to take into account the following points when planning treatment. First, the symbolic goal of walking independently, although very important, should be considered just one of a number of means of motor independence. This is further underlined by the current knowledge concerning the evolution of independent walking in adults with cerebral palsy: Those who achieve independent walking often lose it (Bottos, Feliciangeli, et al., 2001; Murphy et al., 1995; Pimm, 1992). Hence, independence cannot be based exclusively on the achievement or nonachievement of walking. Different solutions such as powered mobility and/or architectural modifications should be considered to achieve the highest level of independence. Even though wheelchairs are still considered to be the antagonists of locomotion, they should be viewed as useful devices for people who do achieve independent walking to help to maintain it as long as possible. Inasmuch as a number of adults with cerebral palsy lose independent walking because of joint pain, the best way to get optimal functional results would probably be to combine wheelchair use with some continuous, but limited, walking.

Second, the functional prognosis of children with cerebral palsy can be established quite early. Several reports suggested that the nature and timing of early locomotor patterns (e.g., crawling) are crucial predictors for the acquisition of independent walking (Badell Ribera, 1985; Bleck, 1975; Bottos et al., 1995; Campos da Paz et al., 1994; Crothers & Paine, 1988; Fedrizzi et al., 2000; Souza & Ferraretto, 1992; Trahan & Marcoux, 1994; Watt et al., 1989). The age of 3 years seems to be a turning point: Children who do not acquire a locomotion pattern such as crawling, bunny hopping, or shuffling—or at least independent sitting, which requires satisfactory trunk control—by that age have very little chance of later developing a functional independent walking pattern, at least in the case of spastic syndromes (Bottos et al., 1995).

Third, principles guiding early intervention in childhood neuromotor disabilities should be critically revised. The acquisition of motor skills still has to be encouraged, but professionals should no longer wait for years to see if a child will eventually become an effective walker because of physiotherapy or orthopedic interventions. Powered mobility should be used as a means of providing efficient, autonomous locomotion for children with severe motor disabilities, enabling them to become active participants in their own lives rather than allowing them to remain mere spectators (Bottos, Feliciangeli, et al., 2001; Butler, 1986, 1997; Tefft, Furumasu, & Guerette, 1997; Wright, 1997).

EARLY INTERVENTION FOR CHILDREN WITH DISABILITIES IN THE AUTONOMOUS REGION OF SICILY

According to the most recent (2001) Italian epidemiological and statistical survey,[2] the region of Sicily has an estimated population of 5,076,700 individuals (i.e., 8.8% of the entire Italian population) of whom 51.5% are men and 48.5% are women. In Sicily, there are 160,012 children (individuals who are under 3 years of age), representing 3.2% of the entire Sicilian population—the latter figure is higher than the average national figures for children of the same age, which is 2.8%. Children in general (i.e., all those under 18 years of age) represent 21.6% of the entire Sicilian population when compared with the average national figures of 17.4% for individuals in the same age group. Overall, Sicily has a higher percentage of individuals who are under 18 years of age compared with the rest of the national population, thus showing a younger population. In 1991, 64,522 children were born for a birth rate of 13 children in 1,000 individuals—higher than the national birth rate, which is 9.6 in 1,000. The rate of people with disabilities for Sicily is estimated to be around 62.8 in 1,000 individuals compared with the general Italian population, which is 48.5 in 1,000. However, the rate of developmental delay in children at 1 year of age—if one considers the various developmental areas (i.e., visual, motor, fine and gross motor, coordination, psychosocial, language [expressive and receptive])—ranges from 1% to 2% and is similar to that in other Italian regions.

A program developed by the local government of Sicily aims at integrating social and health services in order to serve children with severe disabilities[3]. Social and health services include the participation (by law) of the following: 1) families, 2) lay and support groups, 3) professional associations, and 4) volunteers (all of whom are at regional and national levels). The flow chart for diagnosis and treatment of children with developmental disabilities in the Sicilian region starts from the office of the

---

[2]Linee guida per l'attuazione del piano socio-sanitario della Regione siciliana. Supplemento ordinario n.1 alla Gazzetta Ufficiale della Regione Siciliana (p. 1) n. 53, 22 Novembre 2002 (n. 37) [Guidelines for the implementation of the health project of the Sicilian region. Ordinary supplement no. 1 to the Official Gazette of the Sicilian region (part 1) no. 53, 22 November 2002 (no. 37)].
[3]Ibid.

family pediatrician who refers the child with a disability or the child with a suspected problem to a tertiary level center (e.g., a university- or hospital-based center). Once the condition has been fully characterized, the child is referred to the rehabilitation department of the local health district corresponding with the family's permanent address. A forensic medical committee including a social worker and a professional nominated by the health district (usually a child neuropsychiatrist or a physiatrist) will then further evaluate the degree of disability and establish which kind of intervention should be planned. For infants at high risk, such as premature or very low birth weight infants, intervention starts during their stay in the intensive care unit and continues after discharge from the hospital. In this latter instance, intervention programs are provided even in the absence of clear abnormalities. Subsequently, habilitative treatments are carried out in regional or local centers with permission granted by the local health district in which the infant resides. The local or regional team is composed of child neuropsychiatrists, psychologists, social workers, and rehabilitation therapists, namely physiotherapists, SLPs, OTs, and psychotherapists. The provision of rehabilitative services is regulated by national as well as regional laws: Health expenditures in the region of Sicily are charged either to the national, regional, or local health system in variable percentages (usually from 40% to 70% is charged to the national health system, and the remaining part is divided between the regional and local systems) according to the current national and regional regulation. The health care system for developmental disabilities is regulated by specific regional laws and, for better organization, is divided into three main metropolitan areas, namely the cities of Palermo (for western Sicily), Catania, and Messina (for eastern Sicily). These larger districts act as coordinating and integrating centers for 55 local social and health districts covering referrals from the nine main Sicilian provinces: Agrigento, Caltanissetta, Catania, Enna, Messina, Palermo, Ragusa, Siracusa, and Trapani.

CONCLUSION

It is mandatory to look at Italy as an exquisitely nonhomogenous country—a fact that undoubtedly surprises the reader, especially when comparing Italy with much bigger nations such as the United States. Several inconsistencies and inequalities—particularly between the north and the south of Italy—are obvious, both in the health status of the people and in the provision of health care. It would be necessary to bear this in mind in order to understand and correctly interpret social and health policies. As discussed, what is going on in the autonomous region of Sicily provides a good example. Even though systematic legislation concerning early intervention has not yet been put forth, a strong cultural tradition toward early diagnosis and treatment of childhood developmental disabilities still exists. The discussion of early intervention for neuromotor disabilities in northern Italy underlines the important contributions by Milani Comparetti. Other sections of this chapter have shown advances in designing an original instrument for both diagnosis and intervention that combine good Italian (Milani Comparetti) and American (Brazelton) intuitions. Furthermore, much stress has been placed on the importance of a global functional approach to the child with a disability, emphasizing the role of assistive technology, which aside from physical therapy may help the child achieve as much independence as one can reasonably expect. An overview of the available services for early intervention was provided in light of the Developmental Systems Model (Guralnick, 2001). Finally, a brief survey has also been provided on the few experiences with home-based and parent-implemented curricula that have attempted to replicate an already validated and fruitful model of early intervention.

REFERENCES

Allen, M.C., & Capute, A.J. (1988). Neonatal neurodevelopmental examination as a predictor of neuromotor outcome in premature infants. *Pediatrics, 83*, 498–506.

American Academy of Pediatrics. (1999). The treatment of neurologically impaired children using patterning. *Pediatrics, 104*, 1149–1151.

Amiel Tison, C. (1988). Cerebral handicap in full-term newborns related to late pregnancy and/or labor. *European Journal of Obstetrics, Gynecology, and Reproductive Biology, 28*, 157–163.

Armstrong, R. (2001). Social success of children with cerebral palsy: What we learn from those who do well. *Developmental Medicine and Child Neurology, 43*(89), 3.

Badell Ribera, A. (1985). Cerebral palsy: Postural-locomotor prognosis in spastic diplegia. *Archives of Physical Medicine and Rehabilitation, 66*, 614–619.

Bierman-Van Eendenburg, M.E., Jurgens-Van Der Zee, A.D., Olinga, A.A., Hiusjes, H.H., & Towen, B.C. (1982). Predictive value of neonatal neurological examination: A follow-up study at 18 months. *Developmental Medicine and Child Neurology, 27*, 139–145.

Bleck, E.E. (1975). Locomotor prognosis in cerebral palsy. *Developmental Medicine and Child Neurology, 17*, 18–25.

Boccardi, S. (1987). Diagnosi precoce e trattamento tempestivo. [Early diagnosis and treatment]. In M. Bottos (Ed.), *Paralisi cerebrale infantile* [Cerebral palsy] (pp. 337–348). Milan: Libreria Scientifica Editrice.

Boccardi, S. (2003). Dalla "guarigione" all'autonomia. Diagnosi e proposte riabilitative. [From "recovery" to autonomy. Diagnosis and rehabilitative proposals]. In M. Bottos (Ed.), *Paralisi cerebrale infantile* [Cerebral palsy]. Milan: Libreria Scientifica Editrice.

Bottos, M. (1987). *Paralisi cerebrale infantile: Diagnosi precoce e trattamento tempestivo.* [Cerebral palsy: Early diagnosis and treatment]. Milan: Libreria Scientifica Editrice.

Bottos, M. (2003). Dalla "guarigione" all'autonomia. Diagnosi e proposte riabilitative. [From "recovery" to autonomy. Diagnosis and rehabilitative proposals]. In Paralisi cerebrale infantile [Cerebral palsy]. Milan: Libreria Scientifica Editrice.

Bottos, M., Biolcati, C., Sciuto, L., Ruggeri, C., & Feliciangeli, A. (2001). Powered wheelchairs and independence in young children with tetraplegia. *Developmental Medicine and Child Neurology, 43,* 777–779.

Bottos, M., Dalla Barba, B., D'Este, A., & Tronick, E.Z. (1996). The neurobehavioral assessment scale as an instrument for early long-term prognosis and intervention in major disability in high-risk infants. *Journal of Pediatric Psychology, 21,* 755–769.

Bottos, M., Feliciangeli, A., Sciuto, L., Gericke, H., & Vianello, A. (2001). Functional status in adults with cerebral palsy and its implications for treatment of children. *Developmental Medicine and Child Neurology, 43,* 516–528.

Bottos, M., & Orlandi, L. (1997). Services for children with disabilities in Italy. In H. McConachie, D. Smyth, & M. Bax (Eds.), *Services for children with disabilities in European countries* (pp. 52–54). Oxford, London: McKeith Press.

Brazelton, T.B. (1984). *Neonatal behavioral assessment scale: Clinics in developmental medicine.* Philadelphia: Lippincott.

Brunet, O., & Lézine, I. (1955). *Echelle de developpement psychomoteur de la premiere enfance* [Psychomotor development scales]. Clamart, France: Editions Scientifiques et Psychotechniques.

Brunet, O., & Lézine, I. (1967). *Scala di sviluppo psicomotorio della prima infanzia* [Psychomotor development scales]. Florence: Organizzazioni Speciali.

Butler, C. (1986). Effect of powered mobility on self-initiated behaviours of very young children with locomotor disability. *Developmental Medicine and Child Neurology, 28,* 325.

Butler, C. (1997). Wheelchair toddlers. In J. Furumasu (Ed.), *Pediatric powered mobility* (pp. 1–6). Arlington, VA: Rehabilitation Engineering Society of North America (RESNA).

Butler, C., & Darrah, J. (2001). Effects of neurodevelopmental treatment (NDT) for cerebral palsy: An AACPDM evidence report. *Developmental Medicine and Child Neurology, 43,* 778–790.

Campos da Paz, Jr., A., Burnett, S.M., & Braga, L.W. (1994). Walking prognosis in cerebral palsy: A 22 year retrospective analysis. *Developmental Medicine and Child Neurology, 36,* 130–134.

Crothers, B., & Paine, R.S. (Eds.) (1988). The natural history of cerebral palsy (Classics in developmental medicine series). London: Cambridge University Press. (Reprinted from *The natural history of cerebral palsy,* by B. Crothers & R.S. Paine, Ed., 1959, Oxford, England: Blackwell Scientific Publications)

Del Giudice, E., Titomanlio, L., Brogna, G., Bonaccorso, A., Romano, A., Mansi, G., et al. (in press). Early intervention for children with Down syndrome in Southern Italy: The role of parent-implemented developmental training. *Infants & Young Children.*

Fattore, G. (1999). Clarifying the scope of Italian NHS coverage. Is it feasible? Is it desirable? *Health Policy, 50,* 123–142.

Fedrizzi, E., Facchin, P., Marzaroli, M., Pagliano, E., Botteon, G., Percivali, M., et al. (2000). Predictors of independent walking in children with spastic diplegia. *Journal of Child Neurology, 15,* 228–234.

Ferrari, F., Cioni, G., & Prechtl, H.F.R. (1990). Qualitative changes of general movements in preterm infants with brain lesions. *Early Human Development, 23,* 193–231.

Guralnick, M.J. (2001). A developmental systems model for early intervention. *Infants & Young Children, 14,* 1–18.

Johnson-Martin, N.M., Jens, K.G., Attermeier, S.M., & Hacker, B. (1991). *The Carolina Curriculum for Infants and Toddlers with Special Needs* (2nd ed.). Baltimore: Paul H. Brookes Publishing Co.

Johnson-Martin, N.M., Jens, K.G., Attermeier, S.M., & Hacker, B. (1997). *Il programma educativo individualizzato precoce per bambini con anomalie dello sviluppo psicomotorio.* [Early treatment for children with developmental disabilities]. Rome: Verducci Editore.

Legge 5 febbraio 1992, n. 104 (1992). "Legge quadro per l'assistenza, l'integrazione sociale e i diritti delle persone handicappate" [Law 5 February 1992, n° 104. "Comprehensive law for the assistance, social integration and civil rights of handicapped people."] *Gazzetta Ufficiale della Repubblica Italiana* [Official Gazette of the Republic of Italy] n° 39, 17 February 1992 (Ordinary Supplement).

Legge 8 novembre 2000, n. 328. (2000). "Legge quadro per la realizzazione del sistema integrato di interventi e servizi sociali" [Law 8 November 2000, n° 328. "Comprehensive law for the implementation of an integrated system of social interventions and services."] *Gazzetta Ufficiale della Repubblica Italiana* [Official Gazette of the Republic of Italy] n° 265, 13 November 2000 (Ordinary Supplement).

Legge 15 marzo 1997, n. 59. (1997). "Delega al governo per il conferimento di funzioni e compiti alle regioni ed enti locali, per la riforma della pubblica amministrazione e per la semplificazione amministrativa" [Law 15 March 1997, n° 59. "Commitment to the government for the assignment of duties to the regions, for the reform of state administration, and for the simplification of bureaucratic procedures."] *Gazzetta Ufficiale della Repubblica Italiana* [Official Gazette of the Republic of Italy] n° 63, 17 March 1997.

McCormick, M.C., McCarton, C., Tonascia, J., & Brooks-Gunn, J. (1993). Early educational intervention for very low birth weight infants: Results from the infant health and development program. *Journal of Pediatrics, 123,* 527–533.

Milani Comparetti, A. (1965). La natura del difetto motorio nella paralisi cerebrale infantile. [The nature of motor deficit in cerebral palsy]. *Infanzia Anormale, 64,* 587–628.

Milani Comparetti, A. (1981). Le proposte del bambino. [The proposals of children]. In A. Milani Comparetti (Ed.), Il bambino come comunicazione. [Communication and the child]. Milan: Franco Angeli Editore.

Milani Comparetti, A. (1982a). Semeiotica neuroevolutiva. [The neurodevelopmental examination of children]. *Prospettive in Pediatria, 12,* 305–311.

Milani Comparetti, A. (1982b). La riabilitazione del bambino handicappato nella medicina della salute. [The rehabilitation of handicapped children]. *Prospettive in Pediatria, 12,* 301–304.

Milani Comparetti, A., & Gidoni, E.A. (1971). Significato della semeiotica reflesso-logica per la diagnosi neuro-evolutiva. [The meaning of primitive reflexes in the context of the neurodevelopmental examination]. *Neuropsichiatria Infantile, 121,* 252–271.

Milani Comparetti, A., & Gidoni, E.A. (1976). Dalla parte del neonato: Proposte per una competenza prognostica. [Proposals for a correct prognosis in the newborn at risk]. *Neuropsichiatria Infantile, 175,* 5–18.

Murphy, K.P., Molnar, G.E., & Lankasky, K. (1995). Medical and functional status of adults with cerebral palsy. *Developmental Medicine and Child Neurology, 37,* 1075–1084.

Nugent, J.K. (1985). *Using the NBAS with infants and their families: Guidelines for intervention.* White Plains, NY: March of Dimes Birth Defects Foundation.

Pimm, P. (1992). Cerebral palsy: A non-progressive disorder? *Educational and Child Psychology, 9,* 1.

Prechtl, H.F.R., Ferrari, F., & Cioni, G. (1993). Predictive value of general movements in asphyxiated full-term infants. *Early Human Development, 35,* 91–120.

Sala, D.A., & Grant, A.D. (1995). Prognosis for ambulation in cerebral palsy. *Developmental Medicine and Child Neurology, 37,* 1020–1026.

Souza, A.M., & Ferraretto, I. (1992). Factors involved in the prognosis of walking in cerebral palsy. *Arquivios de Neuropsiquiatria, 50,* 80–83.

Tefft, D., Furumasu, J., & Guerette, P. (1997). Pediatric powered mobility: Influential cognitive skills. In J. Furumasu (Ed.), *Pediatric powered mobility* (pp. 70–82). Arlington, VA: RESNA.

Trahan, J., & Marcoux, S. (1994). Factors associated with the inability of children with cerebral palsy to walk at six years: A retrospective study. *Developmental Medicine and Child Neurology, 36,* 787–795.

Watt, J., Robertson, C.M.T., & Grace, M.G.A. (1989). Early prognosis for ambulation of neonatal intensive care survivors with cerebral palsy. *Developmental Medicine and Child Neurology, 31,* 766–773.

Wright, C. (1997). The transitional powered mobility aid: A new concept and tool for early mobility. In J. Furumasu (Ed.), *Pediatric powered mobility* (pp. 58–69). Arlington, VA: RESNA.

CHAPTER 22

EARLY INTERVENTION IN SPAIN

An Overview of Current Practices

CLIMENT GINÉ GINÉ, M. TERESA GARCÍA-DÍE,
MARTA GRÀCIA GARCIA, AND ROSA VILASECA MOMPLET

This chapter provides an overview of the state of early intervention in Spain for children who have or are at risk for developmental disorders. Spain is a country with a plural system of government and public administration. Following the adoption of the new constitution in 1978, the central government gradually devolved various powers to the governments of the newly constituted Autonomous Communities. This means that the social welfare, health, and educational policies of each Autonomous Community result in early intervention programs being implemented in different ways, even though many aspects of what they do are similar. The situation in Catalonia is described and the differences between it and the situation in other Autonomous Communities are pointed out.

EARLY INTERVENTION IN SPAIN SINCE THE 1970s

The first early intervention services were set up in Spain in the 1970s, and they have now spread across the whole country. In 2000, on the basis of many years of experience, a group of professionals from different Autonomous Communities (GAT [Early Intervention Group]) drew up a report titled *Libro Blanco sobre Atención Temprana* (Early Intervention White Paper), and it was hoped that the report would become a reference framework that would help to harmonize differences and unify care models for government bodies and professionals.

In the 1970s, the decade commonly thought to represent the start of early intervention in Spain, teachers with experience in early intervention from countries such as the United States and Argentina ran a series of training courses. These all were private initiatives organized by profession-als who, following this training, set up the first early intervention services, some of which were supervised directly by the University of Washington. In addition to these initiatives taken by professionals, there were others promoted by parents' associations, special schools, health services, and other similar organizations.

The political context in Spain at that time, which helped to encourage diverse origins in keeping with the diverse conceptual frameworks under-pinning them, is worth mentioning. In the 1980s, the political and social changes in the country led to government agencies taking responsibility for early intervention. Although this resulted in services that were quite diverse, the commitment to provide funds for privately run centers or to set up centers within the public sector did mean the start of a network of early intervention services. In 2004, this network comprises around 350 centers with some 2,000 professionals working in them. All of the centers started out in a similar fashion, with an interdisciplinary team generally consisting of psychologists, neuropediatricians, physiotherapists, speech-language pathologists, and social workers. Despite the fact that this multi-disciplinary setup proved to be extremely useful in ensuring a comprehen-sive approach to the intervention, it also had the effect of enhancing the differences resulting from the variety of academic fields in which the different professionals involved had been trained.

Changing Models and Practices

During this period, intervention models based on different theoretical approaches existed in other centers throughout Spain. Moreover, not all involved always used the predominant model in each team because profes-sionals comprising the teams came from varied backgrounds. Nevertheless, communication among contrasting teams gradually developed quite spon-taneously, and conferences were arranged that facilitated the exchange of experiences. It should be pointed out, however, that the most widely employed theoretical model to begin with was neobehaviorist. The goals that the teams set for themselves were also similar: the provision of care for the child and family, as well as information and continuous training for the professionals involved. The teams focused their activity on the care of the child, although they obviously also took into account the need to provide the family with information and support. And when the child started to attend school, the process was supervised to ensure that the integration was successful (Beà, 2001; FEAPS [Spanish Federation of Par-ent Associations on Intellectual Disability], 2001; GAT, 2000).

Later on, an approach based essentially on psychodynamic theory was gradually adopted. This meant the model took on similar characteristics to those described by Cunningham and Davis (1988) in which the profes-sional is seen as an "expert," and the parents are given guidance so that they can carry out instructions in relation to the goals being pursued. One of the factors that may well have influenced this change was the decline in the number of children born with disabilities detectable during pregnancy following an act passed by the Spanish parliament in the 1980s allowing abortions to be performed in certain cases, such as malformation of the fetus. This decline has gradually led to early intervention becoming available to children at risk of experiencing disorders as a result of social or family circumstances.

In 2004, there are teams whose theoretical framework is, for the most part, shared by all of their members, and there are different theoretical models including psychodynamic, neobehaviorist and systemic, and ecological. Little by little, a change of paradigm has been put forward (Giné, 1998; Giné, García-Dié, Gràcia, & Vilaseca, 2001), especially by those involved in research based on the suggestions contained in the work of Guralnick (1997, 2001), Peterander (2000a; Peterander, Speck, Pithon, & Terrisse, 1999), and others, that would replace a child-focused model with a family-focused approach with rehabilitation as its fundamental goal.

Every paradigm shift, however, takes time because the ideas originating in other countries need to be adapted to the social, economic, political, and cultural reality of Spain. This explains why the child continues to occupy center stage in the definition of *early intervention* in the *Libro Blanco*:

> [Early intervention] is the full range of interventions aimed at the child population between 0 and 6 years of age, the family, and the environment, whose purpose is to respond as soon as possible to the temporary or permanent needs presented by children with disorders in their development or who are at risk of suffering such disorders. A team of professionals with an interdisciplinary or transdisciplinary approach must plan these interventions, which must take into consideration the child's overall situation. (GAT, 2000, p. 13)

Although intervention has been fundamentally child focused, the parents seen at the early intervention centers regard their relationship with the professionals dealing with their children as adequate and are satisfied with the job they do (Giné, García-Dié, Gràcia, & Vilaseca, 2002). There is no doubt, however, that Spain is slowly moving toward a family-focused model incorporating all of the parameters that help to make it suitable and effective for each particular social situation while offering parents an early opportunity to decide for themselves once they have received all of the information that a professional team can and should provide.

Political, Economic, and Financial Considerations

It is hard to understand the beginnings of early intervention and the path it has followed in Spain unless due account is taken of the situation in the country during the 1970s, the decade in which the first early intervention programs were set up. Democracy was reinstated in Spain in 1976. As one

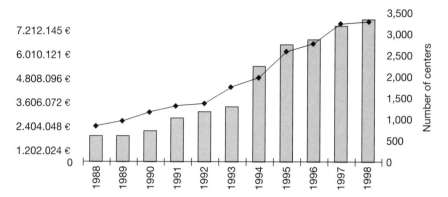

Figure 22.1.   Evolution of early intervention, 1988–1998. (From the web site of the Early Intervention Programme of the Department of Social Welfare and the Family of the Generalitat de Catalunya; http://www.gencat.net/benestar. *Key:* shaded bars represent number of centers, and black diamonds represent euros.)

might expect, however, this was preceded by several years during which institutional change was in gestation, with all of the difficulties involved in making a definitive break from a long period of being in a dictatorship. The first general elections to the Spanish parliament since the end of the Civil War in 1939 were held in 1977, and the governments of the Autonomous Communities were constituted from 1979 onward. There is absolutely no doubt that this change facilitated dialogue with the various levels of government and coincided with the emergence of a willingness to structure and consolidate social resources.

In Catalonia, for example, a decree was issued on July 29, 1985,[1] setting up a network of early intervention centers that are now entirely funded by the autonomous government; users do not have to pay anything. This model, however, has not been implemented in the other Autonomous Communities, and the general picture is one of fragmented care provision with different types of dependence on the governments in question—fully funded public services and private sector services, some with and some without government-funded places (Giné et al., in press).

Figures 22.1 and 22.2 illustrate how early intervention has evolved since the 1980s in terms of budget allocation, the number of early intervention sites funded by the Catalan Autonomous Government, and the number of early intervention centers. Figure 22.1 shows that the number of early intervention places funded by the Generalitat (Catalan Autonomous Government) increased from around 500 to more than 3,500, whereas the

---

[1]Official Gazette of the Catalan Autonomous Government (DOGC 579, 29/7/85).

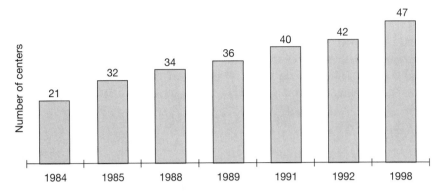

Figure 22.2. Evolution of the number of centers, 1984–1998. (From the web site of the Early Intervention Programme of the Department of Social Welfare and the Family of the Generalitat de Catalunya; http://www.gencat.net/benestar.)

budget allocated to early intervention programs by the Generalitat grew from 2.404.048,42 to 7.212.145,25 €. Figure 22.2 shows the growth in the number of early intervention centers in Catalonia between 1984 and 1998 from 21 to nearly 50, a figure that has remained stable.

In the early years, early intervention centers were funded in a number of different ways depending on the type of center and who owned it. Funding, however, had one thing in common: to a greater or lesser extent, the parents contributed financially to the provision of the service. Slowly, the recognition of early intervention as a public service gained support, and the autonomous governments have eventually come to bear virtually the whole cost.

The *Libro Blanco* (GAT, 2000) insists on the need for coordination at both the all-Spain and Autonomous Community levels to design a common policy among the ministries with responsibilities in the early intervention sphere: health, labor, social affairs, and education. This is similarly necessary at the level of each Autonomous Community government. The creation of professional early intervention associations, however, paved the way for the setting up of a national early intervention group (GAT) that would be able to exert permanent pressure on official bodies to facilitate the work of coordination.

Whatever the path traveled over this period, Spain has an appreciable early intervention culture. Professional practice, university teaching, and research together make up a firmly established service base. The services in place provide care from birth for all families requiring professional advice and support to achieve the most normal possible development for their children.

CONCEPTUAL FRAMEWORK

As mentioned in the previous section, both the organization and conceptual underpinning of early intervention in Spain have gradually evolved since the 1980s, and the field is still in the midst of a transformation process that is moving toward an intervention model that is more family focused and more integrated into the community's services network, in spite of the administrative, financial, and professional training difficulties that still remain. This section describes the basic principles and components characterizing the intervention model that is slowly gaining ground in Spain. Before doing so, however, a word of warning is in order: What follows should be taken with a certain amount of caution. It is extremely difficult to generalize about a whole country. Spain is divided up into 17 Autonomous Communities, often with not only different administrative setups regarding early intervention but also different ideological and professional traditions. Even though the professionals working in early intervention services all over Spain have reached a series of agreements contained in the *Libro Blanco* (GAT, 2000), a look at actual practice is likely to reveal considerable differences among the different Autonomous Communities and also within each of these communities.

The principles outlined here, therefore, correspond with a consensus theoretical framework that is intended to gradually guide the way early intervention services operate in Spain, even though they have hitherto followed quite different paths. The principles in question are slowly generating increased support among professionals regarding concepts, day-to-day practice, and training priorities. Consequently, it is not yet a conceptual framework shared by all those working in the field but rather a signpost directing where it is hoped professional practice will go in Spain.

This conceptual framework can be summarized in the following components: 1) adopting social and ecological perspectives of development, 2) adopting a concept of family-focused intervention, 3) adopting a model for working with families based on collaboration between professionals and parents, 4) promoting child involvement, 5) promoting community-based intervention, 6) promoting an interdisciplinary approach, and 7) promoting competence among professionals and the development of efficient organization.

Adopting Social and Ecological Perspectives of Development

This section refers to the gradual acknowledgment that human development is of a social nature (Bronfenbrenner, 1987; Bruner, 1977; Coll,

Colomina, Onrubia, & Rochera, 1992; Rogoff, 1993; Schaffer, 1977, 1993; Wertsch, 1979, 1988). Despite their different approaches and viewpoints, these authors (following Vygotsky, 1978) agree on perceiving human development as a social activity in which children take part in actions beyond their competence with the help of adults or more experienced peers. Children develop superior psychological processes from opportunities to communicate with adults.

The study of the development of children at biological and/or social risk, as well as the study of those with disabilities, shares this theoretical framework. Consequently, the context (opportunities, conditions, and values present in the interaction) plays a decisive part in determining the direction that the development of these children will take (Bernheimer & Keogh, 1995; Gallimore, Weisner, Bernheimer, Guthrie, & Nihira, 1993; Gallimore, Weisner, Kaufman, & Bernheimer, 1989; Guralnick, 1997, 2001).

As Bronfenbrenner (1987) stated, development can only be understood on the basis of the interrelations and interactions within and between the different circles that the model suggests. These circles reflect the different environments that are present throughout a person's life. As Bronfenbrenner pointed out, however, for the environment to be considered a context of development, it has to satisfy two conditions. First, it has to allow the child to observe patterns of activity that are progressively more complex, and the child has to be able to participate with the help of those with more experience. Second, it has to offer the child the possibility of performing these activities independently at a later time.

Adopting a Concept of Family-Focused Intervention

The fact that human development has an interactive nature implies that the family is responsible for the development of their child because they are the basic context in which the interaction takes place. As Kaye (1986) noted, professionals should not expect to discover an explanation of development in the child; part of the responsibility belongs to the adults who organize the experiences for the child. This statement has greater force for families who have children with disabilities. These families can be more fragile because they have to deal with numerous problems and excessive demands. Another reason for family-focused intervention is to provide support in the natural settings in which the children live and develop.

The family becomes the child's natural context, so strengthening the family and increasing its competence becomes the goal of every intervention and the focus of different support initiatives. This is why professionals have to consider finding a professional–parent style of collaboration that meets the needs of parents and the characteristics of each team; it has to be a style that is fully satisfactory for both sides. It is a question of progressing toward a new concept of focusing more on the family than on the child and of giving priority to supporting the solid aspects of the family rather than caring only about the treatment of the impairments.

Focusing on the solid aspects of the family is the key to success. Professionals have to take into account that the family is the center and that the professionals of the early intervention service therefore collaborate and interact with the family during the entire process of identification, planning, access to, and evaluation of the resources. There are different styles of collaboration, and a single definition does not exist.

Adopting a Model for Working with Families Based on Collaboration Between Professionals and Parents

Neither the process of identifying the needs of the child and its family nor intervention is alien to the way that professionals' work with families is conceived. The relationship between professionals and families has a long and extensive tradition and has been the subject of constant research to find a more effective and positive way to conduct it. It is important to acknowledge that this relationship has not been easy.

A new concept based on collaboration between parents and professionals, in which the parents are not only recipients but also suppliers of information, seems to impose itself. Turnbull, Blue-Banning, Turbiville, and Park called it

> Partnership Education: An ecological perspective of the quality of the lives of children and families implies the admission that not all the expertise belongs to the professionals . . . ; therefore, the professionals need, to a great extent, not only the expertise of the parents but also the expertise of other key members of the community. (1999, p. 168)

Winton, Sloop, and Rodriguez added, "The professionals will never know how to help parents unless they have devoted a certain amount of time to learning the facts, situations or behaviors from them that are the object of collective attention" (1999, p. 159). Therefore, from this perspective, it will be possible to carry out the process of identifying the needs of a family only if the professionals work in close collaboration with the parents and other members of the community and display an attitude more disposed to listening than to merely reproducing knowledge and preconceived ideas.

Promoting the Child's Involvement

This component needs to be understood from two standpoints: psychological and social. From the psychological point of view, in order for learning to take place, the child must actively take part in culturally valued activities with the help of adults or more skilled peers (Vygotsky, 1978). Therefore, all initiatives aimed at advising and guiding the family, as well as those aimed at focusing on the child, must be designed to promote the child's direct involvement in the diverse activities of daily life. The young child must gradually move from the role of *spectator* to the role of *actor* if the child's development is to be stimulated. Therefore, the family needs help to create a climate that will optimize the child's opportunities and conditions.

From the social point of view, every effort must be made to encourage the child's maximum involvement in the common activities proper to the community in which the child lives and, above all, in the school environment (nursery, primary, and secondary school). Interaction with peers and adults in both formal and informal contexts will become a decisive factor in the child's progress, in spite of the difficulties and reluctance that still exist.

Promoting Community-Based Intervention

Intervention must always be aimed at achieving maximum integration of children and their families into the community's services network and optimizing the possibilities that the community offers them to further their progress—associations and clubs; the social fabric; and the cultural, educational, sports, and recreational resources present in the community that always have a normalizing value and a clear influence on the quality of life of all those concerned.

Viewed from another angle, the quality of an early intervention system depends on the existence and efficiency of the coordination of applications at a local, national, and international level. Work can no longer be understood in an isolated way because it is quite obvious that the exchanges among professionals enrich, stimulate, and ensure the updating of knowledge. In this new century, given the progress in information technologies, it seems impossible to renounce the advantages of having reliable and up-to-date information regarding the different experiences of work carried out in Spain as well as abroad.

Promoting an Interdisciplinary Approach

Delivering an adequate service to children and families requires joint work by professionals from different disciplines at various points in the process: making the diagnosis, planning the intervention, and implementing the program. Moreover, such interdisciplinary cooperation is needed at two levels: among the different services involved and within each service. In practice, the response to a child's needs is often provided by a number of services (e.g., health, social, educational) run by different government departments and even different levels of government whose coordination is essential.

Similarly, it is important to ensure that within each service the different specialists comprising the early intervention team work together in making the diagnosis and initial assessment, observing the child and family, and intervening and collaborating with the family. Without doubt, the possibility of being able to analyze each case or family situation from different points of view originating from a diversity of professional fields, as well as being able to reach collective agreement on what needs to be done, are aspects that determine the quality of any service.

Promoting Competence Among Professionals and the Development of an Efficient Organization

The last component of the conceptual model is the need to promote competence among professionals who specialize in different areas (e.g., psychology, pedagogy, physiotherapy, neuropediatrics, speech-language pathology) but work together. Several conditions can have a decisive effect on this.

First, there is the need to find regular opportunities during work time for professionals to reflect together on their practice and compare their different points of view regarding the diagnosis, intervention, and assessment (commenting on their observations, watching video recordings, analyzing difficulties, looking at successful solutions).

Second, specific training activities need to be planned in conjunction with an outside consultant for the team to engage in as a matter of priority, without individual team members having to forego taking part in training activities suited to their particular needs and the characteristics of their discipline.

Third, it is important to consider the promotion of investigation and research. Indeed, for a long period of time, research in this field has been centered almost exclusively on showing the effectiveness of intervention as opposed to nonintervention (Guralnick, 1997). There is a need to advance from here and move on to showing which interventions might be more useful than others, which specific aspects of intervention achieve the best results, and which programs might be better than others. In short, professionals need to continue promoting practical and applied research in early intervention, especially from an interdisciplinary point of view.

Professionals also need to look at how teams are organized. An early intervention center needs to have explicit criteria regarding its organization, which all members of the team have been involved in drawing up and are therefore familiar with. Furthermore, an early intervention center needs to have the necessary mechanisms enabling it not only to make the families aware of the organization but also to get them to participate in it to the greatest extent possible. Moreover, an early intervention center, as a system, needs to be flexible enough to allow it to adapt to any changes that may arise and modify the organization in response to such change. The organizational criteria should be decided on collectively by all members of the professional team and shared with other centers and the families, which could help to improve the criteria. There is no doubt that the role of the family in this organization is important and needs to be included from the beginning. Finally, one of the conditions for ensuring a quality service is periodic self-assessment and external assessment of the team—allowing the team to identify its strong and weak points and to train on the weak points as part of the improvement process.

EMERGING QUALITY MODEL IN EARLY INTERVENTION

The following pages provide a description of the early intervention system in Spain that follows, as much as possible, the Developmental Systems Model (Guralnick, 2001). Each section begins with a description of the current situation and is followed by a subsection titled "What needs to be done," which is designed to illustrate that the Developmental Systems Model constitutes only one step in a process of development and refinement, the details of which remain to be established (see Figure 1.3).

Screening and Referral

In Spain, children and their families usually enter the system via a screening and referral process. Screening refers to regular checkup and monitoring programs for all children. Pediatricians or their nurses, that is professionals from the health care sphere, normally carry out these checkups, which are very general. Nevertheless, there are certain differences between the public and the private sector. In the private sector, pediatricians more often carry out the checkups, whereas in the public sector, the pediatric nurses normally carry them out. The instruments they generally use to perform the checkups are protocols enabling them to detect whether there are any warning signs for disabilities or delays,[2] and the checkups are accomplished through direct observation of the children and information gathered by

---

[2]In Catalonia, the *Taula de Desenvolupament Psicomotor* (Psychomotor Development Table) is commonly used. It is published by the Generalitat de Catalunya and is based on a piece of research known as the *Estudi Llevant*.

interviewing the parents. If the parents detect a problem that the pediatrician or pediatric nurse has failed to pick up, then they can go to the early intervention center themselves and request an appointment. They will be either seen at the center or referred to the appropriate assessment and diagnostic service, which comes under the Autonomous Community government, and the child will be assessed there.

The same thing happens with the social services and the educational services (kindergartens, crèches, or nursery schools). Whenever they detect a possible problem in a child, they can ask for the child to be examined by a professional at an early intervention center. Once the child has been seen, irrespective of whether the referral came from a professional in the health, social services, or education sphere or from the parents, a decision is made to either monitor the child or enter the child into an intervention program at an early intervention center.

If the child is referred to an assessment and diagnostic service for an assessment, then the child will usually enter an early intervention program. Sometimes, certain circumstances to do with the child and family—such as premature birth or low birth weight, siblings with a congenital pathology (health care sphere), or a history of abuse or neglect (social services sphere)—mean that inclusion in a monitoring program is automatic. This often leads to the child being referred directly to an early intervention program.

The value of parents' concerns and worries about the development and behavior of their children should not be underestimated. Data show that parents are the first to detect problems in their children in a high percentage of cases (Giné et al., in press). For the most part, scant attention is paid to parental concerns, and no instruments in general use enable, for example, problems in the development of communication and language to be identified, although a proposal regarding this has been made (Galván-Bovaira, Gràcia, & del Rio, 2002).

In spite of the importance that professionals attach to the screening carried out mainly by pediatricians or pediatric nurses and the information, albeit imprecise, provided by parents, the process is by no means simple. In fact, it has been shown statistically that the instruments currently available and in use in many countries, a minority of which are employed in Spain, fail to pick up many of the developmental problems that emerge later on. Also, as Guralnick (2001) has pointed out, they are not sensitive to cultural differences.

What Needs to Be Done

The examinations performed on children during the early stages of their lives often are quite different depending on whether the children are treated by the public or private health system and depending on the Autonomous Community in which they live. There is a need to improve the checkup system and make it more similar across the different Autonomous Communities (GAT, 2000). There is likewise a need for instruments to be used that are capable of picking up possible developmental problems, even though protocols enabling warning signs to be spotted are being increasingly employed.

It may also be necessary to review certain matters such as the frequency, risk criteria, cost, and effectiveness of the checkup and monitoring system. Pediatricians and pediatric nurses need to make a greater effort in this regard because they are the professionals who are in contact with children from an early age, often 1 or 2 years before any other professional comes on the scene. Spain, perhaps unlike other countries, needs a campaign—which could include the provision of training—to raise awareness among these professionals about certain aspects of psychological development. The screening process often focuses on food and the child's physical condition while tending to ignore other aspects that are fundamental for the child's psychological development such as language, reasoning, habits, emotional matters, temperament, and attitude. A campaign to raise awareness among professionals—essentially pediatricians and pediatric nurses in the public sector—about early signs that may be key to detecting a developmental problem was begun several years ago in Catalonia.

Raising professionals' awareness, however, is certainly not enough. Campaigns also are required to improve professionals' knowledge in this regard, whether they work in the educational sphere (as nursery nurses and infant school teachers) or the social services sphere with very young children. Likewise, the education and training available to parents before they have a child and during the first few years of their child's life also needs to be improved. Professionals and parents could help to ensure that problems are detected at an earlier stage, which would mean an improvement in primary and secondary prevention.

Monitoring

In Catalonia, children not referred to an early intervention center but who are suspected of experiencing some disorder in their development are placed on a monitoring program and are seen periodically by an early intervention professional at the early intervention center, at school, or at the health center. Children with an evident pathology that is detected at birth or prior to birth or who are at risk for biological or social reasons are entered into early intervention programs right away. This monitoring by an early intervention professional is sensitive to psychological consequences. If at any time during the monitoring process there is concern over anything that early intervention specialists regard as requiring treatment, then the child is immediately passed on to an early intervention center for appropriate care.

What Needs to Be Done

Although children in Catalonia who are suspected of having developmental disorders are monitored by a professional from an early intervention center and participate in the usual process of periodic checkups performed by health care professionals, this practice is not sufficiently widespread. Monitoring of children by early intervention center professionals does not occur in all services or Autonomous Communities, nor is it carried out frequently enough or with sufficiently sensitive instruments to ensure a well-grounded decision as to whether the child in question needs to be entered into an early intervention program.

Point of Access

In Spain, there is no clearly defined common point of access, but there is a moment in the process. When a child is regarded as being at risk on the basis of the screening and referral or monitoring process, the child is at the point of access and the family is then advised to go to one of the official assessment and diagnostic centers set up by the autonomous governments.

What Needs to Be Done

Families in Spain ought to have the opportunity to take a more active part at this stage in the decision to move the child from being monitored to being assessed and entered into an early intervention program.

Comprehensive Interdisciplinary Assessment

The assessment is certainly a key stage in early intervention, and it is also one of the most time-consuming stages. In Spain, professionals belonging to the assessment and diagnostic services perform assessment. In Spain, however, depending on the particular Autonomous Community in question, the team of professionals in charge of the psychological, medical, and social aspects of the assessment at the assessment and diagnostic centers may not be child specialists. They are assessment specialists, but they do not necessarily specialize in dealing with very young children. In fact, what these professionals do is assess the disability with a view to determine the degree of disability in each of the three areas just mentioned (i.e., psychological, medical, social). In addition, they also determine the length of the intervention required by the infant. In short, the assessment has a legal focus and enables families to be included in an early intervention program and apply for financial assistance for their children.

Once the degree of disability has been determined, the child is referred to an early intervention center. Even though the early intervention center takes into account the assessment made by the assessment and diagnostic service, the early intervention center also carries out its own assessment of the child's level of development in each of the different areas. In this case, the assessment is closely linked to the intervention plan. The early intervention centers use specific tests to evaluate the child's overall development as well as the child's development in particular spheres such as language and cognition. A psychologist at the center usually performs this latter assessment, although the psychologist may also seek the opinion of other professionals such as speech-language pathologists, physiotherapists, educational psychologists, social workers, and neuropediatricians.

This assessment process generates a profile of child health and development. In addition, depending on the particular service and Autonomous Community, this process may describe the ways in which the family, neighborhood, and community function. The assessment team seeks to produce a diagnosis, often labeling the child (e.g., cerebral palsy, developmental delay), containing enough information to establish biological, environmental, or multiple etiology. Families ought to benefit a great deal more from this information because in certain Autonomous Communities and services in Spain this information is not passed on in a way that is desirable. In practice, the information is used by the professionals of the assessment and diagnostic service to inform the professionals at the early intervention center of their diagnosis and the child's degree of disability. However, the family often is given no information or the information is passed on to them in an extremely summarized form, sometimes employing terminology and procedures that considerably diminish the usefulness that the information could have for the family. Unlike what happens in other countries, such as the United States, families have to wait for the assessment process to be completed by the assessment and diagnostic services before entering into an early intervention program, even though this assessment stage usually does not take very long. Intervention usually begins, however, during the assessment by the professionals at the early intervention center. This means that, generally speaking, children and their families receive some initial intervention that, as is described in the following section, is gradually shaped as the assessment process is completed.

What Needs to Be Done

Professionals who make the assessments within the assessment and diagnostic services should be early childhood specialists, which means that they should have the necessary knowledge about typical development, pathologies, and various relevant assessment tools as well as knowledge about how to relate to the family so that the family is equipped to work with the specialist. Once this has been achieved (i.e., when Spain reaches the stage of having specialist assessment teams), the next step or requirement would be for the interdisciplinary teams to gradually specialize in different types of disorders such as autism spectrum disorders or metabolic disorders, or abuse and neglect.

The ideal situation would be to have relatively small teams made up of specialists working together (e.g., psychologists specializing in infant special education, speech-language pathologists, social workers) who could gather information from another team comprising other specialists (e.g., geneticists, psychologists, occupational therapists). Although this is an interesting idea, the particular training of all of these professionals and the tradition in each country (and region) regarding the type of work they do would be necessary to take into account.

In Spain, the first step that ought to be taken is to reflect on the need for the professionals who assess the infant in the assessment and diagnostic service and the professionals who assess the child again at the early intervention center to work together. The families would probably be glad to have these two stages merged into one.

Program Eligibility

Depending on the assessment process that has been carried out at the preceding stage, the criteria that can be gleaned from it with a view to finding the most suitable program may vary. Moreover, neither the screening instruments nor clinical judgment are infallible. In Spain, no specific programs are designed for different types of problems, and there are still fewer criteria on which professionals working in the different centers and different Autonomous Communities have reached a consensus. The current criteria are completely implicit and, in many cases, closely tied to specific psychological theories that accord a great deal of importance to certain aspects and little to others. In other cases, the criteria are heavily based on physical aspects of development and a medical model. They take little account of factors beyond the child, such as the family environment, the parents' expectations and ideas, the local context, and the community.

In Spain, families are allocated to an early intervention center on a catchment area basis and are not able to choose either the center or a specific early intervention program. The public administrators justify this on the grounds that all of the centers are capable of providing the child and family with the same service because they do not specialize in any specific disorder or problem. The early intervention centers should specialize in major areas such as mental retardation, motor disabilities, visual impairments, and hearing loss and design dedicated programs to deal with them as well as acting as a consultancy and resource center for other early intervention professionals. Nevertheless, it should be said that early intervention centers specializing in certain problems, such as children with motor difficulties and visual and hearing impairments, do exist in some Autonomous Communities. A good example is the Joan Amades Center in Barcelona run by the ONCE (Spanish National Organization for the Blind), which caters specifically to children with visual impairments and provides support for other early intervention professionals and those working in the educational sphere. Most children enter a center based on the catchment area in which they fall, but in some cases, the professionals concerned are able to refer them for monitoring.

What Needs to Be Done

The different Autonomous Communities need to lay down criteria for admission to an intervention program that will ensure that each child receives the care and attention that he or she requires. The first step in this direction would be to set up specific intervention programs for different problems, similar to the ones mentioned previously, on the basis of criteria serving to guide the assessment. These criteria would also make it possible to choose the most suitable program for each child and family. In short, although the starting point has to be the needs of each child and each family, getting to this point requires that specific programs be put in place based on criteria that will subsequently be useful in selecting the most suitable program for a particular child and family.

Admission to Preventive and Early Intervention Programs

In Spain, admission of a child and his or her family into an intervention program is not based on an assessment of stressors that may influence family interaction patterns. A preliminary intervention program is put in place that is gradually adapted and adjusted as the team gets to know the child better. Although some of the factors that may unintentionally influence the changes made in the characteristics of this initial program have to do with the family, the assessment of the stressors needs to be considerably improved.

What Needs to Be Done

Communities should have a broad range of early intervention centers and programs available, and they ought to have the ability to place children in different programs quickly, set up a preliminary intervention program, elect a service coordinator, and begin to organize the assessment of the stressors. Spain is a long way from such a goal, which means that certain aspects have to be prioritized. Designing specific intervention programs focusing on different problems would probably be a necessary first step that still needs to be taken in many Autonomous Communities, whereas improvements need to be made in other Autonomous Communities that already have a number of dedicated centers. The second step is raising awareness among the professionals in Spain of the need to assess the stressors that may be perturbing family interaction.

What has been discussed about early intervention programs is equally applicable to preventive intervention programs, particularly regarding the need to identify and design specific types of programs for different problems. The biggest challenge for communities is to identify relevant services ranging from short-term counseling options to intervention-oriented child care. It is also necessary for the intervention and prevention programs to be linked and integrated. Nevertheless, a first step needs to be taken concerning prevention programs, which consists of making the decision for such preventive intervention programs to be defined and put in place. Presently, they are barely distinguishable from the monitoring process.

Assessment of Stressors

The assessment of stressors is specially designed to acquire information to identify optimal family patterns of interaction. In Spain, both the families of children with a clearly diagnosed pathology and the families of children with a biological or environmental risk go through an initial information-gathering process normally involving oral interviews with the parents. In these interviews, special care is taken in assessing how the family perceives the child's problem, how it affects them, and how they function in everyday life. For the most part, written questionnaires and standard protocols are not used the way they are in other countries. Generally speaking, the preferred option is to establish a good rapport between the professional and the family, which allows different matters that might affect the family to be broached. The child is often present at these interviews so that the pattern of interaction between parents and child can be observed directly.

In these interviews, it is usually important to reach an agreement with the family about which characteristics of the child or which of their own characteristics affect them and which do not, what attitudes might be changed, and where to start working. A good deal of importance is attached to seeking further information from other specialists at the early intervention center or through outside specialists as an aid to better identify the stress factors involved.

The social support and financial resources available are important subjects for these interviews to deal with, although, in Spain, this is something usually done by the social worker in the team or by someone belonging to the management side of the center. This should be included in the general assessment of the stressors so there is a more comprehensive view of the family's characteristics. Communication and relaying information between the family and the professionals involved is regarded as a fundamental aspect that still has to be improved in Spain.

What Needs to Be Done

There is no doubt that a set of protocols, surveys, and questionnaires that can identify possible stressors affecting the family patterns of interaction must be developed in Spain. The assessment of stressors associated with child and family characteristics must be carried out with great care and sensitivity, but Spain is a long way from performing this task systematically in a way agreed on by all professionals working in the early intervention field.

Nevertheless, since the late 1990s, some centers have started to consider involving the parents at this stage as a priority. As a result of taking part in conferences and learning about approaches that were beginning to be employed in other countries (Björck-Åkesson & Granlund, 1995, 1997; Guralnick & Neville, 1997), some centers have started to realize that the information parents can furnish about their own children, about themselves, about the children's participation in other care or therapeutic processes, about how the problem was detected, about their coping experiences following detection, and about how they see their own involvement (Guralnick, 2001) is of fundamental importance. The professionals dealing with the child ought to be aware of these things so they are able to make a much more accurate and fuller assessment of the situation. In an attempt to gradually move away from the expert model hitherto prevalent in this part of the world, there has been a growing realization that a joint assessment, taking into account the information mentioned as well as the tests carried out on the children and the observations made, provides the basis for setting the goals of the program. These goals cannot be set without taking into consideration the families' characteristics, their expectations, the way they see the problem, and their attitude toward it. This means that it is essential for parents to collaborate actively in setting the goals of the program through joint work on the child's characteristics, the parents' own characteristics, and the results of the initial assessments, although this approach is by no means applied in practice by the majority of centers.

Developing and Implementing a Comprehensive Program

Once the initial interviews have been completed, an agreement is reached with the family for the child with clearly established difficulties or the child who is at risk to be entered into an early intervention program. The professionals usually make a specific intervention proposal, which in most cases focuses on direct attention to the child with difficulties.

Although most authors agree that the family is the natural context for any child, with or without disabilities, and that parents need to be involved in early intervention programs (Bromwich, 1981; Fornós, 1997; Gray & Wandersman, 1980; Guralnick & Neville, 1997; Shearer & Shearer, 1976; Worobey & Brazelton, 1986), such involvement is tackled in many different ways at the various early intervention centers in Spain. In fact, generally speaking, early intervention in Spain remains almost entirely focused on the child (Giné et al., 2001).

The results of a pilot study (Giné et al., 2001) show that professionals devote most of their time to dealing with children at the center, usually on an individual basis, and have little time to carry out family assessments in the home or at the center. In any case, family assessments in the home often consist of giving the family guidelines on what they should do, particularly in relation to the more psychomotor and physiotherapeutic spheres. In most cases, work with families at the centers, in spite of being an objective (Fornós, 1997), is in the form of *one-way* counseling: The parents are given information and guidelines by the professionals on how they should behave in certain situations, without their role in the intervention process being taken sufficiently into account. Moreover, the parents see the professionals as experts and therefore they regard themselves as mere receivers of the information given to them, which they must then try to act on for the benefit of their child.

One common activity performed at the early intervention centers in Spain is the work done with parent groups (Fornós, 1997; Fuertes & Palmero, 1995). The aims of such groups include helping to balance the emotional relationship between parents and their children, exchanging experiences with other parents, and enabling parents to discover their own resources.

Offering parents all of the information on the prospects for their child's development is another of the most effective forms of cooperation in regard to the intervention. As Peterander (2000b) pointed out, information helps parents to establish a dialogue with the professionals that facilitates the acquisition of skills and enables them to cope better with the problems of everyday life. According to the findings of a pilot study (Giné et al., 2001), the early intervention center professionals devote part of their time to enhancing the child's independence (e.g., dressing, eating), but they do not pay much attention to the parents' role as necessary active participants and mediators in the child's development in each and every one of the other areas of the child's life.

Again, the early intervention centers do not appear to provide parents with ongoing information on their child's progress. Customary practice is to produce an annual report on the child's progress during the school year that does not include any aspects of the way the family functions because this is not part of the intervention. There is, however, usually a more informal, although rather shallow, exchange of information at the end or at the start of the sessions with the child that often depends on the family's interest in finding out whether the child is improving in the course of treatment.

What Needs to Be Done

A lot remains to be done to improve parents' *educational* skills and bring about a change of paradigm that will assign a leading role to the family. Many professionals point to the need to have more time to be able to interact with families than they do now.

The process of identifying a family's needs and the intervention process itself (with the family and the child) can only be carried out in close collaboration with the parents and other members of the community on the basis of an attitude more akin to listening than merely reproducing knowledge and preconceived schemas. Research (Giné et al., 2001) has shown that this is certainly one of the areas in which progress needs to be made in Spain. The relationship that professionals have with parents, although established in terms of trust and open friendliness, cannot be described as one of close collaboration.

Monitoring and Outcome Evaluation

Throughout the period in which the intervention with the child takes place at the early intervention center, the professionals periodically hold interviews with the family every month or two. In these interviews, the child's progress is evaluated in relation to the goals that were set at the beginning of the intervention, and it may be possible to work on some guidelines with the family. In most cases it is a one-way assessment.

As a general rule, when it comes to the outcome evaluation, the professional again performs a battery of assessment tests, most of them on the child, in order to determine the child's level of development in different areas. These results are communicated to the family, and a decision is made on whether to continue the treatment. In some cases, parents and professionals decide to terminate the treatment because the child has reached the goals that were established. In other cases, parents and professionals decide to discontinue treating the child directly but to monitor the child for a certain length of time, which involves planning three or four visits over a period of approximately 6 months. This is not an option in every Autonomous Community. In many instances, however, it is the child's age that determines the end of the treatment received from the early intervention center because of the relevant government regulations.

In Spain, the family is not given any written report at these monitoring interviews. The usual practice is for a final report about the level attained by the child to be drawn up. This report does not normally include previously evaluated factors because they are not explicitly part of the intervention.

What Needs to Be Done

The monitoring and outcome evaluation processes need to become less child focused and take greater account of the stressor factors on families caused by child characteristics. A stronger evaluation culture is needed that takes into consideration the progress of both the child and the family. Making a satisfactory evaluation requires taking into account the family patterns of interaction that together with the child's characteristics produce child developmental outcomes. This applies to children with established disabilities, at biological risk, or with social risk, as well as to all children who exhibit delayed development. In Spain, early intervention professionals are required to adopt a change of paradigm that entails rigorous work with the family not only in the stages described previously but also during the monitoring and outcome evaluation processes.

Transition Planning

In Spain, there are a variety of types of transition: from hospitals to early intervention centers; from health centers to early intervention centers; or from early intervention centers to nursery schools, special schools, and other children's services. First, all transitions between health care, social, and educational services and early intervention centers are described before discussion on transitions between early intervention centers and other services.

The children and their families coming from hospital neonatal units are usually referred to the early intervention centers directly on account of a patent organic pathology. According to a survey carried out in the Autonomous Community of Catalonia (Giné et al., in press), 50% of hospitals do not know how to refer families to the early intervention services. There is a certain tendency to delay referral of infants and their families to early intervention services or to make the referral via the child's pediatrician. Such transitions are usually accompanied by written reports concentrating on such factors as the physical characteristics, the etiology, and the diagnostic tests that have been performed on the child.

Another moment of transition is when professionals in the health care service refer children and their families to early intervention services. According to the same survey, when health care professionals refer a family to an early intervention center, they do so in writing in only 35% of cases. The reason for the referral is listed in only 44% of these reports, and general reference is made to the family situation in just 35% of the reports.

Transitions to early intervention centers from education agencies (most commonly nursery schools and educational psychology school support services) are generally better coordinated. The Giné et al. (in press) study found that 62% of the professionals working in the educational sphere said they had regular liaison channels with the early intervention center and were extremely satisfied with them.

Final transitions or discharges from the early intervention center to other external services are also an important part of the process that needs to be evaluated in order to get a full picture of the quality of early intervention in Spain. As the *Libro Blanco* (GAT, 2000) points out, when a child reaches the statutory age limit but is judged to be in need of ongoing psychological and/or educational care, the transition is made to mainstream schools with pedagogical support or to special schools. According to the Giné et al. (in press) study, the professionals in the early intervention centers set up agreements with the educational services prior to enrollment in 90% of cases. This is regarded as being extremely positive for both the children and their families. Most children enter mainstream schooling, some attend special schools, and a few split their time between mainstream and special schools.

When the time comes for transition to a mainstream or special school, a process is generally set in motion that involves the professionals from the early intervention center visiting the new setting, meeting the professionals working at the school to explain the child's educational needs, and helping the family to choose the best school for their child until the professionals from the early intervention center are sure that the transition has been completed.

The survey by Giné et al. (in press) also found that when children have to leave the early intervention service as a result of their age, some

65% still require ongoing educational and/or health care. Existing public sector resources are clearly insufficient to meet this demand, particularly in the health care domain (e.g., speech-language pathology, psychotherapy).

What Needs to Be Done

These transitions require a properly planned process. This already happens to some extent in Spain, although the goal of planned processes in all cases and all Autonomous Communities is still a long way off. In fact, there are manifest limitations at these transition points. Some of these deficiencies stem from the fact that the professional functions involved in early intervention (medical, educational, and social) belong to different agencies, which hampers rapid and efficient coordination.

Regarding transitions from health care to the early intervention sphere, greater knowledge of the early intervention centers needs to be promoted among health care professionals and more attention should be paid to developing efficient interagency coordination. In the first place, the pediatric and neonatal units in the hospitals need to be able to refer the families of the children they are treating as soon as they feel it is appropriate to start work with the family and without having to wait until the child is discharged from the hospital. This would certainly improve coordination and ensure continuity of the health care received.

Although some referrals are made from health centers to early intervention centers, there is also much room for improvement here. The pediatricians need to be more aware of the function of the early intervention center and bear in mind that the referrals do not involve only children and that such centers can also provide assistance to their families. It is also necessary to make sure that referrals are made in liaison with the professionals at the early intervention center. Better communication between pediatricians and early intervention center professionals is also needed, especially in establishing joint criteria concerning warning signals so that the problem can be dealt with as soon as possible.

Coordination between the educational services and the early intervention centers needs to be encouraged and improved. Although the referral network operates quite well, it would be useful to ensure that when a nursery school admits a child with suspected developmental delay, a professional from an early intervention center is called in to make a joint assessment of the advisability of a referral to the early intervention center.

The most important shortcoming of the existing early intervention network, however, has to do with the transitions at the point of discharge from the early intervention center to other services. Continuity of care must be ensured when children reach the end of the early intervention phase, especially in the case of state-run services. Poor liaison among the different health care, educational, and social services bodies, coupled with the lack of public sector provision to meet demand, means that transition planning is often slow and therefore involves a certain waiting time in order to gain access to the other services that are required. If access to such services were set up earlier and there was a well-coordinated network, then the continuity of care received by children and their families would no doubt be improved.

CONCLUSION

This chapter described the situation of early intervention in Spain, with special reference to Catalonia, in spite of the difficulties of such a task and given the diversity inherent in the political and administrative system and in the traditions of training and professional practice.

It has to be acknowledged that early intervention has made considerable progress in Spain since the 1970s. In the first place, early intervention is within reach of practically all families. Both the central government and the governments of the Autonomous Communities have incorporated it into their network of services, and some of the latter fully fund it. Second, this progress has been made possible by a broad sector of professionals across the country that have gradually acquired training and experience and built up a network structured around professional associations that has enabled them to exchange experiences and reflect together on certain aspects of the future development of this field. Third, there has been an obvious increase in awareness in society as a whole and in the professional sectors involved regarding early intervention. Nevertheless, there still remains a great deal of work to be done to bring Spain's practices for the care of families and children up to the quality standards of the Developmental Systems Model (Guralnick, 2001) for early intervention.

It seems appropriate, however, to stress the following points. First, although progress has been made in the availability and funding of early intervention, it still needs to be made accessible and free to families in many places. Second, efficient care depends on supplying families with clear information; heightening awareness; enhancing the training of health care professionals in relation to the psychological and educational problems of the children and their families; and ensuring better coordination between the health care network and early intervention services, which in Spain are largely within the realm of social welfare departments. Third, it would seem necessary to effectively incorporate monitoring into the conception and development of early intervention in Spain, implementing it both prior to attendance at an early intervention center to enhance prevention and while any early intervention program is being carried out. Fourth, and this is probably the most far-reaching change proposed, it is necessary to promote a shift away from a child-focused model to a family-focused model that includes the parents as major actors at every stage of the process. A model of collaboration with families that recognizes that *expertise* resides not only in the professionals but also in the parents must gradually be adopted. The parents must be involved in making the diagnosis and in selecting and implementing the program. To ensure that this happens, it is essential to have instruments and protocols that make it possible to evaluate the family's stressors with their active participation and promote improvements in their educational competencies and skills in the home. Fifth, an assessment culture needs to be promoted and disseminated among professionals and agencies regarding the outcome from both the child's and the family's point of view and of the organization involved in the intervention. There is little doubt that early intervention will improve in so far as we are able to not only plan and evaluate on the basis of the results and progress achieved but also reflect on our own practice.

Finally, one of the fields in which the need for improvement in Spain is most evident is in the transition and continuity of services when a child reaches the end of the early intervention stage, especially when the needs are in the health care sphere. Generally speaking, educational services are accessible to all children, and there is normally a good relationship and liaison between these services and the early intervention centers. When the child requires psychiatric care, speech-language therapy, or rehabilitation, however, the parents are often forced to resort to privately run services, which they have to pay for themselves because public provision is quite insufficient. The points here indicate the main direction that changes should take to ensure future improvements in early intervention in Spain.

REFERENCES

Beà, N. (2001). L'atenció precoç: Dels primers centres a la coordinadora. [Early intervention: From early centers to the association]. *Revista de l'Associació Catalana d'Atenció Precoç* [Journal of the Catalonian Association of Early Intervention]. Monogràfic. Desè Aniversari.

Bernheimer, L.P., & Keogh, B.K. (1995). Weaving interventions into the fabric of everyday life: An approach to family assessment. *Topics in Early Childhood Special Education, 15*(4), 415–433.

Björck-Åkesson, E., & Granlund, M. (1995). Family involvement in assessment and intervention: Perceptions of professionals and parents in Sweden. *Exceptional Children, 61*(6), 520–535.

Björck-Åkesson, E., & Granlund, M. (1997). Changing perspectives in early intervention for children with disabilities in Sweden. *Infants and Young Children, 9*(3), 56–68.

Bromwich, R. (1981). *Working with parents and infants: An interactional approach.* Baltimore: University Park Press.

Bronfenbrenner, U. (1987). La ecologia del desarrollo humano. [The ecology of human development]. Barcelona, Spain: Paidós.

Bruner, S.J. (1977). Early social interaction and language acquisition. In H.R. Shaffer (Ed.), *Studies in mother–infant interaction* (pp. 271–289). London: Academic Press.

Coll, C., Colomina, R., Onrubia, J., & Rochera, M.J. (1992). Actividad conjunta y habla: Una aproximación al estudio de los mecanismos de influencia educativa. [Joint activity and speech: An approach to the study of educative influence mechanisms]. *Infancia y Aprendizaje, 59–60,* 189–232.

Cunningham, C., & Davis, H. (1988). Trabajar con los padres. Marcos de colaboración. [Working with parents. Frameworks for collaboration]. Madrid: MEC/ Siglo XXI Editores.

FEAPS [Spanish Federation of Parent Associations on Intellectual Disability]. (2001). Atención temprana para personas con retraso mental. Orientaciones para la Calidad. [Early intervention for mentally retarded persons. Guidelines for quality]. Manuales de Buena Práctica. Madrid, Spain: Author.

Fornós, A. (1997). El modelo asistencial de la atención precoz en Cataluña. [The care model in early intervention in Catalonia]. In J. Tomàs (Ed.), Reeducación psicomotriz, psicoterapia y atención precoz (pp. 100–104). [Psychomotor reeducation, psychotherapy and early intervention]. Barcelona, Spain: Laertes.

Fuertes J., & Palmero, P. (1995). Intervención temprana. [Early intervention]. In M.A. Verdugo (Ed.), Personas con discapacidad [Persons with disabilities] (pp. 925–970). Madrid, Spain: Siglo XXI Editores.

Gallimore, R., Weisner, T.S., Kaufman, S.Z., & Bernheimer, L.P. (1989). The social construction of ecocultural niches: Family accommodation of developmentally delayed children. *American Journal on Mental Retardation, 94*(3), 216–230.

Gallimore, R., Weisner, T.S., Bernheimer, L.P., Guthrie, D., & Nihira, K. (1993). Family responses to young children with developmental delays: Accommodation activity in ecological and cultural context. *American Journal on Mental Retardation, 98*(2), 185–206.

Galván-Bovaira, M.J., Gràcia, M., & del Rio, M.J. (2002). Una propuesta de evaluación de las interacciones comunicativas madre-hijo: La prueba mother-infant communication screening (MICS). [An evaluation proposal of the mother-child communicative interactions: The mother-infant communication screening test (MICS)]. *Revista de Logopedia, Foniatría y Audiología, 1*(XII), 15–23.

GAT [Early Intervention Group]. (2000). *Libro blanco de la atención temprana.* [Early Intervention White Paper]. (Real Patronato de Prevención y de Atención a Peronas con Minusvalía Documentos 55/2000). Madrid, Spain: Ministerio de Trabajo y Asuntos Sociales.

Giné, C. (1998). Repensar l'atenció primerenca. [Rethinking early intervention]. *Desenvolupament Infantil i Atenció Precoç. Revista de la Associación Catalana de Atención Precoz, 11–12,* 19–39.

Giné, C., García-Dié, M.T., Gràcia, M., & Vilaseca, R. (2001). *Un model d'avaluació de la qualitat dels centers de desenvolupament infantil i atenció precoç.* [An evaluation model of the quality of early intervention services]. Unpublished article.

Giné, C., García-Dié, M.T., Gràcia, M., & Vilaseca, R. (2002, October). La participación de los padres en la atención temprana en Catalunya. [Parents' participation in early intervention in Catalonia]. Paper presented at the I Congreso Nacional de Átención Temprana, Murcia, Spain.

Giné, C., Fornós, A., del Rio, M.J., Zaurín, L., Miró, M.T., Beà, N., et al. (in press). L'atenció precoç a Catalunya. Serveis i qualitat. [Early intervention in Catalonia. Services and quality]. Barcelona Institut Català d'Assistència i Serveis Socials.

Gray, S.W., & Wandersman, L.P. (1980). The methodology of home-based intervention studies: Problems and promising strategies. *Child Development, 51*, 993–1009.

Guralnick, M.J. (1997). Second-generation research in the field of early intervention. In M.J. Guralnick (Ed.), *The effectiveness of early intervention* (pp. 3–20). Baltimore: Paul H. Brookes Publishing Co.

Guralnick, M.J., & Neville, B. (1997). Designing early intervention programs to promote children's social competence. In M.J. Guralnick (Ed.), *The effectiveness of early intervention* (pp. 579–610). Baltimore: Paul H. Brookes Publishing Co.

Guralnick, M.J. (2001). A developmental systems model for early intervention. *Infants and Young Chidren, 14*(2), 1–18.

Kaye, K. (1986). *La vida social y mental del bebé. Cómo los padres crean personas.* [The mental and social life of babies]. Barcelona, Spain: Piados.

Peterander, F. (2000a). The best quality cooperation between parents and experts in early intervention. *Infants and Young Children, 12*(3), 32–45.

Peterander, F. (2000b). *Quality indicators in early intervention.* Paper presented at the Novenes Jornades Internacionals d'Atenció Precoç. Desenvolupament Infantil i Atenció Precoç [IX International Early Intervention Conference on Child Development and Early Intervention], Barcelona, Spain.

Peterander, F., Speck, O., Pithon, G., & Terrisse, B. (Eds.). (1999). Les tendances actuelles de l'intervencion précoce en Europe. [Current trends in Early Intervention in Europe]. Sprimont, Belgium: Mardaga.

Rogoff, B. (1993). *Aprendices del pensamiento. El desarrollo cognitivo en el contexto social.* [Apprenticeship in thinking. Cognitive development in social context]. Barcelona, Spain: Paidós.

Schaffer, H.R. (1977). Early interactive development. In H.R. Schaffer (Ed.), *Studies in mother–infant interaction* (pp. 3–16). London: Academic Press.

Schaffer, H.R. (1993). El contexto sociofamiliar en la educación de la infancia. [Sociofamiliar context in education of childhood]. In H. R Schaffer (Ed.), *Temas de infancia* (pp. 38–65). Madrid, Spain: Centro de Publicaciones del MEC y A.M. Rosa Sensat.

Shearer, D.E., & Shearer, M.S. (1976). The portage project: A model for early childhood intervention. In T.D. Tjossem (Ed.), *Intervention strategies for high risk infants and young children* (pp. 338–350). Baltimore: University Park Press.

Turnbull, A.P., Blue-Banning, M., Turbiville, V., & Park, J. (1999). From parent education to partnership education: A call for a transformal focus. *Topics in Early Childhood Special Education, 19*(3), 164–172.

Vygotsky, L.S. (1978). *Mind in society: The development of higher psychological processes.* Cambridge, MA: Cambridge University Press.

Wertsch, J.V. (1979). From social interaction to higher psychological processes: Clarification and application of Vygotsky's theory. *Human Development, 22*, 1–22.

Wertsch, J.V. (1988). *Vygotsky y la formación social de la mente.* [Vygotsky and the social formation of mind]. Barcelona, Spain: Paidós.

Winton, P.J., Sloop, S., & Rodriguez, P. (1999). Parent education: A term whose time is past. *Topics in Early Childhood Special Education, 19*(3), 157–161.

Worobey, J., & Brazelton, T.B. (1986). Experimenting with the family in the newborn period: A commentary. *Child Development, 57*, 1298–1328.

CHAPTER 23

EARLY INTERVENTION IN SWEDEN

A Developmental Systems Perspective

EVA BJÖRCK-ÅKESSON AND MATS GRANLUND

When early intervention is based on a systems theory perspective, prediction and control must be viewed in a probabilistic manner (Guralnick, 2001; Wachs, 2000). Several influences act in addition or co-vary to influence the developmental and functional trajectory of a child and a family. The probabilistic nature of these processes makes it difficult to design descriptive, coherent early intervention treatment packages that are effective for all children. Interventions on a societal system level (e.g., laws, regulations, curricula), designed to increase the probability of well-being for all children, will only have a minimal effect on the well-being for individual children identified in need of special support. According to Wachs, effective assessment and intervention for individual children may be most functional when it is consistent with what is known about the role of multiple developmental influences and system processes. Wachs identified eight principles for intervention based on this knowledge:

1. The focus of assessment should be multidimensional.

2. The structural linkages between influences and dimensions make it necessary to assess and analyze the patterns of co-varying positive and negative factors before intervention.

3. Context must be brought into assessment and intervention. Interventions that work well in one context may not work well in another context.

4. Build on specificity when designing interventions; avoid the assumption that a specific intervention will apply equally well to all outcomes.

5. Build on system and niche characteristics when designing interventions; interventions must be focused on individual and contextual characteristics that maximize the child's ability to place him- or herself in contextual niches that enhance development and well-being.

6. Build intervention strategies that are tailored to a co-varying cluster of influences rather than to single factors taken in isolation.

7. Build on individual differences in reactivity to environmental influences; interventions must be tailored to an individual child's particular characteristics.

8. Intervention efforts operate over a background of time. Interventions should ideally break the operation of negative causal chains and enhance the operation of positive causal chains.

In this chapter, information about early intervention services in Sweden is presented, followed by an analysis of the extent to which the services apply to the eight principles for systems-based early intervention services suggested by Wachs (2000). Finally, the findings are related to Guralnick's (2001) Developmental Systems Model for early intervention.

EARLY CHILD CARE AND EDUCATION IN SWEDEN

Sweden is a country situated in Scandinavia in the north of Europe. Despite the northern location at the polar circle, the climate is tempered with four distinct seasons. It has approximately 9 million inhabitants, and Swedish is the native language. Approximately 80% of the adult population vote in the national elections, held every fourth year, which is an indicator of interest in civic matters. Sweden is changing into a diverse, multicultural society. Since the 1970s, the proportion of the population with an immigrant background has increased dramatically. As of 2002, immigrants formed about 10% of the population, and 24% of children birth through age 17 years had at least one parent with a foreign background (Barnombudsmannen [BO], 2002). About 15% of all students in compulsory school come from foreign backgrounds; either they were born abroad or their parents were born abroad (Swedish National Agency for Education, 2004a).

In Sweden, childhood has its own value and is not merely seen as a time of preparation for adult life and investment in the future. Play is considered highly important in Swedish child care. The national curriculum for compulsory schools emphasizes play as a means for development and learning in all children (The Swedish Ministry of Education, 1998). An important role for the early childhood educator is to create possibilities for children to play (Björck-Åkesson & Granlund, 2003). As in other countries, the natural context for children is dependent on the culture and social contexts and shifts with age. During the first years, two natural contexts in the proximal environment emerge for most children—the family and child care/preschool. The social insurance system governed by the Swedish state guarantees that one parent is entitled to stay home and care for the child for 480 days from the time the child is born until the child is 8 years old. One of the parents (or divided between the parents) can draw the child benefit for the first 390 days with 80% of his or her wages. For the last 80 days, the payment is 60 Swedish crowns (SEK) per day (less than $10 per day). Thus, the natural context for most children for the first 18 months is in the home with one biological parent (still primarily the mother). From about the age of 18 months, most children (approximately 80%) transition into preschool activities or family child care. Thus, child care becomes the second important natural context for most children.

Swedish child care has twin aims. One is to make it possible for parents to combine parenthood with employment or studies. The other is to support and encourage children's development and learning and help them grow up under conditions that are favorable to their well-being (Swedish National Agency for Education, 2004b). In 1996, responsibility for public child care was transferred to the Ministry of Education. Child care for young children from 1 to 6 years is the responsibility of the municipality. Municipalities have an obligation to provide preschool activities for children whose parents work or study, or for children with a particular need for such activities. This obligation extends also to children of unemployed caregivers or caregivers on parental leave, for a minimum of 3 hours per day or 15 hours per week. A child shall be offered a place without unreasonable delay (i.e., normally within 3–4 months of the parents having requested a need for a place). A place shall be offered as near the child's home as possible (Swedish National Agency for Education, 2004c). The concept of child care encompasses preschool, family child care homes, and open preschools. The activities may be run by the municipality or privately. In the fall of 2003, the number of children who attended preschool was 351,700, which is an increase of 18,000 children compared with 2002. This means that 75% of children ages 1–5 years attend preschool. Seven percent of children attend family child care (Swedish National Agency for Education, 2004c).

The preschool cares for children while parents are working or studying or if the children have special needs of their own. Preschools are open year round, and daily opening times vary to fit parents' working hours. Children are registered and the parents pay a fee that in most areas is linked to the family's income and the child's attendance. From 2002, municipalities may apply a maximum fee for preschool activities and child care for schoolchildren. Those municipalities that use maximum fees receive a government grant. For preschools, families are charged a maximum of 3%, 2%, or 1% of the combined household income for the household's first, second, and third child, respectively. The monthly fee must, however, not exceed 1260 SEK (about $950) for the first child, 840 SEK (about $630) for the second child, and 420 SEK (about $315) for the third child in preschool activities. Virtually all of the country's municipalities applied the maximum fee system in 2003 (Swedish National Agency for Education, 2004d). Children are generally divided into groups of between 15 and 20. As a rule, three employees, preschool teachers, and child care attendants are allocated to each group of children. A municipality can grant permission to a private preschool if the program meets the set standards for safety and quality. The municipality is responsible for supervision of such activities.

The family child care is in-home care in which a child-minder takes care of enrolled children while the parents work or study. Activities are generally located in the child-minder's home. The children are registered, and opening hours vary to fit the parents' schedules. The family pays a fee in the same way as for preschool attendance. Family child care complements preschool and, in particular, children who need small groups or who live far from the nearest preschool. Family child care is more common in rural areas than in metropolitan areas.

The open preschool is an alternative to general preschool for the children of parents who are at home during the day. It also supplements family child care. Together with their parents or municipal child-minders, children are offered pedagogical group activity. Open preschools may collaborate with the social welfare services, maternity care, and child health care services. The children are not registered and are not required to attend regularly. Most open preschools are free of charge. In 1999, there were about 900 open preschools in Sweden; however, the number of open preschools is decreasing. In fall 2003, there were 550 open preschools (Swedish National Agency for Education, 2004c).

All children in Sweden grow up in a family context, and there are almost no institutions for children in need of special care. However, some children in need of special medical care may spend more time in hospitals and hospital-like environments. A majority of mothers and fathers in Sweden are employed in the work force—70% of mothers and 73% of fathers (BO, 2002)—or in higher education. Having a system that supports parental leave and low-cost child care, kinship care, or private child care/preschool for young children is relatively uncommon. In 2001, 43% of 1-year-olds attended child care. Of those, 37% were in community preschools, and 6% were in private care. The time the children spend per week at the preschool varies. Half of them spend less than 20 hours each week in preschool, whereas 25% spend more than 36 hours each week (Swedish

National Agency for Education, 2004b). This means that for a smaller group of children, preschool may be the natural context in which children spend most of the time awake.

THE EARLY INTERVENTION SYSTEM IN SWEDEN

When early childhood intervention services are compared among countries, the difference between care and education provided to all children and early intervention provided to children identified as in need of special support is crucial from a systems perspective. In the United States, for example, a general early child care/preschool system providing services to all children does not exist. Many of the specific early intervention services in North America provided to children at risk (e.g., Head Start) are more or less similar to general services provided to all children within many European countries (Kamerman, 2000). In Sweden, children at risk for socioeconomic reasons are commonly not identified in the general system as a specific risk group, and no special services for these children are provided outside of the community child care and social service system. However, children in need of special support (i.e., children with disabilities, children with more diffuse problems such as difficulty concentrating or known psychosocial problems) are entitled to a place at a preschool. High overall quality in the preschool is viewed as the best kind of support for many of these children, and their needs are intended to be met in regular activities and not by special treatment. The general system has been reported to be beneficial to all children (Andersson, 1989), especially for children with a low socioeconomic background in terms of school preparedness and social competence. Children who have preschool as a natural context in young age tend to have a better outcome in the school years than children who do not spend time in child care/preschool.

Most research efforts concerning early education of young children in Sweden have focused on how to improve the quality of general child care (Williams, Sheridan, & Pramling-Samuelsson, 2000). From a systems theory perspective, this implies that support is aimed at improving children's well-being by interventions on a societal level focused on changing the quality of the general service systems. Such interventions probably result in a decreased number of children at risk in general but might not help a specific child in a specific context. They do not lead to increased knowledge or skills in how to intervene with children who do not benefit from the interventions provided in general activities. For these children, specific early childhood intervention services are needed. This chapter primarily discusses specific early intervention services as provided to children identified to be in need of special support.

Early childhood intervention in Sweden can be defined as intervention practices with children in need of special support from birth to the start of school at age 6 years. Early childhood intervention is primarily implemented in one of the natural contexts for young children—the family and/ or in the community-based child care/preschool. Communities and county councils both are involved in the provision of services. The community has the primary responsibility to provide services to enhance the well-being of all children and families. This responsibility includes specific interventions in the preschool or family child care, personal assistance, and respite care for children identified as in need of special support and their families. The county council is responsible for providing general services related to medical conditions to all citizens (including children) through a family physician system and hospitals, general services related to children's health through Children's Health Services (CHealthS), and services related to children identified as having a disability through Children's Habilitation Centers (CHabC).

In the International Classification of Functioning, Disability, and Health (ICF; World Health Organization, 2001), aspects of an individual's health and health-related factors are classified in the dimensions of body function and body structures, activity, participation, and factors related to the environment. The ICF can be used to describe the organizational structure of services provided to young children in need of support. Services provided by the county councils are primarily focused on body function (CHealthS) and on performing activities (CHabC). If a child is identified as having problems with body functions, then he or she is referred to medical services for children through the CHealthS. The child and the family will meet professionals in an organization based on the medical model and focused on body functions (e.g., eye clinic, internal medicine, orthopedic clinic). If a child is identified with developmental delays and does not perform activities as expected, then he or she is referred to a CHabC. Habilitation services are aimed at children with disabilities and their families and on a living dialogue between service users and professionals (Granat, Lagander, & Börjesson, 2002). Professionals represent the medical field, education, psychology, and the social field and are organized according to their domain (e.g., the physiotherapist represents body functions and activity; the special educator focuses on activity, participation, and environmental factors). The services provided by the communities are primarily focused on enhancing the participation of the child in the context of everyday life in the family and the preschool. Community experts are often organized according to the role or system they are meant to support (e.g., family support, preschool consultant). After identification, experts from the different organizations often are involved in providing services to children in need of special support. Thus, a key issue in collaborating around children in need of special support is how to coordinate recommendations and services from experts with different perspectives on early intervention working in different systems.

Screening Program or Referral

A child will enter the early childhood intervention system after being identified as needing special support. Children in need of special support include children with established disabilities (e.g., Down syndrome), children with medical conditions (e.g., asthma), and children at psychosocial risk (e.g., referred by social workers). Children without established conditions often are those considered to have developmental delays and be in need of special support by the family or preschool personnel. The identification process takes different routes and tends to have different content depending on who identifies the child as in need of special support and in what system. Parents, professionals at CHealthS, preschool professionals, or social workers in community services may initiate developmental screening or referral. The parents must have given their consent before the process is started, and measures cannot be taken without parent consent. An exception is cases in which community social authorities have decided that the children need special support to compensate for deficiencies in the parents' ability to fulfill their parental roles.

Factors affecting the route of the identification process are the type of problem identified, the age of the child, and the manner in which the services are organized. Children diagnosed with established disability conditions such as Down syndrome are most often identified at birth. Children with severe forms of cerebral palsy are identified within the first months of life. Children with these types of disabilities are provided with services from CHealthS and CHabC. When entering community child care or preschool, contact with CHabC has already been established for these children, and frequently, in conjunction with starting in child care or preschool, the community provides a resource person or personal assistant. For children with medical conditions (e.g., diabetes), the identification process is more diffuse both in terms of time of identification and in terms of content of the process. Frequently, only professionals at the hospital and CHealthS are involved. If judged necessary because of caregiving demands (e.g., special diet), a personal assistant may be provided when the child starts in community child care/preschool. Community child care/preschool staff often identify children with more diffuse psychosocial problems based on the observation that they do not adjust to the group of children or suspect developmental delays. Social workers may identify children as at psychosocial risk because of "family problems." The time of identification is commonly between 3–5 years of age. However, there is a tendency to wait and see if problems are difficult to assess or the parents are reluctant to consider a delay in development.

The content of the screening program is related to the route of identification. Children with established disability conditions identified early in life are commonly screened and monitored by CHabC professionals. They may use functional assessments, but use of norm-referenced assessment instruments focused on typical development of the child is common. Interaction and environment variables are frequently not a part of the formal assessment procedure (Björck-Åkesson, Granlund, & Simeonsson, 2000), despite the request for such instruments and an increased use of instruments such as WeeFIM and Pediatric Evaluation of Disability Inventory (PEDI). When the child enters the social and cultural arena of preschool, a shift of focus can be discerned toward problems with interacting with same age peers and inclusion (Jansson, 2003). In ICF terms, the focus shifts from body function and activity toward participation. For children with medical conditions, screening and assessment are primarily implemented by medical professionals and focus on body functions related to the identified condition (The National Board of Health and Welfare, 2003). Medical professionals generally do not deal with functions important for general adaptation (e.g., self-regulative functions, social competence). Children exhibiting psychosocial problems are frequently identified by child care/preschool personnel, and their problems often are described in terms of "lacking social competence," "aberrant behavior," or "does not fit into the group" (Almqvist, Hellström, Häggqvist, & Granlund, in preparation). After identification, children are referred for assessment, often focused on norms for typical development and/or body function. An exception is children identified as having parents who cannot fulfill their parental role. For these children, assessments conducted by the social authorities are frequently focused on parent–child attachment patterns and family environment.

In child assessment, the parents often are invited to passively observe professionals implement formal assessment with norm-referenced or standardized tests, regardless of the child's problem (Arman & Frölander, 2001; Björck-Åkesson et al., 2000). The role of parents in other parts of the identification/screening process is related to the type of problem the child exhibits and the age of the child. In the continuous screening/monitoring process, parents of children who have an early diagnosis of an established disability frequently are provided with formal support from CHabC, aimed at supporting the parents in dealing with the crisis of having a child with a disability and providing training and support to the child. A majority of these centers propound that they have adopted a family-centered approach in which families are assigned an active role in the intervention process, both as decision makers and implementers of child-focused intervention (Carlhed, 2003). However, many parents do perceive their role as paradoxical. They expect the professionals to "know the truth" and come up with recommendations for treatment, and at the same instance, they like to be provided with options and "stay in control" of treatment decisions (Carlhed, Björck-Åkesson, & Granlund, 2003; Granat et al., 2002). Parental preferences typically shift with time with a tendency for parents of older children to prefer "options" and "stay in control" to professionals as decision makers (Adolfsson & Resare, 2000).

After entering the community child care/preschool system, the monitoring by CHabC staff of activities concerning the development of children with a disability occurs in the child care/preschool setting. In this context, child care/preschool personnel and personal assistants are present in the everyday life activities of the child. This means that the parents cannot have as much control and information as when interventions occur in the family context. It is not known how this affects parental involvement in the screening/monitoring process. Parents do report that if informal information exchanges with preschool personnel are functioning well in conjunction with leaving and picking up the child at child care/preschool, then they perceive the services as functioning well (Roll-Pettersson, Granlund, & Steénsson, 1999). The role in the screening/monitoring process of parents to children with established medical conditions or established psychosocial risk conditions is not well known.

Early Childhood Intervention Program

Most of the early intervention activities of young children in need of special support are, as previously mentioned, implemented in natural contexts (family, community child care/preschool). For most children with established disability conditions, the child and the implementation of child-focused interventions shift from home to community child care/preschool around the age of 18–24 months with the rationale that parents should only fulfill the role of parents, not the role of trainers (Granlund, Björck-Åkesson, Olsson, & Rydeman, 2001; Möller & Nyman, 2003). As a consequence, information about training procedures and instructions tend to be provided more to personal assistants and preschool staff and less to parents from this age and older. Another reason for the shift of instructional focus is that, with increased age, children's problems tend to be described more in terms of social competence and participation in social activities at child care/preschool and less in terms of deviances from typical development. Interventions focused on inclusion in activities at child care/preschool can only be implemented by personnel present at the preschool. Interventions focused on body function (e.g., medication, physical therapy) tend to be implemented both in the family setting and the child care/

preschool setting and some time at hospitals. Specific care programs for problems with body function exist for some established disability and medical diagnoses. The responsibility of the personal assistant to implement individual treatment for the child in need of special support within the child care/preschool setting sometimes isolates the assistant and the child as a subsystem within child care/preschool, who partly live a "life of their own" parallel to the activities of other children and staff (Rabe, Hill, & Andersson, 2001).

Children identified by child care/preschool personnel as exhibiting psychosocial problems are frequently provided with intervention only at child care/preschool. The aim of the intervention is to include the child in the group by providing support in interacting with peers. If the social authorities also identify the child as at risk because of parents who cannot fulfill their parental roles, then treatment may be provided at home in terms of family support or family therapy. A small number of families at psychosocial risk, who also have a child with an established disability, receive a large number of services.

It has been reported that in child care/preschool, children in need of special support do not participate in the social process of play to the same extent as other children (Almqvist, 2001; Jansson, 2002; Preisler, Tvingstedt, & Ahlström, 2002). Participation in adult-structured activities is not restricted to the same extent (Almqvist, 2001). The participation restrictions in peer interaction and play seem to be related to differences between children in regard to physical information about the context, ability, and opportunities to manipulate the physical environment; ability to interpret the meaning of symbolic action; and ability to share the socio-communicative system created in play. The pattern of difficulties observed varies among individual children (Jansson, 2003).

The assistant and other child care/preschool personnel under the supervision of professionals from CHabC or community child care/pre-school special education consultants mostly implement interventions provided at child care/preschool with the aim to increase social participation and peer interaction of children in need of special support. The interventions are focused on the identified child and the context of play; peer-mediated interventions do not frequently occur. Ideally, intervention methods should be focused on compensating for the child's lack of information about the physical environment, supporting the child in interpreting the meaning in social events, and supporting the child in social interaction (Jansson, 2003). However, such interventions are difficult to implement. Peer group play is an activity easily disturbed when targeted for intervention (Jansson, 2003; Preisler et al., 2002). According to Jansson (2003), peer cultures have a tendency to defend themselves from interference from the outside. They act as a partially closed system that might break down if adult intrusion disturbs the play script and is replaced by adult–child dyadic interaction. Adult interventions in play contexts have been observed to frequently result in a breakdown of the play activity (Jansson, 2002). A basic rule for successful adult-implemented intervention in play activities seems to be to confirm the rules for play set by the children and intervene within the frame of the play script set by the children.

Transition Planning

In Sweden municipalities are obligated to provide a place in a preschool class for all children beginning the fall term of the year the child turns 6 years. The preschool class can be situated either at child care/preschool or at school. At the same chronological age, the CHealthS responsibility for a child's physical well-being and health ends. From then on, the child and family have to use the family physician medical services provided by the county council for questions regarding physical well-being. For children with established disability conditions, the CHabC continues to have responsibility for the special services provided to the child until the age of 18 years when the individual moves into adult habilitation care (AHabC). For children with established medical conditions, the hospital child clinic continues to have responsibility for the special services provided to the child until he or she turns 18. Thus, continuity in specialized services is provided to children with established disability or medical conditions through the whole developmental period until adulthood. This is not the case for children in need of special support because of psychosocial problems. Many times, an assessment of these children is conducted before school starts with the aim to provide the child with a medical diagnosis and thus make the child eligible for more continuous specialized services. However, parents of children with established disabilities also report a discontinuity of specialized child-focused services and/or less information about and control over the services provided in conjunction with the start of school (Stenhammar & Ulfhielm, 1998; The National Board of Health and Welfare, 2003). Explanations might be that CHabC professionals tend to prioritize younger children in providing services (The National Board of Health and Welfare, 2003) and that the daily informal contacts between parents and school become fewer than they were at child care/preschool.

In conjunction with the transition from child care/preschool to school, a developmental assessment of children with established disability conditions is conducted frequently with the official aim to facilitate school placement of the children. If the child has or is suspected to have an intellectual disability, then the assessment must contain intelligence testing conducted by a licensed psychologist as a basis for an eligibility decision to determine if the child should be offered education according to the specific curricula for children with intellectual disability. The same assessment procedure is used many times as a basis for intervention recommendations provided to CHabC professionals other than psychologists and school professionals (Arman & Frölander, 2001). However, these professionals often adhere to theories other than theories of intelligence when designing interventions for children with intellectual disability and report that they have no use for the information provided by the psychologist (Widuch-Berg, 2002).

DO EARLY INTERVENTION SERVICES IN SWEDEN HAVE A BASIS IN SYSTEMS THEORY?

According to systems theory, the influences that affect the outcome of interventions are specific and may vary between system levels (Rutter, 2000; Wachs, 2000). What may be an effective intervention element with an established cause and effect relation on societal level (e.g., opportunities to free play, group size in child care) may not be an effective intervention mechanism for an individual child. Intervention elements effective on a societal level do, however, affect the probability of a good outcome of interventions on an individual level. The way the society has formed early intervention services will thus set the frame within which outcomes of intervention for individual children can be expected and within which early intervention method elements for individual children are formed. Differences between countries in how early intervention plans for individual children are formed and in goals for interventions may indicate that macro system factors influence form and effects of early intervention for individual children. A basic difference on a societal level between early intervention services in the United States and Sweden is whether they are based on rights or needs (Carlhed et al., 2003). In the United States, services are based on an individual's right to obtain services if he or she is identified as eligible for services for specific reasons. Children are not routinely provided with early childhood education or early intervention services. Arrangement of child care and early childhood education is up to the individual family. Children have the right to obtain services if they are identified as at risk or if they have established developmental or medical problems. Thus, most early childhood education services and early intervention services provided by the United States are specialized and focused on specific groups of children and/or individual children. Few services are obtained unless the family speaks for their rights.

Many specialized services are implemented within the family as the natural context. In Sweden, the society provides early childhood education and care to all children, including children in need of special support. Additional services are provided to children identified as in need of special support. Societal resources are allocated to children according to needs, based on decisions made by the society. Children have the right to services within the resource frames set by society. Parents of an individual child cannot legally question whether the resources necessary for an individual child exist. The natural context for implementing child-focused services is most commonly child care. Consequences of these societal differences can be discerned in terms of parents' involvement in the interventions, the person who is implementing interventions, and the kind of problems dealt with in intervention. Parents in the United States are probably more involved in intervention decision making than Swedish parents because of the societal requirement of expressing rights. If the family context or kinship care is more of a natural context for young children in the United States compared with Sweden, then parents probably are also more frequently implementers of treatment recommendations. If children in Sweden more frequently attend community child care from an early age, then problems with peer relations are identified and dealt with at an earlier age. Within the frames set by societal differences, the degree to which early intervention services for individual children are based in principles grounded in systems theory can be analyzed.

As mentioned in the beginning of this chapter, when early intervention is based on systems theory, effective assessment and intervention for individual children and their families must be consistent with what is known about the role of multiple developmental influences and system processes. Based on the eight principles for systems-theory–based interventions suggested by Wachs (2000), the following can be said about early intervention in Sweden:

1. *The focus of assessment should be multidimensional.* Assessment practices in early intervention cannot be considered as multidimensional to a great extent even though there is a tendency toward multidimensionality. The content of assessment is primarily child focused with an emphasis on measures related to typical development (Arman & Frölander, 2001; Björck-Åkesson et al., 2000). The exact content of assessment is related to the first type of problem identified for the child and thus to the type of organization conducting the assessment. The probability of an assessment procedure containing assessment of child participation in social activities and environment is greater if professionals within the child care system conduct the assessment.

2. *The structural linkages between influences and dimensions make it necessary to assess and analyze the patterns of co-varying positive and negative factors*

before intervention. Different organizations within early intervention have their focus on different types of problems and thus collect different kinds of assessment information. No organization is responsible for gaining a comprehensive overview of the collected assessment information that sometimes leads to fragmented intervention decisions and service provision for the child in need of special support and the family. Parents report that they perceive their most challenging task to be coordinating the recommendations and services provided (Carlhed et al., 2003; Stenhammar & Ulfhielm, 1998).

3. *Context must be brought into assessment and intervention; interventions that work well in one context may not work well in another context.* Most assessment efforts are child focused and collect information regarding developmental status. Formal assessment of interaction and environmental factors are less common (Björck-Åkesson et al., 2000). Family environment, family factors, and family goals are informally discussed with the family. Most interventions are child focused and implemented within the child care setting by personal assistants or child care staff. If the identified problem for which intervention is provided is formulated in terms of social competence or peer relations, then the probability that contextual factors are included in assessment and intervention increases.

4. *Build on specificity when designing interventions; avoid the assumption that a specific intervention will apply equally well to all outcomes.* Many of the treatment suggestions given to parents of young children in need of special support are proactive intervention methods focused on specific problems with body function or the performance of activities (e.g., physiotherapy for children with spina bifida, manual sign training for children with Down syndrome). Professionals from hospitals or CHabC are responsible for these suggestions. With age, individual differences are revealed, especially in conjunction with the child's transition to preschool and interaction with peers. Such participation problems frequently require a more individualized assessment and intervention process. Since the late 1990s, a trend can be discerned that children with psychosocial problems are given diagnoses such as attention-deficit/hyperactivity disorder (The National Board of Health and Welfare, 2003). Children within these categories sometimes are given treatment recommendations based on general recommendations rather than an individual assessment (Enbom, 2004). Such general recommendations usually are related to small group size and strict routines.

5. *Build on systems and environmental niche characteristics when designing interventions; interventions must be focused on individual and contextual characteristics that maximize the child's ability to place him- or herself in contextual niches that enhance development and well-being.* Depending on the type of problem and the type of organization providing supervision to implementers of interventions, the degree to which systems and environmental factors

are taken into consideration in the treatment suggestions vary. Treatment suggestions related to body function and performance of activities often are implemented without considering the child's personality or environmental factors. Treatment suggestions concerning a child's everyday function (e.g., interacting with peers) take personality and environmental characteristics into consideration to a greater extent (Granlund & Sundin, 1999).

6. *Build intervention strategies that are tailored to a co-varying cluster of influences rather than to single factors taken in isolation.* The lack of clear service coordination and integration of assessment information concerning body function, the performance of activities, participation, and contextual factors makes it difficult to build intervention strategies tailored to a co-varying cluster of influences. Generally, the more a child's problem is addressed in terms of a child's everyday functioning, the more the treatment suggestions are tailored to clusters of influences (Granlund & Olsson, 1999).

7. *Build on individual differences in reaction to environmental influences; interventions must be tailored to an individual child's particular characteristics.* As with Principle 5, lack of structured assessment information regarding the child's personality and contextual factors frequently makes it difficult to individualize treatment suggestions. The probability that the treatment suggestion is individualized is greater when the parents and the personal assistant are actively involved in formulating and designing the intervention plan (Granlund, Björck-Åkesson, & Alant, in press). A family's individual reactivity is related to the number of services obtained. Families with several identified child and family problems receive more services.

8. *Intervention efforts operate over a background of time; interventions should ideally break the operation of negative causal chains and enhance the operation of positive causal chains.* A key issue is related to the fact that intervention efforts operate over time, thereby requiring that continuity in the services occurs. In Sweden, continuity in services is provided to children with established disability conditions or medical conditions in terms of the organization providing services. Parents of these children do, however, report that the staff turnover rate makes it difficult to maintain continuity (Stenhammar & Ulfhielm, 1998). In addition, continuity is easier for the kind of problems (i.e., problems with body function and/or the performance of activities) that specialized services provided by hospitals and CHabC deal with. Problems with participation are by definition more strongly related to context and will therefore vary to a greater extent over time. To enhance positive causal chains operating in several contexts, child-focused factors related to self-regulation, autonomy, and self-determination must be the focus of interventions to a greater extent than what is common today (Seligman & Csikszentmihalyi, 2000). Another means for enhancing the operation of positive chains is to provide support to

parents in taking on the role of service coordinator by providing the necessary information about the child and family to obtain continuity in the goals set and the measures taken (Möller & Nyman, 2003).

CONCLUSION

In the Developmental Systems Model, a framework for community-based early intervention services and supports for children who are vulnerable and their families is provided (Guralnick, 2001). It is based on three core principles: a developmental framework, integration/collaboration at every level, and inclusion of support in natural environments (see Section I of this book). A fundamental idea is that practices are developed consistent with those principles. If the Developmental Systems Model suggested by Guralnick is combined with Wach's principles for systems-theory–based intervention and applied to a Swedish setting, it becomes evident that the Swedish early intervention system only partly applies system principles and characteristics (see Table 23.1).

According to the Developmental Systems Model (Guralnick, 2001), experientially based child developmental outcomes are related to family patterns of interaction. The first family pattern of interaction is the quality of parent–child transactions; the second relates to family-orchestrated child experiences; and the third relates to providing for the child's health and safety. Those patterns of interactions are carried out in everyday life contexts in the proximal environment of the child. Thus, interventions implemented in the natural contexts of the child must integrate; coordinate services at all levels; and be based on a developmental framework including the child, the interaction, and the environment.

In Sweden, the natural contexts for young children include both the family and the preschool. An ideal aim of early intervention programs in Sweden should be to address stressors to promote optimal patterns of interaction at home and in preschool and thus child development. At the same time, such programs should provide support to obtain needed resources, social support, and information and services adapted to each family's and preschool's needs. On a general level, the aim is partially fulfilled through the services provided to all young children. In reality, for children in need of special support, the individual tailoring of assessment and intervention can be difficult to fulfill. Many times, assessment efforts are formally focused only on the child, with assessment of interaction and environment being performed informally. Most interventions are child focused and implemented by personal assistants or resource staff at preschool, thus decreasing parental knowledge and control over treatment

Table 23.1. Early intervention in Sweden in relation to the Developmental Systems Model's (Guralnick, 2001) core principles and systems-theory–based (Wachs, 2000) intervention principles

Elements of systems theory	Developmental framework	Integration/ collaboration at every level	Inclusion and support in natural environments
Multidimensional assessment	Assessment is primarily focused on the child.	Each organization assesses according to its role and perspective. There is no explicit responsibility for coordination.	Natural environments are the home and preschool. Assessment may be done at preschool.
Assessment of patterns of co-varying factors	Assessment information is fragmented.	Different dimensions of International Classification of Functioning, Disability, and Health are covered by different organizations; there is little explicit coordination.	Interaction and the environment are only informally and implicitly assessed.
Context brought into assessment	Organizational focus rather than child's environmental context regulates the assessment content.	Organizations are responsible for assessing a child's body function and activity; they are not responsible for assessing preschool context.	Context seldom is assessed both in preschool and in the home.
Assessment built on specificity	Services are only partly individualized and partly based on diagnosis.	Specificity is tied to the type of service provided by an organization rather than to intervention goals for the child.	The focus of goals varies between organizations, independent of the context for intervention.
Assessment built on systems and environmental niche characteristics	Interventions are partly based on child characteristics.	Intervention content varies among organizations.	Interventions focused on body function or activity seldom are based on environmental niche characteristics.
Interventions tailored to co-varying clusters	Interventions are mostly based on single identified problems.	There seldom is explicit coordination of intervention efforts from different organizations.	Preschool staff and/or parents have a primary responsibility for coordinating interventions.
Individual differences in reactivity	Differences in reactivity seldom are measured or intervened with in an explicit manner.	Individual differences in reactivity between families affect collaboration between organizations. Multiproblem families receive more services.	Variability in reactivity between natural environments is implicitly dealt with.
Intervention operates over a background of time	Staff turnover in preschools is a risk to decreased stability and continuity.	Continuity in coordination of service provision is difficult due to staff turnover and organizational changes.	Relatively few ecological transitions facilitate continuity and stability.

fidelity and outcome. Several organizations are involved in providing services, and there is not an organization responsible for integrating services. "Strong" families can coordinate this system in an optimal manner, whereas "weak" families receive fragmented services. Inclusion of support in natural contexts is seldom coordinated between family and preschool. The child's health and safety is typically taken care of due to the social security system, and a high degree of continuity is guaranteed due to the small number of organizations involved in intervention up to adulthood. Optimal patterns of interaction are seldom the focus for intervention in the family and the preschool. Family- and preschool-orchestrated child experiences often are provided but are not always individualized and coordinated. Young children in need of special support at preschool are often provided with the same experiences as other children but are reported to participate to a lesser extent. Key issues for enhancing the further development of the Swedish early intervention system are multidimensional assessment, including patterns of interaction and environmental factors, as well as service coordination.

REFERENCES

Adolfsson, M., & Resare, E. (2000). *Samarbete—en förutsättning. Hur utveckla ett gott samarbete mellan habiliteringssjukgymnast och föräldrar till barn med rörelsehinder.* (Collaboration—a prerequisite. How to develop good collaboration between physical therapist at habilitation centers and parents to children with physical disability.) Master's thesis, Internationella Mastersprogrammet inom Habilitering/Early Intervention and Family Support. Institutionen för Samhälls- och Beteendevetenskap, Mälardalens Högskola.

Almqvist, L. (2001). *Delaktighet i skolaktiviteter för barn med funktionshinder.* (Participation in school activities for children with disability.) Master's thesis, psychology. Institutionen för Samhälls- och Beteendevetenskap, Mälardalens Högskola.

Almqvist, L., Hellström, D., Häggqvist, E., & Granlund, M. (in preparation). *Preschool staffs' perception of health in young children.* Institutionen för Samhälls- och Beteendevetenskap, Mälardalens Högskola.

Andersson, B.E. (1989). Effects of public day care: A longitudinal study. *Child Development, 60,* 857–866.

Arman, K., & Frölander, H.E. (2001). *Utvecklingsbedömning av små barn med hörselskada och utvecklingsstörning.* (Developmental assessment of young hard of hearing children with intellectual disability.) Master's thesis, Internationella Mastersprogrammet inom Habilitering/Early Intervention and Family Support. Institutionen för Samhälls- och Beteendevetenskap, Mälardalens Högskola.

Barnombudsmannen (BO). (The children's ombudsman.) (2002). *Många syns inte men finns ändå.* (Many of them are invisible but they are still there.) Retrieved May 16, 2004, from http://www.bo.se/files/publikationer,%20pdf/arsrapport2002.pdf

Björck-Åkesson, E., & Granlund, M. (2003). Creating a team around the child through professionals continuing education. In S. Odom, M.J. Hanson, J.A. Blackman, & S. Kaul (Eds.), *Early intervention practices around the world* (pp. 171–190). Baltimore: Paul H. Brookes Publishing Co.

Björck-Åkesson, E., Granlund, M., & Simeonsson, R.J. (2000). Assessment philosophies and practices in Sweden. In M.J. Guralnick (Ed.), *Interdisciplinary clinical assessment of young children with developmental disabilities* (pp. 391–411). Baltimore: Paul H. Brookes Publishing Co.

Carlhed, C. (2003). Defining dimensions in family-oriented services in early childhood intervention. *Scandinavian Journal of Disability Research, 5*(2), 185–202.

Carlhed, C., Björck-Åkesson, E., & Granlund, M. (2003). Parent perspectives on early intervention: The paradox of needs and rights. *The British Journal of Developmental Disabilities, 49*(97), 79–89.

Enbom, B. (2004). *Liten grupp, struktur och assistent.* (Small group, structure and assistant.) Master's thesis, The Masterprogram Children: Health–Development–Learning–Intervention Institutionen för Samhälls- och Beteendevetenskap, Mälardalens Högskola.

Granat, T., Lagander, B., & Börjesson, M.C. (2002). Parental participation in the habilitation process: Evaluation from a user perspective. *Child: Care, Health & Development, 28*(6), 459–467.

Granlund, M., Björck-Åkesson, E., & Alant, E. (in press). Family centered early childhood intervention: New perspectives? In E. Alant (Ed.), *Beyond poverty: Severe disabilities and AAC intervention.* London: Whurr Publishers.

Granlund, M., Björck-Åkesson, E., Olsson, C., & Rydeman, B. (2001). Working with families to introduce augmentative and alternative communication systems. In H. Cockerill & L. Carrol-Few (Eds.), *Communication without speech: Clinics in developmental medicine* (pp. 88–102). London: McKeith Press.

Granlund, M., & Olsson, C. (1999). Efficacy of communication intervention for presymbolic communicators. *Augmentative and Alternative Communication, 15,* 25–37.

Granlund, M., & Sundin, M. (1999). Funktionalitet i mål och metoder. (Functionality in goals and methods.) In M. Granlund, A.-L. Steénsson, L. Roll-Pettersson, E. Björck-Åkesson, M. Sundin, & A. Kylén (Eds.), *Barn med flera funktionsnedsättningar i särskolan* (Children with multiple disabilities in the special school) (pp. 45–104). Stockholm: Stiftelsen ALA.

Guralnick, M.J. (2001). A developmental systems model for early intervention. *Infants and Young Children, 14*(2), 1–18.

Health and Medical Services Act of 1982 (HSL:SFS:1982:763). Sweden.

Jansson, U. (2002). Aspects of social competence in preschool interaction between children with and without disabilities. In M. Karlsson Lohmander (Ed.), *Social competence and communication* (Vol. 4, pp. 97–118). Göteborg, Sweden: Göteborg University, Researching Early Childhood.

Jansson, U. (2003). *Social processes in pre-school play: Interaction patterns between children with functional differences in inclusive settings.* Presentation at the 2003 ISEI Congress, Rome, Italy, September 17–20, 2003.

Kamerman, S. (2000). Early childhood intervention policies: An international perspective. In J.P. Shonkoff & S.J. Meisels (Eds.), *Handbook of early childhood intervention* (2nd ed., pp. 613–629). New York: Cambridge University Press.

Möller, A., & Nyman, E. (2003). *Barn, familj och funktionshinder—utveckling och habilitering.* (Children, families, and disability—development and habilitation.) Stockholm: Liber.

The National Board of Health and Welfare (Socialstyrelsen). (2003). *Tillgång till habilitering och rehabilitering för barn och ungdomar med funktionshinder—en kartläggning.* (Accessability to habilitation and rehabilitation for children and youth with disability—a survey.) Stockholm: Socialstyrelsen.

Preisler, G., Tvingstedt, A.L., & Ahlström, M. (2002). A psychosocial follow-up study of deaf preschool children using cochlear implants. *Child: Care, Health & Development, 28*(5), 403–418.

Rabe, T., Hill, A., & Andersson, B. (2001). *Boken om integrering: Idé, teori, praktik.* (The book about integration: Idea, theory, practice.) Lund, Sweden: Studentlitteratur.

Roll-Pettersson, L., Granlund, M., & Steénsson, A.-L. (1999). Upplevda behov av råd och stöd hos familjer och klasslärare till barn i särskolan. (Needs of support and service of families and teachers to children in the special school.) In I.M. Granlund, A.-L. Steénsson, L. Roll-Pettersson, E. Björck-Åkesson, M. Sundin, & A. Kylén (Eds.), *Barn med flera funktionsnedsättningar i särskolan* (Children with multiple disabilities in the special school) (pp. 105–180). Stockholm: Stiftelsen ALA.

Rutter, M. (2000). Recilience reconsidered: Conceptual considerations, empirical findings, and policy implications. In J.P. Shonkoff & S.J. Meisels (Eds.), *Handbook of early childhood intervention* (2nd ed., pp. 651–682). New York: Cambridge University Press.

Seligman, M.E.P., & Csikszentmihalyi, M. (2000). Positive psychology: An introduction. *American Psychologist, 55,* 5–14.

Shonkoff, J.P., & Meisels, S.J. (Eds.). (2000). *Handbook of early childhood intervention* (2nd ed.). New York: Cambridge University Press.

Stenhammar, A.-M., & Ulfhielm, K. (1998). *How can we get what we need?* Report from National Swedish Board of Welfare 2.

Support and Service Act (LSS, SFS:1993:387). Sweden.

The Swedish Ministry of Education (Utbildningsdepartementet). (1998). *Läroplan för det obligatoriska skolväsendet, förskoleklassen och fritidshemmet.* (Curriculum for the general school system, the preschool class and leisuretime class). LpFÖ 98. Stockholm: Fritzes.

Swedish National Agency for Education (Skolverket). (2004a). *Gruppstorlekar och personaltäthet i förskola, förskoleklass och fritidshem.* (Group size and staff in preschool, preschool class and leisuretime home.) Stockholm: Fritzes.

Swedish National Agency for Education (Skolverket). (2004b). *Beskrivande data om barnomsorg, skola och vuxenutbildning.* (Descriptive data about early education, school and adult education.) Stockholm: Fritzes.

Swedish National Agency for Education (Skolverket). (2004c). *Barn, elever, personal och utbildningsresultat. Kommunal nivå—avseende år 2003.* (Children, staff and the results of education. Community level—year 2003.) Report 241 from the Swedish National Agency for Education (Skolverket). Retrieved May 16, 2004, from http://www2.skolverket.se/BASIS/skolbok/webext/trycksak

Swedish National Agency for Education. (2004d). *Facts. Preschool activities.* Retrieved May 16, 2004, from http://www.skolverket.se/fakta/faktablad/english/pre-school.shtml

Wachs, T.D. (2000). *Necessary but not sufficient: The respective roles of single and multiple influences of individual development.* Washington, DC: American Psychological Association.

Widuch-Berg, E. (2002). *Hur begåvning och utvecklingsstörning definieras och tillämpas inom Barn- och Ungdomshabiliteringen.* (How the concepts intellectual ability and disability are defined and applied in habilitation for children and youth.) Master's thesis, Internationella Mastersprogrammet inom Habilitering/Early intervention and family support. Institutionen för Samhälls- och Beteendevetenskap, Mälardalens Högskola.

Williams, P., Sheridan, S., & Pramling-Samuelsson, I. (2000). *Barns samlärande—en forskningsöversikt.* (Children learning together—a review of research.) Stockholm: Skolverket.

World Health Organization. (2001). *International classification of functioning, disability and health* (ICF). Geneva: Author.

CHAPTER 24

EARLY INTERVENTION AND CHILDREN WITH SPECIAL NEEDS IN DEVELOPING COUNTRIES

HENNING RYE AND KARSTEN HUNDEIDE

DEVELOPMENT OF EARLY INTERVENTION PROGRAMS

In the 1970s and early 1980s, existing theory development and research related to *attachment* (Ainsworth, Blehar, Waters, & Wall, 1978; Ainsworth & Eichberg, 1971; Bowlby, 1969), *communication* in young children (Bateson, 1975; Stern, 1985, 1996; Trewarthen, 1988), and the importance of social context and *mediation of learning experiences* (Bronfenbrenner, 1979; Feuerstein, 1979, 1980; Feuerstein, Klein, & Tannenbaum, 1991; Vygotsky, 1978) created a growing awareness of how important the caregiver–child relationship is for a child's development. The available knowledge was, however, not yet sufficiently concrete and well defined to provide a basis for the more sophisticated early intervention programs that were to appear later. The first early intervention programs were based on the existing knowledge at the time; the importance of the mother's involvement in teaching the child and the mother's expectations and ways of interacting with the child all were variables considered to be of crucial importance to the child's development. The first early intervention programs adopted a rather instructional approach to improving caregivers' interactions with their children, which was soon revealed to have some drawbacks: Caregivers reported feeling devalued and inadequate; using specified types of material at set times of the day felt strange; and some reported a growing feeling of dependence on program instructions and material (Lombard, 1981). Obviously, the new ways of interacting were not integrated into the caregivers' natural, individual ways of being with their children.

In response to these shortcomings, a new generation of early intervention programs was launched in the 1980s. These programs built on modern empirical infant research, particularly on knowledge about the emotional and communicative development of children and the mediation of learning experiences that normally develop between caregivers and their children. The most well-known programs from these traditions are the ORION program from Holland, now better known as the Marte Meo program; the SPIN program (Biemans, 1990); and the More Intelligent Sensitive Child (MISC) program from Israel (Klein, 1992, 1996, 2001). In the 1990s, the authors of this chapter developed the International Child Development Programs (ICDPs), which integrate in their approach the same communicative and mediation qualities from modern research that provide the basis for Marte Meo and the MISC programs, respectively.

The new generation of early intervention programs represented by Marte Meo, MISC, and ICDP is special in that the programs build on specified qualities of interaction described in modern empirical research. Through intervention, these programs aim to augment the caregivers' interaction by building on the caregivers' own available ways of interacting within the context of everyday situations. In other words, these programs are primarily *directed at the caregivers*. They are primarily *community based* in that they recruit and train existing resource people inside the community. They also are basically *preventive*, although they can also be used clinically when the need arises.

The collaboration with caregivers based on their own functioning and resources represents a way of *joining forces* with the caregivers from within their available personal repertoire of interaction in their own social and cultural contexts. It is not an instructional approach but rather helps the caregivers discover their own ways, resources, or potential for helping their children's development by extending and further developing the positive qualities of interaction they already possess in daily life situations. This collaboration from within the caregivers' available repertoire of interaction is achieved by focusing on increasing the caregivers' awareness of their own ways of interacting, on how the interactions affect the child's response and functioning, and on how this repertoire can be extended and enriched by including more of the qualities that are used less often. Sensitization of the caregivers to the child's situation, needs, and wishes also is important in this way of working.

The qualities described next represent what seem to be universal intentions and meaningful qualities of interaction expressed in ways caregivers and children interact across cultures. Despite the fact that the behaviors of caregivers and the context and cultural traditions through which these interactive qualities are expressed vary across cultures, the intent and meaning experienced in the qualities of interaction focused on in these programs seem to represent some essential preconditions for human survival, psychosocial development, and learning.

Since the 1980s, Western countries have seen a change in the attitudes of professionals and the ways in which they work with parents and other caregivers—signaled by concepts such as *empowering* and *enabling* in the professional literature and shifts in professional approaches from *professional centered* through *family oriented* to *family centered* (Remick, 2002)—and this change in attitude, although much needed for development of collaboration, is, in these authors' personal clinical experiences, not enough to secure a lasting change in daily interaction and building of relationships. The development toward a more positive caregiver–child relationship and interaction appears to go through the following three phases of the caregiver's personal experience: 1) becoming conscious of the positive qualities in the caregiver's own interaction, 2) exploring new possible ways of extending these qualities in everyday life situations, and 3) further developing and integrating these qualities into the caregiver's own personal way of being with others.

To make this new approach to early intervention more easily understandable, this chapter presents some examples of its implications for practical work. This is illustrated through summaries of some projects that the authors have been involved in to a greater or lesser degree as consultants or project leaders. The final section of the chapter discusses Guralnick's (2001) Developmental Systems Model in relation to the ICDP.

MARTE MEO:
THE EMOTIONAL–COMMUNICATIVE APPROACH

The developmental work of what became the Marte Meo program was started in Holland in the 1980s. After being appointed as a leader of a day treatment center for children with severe developmental problems, known in 1978 as ORION, Maria Aarts began developing a way of working with parents that focused on the kind of help parents frequently asked for. It had become increasingly clear that the professional information that parents received did not apply to everyday situations and was of little help in restoring or further developing parents' parenting relationship with their children. This was the background for establishing ORION Video Home Training in 1985, which Maria Aarts and Harrie Biemans developed into a new and practical approach to improving caregiver–child relationships in cases of child developmental problems. In 1987, Maria Aarts left ORION Video Home Training and started her own organization, called Marte Meo, which means "on one's own strength." The Marte Meo program has developed strategies for supporting families with children and adolescents who are struggling with various kinds of psychosocial problems.

The method has proved to be applicable to improving caregiver–child interaction in institutions, kindergartens, schools, and even in homes for the elderly (Aarts, 2000).

To summarize, the Marte Meo program focuses on the following qualities: 1) following the initiatives of the child, 2) expressing positive affect, 3) naming with acceptance what the child is focusing on, 4) reflecting positively what the child does well, 5) taking turns, and 6) expressing the feeling of joy. This approach is not based on teaching caregivers new ways of behaving but rather on helping them discover how these qualities of interaction, when present, have a beneficial influence on both the children's emotional state and behavior and the interactive relationship between caregiver and child and how to augment the presence of these qualities in the interactions of daily life situations. Use of videotaping has proved to be very effective in this process of awareness development—increasing self-confidence—and active searching for ways to improve the caregiver–child interaction. The communicative focus of the Marte Meo program is based on the assumption—supported by empirical child development research—that parents and young children possess a natural competence for building a reciprocal relationship through communication. Supportive dialogue in early development—when fostered in the caregiver–child interaction—not only is central to establishing a positive attachment/bonding relationship but also provides the child with relevant information and understanding that supports both the child's expanding relationship with the child's environment and the child's early mental development. The complexity and comprehensiveness of this caregiver–child communication has been described as a developmental *spiral* that—when based on sensitively adjusted communication and interaction—supports and extends the child's interactive mastery of the environment (Hundeide, 2001; Øvreide & Hafstad, 1996; Rye, 1996, 2001). It is based on this understanding that the Marte Meo program has developed a systematic psychosocial intervention, which is used widely in clinical psychology and child psychiatry practices, in child protection services in several Western countries, and in projects for children with special needs in some developing countries.

CHILDREN WITH CEREBRAL PALSY IN ARMENIA

In the project chosen to illustrate the Marte Meo approach, the emotional and communicative qualities were modified to meet the social and practical developmental needs of children with cerebral palsy who were living in a community in Armenia. Gayane Gavril Zakaryan from Armenia carried out this project for her master's degree thesis in special needs education (Zakaryan, 1998).[1] This short presentation of some of her findings is presented with the generous permission of the researcher.

Zakaryan was trained as a medical doctor and had been working with children with disabilities and their families for several years when she began studying for her master's degree. Her motivation for doing this project on improving communication and interaction in caregiver–child relationships with children with cerebral palsy was rooted in her experience that this was a much neglected issue in the services for habilitating children with disabilities in Armenia. According to Zakaryan, a common problem in Armenia, as in many other countries, is that families with a child with a severe disability are likely to be socially isolated. Parents and other family members feel ashamed of having a child with a disability and consider the disability a disgrace that should be hidden from the social environment—a feeling that easily may add to a child's overprotection or rejection and isolation. In the Armenian tradition of maternal protective nurturing during the early years, soothing the child is considered more important than stimulating the child's interest in new experiences.

It is well known from international studies since the 1970s that children with severe cerebral palsy are at risk for serious delays in developing communication and interaction skills. In Armenia, as well as in many other countries, the main focus of the habilitating services is on the physical training and management of daily routines. The inability of many of these children to adequately communicate their needs and intentions often leads to misunderstanding, crying, and conflicts. This experience may easily leave behind a feeling of guilt and helplessness in the parents, as well as in the child. In some cases, the interaction gets stuck and results in a deterioration of the caregiver–child relationship to the extent that the interaction is limited to what can be described as *administration of care* with little reciprocal communication and feelings of love.

According to Zakaryan, this is the main reason she chose to implement this home-based study of mother–child interaction with young children with cerebral palsy. The main question in this investigation was to what extent communication and interaction could be improved by helping the mothers become more conscious of how to use the qualities spelled out in the Marte Meo program in their interactions with their children.

---

[1]The international master's degree program in special needs education is coordinated by the International Division, which Professor Henning Rye directs. The students all are doing the project work for their theses in their respective home countries. Because Gayane Zakaryan is from Armenia, her project was carried out there.

Project Design

The sample in this case study includes six children with different forms of cerebral palsy and their mothers; the children range in age from 12 to 28 months. The methods include interview, observation in daily life situations, and video recording of the mother–child interaction. The information was gathered before, during, and after the intervention. The intervention period lasted for about 3 months, including six individual sessions of $1^1/_2$ hours each with each mother–child pair and three group sessions of $2^1/_2$ hours each.

Before the intervention, the mothers in the six mother–child pairs typically exhibited the following needs and problems:

1. They could not remember receiving any information about the impact that cerebral palsy might have on their child's psychosocial development, only about the impact on the child's physical development.

2. They did not find interaction with their child enjoyable because the child did not show interest in interacting and did not express pleasure.

3. They lacked confidence in their mothering skills.

4. They had difficulty understanding the child's weak signals. Only 36% of the initiatives from the child were met with positive responses by the mother, and only 44% of the initiatives from the mother were met by positive responses from the child. This kind of asynchronous and disturbed interaction dominated the mother–child interaction.

5. They showed a high frequency of directive, insensitive, and overstimulating behavior.

6. They were not aware of the importance of dialogue and pauses in turn taking.

7. They were not aware of the importance of eye contact.

8. They were not aware of the child's needs for play and pursuit of individual interests.

9. The child seldom initiated activities in play or any other situation and was mostly a passive observer. In the preintervention study, the mother was responsible for 77% of initiatives in the interactions.

10. They were not aware of the importance of praising the child.

11. They were concerned about the child's delayed motor development.

12. They did not value the motor skills that were not gross motor milestones, such as sitting, crawling, or walking.

13. They tried to teach the child to walk long before the child's motor development was ready for it.

During the intervention, the main qualities of interaction were divided into three broad categories: 1) the *initiation* of interaction (the child's initiation and the mother's response to the child's initiative), 2) *involvement* (eye contact, dialogue, turn taking, imitation, infantile speech, and naming during activity), and 3) the *ending* of sequences of the interaction (mutual satisfaction; praising of the child; the mother shows how she enjoys being with the child; and playful, joyful engagement). The main objective was to increase the mother's awareness of how these qualities could be used to improve communication.

The intervention was related to three daily activities: playing, feeding, and bathing. With respect to the mother, the main activities of the facilitator were as follows:

1. To listen with empathy to the mother, which means seeing things from her perspective and understanding her feelings and perceptions of the child

2. To provide the mother with information and act as a consultant, which implies giving the mother information about the effect of cerebral palsy on her child's development and explaining how the mother can positively influence her child's development through supporting enjoyable interaction between mother and child

3. To communicate positively, which means commenting on concrete observable behaviors that showed that the mother was in tune with the child and that she understood and met the child's needs by using the qualities of interaction focused on in this study. In this way, the mothers became conscious of and started to value their own skills as mothers and began to see how their way of meeting the child's needs was beneficial to the child

4. To experiment and model, which implies involving the child in interaction and activities that the mother might try with the child herself and experimenting with how she could involve the child in new activities in a positive manner

Findings

The intervention resulted in a number of visible improvements. First, after the mothers received information about how cerebral palsy may hamper or inhibit their child's ability to collaborate or communicate, as well as influence the mother's interpretation of the children's behavior, the mothers changed their attitudes and expectations. They became more realistic and more confident in their capacity as caregivers. Second, the children and mothers were significantly more synchronized and reciprocal in their interactions. The mothers understood, confirmed, and expanded on the children's initiatives. Children's initiations of interaction had increased from 33% to 48%, and the mothers' initiations were reduced from 77% to 52%. The mothers' positive responses to children's initiatives had gone up from 36% to 77%, and the children's positive responses to mothers' initiatives went up from 44% to 73%. Third, the children had become more aware of the fact that their initiatives to interact could guide the mothers' behavior, which was in turn described as much more *facilitative*. Fourth, the mothers were more able to *read* the child's initiations and intentions and were better able to express their responses through a mode of interaction and communication that was meaningful to the child. Fifth, the mothers more often labeled the objects and actions in which they and their child were involved and explained what they were doing together. Mothers also more often imitated the child's behavior and linked it to other activities in order to sustain the child's interest and extend the scope of activities. Sixth, in spite of the children's motor problems with imitating sounds or motor acts, the imitation dramatically increased in the postintervention phase. The overall interaction was improved in terms of reciprocity, communication, social-emotional adjustment, balance in initiations, and steering joint activities. Finally, the improvement in communication and interaction between mothers and children led not only to a more meaningful interaction but also to a more affectionate relationship, which increases the potential for learning and development.

THE MISC PROGRAM: THE MEDIATIONAL APPROACH

The strategies and principles of implementing the interaction qualities outlined in the MISC program integrate and build on the qualities of communication described previously as a main focus of the Marte Meo program. In brief, the approach to intervention in the MISC program is to promote the following five qualities in the child–caregiver interaction: 1) focusing the child's attention on what the caregiver wants the child to experience, 2) expanding the child's understanding of what he or she is experiencing, 3) mediating meaning and excitement through verbal or nonverbal appreciation or affect in relation to shared experiences, 4) rewarding by mediating feelings of competence, and 5) regulating behavior by helping the child adjust to the needs of the situation and plan before acting.

Based on previous positive reports from intervention projects using the MISC program with socially disadvantaged children, as well as with children with disabilities and their caregivers, several projects based on the MISC program were carried out by international students pursuing their master's or doctoral degrees, coordinated by the International Division, Department of Special Needs Education, University of Oslo. This section of the chapter briefly provides a description of two of these studies: one on young deaf children and their hearing mothers in Zimbabwe and one on impoverished children in Ethiopia.

DEAF CHILDREN AND THEIR HEARING MOTHERS IN ZIMBABWE

The study "Hearing Mothers and Their Deaf Children in Zimbabwe: Mediated Learning Experiences" was carried out by the late Maria Chiswanda (1997, 1999) for her doctoral degree thesis in special needs education. Dr. Maria Chiswanda was born and raised in the Shona culture in Zimbabwe, where the study was carried out. The purpose of the study was to explore and describe interactions between hearing mothers and their deaf children in order to detect the presence or absence of mediated learning experience and to determine the effects of showing mothers how and helping them to detect and practice mediated language experience. The various criteria for mediated learning experience were modified to meet the needs of the Shona daily living experiences. As a Shona-speaking person with experience as a teacher of deaf children, the researcher herself was able to undertake not only the language translation but also the *translation* of the qualities of mediated learning experience into the social and cultural context in which this study was undertaken.

Teaching and learning through sensitization of children's experiences and needs, as well as developing the caregivers' consciousness of their own behavior through modeling, encouragement, and application of mediation behavior with the participants, were important ingredients in helping the mothers develop their use of the mediation qualities in their interaction with their children. A main focus of the intervention was to help the mothers become more aware of the positive aspects of their child-rearing practices and did not conflict with the mothers' own traditions of child rearing.

Although it is not possible to detail here the child-rearing practices in Zimbabwe, it is important to note that children are traditionally highly valued in Zimbabwe, except for children with disabilities, who are considered to be a misfortune. In addition to the rather negative perception of children with disabilities, children who are deaf may be at particular risk for developmental problems because most of the teaching of young children is conducted orally. Moreover, given the importance of face-to-face inter-action for development of communication and meaningful interaction, the tradition of carrying children on the back may make this learning even more difficult for deaf children.

Project Design

In this study, six hearing mothers and their deaf children ranging in age from 9 to 40 months at the time of intervention participated. In this project, the term *deaf* refers to children who do not benefit from auditory stimuli and who therefore prefer a manual way of communicating. In addition, two deaf mothers of hearing children participated as language models. These language models used speech—Shona and basic English— with hearing and speaking people, but otherwise, ZimSign was used as their basic means of communication.

In the preintervention phase, interviews and videotaping of interaction during daily activities—feeding, bathing, and playing—were used to describe the existing interaction behaviors. The same approach was used in the postintervention evaluation of the quality of interaction and the mothers' experiences of the intervention.

The intent of the intervention was, in practical terms, to focus on increasing the communication skills and interaction strategies between mother and child to overcome the typical problems of impoverished lan-guage and communication skills of deaf children in hearing families. The training consisted of individual and group sessions, as well as meeting with and learning from the deaf adults in the project. The intervention extended over a period of 3 months, including three sessions with each mother–child pair and three sessions with the mothers' group.

In this study, the mothers learned primarily through three types of experiences: 1) individual training sessions, in which videotaped examples were used to increase the mothers' awareness of their own competence in using the five qualities of mediation mentioned previously; 2) group discussions, in which mothers were encouraged to share their experiences by showing videotaped interactions with their children; and 3) modeling, in which the deaf adults acted as models for sign language and communica-tion. One of the important contributions of the deaf adults was their function as cultural role models for communication with the deaf children.

Findings

Analysis of videotaped interaction before and after intervention clearly indicated that all six mothers showed a substantial increase in mediation competence on all of the different qualities focused on in the MISC program. The mothers' mediation of learning experience varied, however, according to communicative competence in mothers and children. The main findings can be summarized as follows:

1. When mothers acquired better means of communicating with their deaf children through linguistic symbols and sign language, they also more easily improved their mediation of learning experiences.

2. The improved ways of communicating and the increased awareness of how mothers could expand their mediation of learning experiences seemed to clearly improve the quality of contact as well as the social-emotional interaction between mothers and children.

3. By increasing their ability to communicate and helping them to better understand what to do, how to do it, and when to do it, the children became more capable of regulating and adapting their behavior to daily situations.

4. As the mothers learned to communicate with their children, they seemed to become more relaxed, less controlling, more sensitive to the children's needs and situation, and more competent in their interaction. This led to positive motivation for collaboration on the children's side.

5. The mothers' increased verbal communication and comments that rewarded the children's success or attempts to be independent clearly contributed to the children's increased belief in their own competence, feeling of success, and increased motivation for further interaction.

Of note, Dr. Chiswanda's observed how the growing awareness in each of the mothers of their child's capabilities contributed to their increased respect for the child as a partner of interaction and collaboration.

Dr. Chiswanda concluded that the results across all six dyads concur with a basic proposition of MISC: When parents are sensitized to what they can do to affect their children's development, they will try to improve their way of interacting with the child. The mothers initially expressed doubt about their ability to influence their deaf child's cognitive development, but through the intervention, they both learned how to influence their child's language development and became aware of their children's competence for communication and learning.

IMPOVERISHED CHILDREN IN ADDIS ABABA, ETHIOPIA

The examples of the children with cerebral palsy in Armenia and the deaf children in Zimbabwe exemplify an approach to psychosocial intervention when a disability or dysfunction threatens to disturb the development of normal caregiver–child interaction. Problems related to interaction and learning frequently stem from the long-term consequences of living under conditions of staggering poverty and the struggle for survival. To illustrate the effects of early psychosocial intervention under such conditions, the authors of this chapter, together with colleagues at Addis Ababa University, Ethiopia, started a project in a slum area of Addis Ababa in 1989. The project, "Child Development Research," was initiated as a collaborative effort between Addis Ababa University and the University of Bergen, Norway. In 1993, the Department of Special Needs Education, University of Oslo, Norway, also joined in this collaboration; at that time, Professor Henning Rye was the appointed director of the International Division at the Department of Special Needs Education, University of Oslo. The project was directed jointly by Professor Tirussew Teferra, Addis Ababa University, and Professor Henning Rye, University of Oslo. The main report from this study, *Seeds of Hope: Twelve Years of Early Intervention in Africa*, was published in December 2001. The book also contains references to three doctoral theses and a number of articles published internationally (Klein, 2001).

The research strategy for this project was based on the following aims: 1) to develop methods to map the existing conceptions of needs and practices in the field of child rearing in the population of the area to be studied; 2) to develop an intervention strategy based on local conceptions of needs priorities, existing relevant professional knowledge, and a combined demographic, ethnographic, and psychological approach; 3) to introduce a micro-oriented approach to analysis of interaction through video recording and systematic observation of daily life routines and children's family-based experiences in order to map the complex set of factors and relationships that directly or indirectly influence the interactive experiences of children; 4) to investigate local conceptions and practices of child-rearing priorities and systems of care within the community targeted for intervention; and 5) to begin a pilot project in which all of the previous issues could be explored and clarified and establishment of a long-term prospective research and early intervention project with follow-up studies that would focus on the effects of intervention in children who were not yet school age.

All of the previous aims were realized in the practical implementation of this research program, which finally ended in December 2001. The overarching objective of this project from the beginning was to develop strategies of intervention that could reduce the deleterious impact of environmental risk factors on children's psychosocial development—factors such as poverty, malnutrition, overcrowded living conditions, illness, the family's struggle for survival, and illiteracy or low level of education. Therefore, the practical implementation of this project was carried out in an area of Addis Ababa called Ketchene, which exemplifies a high prevalence of the risk factors mentioned. The psychosocial intervention was based on the MISC program with a focus on sensitizing the mothers regarding their children's psychosocial needs and raising the mothers' awareness of their opportunities and abilities to support their children's development through positive communication and mediation of learning experiences in daily life interactions.

Project Design

A full-scale pilot study that included both studies of 26 children (ranging in age from 6 to 36 months) and their mothers (13 in the experimental group and 13 in the control group), as well as a study of children in an orphanage, provided important experiences for implementing the main study. In the main study, 50 families participated in the experimental group and 50 in the control group, and all were from the Ketchene area. The children who were from 12 to 36 months of age and their mothers were randomly assigned to the experimental and control groups. The numbers of boys and girls were approximately the same in both groups. The groups were comparable with regard to socioeconomic situation, cultural background, living conditions, and health. The intervention was home based and group based every second week and lasted for 3 months. Social and health workers, trained in the project to carry out the intervention and who also lived and worked in the area, carried out the intervention. The professional research team from Addis Ababa University supervised their work. The information was collected through systematic observation, interviews, and systematic analysis of video recordings before and after the intervention.

Findings

Even though there were no systematic differences between the experimental group and the control group in the preintervention study, the results presented next show clear differences between the experimental and the control group regarding the results of the immediate postintervention study and the long-term impact of the intervention on children's psychosocial development revealed after 1 year in school-age children. Specifically in the postintervention study, the mothers in the experimental group showed the following: 1) better understanding of their children and a more positive interaction with less harsh and strict correction; 2) more interest in the children's activities, more use of verbal communication, and the ability to guide the children in a more positive manner, explain more, and help the children experience a more meaningful interaction; 3) more pleasure and enthusiasm in their interaction, more feelings of competence, and an evaluation of their children as intelligent and obedient; and 4) changed attitude from being mainly preoccupied with raising obedient, polite, respectful, and quiet children to valuing children's initiatives and allowing them more independence in daily activities.

Results from the Follow-Up Studies

The first follow-up study of the children's development was carried out 1 year after the intervention. The children in the experimental group, compared with those in the control group, were significantly more developed with regard to language development, more advanced in social and emotional development (e.g., regarding ability to cooperate and share with others), and more advanced in general motor development. In the second follow-up study, when the children were in first or second grade, the results related to psychosocial development underpinned the main conclusions regarding the differences between the children in the experimental group compared with those in the control group. The children in the experimental group were more advanced in academic skills; showed better social-emotional adjustment to the school situation; and were less aggressive, hyperactive, and anxious or fearful in their behavior. It is important to note that the extracts of the results presented cannot in any way do justice to the comprehensive material collected in this long-term study. Interested readers are referred to the publications mentioned previously.

ICDP: INTEGRATING
EMOTIONAL-EXPRESSIVE AND MEDIATION QUALITIES

The ICDP is partly an integration of the two previous programs, Marte Meo and MISC, and it is partly new in the sense that other components are introduced that are not present in either of its two predecessors. The integrative part is represented by what is described as the *eight guidelines* of good interaction or the *three dialogues*. These guidelines of good interaction largely integrate Marte Meo's emphasis on *emotional-expressive communication* and the MISC's emphasis on the *mediational qualities of interaction* between caregiver and child. However, when these guidelines were selected, it was with the awareness that the target group might be caregivers with minimal education who needed simple labels to direct their attention to those aspects that are known as essential for good interaction. The eight guidelines are split into three categories or dialogues: the *emotional-expressive*, the *meaning-oriented* and *expansive* or *mediational dialogue*, and the *regulative* and *limit setting dialogue*. These dialogues contain the interactive qualities that can be found in the other two programs. The ICDP contains four more components that are new: 1) the caregiver's definition of the child and of him- or herself as caregiver, 2) the zone of intimacy and empathic identification—inclusion and expulsion of the child, 3) the principles of sensitization training of caregivers, and 4) principles of implementation and sustainability. These components are described in more detail next.

The Caregiver's Definition of the Child

The way caregivers see and define their child is basic to the caregiving process. When a child's utterances and actions are taken as expressions of feelings, experiences, wishes, and initiatives that the caregiver can recognize from her own experience in similar situations, this may invite an empathic response in the caregiver so that she can join in and participate in the child's experience. The capacity to observe and empathize with the child's initiatives, experiences, and mental states is therefore essential and is called *empathic identification*. There are other terms that mean roughly the same thing, for example, *empathic responsiveness* (Emde, 1989) and *sympathy* (Trevarthen, 1996).

Caregivers will respond to a child as a person with special qualities, and they will adapt their thoughtful responses accordingly. Therefore, when a child is neglected or abandoned, this is not necessarily because of lack of caring skills; it is just as likely that this is a consequence of being negatively defined by the caregivers. When a child is seen as bad, psychopathic, or evil and possessed, this will naturally invite a nonempathic objectified relationship, which may prevent the caregiver's potential for positive caring. Such negative labels may initiate and fixate a negative self-fulfilling developmental process in the caregiver–child relationship (Woodhead, 1990). To prevent this from happening, a different approach is needed that emphasizes identifying and pointing out positive features and resources in the child rather than pointing out the deficiencies and the deviant features, which is the traditional way assessment functions (Hundeide, 1992, 1995). It is assumed that empathic identification is the underlying mechanism behind sensitive human care and companionship (Braaten, 1996; Stern, 1996; Trevarthen, 1990). The question then becomes one of figuring out how to promote or facilitate an emphatic identification in caregivers who do not seem to possess or express this capacity. This is probably one of the most central issues in early care and psychosocial intervention in caregiver–child relationships.

Zone of Intimacy

These conditions could be conceptualized as entrance criteria for what is called the *zone of intimacy* (Hundeide, 2001). Those who are inside that zone are those with whom people more easily feel empathy, participation, companionship, and compassion, whereas people tend to feel more indifferent toward those who are outside that zone. Although individuals can cognitively recognize the suffering of strangers who are *outside* the zone of intimacy, this experience does not have the same emotional, direct quality as it does when individuals empathetically share the emotional experience and purposes of someone close to them (Hundeide, 1996a, 1996b, 2001).

The zone of intimacy model also integrates the conception of the child as a person, empathic identification, and the four emotional-expressive guidelines. These four guidelines make up the early *emotional-expressive dialogue* between caregiver and child in which the caregiver sensitively follows and responds to the expressive initiatives and body language of the child, confirming the child's signals by commenting approvingly on what the child is doing. A real dialogue of emotional expressive intimacy may develop in which a feeling of trust, joy, and companionship is shared between caregiver and child (Braaten, 1996; Stern, 1985, 1996; Trevarthen, 1996). This early emotional-expressive dialogue seems to be the key to the formation of affectionate relationships and to the child's ability to open up to people.

As indicated, the four emotional guidelines will appear as natural responses when there is an empathic identification with the child's feelings. This is illustrated in the following way: When the child, inside the zone of intimacy, is seen as a sensitive, tender person, the four emotional guidelines of *showing love, responding to initiatives, establishing a dialogue*, and *giving praise* follow naturally when there is a need for them because this is the way individuals naturally communicate with insiders. This works both ways: By communicating with the child in this sensitive, emotional way, empathic identification and the intimate relationship are strengthened, and a positive cycle of care is started. If the child is not included within the zone, however, then this type of intimate communication is neither easy nor natural. The starting point of getting through the border into a positive intimate relationship may, in fact, be achieved by listening to the child's story; being attentive and responsive to the child's initiative; and establishing positive, face-to-face expressive dialogue. This may bring the child inside the zone of intimacy so that the four guidelines occur as a natural consequence of the intimate relationship. Similarly, the other two dialogues (mediational and regulative) can be integrated into the zone of intimacy through emphatic identification and parental availability to the child's needs.

PRINCIPLES OF SENSITIZATION IN THE TRAINING OF CAREGIVERS

In line with the theoretical conceptions developed in the previous section, the problem of sensitizing the caregiver is first and foremost one way to activate the caregiver's mechanism of empathic identification with the child. It is only when this process is operative that one can expect a more sustainable change in the relationship. The question is, then, how to achieve sustainable change.

A first step is to train caregivers to achieve a positive redefinition of the child. As already indicated, the caregiver's perception of the child is essential for whether feelings of empathy and understanding may be released, starting a positive cycle of caring. The ICDP has adopted the following three strategies to promote a more positive image of the child:

1. *Pointing out the child's positive features and qualities.* It is important to always try to point out some positive feature in each child. It can be anything from beautiful hair and eyes to how sensitively the child responds to a gentle touch. Talk about the child should be done with respect and in a positive way, which may influence the caregiver's attitude. This is a very simple but powerful technique.

2. *Relabeling the child's negative features by putting them in more positive terms.* In many cases, there are obvious negative features in the child's behavior, such as aggression and disruptive, disturbing behavior. In such cases, it is sometimes possible to promote a more positive definition of the child by relabeling the negative behavior from *aggressive* and *self-centered* to *attention seeking*. This then raises the question of why the child is always trying to be the focus of attention and opens up the dialogue for a more positive way of looking at the child's problem (e.g., How can we give the child more attention and love so that the disruptive behavior diminishes?). There are other examples, including the child's physical appearance; it is always possible to see a tender beauty in most children, whatever their physical appearance. When caregivers see the tender helplessness of a child when he or she struggles to win his or her parents' love and acceptance, empathic identification with the child tends to be released by the caregiver.

3. *Reactivating good memories of an earlier positive relationship with the child.*
   This recommendation applies particularly to parents who, through
   the stresses of life, have developed a negative or abusive relationship
   with their children. In such cases, it may be helpful to go back to
   positive memories from when the relationship was good. Asking the
   caregiver to describe his or her feelings and tell stories about the child
   during this period may help bring back a positive image of the child.

A second step is to learn how to talk to caregivers in a way that will
achieve the best results. As pointed out by Fonagy (1996), the *capacity for
mentalizing*, that is the caregiver's capacity to observe the moment-to-
moment changes in the child's mental state, is critical for adequate care.
Seeing the child as a person and as an intentional being with normal human
feelings is part of that, but the issue is how to promote the caregiver's
sensitivity to the child's mental states, emotions, and intentions. How
professionals talk to the caregivers about the child is important in this
connection. Using an empathic interpretive way of talking, in which the
focus is on the child's subjective feelings and experiences, opens up the
child's subjectivity as a legitimate topic of discourse. In typical situations
of neglect and child abuse, the child's subjective feelings often are ignored
and rejected as an acceptable subject for discussion (Ryan & Thomas,
1980). Therefore, using an *empathic interpretive style of speech (genre) focusing
on the child's feelings, intentions, and experiences* may help to sensitize and
raise the caregiver's awareness in this field. To achieve this, one sometimes
has to pretend that one knows what the child is feeling (e.g., "You know
when you praise your child for what he has done, he will feel much more
confident and will know that you appreciate what he does."). The point
is not whether the child really feels this; the point is that this type of
discourse opens up and legitimizes the child's mental state as a reality that
the child has to deal with. For some caregivers, the simple acceptance of
talking about the child's feelings in this way is already an important step
toward a more humanized and sensitive relationship. When promoting a
positive conception of the child is combined with sensitive talk about the
child's emotional state, a powerful tool to promote a more empathic attitude toward the child is put in place.

A third step in sensitizing caregivers is to teach them to activate and
personalize their own experience and tacit understanding. By requesting
caregivers to exemplify and tell stories about their experience in some
field, they have to put their experience into words and a story and that is
a consciousness-raising and interpersonal achievement that structures their
own understanding (Brown & Palincsar, 1988). In relation to the guidelines
of good interaction, the following are three techniques used for activation
and personalization:

1. *Exemplification of one's own interactions with the child.* The caregivers
   are asked to bring examples and tell stories about their own experiences

with their children that illustrate the eight guidelines. This is another active educative principle that forces the caregivers to select and verbalize samples from their own interactions.

2. *Observational tasks relating to the child.* These are simple observational tasks that the caregivers bring home and share with the rest of their family, which include asking the caregivers to answer questions designed to touch on the four emotional guidelines, such as "How does your child react when you . . . ?", or to describe the qualities that they appreciate most in their child. These tasks are quite popular and seem to help caregivers discover their child as a psychological person with an entire range of human qualities and competencies.

3. *Self-assessment of caregivers' own interaction.* This is used as an educational technique. By assessing their own interactive practice, caregivers are brought into an active position in relation to the guidelines. This is important because these guidelines are simple, and their significance may be overlooked. It is not until these guidelines are applied in a practical context of caregiver self-assessment that their importance as guidelines for action becomes apparent.

A fourth step in sensitizing caregivers involves teaching them to use the eight guidelines as a basis for self-assessment and exemplification. The eight guidelines of good interaction are useful when employed as a frame of reference for caregivers to activate their own experiences for self-monitoring and for analysis of observations, either directly or on video. These guidelines may appear simplistic to an educated psychologist but for an undereducated caregiver they provide a vocabulary and a topicalization of experiences that caregivers can recognize from their own childhood. By providing them with a booklet of these guidelines with some exercises, caregivers can then anchor experiences that might otherwise appear to them to be fleeting and vague. Experience has shown that booklets with illustrations of the eight guidelines are important, particularly for those who need it most, namely, those with a limited educational background.

A fifth step focuses on pointing out the positive features of the caregiver's existing practice. As mentioned earlier, the sensitization approach starts by taking for granted that most caregivers have a repertoire of personal caregiving skills and that pointing out and activating these skills rather than instructing them in new skills can generate better results.

The sensitization approach starts with the facilitator pointing out positive features in each caregiver's interaction with his or her children and explaining why they are positive. This can be done by using videotaping with replay and feedback. Seeing themselves on video, doing something that the facilitator sees as positive, always has a strong impact on caregivers (Biemans, 1990). The ICDP has used video feedback only to a limited extent because it requires special training, and videos may not always be available. The same principles of positive feedback have also been used while observing the caregivers in action with their children. The ICDP has started using pictures from the caregiver's everyday setting, where the action is, and this provides useful clues for the caregivers about their own narrative constructions of how good interactions may take place in a concrete situation from their own daily lives (Hundeide, 2001).

Finally, a sixth step in sensitizing caregivers involves having them share their experiences in a group setting. Sharing experiences by telling each other personal stories about their children makes an impact, and it is a popular exercise that clearly has more social functions than just to confirm the caregivers' understanding of child care. Sharing experiences in a group is another way of raising the caregivers' awareness; when they see that other participants with similar backgrounds have similar experiences, there is a special effect that is different from that of being taught by an instructor. However, in order for equal sharing to take place, it is important that the facilitator let the participants speak out. Thus, the facilitator's role should be to guide the group by following their initiatives to focus on the relevant issues to be discussed and let the participants do the talking.

In summary, the whole idea of sensitization is to raise awareness and allow caregivers to see the qualities of care and interaction that are already available in their own repertoire. *Sensitization is, therefore, different from behavioral instruction and direct guidance.* Sensitization tries to reactivate what is already present by raising the caregiver's consciousness of his or her own activities through a sequence of exercises combined with storytelling and the exchange of experiences in groups, by pointing out what they already do positively, and by reactivating their own experiences of situations in which empathic identification with the child has been aroused.

PRINCIPLES OF IMPLEMENTATION AND SUSTAINABILITY

The impact of a program depends not only on its nature but also on the quality and intensity of its implementation. Even a high quality program may be implemented sloppily and with low intensity; in addition, there may be different kinds of resistance factors ranging from opposition from the leadership of the institution or political authorities to deficient motivation of the facilitators or staff or among the caregivers themselves. All of these contextual and framing conditions may contaminate the impact of the program. Factors of importance are 1) support from and cooperation with local authorities; 2) clarification of institutional and administrative/economic space; 3) staff willingness and motivation for the training; 4) plan of action; 5) quality and intensity of the implementation (including number of interventions); 6) facilitation of positive interaction by changing daily routines; and 7) plan for follow-up, self-evaluation, and an internal reward system (Hundeide, 2001).

It is important to introduce internal monitoring of quality in order to sustain the quality of the implementation. This could be done either by filling out a questionnaire every month or getting regular video feedback showing the participants' interaction with the caregivers in which—as training—they present themselves in regular meetings for the rest of the staff. Finally, regular reporting about the progress of the implementation to the authorities that support the program is important.

These principles of implementation in connection with evaluation also are important because they specify the ideal conditions under which the program should be implemented. *If a program is implemented under low quality conditions, then it becomes difficult to determine whether the mediocre effect of the program is due to the program itself or the conditions under which it has been implemented.* For this reason, any intervention should have some indicator that expresses the quality and intensity of the intervention, which is the point of having principles and indicators of implementation.

STUDIES ON THE EFFECTS OF THE ICDP

The ICDP has been developed as a humanitarian response to the needs of children living under extreme conditions. For this reason, scientific evaluation of the program has not been a primary concern. Within the scope of what has been possible regarding staff and resources, a series of studies has been carried out. Despite methodological weaknesses with some of the studies, the general impression is that the program has had the following expected positive effect. Participants who were asked reported that they benefited *much* or *very much;* none reported that they did not benefit. The program also seemed to have a significant impact both on the caregivers' attitudes toward children and on caregivers' interaction with and relationship with their children, as revealed in the analysis of video recordings of their interactions. There have not been any direct studies on the effects on children; there is only vague observational indications reported by caregivers. A longitudinal controlled study would be required to assess the long-term effects on children. Until now, the main concern has been to improve the child's quality of care, caregiver–child interaction, and caregivers' relationship with their children, and the preliminary findings seem to indicate that the program is achieving these goals.

It is important to pursue more studies such as qualitatively oriented microstudies in order to assess in more detail changes that are taking place and the conditions that arrest these changes. Furthermore, it is important to pursue more controlled longitudinal studies with pre- and postexperimental and control group design to investigate the changes that may be taking place in the four areas that have been the focus of our program, namely 1) the perceived reception of the program and to what extent the participants experienced benefit from participation and why, as well as how the program can be implemented conveniently and practically in different settings; 2) the extent of any changes, in line with the objectives of the program, in the caregivers' conception of the child and child care; 3) the extent of recordable changes in the quality of interaction and relationship between the caregiver and child as manifested on video recordings; and 4) the extent of developmental changes in the child in line with what should be expected from the caregivers' participation in the ICDP.

ICDP IN OPERATION

The ICDP is now in operation in more than 14 countries in Europe, Africa, Latin America, and Asia. Different versions of the program are developed for different target groups of caregivers from those working in health clinics, preschools, schools, camps with dislocated children who may be traumatized, with immigrants, and with children with special needs. Because the core program is based on universal aspects of care, like those expressed in the three dialogues, these aspects will also reappear in any context in which children's psychosocial care is at stake. The strength of this program is therefore its simplicity, wide applicability, and focus on the basic process of human care. Sensitization, not instruction, is the methodology for training caregivers; local cultural practices are also reactivated in different settings and communities, and this does not represent a conflict with the underlying universal pattern of the program represented by the three dialogues. In some way, they seem to express universal aspects of human socialization and care.

COMMENTS ON THE DEVELOPMENTAL SYSTEMS MODEL

Guralnick (2001) has provided an impressive and broad model for assessment of stressors and risk factors linked to children who are vulnerable and their families. These stressors to family patterns of interaction need to be compensated with monitored intervention based on this assessment. A detailed action program is suggested from initial assessment to intervention and family support. How does ICDP fit into this framework?

1. The ICDP considers the basis for human care to originate from the human capacity for emphatic identification with the child and sensitivity to the child's needs, states, feelings, intentions, and initiatives. These are human qualities in the caregiver that can be promoted, and this is considered an essential part of the interventions: to strengthen—in general—the empathic capacity and sensitivity of the caregiver. Such sensitivity has to be open and adjustable to the ongoing needs and transactions of the situations. It is assumed that long-term sustainability of behavioral change through intervention has to be based, at least partly, on the caregiver's new perception or conception of the child, the child's new sensitivity, empathic identification with the child, and the child's common sense understanding of what is a good interaction.

2. Therefore, to promote the caregiver's empathic identification with a child, much of the work is focused on modifying and redefining the caregiver's conception or naive diagnosis of the child. Through negative stigmatizing and a static conception of the child, the natural process of empathic identification may be blocked, and the work is directed toward redefining and opening up the caregiver's negative conceptions before any further interventions are implemented.

3. In Guralnick's (2001) framework, quality of parent–child transactions plus family orchestration of child experiences are central components in his model. In this respect there is consensus—the basis for a child's development is the quality of interaction with dominant caregivers. However, the emphasis here is slightly different: In the Guralnick framework, one focus is on *how quality of parent–child transactions can be disturbed through various stressors, risks, and threats*. In the ICDP, the emphasis is more simplistic with an emphasis on *what the positive qualities of good interaction and good care are* that are required for healthy development. This chapter pointed out three dialogues and eight guidelines that are considered essential (Klein, 2000; Schaffer, 1996). Through this direct emphasis on the positive qualities of good care, the ICDP achieves a simple method of describing and communicating with uneducated caregivers about the qualities that should be promoted in daily interactions with their children. This is something to which they can easily assimilate and relate.

4. In the ICDP, the emphasis is on the qualities of parent–child interaction and transactions and how these can be disturbed or promoted. An essential feature of this program is to specify what qualities should ideally be present in the interactions between counselors and caregivers. The approach is one of facilitating and punctuating those qualities, inside the repertoire of existing qualities that are already present in the interaction between caregiver (parent) and child (Hundeide, 2001).

5. Like Guralnick's model, the ICDP is aware of the situational, economic, and ecological conditions that need to be in place for a sustainable intervention to take place. In the ICDP, these are operationalized into seven principles of implementation that are established before any intervention is started.

Finally, there are many problems and obstacles when working in developing countries. The discrepancy between what is known and what can be done in Western countries could be substantially reduced with available knowledge and financial resources. This is not yet the case in developing countries. The lack of professional competence, established public services for most people with special needs, financial resources, and political determination to develop a society for all are still major obstacles to an inclusive society. In most developing countries the important components described in Guralnick's (2001) model represent services that are not available to most citizens. Screening of children whose parents are concerned about their children's development, further monitoring of children's development who are not referred for further examinations, comprehensive interdisciplinary assessment, and programs of early intervention to improve children's development and family welfare are still not available as public services in most developing countries. Most of the services available for assessment and treatment of children with special needs are established and run by local or international organizations. These services, however, may have relatively high professional standards. In some countries, however, community-based services are implemented as national programs (e.g., Uganda, Ghana, Palestine) where health and social services are organized on regional and local levels. The health and social workers serving the local communities in these programs do have only limited professional training and therefore mainly offer physical training and help with solving practical problems of daily life. This kind of service, however, should not be underestimated. Health and social workers represent a welcome recognition and social acceptance of the special needs of many children and families, as well as encouragement and belief in a better future.

The situation in developing countries as exemplified by the projects presented in this chapter should not be seen as arguments against the Developmental Systems Model (Guralnick, 2001). This model encompasses, in an excellent manner, the most important principles and components of services for children with special needs and their families, and it should be implemented everywhere—in Western and developing countries. The projects presented in this chapter, the intervention programs that were implemented, and the described outcomes of the interventions are very much in line with the core components in this model. In developing countries, the model should be presented as an example of how to meet important special needs in children and families and how future services for children and families with special needs should be organized.

The model's emphasis on supporting family patterns of interaction and strengthening families as the best way of promoting children's development, combined with the core principles of integration and inclusion, is essential to developing a system of services that encourage full participation of children and families in all aspects of community life. The model's emphasis on the importance of sensitivity to cultural differences and their developmental implications is essential to implementing early intervention programs in different cultural, social, and economic contexts. The authors of this chapter want to express their belief that the Developmental Systems Model for early intervention may be of great help in planning integrated and coordinated early intervention programs, and it is recommended that the model be promoted as a guideline for the future development of services for children at risk and children with disabilities and their families in industrialized, as well as developing, countries.

REFERENCES

Aarts, M. (2000). *Marte Meo: The basic manual.* Harderwijk, Holland: Aarts Productions.

Ainsworth, M.D.S., Blehar, M.C., Waters, E., & Wall, S. (1978). *Patterns of attachment.* Mahwah, NJ: Lawrence Erlbaum Associates.

Ainsworth, M.D.S., & Eichberg, C. (1971). *Effects on infant–mother attachment: A psychological study of the strange situation.* Mahwah, NJ: Lawrence Erlbaum Associates.

Bateson, M.C. (1975). Mother–infant exchanges: The epigenesis of conversational interaction. *Annals of the New York Academy of Sciences, 263,* 101–113.

Biemans, H. (1990). *Theory, method and organization of SPIN.* From the seminar "The Power of Change" [Video home training]. (Available from the Ministry of Welfare, Rijswijk, Holland).

Bowlby, J. (1969). *Attachment.* New York: Basic Books.

Braaten, S. (1996). When toddlers provide care: Infant's companion space. *Childhood, 3*(4).

Bronfenbrenner, U. (1979). *The ecology of human development: Experiments by nature and design.* Cambridge, MA: Harvard University Press.

Brown, A.L., & Palincsar, A.S. (1988). Guided cooperative learning and individual knowledge acquisition. In L.B. Resnick (Ed.), *Cognition and instruction: Issues and agenda* (pp. 393–451). Mahwah, NJ: Lawrence Erlbaum Associates.

Chiswanda, M. (1997). *Hearing mothers and their deaf children in Zimbabwe: Mediated learning experiences.* Unpublished doctoral dissertation, Oslo University, Norway.

Chiswanda, M. (1999). Hearing mothers and their deaf children in Zimbabwe: Mediated learning experiences. Infant and toddler intervention. *The Transdisciplinary Journal, 9,* 391–406.

Emde, R. (1989). Infants' relationship experience. In A. Sameroff & R.N. Emde (Eds.), *Relationship disturbance in childhood* (pp. 33–51). New York: Basic Books.

Feuerstein, R. (1979). *The dynamic assessment of retarded performers.* New York: University Park Press.

Feuerstein, R. (1980). *Instrumental enrichment: Redevelopment of cognitive functions of retarded performers.* Baltimore: University Park Press.

Feuerstein, R., Klein, P.S., & Tannenbaum, A.J. (1991). *Mediated learning experience (MLE): Theoretical, psychosocial and learning implications.* London: Freund Publishing House.

Fonagy, P. (1996, July). *Prevention, the appropriate target of infant psychotherapy.* In Plenary address. Sixth World Conference of the Association for Infant Mental Health, Tampere, Finland.

Guralnick, M.J. (2001). A developmental systems model for early intervention. *Infants and Young Children, 14,* 1–18.

Hundeide, K. (1992). *Helping disadvantaged children.* Oslo, Norway: Sigma Forlag.

Hundeide, K. (1995). Facilitating cultural mediation. In P. Klein (Ed.), *Early intervention* (pp. 113–134). New York: Garland.

Hundeide, K. (1996a). *Ledet samspill. [Guided Interaction].* Nesbru, Norway: Vett og Viten.

Hundeide, K. (1996b). *Manual for the ICDP programme.* Unpublished manuscript.

Hundeide, K. (2001). *Ledet samspill fra spedbarn til skolealder. [Guided interaction from infancy to school age].* Oslo, Norway: Vett og Viten.

Klein, P.S. (1992). Cognitive and emotional interplay in early development: Mediational role of parents. *Advances in Cognition and Educational Practice, 1A,* 169–194.

Klein, P.S. (1996). *Early intervention: Cross-cultural experiences with a mediational approach.* New York: Garland Publishing.

Klein, P.S. (2000). A developmental mediation approach to early intervention: Mediational intervention for sensitizing caregivers (MISC). *Educational and Child Psychology, 17*(3), 19–31.

Klein, P.S. (2001). A mediational intervention for sensitizing caregivers (MISC). In P.S. Klein (Ed.), *Seeds of hope: Twelve years of early intervention in Africa* (pp. 29–93). Oslo, Norway: Unipub Forlag.

Lombard, A. (1981). *Success begins at home.* Lexington, MA: D.C. Heath & Co.

Øvreide, H., & Hafstad, R. (1996). *The Marte Meo method and developmental supportive dialogues.* Harderwijk, Netherlands: Aarts Productions.

Remick, L. (2002). *Early intervention services in the United States and Norway.* Unpublished manuscript.

Ryan, J., & Thomas, F. (1980). *The politics of mental handicap.* New York: Penguin.

Rye, H. (1996). *Early intervention in psychosocial development: Experience from a project in Ethiopia* (Rep. No. 1). Norway: Oslo University, Norwegian Research Council.

Rye, H. (2001). Twelve years of early intervention in Ethiopia. In P.S. Klein (Ed.), *Seeds of hope: Twelve years of early intervention in Africa* (pp. 7–28). Oslo, Norway: Unipub Forlag.

Schaffer, H.R. (1996). Joint involvement episodes as context for development. In H. Daniels (Ed.), *An introduction to Vygotsky* (pp. 251–281). London: Routledge.

Stern, D. (1985). *The interpersonal world of infants.* New York: Basic Books.

Stern, D. (1996). *The motherhood constellation.* New York: Basic Books.

Trevarthen, C. (1990). Infants' motive for speaking and thinking in the culture. In A. Heen Wold (Ed.), *The dialogue alternative* (pp. 99–137). Oslo, Norway: University Press.

Trevarthen, C. (1996). *Mother–child communication as a paradigm.* Manuscript submitted for publication.

Trevarthen, C. (1988). Universal co-operative motives: How infants begin to know the language and culture of their parents. In G. Jahoda & I.M. Lewis (Eds.), *Acquiring culture: Cross-cultural studies in child development* (pp. 35–90). London: Croom Helm.

Vygotsky, L.S. (1978). *Mind in society.* Cambridge, MA: Harvard University Press.

Woodhead, M. (1990). Transactional models of early education effectiveness: What is the message for policy? *Early Child Care and Development, 58,* 129–141.

Zakaryan, G.G. (1998). *Mothers and their children with cerebral palsy in Armenia: Early intervention.* Unpublished master's thesis, Oslo University, Norway.

Author Index

Page numbers followed by *f*, *t*, and *n* indicate figures, tables, and footnotes, respectively.

Aarts, M., 595, 596
Aber, J.L., 315
Abidin, R.R., 188, 197, 198*f*, 201, 240
Achenbach, T.M., 246, 247
Achilles, C.M., 294
Adam, E., 488
Addenbrooke, M., 468
Addington, J., 485
Adolfsson, M., 579
Affleck, G., 323
Ahlström, M., 580
Ainsworth, M.D.S., 593
Akers, A.A., 322
Akers, A.L., 32, 34, 36
Akers, J., 189
Alamprese, J., 117
Alant, E., 585
Albano, M.L., 489
Albers, A.B., 239
Aldwin, C., 241
Alexander, K., 269
Alexander, K.L., 270
Allanson, A., 174
Allen, M.C., 352, 529
Allen-Meares, P., 106, 216
Allred, K.W., 160*f*, 168*f*
Almqvist, L., 578, 580
Alper, J.S., 170
Alpern, G.D., 82, 84*f*
Alspaugh, J.W., 271, 294
Altemeier, W., 74
Alwin, J., 282
Al-Yagon, M., 508, 516, 517, 518
Amato, P.R., 242
Ambikapathy, P., 407
Amdur, J.R., 84*f*
Amiel Tison, C., 529
Anderson, B., 353
Andersson, B.E., 575, 580
Ankonina, D.B., 193
Antonovsky, A., 516
Apfel, N.H., 200
Appel, A.E., 242
Appelbaum, M., 193, 240, 276
Applequist, K.L., 358

Appleton, P.L., 468
Arman, K., 578, 582, 583
Armbruster, B.B., 270
Armsden, G.C., 323
Armstrong, K., 281
Armstrong, R., 528
Ashby, G., 412
Ashford, L.G., 77, 79
Ashman, A., 403–404
Aslin, R., 278
Assel, M.A., 11
Atkins-Burnett, S., 78, 106, 216, 448, 511
Atkinson, E., 242
Atkinson, L., 193, 313, 323
Attermeier, S.M., 526
Attfield, E., 468
Atwater, J.B., 389, 390
Au, K., 291
Aylward, G.P., 83*f*

Babani, L., 247
Bachu, A., 353
Bacoula, C., 489
Badell Ribera, A., 533, 534, 535
Bagnato, S.J., 85*f*, 114, 115
Bagni, C., 172
Bailey, D., 108, 109, 115, 308, 338
Bailey, D.B., 30, 45, 47, 66, 115, 151, 154, 156, 157, 158, 159, 160*f*, 162, 163*f*, 165, 168*f*, 174, 178, 186, 192, 197, 200, 207, 219, 249, 327, 334, 357, 383, 417
Bailey, J., 403, 409, 414
Bain, J., 78
Baird, S.M., 34, 38
Baker, B.L., 187, 190, 192, 193, 199, 202, 203, 205
Baldwin, A., 314
Baldwin, C., 314
Baldwin, L., 270
Baldwin, L.M., 255
Ball, E.W., 288
Ballard, L., 464

Bandura, A., 365
Bangs, T.E., 83*f*
Banis, H.T., 247
Barakat, L.P., 323
Barker, W., 494
Barnard, K.E., 187, 246, 249, 513
Barnes, H., 272
Barnett, D., 12, 323, 324
Barnett, W.S., 360, 494
Barocas, R., 15, 61, 73
Barr, D.M., 331
Barratt, M.S., 13, 187
Barrera, I., 338
Barron-Sharp, B., 162, 254
Barton, K., 472
Basham, R., 323
Basil, C., 466
Bates, J.E., 245
Bateson, M.C., 593
Bausano, M., 218
Beà, N., 544
Beamish, W., 411, 414
Beck, A.T., 198*f*, 202, 203
Beck, R.W., 198*f*, 202, 203
Beckman, P.J., 176, 186, 187, 188, 189, 190, 195, 199, 200, 205, 377, 378, 380, 385, 386, 388, 391, 466
Beckman Boyes, G., 466
Behl, D., 32, 34, 189
Behrman, R., 90, 281
Belcher, H.M.E., 16
Bell, R.Q., 257
Bella, J.M., 50
Belsky, J., 237
Belt, P., 314
Benchaaban, D., 330
Bennett, F.C., 494
Bentovim, A., 238
Berlin, L.J., 63
Bernheimer, L.P., 8, 12, 13, 44, 60, 65, 67, 218, 549
Bernier, K.Y., 45, 360
Bernstein, B., 74
Betel, J., 246
Bethell, C., 337

Bettison, S., 404, 412
Bickett, L., 84*f*
Biemans, H., 594, 595, 611
Bierman-Van Eendenburg, M.E., 529
Bigras, M., 201
Biolcati, C., 535
Birch, S., 294
Birenbaum, A., 196
Birnbaum, R., 136
Bishop, D.S., 255
Bishop, N., 389
Bizzell, R., 286, 289
Björck-Åkesson, E., 561, 572, 578, 579, 583, 584, 585
Blacher, J., 151, 190, 323
Blachman, B.A., 288
Black, M.M., 199
Black, R., 288
Blackman, J.A., 223, 339, 507
Blair, C., 404
Blank, M.J., 37
Blasco, P.M., 159, 160*f*, 162, 168*f*, 200
Bleck, E.E., 533, 534, 535
Blehar, M.C., 593
Block, J.H., 258
Bloom, F.E., 314
Blue-Banning, M., 550
Blum, N., 141
Blumenthal, J.B., 37
Blums, G.J., 242
Blyth, D., 278
Boavida, J., 216
Bobrow, M., 174
Boccardi, S., 527
Bochner, S., 404
Bolger, N., 241
Boll, T.J., 82, 84*f*
Bologna, T.M., 31, 34, 37, 48, 114, 498
Boone, H.A., 43, 361
Booth, A., 289
Booth, C.L., 246, 353
Borges, L., 216
Börjesson, M.C., 576
Bornstein, M.H., 312
Borowitz, K.C., 12, 63
Botein, S., 239
Botting, N., 314
Bottos, M., 527, 528, 531, 533, 534, 535, 536

Bottroff, V., 412
Bowdery, S., 465
Bowe, F.G., 15, 379
Bowlby, J., 593
Bowman, B.T., 126, 292
Bowman, T., 193
Boyce, G.C., 189, 190, 197, 200, 204, 312, 315
Boyce, L.K., 312
Boyd, K., 50
Boyles, C., 289, 291
Braaten, S., 607, 608
Bradbury, H., 362
Braddock, D., 37
Bradley, F.H., 12
Bradley, R.H., 246, 312
Brady, S.J., 334
Braga, L.W., 533
Braithwaite, J., 404
Brand, K.L., 189
Brassard, J.A., 324
Bray, A., 464
Brazelton, T.B., 531, 532, 538, 562
Bredekamp, S., 287, 305
Brennan, E.L., 379
Brennan, K.A., 203
Breuning, P., 189
Bricker, D., 16, 78, 187, 197, 329, 331, 447, 494
Bristol, M.M., 186, 187, 192, 193, 194, 200, 202, 203, 204, 205, 243, 323
Britner, P.A., 12, 63, 188, 192, 199, 202, 205
Bromwich, R., 562
Bronfenbrenner, U., 37, 111, 153, 218, 235, 316, 324, 354, 375, 376, 548, 593
Bronheim, S., 124
Brookfield, J., 50
Brooks, J., 268
Brooks-Gunn, J., 15, 63, 246, 247, 271, 272, 275, 293, 314, 315, 418, 504, 526
Brown, A.L., 610
Brown, J., 292
Brown, S., 139
Brown, S.E., 45
Brown, T., 192, 195
Brown, W.H., 331
Browning, K., 78

Bruce, E.J., 323
Bruce, M.L., 239
Bruder, M.B., 7, 8, 9, 31, 33, 34, 37, 42, 43, 44, 45, 46, 48, 59, 65, 67, 114, 133, 134, 305, 329, 333, 360, 498
Bruder, M.E., 394
Bruer, J., 278
Bruner, S.J., 548
Brunet, O., 526
Bryant, D., 275, 293
Bryant, F.B., 314
Bryer, F., 411, 414
Bryne, E.A., 464
Brynelsen, D., 441, 442, 443, 444, 445, 448, 451
Buchanan, C.M., 242
Buck, D., 114
Buck, M.J., 245
Bucy, J.E., 218
Buehler, C., 242
Buehlman, K., 248
Buell, M., 284
Buhs, E.S., 294
Buka, S.L., 328
Bull, W., 40
Burack, J., 313
Burchinal, M., 12, 15, 18, 60, 272, 283, 312
Burgeson, R., 278
Burmeister, J., 276
Burnett, S.M., 533
Burns, M.S., 292
Burns, S., 289
Burr, W.F., 237
Burrell, B., 161*f*, 168*f*, 197
Burris, M.A., 362
Burton, S., 82
Butler, C., 533, 536
Butler, M., 141
Butter, E.M., 326
Button, S., 187, 199, 205
Buysse, V., 34, 45, 330, 360, 383
Byrd, M.R., 388
Byrne, K.E., 77, 79
Byrnes, J., 289

Caldas, C., 170
Caldwell, B., 246
Cameron, R.J., 455, 485, 494
Cameto, R., 5, 45, 62

Campbell, A.A., 85f
Campbell, F.A., 74, 245, 246, 272, 273, 293
Campbell, P.H., 34, 45, 362
Campbell, S.B., 517
Campos da Paz, A., 533, 534, 535
Cannon, B.O.M., 311
Cannon, G.S., 42
Capodilupo, A., 290
Capute, A.J., 529
Caracelli, V.J., 356
Carlhed, C., 579, 582, 584
Carlson, C., 289
Carlton-Ford, S., 278
Carpenter, B., 459, 463, 465, 466, 467, 468, 476
Carruthers, A., 411, 414
Carta, J.J., 15, 45, 47, 389
Carter, A., 331
Carter, M., 411, 418
Casby, M.W., 330
Case, L., 246
Case, R., 290, 315
Cass, H., 135, 136
Cassidy, D., 284
Casto, G., 315
Catlett, C., 48
Cawley, J., 290
Ceci, S., 271
Cecil, H., 494
Chadury, Y., 135
Chadwick, D., 418
Chait, R., 307
Chalk, R., 239
Chall, J.S., 270
Chamberlin, R., 281
Chandler, L.K., 45, 46, 377, 388
Chandler, M., 111
Chang, B., 79
Chase-Lansdale, P.L., 284
Chen, J., 160f, 168f
Chen, Y., 358
Chiswanda, M., 601, 603
Christian, K., 314
Christy, D.S., 156
Cicchetti, D., 12, 242, 507, 508, 512, 516
Cioni, G., 531
Clarkson, J., 464
Clarren, S., 140, 323
Clay, M., 280
Clayton, P.E., 276

Clements, D., 290
Clements, M., 12, 323
Clifford, R., 308
Coatsworth, J.D., 279, 281
Cobb, S., 237
Cochran, M., 243, 244, 324
Cocks, E., 409, 412
Coffman, J., 293
Cohen, J., 310, 315
Cohen, P.D., 124
Cohen, S., 218
Cohler, B.J., 258
Coie, J.D., 314
Cole, D.A., 216
Cole, R., 269
Coleman, J., 290
Coleman, P.K., 195, 335
Colker, L., 287
Coll, C., 12, 312, 548–549
Collins, F.S., 170
Colomina, R., 549
Conn-Powers, M.C., 388
Connell, D.B., 239
Connell, M.C., 389
Connor, R.T., 330
Conrad, P., 171
Conroy, M.A., 331
Conway, S., 466, 468
Cook, L., 35
Cooke, R.W.I., 314
Cooley, W.C., 32
Cooper, C.S., 160f, 168f
Cooper, J., 136
Coots, J., 153
Copeland, I., 411
Copple, C., 287, 305
Corning, A., 171
Cornwell, J.R., 34
Correa, V., 160f, 165, 168f
Corso, R.M., 338
Corwyn, R.F., 12, 312
Costello, E.J., 79
Cousins, J.B., 365
Covey, T.J., 315
Covington, M.V., 294
Cox, B., 489
Cox, M.J., 21, 199, 242, 308, 383, 515
Coyne, J.C., 239
Crawford, W., 43
Crittenden, P.M., 243
Crnic, K.A., 15, 187, 189, 190, 238, 323, 324
Crockenberg, S., 243

Crombie, M., 315
Crothers, B., 533, 534, 535
Crouter, A.C., 247
Crowley, S.L., 192, 195, 200, 204
Csikszentmihalyi, M., 585
Cullen, F.T., 205
Culligan, A., 188
Culross, P., 281
Cummings, E.M., 242
Cummings, H., 441
Cunningham, C.C., 464, 544
Currie, J., 293
Currier, R.O., 199
Cuskelly, M., 217
Cynader, M.S., 406

Dadds, M.R., 242, 281
Daggett, J., 245
Dale, D., 32
Dale, N., 464, 468
Dalla Barba, B., 531
Daly, B., 485
Damianou, S., 489
Daniele, R.J., 193, 241
Daniels, D., 288
Darling, R.B., 464
Darlington, R., 270
Darrah, J., 533
Dauber, S.L., 270
Davies, J., 464
Davies, L., 242
Davies, P., 242
Davillier, M., 189
Davis, H., 544
Davis, R.H., 78
Deal, A., 113, 116, 157, 215, 494
Deal, A.G., 111, 116, 192, 244, 254, 255, 319, 360
Deal, J.E., 245
Deck, D., 274
Deiner, P.L., 187
DeKlyen, M., 517
Del Giudice, E., 526
del Rio, M.J., 554
DeLongis, A., 241
Demo, D.H., 308
Dempsey, I., 411, 414, 465
Denham, S.A., 517
Denton, D., 285
Denton, K., 289
Derogatis, L.R., 198f, 202, 203

DesJardin, J.L., 175
D'Este, A., 531
DeVellis, R., 205
DeWolfe, D.J., 241
Diamond, K.E., 79, 376, 384
Dickinson, D.K., 289, 290, 291
Diller, L., 193, 241
Dinnebeil, L.A., 9, 31, 34, 38, 308, 383, 386
Dobbins, D., 105
Dobos, A., 74
Dobrez, D., 8
Dobson, B., 461
Dodds, J., 105
Dodge, D., 287
Dodge, K.A., 245
Dodson, S., 83f
Doherty, G., 445
Donaldson, M., 278
Donenberg, G., 187, 190, 192, 193, 199, 202, 203, 205
Donker, D., 460
D'Onofrio, B., 270
Donovan, M.S., 292
Donzella, B., 282
Downey, G., 239
Drew, B.S., 43, 361
Dromi, E., 514, 515
Drossinou, M., 482, 485, 490
Drotar, D., 323
Drucker, A., 32
Drummond, J., 440
du Plessis, D., 403, 409, 414
Dudley, J.R., 196
Dumas, J.E., 188, 190, 193, 199, 201, 203
Duncan, G., 270, 271, 315
Duncan, G.J., 246
Dunkel-Schetter, C., 241
Dunn, J., 242
Dunn, L.M., 274
Dunst, C.J., 8, 30, 31, 34, 38, 44, 48, 50, 59, 65, 67, 106, 111, 113, 115, 116, 151, 153, 155, 156, 157, 192, 199f, 200, 201, 204, 205, 215, 216, 218, 244, 254, 255, 257, 319, 324, 333, 360, 364, 386, 443, 494, 498
Dworkin, P.H., 40, 73, 74, 78

Dwyer, C., 117
Dwyer, M.C., 307
Dyer, J., 286
Dykes, M.K., 83f
Dyson, L.L., 13, 187, 188, 192, 200

Earl, L.M., 365
Early, D., 383
Easterbrooks, M.A., 205, 245
Eccles, J.S., 294
Edelbrock, C., 190
Edelbrock, C.S., 246, 247
Edelman, L., 48, 386
Edmonds, E., 287, 290
Edmonds, L., 40
Efstathiou, M., 483, 485
Egeland, B., 245
Eggbeer, L., 337
Ehlers, S., 352
Ehrle, J.L., 239
Eichberg, C., 593
Elder, J., 30, 37
Elkins, J., 403–404
Elliott, M., 388, 389
Ellis, B.J., 242
Ellis, J.T., 160f, 168f, 311
El-Sheikh, M., 242
Emde, R., 607
Emilien, G., 170
Enbom, B., 584
Endo, S., 330
Engelmann, S., 287
Entwisle, D.R., 269, 270, 293, 294
Epstein, J., 50
Epstein, N.B., 255
Erickson, M., 194, 205, 360
Escalona, S., 314
Escobar, C.M., 494
Espe-Sherwindt, M., 216
Esses, L.M., 464

Factor, D.C., 190, 200
Fadiman, A., 352
Falcon de Vargas, A., 170, 177
Fante, M., 415
Farber, E.A., 245
Farel, A.M., 40
Farran, D.C., 74, 115, 245, 270, 271, 272, 278, 287, 289, 292, 418
Farrell, S.E., 62
Farrow, F., 123
Fattore, G., 522

Fedrizzi, E., 533, 534, 535
Feeney, J.A., 242
Feiler, R., 288
Feldman, M.A., 15, 246
Feliciangeli, A., 528, 533, 535, 536
Fendt, K., 275
Fenichel, E., 41, 137
Ferguson, A., 43, 113
Ferguson, R.F., 292
Fergusson, D.M., 242
Ferraretto, I., 533, 534, 535
Ferrari, F., 530
Feuerstein, R., 593
Fewell, R.R., 83f, 192, 194, 195, 200, 203, 205
Fialka, J., 12, 323, 468
Fidler, D.J., 323
Fiechtl, B.J., 389
Fiese, B., 111
Fiese, B.H., 7, 60, 153, 312, 314, 503, 508
Filer, J., 217
Filipek, P.A., 8, 18, 19
Fincham, F.D., 242
Findler, L., 323
Finn, J.D., 294
Finn-Stevenson, M., 311
Fischer, C.L., 244
Fisman, S.N., 188, 190, 192, 193, 194, 199, 203
Fleer, M., 410
Fleming, D., 440
Fletcher, J., 289
Florian, V., 323
Flynn, C., 124
Foley, D., 406, 411, 415
Foley, T., 290
Folkman, S., 198f, 203, 240, 241
Folsom, R.C., 40
Fonagy, P., 610
Fontana, A.F., 241
Foorman, B., 289
Forbes, J., 157
Ford, T., 462
Fornós, A., 562
Foster, M., 78
Foster, P.J., 276
Fowler, S.A., 45, 377, 381, 382, 391, 393
Fox, C., 383
Fox, E., 104
Fragulitaki, A., 483
Francis, D., 289
Frank, A., 114
Frank, N., 176

Frankenburg, W., 83*f*, 105
Fraser, J., 281
Frea, W.D., 334
Freeman, H.E., 367
Freeman, N.L., 190, 191, 199, 200
Freire, P., 362
French, D., 174
Frey, K.S., 192, 193, 194, 195, 200, 203, 205
Friedrich, W.N., 187, 238
Friend, M., 35
Frölander, H.E., 578, 582, 583
Frost, B.J., 406
Fuertes, J., 562
Fujiura, G.T., 308
Funk, S.G., 78
Furumasu, J., 536
Fusco, J., 323
Fyffe, C., 409, 411, 414

Gabard, D., 32
Gallagher, J.G., 62, 485
Gallagher, J.J., 5, 34, 100, 121, 126, 127, 192, 203, 243, 323, 326
Gallimore, R., 13, 44, 60, 67, 153, 291, 549
Galván-Bovaira, M.J., 554
Gamel-McCormick, M., 334
Ganzel, B., 316
Garbarino, J., 316
Garber, J., 242
Garcia Coll, C., 352
García-Dié, M.T., 545
Gardener, L., 117
Garfinkle, A.N., 331
Garland, C.W., 114, 126, 466
Garmezy, N., 240
Garner, H., 153
Garretson, J., 19
Garshelis, J.A., 160*f*, 168*f*
Gartner, A., 154
Gatward, R., 462
Gauntlett, E., 411
Gavidia-Payne, S.T., 409, 411
Geffken, G.R., 187
Geiger-Benoit, K., 276
George, E., 35
Gericke, H., 528
Gerlach-Downie, S., 334
Gershman, K., 323
Giangreco, M.F., 489

Gidoni, E.A., 527, 529, 530
Gilkerson, L., 417
Gill, M.J., 194, 203, 276
Gillberg, C., 352
Gilliam, W.S., 3, 45, 48, 77, 81, 82, 92, 273, 292, 307
Giné, C., 541, 542, 550, 562, 563, 565
Giorgetti, K., 329
Glascoe, F.P., 18, 74, 76, 77, 78, 79
Glasser, P., 245, 257
Glenwick, D.S., 188, 199
Glynne-Rule, L., 464
Goelman, H., 445
Goetze, L.D., 31, 156
Goffin, S., 286, 287
Goffin, S.G., 32
Goffman, E., 13, 187, 196
Goldberg, W.A., 205, 245
Goldenberg, C.N., 44
Goldenberg, D., 83*f*
Goldhammer, K., 359–360
Goldman, B.D., 193, 240
Golub, S.A., 32
Gomby, D., 281
Gonzalez, V., 441
Goodfellow, J., 409
Goodman, J.F., 313, 494
Goodman, R., 462
Gordon, D., 461
Gordon, N.J., 34, 115
Gordon, R.M., 193, 241
Gottesman, I., 270
Gottman, J.M., 243
Gottwald, S.R., 34
Gowen, J.W., 156, 167, 193, 195, 203, 205, 240
Grace, M.G.A., 533
Gràcia, M., 545, 554
Graczyk, P., 239
Graham, M.A., 389
Granat, T., 576, 579
Granlund, M., 561, 572, 578, 579, 585
Grant, A.D., 533
Grant, S., 330
Graves, C., 160*f*, 168*f*
Gray, C.W., 272
Gray, D.E., 196
Gray, S.W., 562
Green, I., 418
Green, J.A., 78
Green, M., 48
Green, R.B., 174
Green, S., 196, 205

Greenberg, M.T., 187, 189, 193, 194, 195, 200, 205, 238, 314, 323, 517
Greenberger, E., 247
Greene, J.C., 356
Greenland, B., 48, 386
Greenspan, S., 15, 61, 73, 76
Greer, M., 359–360
Griffin, P.M., 84*f*, 289
Griffin, S., 290, 315
Gross, R., 275, 314
Groves, B.M., 12
Gruen, R.J., 241
Grunebaum, H.U., 239, 258
Grych, J.H., 242
Guerette, P., 536
Guidubaldi, J., 83*f*
Gunn, P., 315
Gunnar, M., 282
Guralnick, M.J., 3, 7, 8, 9, 10, 11, 11*f*, 12, 13, 14, 14*f*, 15, 16, 17*f*, 19, 21, 30, 31, 37, 48, 59, 60, 61, 62, 63, 64, 65, 66, 67, 74, 75, 101, 102, 105, 110, 112, 114, 125, 134, 135, 138, 145, 151, 185, 186, 215, 235, 236, 268, 305, 310, 313, 315, 317, 329, 330, 337, 351, 354, 355, 357, 368, 376, 384, 401, 402, 407, 408, 414, 416, 417, 418, 419, 425, 431, 439, 448, 452, 458–459, 468, 485, 486, 491, 494, 503, 504, 508, 510, 512, 513, 515, 518, 523, 524, 538, 545, 549, 552, 554, 561, 562, 567, 571, 572, 586, 587*t*, 595, 614, 615, 616
Guthrie, D., 13, 44, 60, 153, 549
Gutierrez, S., 379
Gutman, L., 269

Hack, M., 314, 315
Hacker, B., 526
Hadadian, A., 217
Hafstad, R., 596
Hagerman, P.J., 174
Hagerman, R.J., 141, 174
Häggqvist, E., 578
Hains, A.H., 45, 374, 377, 381, 382, 384, 386, 389, 392

Halbert, J., 34, 45, 362
Hale, L., 31, 34, 308, 386
Haley, A., 270
Hall, N.W., 311
Halpern, L.F., 189, 199, 205
Halverson, C.F., Jr., 245
Hamby, D.W., 50, 65, 106, 113, 115, 216, 256, 257, 333, 360
Hammer, D., 240
Hammond, M.A., 246, 330
Hancock, T.B., 152, 331
Handleman, J.S., 310
Hanft, B.E., 8, 44
Hanline, M.F., 189, 199, 387, 389, 392
Hanrahan, P., 376
Hansen, D.F., 79
Hanson, C.R., 114
Hanson, M.J., 15, 33, 37, 45, 189, 199, 338, 377, 378, 379, 380, 383, 385, 386, 388, 391, 394
Harbin, G.L., 5, 7, 8, 19, 34, 35, 38, 40, 44, 62, 100, 104, 105, 106, 111, 117, 118, 121, 123, 126, 127, 216, 318, 326, 327, 329, 332, 335, 360, 386, 485
Harik, V., 12
Haroupias, A., 483
Harris, F., 268
Harris, S.L., 194, 203, 310
Harrison, M.J., 187, 199, 202
Harrison, P.L., 84f, 86
Harry, B., 154, 393
Hart, B., 288
Hart, C.H., 12
Hart, H.T., 333
Harter, K., 242
Hartman, A., 254
Haskins, R., 282
Hastings, R.P., 192, 195
Hauch, C., 192, 202, 203
Hauser-Cram, P., 45, 166, 191, 192, 197, 200, 235, 323, 352, 353, 356, 363–364, 494, 514
Hautmäki, A., 463
Hawke, A., 418
Hawkins, S., 189
Hayes, A., 217, 403, 406, 409, 411, 412, 413, 418
Hayes, V.E., 160f, 168f

Haynes, C.W., 314
Hebbeler, K., 5, 35, 38, 45, 62, 308, 321, 328, 331, 332, 334, 335, 336, 338, 352
Hecht, L., 48
Hedges, L.V., 294
Heffernan, J., 19
Hegarty, S., 518
Heibert-Murphy, D., 190, 203
Heiges, K.L., 242
Heinen, H., 458, 498
Helders, P.J.M., 333
Hellström, D., 578
Helmerhorst, F., 460
Hemmeter, M.L., 45, 331, 334, 388
Hemp, R., 37
Henderson, C., 281
Henderson, D., 200
Henderson, L.W., 78, 79, 84f, 157, 186, 197, 207
Hendricks, L., 467
Henry, G., 274, 285
Herbert, E., 463
Hermanussen, M., 276
Heroman, C., 287
Herrmann, S., 105
Hertzman, C., 269
Heslop, P., 461
Hicken, M., 40
Hiebert-Murphy, D., 192, 202, 204
Hill, A., 580
Hill, J., 276
Hill, R., 237
Hinton, C., 49
Hirshberg, L.M., 250, 253
Hiusjes, H.H., 529
Hodapp, R.M., 175, 313, 323
Hoff-Ginsberg, E., 247
Hofferth, S., 293
Hogarty, P., 276
Holburn, S., 388
Holden, G.W., 242, 245
Holroyd, J., 188, 200
Holt, K.D., 203
Homatidis, S., 190, 191, 200
Hooper, S., 15, 61
Hooven, C., 243
Horn, E., 331, 380
Hornby, G., 463
Horwood, L.J., 242
Houston, H.L.A., 78

Howard, L.M., 134, 135
Howarth, J., 472
Howell, A., 352
Howell, F., 281
Howes, P.W., 242
Howse, R., 291, 294
Hoyson, M., 330
Hresko, W., 82
Hughes, C., 333
Hughes, M.A., 191
Hugman, R., 411
Huh, K., 189
Humphries, T., 8, 65
Hundeide, K., 596, 604, 607, 608, 612, 613, 615
Husband, P., 43
Hutcheson, J.J., 199
Hutchison, T., 78
Huttenlocher, J., 289
Hwang, B., 333

Imvrioti, R., 482
Ingber, S., 514, 515
Ingstad, B., 154
Innocenti, M.S., 31, 34, 156, 189, 197, 199, 389
Ireton, H., 79, 85f
Irish, K., 329
Isacson, O., 170

Jacob, A., 404
Jacobs, F.H., 186, 356, 366, 366f
Jacobs, V.A., 270
Jacobson, J.W., 326
Janko-Summers, S., 37
Jansson, U., 578, 580, 581
Jenkins, V., 200, 257
Jens, K.G., 525
Jessop, D.J., 199
Jimenez, M.V., 336
Jodry, W., 244, 324
Johansen, C., 113
Johanson, C., 386
Johnson, K.L., 77
Johnson, L.J., 35, 38, 45
Johnson, L.L., 79
Johnson, S.A., 38
Johnson, Z., 281
Johnson-Martin, N.M., 193, 240, 525
Johnston, C., 187, 199f, 205
Jones, K., 140
Jones, L., 472
Jones, M., 337
Jones, S., 315
Jones, S.D., 35

Jordan, N., 289
Joseph, G., 37
Juchartz-Pendry, K., 383
Judge, S.L., 216, 241
Jung, L.A., 34, 38
Jurgens-Van Der Zee, A.D., 529

Kaderoglou, E., 489, 494
Kagan, S.L., 30, 31, 32, 37, 51, 126, 235, 339, 374
Kahn, G., 157
Kaiser, A., 9
Kaiser, A.P., 152, 331, 333
Kalantzi, K., 482
Kalmanson, B., 385
Kameny, R., 104
Kamerman, S., 575
Kaminer, R., 41
Kaplan-Estrin, M., 12, 323
Kappi, C., 488
Kapuscik, J.L., 356, 366, 366f
Karlan, G.R., 466
Karraker, K.H., 195
Kasari, C., 188, 199
Kates, D.A., 37
Katon, W., 241
Katz, I.F., 243
Kaufman, S.Z., 549
Kaye, K., 549
Kazak, A.E., 194
Keilty, B., 305
Keirse, M., 460
Keith, B., 242
Kelly, J.F., 246, 248, 249, 250, 353, 513
Kelly, W., 315
Kemp, C., 409, 411, 418
Kemper, K.J., 79
Kennedy, M.M., 365
Kenyon, P., 411
Keogh, B.K., 8, 12, 13, 65, 67, 218, 549
Kerfoot, S., 485
Kerig, P., 242
Ketelaar, M., 333
Kettler, K., 249
Keyes, L., 290, 383
Kilgo, J.L., 31, 42, 384
Kitsul, Y., 104
Kitzman, H., 281
Klass, C.S., 334
Klaus, R., 272
Klebanov, P.K., 246, 272
Kleckner, M., 117
Klein, A., 290

Klein, N.K., 314, 417
Klein, P.S., 593, 594, 604, 615
Knitzer, J., 32, 37, 92, 308
Knowlton, A., 392
Kobe, F.H., 240
Kochanek, T.T., 107, 328, 360
Koegel, R.L., 188, 192, 200, 202
Kofman, O., 239
Kohen, D.E., 15
Kohn, M.L., 247
Konstantareas, M.M., 190, 191, 200
Konstantopoulos, S., 294
Konstantopoulou, P., 492
Kontos, S., 290, 292, 329
Koppelman, J., 82
Kornfein, M., 218
Kottaridi, Y., 488
Kovacs, M., 240
Kraemer, H., 275
Krais, R., 435
Kramer, L.I., 189, 191
Krausert, P.L., 442
Krauss, M.J., 13
Krauss, M.W., 151, 166, 186, 193, 197, 235, 248, 249, 254, 323, 353, 363–364
Kreisman, M., 271
Krietzmann, J.P., 322
Krishnakumar, A., 242
Kropf, N.P., 62
Kuehl, J., 425
Kurdek, L., 288
Kusch, M., 431
Kysela, G.M., 440

La Paro, K., 293
Ladd, G.W., 12, 294
LaFasto, F.M.J., 42
LaFreniere, P.J., 201
Lagander, B., 576
LaGrange, A., 445
Laird, J., 254
Lam, W., 105
Lamias, M., 171
LaMontagne, M.J., 35, 38
Land, D., 270, 271, 294
Landry, S.H., 11
Lange, G., 289, 291
Langley, M.B., 83f
Lankasky, K., 533
Lanners, R., 498
LaPointe, N., 157

Larner, M., 90, 287
Larson, C.E., 42
LaVange, L., 275
Lavee, Y., 256
Lavigne, J.V., 142
Law, J., 323
Layzer, J.I., 269
Lazar, I., 270
Lazarus, R.S., 198f, 203, 240, 241
Leaf, P., 239
Leavitt, A., 19
Lee, S.K., 199
Lee, V., 293
Leet, H.E., 254, 319
Lefebvre, D., 389
Legters, N., 270, 271, 294
Leiter, V., 45, 48, 353
LeMay, D., 84f
Lender, W.L., 313
Lendich, B., 242
Lengua, L.J., 314
Lerner, E.P., 50, 167, 176
Lerner, R., 354
Lero, D., 445
Levine, P., 322
Levine, S., 289
Levy, S.E., 352
Lewis, C.C., 79, 141
Lézine, I., 526
Li, S.M., 331
Liaw, F.R., 78, 270, 272
Lieber, J., 331, 380
Lieberman, H., 157, 162
Limber, S.P., 393–394
Limbrick, P., 465
Linder, T.W., 114, 126, 134, 221
Linfoot, K., 161f, 168f, 404
Link, B.G., 205
Linn, M.I., 313
Linney, J.A., 323
Linver, M.R., 15, 247, 293
Lippman, C., 48
Lipsey, M., 287
Lipsky, D., 154
Lishner, D.M., 322
Littman, C.L., 337
Llewellyn, G., 415
Lobach, K.S., 37
Locke, H.J., 202
Loeb, S., 293
Logan, K.R., 417
Logan, P., 411
Logan, S., 135
Lombard, A., 593
Lombardi, J., 90

Longstreth, L.E., 246
Lopez, S.R., 151, 323
Losardo, A., 9
Loughran, F., 461
Lovaas, O.I., 310, 455
Love, J., 282
Lovejoy, C., 239
Lowman, B., 158
Luiselli, J.K., 311
Lukemeyer, A., 352
Lundy, B., 239
Lunenberg, F., 287
Luthar, S.S., 507, 508, 512, 516
Lutz, S., 389
Lutzer, C., 59
Lynch, E.W., 338, 391, 393
Lynch, M., 12
Lyon, S.R., 389
Lyons-Ruth, K., 239

Mackey-Andrews, S., 359
MacLean, E., 74
MacLean, W.E., Jr., 189
MacPhee, D., 246
Macy, M., 331
Maddux, R.B., 133
Maeder, D., 404
Magill-Evans, J., 187, 199, 202
Magnuson, K., 270, 352
Magrab, P.R., 30, 37, 124
Mahoney, G., 50, 217, 332, 333
Mainland, M.K., 84f
Maiuro, R.D., 241
Majnemer, A., 136
Malinowski, M., 334
Mallik, S., 308, 328, 331, 338
Malone, A.F., 189
Malone, D.M., 417
Maloteaux, J.M., 170
Manuel, P., 462–463
Marcoux, S., 533, 534, 535
Mardell-Czudnowski, C.D., 83f
Marfo, K., 440, 441
Margalit, M., 193, 195, 200, 507, 508
Markakis, E., 483
Marlow, N., 314
Marlowe, D., 43
Marquis, J., 50, 176
Marquis, J.G., 167, 217
Marsden, D.B., 78, 84f

Marsh, D.T., 151
Marshall, P.C., 314, 406, 508
Marsland, K.W., 82
Martinea, T.M., 174
Marvin, R.S., 12, 63, 187, 188, 251f
Mash, E.J., 187, 199f, 205
Maslow, A., 174
Masten, A., 279, 281
Mayes, L.C., 77
Mazzucchelli, T., 312
McAdoo, H.P., 12, 312
McAllister, J.W., 32
McArthur, D., 188, 200
McBride, B.J., 330
McBride, S.L., 43, 218, 361
McBrien, D., 139, 140
McCall, R., 276
McCarton, C., 275, 314, 526
McCathern, R.B., 333
McCollum, J.A., 31, 36, 45, 48, 191, 358
McConachie, H.R., 134, 135, 462, 465
McConkey, R., 463
McConnell, S.R., 160f, 168f, 330, 389
McCormick, M., 314
McCormick, M.C., 526
McCoy, S.J., 288
McCubbery, J., 409
McCubbin, H.I., 204, 237
McDermott, P.A., 270
McDonald, L., 241, 440
McDowell, A.D., 190, 194, 197, 204
McEvoy, M.A., 389, 494
McGonigel, M.J., 114, 116, 466
McGraw, C.K., 288
McGurk, K., 283
McHale, S.M., 247
McInerney, W., 383
McKee, C., 362
McKee, P., 307
McKenna, P., 3, 5, 45, 62, 327
McKinney, B., 323
McKnight, J.L., 322
McKusick, V.A., 170
McLachlan, A., 135
McLean, M.E., 9, 40, 41, 113, 115, 305, 329, 380
McLoyd, V.C., 314

McNab, T.C., 339
McNulty, B.A., 123
McRae, D., 412, 413, 414
McWilliam, P.J., 115
McWilliam, R.A., 5, 8, 34, 38, 42, 43, 44, 45, 50, 62, 100, 104, 106, 108, 109, 113, 114, 115, 117, 121, 126, 127, 215, 216, 217, 218, 219, 326, 332, 335, 351, 360, 386, 485
Meisels, S.J., 3, 41, 73, 74, 75, 76, 77, 78, 79, 84f, 86, 101, 107, 115, 137, 270, 305, 440, 448, 451, 494, 511
Melaville, A.I., 37
Melton, G.B., 393–394
Melzer, D., 462
Melzer, H., 462
Merbler, J., 217
Mesibov, G., 467
Meyer, D.J., 464
Meyer, E.C., 203
Meyer, L.H., 216
Meyer, R.E., 40
Meyers, C.E., 191
Meyers, M.K., 352
Mezey, J., 329
Michie, S., 174
Middleton, S., 461
Miguel, S., 82
Mikus, K.C., 468
Milani Comparetti, A., 527, 528, 529, 530, 531, 538
Milburn, S., 288
Miller, A.C., 193, 194, 203, 205, 241
Miller, H., 215
Miller, L., 286, 289
Miller-Johnson, S., 272
Miller-Loncar, C.L., 11
Mills, B.L., 48, 386
Minchcom, P.E., 468
Mink, I.T., 191
Minnes, P., 151
Minton, H.L., 193
Mirfin-Veitch, B., 464
Mitchell, D., 218
Mittler, H., 463, 464–465
Mittler, P., 460
Moes, D.R., 334
Möller, A., 579, 586
Molloy, B., 281
Molnar, G.E., 533
Mombaerts, D., 498

Monashkin, I., 258
Moore, D., 329
Moore, K.A., 239
Moore, S., 43, 361
Moore, T., 404, 412
Moos, B.S., 200, 256
Moos, R.H., 200, 256, 257
Morgan, J., 30, 34
Morgan, M., 379
Morgan, S.B., 187
Morisset, C.E., 187, 246
Morog, M.D., 188
Morris, J., 281
Morris, J.K., 178
Morrison, F.J., 314
Morrison, R.S., 21, 67, 330, 382, 383, 390
Mortensen, L., 189
Mott, S.E., 186
Mowat, D., 171
Mulick, J.A., 326
Mullan, J., 238
Murphy, K.P., 533, 535
Murphy, L.O., 79, 141
Murray, S., 274
Myers, B.A., 151

Nagel, S.K., 247
Nakamoto, D., 389
Neas, K.B., 329
Neisworth, J.T., 85*f*, 114, 115
Nelisaratos, N., 202
Nelson, C.A., 314, 406
Neuberger, S., 508
Neuman, G., 239
Neuman, M.J., 32, 374
Neville, B., 518, 561, 562
Neville, P.R., 30, 31, 32
Newborg, J., 83*f*
Newcomb, S., 176, 249
Newport, E., 278
Newson, E., 464
Niccols, A., 313
Nickel, R.E., 32, 40, 78, 176
Nicoll, A., 78
Niebank, K., 431
Niegro, S., 243, 244
Nihira, K., 13, 44, 60, 191, 549
Noh, S., 188, 190, 199
Noller, P., 242
Noonan, M.J., 382, 384, 389
Nugent, J.K., 533

Nye, B., 294
Nyman, E., 579, 586

O'Brien, M., 245, 376
O'Connell, M., 353
Odom, S.L., 115, 330, 331, 389, 494
Offord, D., 279, 280, 284
O'Hara, M., 239
O'Hare, E., 239
Ohlson, C., 37
O'Keeffe, F., 404
Oldfield, J., 442
Olds, D., 281, 282, 282*n*
Olinga, A.A., 529
Oliver, M.N.I., 199
Olson, D.H., 198*f*, 200, 204, 256
Olson, H.C., 404
Olsson, C., 579, 585
Olswang, L.B., 333
Oltean, M., 258
O'Neal, C.R., 63
O'Neil, R., 247
Onrubia, J., 549
Opitz, J., 171
Orlandi, L., 527, 534
O'Rourke, M., 352
Orsmond, G.I., 13, 187
Orth-Lopes, L., 388, 389, 390
Osborn, L.M., 79
Oser, C., 310
Osofsky, J.D., 12
Ottaviano, S., 525, 526
Øvreide, H., 596

Page, S., 37
Paget, K.D., 386
Pagliano, P., 467
Paine, R.S., 533, 534, 535
Paino, K., 406
Paley, B., 404
Palincsar, A.S., 610
Palmer, F.B., 404
Palmero, P., 562
Palsha, S.A., 44
Pantell, R.H., 79, 141
Park, J., 15, 34, 38, 352, 550
Parker, J., 467
Parker, K.C.H., 84*f*
Parker, R., 461
Parmar, R., 290
Pascoe, J.M., 79
Patrick, D., 322

Patterson, D.L., 246
Patterson, J.M., 204, 237, 503, 516, 517
Patton, M.Q., 356
Pearce, D., 268
Pearlin, L., 238
Peerquin, D., 460
Peisner-Feinberg, E., 283
Pellin, B., 287, 290
Pelosi, J., 104
Penner, P.L., 199
Pepin, L., 483
Pepler, D., 313
Perales, F., 333
Perez, J., 79, 162, 254
Perfetti, C., 289
Perrin, E.C., 135, 141, 142
Perry, A., 190
Perry, B.F., 359–360
Perry, D.F., 37
Pesetsky, D., 289
Peterander, F., 486, 498, 545, 562
Petermann, F., 431
Peters, D.L., 334
Petersen, A., 171
Peterson, C., 218, 242
Peterson, R.A., 323
Petit, G.S., 245
Petterson, S.M., 239
Peyton, V., 245
Phillips, D., 74, 115, 305, 310, 339, 406
Phillips, M., 269, 270, 293
Pianta, R.C., 12, 21, 63, 187, 188, 251*f*, 288, 293, 383, 393, 515
Pierce, L., 45, 374
Pieterse, M., 404, 411
Pilkington, K.O., 8, 44, 334
Pimentel, A.E., 62
Pimm, P., 533, 535
Pinder, G.L., 333
Pinderhughes, E.E., 245, 314
Pithon, G., 545
Plowright, C.M.S., 200
Pokorni, J.L., 187, 189, 195, 200, 205
Polglaise, L., 406
Ponchon, M., 170
Portner, J., 256
Poston, D., 201
Powell, D.R., 270
Powers, L.E., 323
Powls, A., 314

Pramling-Samuelsson, I., 575
Prechtl, H.F.R., 531
Preisler, G., 580
Preskill, H., 365
Press, F., 406, 418
Pretis, M., 425, 426, 427t–428t, 429t, 430, 430t, 431, 432t, 433t–434t, 434, 435t, 436
Pretti-Frontczak, K.L., 331
Price, D.A., 276
Price, K., 135
Pritchard, E., 32, 339
Pritchard, P., 406
Profilet, S.M., 12
Provence, S., 79, 107, 115, 200
Pugach, M.C., 35
Pugh-Hoese, S., 284
Pulman, L., 217
Pungello, E., 272

Quick, A.D., 85f
Quinn, M.E., 241
Quinton, D., 277

Raab, M., 8, 65, 333, 360
Rabe, T., 580
Radin, N., 245, 257
Radloff, L., 202
Ragozin, A.S., 323
Rainforth, B., 489
Ramey, C.T., 74, 245, 246, 272, 275, 404
Ramsey, B., 272
Randall, C.C., 389
Randall, P., 467
Rapp, N., 389
Rappaport, J., 156
Rapport, M.J.K., 42
Ratokalau, N.B., 382
Raviv, A., 193
Rayner, K., 289
Reason, P., 362
Reich, K., 90
Reid, R., 312
Reilly, S., 135
Reitman, D., 199, 203
Remick, L., 595
Resare, E., 579
Reuter, J., 84f
Revenson, T.A., 241
Reynell, J., 85f
Reznikoff, M., 241
Rheams, T., 79, 162, 254

Ricci, L.A., 175
Rice, M.L., 376
Richards, E., 37
Richardson, G.E., 516
Richardson, M., 322
Ripple, C.H., 81, 92
Risley, T.R., 288
Roach, M.A., 13, 187, 188, 190, 191, 199
Robbins, S., 48
Roberts, C., 312
Roberts, J.E., 15, 61
Roberts, R.N., 31, 32, 34, 36, 44, 45, 47, 49, 156, 322
Robertson, C.M.T., 533
Robinson, N.M., 323
Rochera, M.J., 549
Rodrigue, J.R., 187, 190, 192, 194, 195, 199, 200, 202, 204, 205
Rodriguez, I., 104, 117
Rodriguez, P., 357, 550–551
Rodriguez, P.B., 216
Rogers, C., 123
Rogoff, B., 549
Rogosch, F.A., 242
Roizen, N.J., 339
Roll-Pettersson, L.R., 161f, 168f, 579
Rollins, K.B., 293
Romer, E.F., 48, 361
Roper, N., 8, 65
Rosenblatt, B., 136
Rosenkoetter, L.I., 382
Rosenkoetter, S.E., 45, 46, 374, 377, 381, 382, 386, 391, 392
Rosin, P., 34, 48
Rosman, E.A., 32, 37, 308
Ross-Allen, J., 388
Rossi, P.H., 367
Roszmann-Millican, M., 114, 116
Roth, J., 293
Rounds, K., 48
Rous, B., 45, 46, 59, 388, 391, 393
Rouse, J., 409, 412
Rowland, C., 9
Roy, S., 290
Ruble, L., 139
Ruggeri, C., 535
Ruiz, D.M., 35
Rule, S., 9, 31, 34, 308, 386, 389
Russell, P., 461–462, 465

Russell, S., 284
Russo, J., 241
Rutter, M., 240, 277, 512, 582
Ryan, J., 610
Ryan, R.H., 269
Rydeman, B., 579
Rye, H., 596, 604

Saffran, J., 278
Safran, S.P., 352
Sainato, D.M., 21, 67, 330, 382, 383, 390
Sainsbury, K., 466–467
St. Pierre, R.G., 269, 274, 275
Sala, D.A., 533
Salisbury, C.L., 43, 44, 390
Salmon, S., 290
Salt, A., 135
Saluja, G., 308
Sameroff, A.J., 7, 15, 61, 73, 111, 153, 195, 269, 312, 314, 503, 508
Sameroff, S., 111
Samson-Fang, L., 32
Sandall, S., 9, 113, 115, 305, 329, 331, 380
Sandoval, D., 248
Sanford, A., 84f
Santelli, B., 50, 167, 176
Sarama, J., 290
Sarkis, L., 157
Saylor, C.F., 190
Scarborough, A., 35, 166, 308, 338
Scarpa, J., 239
Scarr, S., 246
Schacht, R., 156, 167, 169
Schaefer, E.S., 257
Schaffer, H.R., 549, 615
Schatschneider, C., 289, 314
Schooler, C., 247
Schopler, E., 192, 243, 323
Schroeder, C.S., 142
Schuck, L.A., 218
Schultz, C.L., 323
Schultz, N.C., 323
Schuster, J., 388
Schwartz, I.S., 216, 329, 330, 331, 389
Schweinhart, L., 272, 287
Sciuto, M., 528, 535
Scorgie, K., 241
Scott, B.S., 193, 203
Scott, D., 275

Scott, S., 215, 217
Scott-Little, C., 308
Seid, M., 294
Seidenberg, M., 289
Seifer, R., 15, 61, 73, 195, 314
Seligman, M., 464
Seligman, M.E.P., 585
Seligman, S., 385
Selzer, M.M., 151
Semple, S., 238
Sergeant, J., 167
Sexton, D., 79, 161f, 162, 168f, 197, 200, 254, 256
Shapiro, J., 151, 323
Sharp, L., 79, 141
Sharpton, W.R., 197
Shaver, P.R., 203
Shearer, D.E., 562
Shearer, M.S., 82, 84f, 562
Shechtman, F., 249
Sheehan, G., 242
Sherbenou, R., 82
Sheridan, S., 575
Shevrin, H., 249
Shields, G., 161f, 168f
Shields, J., 456
Shonkoff, J.P., 3, 47, 74, 101, 115, 166, 197, 235, 271, 305, 310, 314, 323, 327, 339, 355, 363, 406, 440, 448, 451, 494, 508
Shore, R., 74, 508
Shotts, C.K., 382, 383, 392
Shuster, J., 45
Siegler, R., 289
Sigafoos, J., 312
Sigman, M., 188, 199
Sigston, A., 485
Simeonsson, R.J., 35, 108, 109, 115, 158, 160f, 162, 163f, 168f, 186, 192, 197, 200, 308, 578
Simmons, R., 278
Simpson, K., 242
Sims, M., 411
Sinclair, R., 288
Singer, E., 171
Singer, L.T., 189, 193, 194, 195, 199, 202
Siperstein, G.N., 507
Sippell, W.G., 276
Sisson, R.W., 311
Skaff, M., 238
Skelton, E.J., 464
Skinner, D., 154, 160f, 165, 168f, 174, 293, 330, 357

Slentz, K.L., 187, 197
Sloop, S., 550–551
Sloper, P., 464, 472
Slough, N.M., 189
Smeeding, T., 352
Smith, B., 9, 327
Smith, B.J., 3, 42, 113, 115, 305, 329, 380
Smith, C.M., 323
Smith, K., 32
Smith, K.E., 11
Smith, L., 277
Smith, M., 290
Smith, R., 516
Smith, S., 278
Smith, T., 310
Smith, T.B., 199, 315
Smyrnios, K.X., 323
Snow, C., 289, 290
Snyder, P., 162, 254
Son-Yarbrough, W., 292
Sontag, J.C., 156, 167, 169
Souza, A.M., 533, 534, 535
Spanier, G.B., 198f, 202
Sparkman, K., 174
Sparling, J., 156, 158, 272, 275
Speck, O., 425, 545
Speechley, M., 188
Speltz, L., 517
Speltz, M.L., 323
Spencer, M.B., 37
Spiegel, H., 436
Spiegel-McGill, P., 376
Spieker, S., 187
Spiker, D., 5, 8, 45, 62, 275, 309, 312, 313, 314, 332, 336, 338
Squires, J., 16, 78, 79, 447
Srinivasan, B., 466
Staff, I., 43
Stancin, T., 323
Starkey, P., 290
Starnes, A.L., 34, 115
Stayton, V., 31, 44, 48, 133
Steénsson, A.-L., 579
Stefou, M., 489
Stegelin, D.A., 35
Stein, R.E.K., 199
Steinberg, M.S., 293
Stenhammar, A.-M., 581, 584, 585
Stepanek, J.S., 249
Stern, D., 593, 607, 608
Sterzin, E.D., 114
Stewart, M., 442
Stickle, T.R., 199

Stipek, D.J., 269, 288
Stock, J., 83f
Stockdale, A., 177
Stokes, S.J., 190
Stoneman, Z., 60
Stormshak, E., 15, 324
Strain, P.S., 330, 389
Straka, E., 417
Streufert, C.A., 382
Streuning, E.L., 205
Striffler, N., 37
Strothmann, M., 435
Sturner, R.A., 78
Summers, J.A., 31, 32, 34, 38, 196
Sundin, M., 585
Svanberg, P.O.G., 517, 518
Sviberg, B., 194, 204
Svinicki, J.S., 83f
Swan, W., 30, 34
Swank, P.R., 11
Swann, D., 43, 361
Swartz, J., 274, 275
Szczepanski, M., 145

Tabors, P.O., 289
Tam, B.K.Y., 38
Tangel, D.M., 288
Tannenbaum, A.J., 593
Tardif, T., 247
Tarr, J.E., 360
Tatelbaum, R., 281
Taylor, H.G., 314, 323
Taylor, J., 412
Taylor, K., 312
Taylor, L., 12, 383
Taylor, M.J., 190, 192, 195, 200, 204
Teague, T.L., 393–394
Teasdale, G.R., 404
Teferra, T., 604
Tefft, D., 536
Ten Have, T., 78
Tennen, H., 323
Terrisse, B., 545
Terry, S.F., 177
Thalange, N.K., 276
Tharp, R., 291
Thelen, E., 277
Thomaidis, L., 489, 494
Thomas, D., 293
Thomas, F., 610
Thompson, B., 79, 161f, 168f, 197
Thompson, K., 415
Thompson, L., 50
Thompson, R.J., 136, 203

Thompson, T., 141
Thorp, E.K., 48
Thurman, S.K., 34
Thyer, B.A., 62
Tjossem, T., 110
Tobing, L.E., 188, 199
Toccafondi, S., 187
Tocci, L., 38, 50, 106, 117, 216, 386
Tonascia, J., 526
Torgesen, J., 289
Torres, R.T., 365
Toth, S.L., 242
Tougas, J., 445
Towen, B.C., 529
Towns, F., 246
Trahan, J., 533, 534, 535
Trahms, C.M., 19
Trause, M.A., 189, 191
Treloar, R., 463
Trevarthen, C., 593, 607, 608
Triggs, S., 472
Tritt, S.G., 464
Trivette, C.M., 8, 34, 48, 50, 65, 106, 107, 111, 113, 115, 116, 127, 157, 192, 200, 215, 216, 244, 254, 255, 257, 319, 321, 322, 324, 333, 360, 386, 443, 494
Trommsdorff, G., 278
Tronick, E.Z., 531
Trute, B., 190, 192, 202, 203, 204, 243
Tuchman, L., 48
Turbiville, V., 100, 113, 156, 217, 550
Turkheimer, E., 270
Turnbull, A.P., 15, 30, 34, 38, 50, 100, 113, 115, 151, 154, 156, 167, 176, 352, 507, 550
Turnbull, H.R., 15, 30, 100, 113, 115, 156, 352
Turnbull, R., 507
Turner, C., 242
Tvingstedt, A.L., 580
Twardosz, S., 389
Tyndall, S., 34

Udy, G., 410
Ulfhielm, K., 581, 584, 585
Umbreit, J., 48, 361
Upshur, C.C., 45, 187, 191, 194, 197, 205, 323, 356, 363, 514

Uttaro, T., 157

Vadasy, P.F., 192
Van Dyke, D.D., 352
Van Horn, J., 124
Vandenberg, B., 200
Vandivere, S., 239
Varni, J.W., 247
Vayona, S., 489
Vellet, S., 11
Venuto, N., 334
Vermeer, A., 333
Vianello, A., 528
Vig, S., 41
Vilaseca Momplet, R., 545
Vincent, L.J., 389
Vitaliano, P.P., 241
Voysey, M., 196
Vygotsky, L.S., 549, 551, 593

Wachs, T.D., 571, 572, 582, 583, 586
Wade, S.S., 323
Wagner, M., 5, 45, 62
Wakeley, A., 290
Wald, N.J., 178
Waldfogel, J., 275
Waldron, M., 270
Walker, E., 239
Walker, L., 46
Wall, S., 593
Wallace, K.M., 202
Wallander, J.L., 247
Walsh, S., 59
Wampler, K.S., 245
Wandersman, L.P., 562
Wang, C., 362
Wang, P., 141
Warfield, M.E., 45, 166, 197, 235, 323, 353, 356, 363, 364, 514
Warren, S.F., 333
Wasik, B., 75, 105, 275, 494
Watamura, S., 282
Waters, E., 593
Watson, J.D., 170, 171
Watt, J., 533, 534, 535
Watts, B.H., 412
Waxman, S., 289
Weikart, D., 272, 287
Weil, M., 48
Weisner, T.S., 13, 44, 45, 60, 218, 356, 514, 549
Weiss, C.H., 355, 356, 365
Weiss, H., 434

Weiss, J.L., 258
Weissbourd, B., 235
Weissman, M., 239
Wells, N., 353
Wenz-Gross, M., 507
Werner, E.E., 73, 278, 512, 516, 517
Wertheimer, R., 315
Wertsch, J.V., 549
Wesley, P.W., 34, 44, 383
West, J., 289, 315
West, J.F., 42
West, S., 464
West, T., 35, 38, 318
Whaley, K.T., 45, 374
White, S.H., 276
Whitehead, A.D., 34
Whitehead, L.C., 187, 189, 190, 192, 197, 200, 204
Whitehurst, G., 287, 288
Whitelaw, A.J., 404
Whitmore, E., 362
Whyte, S., 154
Widen, J.E., 40
Widuch-Berg, E., 582
Wiesner, T., 153
Wigfield, A., 294
Wilcox, B.I., 194
Wilcox, K.T., 247
Wilcox-Herzog, A., 290, 292
Wilgosh, L., 241
Williams, P., 575
Williams, W., 271
Williamson, G.G., 145
Wills, T.A., 218
Wilson, J., 389
Winett, R.A., 518
Wing, L., 352
Winton, P.J., 48, 186, 197, 219, 338, 417, 550–551
Wisbeach, A., 135
Wischnowski, M.W., 45, 46
Wiske, M.S., 78, 84f
Wnek, L., 83f
Wolery, M., 43, 45, 46, 47, 115, 154, 328, 376, 382, 391, 392
Wolf, L.C., 188, 190, 192, 193, 194, 199, 203
Wolfendale, S., 458
Wolraich, M.L., 78
Wolverton, A., 442
Woodgate, A., 466
Woodhead, M., 607
Woodruff, G., 114, 116

Woods Cripe, J.J., 494
Worobey, J., 562
Wright, C., 536
Wu, C.L., 217, 219

Xanthopoulos, X., 483, 485

Yamaki, K., 308
Yamashita, L., 389
Yamashita, T.S., 189
Yeates, K.O., 246, 323
Yeung, W.J., 247
Yoder, D., 335

Yoder, P.J., 333
York, J., 489
York, R., 489
Yoshikawa, H., 308
Young, K.T., 82
Young, M., 90

Zakaryan, G.G., 596–597
Zalfa, F., 172
Zanolli, K., 245
Zax, M., 15, 61, 73
Zeanah, C.H., 305
Zeisel, S.A., 15, 61

Zeitlin, S., 145
Zelli, A., 245
Zercher, C., 379
Zeschitz, M., 435
Zigler, E.F., 3, 82, 273, 292, 307, 311, 313
Zill, N., 289, 315
Zinkin, K., 85f
Zipper, I.N., 48
Zorn, D., 38
Zoukis, N., 483
Zucherman, T.G., 248
Zuckerman, B., 12
Zuckerman, M., 257

Subject Index

Page numbers followed by *f* indicate figures; those followed by *t* indicate tables.

Aaron De Lowe Early Intervention Center
    (Israel), 505, 510, 511, 514
Abecedarian Project and Project Care as
    prototype for Infant Health
    and Development Program,
    275
Abecedarian Study on early intervention
    services, 74–75, 272
Aboriginal Head Start (Canada), 441
Abt Associates' evaluation of Even Start,
    274
Academic achievement of children living in
    poverty, 269–272
  fourth-grade slump, 270
  gender differences, 271–272
  grade retention and referral to special
    education, 270–271
  school completion rates, 271
Access, *see* Point of access (POA)
Activity settings, 43–44
Activity-based intervention, 331
Advocacy groups, 177
Ages & Stages Questionnaires®, 447
Area Special Educational Needs
            Coordinators (SENCOs;
            United Kingdom), 457
Armenia
  cerebral palsy, use of Marte Meo
            approach for children with,
            596–600
Assessment, 136–148
  Austrian developmental communications
            model and diagnostics issues,
            430–432, 432*t*
  British Columbia Infant Development
            Program, 445–448
  changing diagnostic procedures for, 352
  definition of, 41
  family assessment, 186–187
  of family characteristics, *see* Family
            characteristics
  of family's information needs, *see*
            Information needs of families
  of family's resource needs, *see* Resource
            needs of families
  instruments for, 137
  in Italy, for infants, 528–529
  medical assessment, 138–141, 336

needs assessment, 357–358, 358*t*
  psychological assessment, 141–143
  special education assessment, 143–148
  of stressors, *see* Assessment of stressors
  structuring relationship-focused
            assessment, 249–254
    conversation and discussion, 252–254
    questions for discussion, 250–252
  Sweden, 578, 583
  United Kingdom multi-agency
            assessment, 472–473
  see also Comprehensive interdisciplinary
            assessment; Screening and
            surveillance
Assessment of stressors, 20, 185–213
  considerations and issues in conducting,
            196–197
  coping skills, 193–194, 323–324
    instruments to measure, 198*t*, 203–204
  emotional stress, 192–193
    instruments to measure, 198*t*, 202–203
  family cohesiveness and, 191–192
  Greece, 491–492, 496–497
  inclusion and, 64–65
  Israel, 513–514
  marital stress, 192
    instruments to measure, 198*t*, 202
  parenting stress, 188–193
    child-rearing attitudes of parents,
            245–246
    differences between mothers and
            fathers, 190–191, 193, 195
    instruments to measure, 197–202, 198*t*
    in parents of children at biological risk
            for disability, 189, 193
    in parents of children in early
            intervention, 189–190
    in parents of children with established
            disabilities, 188–189
  screening instruments for, 197–202
    questions for, 198–199*t*
    recommendations, 201–202
  social support, 194–195, 323
    instruments to measure, 199*t*, 204–205
  Spain, 560–562
  threats to confident parenting, 195–196
    instruments to measure, 199*t*, 205–206

Assistive technology versus physiotherapy
    in Italy, 533–534
Attention-deficit/hyperactivity disorder
    (ADHD), 460, 469
Australia, 401–423
    Developmental Systems Model and,
        401–402, 407–408
        establishment and maintenance of,
            414–416
    evolution of early intervention, 405–408
    inclusion issues, 415
    population and government, 403
    research, program evaluation, and
        training, 416–418
    service provision, 408–414
        coordination of, 412–414, 415
        models of service delivery, 408–409
        quality of, 411–412
        referral to services, 408
        service providers, 409–411
    target population, 403–405
        funding systems, effect on, 404–405,
            415
        traditionally targeted populations, 404
Australian Network for Promotion,
    Prevention, and Early
    Intervention Network for
    Mental Health in Young
    People (AUSEINET), 406
Australian provision of services for autism,
    409
Australian Research Alliance for Children
    and Youth (ARACY), 419
Austria, 425–437
    developmental communications model,
        426–436
        attachment-related strategies,
            428–430, 430t
        diagnostics issues, 430–432, 432t
        final evaluation, 434–435
        first contact, 428, 429t
        goal-oriented work, 432–434, 433t
        hierarchical steps in, 426, 427t
        reflection process, 434, 435t
    Developmental Systems Model and, 425
Autism
    benefits of early intervention for, 467
    diagnostic procedures for, 352
    early identification of children with, 8,
        139
    increase in diagnosis of
        British Columbia, 451, 469
        United Kingdom, 460
    LEAP model of intervention for, 330
    litigation for services brought by parents
        of children with, 326

parent–child interaction strategies and,
    333
parenting stress associated with, 188
    Beck Depression Inventory, use of,
        203
    Carolina Parent Social Support Scale,
        use of, 205
    Center for Epidemiological Studies
        Depression Scales, use of, 203
    Coping Health Inventory for Parents,
        use of, 204
    coping skills, 194
    differences between mothers and
        fathers, 190
    Dyadic Adjustment Scale, use of, 202
    emotional stress and, 193
    Family Adaptability and Cohesion
        Scale, use of, 200
    Family Environment Scale, use of, 200
    Family Impact Questionnaire, use of,
        199
    Marital Adjustment Scale, use of, 202
    marital stress and, 192
    Parenting Sense of Competence Scale,
        use of, 205
    Questionnaire on Resources and
        Stress, use of, 200
    social isolation and, 194
    stigma of having child with autism,
        196
    threats to confident parenting, 195
    Ways of Coping Scale, use of, 204
    point of access and, 121
    specialists in assessment process, 148

Back to Sleep Awareness Campaign
    (Canada), 441
Beck Depression Inventory (BDI), 202,
    203
Biological factors in child development,
    314–315
Birth defects registry, 40
Birth screening, 88–90
    state programs for birth defect
        surveillance, 40
Birth-to-three age group
    legislation to provide early intervention
        for, 4
    see also Part C services for infants and
        toddlers (IDEA '97)
Blindness, see Vision impairment
Brain, assessment of, 140–141
Brief Symptom Index (BSI), 202–203
Brighter Futures (Canada), 441
Britain, see United Kingdom
British Columbia, 439–454

background on early intervention
   services, 440–441
funding issues, 442, 452
future trends, 450–452
Infant Development Program, 439,
   441–445
   children's characteristics, 443–444
   collaborations, 443
   cultural and related issues, 444–445
   Developmental Systems Model and,
      439, 448–450
   early assessment and intervention,
      445–448
   professional training, 445
Integrated Service Delivery and
   Integrated Case Management,
   445

Canada, see British Columbia
Canada Prenatal Nutrition Program
   (CPNP), 440
Caregiver reports of developmental
   concerns, 81, 82
   starting point for diagnosis, 139
Caregiver's definition of child, 607–608
Carolina Curriculum for Infants and
   Toddlers with Special Needs
   (CCITSN), 525–526
Carolina Parent Social Support Scale, 205
"Celebrating Families" program (United
   Kingdom), 468
Center for Epidemiological Studies
   Depression Scales (CES-D),
   202, 203
Center for Rehabilitation of Spastic
   Children (KASP; Greece), 489
Center for the Education and
   Rehabilitation of the Blind
   (KEAT; Greece), 489
Center-based programs, 327, 328, 360
   Australia, 415
   efficiency, compared with home-based
      services, 364
   Italy, 525, 527–528
   Spain, 562
Centers for Diagnosis, Assessment,
   Evaluation, and Support
   (CDAES; Greece), 484–485,
   487, 490, 494–496
Cerebral palsy
   Armenian provision of services for,
      596–600
   Australian provision of services for, 409
   neonatal problems and low birth weight
      associated with, 315
   parenting stress associated with

Dyadic Adjustment Scale, use of, 202
   Family Support Scale, use of, 205
   Swedish early childhood intervention
      for, 577
Charitable agencies' prekindergarten
   programs, 284, 285
Child abuse and neglect, 94, 314
Child care
   developmental screening in, 90–92
   resource and referral agencies, 121
   screening and surveillance in, 90–92
   instruments for, 88
   licensure laws and, 90–91
   universal programs through age 2,
      282–284
   see also specific countries
Child Care Development Fund (CCDF),
   quality set-asides, to develop
   screening systems, 91
Child development
   biological factors in, 314–315
   family patterns of interaction and, 7, 11
   holistic approach to, 311–312
   social skills in, 331, 335, 389
   social support as factor, 324
   social-environmental factors in, 314–315
Child neuropsychiatrist role in Italy, 524,
   530
Child Protective Services (CPS)
   point of access and, 120
Child-find systems, 80–81
Child-rearing attitudes of parents,
   245–246, 312–314
Children With Special Health Care Needs
   (CSHCN) program
   point of access and, 120
   referrals of children to specialized
      services, 106
Children's Trusts (United Kingdom), 475
Class size, 294
Collaboration and partnerships, 113–115,
   117
   British Columbia Infant Development
      Program, 443
   caregivers, effect on, 594
   collaborative consultation during
      assessment, 42
   Spain and parental-professional
      partnerships, 550–551, 568
   in successful transition process, 385–386
   United Kingdom transdisciplinary
      approach, 467–468
Committee on Integrating the Science of
   Early Childhood Development,
   National Academy of Sciences,
   5–6, 9

Commonwealth Government Stronger Families and Communities Strategy (Australia), 414
Communication
developmental communication model in Austria, 426–436
in successful transition process, 385–386
Community Action Program for Children (CAP-C; Canada), 441
Community environment as risk factor, 315–316
Community maps of resources, 322
Community support groups, 176–177
Community-based programs and resources
child care resource and referral agencies, 121
home visits by public health nurses, 281–282
nature and availability of, 316, 322
new generation of programs as, 594
preschool programs for poor families, 281–286
screening, recommendations for, 88–94, 89f
Spain, 551–552
Sweden, 576
use of, 8, 216
Competencies of staff, see Staff competencies
Components of Developmental Systems Model, 16–21
see also Developmental Systems Model
Comprehensive interdisciplinary assessment, 133–150
advantages of, 134–135
assessment portion, 136–148
checklists used for, 146
community resources as limitation on, 148–149
cross/transdisciplinary, defined, 134
Greece, 488–489, 495–496
inclusion and, 62–63
interdisciplinary approach, 133–135
Israel, 510–511
medical assessment, 138–141
multidisciplinary, defined, 134, 221
as part of Developmental Systems Model, 19, 148–149
problems with, 135
psychological assessment, 141–143
report to be created for family, 147–148
service coordination and integration, 40–42
Spain, 556–558
special education assessment, 143–148
tools used for, 145
Comprehensive program, see Developing and implementing comprehensive program

Computerized axial tomography (CAT) scans, 140
Congenital hyperthyroidism, 139
Consistency of programs, need to improve, 9–10
Continuity of services as transition issue, 382, 391–392
see also Transition issues
Coordination among services, see Interagency organizational structure and coordination; Point of access; Service coordination and integration
Coping Health Inventory for Parents (CHIP), 204
Coping skills, 193–194, 238, 323–324
as family characteristic, 240–241
instruments to measure, 203–204
Cost effectiveness and gains made by children with disabilities, 364
United Kingdom, 459–462
Cultural background of family, 153–154, 352
in British Columbia Infant Development Program, 444–445
in United Kingdom, 466
see also Ethnic background of family
Curriculum for prekindergarten, 286–292

Developmentally appropriate practice (DAP) for preschool education
Darcee program, 286–287
Databases
integrated databases, development of interagency data, 121–123
need for, 127
resource directory, 123–124
state variances in collecting Part C data, 44–45
Deafness, see Hearing impairment
Demographics
Australia, 403
changing nature of, 352
gathering information about child and family, 108, 112, 122–123
Sweden, 572
United Kingdom, 460
see also Ethnic background of family; Socioeconomic status of family
Depression of parents, 192–193, 195, 239–240, 323
instruments to measure, 202–203
Devaluation-Discrimination scale, 205
Developing and implementing comprehensive program, 305–349
biological and social-environmental factors, 314–315

in context of early intervention, 307–310
ecological model, need for, 315–316
Greece, 492, 497
inclusion and, 65–66, 329–331
information needs of families, 325–327
instructional services, 328–334
  center-based, 328–331
  home-based, 331–334
Israel, 514
parenting attitudes, behavior, and
    interactions, effect of, 312–314
part of Development Systems Model,
    20–21, 306, 316–337
resource supports and, 319–323
respite services and, 336
for service coordination and integration,
    42–44
social support and, 323–325
Spain, 562–563
therapy services and, 327t, 334–335
timing and intensity of intervention,
    310–312
Developing countries, 593–619
  Armenia and Marte Meo approach for
      children with cerebral palsy,
      596–600
  background, 593–595
  Ethiopia, and More Intelligent Sensitive
      Child program, 603–606
  Zimbabwe and More Intelligent
      Sensitive Child program,
      601–603
Developmental screening, 77–80
  accuracy of, 78–79
  in child care and state prekindergarten
      settings, 90–92
  costs of, 78
  Greece, 486–487
  pediatrician's role, 336–337
  physical examination as part of, 140
  tests used in, 82–88, 83t
  see also Screening and surveillance
Developmental Systems Model
  application of, 22
  compared with British Columbia Infant
      Development Program,
      448–450
  compared with Swedish system, 587t
  components of, 16–21, 17f
    assessment of stressors, 20, 185–213
    see also Assessment of stressors
    comprehensive interdisciplinary
        assessment, 19, 133–150
    see also Comprehensive
        interdisciplinary assessment
    developing and implementing of
        comprehensive program,
        20–21, 306, 310–337

see also Developing and
    implementing comprehensive
    program
  eligibility, 19–20
  monitoring and outcome evaluations,
      21, 351–372
    see also Evaluation
  point of access, 18–19
    see also Point of access (POA)
  screening program and referral, 16–18
    see also Screening and surveillance
  transition planning, 21, 373–398
    see also Transition issues
framework of, 11–12
inclusion as core principle of, 7, 59–69
  see also Inclusion
intent of, 15–16
overview, 10–16
preventive intervention component, 15
principles of early intervention relevant
    to, 6–7, 6t
for service coordination and integration,
    38–46
stressors and, see Assessment of stressors;
    Stressors
see also specific countries for foreign
    application of model
Developmentally appropriate practice
    (DAP) for preschool education,
    287
Devereaux Social-Emotional Scale for
    Preschool Classrooms, 88
Diagnosis, see Assessment; Comprehensive
    interdisciplinary assessment
Disability Discrimination Act 1995 (United
    Kingdom), 457
Disability Rights Commission (United
    Kingdom), 470, 475
Discrimination issues associated with
    genetic information, 177–178
Distress, see Assessment of stressors;
    Stressors
Down syndrome
  attachment problems and, 429
  early intervention for, 93, 315
  family patterns of interaction and, 13,
      313
  genetic testing for, 141
  Italian study of home-based program
      for, 526
  language development, directives for,
      332–333
  monitoring following diagnosis, 139
  mothers as primary caregivers of
      children with, 463
  not inherited, 173
  number of children with, 338

Down syndrome—*continued*
  parenting stress associated with, 188
    Beck Depression Inventory, use of,
      203
    differences between mothers and
      fathers, 191
    emotional stress and, 193
    Family Adaptability and Cohesion
      Scale, use of, 200
    family cohesiveness and, 192
    Family Support Scale, use of, 205
    Impact on Family Scale, use of, 199
    marital stress and, 192
    Parenting Sense of Competence Scale,
      use of, 205
    Questionnaire on Resources and
      Stress, use of, 200
    threats to confident parenting, 195
    Ways of Coping Scale, use of, 204
  physical examination for, 140
  point of access and, 121
    classification of children with
      developmental delays, 110
    referral to, 106
  Swedish early childhood intervention
    for, 577
Drug treatment for genetic disorders, 171,
    175–176
Dyadic Adjustment Scale (DAS), 202

Early and Periodic Screening, Diagnosis
    and Treatment (EPSDT)
    services, 80
  point of access and, 108, 120
Early Childhood Coordination Project
    (Australia), 413
Early Childhood Development Agreement
    (Canada), 440
Early childhood education and care
    settings
  learning in, 328–331
  screening and, 81–82
Early Childhood Outcomes Center, 47
Early childhood special educators, role of,
    144–148
Early Head Start
  empowerment of parents as part of, 235
  point of access and, 121
  screening requirements of, 81, 91
Early identification
  of children at substantial risk, 8
  multiple points of access preventing, 101
  rationale for, 74–75
  see also Newborn screening programs;
    Screening and surveillance

Early Intervention Collaborative Study
    (EICS), 363
Early intervention programs
  characteristics of children in, 308–310,
    609–610
  comprehensive program, *see* Developing
    and implementing
    comprehensive program
  definition of early intervention
    Australia, 403–404, 405
    EC countries, 485
    United Kingdom, 458–459
  family characteristics assessment and,
    247–254
    see also Family characteristics
  federal special education laws and, 80
  inclusion and, 64
  litigation for services, 326
  matching needs with services, 249
  mental health specialists in, 255
  number of children receiving services,
    305
  parenting stress associated with, 189–190
  principles of, 6–9, 6*t*
  see also Developmental Systems Model;
    Preventive intervention
    programs; *specific countries and
    programs*
Early Screening Inventory–Revised (ESI-
    R), 86
Early Screening Profiles (ESP), 86–87
Early Screening Project, The, 88
Ecological approach, 37–38, 315–316
  monitoring and outcome evaluations in
    context of, 354–355, 360
  point of access and, 111–112, 111*t*
  Spain, 549
Ecomap, development of, 109, 112
Education, state department of, as lead
    state agency, 33
Education, U.S. Department of, and Title
    I, 273–274
Education for All Handicapped Children
    Act of 1975 (PL 99-142), *see*
    Individuals with Disabilities
    Education Act (IDEA)
Education of the Handicapped Act
    Amendments of 1986 (PL 99-
    457), 4, 46, 351
  Part H (now Part C), 33
  see also Part C services for infants and
    toddlers (IDEA '97)
Educational level of parents, *see*
    Socioeconomic status of family
Electroencephalograms (EEGs), 141

Elementary and Secondary Education Act
    of 1965 (PL 89-10), 274
ELEPAP, *see* Hellenic Society for the
    Protection and Rehabilitation
    of Disabled Children
Eligibility, 19–20
    see also specific countries and programs
Embedded instruction, 331
Emerging Findings (Children's National
    Service Framework), 460
Emotion coaching parenting style, 243
Emotional stress, 192–193
    instruments to measure, 198*t*, 202–203
Empowerment, 113, 156–157, 235, 465,
    468, 595
Environmental risk, 14–16, 14*f*, 314–315
    of children in early intervention
        programs, 309–310
Ethiopia, More Intelligent Sensitive Child
    (MISC) program, 603–606
Ethnic background of family, 153–154
    academic achievement of children and,
        269
    Australia's target population, 404
    in British Columbia Infant Development
        Program, 444–445
    in early intervention programs, 309, 338,
        352
    grade retention and, 270
    immigrant absorption, multicultural
        approach to (Israel), 507
    poverty and, 268
    school completion rates and, 271
    special education placements and, 270
    spoken language of family and child's
        educational placement, 378–379
    transition process and, 379
    in United Kingdom, 466
Etiology-specific information and
    treatment, 175
European Association on Early
    Intervention (Eurlyaid), 458
Eurydice Program (Greece), 483
Evaluation
    Australian programs, 416–418
    Austrian programs, 434–435
    components of, 366–368, 366*f*
    definition of, 356
    in ecological context, 354–355, 360
    Greece, 492–493, 497–498
    inclusion and, 66
    Israel, 514–515
    multi-tiered approach to, 355–364
        achieving outcomes (Tier IV),
            362–364, 363*t*

monitoring and accountability (Tier
    II), 358–360, 359*t*
needs assessment (Tier I), 357–358,
    358*t*
quality review and program
    clarification (Tier III),
    360–362, 361*t*
participatory evaluation, 364–365
of point of access, 125
in service coordination and integration,
    44–45
Spain, 563–564
Even Start
    point of access and, 121
    scope of, 274–276
Every Child Matters (United Kingdom),
    457, 459, 461, 476
Exemplary models, 8

Families First project (Australia), 407, 408
Family Adaptability and Cohesion
        Evaluation Scales (FACES III),
        200, 202, 256
Family assessment, 186–187
Family characteristics, 235–266
    coping skills/problem solving, 240–241
    depression, 239–240
    early intervention and, 248–254
        matching needs with services, 249
        sensitive assessment of, 248–249
        structuring relationship-focused
            assessment, 249–254
    focused measures of, 253–258
    literature review as background for
        assessing, 236–238
    parenting attitudes toward child rearing,
        245–246
    psychosocial concerns, 254–258
    relation to child and family outcomes,
        239–247
    social support, 242–245
    socioeconomic status, 246–247, 254–255
Family cohesiveness, 191–192, 241
Family Coping Strategies Scale (F-
        COPES), 204
Family distress, *see* Stressors
Family Environment Scale (FES), 200,
        256–257
Family financial resources, 321–322
    see also Socioeconomic status of family
Family Functioning Style Scale (FFSS),
        255–256
Family Impact Questionnaire (FIQ), 199

Family needs
  assessment instrument for, 157–169
    see also Family Needs Survey
  community service needs, 158
  explaining to others, 158
  family functioning, 158–159
  financial needs, 158
  focus on child's unique needs and
    treatments, 175–176
  information needs, see Information needs
    of families
  parental support groups, 176–177
  resource needs, see Resource needs of
    families
  respite services, 336
  support needs, 158
  types of, 158
  see also Fathers' needs
Family Needs Survey, 108, 109, 112, 179
  British Columbia Infant Development
    Program, use of, 443
  development of, 157–167
  Family Functioning domain of, 200
  form, 163–164f
  summary of studies reporting data using,
    160t
Family patterns of interaction
  child development and, 11
  environmental risk and, 14–16
  integrating early interventions within,
    7–8
  relationship to child's development and
    well-being, 7
  stressors to, 11f, 12–14, 14f, 60, 236
  see also Parent–child interactions
Family Quality of Life Scale, 201
Family Resource Scale, 254
Family support and goals for early
    intervention, 154–157
Family Support Scale (FSS), 204–205, 257
Family-centered approach, 155, 595
  British Columbia Infant Development
    Program, 442
  Greece, 485, 486
  Israel, 517
  Spain, 545, 549–550, 568
  Sweden, 573–575, 582–583
  United Kingdom, 466
  see also Home-based programs
Family-Centered Maternity and Newborn
    Care: National Guidelines
    (Canada), 440
Family-orchestrated child experiences, 11
Fathers' needs
  reflection on, 434
  separate recognition of, 217, 463–464
  see also Assessment of stressors

Federally mandated screening and child-
    find systems, 80–81
Fetal alcohol syndrome (FAS)
  physical examination for, 140
  psychological aspects of, 143
Fetal Alcohol Syndrome/Fetal Alcohol
    Effects Initiative (Canada),
    440–441
First Nations and Inuit Child Care
    Initiative (Canada), 441
First Steps program (Israel), 506–507
Folic Awareness Campaign (Canada), 441
Follow-in directives, 332–333
Food stamps, 321
Foreign language, interpretation and
    translation services, 379
Fragile X syndrome, 141, 172–173
  drug treatment for, 175–176
  gene therapy for, 176
  inherited disorder, 173–174
  newborn screening for, 177
  support and advocacy groups, 177
Free choice pediatrician (FCP, Italy),
    523–524
Funding, see Government funding
Future trends
  in service coordination and integration,
    47–51
  systems change and, 9–10
  see also specific countries

Gender differences in academic
    achievement, 271–272, 289
Gene therapy, 171, 176
General Accounting Office study on
    EPSDT services, 80
Genetics, 169–179
  causes of disability from, 171–172
  drug treatment based on genetic profiles,
    171, 175–176
  family needs for information about,
    169–173, 179
  inherited disorders, 173–174
  privacy and discrimination issues,
    177–178
  survival rates for children with genetic
    conditions, 352
  testing, 141
Georgia preschool education, 274, 280,
    284
Getting to Know Me and My Family, 108
Good Beginnings organization (Australia),
    406, 408
Government funding
  Australia, for early childhood services,
    404–405, 415
  British Columbia Infant Development
    Program, 442, 452

for early childhood education and care
    settings
    screening in, 81–82, 92–93
for educational programs and job
    training, 269
Spain, for early intervention centers,
    546–547
see also specific programs
Grade retention, 270–271
Grandparents' role in early intervention
    programs, 464
Greece, 481–501
    assessment of children, 484
    assessment of stressors, 491–492,
        496–497
    background of special education,
        481–482
    comprehensive interdisciplinary
        assessment, 488–489, 495–496
    Constitution of, 481–482
    developing and implementing programs,
        492, 497
    Developmental Systems Model and,
        485–486
    eligibility, 489–491, 496
    entrance into early intervention
        programs, 490–491, 496
    evaluation, 492–493, 497–498
    future trends, 494–498
    Law 1566 (general education), 482
    Law 2817 (special education), 483–485,
        494
    Law 3106 (decentralization of services),
        493–494
    monitoring, 487, 495
    placement, 484
    point of access, 487–488, 495
    preventive intervention programs, 491,
        496
    referrals to freelance therapists, 490
    screening, 486–487, 494–495
    target population, 483–484
    transition process, 493, 498
    see also Centers for Diagnosis,
        Assessment, Evaluation, and
        Support (CDAES); *entries
        starting with "Hellenic"*

Hawkins-Stafford Elementary and
    Secondary School
    Improvement Amendments of
    1988 (PL 100-297), 274
Head Start
    administration of funds, 285
    connections with kindergarten, 293
    coordination among agency services
        needed for, 100

creation of, 267
gender differences in, 271–272
literacy programs added to, 288
point of access and, 120–121
scope of, 273, 284, 285
screening and surveillance in, 81, 90–92
Health and safety of child, 11, 12
Health care and medical services, 336–337
    Italy, 522
    see also Pediatrician's role
Health, state department of, as lead state
    agency, 33
Healthy Pregnancy Marketing Strategy
    (Canada), 441
Hearing impairment
    Australian provision of services for, 409
    Institution for the Deaf (Greece), 489
    Israeli center for, 504–505, 510, 512
    More Intelligent Sensitive Child
        program (Zimbabwe), 601–603
    number of children with, 338
Hearing screening, 40
    for children with Down syndrome, 139
    early intervention, advantages of, 75
Hellenic Ministry of Education and
    Religious Affairs (HMERA),
    482, 483–485, 487, 494
    Special Education Directorate, 482, 490
Hellenic Ministry of Health and Social
    Solidarity (HMHSS), 498–499
Hellenic Ministry of Health and Social
    Welfare (HMHSW), 487,
    493–495, 497–498
Hellenic Portage Association, 489
Hellenic Society for the Protection and
    Rehabilitation of Disabled
    Children (ELEPAP), 489
High-risk registry, 106
Hispanics, *see* Ethnic background of family
Holistic approach to child development,
    311–312
    in Europe, 432
Home Start (United Kingdom), 465
Home visits
    British Columbia Infant Development
        Program, 442
    by public health nurses, 281–282
Home-based programs, 327, 331–334, 360
    efficiency compared with center-based
        services, 364
    Italy, 525–526
    see also Family-centered approach; Home
        visits
Hospital-based prenatal and birth
    screening, 88–90
Human Genome Project, 170
Hydrocephalus, 140

Immigrant absorption, multicultural
    approach to (Israel), 507
Impact on Family Scale (IFS), 199
Inclusion
    assessment of stressors, 64–65
    Australia, 415
    British Columbia, 451
    comprehensive interdisciplinary
        assessment, 62–63
    as core principle in early intervention, 7,
        59–69, 351
    developing and implementing
        comprehensive program,
        65–66, 329–331
    early intervention program, 64
    Greece, 485
    Italy, 527–528
    legal status of principle of, 59–60
    monitoring and outcome evaluations, 66
    point of access and, 62, 112–113
    preventive intervention program, 63–64
    screening program or referral, 61
    surveillance, 61–62
    transition planning and, 66–67, 393
Individualized education program (IEP)
    principles of intervention and, 6
    Routines-Based Interview for, 221, 223
Individualized family service plan (IFSP)
    age of child needing, 309
    assessment necessary for, 137
    collaborative and comprehensive
        approach, 42–43
    family involvement in development of,
        155
    legal requirements of, 33
    principles of intervention and, 6
    Routines-Based Interview for, 221, 223
Individuals with Disabilities Education Act
    (IDEA) Amendments of 1997
    (PL 105-17), 4, 9, 30
    services under, 327
    transition plan required, 380–381
    see also Part B services for preschool
        special education (IDEA '97);
        Part C services for infants and
        toddlers (IDEA '97)
Individuals with Disabilities Education Act
    (IDEA) (PL 99-142)
    inclusion as principle of, 59
Infant Development Program (IDP; British
    Columbia), 439, 441–445
Infant Developmental Assessment (IDA),
    87
Infant Health and Development Program
    (IHDP), 274–276

Infant-Toddler and Family Instrument
    (ITFI)
    Family Issues and Concerns portion of,
        200
Infant-toddler program of Part C, see Part
    C services for infants and
    toddlers (IDEA '97)
Infant-Toddler Social-Emotional
    Assessment (ITSEA), 87
Information gathering
    for diagnosis, 139–140
    at point of access, 107–109, 112,
        122–123
    in relationship-focused assessment of
        family, 253
    special education assessment, 143–144
    transition's need for information
        exchange, 392
    see also Assessment; Databases; Registries
Information needs of families, 151–183,
        325–327
    assessment of, 157–169
    empowerment aspect of, 156–157
    genetics information, 169–173
        case study, 169–171
    information broker assigned for, 326
    Internet searching for information, 326
    pediatrician's role in meeting, 336–337
    privacy and discrimination issues
        associated with genetic
        information, 177–178
    studies rating as highest need, 167
        difficulty of predicting, based on
            demographic variables, 169
        expressed needs, 167–169, 168t
    see also Family Needs Survey
Information needs of parents
    Spain, 563
    Sweden, 579
Infrastructure
    of point of access, 117–125
    service coordination and, 37–38
Inherited disorders, 173–174
Institution for the Deaf (Greece), 489
Intake
    information gathered at, 108
    paradigm shift away from, 107, 126
    see also Point of access (POA)
Integration of services, see Service
        coordination and integration
Intensity of intervention, 310–312,
        612–613
Interagency agreements, creation of,
        123–124

coordination of agency policies with, 123–124
Interagency coordinating councils (ICCs), 33
Interagency organizational structure and coordination, 117–122, 322–323, 391–392
individualized family service plan (IFSP) and, 43
Interdisciplinary assessment, see Comprehensive interdisciplinary assessment
Interdisciplinary teams, see Team approach
International Child Development Programs (ICDPs), 594, 606–609
caregiver's definition of child, 607–608
components of, 607–609
Developmental Systems Model and, 614–617
implementation and sustainability principles, 612–613
in operation, 614
sensitization principles in training of caregivers, 609–612
studies on effects of, 613–614
zone of intimacy, 608–609
International Society on Early Intervention (ISEI), 24
Internet
Israeli support center for parents of children with special needs, 506
Israeli technology integration and Internet challenges, 517–518
searching for information on, 326
Interpretation and translation services, 379
Intersubjectivity, 291
Intraventricular hemorrhage (IVH), 315
Introductions as directives for language development, 333
Isolation of families with children with disabilities, 194–195
Israel, 503–520
Aaron De Lowe Early Intervention Center, 505, 510, 511, 514
assessment of stressors, 513–514
background, 503–504
comprehensive interdisciplinary assessment, 510–511
Developmental Systems Model and, 508–515
early intervention programs for developmental disabilities, 504–506

eligibility, 512
entering early intervention program, 512–513
evaluation, 514–515
family-centered approach, 517
First Steps program, 506–507, 510
future trends, 515–519
immigrant absorption, multicultural approach to, 507
Maagan (support scheme and preschool/child care center), 506
Makom Meyuchad (Internet support center for parents of children with special needs), 506, 517
Micha (national counsel for the education of children who are hearing impaired), 504–505, 510, 512, 514
monitoring, 509–510
More Intelligent Sensitive Child (MISC) program, 594
"Or" preschool intervention project, 507, 510
point of access, 510
resilience models, 507, 516–517
screening and referral, 508–509
Shalva, 505, 510, 514
SPIN program, 594
targeting family vulnerabilities, 506–507
teacher and professional training programs, 518–519
technology integration and Internet challenges, 517–518
transition process, 515
well-baby care centers, 509
Italian National Health Service (INHS), 522
standard treatment approach of, 526
Italy, 521–540
assessment, 528–529
assistive technology versus physiotherapy, 533–534
background, 521–522
center-based programs, 525, 527–528
child neuropsychiatrist role, 524, 530
Developmental Systems Model and, 523–526
disabilities, early intervention for, in Sicily, 535–537
early intervention programs, 523–526, 523f
free choice pediatrician (FCP), 523–524
home-based programs, 525–526
inclusive programs, 527–528

Italy—*continued*
  infant screening, 528
  institutional approach of, 527–528
  Law 104/92 (for people with
      disabilities), 522
  Law 328/00 (for integrated system of
      social services), 522, 524
  local health agency (LHA) role, 522, 523
  Neurobehavioral Assessment Scale
      (NAS), use of, 531–532
  neuromotor disabilities, early
      intervention for, 527–535
    choice of intervention, 533–534
    conceptual framework for diagnosis
        and intervention, 530–533
    functional organization for services,
        529–530
    historical review, 527–529
    parental involvement, 525
    private charity services, 529–530
    psychomotricity therapists, 525
    speech-language pathologists (SLPs),
        525, 530
    transition process, 525
    university-based centers for services, 530

Joan Amades Center (Spain), 559

Kamehameha Early Education Program
    (KEEP), 291
KASP, *see* Center for Rehabilitation of
    Spastic Children (Greece)
KEAT, *see* Center for the Education and
    Rehabilitation of the Blind
    (Greece)
Kindergarten
  connections with prekindergarten,
      292–294
  Greece, 483
  transition to, programs to enhance, 389

Language development
  directives for, 332–333
  see also Speech-language pathologists
      (SLPs)
Lead state agencies, 33
Leadership
  for community preschool programs, 285
  point of access and, 126–127
LEAP model of intervention, 330
Libro Blanco sobre Atención Temprana (Early
    Intervention White Paper;
    Spain), 543, 545, 547, 548, 565
Lifelong support in United Kingdom,
    465–467
Literacy programs
  point of access and, 121
  in prekindergartens, 288–289
Litigation for services, 326

Low birth weight, *see* Premature and low
    birth weight infants
Low-incidence disabilities
  families of children with, and specialized
      programs, 105
Low-income programs
  screening and, 81–82, 92–93
  see also Poverty; *specific programs*

Maagan (Israeli support scheme and
    preschool/child care center),
    506
Magnetic resonance imaging (MRI), 140
Makom Meyuchad (Israeli Internet support
    center for parents of children
    with special needs), 506, 517
Maple syrup urine disease testing, 141
Marital Adjustment Scale (MAS), 202
Marital stress, 192, 242–243
  instruments to measure, 198*t*, 202
Marte Meo program, 594, 595–596
  Armenia, use of with children with
      cerebral palsy, 596–600
  integrated into International Child
      Development Programs, 606
Maternal depression, 239–240
Maternal employment, 352–353
Maternal intelligence, 246
Mathematics programs in prekindergarten,
    290
McMaster Family Assessment Device, 255
"Me and My Mommy" program (Israel),
    505
Medicaid EPSDT services, *see* Early and
    Periodic Screening, Diagnosis
    and Treatment services
Medical assessment, 138–141
Medical model, 138
Medical services, *see* Health care and
    medical services
Medications for behavioral symptoms, 336
Mentalizing, caregiver's capacity for, 610
Meta-emotion, definition of, 243
Micha (Israeli national counsel for the
    education of children who are
    hearing impaired), 504–505,
    510, 512, 514
Michigan service rates for early
    intervention, 75
Milieu teaching, 331
Minorities, *see* Ethnic background of
    family
Monitoring
  developmental, *see* Developmental
      screening; Screening and
      surveillance
  Greece, 487, 495
  Israel, 509–510

outcome evaluations, 21, 351–372
  see also Evaluation
Spain, 555–556
Montessori curriculum, 286–287, 292
More Intelligent Sensitive Child (MISC)
    program, 600–606
  development in Israel, 594
  integrated into International Child
    Development Programs, 606
  use in Ethiopia for impoverished
    children, 603–606
  use in Zimbabwe for deaf children with
    hearing mothers, 601–603
Multidisciplinary assessment, *see*
    Comprehensive
    interdisciplinary assessment
Multidisciplinary model of service delivery,
    33, 41–42
  see also Staff competencies
Multipower Resource Centers of Special
    Education (MRCSE, Greece),
    485

National Academy of Sciences
  Committee on Integrating the Science
    of Early Childhood
    Development, 5–6, 9
  on preschool education, 292
National Association for the Education of
    Young Children (NAEYC), on
    developmentally appropriate
    practice, 287
National Center for Education Statistics
    (NCES), data on academic
    achievement, 269, 271
National Centre for Early Intervention
    (United Kingdom), 456, 459
National Centre for Excellence in Early
    Intervention (United
    Kingdom), 476
National Children's Agenda (Canada), 440
National Early Intervention Longitudinal
    Study (NEILS)
  on child characteristics, 308
  on environmental risk factors, 315
  on instructional home-based services,
    331
  on instructional services, 328
  on number of hours of service typically
    received, 328
  overview, 307
  on program variation, 5
  on service coordination, 35
  on therapy services, 335
National Education Goals Panel (NEGP),
    priorities to have children start
    school ready to learn, 267, 383
National Fragile X Association, 177
National Institute for Child Health and
    Human Development

(NICHD) study on child care,
    282, 283
National Service Framework External
    Working Group on Disabled
    Children, 472
National Service Framework (NSF, United
    Kingdom), 471–472
Naturalistic teaching approaches, 330–331
Needs of families, *see* Family needs;
    Information needs of families;
    Resource needs of families
Neobehaviorist model, use of (Spain), 544,
    545
Neonatal intensive care unit (NICU)
  Italy, 529
  see also Premature and low birth weight
    infants
Netherlands
  Marte Meo program, 594, 595–596
  ORION program, 594, 595
Neurobehavioral Assessment Scale (NAS),
    531–532
Neuromotor disabilities and early
    intervention in Italy, 527–535
New South Wales Early Intervention
    Coordination Project
    (Australia), 414
Newborn screening programs
  for fragile X syndrome, 177
  hearing screening, lack of coordination
    in programs, 40
  point of access referrals to, 106
  scope of, 75–76
North Carolina
  integrated data system for child services,
    127
  prekindergarten programs, 285–286
  T.E.A.C.H. program, 283–284
Northern Metropolitan Early Intervention
    Interdepartmental Working
    Party (Australia), 413
Nutritional deficiencies, 314

Occupation of parents, *see* Socioeconomic
    status of family
Office of National Statistics (United
    Kingdom), 462
Open preschools (Sweden), 574
Opportunistic surveillance, 77–78
"Or" preschool intervention project
    (Israel), 507
ORION program (Holland), 594, 595
  see also Marte Meo program
Outcomes, *see* Evaluation

Parent empowerment, 7
  in transition process, 392–393
Parental Attitude Research Instrument
    (PARI), 257–258
Parental substance abuse as risk factor, 94,
    314, 460

Parental substance abuse as risk
factor—*continued*
Fetal Alcohol Syndrome/Fetal Alcohol
Effects Initiative (Canada),
440–441
Parental support groups, 176–177
Parent–child interactions
quality of, 11, 312–314
strategies for, 333
Parent–Child Mother Goose (Canada),
443, 446–447
Parenting Attitude Research Instrument
(PARI), 257–258
Parenting attitudes toward child rearing,
245–246, 312–314
Parenting Attitudes Towards Childrearing
Questionnaire, 205
Parenting Sense of Competence Scale
(PSCS), 205
Parenting stress, *see* Assessment of stressors
Parenting Stress Index (PSI), 188, 197,
199, 201, 240
Parent–professional partnerships, 7
see also Collaboration and partnerships
Parent Checklist for Home Visit (Canada),
443
Part B services for preschool special
education (IDEA '97)
coordination among agencies, 100–102
early identification issues of, 101
point of access and, 120
referral service of, 89f, 92
specialized services of, 327, 327t
Part C services for infants and toddlers
(IDEA '97)
coordination among agencies, 35,
100–102
creation of, 30, 33–34, 306
data collection and organization,
variances in, 45
directory of services to be created by
states, 123
early identification issues of, 101–102
educational and therapeutic focus of,
111, 118
empowerment of parents as part of, 235
entry system's shortcomings, 118, 121
goals of, 305–306
outcomes of, 47–48, 49f
point of access and, 120
classification of children with
developmental delays, 110
co-location of staff from different
agencies recommended for,
117–118
integrated and comprehensive POA
recommended for, 121

recommendations for changes to law,
89–90
referral service of, 89f, 92
specialized services of, 327–328, 327t
variation among states, 31–32, 89
Participatory evaluation, 364–365
Partnerships, *see* Collaboration and
partnerships
Pediatrician's role, 336–337
Italy, 523–524
Spain, 553–554, 555
see also Assessment; Health care and
medical services
Peer interactions of children, 293, 330,
580–581, 583
Personal assistant's role (Sweden), 577,
579, 580
Pharmacogenetics, 171, 175–176
Phenylketonuria (PKU)
diagnosis of, 139, 141
early intervention, advantages of, 75
specialists in assessment process, 148
Physical examinations, *see* Assessment
PL 89-10, *see* Elementary and Secondary
Education Act of 1965
PL 99-142, *see* Individuals with Disabilities
Education Act (IDEA)
Amendments of 1997 (PL 105-
17)
PL 99-457, *see* Education of the
Handicapped Act Amendments
of 1986
PL 100-297, *see* Hawkins-Stafford
Elementary and Secondary
School Improvement
Amendments of 1988
PL 105-17, *see* Individuals with Disabilities
Education Act (IDEA)
Amendments of 1997
Play
as context for intervention activities,
330, 580–581
importance of, 572
Point of access (POA), 18–19, 99–131
co-location of staff, 117–118
coordination among services needed,
39–40, 100, 105, 118–120
coordinator assigned to child and family,
40, 114–115
designing integrated approach, 102–125
easy access needed, 101
ecomap, development of, 109, 112
exemplary
conceptual framework of, 102, 103f
providing multiple paths to
coordination, 118–120, 120f
full access needed, 101–102

Greece, 487–488, 495
inclusion and, 62
infrastructure, 117–125
integrated databases, development of
interagency data, 121–123
need for, 127
resource directory, 123–124
interagency agreements, creation of,
123–124
coordination of agency policies with,
123–124
interagency organizational structure,
117–122
Israel, 510
leadership, effect of, 126–127
monitoring and evaluation of
effectiveness of, 124–125
problems with federal and state
categorical programs and,
100–102
purposes and goals of, 102–104
Spain, 556
staff competencies, 115–117
interpersonal characteristics, 116–117
interpersonal skills, 116
knowledge, 115–116
linkages in integrated approach, 119
selection and development, 124–125
training, 116, 127
tasks to achieve goals of, 104–111
division of children into three broad
groups, 109–111
information gathering, 107–109, 112,
122–123
public awareness, creation of,
104–106, 110
trust, development of, 106–107
timely access needed, 101
values underlying, 111–115
collaboration and partnerships,
113–115, 117
developmentally appropriate, 113
ecological, 111–112, 111*t*
empowering, 113
inclusion, 112–113
Portage Home Teaching Programmes
(United Kingdom), 475
Positron emission tomography (PET) scan,
141
Postpartum Parent Support Program
(PPSP; Canada), 441
Poverty
academic achievement of children living
in, 269–272
depression of parents and, 239
developing preventive intervention
programs for, 267–304

clinical level of intervention, 279–280
connections with kindergarten,
292–294
difficulty of large-scale
implementation, 273–276
educational curriculum, 286–294
levels of intervention, 279–281
literacy programs, 288–289
mathematics curriculum, 289–290
motivation of children and, 294
recommendations and principles for,
276–281
results of earlier studies on, 272–273
targeted intervention, 280
teaching format, 290–292
More Intelligent Sensitive Child
program (Ethiopia), 603–606
nature and extent of, 268–269
as risk factor, 94, 314–315
United Kingdom, 461
see also Socioeconomic status of family
Prader-Willi syndrome, 141
Prekindergarten
for children from low-income families,
284–286
connections with kindergarten, 292–294
curriculum for, 286–292
Darcee program, 286–287
literacy emphasis, 288–289
Montessori program, 286–287
screening and surveillance, 88, 90–92
state-funded programs, 273–274
teacher training, 91–92
Prelinguistic communication, 313
Premature and low birth weight infants
early intervention for, 93, 309
advantages of, 75
identification of, 76
Infant Health and Development
Program targeting, 275
Italian organization of services for,
529–530
parenting stress associated with, 189
Brief Symptom Index, use of, 203
Carolina Parent Social Support Scale,
use of, 205
coping skills and, 194
differences between mothers and
fathers, 191
Dyadic Adjustment Scale, use of, 202
emotional stress and, 193
Impact on Family Scale, use of, 199
Parenting Attitudes Towards
Childrearing Questionnaire,
use of, 205
Questionnaire on Resources and
Stress, use of, 200

Premature and low birth weight
infants–*continued*
social support for parents and, 195
Symptoms Checklist 90–Revised, use
of, 203
threats to confident parenting, 195
as risk factor for developmental
difficulties, 314, 315
screening and assessment in Israel, 509
survival rates for, 352, 451
Preschool special education program, *see*
Part B services for preschool
special education (IDEA '97)
Preventive intervention programs
for children living in poverty, 267–304
difficulty of large-scale
implementation, 273–276
recommendations and principles for,
276–281
summary of studies' results, 272–273
see also Poverty
as Developmental Systems Model
component, 15
Greece, 491, 496
growth of, 3
inclusion and, 63–64
Israel, 518
Spain, 559–560
Principles of early intervention, 6–9
Privacy issues associated with genetic
information, 177–178
Private charity services, role in Italy,
529–530
Problem solving, *see* Coping skills
Professional organizations, role of, 8–9
Project SLIDE (Skills for Learning
Independence in Diverse
Environments), 389
Psychodynamic theory, use of (Spain), 544
Psychological assessment, 141–143
Psychometric screening, 76, 86
Psychomotricity therapists (Italy), 525
Psychosocial concerns of family, 254–258
Public awareness of point of access,
104–106, 110
Public-funded early childhood education
and care settings
screening in, 81–82, 92–93
see also Government funding; *specific
programs*

Quality Protects (United Kingdom), 469
Quality review and program clarification,
360–362, 361*t*
Questionnaire on Resources and Stress
(QRS), 200

Redirectives, 333

Referrals, *see* Screening and surveillance
Registries
birth defects registry, 40
high-risk registry, 106
prenatal and birth risk registry, 88
Research and Training Center on Service
Coordination, 34, 35, 48, 49*f*,
50
Research Institution for the Child–Spiros
Doxiadis (Greece), 489
Resilience models, 507, 516–517
Resource needs of families, 215–234
community-based resources, use of, 216
comprehensive program including
resource supports, 319–323,
320*f*
definition of resources, 215–216
emotional support, 216–217
external versus internal resources, 216
informational support, 217
material support, 217
routines-based assessment, 217–224
conceptual framework for, 218–219
definition of routines, 218
routines-based interview, 219–224, 220*f*
examples of needs detected through,
224–232
see also Routines-Based Interview
(RBI)
types of support, 216–217
Respite services, 336
Risk factors, *see* Environmental risk
Risk status and program eligibility as
prescreening methods, 92–93
Routines-Based Interview (RBI), 108–109,
112, 219–224
examples of needs detected through,
224–232
apparently low-complexity example,
227–232
high-complexity example, 224–227,
231–232
Family Preparation Form, 222
implications for intervention planning
and service delivery, 223–224
interviewer for, 222
number of persons involved in, 222–223
options for settings and people, 219–221
preparation for, 219
Report Form, 220*f*
stages of interview, 223
timing of, 221–222
Rural communities and resources available,
322

Screening and surveillance, 16–18, 73–98
basis of surveillance, 73–74

from birth to age 3 or 4, lack of, 76
British Columbia Infant Development
    Program, 445–448, 446f, 452
child care, prekindergarten, and Head
    Start systems, 90–92
definition of screening, 73
developmental, 77–80
federally mandated screening and child-
    find systems, 80–81
graduated follow-up system, 93–94
Greece, 486–487, 494–495
hospital-based prenatal and birth
    screening, 88–90
inclusion and, 61–62
information gathering and transmission
    to point of access, 107–108,
    110
Israel, 508–509
Italy, for infants, 528, 529
principles of effective screening systems,
    75–77
public-funded early childhood education
    and care settings, 81–82, 92–93
rationale for early identification, 74–75
recommendations for effective
    community-based screening,
    88–94, 89f
review of screening measures, 82–88
risk status and program eligibility as
    prescreening methods, 92–93
sensitivity of, 76–77
in service coordination and integration,
    39–40
of siblings of children with
    developmental delays or genetic
    conditions, 93, 94
Spain, 553–555
specificity of, 76–77
Sweden, 577–579
systems and settings in which to embed,
    80–82
tests used in, 82–88, 83t
Self-efficacy of parents, 195
    instruments to measure, 205–206
SENCOs, see Area Special Educational
    Needs Coordinators (United
    Kingdom)
Sensitivity of screening process, 76–77
    assessment of family characteristics,
    247–249
    Early Screening Inventory–Revised, 86
    Early Screening Profiles, 87
Sensitization principles in training of
    caregivers, 609–612
Service coordination and integration,
    29–58
    activity settings, importance of, 43–44

advantages of, 30–31
Australia, 412–414, 415
British Columbia Integrated Service
    Delivery and Integrated Case
    Management, 445
definition of coordination, 35
definition of integration, 32
developmental systems approach to,
    38–46
    comparison to service coordination
    tasks, 39, 39t
    comprehensive interdisciplinary
    assessment, 40–42
    developing and implementing
    comprehensive program, 42–44
    monitoring and outcome evaluations,
    44–45
    screening, referral, and access, 39–40
    transition planning, 45–46
difficulties in implementing, 34, 339
in early intervention, 30–32
framework for, 37–38
future trends, 46–50
    clarification of intention, 46–47
    training needs for early intervention
    preparation, 48–50
interactive variables that facilitate, 38
interagency collaboration issues for, 31,
    32t
Italian early intervention program in
    Sicily, 535–537
in Part C of IDEA, 33–34
point of access and, 40, 102–125
    see also Point of access (POA)
Sweden, 583–584, 585
Service coordinators
    individualized family service plan (IFSP)
    role, 33, 41–43
    in information broker role, 326–327
    Israel, 513
    Part C role, 35–36, 36t, 38, 41, 45
    point of access coordinators, 40,
    114–115
    as team coordinator, 41–43
    training of, 48, 50
    in transition process, 387
Shalva (Center for Children Who Are
    Mentally and Physically
    Challenged; Israel), 505, 510,
    514
Siblings of children with developmental
    delays or disabilities
    role in early intervention programs, 464
    screening and surveillance of, 93, 94
Sicily early intervention programs,
    535–537

"Significant others" in early support and
intervention, 464–465
see also Social support
Social isolation of families with child with
disabilities, 194–195
stigma of having child with disabilities,
195–196
Social support, 194–195, 323–325
as family characteristic, 242–245
importance for reducing stressors, 237
instruments to measure, 204–205
Social-environmental factors in child
development, 314–315
Society for Children and Youth of BC
(Canada), 451
Socioeconomic status of family, 246–247
depression and, 239–240
in early intervention programs, 309, 352
instruments used to create hierarchy of
family needs, 254–255
as risk factor, 314–315
transition process and, 392–393
see also Poverty
Sotos syndrome, 140
Spain, 543–570
assessment of stressors, 560–562
background, 543–544
center-based programs, 562
changing models and practices, 544–545
comprehensive interdisciplinary
assessment, 554–558
conceptual framework, 548–553
child's involvement, 551
collaboration between professionals
and parents, 550–551, 568
community-based intervention,
551–552
family-focused intervention, 549–550
interdisciplinary approach, 552
social and ecological perspectives of
development, 548–549
training and promotion of competence
among professionals, 552–553
developing and implementing
comprehensive program,
562–563
Developmental Systems Model and,
553–567
educational and social services, 554
eligibility, 558–559
entrance to preventive and early
intervention programs,
559–560
evaluation, 563–564
family-centered model, 545, 568
information for parents, 563

Libro Blanco sobre Atención Temprana
(Early Intervention White
Paper; Spain), 543, 545, 547,
548, 565
monitoring, 556
neobehaviorist model, use of, 544, 545
parental involvement, 545, 562
pediatrician's role, 553–554, 555
point of access, 556
political, economic, and financial
considerations, 545–547, 546f,
547f
psychodynamic theory, use of, 545
screening and referral, 553–555
transition planning, 564–567, 568
Special education
assessment, 143–148
placement related to gender, ethnicity,
and social class, 271
preschool provision of and screening, 82
see also Part B services for preschool
special education (IDEA '97)
state provision of services, 80
Special Education Needs Code of Practice
(United Kingdom), 457
Special Education Needs and Disability
Act 2001 (United Kingdom),
457
Special Educational Needs Action Plan
(United Kingdom), 469
Special Educational Needs Strategy
(United Kingdom), 475, 476,
477
Specificity of screening process, 76–77
Early Screening Inventory–Revised, 86
Early Screening Profiles, 87
Speech-language pathologists (SLPs), 100,
525, 530
in assessment team, 138, 142–143
British Colombia, 443
SPIN program (Israel), 594
Spina bifida, 194–195
Staff competencies
from numerous fields, need for, 31
point of access, 115–117
interpersonal characteristics, 116–117
interpersonal skills, 116
knowledge, 115–116
linkages in integrated approach, 119
selection and development, 124–125
training, 116, 127
service coordinator to assess, 41–42
State Children's Health Insurance Program
(SCHIP), 92
State services
for birth defect surveillance, 40

for children at risk for developmental
  delays, 4–5, 80
for early intervention, 307–308
models of service coordination, 34–35
prekindergarten programs, 273–274,
  284, 285
  teacher licensing, 292
screening systems, need to develop,
  90–92
variation in Part C services, 31–32, 89
Stigma of having a child with disabilities,
  195–196
Stressors, 185–213
  to family patterns of interaction, 11f,
    12–14, 14f, 60, 236
  social isolation as, 194–195
  see also Assessment of stressors
Substance abuse of parent as risk factor,
  94, 314, 460
Sudden Infant Death Syndrome (SIDS),
  441
Supplemental Nutrition Program for
  Women, Infants, and Children
  (WIC)
  point of access and, 108, 120
  screening and, 82, 92
Supplemental Security Income (SSI),
  321–322
Sure Start (United Kingdom), 469, 471,
  473–475, 476
Surveillance, see Screening and surveillance
Sweden, 571–591
  assessment, 578, 583
  background, 571–572
  child care, 573–575, 583
  Children's Habilitation Centers, 576,
    580, 581
  Children's Health Services, 576, 581
  community-based support, 576
  demographics, 572
  Developmental Systems Model and,
    586–588, 587t
  early intervention system, 575–582
    implementation of, 579–581
  environmental factors, 584–586
  family-based care, 573–575, 582–583
  information needs of parents, 579
  open preschools, 574
  parental involvement, 579
  peer interactions of children with
    disabilities, 580–581, 583
  personal assistant's role, 577, 579, 580
  play, focus on, 572, 580–581
  screening and referral, 577–579
  service coordination and integration,
    583–584, 585

state support of parents to stay home
  with children, 573
systems theory and, 582–586
transition planning, 581–582
Symptoms Checklist 90–Revised (SCL-
  90-R), 202, 203

T.E.A.C.H. program (North Carolina),
  283–284
Teacher education, 292
  Israel, 518–519
  see also Training
Teachers' role in transition process, 380,
  387, 391
Team approach, 133–135
  during assessment, 40–42
  Greece, 488–489
  Israel, 510–511
  meetings as important part of, 44
  participatory evaluation, 364–365
  problems with interdisciplinary teams, 8
  Spain, 552
  see also Collaboration and partnerships;
    Comprehensive
    interdisciplinary assessment;
    Point of access (POA)
Technology
  integrated databases, development of
    interagency data, 121–123
  need for, 127
  resource directory, 123–124
  see also Internet
Temporary Assistance for Needy Families
  (TANF)
  importance of, 321
  point of access and, 108, 120
Therapy services, 327t, 334–335
Three- to five-year-old children
  legislation to provide early intervention
    for, 4–5
  see also Part B services for preschool
    special education (IDEA '97)
Timeliness of access to services, 101
Title I and U.S. Department of Education
  administration of funds, 285
  scope of, 273–274, 284
Together from the Start (United Kingdom),
  458, 469–473, 475
Training
  in Australian programs, 416–418
  in British Columbia Infant Development
    Program, 445
  of child care providers and preschool
    teachers
    on inclusion, 330

Training–*continued*
of Israeli teachers and professionals,
518–519
for naturalistic teaching, 330–331
of point of access staff, 116, 127
of prekindergarten teachers, 91–92
sensitization principles in training of
caregivers, 609–612
in service coordination needs, 47–50
in Spain, 552–553
as transition implementation issue, 383,
390–391
see also Teacher education
Transition issues, 21, 373–398
child characteristics and experiences,
377–379
components of, 377–381, 378*f*
contexts for service transitions, 375–376
creating successful transitions, 383–393,
384*f*
communication and collaboration,
386–388
preparation of children, families, and
professionals, 388–391
support services for, 391–393
definition of transition, 46, 376
family characteristics and experiences,
379
Greece, 493, 498
horizontal transition, 374
implementation issues, 381–383
continuity of services, 382, 391–392
philosophical issues, 382–383
training and personnel preparation
issues, 383
inclusion and, 67, 393
information exchange for, 392
Israel, 515
Italy, 525
to more child-centered services, 385
parental involvement in, 392–393
procedural variables, 381
as process, 376–377, 384–386
relationships among participants, 380,
385–386
in service coordination and integration,
46
service provider characteristics and
experiences, 379–380
Spain, 564–567, 568
spoken language of family and, 378–379
support for, 381
Sweden, 581–582
vertical transition, 374
Trust, development of, 106–107

Uniformity of programs, need to improve,
9–10

United Kingdom, 455–480
Area Special Educational Needs
Coordinators (SENCOs), 457
"Celebrating Families" program, 468
childhood disability, changing patterns
in, 459–461
Children's Trusts, 475
development of role of key worker,
471–472
developmental monitoring introduced in,
78
Disability Discrimination Act 1995, 457
Disability Rights Commission, 470, 475
early intervention defined, 458–459
efficacy debates, 459–462
Every Child Matters, 457, 459, 461, 476
Family Service Plan, 472–473
family support, 465
framework for positive early
intervention, 468–475
future trends, 476–477
impact of disability on families, 462–468
family contributions, 463–465
professional perspectives, 463
"significant others" in early support
and intervention, 464–465
lifelong support, 465–467
mental health of young children, 462
multi-agency assessment and support,
472–473
national policy context, 456–458
National Service Framework, 471–472
neonatal care improvements, 460
social exclusion, 459–461
Special Education Needs Code of
Practice, 457
Special Education Needs and Disability
Act 2001, 457
Special Educational Needs Action Plan,
469
Special Educational Needs Strategy, 475,
476, 477
survey on fathers' needs, 217
Together from the Start as program
guidance, 458, 469–473, 475
transdisciplinary approach, 467–468
see also Sure Start (United Kingdom)
Universal programs
advantages of, 126
British Columbia, 451
child care through age 2, 282–284
prekindergarten systems, 81, 280, 284
screening, 88, 107
University-based centers for services
(Italy), 530
U.S. General Accounting Office study on
EPSDT services, 80

Vision impairment
   Australian provision of services for, 409
   Center for the Education and
             Rehabilitation of the Blind
             (KEAT; Greece), 489
   Joan Amades Center (Spain), 559
   number of children with, 338

Ways of Coping Scale (WCS), 203–204
Welfare programs, 269, 321

see also specific programs
Well-baby care centers (Israel), 509
WIC, *see* Supplemental Nutrition Program
             for Women, Infants, and
             Children

Zimbabwe, and More Intelligent Sensitive
             Child program, 601–603
Zone of intimacy, 608–609